The Sailing Encyclopedia

The
Sailing
Encyclopedia

Edited by
Michael W. Richey

Advisory Editor
Donald M. Street

Lippincott & Crowell
Publishers *New York*

First U.S. edition.

This book was designed and produced by
The Rainbird Publishing Group Limited,
36 Park Street, London W I Y 4DE.

House Editors: Peter Coxhead and Raymond Kaye
Assisted by Edward Taney
Designer: Alan Bartram

For information address Lippincott & Crowell, Publishers,
521 Fifth Avenue, New York, N.Y. 10017.

ISBN 0-690-01922-X

Library of Congress No. 79-3821

Text photoset by Jolly & Barber Limited,
Rugby, England
Printed and bound by Dai Nippon Printing Company Limited,
Hong Kong

Contents

List of Color Plates

Contributors

G. E. Beck
Assistant chief scientist to a leading electronic-instrument company

Andrew Bray
Assistant editor of *Yachting Monthly*

Adlard Coles
Author of *Heavy Weather Sailing* and many works on yacht pilotage, chairman of a nautical publisher; Gold Medallist, Royal Institute of Navigation

Captain Charles H. Cotter
Author of books on nautical astronomy; formerly senior lecturer Department of Maritime Studies, University of Wales Institute of Science and Technology

Professor A. D. Couper
Head of the Department of Maritime Studies, University of Wales Institute of Science and Technology

R. Michael Ellison
Master Mariner and specialist in self-steering devices

J. Ewing
Institute of Oceanographic Sciences

Bob Fisher
Yachting correspondent of the *Guardian*

R. N. B. Gatehouse
Designer of electronic navigation equipment for small craft; Gold Medallist, Royal Institute of Navigation

Frank George
Sometime editor of *The Geographical Journal*; assistant editor of the *Journal of Navigation*

A. Gwynn Jones
Nautical historian

Commander Gregory Haines
Formerly consultant to a leading sonar manufacturer

James Grogano
High-speed sailing enthusiast

Alban Harrison
Formerly chief scientist of a leading radar manufacturer

Rear-Admiral D. W. Haslam
Hydrographer of the Navy

H. G. Hasler
Marine consultant and designer, pioneer of self-steering and the Western version of the Chinese rig

J. N. Howard-Williams
Yachtsman; author and managing editor of a nautical publisher

Colin Jarman
Yachting journalist; staff member of *Yachting Monthly*

David L. Jenkins
Yachting journalist and author of books on sailing

Sir Peter Johnson, Bt
Author of yachting books; director of a nautical publisher

Captain John F. Kemp
Head of the School of Navigation, City of London Polytechnic

G. W. Lennon
School of Earth Sciences, The Flinders University of South Australia

C. A. Marchaj
Author of theoretical works on sailing; Honorary Research Fellow, Department of Aeronautics and Astronautics, Wolfson Marine Craft Unit, University of Southampton

W. E. May
Formerly Assistant Director of Admiralty Compass Observatory

Captain A. B. Moody
Formerly Head of Navigational Science Division, US Hydrographic Office; sometime President of US Institute of Navigation

Colin Mudie
Naval architect, yacht designer and author of books on the subject

Richard C. Newick
Multihull designer and builder of Massachusetts, USA; contributor to American yachting magazines

David Pelly
Formerly assistant editor of *Yachting World*

Douglas Phillips-Birt (deceased)
Naval architect; author of books on yachts and yachting

Barry Pickthall
Editor of *Dinghy Magazine*

H. Quill
Horologist and nautical historian

John E. Powell
Director of a mast-manufacturing company

Commander J. S. N. Pryor
Superintendent of Sailing Directions, Hydrographic Department, Ministry of Defence

Michael W. Richey
Director, Royal Institute of Navigation; prominent yachtsman

Rear-Admiral G. S. Ritchie
President of the Directing Committee, International Hydrographic Bureau, Monaco; former Hydrographer of the Navy

D. H. Sadler
Astronomer, formerly of the Royal Greenwich Observatory, Herstmonceux; sometime Superintendent H.M. Nautical Almanac Office

Hugh Somerville
Author of books on sailing; yachting correspondent of the *Sunday Times*; formerly editor of *The Yachtsman*

Donald M. Street
Author of yachting books: lives in Grenada, West Indies, where he skippers and charters his yawl *Iolaire*

Lt-Commander D. W. Waters
Formerly Deputy Director and Head of Division of Navigation and Astronomy, National Maritime Museum, Greenwich

Alan Watts
Meteorologist; Lecturer in Physics, North East Essex Technical College, Colchester; author of books on meteorology for small craft

Commander K. J. Wickham
Electrical and mechanical engineer; author of books on boating

Preface

Books about the sea, nowadays, seem to proliferate and on sailing in particular there exists every kind of work: instruction manuals, handbooks on cruising, dinghy sailing, ocean racing, on the weather at sea, navigation, boat design and so on, and of course innumerable accounts of notable voyages. However, there is no single work that covers every aspect of the subject, from, say, the history of sailing craft or of chart making to match racing, or from wave motion to wind-vane steering. The aim of the present volume is to provide a standard work that will cover every subject likely to interest those concerned with sail. Essentially it is a work of reference, but addressed to the general reader rather than the specialist.

The compilation of such a comprehensive volume has inevitably involved some editorial decisions of an arbitrary kind, both as to how wide to cast the net and how to pare the contributions down to reasonable proportions. No doubt the results are open to criticism on that account and some indication of the line of thought pursued may be helpful.

In general, matter to be found in standard textbooks has not been included. Thus there is a useful article about the Collision Regulations, their history and how they are applied, particularly under sail, but the full text of the regulations, so easily obtained elsewhere, is not given. Matter of a generally ephemeral nature (and sailing is no less subject to fashion than are other sports) has generally been ignored, except in passing. The latest trends in deck layout or anti-fouling paint may thus not always be evident from the book and here no excuse is needed. Nor, for obvious reasons, has it been possible to include all yacht clubs and some basis for selection has had to be found. Although some of the clubs included may be smaller and less important than others omitted, all those that do appear have some significance in the social history of yachting and that has been the criterion for their inclusion.

No doubt the book will be found to have its failings and for these the Editor must assume responsibility. To the contributors, whose knowledge on so wide a range of subjects lends the work its authority, must go the credit. In addition I should like to thank many others who have helped in different ways and most particularly Phoebe Mason, whose discerning criticism has much improved certain sections of the text.

London 1980   MICHAEL RICHEY

Editorial Notes

The encyclopedia is arranged in alphabetical sequence. For the purposes of alphabetization, 'the', 'a', and 'an' are ignored, and when the title of an entry consists of more than one word the whole is treated as one sequence of letters. For example, 'sailings, the' is placed between 'Sail design and materials' and 'Sail trim'.

Words in the text printed in SMALL CAPITALS direct the reader to a separate entry where more information may be found. Other useful cross references, also set in small capitals, appear in the alphabetical sequence, and at the ends of many entries.

It is impossible to write about many of the subjects in this encyclopedia without using technical terms. However, when such terms are not self-explanatory, they are either defined at their first use in an entry, or a cross reference to a definition is supplied.

British and American terminology and spelling occasionally vary, but their differences are made clear either in the entry concerned or in the cross references. The abbreviations used are listed below.

Because Britain is in the process of changing to the metric system, the rounded metric equivalents have been given, where appropriate, in parentheses after the Anglo-American units of measure. Conversion factors are given on p. 286, where the reader should note the difference between the values of the ton and gallon as used in Britain and the United States.

Abbreviations

A	ampere(s)
AC	alternating current
ADF	automatic direction finders
ASTO	Association of Sea Training Organizations
AYRS	Amateur Yacht Research Society
bhp	brake horse power
°C	degrees Celsius (centigrade)
CB	centre of buoyancy
cc	cubic centimetre(s)
CCA	Cruising Club of America
CE	centre of effort
CG	centre of gravity
cm	centimetre(s)
CLR	centre of lateral resistance
CORK	Canadian Olympic Regatta Kingston
CQR	plough anchor; plow anchor (from the sound of the word 'secure')
CSK	Choy, Seaman and Kumalae (design team)
CVP	Cercle de la Voile de Paris
CYA	Canadian Yachting Association
DC	direct current
DEC	declination
D.lat.	difference of latitude
DME	distance-measuring equipment
°F	degrees Fahrenheit
ft	foot (feet)
g	gram(me)(s)
GHA	Greenwich hour angle
GMT	Greenwich mean time
GRP	glass-reinforced plastic(s)
hp	horsepower
hr	hour(s)
HWF & C	high water full and change
IALA	International Association of Lighthouse Authorities
in	inch(es)
IMCO	Intergovernmental Maritime Consultative Organization
IOR	International Offshore Rule
IOW	Isle of Wight
IRPCAS	International Regulations for Preventing Collisions at Sea
IYRU	International Yacht Racing Union
kg	kilogram(me)(s)
kHz	kiloHertz
l	litre(s)
lb	pound(s)
LHA	local hour angle
LOA	length overall
LWL	waterline length
MHz	megaHertz
min	minute(s) (time and angle)
mm	millimetre(s)
MORC	Midget Ocean Racing Club
MP	multipulse
NAYRU	North American Yacht Racing Union
NYYC	New York Yacht Club
ODAS	Ocean Data Acquisition System
ORC	Offshore Racing Council
OSTAR	*Observer* Single-handed Transatlantic Race
oz	ounce(s)
PVC	polyvinyl chloride
QE	quadrantal error
RBR	Round Britain Race
RCC	Royal Cruising Club
RNSA	Royal Naval Sailing Association
RORC	Royal Ocean Racing Club
rpm	revolutions per minute
RTYC	Royal Thames Yacht Club
RYA	Royal Yachting Association
RYS	Royal Yacht Squadron
sec	second(s) (time and angle)
SHA	sidereal hour angle
SORC	Southern Ocean Racing Conference
STA	Sail Training Association
TM	Thames Measurement
USYRU	United States Yacht Racing Union
V	volt(s)
VDS	variable depth sonar
VHF	very high frequency
VLF	very low frequency
V_{mg}	speed (velocity) made good
W	watt(s)
yd	yard(s)
YRA	Yacht Racing Association

A

Aback
A sail is said to be aback when it is sheeted to windward or the wind comes on to what should be its lee side.

Abaft
Nearer the stern.

Abeam
On the beam; at right angles to the fore-and-aft line of a craft in the horizontal plane.

About
To go about is to go from one tack to the other.

A-cockbill
The anchor is said to be a-cockbill when it is ready to let go, hanging from the cathead or hawsehole.

Admiral's Cup see YACHT RACING: Major races and series.

Aft
Towards the stern; behind.

Age of the moon
The number of days since new or change of moon. *See* ESTABLISHMENT OF THE PORT

Age of tide
The effect the time interval between new and full moon will have upon the range of the tide or tidal stream.

Agonic line
A line joining places where there is no magnetic variation.

Aground
Said of a vessel touching the bottom.

Ahead
Towards the bows; in front of.

A-hull
A vessel is said to be lying a-hull when all sail is lowered in a gale and she is left to take up her own position in the seas. *See* HEAVY-WEATHER SAILING

Air masses *see* WIND AND WEATHER

A-lee
On the lee side.

All in the wind
Head to wind when going about, the sails shivering.

All plain sail
A vessel is said to be under all plain sail when its working sails only are hoisted. In the case of a twin-headsail yawl, for example, it would mean two headsails, main and mizzen, but no spinnaker, staysail etc.

Altitude
In ASTRONOMICAL NAVIGATION, the angular distance above the horizon. The altitude read off the SEXTANT, corrected only for instrumental errors, is called the sextant altitude. The sextant altitude after correction for refraction, height of eye, and DIP is known as the observed altitude.

Amateur Yacht Research Society
The AYRS was formed in Britain in 1951. It provides a useful exchange of information among amateur sailors. It has published about 80 very interesting books and pamphlets, embracing such subjects as multihulls, self-steering gear, hydrofoils, and solid sails. Anyone interested can apply for membership, which is international.

America's Cup *see* YACHT RACING: Major races and series.

Amidships
The middle part of a vessel. As a helm order: with neither port nor starboard helm.

Amphidromic point
A no-tide point.

Anafront *see* WIND AND WEATHER: Fronts and frontal depressions

Anchors, anchor work *see* GROUND TACKLE

Anemometer
An instrument for measuring wind force.

Anticyclones *see* WIND AND WEATHER

A-peak
The anchor is said to be a-peak just before it breaks out of the ground when weighing, the bows of the vessel being vertically above it.

Apparent noon
The instant the apparent sun is on the meridian.

Apparent time
Time based on the rotation of the earth in relation to the apparent or true sun.

Apparent wind
The wind as measured from a moving body. The resultant of the true wind and the wind due to the vessel's motion.

Apron *see* HULLS: Construction components

Aries, first point of
The point on the celestial sphere at which the DECLINATION of the sun changes from south to north.

Armillary sphere
An instrument incorporating concentric metal circles in several planes, by means of which astronomical problems can be solved without calculation. It is said to have been invented by the Greek astronomer Eratosthenes (*c.* 250 BC) and was elaborated by the later Greek and Arab astronomers.

Arming the lead
Placing tallow in the lower end of a sounding lead to retrieve samples of the bottom.

Aspect ratio
The ratio of the hoist to the length of the foot of a sail.

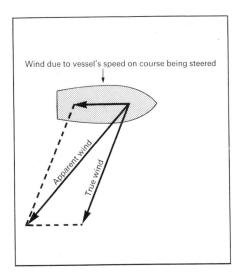
The relationship between apparent and true wind

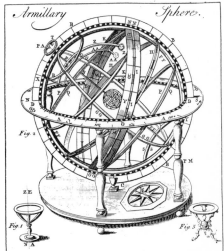
An engraving of an armillary sphere from Nature Displayed *Vol. IV (1740), a translation of la Pluche's* Le Spectacle de la Nature

Association of Sea Training Organizations

ASTO was formed in 1971 by bringing together the increasing number of independent organizations that provide various forms of sea training for young people. The aim of ASTO and its member organizations is to further the personal development of young people and adults by means of training under sail at sea.

Astrolabe *see* MARINER'S ASTROLABE

Astronomical navigation

The practice of guiding a ship on its way using information obtained from observations of the sun, moon, planets, and stars; it is often termed 'astronavigation' or 'celestial navigation'. In many respects the most basic form of navigation, it has had a significant role from the days when men first ventured out of sight of land to the present, when the navigator has many more sophisticated methods at his disposal. Not only is astronomical navigation available to every seafarer (and to land, air, and space travellers), but the changing aspect of the night sky has continued to invite and challenge the navigator's ingenuity. The extent to which he could accept the invitation has depended on the development of astronomy, the design and construction of instruments – particularly marine timekeepers – and techniques of observation and calculation. The successful application of astronomy to the seventeenth- and eighteenth-century problem of determining longitude at sea forms an absorbing chapter in the history of science; and astronomy received a great impetus from the desperate need of navigators to be able to interpret, understand, and predict the positions of the sun and moon for their purposes.

Historically, there have been only three main phases, though techniques and practices greatly improved during each:
1. Before the theory of gravitation enabled the position of the moon to be predicted, essentially to serve as an astronomical clock, the sun and stars could provide only direction and latitude; there was no method of determining longitude.
2. Once the difficulties – theoretical, instrumental, observational, and computational – of using the moon 'to tell the time' by the method of LUNAR DISTANCES and thus to provide longitude, had been overcome the full scope of astronomical navigation could be developed.
3. There is no clear-cut division between the second and third phases. The link is time and the invention and development of the MARINE CHRONOMETER; this eventually made unnecessary the independent determination of time from lunar distances. The third phase, however, became firmly established with the advent of radio time signals; apart from advances in instruments, almanacs and sight-reduction tables, methods of observation and calculation there had been no other basic change. However, in recent years, a considerable simplification has taken place in presentation, understanding, and methods to compensate for the reduced time that a navigator can afford to devote in training to the subject. It is this simplified presentation that is described below.

Astronomers can now predict, with far greater precision than that required for navigation, the positions of all the natural objects visible in the sky as seen from the earth. Navigators are primarily concerned with the directions towards such objects; and the necessary data, in a form suitable for navigation, are given annually in *The Nautical Almanac* (*see* NAUTICAL ALMANACS) and can readily be taken out for any required time. It is here assumed that Greenwich Mean Time (GMT), or its equivalent, is immediately available to appropriate precision (about the nearest second) to all navigators; frequent worldwide radio time signals make this easily possible with the aid of modern watches. A direction is specified by two coordinates and these, referred to the natural coordinate system defined by the earth's north-pointing axis of rotation, or its equivalent the plane of the equator, are:
1. The angular inclination to the axis. The quantity usually tabulated, known as DECLINATION, is the complement $(90° -)$ of this angle and is the inclination to the equator; negative values are usually designated S for south.
2. The angular rotation round the axis from some specified direction or zero point on the equator. Traditionally, this coordinate has been measured eastwards round the circle

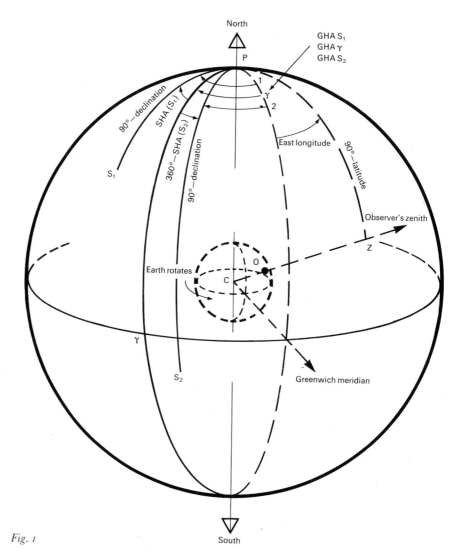

Fig. 1

from the direction to the vernal equinox, and is known as 'right ascension'. This vernal equinox, known to navigators as the First Point of Aries, is the point in the sky (nearly fixed in relation to the stars) occupied by the sun about 21 March when its declination is zero. The quantity required by the navigator, and usually tabulated directly in the almanacs, is, however, measured westwards from the Greenwich meridian; it increases by about $360°$ in a day, or $1'$ in 4 sec, rather more for the stars and less for the moon, and is known as GREENWICH HOUR ANGLE (GHA). For any object, therefore,

GHA object =
GHA Aries—right ascension object

and, for economy of tabulation, the equivalent of right ascension, which changes only slowly with time, is often given instead of GHA. In *The Nautical Almanac*, $360°$—right ascension is tabulated for the stars under the term SIDEREAL HOUR ANGLE (SHA); it is to be added to GHA Aries to give GHA of a star.

The diagram (fig. 1) illustrates how these directions may be indicated by points plotted on the surface of a sphere (the celestial sphere), with the rotating earth at its centre. The directions of the Greenwich meridian and of the ZENITH of the observer, which rotate with the earth, are also shown. P is the north pole, γ the vernal equinox, S_1 and S_2 two objects (sun, moon, planets or stars, S_2 with a negative or south declination) and Z is the observer's zenith.

At any instant of time S_1, S_2 (and as many other objects as may be desired) can be plotted relative to the observer's zenith Z and the pole P. S_1, S_2 move slowly relative to the vernal equinox, while Z rotates rapidly with the earth, but is fixed relative to the rotating Greenwich meridian. The angular distances ZS_1, ZS_2 are the ZENITH DISTANCES of the objects S_1, S_2; these may be observed with a suitable instrument, such as a SEXTANT, provided the observer's zenith can be defined. The zenith is, in fact, defined by the direction of the earth's gravitational field; inversely, the direction defines the observer's position on the earth's surface (latitude and longitude). At sea the horizon provides the most convenient reference, and the marine sextant is designed to facilitate the observation of ALTITUDE ($90°$ − zenith distance) above the visible horizon. The zenith may also be determined directly by means of a bubble or by more sophisticated gyro-stabilized platforms.

As can be seen from fig. 2, knowledge of the zenith distances of two objects serves to determine the position of the zenith, and thus that of the observer. The latitude is obtained directly from PZ, and the longitude from the combination of the local hour angle (LHA) = angle ZPS and the known GHA:

$$LHA = GHA \begin{array}{l} - \text{west} \\ + \text{east} \end{array} \text{longitude}$$

A single known zenith distance, say S_1Z, means that Z must lie on a circle centred at S_1; normally the navigator knows his approximate position and, close to this, the position circle can generally be replaced by a position line. The astronomical spherical triangle P (pole), Z (zenith), S (star or other object) forms the basis of all astronomical navigation; it is necessary by some means (numerical calculation, tabular solutions, graphs, simulators or mechanical devices) to solve the triangle for one or more 'parts' in terms of three others. Many hundreds (possibly thousands) of methods and techniques have been proposed for doing this, the objective being to design procedures that combine: simplicity of principle, universality of application, minimum calculation or table references, adequate precision, and minimum likelihood of error. There is no optimum method.

In principle it suffices to determine the position of the zenith among the stars. Instruments have been designed to do precisely this, pinpointing the zenith with a vertical telescope on a zenithal photograph which is then calibrated by a star chart; but this is not practicable, either observationally or computationally. An equally difficult practical method is to point two (or more) telescopes simultaneously at two stars, thus determining the position of the zenith relative to that of the pole; the coordinates of the zenith (and thus of the observer) can then be measured mechanically – this method can, however, be used with sophisticated equipment, utilizing photoelectric guiding and sighting, a stabilized platform, and automatic computation to provide a continuous record of deduced position. Also simple in principle is the superimposition of precalculated altitude curves (corresponding to the position circles for a range of altitudes) for two or more stars (or other bodies, though this is much more difficult) on a chart; the observer's position can then be pinpointed by plotting the corresponding observed altitudes. The same principle may be appealed to in tabular or computational methods that seek to provide the latitude and longitude of the observer from two (or more) observed altitudes; they require the solution of two spherical triangles ($S_1 S_2 Z$ and $S_1 PZ$ of fig. 2) and generally involve too much calculation.

However, in practice it is usual to regard an observation of the altitude of an object as providing a position line as indicated in fig. 3; each observation is then treated as a separate entity. A single position line cannot of itself provide the navigator with his position, but it can give him information of almost equal value; two or more position lines can be

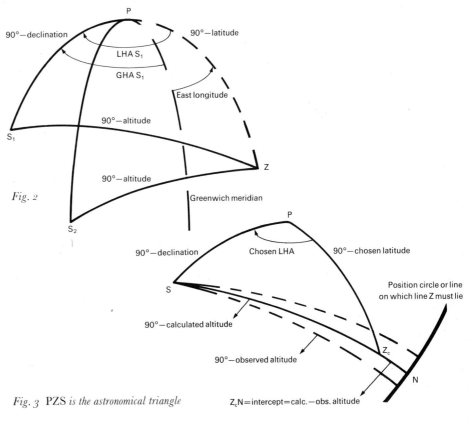

Fig. 2

Fig. 3 PZS *is the astronomical triangle*

combined to provide a determination of position. Almost all methods of deriving a position line from an observed altitude are based on the 'intercept method', introduced by the French admiral Marc Saint-Hilaire in 1879: the altitude (and the direction, or AZIMUTH) that would have been observed from a chosen position (zenith Z_c in fig. 3) is calculated from the spherical triangle PZ_cS and is then compared with the observed altitude to give the 'intercept' Z_cN equal to the difference between SZ and SZ_c. The intercept can then be plotted, on the chart, from the chosen position towards or away from the object and the position line (really part of the position circle) drawn at right angles. This procedure has the enormous advantage that the position can be chosen to simplify the solution of the spherical triangle; it is also of universal application, equally good for any latitude, for any object and any position in the sky. Fig. 4 illustrates how the position lines resulting from observations of the two objects S_1 and S_2 of fig. 2 might be plotted on the chart.

Of the many methods of calculating the altitude and azimuth from a chosen position (that is solving the triangle PZ_cS for the altitude $90° - Z_cS$, the azimuth PZ_cS from a knowledge of the latitude $90° - PZ_c$, the declination $90° - PS$ and the hour angle Z_cPS), undoubtedly the simplest in principle is that of direct tabulation for certain combinations of the three arguments; the required altitude and azimuth can be obtained by simple interpolation, usually for declination only.

With *The Nautical Almanac* and a set of sight-reduction tables the navigator can thus reduce his observations, made relative to his own reference frame of the horizon, to a fix to give him his position. But he can also use the observations to give him useful information more directly: he can steer by the stars either literally or by using them to check his compass; he can 'home' by using the stars to tell him which way and how far to go; he can check his HEADING and speed, and his departure from his intended course; and he can combine this information with that from other sources.

However, there are severe limitations compared with modern methods of navigation.

An essential requirement is being able to see both the horizon and the object to be observed; only a few objects (sun, moon, and the brighter planets) are observable during the day, and the horizon ceases to be useful after twilight; clouds still further reduce visibility. Generally, observations have to be taken at times to suit the stars rather than the navigator's convenience, and require skill and experience. The precision obtainable is probably adequate for almost all purposes, but is lower than some other methods. Even with present-day almanacs and tables the reduction is not trivial and the calculations and plotting require familiarity and care. Even so, it provides adequately for *en route* navigation and gives the navigator an independence of shore-based aids that makes him a master of his environment. It is this that distinguishes astronomical navigation and makes it peculiarly the province of the enthusiast, whether he be professional or amateur.

There are several practical difficulties that have to be overcome in the above ideal presentation. The marine sextant is simple in principle: the light from the star (or other object) is reflected from a plane rotatable index mirror to a fixed half-silvered plane horizon mirror from which it is reflected into a small horizontal telescope through which the observation is made; the star is seen in the same field of view as the horizon (seen through the unsilvered half of the horizon mirror) and the index mirror can be rotated until the star is on the horizon; as seen in fig. 5, the index mirror will then have been rotated through an angle equal to one-half of the altitude of the star. But it is an instrument of precision requiring careful upkeep and use to give the necessary accuracy; in good adjustment, readings of altitude can be obtained to about 0′.2. Apart from the judgment required in observing the timed coincidence of the star with the not-always clear horizon in a vertical plane (the sextant must be swung through a small arc to ensure this), allowance has to be made for the dip of the horizon. The uncertainty of this correction, together with that caused by an ill-defined horizon, forms the main limitation on precision; it arises partly from the uncertainty of the height of eye (an error of 1 m at a height of 10 m means

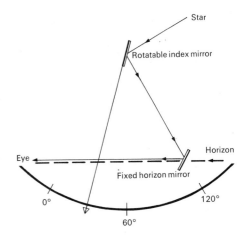

Fig. 5 The principle of the sextant: the angle of rotation of the index mirror is precisely half the altitude of the star being observed

an error of 0′.3) but mainly from uncorrectable variations in the densities of the lower air layers; in excellent conditions total errors might be kept down to a maximum of 0′.5, but in average conditions errors of this size are likely to occur on about half the occasions.

In order that the observed altitude may be compared with that calculated for an ideal observer situated at the centre of the earth, corrections have to be applied for atmospheric refraction, PARALLAX and, where appropriate, SEMI-DIAMETER and phase. These corrections are, however, readily tabulated and are often combined into a single correction. Refraction is due to the slight curvature of the path of a ray of light through the atmosphere, which is caused by the varying air density with height; for all except very low altitudes (say less than 5°), which are not to be recommended in any case because of atmospheric extinction, the correction for refraction is determined with a precision comparable to that of observation.

The correction for parallax arises from the angular displacement of a nearby object against the background of the distant stars between the position as seen by an observer on the surface of the earth and the ideal observer at the earth's centre. It is significant to navigational accuracy only for the moon, for which the correction can reach more than 1°; although it is easily applied, it may be noted that a shift of about 10 km in the observer's position could make a difference of 0′.1 in the correction. In principle, therefore, if a topocentric (i.e., as seen by the observer on the surface of the earth) position of the moon among the stars could be observed to a precision of 0′.1, the shift (in the two coordinates) from the calculated geocentric position would, in the favourable circumstances of the moon being high in the sky, provide data to give the observer's position to within,

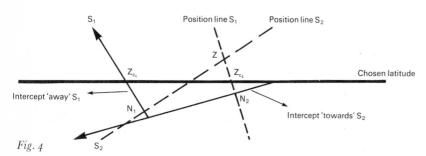

S₁
Position line S₁   Position line S₂
Z
Z_{c_1} Z_{c_2} Chosen latitude
Intercept 'away' S₁   N₁   N₂   Intercept 'towards' S₂
S₂
Fig. 4

say, 15 km, or nearly 10 miles, without recourse to any vertical reference. The method provides much greater potential accuracy when the object observed is a close artificial satellite; the parallactic shift is so large that, provided the satellite is bright enough to be seen, visual estimation of position to, say, $0°.1$ will give the observer's position to within about 1 km. Unfortunately neither of the above procedures is practicable, the first because of the difficulty of observation and the second because geocentric positions of artificial satellites are not generally available to the navigator.

The parallactic method for the moon should not be confused with the historic method of lunar distances, to which it bears a superficial resemblance; lunar distances were used (in broad principle) to give the observed geocentric position of the moon among the stars, the appropriate corrections for parallactic shift being applied in the reduction; this observed position was then compared with the predicted position to give the GMT to which the observation corresponded. An observer may move 10 km due to the rotation of the earth in about 25 sec, in which time the moon will move about $0'.2$, while the parallactic shift could by $0'.1$. This illustrates one of the serious difficulties that made the successful use of the method of lunar distances in the determination of longitude such a triumph for all concerned – not least the navigator.

As with all forms of position-line navigation, optimum results depend on the judgment of the navigator in interpreting information that is always subject to uncertainty – and often internally inconsistent. Techniques for handling such information have been developed, ranging from simple intuitive rules to extreme sophisticated computer programs. Fortunately very few navigators need to have the optimum precision that astronomical navigation can provide: a positional accuracy of a mile or two will suffice for most requirements and this is well within the practical limits. Almost any of the (many) procedures of reduction (almanacs, sight reductions, corrections etc.) will provide adequately for this precision; the critical factor, in respect of precision as well as applicability, lies in the observations. Apart from the possibility of blunders (which occur relatively frequently) in the reductions, it can be said that, for the average navigator, the precision of his fix is directly proportional to that of his observations. The best way of avoiding the effect of blunders is, first, to reduce their occurrence by noting that they tend to arise in the simplest processes over which even greater care should be taken, and, second, always to have more observations than the minimum; it is then that the navigator can exercise his judgement – he will rarely require more sophisticated statistical aids.

The stars are not always available and it is part of the navigator's task to know the sky, by day as well as by night, and to plan his observations to best accord with his requirements. He now receives much help: *The Nautical Almanac* tells him of the availability of the moon and planets, provides him with star charts, and gives him rising, setting, and twilight data. And the *Sight Reduction Tables for Air Navigation* AP 3270 (American: HO 249), volume 1: *Selected Stars* provides the best selection of seven stars at any time or place. Designed for air navigation, and with a tabular unit of $1'$ only, it nevertheless provides the simplest set of star tables for surface navigation – and its limitations are probably acceptable to most.

To use astronomical navigation efficiently the navigator needs to know the sky, to make careful observations with a precision instrument often in poor conditions, to take out data from almanacs and tables, to do some numerical calculations, to plot clearly; he need know little astronomy and requires no great computing skill, but at all times he must exercise skill, care, and judgement.

A number of hand-held calculators and special computers with an astronavigational facility have recently been developed and, because of the speed and simplicity of the solution, may be expected increasingly to supplant or supplement reduction tables at sea. Typically, for the entries latitude, longitude, GHA, declination, and corrected altitude, a calculator may display intercept and azimuth and, in the more advanced models, combine the results of a number of sights to obtain a fix. Even the simplest 'mathematical' calculator will facilitate the extraction of the data and the numerical computation needed to reduce a sight.

See also MARINE CHRONOMETER; NAVIGATION; NAUTICAL ALMANACS

Astronomical triangle
The triangle used in the solution of ASTRONOMICAL NAVIGATION problems.

Athwart
Across, at right angles to the fore-and-aft line.

A-trip
The anchor is a-trip when it has broken out of the ground and is ready for weighing.

A-try
Lying in a gale under trysail only. *See* HEAVY-WEATHER SAILING

Auto-steering devices *see* SELF-STEERING GEAR

Auxiliary engines
Inboard or outboard power units fitted in sailing vessels for occasional use.

– size
An auxiliary engine should be capable of propelling a yacht at not less than 5 knots in smooth water. The tidal stream in many estuaries runs at 3 knots or more, and it may be necessary to motor against this when there is little or no wind. Or, there may be a strong headwind blowing against a favourable tide. In shallow water this will produce short steep seas that have a considerable stopping effect on a displacement hull. The WINDAGE of masts and standing rigging will still further reduce speed.

The designer will calculate the horsepower required to drive a given hull at the desired speed. This will be in the region of 2 hp per ton displacement for hulls in the 25 to 30-ft-range, becoming less for larger sizes. The horsepower arrived at may well have to be increased by 20% to cater for emergencies, but any additional horsepower installed for increasing speed is subject to economic limitations. The economic speed at which a displacement hull may be driven is related to the waterline length. Roughly this works out at 6 knots for 25 ft and 8 knots for 35 ft. The cost of increasing these speeds by just 1 knot is high. An engine of double the horsepower will be needed with a corresponding increase in fuel cost.

– type
The main option is between inboard and outboard. An inboard engine is to be preferred, but it may be difficult to modify an existing hull to take one. On the other hand an outboard motor may be attached to almost any hull designed primarily for sailing. Where either is practicable a balance between economic considerations and personal preference has to be arrived at. For example, the relatively high cost of an inboard diesel engine cannot be justified on account of low fuel cost alone if it will only be used for a few hours or so each day. A petrol (gasoline) engine of the same horsepower will be cheaper and a small outboard which causes no drag when sailing will cost even less. Nevertheless, an inboard diesel may still be preferred for low fire risk, easy starting, and better general reliability due to the absence of spark-ignition equipment.

INBOARD ENGINES
An inboard engine may be sited anywhere along the centreline of the boat to suit the internal layout. Somewhere aft of amidships is desirable to avoid excessive length of shafting with attendant alignment problems. The engine may be inclined at a small angle to the horizontal so that the propeller is placed well below the waterline with the engine at a higher level for better access. The maximum angle of inclination is determined by the lubricating system and must not be exceeded without advice from the engine makers. The V-drive makes it possible for an engine to be

Inboard auxiliary engine. This V8 petrol (gasoline) engine develops 375 bhp and weighs 885 lb (400 kg)

placed well aft and high up without excessive tilt. The engine is fixed with the output shaft facing forward and coupled to a special gearbox that reverses the direction of drive so that the propeller shaft passes back beneath the engine (fig. 1).

An inboard marine engine is similar in most respects to one used for a road vehicle. The principal differences are: the exhaust manifold is usually water cooled, a pump is provided for draining the sump, and a heavy-duty ball bearing is fitted to the output shaft of the reverse or reduction gearbox to transmit propeller thrust to the hull. The engine and reverse gearbox form a single unit to which may be bolted a speed reduction or a V-drive gearbox, which may include speed reduction if required. The equivalent of the clutch in an automobile is built into the reverse gearbox and operates automatically as the gear shift is moved. Reduction of engine speed before each operation is necessary to prevent excessive wear on the clutch element. A single lever controlling speed and gear will ensure that this is done, but separate levers controlling each function will give better control when manoeuvring. This may be of some importance in a twin-screw motor launch. The sailing man who uses his engine only for short periods will prefer the single-lever control.

Some small engines have only a clutch and no reverse gear. Others drive a variable-pitch propeller that might have two or three blades. The propeller shaft rotates in one direction only and the pitch of the blades is altered

by a control rod inside the hollow propeller shaft to give ahead, astern, and neutral drive. No clutch is needed, and reduction of engine speed before each operation is not crucial because the horsepower absorbed by the propeller reduces as the blades move towards the neutral position, and gradually increases as the drive is taken up in the opposite direction.

Propeller drag cannot be entirely eliminated, but will be reduced to a minimum by using a two-bladed folding or feathering propeller on the centreline. Some resistance will still be caused by turbulence set up if the propeller is housed in an aperture between the hull and rudder. The alternative is for it to be offset to one side and as low down as possible. Performance under sail will be good, but the propeller is more exposed to damage and there will be some loss of efficiency due to the thrust not being directly aft, and steering under power will be poor, especially astern. A folding propeller causes the least drag as the two blades are hinged so that they lie parallel with the shaft when not in use and open up to the working position by centrifugal force as the shaft begins to turn. Some trouble may be experienced by the hinges becoming stiff during long periods of idleness, and a blade shape that will lie close to the shaft when folded is far from efficient. This, however, is not of great importance in a low-horsepower installation. A feathering propeller works on the same principle as the variable-pitch type. When sailing the blades are turned past the full-ahead position until

the faces are parallel with the shaft. Under power the efficiency is less than that of a solid propeller because the blade shape has to be modified from the ideal to lessen resistance when sailing. A solid two-blade propeller fitted on the centreline is robust and efficient. To reduce drag when sailing the shaft is locked with the blades vertical. This is only effective so long as the rudder post is thick enough to deflect the flow of water clear past the blades.

The resistance of a solid propeller may be reduced to almost zero if it is free to rotate at a speed to match the flow of water past the hull. For this purpose a sailing clutch is fitted to disconnect the propeller shaft from the engine. At low speeds the friction of the stern gland packing may be enough to prevent the shaft turning at the optimum speed, and performance will be improved by locking the shaft. This will be a matter for experiment in each case. A shaft brake or sailing clutch may be used to protect a hydraulic gearbox that would be damaged if driven by the propeller when the supply of oil from the engine is not available. Another method is to use the equivalent of a sailing clutch operated by oil pressure so that it automatically disengages when the engine stops.

In brief, although a propeller of the correct diameter and pitch may be fitted, some loss of efficiency under power has to be accepted if performance under sail is of prime importance. The additional fuel cost will not be great if the engine is only to be used for an hour or so each day. On the other hand, for a cruising yacht, which is expected to spend more time under power, the need for keeping down fuel cost and the number of hours of use could be more important than fast sailing. The owner must decide which is the more important.

The principal advantages of an inboard engine are: durability due to heavier construction and moderate operating speed, low oil consumption and smooth slow running because, generally, lubricant is not mixed with the fuel, and superior specific fuel consumption. Although heavier than the equivalent outboard motor, the siting of the inboard engine inside the hull makes for better fore-and-aft trim and affords protection for offshore working. The propeller may be sited as far below the waterline as the draught of the boat will permit for efficiency under power and to give some measure of protection against fouling or damage by floating rubbish.

There is a wide choice of petrol (gasoline) and diesel models in the 1.5-hp to 20-hp range, all designed for marine use at speeds ranging from 1200 rpm to 2500 rpm. Others are marine versions of well-tried road-vehicle engines that are often cheaper and lighter, but operate at speeds up to 4500 rpm. Factors to be taken into consideration when deciding between the purpose-built marine engine and an automotive conversion are cost, availability of spares and service, and noise level.

All but the smallest unit may be fitted with 2:1 or 3:1 reduction gearboxes. Propeller thrust is taken by a heavy-duty ball bearing located in the reverse or reduction gearbox (if fitted). A locating bearing should be fitted aft of a sailing clutch.

Against the advantages of an inboard engine must be set the cost of the installation of engine bearers, fuel tanks, propeller shafting, cooling and exhaust pipework. Substantial engine bearers are needed to distribute weight and driving forces inside the hull and to preserve good alignment. A flexible coupling fitted close to the reverse/reduction gearbox will take care of minor misalignment due to flexing of the hull, but a firm engine bed and good initial lining-up are essential to keep down the wear on the stern tube bearing and gland packing. One or more fuel tanks have to be built into the hull with filling connections and vents on the weather deck. Water-cooled engines require hull fittings and associated pipework for the circulating water. Dry or wet exhaust systems are used. The former is similar to that in an automobile with an expansion chamber for silencing. Careful installation is necessary to avoid damage to the surroundings by radiant heat. The wet system is to be preferred. The exhaust gases are silenced and cooled by injecting the engine cooling water discharge into the line as close to the engine as possible. From there onward tough rubber hose is used, installation is simplified, and there are no fire risks or corrosion problems as long as the cooling injection is maintained.

Air-cooled engines up to 100 hp are available that cannot be damaged by frost and can work in shallow weed-infested waters. They may be less than the price of a similar water-cooled model, and the cost of installation is reduced since no hull fittings or pipework is needed. Provision has to be made for a free flow of cooling air which could be inconvenient if the engine is to be mounted under the cockpit sole, and a safe route has to be found for the uncooled exhaust pipe. They are inclined to be more noisy than water-cooled engines.

Outboard engines
The outboard motor is a 1 self-contained power unit designed for clamping or bolting to the transom of a boat, or in a well in the stern or interior. The principal advantages are: ease of installation, low weight per horse-power, and the tilt mechanism or a suitable mounting bracket that allows the propeller to be raised above water for weed clearing, beaching or to reduce drag when sailing; also, they are portable and accessible for service and repair. The range of motors extends

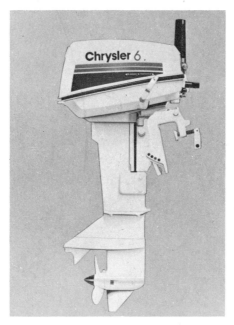

Outboard auxiliary engine. This typical two-stroke unit suitable for smaller boats develops 6 bhp (4.5 kw), weighs 53 lb (24 kg), and has a fuel-tank capacity of 5 British, 6 US gal (23 litres)

from light, low horsepower units for dinghies and inflatables to those developing 150 hp and weighing 400 lb (180 kg) or more. All have the same basic layout of one or more horizontal cylinders with a vertical crankshaft driving the propeller through an extension shaft and bevel gears that give a speed reduction between 1.5:1 and 3:1. The majority have 2-stroke petrol engines, mainly to keep down cost of production.

Ignition
Single- and 2-cylinder motors have a flywheel magneto with a separate coil and contact breaker for each cylinder. For three or more cylinders a distributor-type magneto, battery-operated coil ignition or coil ignition

fed from a flywheel alternator may be used. Part of the rectified alternator output can be used for battery charging so that power is available for engine starting, lighting, and intrumentation. The capacitor discharge (CD) system fitted to larger models permits the use of surface-gap plugs which are largely immune from fouling and need no adjustment. Timing may be by a contact breaker as used in a normal coil ignition system, or a magnetic pick-up is used to trigger a solid state switch controlling the direct current (DC) supply from the capacitor to the coil primary winding (fig. 1).

Lubrication
In 2-stroke motors lubrication is achieved by mixing a controlled amount of oil with the petrol. The proportion varies from 10:1 to 100:1 according to make of engine. The grade and quantity of oil added must be strictly in accordance with the maker's instructions. No other routine attention is needed. A recognized drawback of the system is the fouling of sparking plugs. This may be overcome by using the 4-stroke cycle with crankcase lubrication. Regular oil changes at about 25-hour intervals are, however, needed, and as a rule the units are heavier and more expensive. Underwater gearboxes containing bevel gears are either filled with high viscosity oil or packed with grease, according to make.

Steering and tilt
The engine and propeller leg swivel about a vertical hinge pin so that the full thrust of the propeller is directed right or left for steering. Manoeuvrability is good except at low speeds. When used as an auxiliary the motor can be set in the ahead direction and the boat steered by its own rudder. A second hinge pin, mounted horizontally, allows the unit to tilt for raising the propeller clear of the water and for adjusting the mounting angle so that the propeller shaft lies parallel with the water at different angles of transom or trim. It also allows the motor to lift if the SKEG strikes an

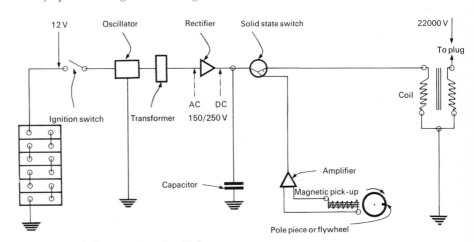

Fig. 1 Schematic diagram of capacitor-discharge ignition system

underwater obstruction. When going astern an automatic lock prevents lifting.

Gears

The smaller motors have no astern gear, but some may be swivelled through 360° to give astern thrust. Most models from 6 hp up have ahead and astern gears with selection by dog clutch in the underwater bevel gearbox. Interlocking of the throttle and gear shift is desirable to prevent damage by changing gear without slowing down.

Installation and control

Whether or not the motor is clamped on the transom or to a bracket the load is concentrated in a small area. To test for strength, lock the tilt gear in the raised position and press down firmly on the propeller. Any flexing of the transom may be cured by fitting a doubling piece to spread the load. A boat-builder should be consulted if there is any movement between the side planking and the transom during this test. When transom mounting is not possible the motor may be hung over one side from a transverse member securely fastened to the deck or both gun-wales. Correct mounting is important. With the boat in seagoing trim the motor should hang vertically so that the propeller shaft lies parallel with the water surface. Thrust directed away from the horizontal wastes power by attempting to push the boat's head up-wards or downwards instead of ahead. In-correct depth setting also wastes power; too shallow and the propeller thrust will be reduced by cavitation, too deep and engine output will be lowered by back pressure on the underwater exhaust. Standard motors are made for transom heights of 15 in and 20 in, measured as shown in fig. 2. When the motor cannot be tilted due to the power head fouling the transom, a bracket mounted on slide rails or swinging links can be used to raise it vertically clear of the water.

Standard motors up to 25 hp are fitted

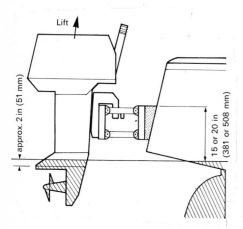

Fig. 2 A mounting bracket is used when a transom is unsuitable for the direct mounting of a standard outboard motor

with tiller steering that carries the throttle control, the gear shift being mounted on the power head. Remote steering, throttle, and gear controls may be fitted to most motors of 6 hp and upwards. Remote steering is considered to be an unnecessary complication for auxiliary use. For most purposes it will be possible to use the yacht's rudder with the outboard set to drive straight ahead. The need for remote throttle and gear control will depend on how easily the motor can be reached from the steering position, in the case of auxiliaries; in power craft remote steering, throttle and gear controls are essential for the safety of the crew and total control of the boat's movement. Unlike an inboard installation, single lever control of both functions is preferred for simplicity.

Starting

Hand-starting is used for engines up to 20 hp and optional electric starting is available on most models from 10 hp up. Recoil or self-rewind starters are easier to use than the simple pull cord and only need a minimum of maintenance.

The electric start is essential for large engines and a convenience on small ones, but there may be some difficulty in keeping the battery charged if the engine is only used for short periods.

Fuel supply

The fuel tank forms an integral part of small outboards. Filling up in a seaway is difficult but at least the spillage falls overboard, though there is a risk of water splashing in the tank. Portable tanks with self-sealing hose connections are in general use. Within the length of hose supplied they may be placed forward of the motor to improve weight distribution. Refuelling at sea is only a matter of unplugging the hose and connecting it to a full tank. Tanks must be properly secured for sea voyages to prevent fuel leaks due to a fractured hose or damaged tank. They should always be refilled ashore in order to minimize fire risk.

Propellers

For best results the outboard motor should run as close to the designed speed (rpm) as possible. This will be determined by the choice of propeller. A small diameter, low-pitch propeller cannot absorb the full engine output without overspeeding; loss of drive due to cavitation and unnecessary wear and tear will result. On the other hand, a large, coarse-pitch propeller will overload the engine so that it cannot reach its designed rpm. High fuel consumption, excessive carbon deposits, and plug failures will follow. Most manufacturers offer a range of standard propellers. Expert advice should be sought as to the one best suited to the weight and underwater shape of the hull that is to be driven.

See also ELECTRICS; HULLS; MAINTENANCE

Avast
The order at sea to stop or hold.

Awash
Just covered by water.

A-weather
On the weather side; to windward.

Azimuth
The direction of a celestial body measured clockwise through 360° in the horizontal plane. *See also* ASTRONOMICAL NAVIGATION

B

Baby stay *see* MASTS AND RIGGING: Glossary

Back
(1) To sheet the clew of a sail to windward;
(2) said of the wind when it shifts against the movement of the sun, or anti-clockwise.

Back splice *see* ROPEWORK: Splices

Backstaff
A modification of the cross staff in which the observer stood with his back to the sun so that the shadow cast by a crosspiece, or 'shade vane', or the bright spot from a pinhole in that vane, fell upon a slit in the 'horizon vane' at the end of the staff and was brought into coincidence with the sea horizon. The backstaff was invented by the Englishman John Davis, or Davys, two forms being described in his *Seaman's Secrets* published in 1594.
In the simpler form the ALTITUDE was read by sliding the crosspiece along the graduated staff; it was only suitable for altitudes up to about 45°. In the 90° backstaff, or Davis quadrant, the horizon vane was viewed through a sight vane on a separate graduated arc below the staff; the shade vane on a graduated arc above the staff was first set to a value some 10° or 20° less than the altitude and the sight vane was then moved along its arc to obtain an exact coincidence between the shadow on the horizon vane and the sea horizon. The altitude is the sum of the two angular settings.
Later improvements included a small lens on the shade vane to focus an image of the sun on the horizon vane and a diagonal scale on the sight vane reading the angle to 1′ of arc. Although only suitable for observing the sun the backstaff, unlike the cross staff, had the great advantage of not requiring the observer to look in two directions at once, or directly at the sun. It continued in use until superseded by the reflecting quadrant and SEXTANT in the eighteenth century. *See also* NAVIGATION: Historical

Backstay *see* MASTS AND RIGGING: Glossary

Backwind
One sail backwinds another when it directs the wind on to its lee side. A boat may be backwinded, accidentally or deliberately, when another boat to windward douses it with this turbulent, or 'dirty' air as it is sometimes called.

Baggywrinkle
Ends of manila rope stranded between lengths of marline to form a bushy protection to prevent the sails from chafing against the rigging.

Bail *see* MASTS AND RIGGING: Glossary

Ballast keel
A shaped keel, generally of lead or cast iron, which is used to give a yacht stability under sail.

Balloon jib
A light-weather jib set for reaching in place of the working jib. *See also* RIGS: Fore-and-aft rigs

Bar
A shoal at the mouth of an estuary or harbour entrance.

Barometer
An instrument for measuring the pressure of the atmosphere, needed at sea as an aid to appreciating the meteorological situation. The mercury barometer was invented by the Italian Evangelista Torricalli in 1643: a long glass tube is filled with mercury and inverted over a vessel, the cistern, also containing mercury. It was soon noticed that changes in the weather were associated with a rise or fall of the mercury column and before the end of the century the Englishman Robert Hooke (1635–1703) had demonstrated a marine barometer to the Royal Society in London. Marine barometers differ from the types used ashore in having a very narrow neck at the bottom of the tube to prevent violent surges in the mercury due to the motion of the ship. The aneroid barometer is, however, more convenient for use at sea. A metallic capsule nearly exhausted of air is prevented from collapsing by a strong spring, the pressure of which in response to changes in pressure is magnified by a train of levers to move a pointer over a scale. Barometers were formerly calibrated in inches or millimetres of mercury, but now generally in millibars: the bar is the meteorological unit of pressure

1000 mb = 750.1 mm = 29.531 in

Until about 1920, when two Norwegian meteorologists, Vilhelm Bjerknes and his son Jakob, developed the theory of frontal depressions, the correlation of the height of the barometer to changes in wind and weather was largely empirical. Admiral Fitzroy's *Remarks on New Zealand* (1846) and the mnemonic verse often inscribed on old barometers summarized the relationship for temperate latitudes; the LAW OF STORMS was for reducing the danger of tropical cyclones. *See also* WIND AND WEATHER: Meteorological instruments

Barque (bark); barquentine (barkentine) *see* RIGS: Square rigs

Baseline *see* HYDROGRAPHIC SURVEYING

Beam
(1) Transverse member of a vessel on which the decks are laid; (2) the extreme width of a vessel; (3) on the beam *see* ABEAM

Beam ends
A vessel is said to be on her beam ends when she is heeled so that her masts are horizontal.

Bear away
To turn further away from the wind.

Bearing
The direction of one point from another in the horizontal plane, measured in relation to true north, compass north, or relative to HEADING (and thus termed true, compass, or relative bearing).

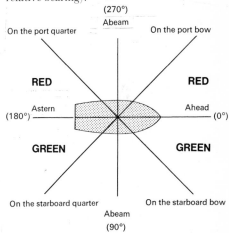

Relative bearings of objects are given in relation to the ship's head

Beat
To sail to windward by tacking, putting the wind first on one bow then the other.

Beaufort wind scale *see overleaf*

Becket (sheet) bend *see* ROPEWORK: Bends and hitches

Bee block *see* MASTS AND RIGGING: Glossary

Beitáss
A luff spar used in Viking ships to enable them to claw to windward.

Belay
To make fast a rope on a bollard, pin, cleat etc.

Belaying pins *see* MASTS AND RIGGING: Glossary

Bend *see* ROPEWORK

Beneaped *see* NEAPED

Bermudian rig *see* RIGS: Fore-and-aft rigs

Beaufort wind scale

Admiral Sir Francis Beaufort (1774–1857), hydrographer to the Royal Navy, originated this system of describing wind force, which in a later form was to find international acceptance. The scale comprises the numbers 0–12, equated with wind strengths as in Table I (*right*). The figures for wave height are the probable average heights in the open sea, away from land; the figures in parentheses are the probable maximum heights in these conditions. Near land, or in enclosed waters, waves will be steeper but not so high.

The descriptions in Table II have been adapted from a table in Alan Watts, *Instant Weather Forecasting* (St Albans, Hertfordshire, and New York 1968). They show the typical conditions the yachtsman will encounter at each wind strength on the Beaufort scale up to the practical limits for dinghies (0–7) and deep-keel vessels (0–10).

Bight

A loop in a rope.

Bilges *see* HULLS: Construction components

Binnacle

The receptacle that houses the compass.

A modern pedestal-mounted, domed binnacle compass

Bitter end

(1) The extreme of a line; (2) the inboard end of a line.

Table I

BEAUFORT NUMBER	DESCRIPTION	MEAN WIND SPEED IN KNOTS	M/SEC	PROBABLE MEAN WAVE HEIGHT IN METRES
force 0	calm	0–1	0–0.5	—
1	light air	1–3	0.5–1.5	0.1 (0.1)
2	light breeze	4–6	2.0–3.0	0.2 (0.3)
3	gentle breeze	7–10	3.5–5.0	0.6 (1)
4	moderate breeze	11–16	5.5–8.0	1 (1.5)
5	fresh breeze	17–21	8.5–10.5	2 (2.5)
6	strong breeze	22–27	11.0–14.0	3 (4)
7	near (US: moderate) gale	28–33	14.5–17.0	4 (5.5)
8	(US: fresh) gale	34–40	17.5–20.0	5.5 (7.5)
9	strong gale	41–47	21.0–24.0	7 (10)
10	storm (US: whole gale)	48–55	24.5–28.0	9 (12.5)
11	violent storm (US: storm)	56–63	28.5–32.5	11.5 (16)
12	hurricane	64 and over	33.0 and over	14 (–)

Table II

BEAUFORT NUMBER	DINGHY CRITERIA	DEEP-KEEL CRITERIA	STATE OF SEA
0	Sails will not fill. Racing flag will not respond. Flies and telltales might just respond	Boom swings idly in the swell. Racing flags and anemometers will not respond. Flies and tell-tales might just	Sea mirror-smooth. Calm enough to preserve shape of reflections of sails, masts etc.
1	Sails fill. Racing flag may not be reliable. Flies and telltales respond. Crew and helmsman on opposite sides of craft	Sails just fill, but little way made. Racing flags and vanes may respond but cup anemometers may not. Flies and tell-tales respond. Spinnakers do not fill	Scaly or shell-shaped ripples. No foam crests to be seen on open sea
2	Useful way can be made. Racing flag reliable. Helmsman and crew both sit to windward. Spinnakers may fill	Wind felt on the cheek. Controlled way made. Spinnakers and sails generally fill. Racing flags and anemometers respond and are reliable	Small short wavelets with glassy crests that do not break
3	Helmsman and crew sit on weather gunwale. Spinnakers fill. Fourteen-footers and above may plane	Good way made. Light flags fully extended	Large wavelets. Crests may break but foam is of glassy appearance. A few scattered white horses may be seen when wind at upper limit
4	Dinghy crews lie out. Twelve-foot dinghies may plane: longer dinghies will plane. The best general working breeze	Best general working breeze for all craft. Genoas at optimum	Small waves lengthen. Fairly frequent white horses
5	Dinghies ease sheets in gusts. Crews use all weight to keep craft upright. Genoas near their limit. Some capsizes	Craft's way somewhat impeded by seaway. Genoas near their limit. Spinnakers still carried. Yachts approach maximum speed	Moderate waves. Many white horses

6	Dinghies overpowered when carrying full sail. Many capsizes. Crews find difficulty in holding craft upright even when spilling wind	Edge of 'yacht gale' force. Cruising craft seek shelter. Reefing recommended to meet gusts when cruising	Large waves form and extensive foam crests are prevalent. Spray may be blown off some wave tops
7	Dinghies fully reefed. Difficult to sail even on main alone. This is the absolute top limit for dinghies – other than *in extremis*	Yacht gale force when most cruising craft seek shelter. Racing yachts may just carry spinnakers. Reefing essential	Sea heaps up and white foam from breaking waves begins to be blown in streaks along the wind direction
8	Dinghies may survive if expertly handled in the seaway on foresail alone	Gale force in any terms. Only necessity or ocean racing keeps craft at sea. Set storm canvas or heave to	Moderately high waves of greater length. Edges of crests begin to break into spindrift. Foam blown in well-marked streaks along the wind
9	Not applicable	Unless ocean racing – and sometimes even then – craft seek deep water. Run towing warps etc. This may be survival force for most	High waves. Dense streaks of foam along the wind. Crests begin to topple, tumble, and roll over
10	Not applicable	Almost the ultimate for yachts. Only chance in deep water and with sea room to run before it or possibly lie to	Very high waves with long overhanging crests. The whole surface of the sea takes on a white appearance. Tumbling of sea heavy and shocklike. Visibility impaired

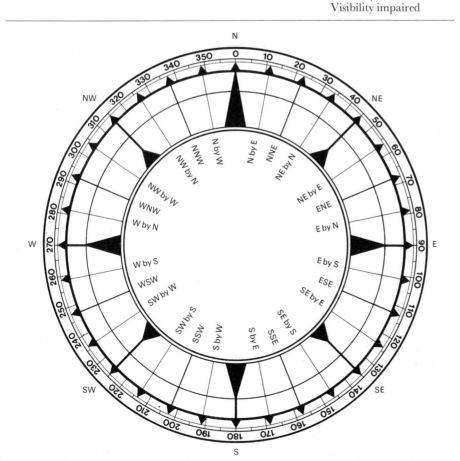

Boxing the compass: the names of the 32 points of the compass are shown here; the names of the half and quarter points vary according to the system used in boxing the compass. In the United States Navy, for example, the next clockwise quarter point from ENE is ENE¼E, but in the Royal Navy it would be called E by N¾N, as it is read back from the next point (E by N)

Blackwall frigate
Name given to the ships built, many of them at Blackwall on the Thames, for trade to the East after the East India Company's exclusive charter had expired in 1833.

Blackwall hitch *see* ROPEWORK: Bends and hitches

Blocks and tackle *see* PURCHASE

Board
A windward leg, or tack, when beating.

Bobstay *see* MASTS AND RIGGING: Glossary

Bollard
A post of iron or timber to which a vessel's warps may be made fast alongside.

Bolt rope
A rope sewn around the edge of a sail to take the strain off the cloth.

Boom *see* MASTS AND RIGGING: Glossary

Boom vang (kicking strap) *see* MASTS AND RIGGING: Glossary

Boot topping
The mixture formerly painted on ships' bottoms to inhibit weed and barnacles; the various anti-fouling paints do this now.

Bottle screw (rigging screw) *see* MASTS AND RIGGING: Glossary

Bower anchor
A ship's principal anchor, lowered from the bows.

Bowline *see* ROPEWORK: Bends and hitches

Bowsprit
A spar projecting over the stem of a sailing vessel to stay the foretopmast, and on which the jibs are set.

Boxing the compass
The recitation in succession of the names of the points, half points, and quarter points of the compass. This was a means formerly

adopted for teaching the young seaman. There are at least three rules for determining from which points the half and quarter points shall be named. For example, in the Royal Navy quarter points are never measured from points whose names begin and end with the same letter; in the British merchant navy measurement is never made from an intermediate point; in the United States Navy measurement is only made from an intermediate point when on the east or west side of it. *See also* MARINER'S COMPASS

Brace
A rope (or wire) that controls the horizontal movement of the yards in a square-rigged vessel.

Brail
A rope, or ropes, whose function is to gather a loose-footed sail into the mast.

Breaking strains *see* MASTS AND RIGGING; ROPEWORK

Breast hook *see* HULLS: Construction components

Breeze, land
A wind blowing offshore, generally by night when the sea is warmer than the land. *See* WIND AND WEATHER: Local winds.

Breeze, sea
A wind blowing onshore, generally by day when the land is warmer than the sea. *See* WIND AND WEATHER: Local winds.

Brig, brigantine *see* RIGS: Square rigs

Bring up
To anchor.

British-American Cup *see* YACHT RACING: Major races and series

Broach to
To fly involuntarily into the wind when running before a heavy sea so that the wind is brought on the beam.

Bulkheads *see* HULLS: Construction components

Bull's eye
A round wooden sheaveless block for altering the lead of a line.

Bulwark
A protection of planking or steel built round the edges of the top deck to prevent people or gear from being washed overboard in heavy weather. *See also* HULLS: Construction components

Buoy
A buoy is a floating object that is generally moored to the sea bed, but may be free-floating. Buoys are mainly used for navigational purposes to mark a channel, shoals and dangers, or to indicate areas of interest to navigation, such as spoil grounds or military firing. The ends of fishing nets, and other equipment lowered into the water, such as scientific instruments, are frequently marked

by buoys, which may be free-floating or moored depending on the purpose for which they are being used.

Buoys can vary in size from a spar of wood to large steel structures with their own power supplies that exhibit powerful lights. Some buoys are now constructed in glass-reinforced plastic. Details of buoys are shown on navigational charts against a buoy symbol where their colours, light characteristics, and sound signal are given according to a standard abbreviation code.

Lanbys and some of the more important landfall buoys are given in lists of lights published by national hydrographic offices. Some authorities publish lists of buoys, but Britain does not do so.

– navigational buoys
A large navigation buoy usually consists of a steel flotation drum about 10 ft (3 m) in diameter and $6\frac{1}{2}$ ft (2 m) in depth, weighing about 6 tons. The shape of the buoy is provided by a lattice superstructure, which may be conical, can, spherical, or pillar. A light, radar reflector, and/or topmarks may be fitted above the superstructure.

Within the drum there are pockets for housing the acetylene-gas cylinders or electric batteries for the light.

Buoys are moored with stout chain to iron or concrete sinkers or clumps of about 6 tons in weight depending on the nature of the sea bed. A bell or whistle FOG SIGNAL is sometimes fitted. These are usually operated by wave action on the buoy; they can therefore be unreliable in calm weather, which often occurs in low visibility. Whistles and the clappers of bells are sometimes worked by compressed gas to give a regular signal.

The majority of lighted buoys have gas-operated lights, the characteristics of which are controlled by an automatic valve, but in some countries electric lights powered by long-life storage batteries are used. Lighted buoys can generally operate for 6 to 12 months without attention.

HIGH-FOCAL-PLANE BUOYS
These are pillar buoys with the superstructure high enough to give the light an elevation of 20 to 27 ft (6–8 m). These buoys are generally used in offshore landfall positions.

LANBY (OR LIGHTHOUSE BUOY)
Lanby is an acronym for *l*arge *a*utomatic *n*avigation *buoy*. These are very large buoys consisting of a steel drum about 40 ft (12 m) in diameter and surmounted by a steel tower about 40 ft (12 m) high. Lanbys display a powerful light and are equipped with a sound signal, and they may also have a radio-beacon. Control of the light and fog signal is entirely automatic and they can continue operating for about 6 months without attention, but their performance is continually monitored from ashore.

Lanbys are replacing manned light vessels

Broach to. The Italian yacht Tarantella *about to broach in stormy conditions off the Isle of Wight*

in some instances as they are much less expensive to maintain and can be moored in depths of up to 330 ft (100 m).

ODAS BUOYS

ODAS is short for *ocean data acquisition system*. These are large special-purpose buoys carrying a number of scientific sensors for monitoring sea temperature, salinity, air temperature, and several other parameters. They can be moored in oceanic depths or they may be free-floating. They generally resemble a pillar buoy and are usually painted in red and yellow vertical stripes if anchored, and in horizontal bands if free-floating.

DAN BUOYS

Small temporary marks consisting of a flotation drum with a wooden spar about 10 ft (3 m) long through the centre. The lower end of the spar carries a ballast weight to keep it upright in the water. A flag, topmark or light may be fixed to the upper end. In deep water extra flotation can be given by adding small floats to the mooring wire. *See also* BUOYAGE SYSTEMS

– mooring buoys

These are used to support the moorings for vessels in harbours where swinging room is restricted, or for greater security than the anchors of a vessel can provide. They vary in size from small plastic floats for boat moorings to steel drums 20 ft (6 m) in diameter that may also have telephone connection to the shore.

In the offshore-oil industry massive mooring buoys have been developed to secure very large tankers at the seaward end of oil pipelines in exposed areas. These can vary from ordinary large-sized mooring buoys a few metres in diameter to huge manned floating structures of several thousand tonnes displacement, which provide special mooring facilities for the tanker as well as the oil hoses to lead to the tanker.

Buoyage systems

In European waters buoys for navigation first came into use in the fifteenth and early sixteenth centuries. A Royal Charter to Trinity House in 1514 regulated the laying of buoys in England. The first buoys were laid in the Thames Estuary about 1538. Early buoys consisted of baulks of timber and later wooden barrels; metal buoys came into use about the same time as ships of iron or steel began to replace wooden ones.

IALA high focal plane buoy (top) *stationed off the east coast of England*

A Lanby buoy (centre) *undergoing trials in the English Channel off Portland Bill*

The ODAS buoy DBI (left) *before being towed to its station in the southern North Sea in Autumn 1975*

In 1882 a conference was held at Trinity House in London to establish a uniform system of colours and shapes for buoys. From this conference a lateral system (*see below*) evolved in which can-shaped buoys had to be left on the port hand, conical buoys on the starboard hand, and spherical buoys were to be used for marking middle grounds. Britain adopted this system and extended it to areas of the British Empire.

In 1889, at an International Marine Conference in Washington attended by most of the maritime nations, another lateral system was recommended. This differed from the British system in that it relied mainly on colour rather than shape, with starboard-hand buoys painted red and port-hand buoys black or parti-coloured.

Thereafter various conferences were convened in an attempt to establish a much-needed common system, but with limited success before the 1970s.

Navigational buoys are generally laid according to one of two main principles, namely lateral or cardinal. By day, the significant features of a mark are its colour, shape, and topmark; by night, the colour and rhythm of its light.

– lateral system

The lateral, or side-marking, system has distinctive shaped or coloured buoys to mark the port (left) or starboard (right) side of the navigable water according to an established direction of navigation; this is usually 'from seaward', 'proceeding with the main flood stream', or an arbitrarily established direction.

– cardinal system

The cardinal, or compass-marking, system has buoys of differing colour, shape, and/or topmark to indicate the compass quadrant in which the buoy is moored relative to the danger or point of interest it marks. Thus a north cardinal buoy is moored on the north side of a danger (i.e. a mariner should pass to the north of it).

– Uniform System of Buoyage (1936)

This international system was drawn up by a League of Nations convention to cater for, and render compatible, lateral and cardinal marking. Unfortunately, many countries had not ratified the system when most of the buoyage in European waters was swept away by World War II. After the war some nations adopted the 1936 recommendations, but with many differences of interpretation; thus, for example, a vessel sailing from the Atlantic to the Baltic may encounter several different national systems, mostly cardinal and with a certain amount of agreement in topmarks. The lateral form is in use in Britain, but conversion to the IALA System 'A' (*see below*) is to be completed by the end of 1981, as well as in other European waters. Some areas of former British interest overseas also use the Uniform Lateral system with local variations.

Briefly, the Uniform System allows for the following main types of buoys:

Starboard-hand marks are conical and painted black, black and white in chequers, or black and yellow in chequers, with white lights showing one of three flashes or occultations.
Port-hand marks are can-shaped and painted red, red and white in chequers, or red and yellow in chequers, with red lights showing up to four flashes or occultations. White lights may be used showing two or four flashes or occultations.
Middle-ground (bifurcation or junction) marks are spherical and painted red and white, or black and white, horizontal bands with various topmarks to indicate on which side the main channel lies.
Mid-channel or landfall marks are pillar buoys painted black and white, or red and white, in vertical stripes. When lit they exhibit lights that cannot be confused with other lights in the vicinity.
Wreck-marking buoys are painted green and may be can, conical, or spherical in shape depending on the side to which they should be left. When lit they exhibit green lights.
North cardinal marks are conical and painted black-white-black horizontally with a cone (point upwards) topmark. When lit they exhibit a white light showing an odd number of flashes.
South cardinal marks are can-shaped and painted red-white-red horizontally with a cone (point downwards) topmark. When lit they exhibit a red light showing an even number of flashes.
West cardinal marks are can-shaped and painted black above white with a two-cone (point to point) topmark. When lit they exhibit a white light showing an even number of flashes.
East cardinal marks are conical and painted red above white with a two-cone (base to base) topmark. When lit they exhibit a red light showing an odd number of flashes.
Spoil-ground marks are painted yellow above black.

– red-to-starboard systems

UNITED STATES SYSTEM OF BUOYAGE
This is essentially a lateral system. It is sometimes referred to as a 'red-to-starboard' system (and contrasts with the red-to-port systems of northwest Europe).

The shapes of the buoys have less significance than the colour, but there are two basic shapes, can and conical (often referred to as 'nun' buoys) as shown in fig. 1.

The direction of buoyage is defined as from seaward towards the head of navigation, but as this definition cannot always be applied, additional assumptions have to be made. In general terms these are: southward along the Atlantic coast; north and west along the

Port-hand marks — Lighted buoy, Can buoy
Starboard-hand marks — Lighted buoy, Can buoy

United States buoyage system – as seen entering from seaward. The port-hand marks are black with odd numbers, and the lights of the lighted buoys are green or white, flashing or quick flashing. The *starboard-hand marks are red, with even numbers, and lights are red or white, flashing or quick flashing*

coasts of Gulf of Mexico; and northward along the Pacific coast.

Buoyage systems in other countries of North and South America are, in general, variations on the United States system, with the common denominators of being entirely lateral, and red to starboard.

CHINESE AND JAPANESE SYSTEMS OF BUOYAGE
Although the buoyage systems used in China and Japan differ considerably in the shapes and colours of the buoys, both countries use a lateral system with red to starboard.

– IALA Maritime Buoyage System 'A'

Despite the many attempts to reach international standardization of the characteristics of buoyage, there were at least 30 different systems in use throughout the world in early 1971 when a series of accidents in the Dover Strait resulted in the loss of 51 lives.

In 1973, the International Association of Lighthouse Authorities (IALA) asked its technical committee to recommend an international system of standardized buoyage. Following successful trials in the Thames Estuary and by the West Germans in the Baltic, a simple unambiguous system known as IALA Maritime Buoyage System 'A' was accepted by almost all maritime countries in northwest Europe.

Alteration to the buoys in northwest Europe began on 18 April 1977 and the whole area from the Bay of Biscay to northern Norway and the Baltic is scheduled to be changed by the end of 1981 (fig. 2). The west coast of Spain, Portugal, and the west of the Mediterranean will probably be converted to System 'A' by 1983. Other areas may also change, although there is no date for a complementary System 'B' to be introduced in the Americas and other countries favouring the red-to-starboard system.

The basic principle of System 'A' is that the lateral and cardinal systems are combined but the link with the direction of main flood-tide is changed to a 'General Direction of Buoyage' that follows a clockwise direction around the great continental landmasses. Fig. 3 shows how, in certain areas, the old

direction of buoyage may be reversed. Within estuarine waters the local direction of buoyage will continue to relate to the direction taken by a mariner when approaching from seaward. The direction of buoyage will be described in SAILING DIRECTIONS and, where doubt might exist, will be clearly shown on charts by a large, magenta arrow.

The system applies to all fixed and floating marks except lighthouses, sector lights, leading marks, light vessels and 'lighthouse buoys', i.e. very large, navigational buoys. It thus includes almost all lighted and unlighted beacons (except leading marks) that will use the same shaped and coloured topmarks as buoys.

The main features of the system are its simplicity and lack of ambiguity. It includes only five types of marks, which may be used in any combination:
Lateral marks to show port and starboard sides of well-defined channels.
Cardinal marks to show where deep water lies relative to the mark.
Isolated danger marks to indicate dangers of limited extent with navigable water all round.
Safe-water marks to indicate navigable water all round and under the mark.
Special marks to mark special areas or features rather than to assist navigation.

The system includes no special buoys for marking wrecks and so all new dangers will be indicated by the internationally agreed marks; mariners must refer to charts and other documents to find out the significance of special marks.

LATERAL MARKS
A port-hand lateral mark must be a solid red, can-shaped buoy and/or topmark; a starboard-hand, lateral mark must be a solid green (or, exceptionally, black) conical (point upwards) buoy and/or topmark. Apart from the change from black to green for starboard-hand marks, an important feature of a System 'A' lateral mark is its light. No white lights are used but, as red and green lights are strictly reserved for port and

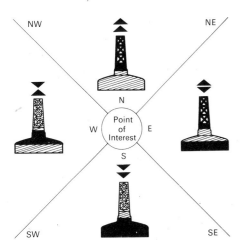

Port-hand marks · Starboard-hand marks

Navigable channel

Direction of buoyage

Lateral marks: port-hand marks are red; starboard-hand are green (exceptionally black). Topmarks are always fitted if the buoy is not can or conical. The lights are the same colour as the buoys and are used in any rhythm

starboard lateral marks, these colours are used in any rhythm (quick flashing, flashing, long flashing, group flashing, occulting, group occulting, etc. *See also* LIGHTS: Characteristics of lights

CARDINAL MARKS
All cardinal marks must be pillar or spar buoys, in combinations of black and yellow colours, with important black double-cone topmarks – as large as is practicable in the prevailing weather conditions. The combinations are:
North cardinal mark Black above yellow with two black cones, pointing upwards (i.e. to the north on charts).

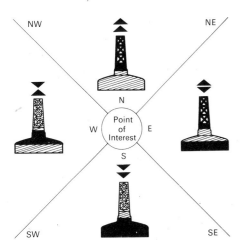

Cardinal marks: topmarks are always fitted, when practicable, and buoy shapes are pillar or spar (the latter is illustrated). White lights distinguish the buoy as a cardinal mark. Their characteristics indicate the mark's quadrant: north – uninterrupted very quick flash or quick flash (V Qk Fl or Qk Fl); east – 3 very quick flashes every 5 seconds (V Qk Fl (3) 5s) or 3 quick flashes every 10 seconds (Qk Fl (3) 10s); south – 6 very quick flashes plus long flash every 10 seconds (V Qk Fl (6) + L Fl 10s) or 6 quick flashes plus long flash every 15 seconds (Qk Fl (6) + L Fl 15s); west – 9 very quick flashes every 10 seconds (V Qk Fl (9) 10 s) or 9 quick flashes every 15 seconds (Qk Fl (9) 15s)

East cardinal mark Black with single, horizontal, yellow band, with two black cones, base to base.
South cardinal mark Yellow above black with two black cones, pointing downwards (i.e. to the south on charts).
West cardinal mark Yellow with single, horizontal, black band with two black cones, point to point.

The lights on cardinal marks are most ingenious; white lights are used, with a group of unique very quick or quick flashes based on a clockface. Thus an east cardinal mark will have 3 flashes in a group; a south mark 6, followed by a long flash to distinguish it from east and west marks; a west mark 9; and a north mark uninterrupted flashes in the group. Adjacent cardinal buoys may use quick- or very-quick-flashing lights to differentiate one from another.

ISOLATED DANGER MARKS
The shape of an isolated danger mark is not significant but, if it is a buoy, it will be a pillar or spar buoy, painted black with one or more horizontal red bands. Each will have two black spheres as a topmark and, if lit, a white light will show a group of two flashes.

SAFE-WATER MARKS
These marks must have red and white vertical stripes; spherical buoys or pillar or spar buoys with a single, red, spherical topmark may be used with an occulting, isophase or single long-flashing white light every 10 seconds.

SPECIAL MARKS
Special marks must be yellow, with a yellow light and sometimes a yellow X-shaped topmark; the shape of the mark usually conforms with that which would be used for a navigational mark in that position, but yellow lights must not have the same characteristics as any used for white lights. Special marks indicate cables, spoil grounds, quarantine or other anchorage areas, ODAS (*see* BUOY) etc. Nautical documents and charts must always be consulted.

Any new danger must be marked by the most appropriate marks and lights; until its details have been adequately promulgated, at least one such mark may be duplicated and may carry a Racon, coded W (· – –) showing a signal length of 1 nautical mile on radar displays.
See also PILOTAGE

Buys Ballot's law
A way of estimating the direction of the centre of a storm from the direction of the true wind. *See* WIND AND WEATHER: Large-scale winds

By the lee
Running with the wind on the lee quarter and, in a fore-and-aft-rigged vessel, the same side as the boom.

Cable *see* GROUND TACKLE

Caique
In general terms, a small Levantine sailing vessel, often with a lateen rig. The name is also applied to skiffs and rowing boats of the region.

Camber
The athwartship curve of a deck.

Cam jammers *see* MASTS AND RIGGING: Glossary

Canadian Olympic Regatta Kingston (CORK) *see* YACHT RACING: Major races and series (Pre-Olympic regattas)

Canadian Yachting Association *see* UNITED STATES YACHT RACING UNION

Cap; cap shroud *see* MASTS AND RIGGING: Glossary

Capetown-Rio *see* YACHT RACING: Major races and series.

Capsize *see* HEAVY-WEATHER SAILING

Capstan *see* GROUND TACKLE

Cardinal system, cardinal marks *see* BUOYAGE SYSTEMS

Carlings *see* HULLS: Construction components

Carrick bend *see* ROPEWORK: Bends and hitches

Carvel *see* HULLS: Construction components

Catamarans *see* HULLS: Hull forms; MULTIHULLS

Cathead *see* HULLS: Construction components

Cat rig
A fore-and-aft rig, generally for small boats, with a single sail set on a mast stepped very far forward.

Catspaw *see* ROPEWORK: Bends and hitches

Celestial meridian
A great circle of the celestial sphere through the zenith and the celestial poles.

Centreboard classes *see* DINGHIES AND CENTREBOARD CLASSES

Centre of effort (CE)
The centre of gravity of a sail plan considered as a plane.

Centre of lateral resistance (CLR)

The point assumed to be the centre of gravity in the plans of a vessel's underwater profile.

Chain plate *see* MASTS AND RIGGING: Glossary.

Chart datum

The tidal datum to which the soundings on a chart refer.

Chartmaking *see* HYDROGRAPHIC SURVEYING

Chart projections *see* MAP AND CHART PRO-JECTIONS

Check

To ease away slowly, as with the sheets under sail.

Chinese rig

The Chinese, or junk, rig may be described as a fully battened, balanced lugsail, and its main features are shown in fig. 1. The mast A is traditionally (and preferably) completely unstayed regardless of the size of vessel, and stands up as a cantilever supported only at the partners B and step C. The sail lies permanently on one side of the mast, in this case on the port side, although many Chinese sails in fact lie on the starboard side.

A proportion of the sail, varying between about 5% and 30% of its area, lies forward of the mast, and this percentage is known as the balance. A halyard D from the masthead raises the yard E that is attached to the head of the sail. A number of stiff, full-length battens F divide the sail into panels and keep it stretched from LUFF to LEECH, thus being attached to the sail along most of their length as well as at their ends.

The sheet G is a single rope forming a purchase whose deck anchorage at M is a treble block. The sheet controls the whole leech through sheet spans H that are secured to the ends of each batten and the boom J. The sheet and its spans may take a great variety of forms, but their purpose remains the same – to control both the incidence of the sail to the boat and its 'twist' (i.e. the difference in incidence between the head and the foot), and to hold the leech of the sail down when REEFED or FURLED.

Each batten is held close to the mast by a batten parrel K, commonly of rope. One or two other running or standing ropes (not shown) hold the yard-sling point close to the mast and the forward ends of the battens and the boom back towards the mast. A system of topping lifts L, which may be either standing or running, passes through eyes under the boom and extends up both sides of the sail to a point at or near the masthead. A 'mast lift' (not shown) serves to support the forward end of the boom. These lifts are slack when under full sail, but as soon as the halyard is started they support the boom and gather the furled part of the sail and its battens automatically, rather like a Venetian blind.

To reef to any required degree it is simply necessary to lower the sail until the desired number of panels have furled themselves in the lifts. The sheet and any hauling parrels (*see* MASTS AND RIGGING: Glossary) will have gone slack as the sail comes down, and these are now set up again to complete the job. Fig. 2 shows the same sail reefed down to two panels (for gales), with four panels furled.

Although simple in conception the geometry of the rig is fairly subtle and imposes a number of limitations on the shape and battening of the sail if it is to reef and furl neatly. Only one sail is set on each mast but any number of masts may be used. Since the sail remains always on the same side of the mast it is sometimes to windward of the mast and sometimes to LEEWARD of it, but unlike the Western lug rig (*see* RIGS: Lateen and lug) it is

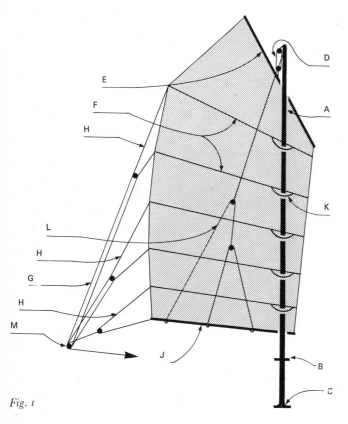

Fig. 1

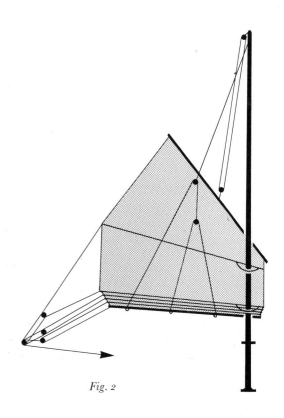

Fig. 2

efficient in either position. If the sheets are arranged to swing automatically clear of the leech of the sail when tacking or gybing, these manoeuvres call for no deck work other than steering; the rig looks after itself, and is notably 'softer' to GYBE than a gaff or Bermudian mainsail.

The history of the rig has remained somewhat conjectural, but recent research by Dr Joseph Needham, *Science and Civilisation in China*, Vol IV: 3, Cambridge University Press, has provided a broad basis of historical fact, some of it rather astonishing to the Western mind. The Chinese lug sail, made of bamboo matting and stiffened by bamboo or pine battens, is believed to have originated in China before AD 300. By 1430 the seagoing junks of the Ming dynasty seem to have been substantially larger than any ships of the Western world and to have voyaged in huge fleets at least as far as the Red Sea and East Africa. The great junks of this time are believed to have reached 500 ft (150 m) in overall length, which is far larger than any seen since and nearly twice as long as the clipper *Cutty Sark*, built in 1869 and now preserved as a museum ship at Greenwich, London. But by the sixteenth century the Ming navy had all but vanished, a victim of political change,

leaving only the smaller coasters and river traders that have continued to develop in design, though not in size, into the twentieth century. These include junks 180 ft (55 m) long with a 30-ft (9-m) beam and with anything up to five masts, some of them over 6 ft (1.8 m) in diameter at the partners and carrying mainsails of over 3000 ft² (280 m²).

From Marco Polo (?1254–1324) onwards, Western observers on the China coast have become fascinated by junks in their endless variety of size and type, and have praised their efficiency as practical sailing craft while struggling to understand the thinking of Chinese shipwrights and sailors which seemed so often to be the exact opposite of their own. The Chinese rig was one of the earliest of the true fore-and-aft rigs, that is to say rigs in which the wind blows against opposite sides of the sail on opposite TACKS. For centuries it may have been the most efficient windward rig in the world, particularly in hard winds where the flat sail develops good drive while inducing minimal leeway. The windward ability of Western rigs has been transformed in fairly recent times by the development of high-quality sailcloth and sophisticated sailmaking. Previously, all large flax sails tended to develop too much 'belly' for

windward work; seamen were continually seeking ways of making them set flatter. The Chinese sail can be made to set very flat in all wind strengths, regardless of whether it is made of good sailcloth, bamboo matting, or indeed old flour sacks. Modern junk sails are made of low-grade cotton cloth, but this is believed to be more a matter of durability and convenience than of aerodynamic efficiency.

There is no standard type of sail in China, and every conceivable variation seems to exist there. Fig. 3 shows some of the shapes of sail recorded in the past 50 years, notably by G. R. G. Worcester in *Junks and Sampans of the Yangtze*, first published in 1947. The square-headed sail (fig. 3a) seems to be the ancient shape and is still widely distributed, particularly on inland waters in the high-aspect-ratio form shown in fig. 3b. The remaining sketches show forms in which the yard is more steeply angled, that of fig. 3f (the foresail of a three-master) having a yard that is actually in line with the luff. It will be seen that the number of battens, and hence the width of the panels, also varies very considerably. As in the West, the different types of sail found in different districts seem to be dictated as much by fashion as by logic, and it is not easy to

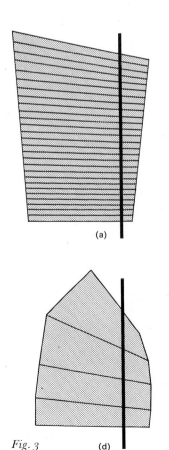

(a)

(d)

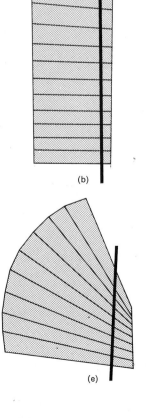

(b)

(e)

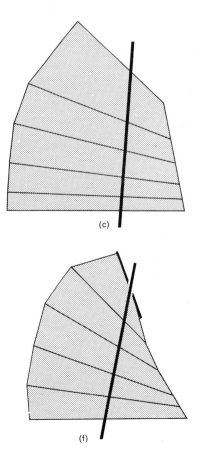

(c)

(f)

Fig. 3

analyse the pros and cons of the different forms.

All native Chinese rigs share a number of common features. They are constructed of cheap and readily available materials with hardly any metal parts. The subdivision of the sail into a number of separate panels, each supported and controlled by its own system of sheets, battens, and parrels, ensures that the stresses are shared between a considerable number of load-carrying members and that no one part takes a heavy load except for the mast and halyard. The loads on sailcloth and sheets are vastly less than with the Western rig, and it is difficult to think of any other rig in which a 3000-ft^2 seagoing sail could be made of bamboo matting and yet be able to sail through a gale without damage. In many ways it is valid to think of a Chinese sail as being a number of much smaller sails joined together.

Because of its balanced area forward of the mast and because the sheet controls the whole leech the sail commonly shows little or no 'twist', whereas Western rigs, particularly the gaff rig, often develop far too much twist in a hard breeze. The hulls of many Chinese work boats have very little lateral resistance, and there is evidence that such hulls go to windward better with the Chinese than with Western rig.

A large Chinese sail is extremely heavy. Junk mainsails may weigh as much as 5 tons and have two or more separate halyards with a yard more than 65 ft (20 m) long. It can take the whole crew over an hour to hoist such a sail, but reefing or furling is a matter of seconds and, if the halyards are kept ready to let go, the rig is almost squall-proof.

Chinese vessels usually carry large and expert crews who are prepared to do a lot of 'fiddling' with the rig, such as flicking the sheet spans clear of the leech when tacking or gybing. By accepting this sort of deck work they are able to use a wide variety of sail shapes and rigging layouts. When the sail is set a Chinese seaman can reach any part of it by climbing around on the battens and parrels, which provide a natural climbing frame. If, through old age or misuse, a Chinese sail becomes torn or lets go a seam, the damage remains localized and the repair may be postponed indefinitely. The Western observer, laughing at the sight of a junk with her sails full of holes, may overlook the fact that she is working briskly to windward through a crowded anchorage.

It is easy to sail tolerably well with the Chinese rig but rather difficult to get the best out of it, since the sail gives little indication of being at a wrong angle of incidence to the wind, or to the boat. On all points of sailing the sheet should be further out than the sheet of a gaff or Bermudian sail. When CLOSE-HAULED, it should be sheeted more like a headsail than a Western mainsail, and boats rigged with a single Chinese sail usually go best to windward with the end of the boom well out over the rail. Even with correct sheeting it is difficult to know how close to sail to the wind, since the sail will go on drawing when the boat is pointing too high and sailing too slowly.

On a REACH in a fresh breeze, with the sheet well off, the sail is particularly efficient, developing plenty of drive with very little heeling force. On a broad reach or run the absence of shrouds enables the sail to be squared right off at right angles to the boat, thereby giving maximum efficiency and greatly reducing the possibility of an accidental gybe.

Since 1960 there has been a marked revival of interest in the use of Chinese rig on Western vessels, but the requirements of Western seamen are different from those of the Chinese in a number of ways. Commercial sail is almost extinct in the West, but there has been an increasing demand for yachts, i.e. vessels (whether of commercial origin or not) used only for recreation or cruising.

Chinese rig: Michael Richey at the helm of Jester.
The self-steering vane gear is clearly seen

Many Western yachtsmen now want to make long open-sea passages in very small boats, an ambition that has never been evident in China. Many also want to sail single-handed, or with a weak crew of family or friends that may not include any other competent seaman. The advent of wind-vane steering gear has made it possible for these short-handed boats to make long passages efficiently, provided that the rig can be easily handled. The Chinese rig has proved incomparable at providing this ease of handling, together with safety and sailing efficiency, with the help of a certain amount of fresh development work that started in 1960 and is likely to go on for some time to come. As developed in Britain, the rig is 'fully automatic' in that all sail handling, including reefing and furling, is done simply by veering or hauling ropes without ever touching the sail itself. All the running ropes may be led to the steering position and there is no need for the watchkeeper to move around the deck – a valuable safety factor in a small boat coping with a gale in open water.

In the 25-ft (7.6-m) *Jester*, which was rigged in 1960 with a single Chinese sail, the cockpit was eliminated and the boat handled from an enclosable control position amidships. The watchkeeper stands waist-high out of a small hatch when handling the rig or the vane gear. By 1978 *Jester* had sailed at least 40 000 miles (74 000 km) of open sea, including nine single-handed crossings of the North Atlantic, four of them as a competitor in the Single-handed Transatlantic Races. Her best time of 37 days 22 hours from Plymouth, England, to Newport, Rhode Island, has only once been beaten by a single-handed boat of less than 26 ft overall.

In the 47-ft (14-m) *Ron Glas* (plate 2), built in 1971 with a two-masted 'Chinese schooner' rig, the control ropes were for the first time led inside a wheelhouse so that all sail handling can be done from a fully enclosed position, thus approaching the watchkeeping conditions of a motor vessel. By 1976 *Ron Glas* had sailed many thousands of miles of open water, including four crossings of the North Atlantic, two of them as a competitor in the Singlehanded Transatlantic Races. Neither of these boats has suffered any trouble with her rig, and their Atlantic crossings have been unusually effortless.

In 1972 Bill King completed a single-handed circumnavigation of the world by way of the Cape of Good Hope and Cape Horn in the 42-ft (13-m) *Galway Blazer II* (see p. 194), believed to be the first Chinese-rigged vessel ever to have sailed down the Roaring Forties. Under a new owner she has since completed the 1976 Singlehanded Transatlantic Race without incident, and has logged over 50 000 miles in 8 years' service.

Ron Glas, *a two-masted 'Chinese schooner'*

In 1975 the Chinese rig was offered for the first time as an alternative to the Bermudian rig on a stock 21-ft (6.4-m) fibre-glass cruising yacht *Pilmer* (plate 4), and the public response was enough to encourage the fitting of the rig to other stock hulls. These boats use unstayed, light-alloy masts of quite small diameter, and have a performance that compares well, on average, with that of the Bermudian-rigged versions while offering extreme ease of handling together with improved accommodation below, since it is no longer necessary to stow spare sails in the fore-cabin. Only one sail is carried with the Chinese rig, and it remains permanently bent. *Pilmer* made a non-stop, single-handed passage entirely under sail from Poole in Dorset, England, to Loch Sween on the west coast of Scotland, a distance of 540 miles in 7 days 7 hours through constantly varying wind conditions including spells of gale-force winds. She logged 64 'sail changes' (i.e. reefing or unreefing), an average of one every 2½ hours, day and night, without exhausting her crew or ever requiring him to get out on deck until she came in to anchor at the end of the voyage.

By facilitating this sort of passage-making the Chinese rig is enlarging the scope of small cruising yachts and setting new standards for short-handed seamanship. In demanding a fully automatic sail the Western designer accepts many more restrictions on the shape of the sail and the layout of the rig than his Chinese counterpart, but his work remains wholly based on the result of 1700 years of continuous empirical development in China.

See also MASTS AND RIGGING; RIGS: Lateen and lug rigs (Balanced lug).

Chock-a-block (two-blocked)

The position when two blocks of a tackle have come together and no further movement is possible.

Choke the luff

A method of jamming a tackle by leading the hauling part across the SHEAVE of the block.

Chronometer *see* MARINE CHRONOMETER

Clamp *see* HULLS: Construction components

Class racing *see* YACHT RACING

Claw off

To sail off a lee shore.

Claw ring *see* MASTS AND RIGGING: Glossary

Cleat *see* MASTS AND RIGGING: Glossary

Clevis pin *see* MASTS AND RIGGING: Glossary

Clew

The lower after corner of a fore-and-aft sail, or the lower corners of a square sail.

Clinker (lapstrake), clincher, clenched
lap *see* HULLS: Construction

Clipper *see* RIGS: Square rigs

Close-hauled

Sailing as close to the wind as possible with the sails full and not shivering.

Close-winded

A vessel is said to be close-winded if she can point well to windward.

Clouds *see* WIND AND WEATHER

Clove hitch *see* ROPEWORK: Bends and hitches

Coaming(s) *see* HULLS: Construction components MASTS AND RIGGING: Glossary

Cocked hat

A triangle formed by three POSITION LINES, adjusted to a common time, that do not meet at a point.

Cold front *see* WIND AND WEATHER

Collision regulations

(International Regulations for Preventing Collisions at Sea)
– early sea laws

The problem of avoiding collisions at sea is almost as old as navigation itself, but the earliest recorded sea laws that mention it are the laws of Rhodes. These appear to date from the third or second century BC. They were certainly incorporated into Roman law

Choking the luff is a quick and simple way of preventing a rope from running through a block in situations like that illustrated. Freeing the hauling part allows further movement to take place

by AD 161, although the earliest known copy dates from Byzantine times, between AD 600 and 800.

The Rhodian laws were mainly concerned with the commercial aspects of shipping, but there is a chapter that provides that when a moving ship collides with a stationary ship, the moving ship should be held to blame. The necessity for keeping a proper lookout and for making warning light and sound signals is also mentioned. The Rhodian laws formed the basis of a number of Mediterranean codes and it has been suggested that knowledge of these was spread through northwest Europe by returning Crusaders.

By about the mid-twelfth century, the laws of Oléron had been written down on the island of that name off the southwest coast of France, near La Rochelle. In these laws, or 'judgments' as they were termed, the provision concerning collisions differed from the Rhodian in that the cost of damage resulting from accidental collision was required to be divided equally between the two parties; the expressed intention was that old ships should not purposely be put in the way of better ships.

The thirteenth-century laws of Visby (the port of Gotland and an important commercial centre in the Middle Ages) were generally similar to the Oléron code, but were based in part at least on earlier practice in the Baltic area.

– naval rules

The early sea laws dealt with the allocation of blame after a collision had occurred but, with the development of sea power in the form of large and highly structured navies, it became necessary to allocate some responsibility for taking preventive action to avoid collision between ships. The convention was then that ships of junior rank should give way to ships of senior rank. Although based on etiquette, this was nevertheless a practical convention in that it generally implied that smaller and handier ships were required to keep out of the way of larger and less manoeuvrable vessels.

At the end of the eighteenth century, the first rule specifying positive action for avoiding collision between ships was introduced by Lord Richard Howe (1726–99) of the Royal Navy. This stated that 'ships of war are to bear up for each other, shorten sail, etc. without regard to the seniority of the Commanders or other claims of distinction, in such manner as shall be found most convenient on either part. But when ships are upon different tacks and must come near to each other the ship on the starboard tack is to keep her wind while that on the larboard tack is always to pass to leeward' The implementation of this rule is illustrated in fig. 1, which shows that it requires the ship on the larboard (port) tack to alter course to starboard. It is important, not only in that it has survived

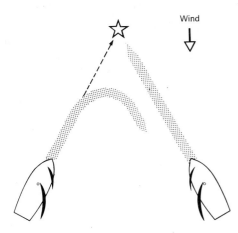

Fig. 1 Lord Howe's Rule

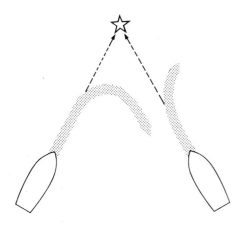

Fig. 2 Port Helm Rule

almost unaltered for sailing ships today, but also in that it has formed the basis for our entire system of rules for preventing collisions between ships.

– steamship rules

Lord Howe's rule was applied by merchant ships as well as warships and seems to have sufficed until steamships began to appear in significant numbers at the beginning of the nineteenth century. At first, steamships were confined to rivers and inland waters, and a variety of local rules were developed to regulate their navigation. As steamships ventured around coasts and eventually across the oceans, a rationalization of the rules became necessary and in 1840 the British Trinity House Corporation took an initiative in promulgating what they considered should be the proper practice of seamen at that time.

The most important of the Trinity House rules was the so-called Port Helm Rule which provided that: 'When steam vessels on different courses must unavoidably cross so near that, by continuing their respective courses there would be risk of collision, each

vessel shall put her helm to Port so as always to pass on the larboard side of each other.' The implementation of this rule is illustrated in fig. 2.

The principal defect of this rule arose in encounters where ships would pass closely but safely if no action were taken on either part. In such cases, one of the ships would sometimes alter course in accordance with the rule and thereby convert a safe passing into a collision. This defect led to the governments of Britain and France developing a completely new system of rules that came into operation in 1863.

– international rules

Although developed bilaterally, the 1863 rules were adopted internationally with extraordinary rapidity so that, by the end of 1864, they had been adopted by over 30 maritime nations, including the United States. In the 1863 rules, for the first time all the collision-avoidance rules, whether steering and sailing rules or rules concerning light and fog signals, were collected together and given equal force of law. Also the rules were recast into a form and expressed in a literary style that remain clearly evident today. Of the radical changes introduced, the most important was the replacement of the universal Port Helm Rule by separate rules covering six circumstances under which ships might come into conflict.

– international conferences

In 1889, a first International Conference to consider the rule of the road at sea was convened on the initiative of the United States government and held in Washington. This conference was notable for the acceptance of two practices already in common use on the United States coast and in inland waters. The first of these was the requirement that vessels altering course to avoid collision should indicate their action by making whistle signals. The second was the adoption, in a permissive form, of a second white masthead light for steamships to give a better indication of their headings. The main recommendations of the Washington Conference were implemented by the end of the nineteenth century and thereafter remained virtually unchanged for over 50 years.

At an International Maritime Conference held in Brussels in 1910, the Collision Regulations were placed on a true international basis. Amendments to the regulations were discussed also at the Safety of Life at Sea conferences in London in 1914 and 1929, but in neither case were the recommendations ratified. A conference in London in 1948 agreed to some minor changes in the regulations and these came into force in 1954. A further conference in 1960 was the first to be held under the auspices of the Intergovernmental Maritime Consultative Organization (IMCO) and it resulted in a

number of important changes to take account of the increasing use of radar as a means of avoiding collisions at sea. These regulations came into force in 1965.

– the current regulations

In 1972, an IMCO Safety of Life at Sea Conference in London agreed on a new set of collision regulations that came into force in 1977. These comprise largely a streamlining and rearrangement of the previous regulations, but there are also some significant changes in principle. A completely new rule was included concerning the conduct of vessels in traffic separation schemes, and the rule requiring that one of two vessels in a crossing encounter should maintain course and speed was relaxed.

The 1972 regulations are arranged in four main parts, lettered A to D. Part A contains rules of a general nature, dealing with applications, definitions, and responsibilities. Part B comprises steering and sailing rules that establish the conventions by which ships should avoid collision under a number of different circumstances. Part C contains rules dealing with identification lights and shapes to be carried by vessels of different classes. Part D contains rules specifying the light and sound signals to be used by vessels when manoeuvring, when in restricted visibility, and when in distress. There are also annexes to the regulations which contain technical specifications of lights and sound signals prescribed in the body of the regulations.

– interpretation

Any practical interpretation of the Collision Regulations should only be made on the basis of a detailed study of the regulations themselves, but a general appreciation of the way in which they operate is as follows:

a. For encounters between two sailing vessels, the principle is that the vessel that has the wind on the port side should give way to the vessel that has the wind on the starboard side (i.e. Lord Howe's rule). If both vessels have the wind on the same side, the vessel to windward is required to give way to the vessel to leeward (*see* fig. 3).

b. When two power-driven vessels are meeting on nearly reciprocal courses each is required to alter course to starboard (*see* fig. 4).

c. When two power-driven vessels are crossing, the vessel that has the other on her own starboard side is required to give way, and should generally avoid crossing ahead of the other. *See* fig. 5 and note the similarity to Lord Howe's rule.

d. A vessel overtaking any other is required to keep out of the way of the overtaken vessel.

e. Where, by any of these rules one of two vessels is to keep out of the way, the other is required to keep her course and speed. Such a vessel *may*, however, take action (other than an alteration of course to port for a vessel on her port side) if it becomes apparent that the

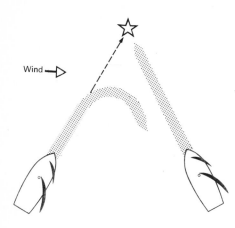

Fig. 3 Two sailing vessels with the wind on the same side

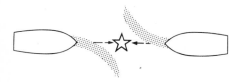

Fig. 4 Power-driven vessels meeting on reciprocal courses

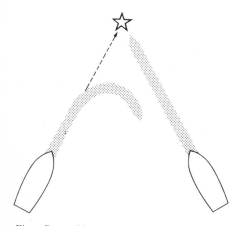

Fig. 5 Power-driven vessels crossing

vessel supposed to keep out of the way is not taking appropriate action. Also, she is *required* to take avoiding action at a late stage when collision cannot be avoided by the action of the give way vessel alone.

f. Since all vessels do not have the same manoeuvring capabilities, an order of precedence is established, ranging from a power-driven vessel, to a sailing vessel, a vessel fishing, a vessel constrained by her draught, a vessel not under command and a vessel restricted in her ability to manoeuvre: the convention being that when two such vessels meet, the vessel higher in order should give

way to the vessel lower in the order.

g. The above provisions (a) to (f) apply when vessels are in sight of one another. In restricted visibility the requirements are less precise and there is no necessity for either vessel in an encounter to maintain course and speed. Every vessel is required to go at a safe speed, to make full use of all available lookout facilities including radar, and to take action if possible to avoid being too close to other vessels. If risk of collision cannot be avoided, ships should reduce speed to bare steerage way and, if necessary, stop.

– application
The International Regulations for Preventing Collisions at Sea are applicable to all vessels upon the high seas and in all waters connected therewith, navigable by seagoing vessels. It is, however, provided that special rules made by appropriate authorities for rivers, harbours, lakes, and inland waters should take precedence over the International Regulations, although it is intended that any such local rules should comply as closely as possible with the corresponding international rules. Thus the rules for avoiding collisions in the inland waterways of the United States and on the Great Lakes are similar in principle to the international rules but have differences in detail to take account of the special navigational conditions in these areas.

Commercial sail *see* TRADING UNDER SAIL

Compass *see* GYROCOMPASS; MARINER'S COMPASS

Compass card
This name replaced the earlier word 'fly' about the mid-seventeenth century. From the end of the fourteenth century a cardboard disk was attached to the compass needle so

that courses other than N and S could be readily determined. The card was at first marked with the points, half points, and quarter points of the compass (*see* WIND ROSE) and these were later supplemented by graduation in degrees.

At first degrees were measured from 0° at N and S to 90° at E and W, but during the last hundred years a change has been made and cards are now usually graduated from 0° at N all the way round clockwise to 360°. In the Royal Navy this change was delayed for magnetic-compass cards until the 1940s: to avoid confusion it was preferred to limit the 360° notation to true courses given by the gyrocompass. The tendency of cardboard to warp led to cards being made of paper-covered mica. With the introduction of the liquid compass a card of mica, plastic, or even metal became a necessity. *See also* BOXING THE COMPASS; MARINER'S COMPASS

Compass point
A division of the compass card: 1/32 of a circle or $11\frac{1}{4}°$. *See also* BOXING THE COMPASS; COMPASS

Compass rose *see* WIND ROSE

Composite Omega
A form of OMEGA in which the differing propagation characteristics of the three frequencies in the system are used to give a first order correction to the position fix in place of the detailed table of predicted variations otherwise used.

Conn, con
To direct a craft by verbal orders, as from the master to the helmsman or quartermaster when manoeuvring.

Consol
A radio aid to navigation in which medium frequencies (192–363 kHz) are transmitted from a shore station in a multilobe pattern sending Morse dashes. The intervals between are occupied by dots coming from a displaced pattern so that in specific equisignal directions a continuous note is heard. These directions recur at 15° intervals and over a period of about one minute the composite radiated pattern is rotated through this angle. An observer within a given sector will thus hear a number of dashes before these are merged into the equisignal tone and changed to dots. By counting the dashes and referring to a chart or table the true bearing of the Consol station is determined. The correct sector must be identified from a prior knowledge of the approximate direction.

A modern compass card marked in points, half points, quarter points, and degrees

The junk-rigged version of the Sunbird 32, designed by Alan Boswell. There is also a sloop-rigged version

An accuracy of $0°.6$ at a range of 300 km is a representative figure; SKYWAVE effects at night and at greater distances degrade this to the order of $2°$ at 1500 km.

Stations are in operation over western Europe, and parts of the Soviet Union. Since the only shipboard equipment is a radio receiver that can be tuned to medium frequencies, the system is of particular use to fishing and pleasure craft.

Construction *see* HULLS

Convergence *see* WIND AND WEATHER: Atmospheric pressure and weather systems

Copper sheathing
A method, first introduced in the eighteenth century, of protecting the bottom of wooden vessels against worm, and weed and barnacles, by sheathing her below the waterline with sheets of thin copper.

Coriolis
The horizontal acceleration at right angles to a GREAT CIRCLE on the earth necessary to enable a moving body to follow that great circle. For example, it affects the direction of circulation of winds and sea currents.

CORK *see* YACHT RACING: Major races and series (Pre-Olympic regattas)

Corner reflectors *see* RADAR REFLECTORS

Corrector (magnet)
A magnet used in the correction, or compensation, of the magnetic compass. *See also* COMPASS: Mariner's compass

Course
The intended direction of movement of a craft in the horizontal plane, generally measured in relation to the true or magnetic meridian; direction to be steered.

Course made good
The mean course actually followed.

Covering boards *see* HULLS: Construction components

CQR *see* GROUND TACKLE

Crane *see* MASTS AND RIGGING: Glossary

Cringle
An eye worked into the bolt rope of a sail and fitted with a thimble.

Two-man Enterprise dinghies. Designed by Jack Holt, they may be constructed of wood, GRP or a mixture, with aluminium spars

Cross staff
An old instrument for measuring the angle between the sun or a star and the sea horizon. The end of the graduated staff was placed against the cheekbone, and a crosspiece was moved along it until one end was seen to coincide with the star when the other end touched the horizon. Under various names – cross staff, Jacob's staff, balestila – it came into general use among Portuguese mariners in the fifteenth century, although it had already been described as an astronomer's instrument by the Provençal, Levi ben Gerson, by 1342. It continued in general use at sea until superseded by the reflecting quadrant in the eighteenth century.

The cross staff was ill adapted to measure ALTITUDES greater than about $60°$, for which the astrolabe was preferred, and for angles below $30°$ a shorter crosspiece was substituted and read against another set of graduations on the staff. One source of error was the PARALLAX introduced by holding the end of the staff at the wrong distance from the eye, but this could be checked by setting the two crosspieces to read the same angle. Another difficulty arose from the excessive brightness of the sun and about 1600 the English mathematician Thomas Harriot, or Hariot, recommended that the end of the crosspiece should just cover the sun's disk; a quarter of a degree was to be subtracted for the SEMI-DIAMETER.

Similar in principle to the cross staff was the *kamal*, possibly in use on the Indian seas in the thirteenth century and still to be found in Arab dhows. The crosspiece is a wooden tablet, at the end of knotted string held between the observer's teeth. Each knot corresponds to a particular altitude; the unit of angular measurement was the *isba*, the 56th part of a right angle. The height of the Pole Star was recorded in the pilot books for principal ports of call but the *kamal* was knotted to identify these latitudes rather than the angles of elevation. The Chinese sailing directions for the Indian Ocean in the fifteenth century employ the same unit of measurement for the altitudes of stars and there is evidence that an instrument closely resembling the *kamal* was used.

Crosstrees (spreaders) *see* MASTS AND RIGGING: Glossary

Crown knot *see* ROPEWORK: Splices

Cruising Club of America
The Cruising Club of America (CCA) owes its origin at least partly to the Royal Cruising Club. It was in 1921 that William Washbourn Nutting, Casey Baldwin, and James Dorsett sailed across to England in the gaff-rigged ketch *Typhoon*, a yacht described in the first of Uffa Fox's 'annuals', published in the 1930s. The object was to arrive at Cowes in time for the Harmsworth Trophy motorboat race, which they did. At Cowes Nutting and his friends met that pillar of the RCC Claud Worth, whose *Yacht Cruising* (1910) was a classic. As a result of conversations with Worth, Nutting had the idea of forming the Cruising Club of America.

On his return a meeting was convened at 'Beefsteak John's' in Greenwich Village. This was followed by a meeting at the Harvard Club, with the 36 charter members who duly formed the Cruising Club of America. Ever since the Club has been something of an equivalent of the Royal Cruising Club and the ROYAL OCEAN RACING CLUB. For instance, the Club organizes cruises, typically to a West Indies port in the winter. It also organizes offshore races such as the biennial Newport R.I. race to Bermuda. The club's rating rule for offshore racers was used for many years until 1970, when the CCA and the RORC amalgamated their rating rules into the International Offshore Rule (*see* HANDICAP SYSTEMS) and the North American Yacht Racing Union (now the UNITED STATES YACHT RACING UNION) took over from the CCA as the administering body for the IOR in North America.

The CCA's Blue Water Medal is one of the most coveted yachting awards, and was given in 1940 to the yachtsmen who assisted in the Dunkirk evacuation.

Cunningham hole
A grommet or eyelet in the luff of a mainsail a short distance above the tack, enabling the bunt of the sail to be flattened by means of a tackle.

Cut, angle of
The angle at which two POSITION LINES intersect.

Cutter
Nowadays, a fore-and-aft-rigged vessel with one mast and two headsails.

D

Dan buoys *see* BUOY: Navigational buoys

Daymark
An unlighted beacon; or a beacon, whether lighted or not, that serves as a daytime navigational mark.

Deadeye
A block, generally of lignum vitae, used formerly to secure the end of a shroud to the chain plate. Rigging screws (turnbuckles) have now replaced deadeyes. *See also* MASTS AND RIGGING: Glossary; PURCHASE

Dead reckoning
Navigation based on direction and distance from a known point.

Deadwood *see* HULLS: Construction components

Decca Navigator
A navigation system giving position by measurement of the phase difference between continuous-wave radio signals from ground-based stations. The line of position from a single observation is hyperbolic and charts are overprinted with the hyperbolic patterns relating to a 'chain' of master stations and red, green, and purple slave stations so designated from the colours in which the patterns are printed.

Transmissions are in the band 70–130 kHz on harmonically related frequencies that are multiplied in the receiver to bring the master and each slave to a separate common frequency for phase comparison. One cycle of phase difference at the multiplied frequency represents one 'lane', a typical width for which would be 352 m (purple) to 586 m (red) along the base line between master and slave stations.

Recurring lanes or phase-difference cycles are indistinguishable and continuous reception after an initial knowledge of position to within half a lane is needed to keep the lane count. Two modes of lane identification are, however, available in which the chain transmissions are momentarily interrupted and regrouped so that the receiver can extract a coarse hyperbolic pattern from which the correct lane is identified. The V-mode includes a vernier pattern for the identification reading and the later MP-mode generates a 'multipulse' signal by simultaneous radiation of all four Decca frequencies from each station in turn for 0.45 sec in a sequence repeated every 20 secs. The multipulse signal is insensitive to phase shifts of its constituents and gives more reliable lane identification than the V-mode under difficult ionospheric conditions.

The phase measurements are displayed on Decometers where a pair of clocklike pointers give the lane number and the lane fraction,

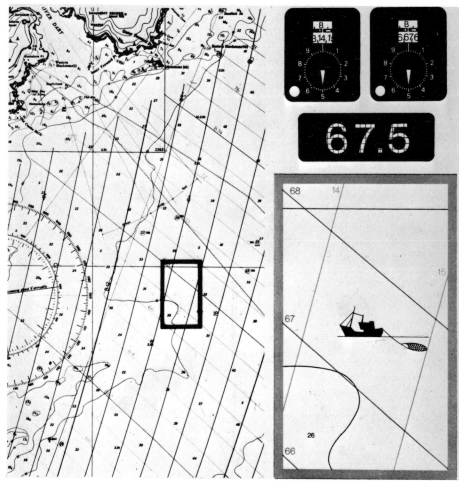

Decca Navigator. The illustration shows a portion of a chart overprinted with the hyperbolic grid. In this example of the system in use the Decometer readings are shown top right. The left-hand instrument (red) indicates to the navigator that his ship is in the group of lanes designated B and, in the lower window, the lane number 14. The rotating pointer below gives the fractional value between each lane. The green Decometer on the right shows a

reading of B67.5. The digital readout beneath the instruments indicates, three times a minute, the lane numbers shown by each Decometer in turn. This is used as a check against the Decometer readings and in the example confirms that displayed by the green Decometer. The intersection of the two lines on the chart corresponding to the readings gives the ship's exact position (enlarged on the right).

or there is a digital indicator for the lane with a single fraction pointer.

In the track plotter a stylus moves in response to the increments in one hyperbolic pattern over a chart carried on rollers drven by the increments in the other.

Position-fixing accuracy ranges from a few tens of metres by daytime in areas where the geometry is favourable to a few kilometres in the presence of SKYWAVE interference by night at extreme range. Decca chains cover most of western Europe and many other parts of the world that have similarly busy coastal waters.

Declination
The angular distance of a celestial body from the celestial equator.

Dectra
A long-range derivative of the DECCA NAVIGATOR that has been operating experimentally in the North Atlantic since 1957.

Deep
(1) An area of exceptional depth in the ocean; (2) on the old lead line, an unmarked point that measures a sounding in fathoms.

Deep-sea lead
A heavy sounding lead, up to 100 lb (45 kg) weight, with a line of 100 fathoms (183 m) or more.

Departure
The east-west component of a RHUMB LINE, measured in NAUTICAL MILES.

Historical introduction

During all but the last few years of the period when sail dominated the seas, the four pillars of scientific naval architecture were missing:
1. The method of calculating displacement in advance was either unknown or crude; the level of flotation was therefore a gamble.
2. Though the power that could drive the ship – the wind – was a function of stability, the facts of stability were not known, i.e. the existence and behaviour of the metacentre.
3. The sources of resistance were not recognized: there was no awareness of the predominant importance of frictional resistance at sailing speeds, and the false analogy of the fish form tended to govern hull shape.
4. There was only vague awareness of the principles of structural strength.

Naval architecture was concerned with the means of preserving and repeating ship shapes by recording basic offsets and proportions in simple numerals, or without writing by means of certain shipyard devices; with assuring fairness of line; later with solving the problem of solid geometry involved in portraying ships' lines on sheets of paper.

The 'mystery' of shipwrightry in ancient to medieval times, and even later, has largely to be guessed. As in other crafts and skills, a high degree of secrecy prevailed. Occasionally a little light was allowed to gleam on the slipways: 'In the name of God and the glorious Virgin Mary I begin this book of measures of galleys both great and light . . .' wrote an Italian Renaissance authority.

It is readily believed, and is to a great extent true, that shipbuilders were not well enough educated to assimilate theoretical and mathematical principles. It must also be appreciated that until well into the eighteenth century the shipbuilders' distrust of theory was too often justified by its evident inadequacy when applied to practical shipbuilding. There were, however, complex problems involved. The mass of interrelated variables in sail propulsion made a rational approach to design far more difficult than it became once engines had replaced sail. The naval architect with today's corpus of knowledge would still be unable to rationalize the design of an eighteenth-century sailing ship; and the modern racing-yacht designer continues to lean heavily on flair and on his intuitive judgement.

The principle of Archimedes (287–212 BC) was still, by the middle of the seventeenth century, applied only sometimes, and uncertainly, to the designing of ships. In May 1666 Pepys wrote of a visit to Anthony Deane (later Sir) a leading shipbuilder of the day: '. . . he fell to explain to me the manner of his casting the draught of water which a ship will draw beforehand; which is a secret the King and all admire in him; and is the first that hath come to any certainty beforehand in foretelling the draught of water of a ship before she be launched.'

As computational methods had not yet been devised for determining the volumes of irregularly shaped solids, such as a ship's underwater body, Sir Anthony Deane must have been using one of the experimental methods that survived well into the nineteenth century. By weighing a solid wooden model of the underwater hull the volume of the hull could be determined when the weight of the wood was known; and thence the volume of the ship's underwater body found by multiplying by the cube of the scale. Or the displacement might be estimated by submerging the model in a full bowl of water and weighing the overflow, again correcting for scale. Such methods were neither closely accurate nor within the competence of the builders of the smaller craft; but they were a means of sometimes applying the principle of Archimedes to ship design pending computational methods.

Leonardo da Vinci applied his questing mind to problems of ship design. Using towed models, he was led to the conclusion that the form of least resistance had the full end leading – the streamlined form. Leonardo had been dead for nearly seventy years when in 1586 a well-known master shipwright, Mathew Baker, in a manuscript *Fragments of Ancient English Shipwrightry*, showed a drawing that compared a ship's underwater body with a fish, and by an analogy arrived at the conclusion Leonardo had reached by experiment. Where the earlier experimenter had been misled by the wholly excusable failure to correlate model with full-scale results, a problem not finally solved until the late nineteenth century, the later analogist, hardly less excusably, failed to detect the fallacy that connected the behaviour of a ship floating at the boundary of two fluid media and a fish wholly submerged in one.

Stages in the development of marine drafting methods, incomplete until the nineteenth century, are a fascinating study, and fundamental to the evolution of scientific naval architecture which, without precise methods of drawing, resembled an intellect without command of a language. In naval architecture methods of drawing did to a great extent keep pace with the growth of ideas, though the problem of delineating a vessel's form on paper, and of enlarging it to full size for the use of the builder, tended for a long time to become the main preoccupation, rather than hydrodynamic theory.

The process was hastened by a revolution in the method of building larger ships that had been proceeding since about the middle of the fifteenth century. Hitherto, in the Mediterranean as well as in the cruder north, the hull planking had been laid up without firm support from transverse frames; these, and other internal structures giving strength to the shell of planking, were inserted wholly or mainly after the planking had been laid. The revolution lay in the pre-erection of the transverse framing to form a skeleton on which to lay the planking, a system of construction that has remained the standard one until the present day, having been carried through from wooden to metal shipbuilding.

The need to establish the form of the frames before laying any planking, without any guidance from the natural fair curves wood planking assumes when laid up by long-practised shipwrights, demanded new and elaborate processes of ship geometry and a ready means of enlarging the drawn frame shapes to full size. At the beginning of the period only the constructionally significant projections – the transverse cross sections giving the shape of the frames, and the rising line (the curves, in plan and elevation, passing through the ends of the floor timbers) appear to have been employed. One practice, which subsequently disappeared in favour of more elastic methods, was to draw the transverse sections from arcs of circles having various radii, these converging or being connected by tangential lines. Such forms could be brought to full size by the use of a straight edge and pegged chalk line for radii. It encouraged elegant draughtsmanship but the shapes evolved were without hydrodynamic significance. The various projections of waterlines, bow and buttock lines, and diagonals came gradually into use for fairing drawings during the course of the seventeenth to nineteenth centuries.

The principles of stability were beyond any commonsense solution. It was once believed that to remain stable a ship's centre of gravity had to be below the centre of buoyancy; but clearly in high-piled, heavily sparred ships the centre of weights was far above the centre of flotation. The level below which the centre of weights must remain if a ship is to be stable is the metacentre. This was not defined until 1746 by the French astronomer and hydrographer Pierre Bouguer (1698–1758) in his *Traité de Navaire*, where he demonstrated a method of finding this centre. He also showed that the condition for the maintenance of stability as the vessel heeled was that the angle of heel should not so alter the underwater form of the hull that the metacentre dropped below the unchanging (provided weights in the ship did not shift) centre of gravity. In effect this meant that the waterplane at which the ship floated should not become appreciably narrower as she heeled, which could be assured by means of adequate freeboard. This accounted for the stability of ships despite their high topsides. The *métacentrique* concept showed that while big beam gave a ship the required resistance to initial heel, adequate freeboard was required to

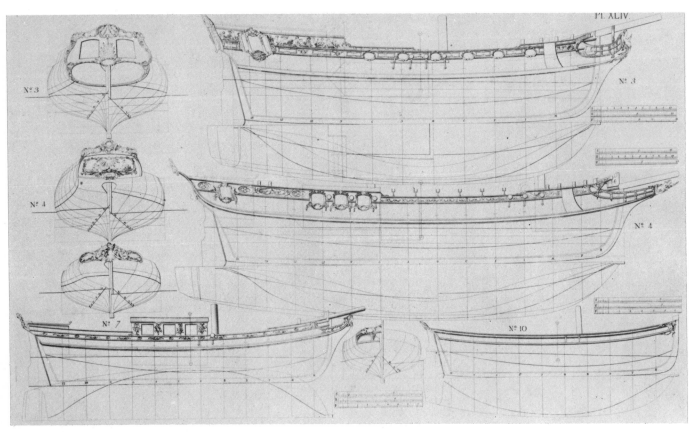

A plate from Chapman's Architectura Navalis Mercatoria *showing the hulls of four yachts ranging in length from 54 ft (16.5 m) to 24 ft (7.3 m)*

assure that stability remained positive when the ship was forced over to big angles. Unfortunately the calculations involved were not put into a form suitable for average ship drawing office work for many years. When the British turret battleship *Captain* capsized in a moderate gale in the Bay of Biscay as late as 1870 it was the outcome of inadequate methods of calculating the heeled metacentric height.

If Pierre Bouguer is accepted as the father of naval architecture, Fredrik Henrik af Chapman (1721–1808), a Swede of English extraction, must be acknowledged as the first naval architect. He was a practical shipbuilder. His *Architectura Navalis Mercatoria* (1768) was a collection of superbly executed ship drawings with the minimum of explanatory text. The *Treatise on Shipbuilding* (1775) was the greatest work on naval architecture, with its blend of theory and practice, yet to have appeared. He began by noting for how long shipbuilding had been practised and how few changes in design had been made in the course of his century. It might be inferred, Chapman suggested, that therefore shipbuilding had been brought to the 'utmost perfection'. But he then proceeded to point out that although

seagoing ships conformed to the same general proportions, some of them performed excellently and others badly. Experiments with small adjustments within the conventional limits sometimes produced happy results, sometimes the reverse. Efforts to correct the faults of one ship in a successor tended to produce a vessel having new faults.

His conclusions indicated disarray in the state of contemporary naval architecture, its casual and empiric nature: 'It thus appears, that the construction of a ship with more or less good qualities, is a matter of chance and not of previous design, and it hence follows, that as long as we are without a good theory on shipbuilding, and have nothing to trust to beyond bare experiments and trials, this art cannot be expected to acquire any greater perfection, than it possesses at present.'

When machinery replaced sails for propulsion, the need to calculate in advance power requirements for a given speed gave new urgency to studies of ship form and resistance. These were conducted mainly in ship-model testing tanks; the laws connecting the resistance of a ship with that of its model to any scale had been worked out by William Froude by 1875. Experiments revealed the

predominant importance of frictional resistance; they also showed that there was no single form of least resistance, but that it varied with the relative speed of the vessel. Furthermore, this demonstrated that a hull form finer forward than aft was superior at average speeds.

The design of fast sailing craft, particularly in the United States, had been moving in this direction during the last days of sail, but this was thanks to experienced judgement rather than scientific experiment, and the fish form continued to dominate the ideas of many smaller builders. The technique of model tank testing was incomplete for application to propulsion under sail until 1932, when Dr K. S. M. Davidson in the United States extended existing model methods to cover the very different motion of a sailing craft (*see* Yacht design *below*). By this time the technique was required only for application to yachts.

Yacht design
The art and science of yacht design has always proceeded on two levels:
1. True architectural developments proceeding from improved knowledge

2. Changes resulting from the prevailing measurement rules.

The latter affect primarily racing yachts, but these are the forcing house of design development and influence strongly, if not always quite logically, the design of all yachts. The two lines of development interact but are essentially separate.

The early yachts of this era, beginning in the early nineteenth century, resembled the best working craft of their day, the revenue cutters, pilot boats, the naval brigs, schooners, and cutters. Yachts had superior accommodation and sometimes lighter scantlings. In Britain the cod's-head and mackerel's-tail theory (see Historical introduction above) dominated design. The yachts had full bows, about 3 to $3\frac{1}{2}$ beams in their length, and full, rounded midship sections of moderate draught. Rule of thumb dominated design: the carving of models rather than the drawing of plans was a usual procedure.

Yachts, carrying no cargo or heavy weights, needed ballast for stability. From the opening of the modern age of yachting until as late as 1880 an important question in design was the mode of ballasting; in the early part of the period it was the dominant one. During this time methods ranged from the historic practice of having all ballast inside the hull, when it might be composed of stones from the beach, metallic ores, iron scrap, or pigs of cast iron or occasionally lead, to the modern fashion of having it all outside the hull in a wide, deep casting of lead bolted below the wood structural keel. This development, unique to yachting, had to fly in the face of cherished and apparently well-founded old beliefs. It was initially considered that the concentration of overmuch weight below the hull would put dangerous stresses on the construction; secondly that the low centre of gravity would give an insupportable motion to the yacht, even endangering her rig. In the use of all-outside ballast racing yachts led the way, and in the larger of them either full composite construction, or at least the employment of steel for transverse framing and some longitudinal members, solved the structural difficulty.

By the mid-nineteenth century, ballast in first-class yachts was cast iron moulded to fit internally between the floors, or alternatively the same in lead. During the first half of the century much attention was paid to what was described as 'elasticity' in a seaway, and 'live' ballast. This was a persistence of a very old nautical belief whose truth is doubtful. The Vikings in the construction of their galleys went to great pains to assure flexibility by lashing, not nailing, the lower planking to the frames. The masters of privateers and revenue cutters, when engaged in chase, sometimes had shot placed in slung hammocks and in the hands of the crew to introduce a

The yacht America *from a coloured lithograph by Brown and Severin, signed by the designer George Steers on 7 November 1851 as being 'correct in every aspect'*

degree of swing into the proceedings. Lord Robert Montague in his *Yacht Architecture* (1850) wrote that ballast should be placed upon springs. Later, the practice of hanging all ballast outside in an external keel killed such ideas for racing yachts, but there remained until the present day some yacht architects who were not displeased when wrinkles in the deck covering, or doors jamming shut below deck when a yacht was beating to windward, indicated that the hull was moving and not dead; and for equally long there were those who believed that for easy motion in a seaway a yacht should carry an appreciable proportion of her ballast internally. But by 1853 those with advanced ideas, such as the American 'Vanderdecken' in his *Yachts and Yachting*, went so far as to suggest that most yachtsmen favoured a high proportion of outside ballast. To make room for this the wooden keel was widened and deepened, and the garboards drawn in a full rounded curve. Thus the traditionally narrow wooden keel was transformed into what for a time was known as a 'lead bottom' and the metal keel itself, along with the wood structural keel above it, grew into a fin appendage of the hull.

There was for a time an enthusiasm for shifting ballast. It was introduced to British waters in 1826 and prohibited in 1856, but continued in popularity for longer in the United States. This ballast might be of lead shot in bags, which would be kept amidships on the cabin sole when sailing with the wind free or when short tacking, and piled up to windward when making a long board. This entailed shifting the ballast bags with all speed from the racks on one side of the hull to the other when putting about; a gruelling task for a squad below deck. In the United States there was a famous breed of sandbagger catboat, and also sloops in which great sail spreads were kept upright by a numerous crew with their ballast bags perched up to weather; such craft were still being sailed in America in the early 1880s. But movable ballast was clearly inimical to good design and dangerous in small craft.

While ballasting developments were following their course amid lively discussion, the form of hulls was changing in other respects. After so many years the fish form was discarded. When the *America* won her race round the Isle of Wight in 1851, and a few days later gave an even more convincing display of her superiority to the best British yachts, this was widely attributed at the time to her long, fine-lined bow with some hollow in the waterlines abaft the stem. A technically most proficient judge of hull form in his day, Dixon Kemp, agreed with this view. Today her success would be regarded as mainly due to the qualities of her sails and rigging, but with some contribution to performance from her unusual hull form.

It was further believed that the *America* had initiated this hollow form of bow. In fact, it had been anticipated in both Britain and America. George Steers, the *America*'s designer, had produced earlier boats with a similar hull form. It was found in the pilot schooners *Mary Taylor* and *Moses H. Grinnell*; the latter came out in 1850 and her lines were refined to produce the *America*. In Britain the yacht *Mosquito*, built in 1848, was given a long, hollow-lined bow, but she was unsuccessful so her shape was not approved. Much earlier, the *Menai* in 1826 had been built with such a bow; it was treated with obloquy. Before even the *Menai*, pilot boats and some frigates had been built in the United States with the greatest beam abaft amidships and a hollow entrance.

In mid-century, the Scottish naval architect John Scott Russell was propounding his wave-line theory of design for application to steamships. This theory produced a hull shape similar to the *America, Mosquito, Menai,*

and similar craft. Russell later designed the yacht *Titania* in accordance with his ideas. She was not successful, which reflected on her defects aloft rather than her hull shape. A smaller British cutter, the *Volante*, which was in the race round the Isle of Wight with the *America*, came out that year with a relatively fine bow. Russell's theory was ingenious though fallacious, but its effect on hull form was not detrimental. The much-publicized *America* focused interest on the hull form and forced a reshaping of design ideas. It would appear that Steers and American designers were following the evidence of practical experience rather than Russell's theories.

After the *America*'s example an appreciable part of the British yachting fleet was virtually rebuilt; the apple bows were removed and the yachts lengthened with long, knifelike forebodies. The partial rebuilding of yachts was fairly common then. There is no doubt that faster and better yachts were often the outcome, though the fine bows should not receive all the credit: it was partly owing to the resultant lengthening of the hulls, though at this time the importance of length for speed was not fully appreciated. In America the fine bow with hollow lines similarly became accepted, but with less enthusiasm and not so quickly.

In 1877 Colin Archer, the Norwegian architect of Scottish descent, advanced his wave-form theory. He adopted Russell's

wave-form curve, with some modifications, but specified that it should be the curve of areas, and not any particular curve in the hull shape, which should conform to it. Archer stated that the curve of areas of the forebody should be a curve of versed sines and that of the afterbody a trochoid; the forebody should extend 0.6 of the waterline length, the afterbody 0.4. The hull lines were thus not stereotyped, only the distribution of the displacement along the length. Various shapes of hull could show the same progression of the volume of the displacement, but the main effect of the system was to produce fine bows and full sterns.

Like Russell's, Archer's theory was hydrodynamically invalid, but the form of hull encouraged had merit. For over half a century the influence of the Archer wave form was potent in sailing-yacht design, despite the fact that it had never been accepted in general naval architecture. Initially it provided a guide for some leading designers. In the United States, Carey Smith was influenced by the Archer displacement curve. Edward Burgess followed the theory in his designs for *America*'s Cup defenders and many other yachts – though he modified Archer's curve of areas in the light of the curves from his own or other American craft that had proved successful. Used in this manner the Archer curve was a not unsatisfactory guide. Its longevity may be seen by the fact that in the

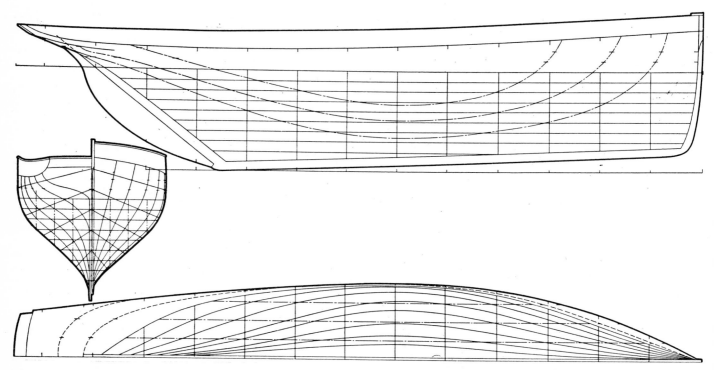

The hull lines of Volante, *designed and built by John Harvey in England. The extreme rake of the sternpost was to reduce tonnage measurement*

1948 edition of Norman Skene's standard *Elements of Yacht Design* it was claimed with apparent confidence that 'there is undoubtedly an advantage in having the curve of areas conform to the wave-form theory', though it was significantly confessed that many successful yachts diverged widely from it. And in a paper entitled 'Sailing Yacht Design' read before the American Society of Naval Architects and Marine Engineers in New York, 1963, the authors pointed out that the wedge-shaped hull resulting from Archer's theories of 1877 grew in popularity and had in fact remained in considerable favour until quite recent times.

In the subsequent discussion of this paper, reference was made to successful craft built to an area curve developed by John Hyslop; this used a sine curve forward and a modification of the sine curve aft. One of these craft was the *Weetamoe*, a J-boat designed by Clinton H. Crane, which came near to success when contending for the defence of the *America*'s Cup in 1930. All theories that involved a standardized distribution of the displacement longitudinally were hydrodynamically unsound: the optimum distribution varies with the speed. This became clear once model tank testing was developed into a reliable technique (*see below*). But as sailing craft cannot be designed for one predetermined speed, the principle of using a displacement distribution represented by a stereotyped curve of areas that had been proved in practice to provide a good form for average conditions was not unsound.

In the United States, as in Europe, the working craft of sail provided the early models for yachts. American yachting had its origin in the shoal waters of New York Bay, Hoboken, South Brooklyn, Long Island Sound, where convenient anchorages were shallow; American yachtsmen had the example, which the British had not, of numerous centreboard working boats that might be converted into yachts or provide design guides for them. The yachting prejudices of Britain and America were in nothing so widely separated as in the former's aversion to centreboards and the latter's general dependence upon them. But extreme beam and extreme lack of draught were not characteristic of early American yachts, and for a number of years moderate proportions were usual in hulls with and without centreboards; the *America* was an example. But gradually the yacht, following its own line of development, became more extreme in beam and shallowness. The trend was not general, but sufficiently so to appear in the nature of a national tradition. During the 1860s and '80s, broad shallow sloops with centreboards became increasingly the dominant type of American yacht. The attainment of more speed was assumed to be a matter of adding

to beam and reducing draught, thus retaining sail-carrying power while producing hulls that became ever-shallower dishes. Though stability in such craft at small angles of heel was great, their range of stability, lacking draught and ballast as they did, was small, and the years were scattered with yachting tragedies. The *Eva* capsized and was lost on Charleston Bar in 1866; the larger schooner *Meteor* capsized in 1869; the *Mohawk*, a schooner of 140 ft (42.7 m) in length and drawing only 6 ft (1.8 m), was lost in 1876 – she was lying at anchor with sails set when a squall threw her over in a violent capsize. Behind the catalogue of disasters was another of narrow escapes, often in quite large craft.

Partly these were the outcome of a failure to understand the laws governing ship stability, the formulation of which was yet uncertain; partly because some designers of yachts were then incapable of understanding even the principles involved. In his *History of American Ships* (New York 1936), the American historian of sail, Howard I. Chapelle, wrote: '. . . the designing of yachts had passed from shipbuilders to boatbuilders in the 1850s, and from boatbuilders to carpenters in the 1860s. In the 1870s, saloon keepers, a hatter, and fishermen, without any training as . . . shipwrights, became the leading modellers and builders of yachts! So the times had changed and the reputation of the profession of naval architecture faded, to be replaced by the whittler and "by guess and by God" methods, until the 1870s and 1880s when yacht designing came into the hands of skilled, trained naval architects, who have guided yacht development in America since then.'

In Britain a prejudice against centreboards, and an old tradition that favoured adequate draught, were reinforced by a series of measurement rules used for classifying racing yachts and assessing them for time allowance, and which heavily taxed beam, to produce a design trend precisely the opposite of the American: towards ever-increasing draught and decreasing beam. And although, once the extremes of this trend were reached, yachts had become uncomfortable and of an irrational form, at least it was not a dangerous one. The measurement rules that in succession governed the shape of British racing yachts, and by the shadow of fashion less specialized yachts also, are shown below reduced to their barest elements:

1. $L \times B \times H$
2. $B^2 \times (L - B)$
3. $B \times (L - B)^2$
4. $L \times S$

In these expressions L is length, B the maximum beam, H the internal depth of the hull, and S the sail area. The first of the above rules appeared in the mid-seventeenth century, when it was used for trading vessels; it

was adopted for yachts in the nineteenth century. This indicated the long arm of tradition that extended over developments in yacht design on the eastern side of the Atlantic. Difficulties of measuring the depth factor led to its being eliminated and replaced by beam, and the length was reduced by a factor equal to the beam to make measurement easier when making an assessment of effective sailing length. The rule emerged in the form of (2) above and was used only for yachting in the mid-nineteenth century. The various devices introduced into it were not unreasonable at the time, but mathematically the result was to measure beam twice by squaring it, thus taxing this dimension heavily. With the developments in ballasting discussed above, it became possible to reduce beam and substitute for it, in terms of ultimate stability, a considerable weight of low-slung metal. The situation was not improved when in 1880 the rule was modified to the form shown in (3) above. Though not intended to do so, this rule had the effect of taxing beam yet more highly than the previous one once a certain smallness of beam in proportion to length became acceptable – an unforeseen mathematical quirk – and the new techniques of ballasting made it acceptable.

The effect of the above rules on British yacht design is indicated in the following table:

1830	Revenue cutter	$2\frac{3}{4}$ beams in length
1847	*Mosquito*	4 beams in length
1873	*Vanessa*	$4\frac{3}{4}$ beams in length
1875	*Jullanar*	6 beams in length
1882	*Chittyee*	$6\frac{1}{4}$ beams in length

The rush to reduced beam accelerated between 1873 and 1886 as confidence in the use of carrying great weights of ballast hung below the hull increased. A 5-tonner at the former date might have had a length of 25 ft 3 in (7.69 m), a beam of 7 ft 3 in (2.21 m), and a displacement of 5 tons; by the latter date it had proved possible to build a yacht, also measuring 5 tons under the above rules, to such extreme dimensions as length 34 ft (10.36 m), beam 5 ft 6 in (1.68 m), displacement 12.5 tons. The comparative weights of ballast would have been 2.6 tons and 7.5 tons. In 1887 voices were raised at the Institution of Naval Architects, London, bewailing 'the extraordinary shape of our yachts', which were described variously as 'monstrosities full of lead' and 'soap boxes standing on edge'.

Before reaching the extremes attributable to the bad mathematics of measurement formulae, the deep, narrow type of yacht represented the best expression of European yacht design, and it had a strong influence on American design. In the United States nothing resembling the British rules with their overweighted beam factors had ever been used. The NEW YORK YACHT CLUB was the main authority for yacht measurement, and after briefly using a Customs House system of tonnage measurement, various methods were devised purely for yachts. In the rudimentary state of scientific yacht design prior to the last quarter of the century, these rules were inevitably defective. Their approach, however, was more rational hydrodynamically than the British, though the rules were not of a nature to curb the tendency to excessive beam and lack of draught. In turn displacement, waterplane area, sail area were used as the criterion of size, and then the measurement of internal capacity – a reversion towards the original Custom House rule. When, slowly, evidence of the comparative merits of the beamy, shallow American type and the deep, narrow British type became available, it was evident that the two radically opposed conceptions of how to shape a sailing yacht did not produce such radically different results out on the water. The 10-ton British cutter *Madge* was very successful during the American season of 1897, when the *Schemer* was one of the fastest sloops of her day in the United States. Their dimensions are given in the table below.

But though *Madge* beat *Schemer* handsomely, it was clear that even such glaring contrasts of form were less important than the details of sails and gear. The American sloop was better in light airs and smooth water, the British cutter in heavy weather and especially in a head sea. On the average there was not much between them in speed compared over a wide enough range of conditions. *Madge* raced with other American sloops of *Schemer*'s type. What particularly was noticeable was that after racing the immaculate *Madge* remained immaculate, while the sloops emerged in various stages of disarray, the outcome of the high stresses generated by their hulls, stiff and unyielding until the moment came when they were in danger of capsizing under the pressure of the massive rigs required to drive them.

In the years following, the American yachts became narrower and deeper, the British beamier and with their lead-mine characteristics modified. A compromise type emerged on each side of the Atlantic, owing much to more rational measurement rules and the advance of scientific design; but there

remained enough difference between the leading racing yachts in Europe and the United States to mark the opposed traditions from which they had sprung.

It was during these years that the profession of the yacht architect was becoming established. The architects were heirs of the builder-designers, proprietors of the smaller commercial yards, who turned to yacht building for occasional work, and some of whom adopted it as a full-time activity with the later nineteenth-century growth of yachting. Others were trained as naval architects and then specialized in yachts. But the profession retained a certain amateur strain, revealing the fact that successful racing-yacht design was in an appreciable degree a matter of flair and was usually, though not invariably, confined to those with sailing experience. Some of the apparent glamour of yachting rubbed off on the yacht architect. While most eminent naval architects and ship designers passed their days unknown beyond their professional circles, yacht architects became small national figures, as did racehorse trainers. Yachts were described as the poetry of naval architecture.

It was not until the 1870s that the English naval architect William Froude, using a technique of ship-model testing devised by himself, was able to prove that at lower and economical speeds the major portion of ships' resistance was due to friction between the hull surface and water. The new knowledge of surface friction opened the way to the second revolution in yacht design. This was the reduction of wetted-surface area, which progressed until the long straight keels common until 1877 had been replaced by the triangular underwater profile and fin-keel entirely modern in appearance.

The first yacht in which wetted surface was drastically reduced was the 126-ton English yawl *Jullanar* of 1875. Designed by an amateur, E. H. Bentall, it is not known to what extent, if at all, he was influenced by Froude's results. It appears that he carved several half models – a method of design by this time regarded as scientifically naïve – until he arrived at a shape that pleased him. But Bentall used drawings also. In place of the deep forefoot and long keel of contemporary yachts, *Jullanar* was cut away forward and

aft, the length of straight keel being less than half that of the waterline, while the sternpost was set well ahead of the after waterline ending. Her lateral plane was thus much reduced while the length on the waterline was retained. *Jullanar* embodied the two first principles of fast yacht design: small wetted surface for the reduction of frictional resistance and as great a length as practicable for the reduction of wave-making resistance at the higher sailing speeds. The yacht was remarkably successful in her first two seasons, winning £796 in prize money. Thereafter, having proved the point, she was raced less frequently; but she was still sailing in 1897.

She was followed five years later by the 10-ton *Evolution*, also by Bentall. She was a brilliant failure. Brilliant because she incorporated in her form the third requirement for speed under sail, the separation of the hull into a canoe body providing the displacement to carry the ballast, and an appendage keel – a fin – to generate lateral resistance; a failure because, built under the tonnage rule then in force, her beam was reduced to an extent that precluded adequate stability. It was lack of enough salient keel area in the *America*'s Cup challenger *Thistle* (1887), designed by the Scottish architect George Lennox Watson, that spoiled the performance of a yacht that was otherwise an advanced conception. The lateral plane of *Thistle* was considerably reduced, but the yacht had full garboards and little depth of salient keel surface; hence she was unable to generate the fin action required for adequate lateral resistance, and the yacht sagged off to leeward. High, tucked-in garboards and sufficient depth of fin-keel surface are the necessary adjuncts of a cutaway profile. This was achieved by Nathanael Herreshoff in America with the *Gloriana* of 1890. Here the forefoot was completely suppressed and the forward endings of the waterlines were full convex curves. This was not a reversion to the full bows of the pre-*America* era, but simply a necessary rounding in of the forward waterlines to enable the hull to be drawn out into a generous overhang forward – an important feature of the design – which gave the hull a long, smooth entry once heeled. The midship section was of the S-form now so familiar, the relatively shallow canoe body carrying below it a deep, flat-sided keel. *Gloriana*'s racing success was enough to kill the class she belonged to.

Herreshoff produced in its most modern form the type of hull with a canoe body and attached fin-keel in the year following *Gloriana*. This was *Dilemma*, a yacht of 26 ft (7.92 m) on the waterline and 38 ft (11.58 m) overall. The shallow hull ran out naturally into overhangs fore and aft, and beneath the hull was a small fin-keel with a bulb of ballast. The rudder was hung independently. With *Gloriana* and *Dilemma* the form of the

Dimensions of Madge *and* Schemer

	Madge	*Schemer*
Length overall	46 ft 0 in (14.02 m)	39 ft 8 in (12.08 m)
Length waterline	39 ft 9 in (12.12 m)	36 ft 10 in (11.23 m)
Beam	7 ft 9 in (2.36 m)	14 ft 0 in (4.27 m)
Draught (hull only)	7 ft 8 in (2.33 m)	3 ft 0 in (0.91 m)
Draught (centreboard)	—	9 ft 0 in (2.74 m)
Ballast on keel	10½ tons	4½ tons

A model of the yawl-rigged yacht Jullanar

The hull lines of Herreshoff's Gloriana *(below),
designed under the Seawanhaka Rule to race in the
46-ft waterline class, shows the modern yacht form
almost fully evolved*

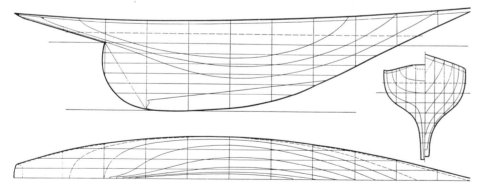

safeguards, could not, in the day of scientific design that had arrived, do other than lead to freak yachts.

The designer of racing yachts is concerned only to produce the fastest possible craft by applying the soundest hydrodynamic and aerodynamic principles within the framework of the prevailing measurement rule. The latter, it has been seen, may force design into undesirable channels. The fact that racing yachts tend to influence yacht types beyond their own restricted sphere, and a certain sense of fitness that demands that a racing yacht should be something more than merely fast, but also an efficient and reasonably elegant seagoing vessel, have always led those who formulate measurement to aim at encouraging an ideal type of yacht. This ideal was once summarized by the English hydrodynamist R. E. Froude as a craft combining speed, seaworthiness, and habitability.

By the 1890s it had become clear that to govern the shape of racing yachts by a simple formula, without safeguarding clauses defining dimensional limits and penalties, could only lead to extremes in design. This was the result of the increasing expertise of the yacht architects, who with ever-growing subtlety were able to play one factor in a rating formula against another, frequently to the detriment of comely design, though speed might be improved. The chief governing factors are length, sail area, and displacement. In the United States the formulation known as the Universal Rule, derived from earlier ones, was adopted in 1903. By limits on draught, sail area, and a certain control of overhanging length, the freedom allowed by the basic formula was restrained. In Britain, and shortly extending to Europe, a series of rating formulae were produced with the same object. In them a spreading growth of safeguarding clauses tried to tempt the adventurous steps of racing-yacht design along ways not too outlandish. The First Linear Rule (1896), the Second Linear Rule (1901), the First International Rule (1906), the Second and Third in 1919 and 1933, all had as their object the production of fast racing yachts that were also of a healthy seagoing type with enough fullness of body to contain adequate accommodation. The Third International Rule, today incorporating a number of amendments and additions, still governs the 12-Metre yachts that contest the *America*'s Cup.

The discovery of the form giving the lowest resistance and maximum speed has been a preoccupation in the design of sailing craft linked like a binary star to that of achieving good balance. The British yacht architect J. Laurent Giles once observed that from the mid-1920s until World War II 'more was written and said about the balance of sailing craft than about any other single technical

modern yacht was established. The passage of some ninety years has failed to make *Dilemma* appear dated. This is emphasized by comparing her with the smaller Soling one-design produced by Jan Linge in 1966.

In 1886 the rule numbered (4) above was adopted in Britain. Beam disappeared as a measurement, and the way was opened for a more rational shape of yacht. Briefly, for a period in the early 1890s, racing yachts passed through an aesthetically beautiful

phase; this imprinted an ideal upon design that persists. Moving from the extreme of the overheavy plank-on-edge cutters of the late 1880s to the overlight skimming dishes of the later 1890s, the one classical form of beauty in yacht design was realized. In Britain it became known as the '*Britannia* ideal' after the royal cutter that was a perfect representative of the type. A rule as simple as (4), however, taking account only of length, waterline, and sail area, and without other

topic connected with yachts and yachting'.

By balance is broadly meant quick respon-
siveness to the helm under all conditions.
Particularly, balance is judged when sailing
to windward, under which conditions a
balanced yacht carries the minimum of
weather helm and continues to steer lightly
at big angles of heel. The English naval architect and writer Dixon Kemp (1839–99),
whose massive body of work did so much to
establish sailing-yacht architecture as an
independent study, advocated a system for
producing a hull shape considered to reduce
hydrodynamic tendencies towards imbalance. It was a geometrical system which
assured that the hull should immerse an
approximately similar volume of topsides
forward and aft on heeling. The form of hull
encouraged by the Archer theory tended
towards the wedge shape, with full stern and
fine bow. Excess of buoyancy in the topsides
aft and lack of it forward made a hull with a
markedly asymmetrical heeled shape, having
a bulk of winged-out buoyancy aft and to
leeward, which could give rise to a horizontal
pressure component and induce hydrodynamic steering effects. The principles
enunciated by Kemp were adapted and
developed in later years to produce various
drawing-table methods (generally known as
'volumetric' hull balance) for producing a
hull shape that tended to run straight when
heeled. Their general effect was to encourage
a more nearly symmetrical hull form than
had become common, with the centre of
buoyancy not far abaft amidships and hence
with nearly equal volumes of displacement in
the fore- and afterbodies. Yacht design in this
respect was much influenced by model-yacht
racing. Models before World War II were
steered by a device known as the Braine gear,
which could not be operated when sailing to
windward, under which conditions models
had to sail with their rudders pinned amidships; a condition that made excellent balance essential to control.

The most sophisticated and elaborately
wrought system of sailing hull balance was
the work of Rear Admiral Alfred Turner. He
evolved the theory by stages, using the experience gained through the numerous model
racing yachts he designed and the analysis of
the lines of many yachts, successful and unsuccessful. The outcome was what became
widely known as the 'metacentric-shelf'
theory of hull balance, the effectiveness of
which in practice, together with Admiral
Turner's terse, elliptical prose style, and
many lectures, aroused wide interest rare for
so technical a matter. Though more complex,
and based on different principles, the
metacentric-shelf system had a similar effect
on hull shape to the volumetric system considered above; the shape demanded had a
relatively fine afterbody and a forebody

approximately matching it. The system thus
also encouraged the trend, which became
general in good design, away from full stern
and fine bows.

Admiral Turner delivered two papers on
what became known as the 'Law of Balance'
before the Institution of Naval Architects in
London in 1937 and 1942. Professional opinion rejected on both occasions the scientific
validity of the theory. This was reasonable in
that the theory depended on the proposition
that the vertical force of buoyancy acting on
the heeled hull could produce a directional
change, though this would demand a horizontal component of the force. However, an
Hon. Vice-President of the Institution, a
naval architect who employed the system in
the design of his own yachts, pointed out that
although the conception of a metacentric
shelf had evoked controversy, it did seem to
offer a reasonably reliable criterion for the
probable steering qualities of a heeled hull;

The successful American yacht Ranger, *designed
by Starling Burgess and Olin Stephens for Harold
Vanderbilt. The jib is double clewed*

and in practice a bad shelf was likely to mean
poor steering with the inclined hull.

In the mid-1930s the science of sailing-yacht
design took a stride forward greater perhaps
than any since Froude's frictional-resistance
formulations were applied to sailing craft.
The new development was in fact the extension of Froude's technique of ship-model
testing to the more complex action of a vessel
under sail.

This was due to the work of Dr K. S. M.
Davidson, begun in 1932 at the Stevens'
Tank, Hoboken, N.J. It had long been apparent that, unlike mechanically propelled
vessels, the straightforward, upright resistance of a sailing hull or its model was no
criterion of her speed in practice except when
running dead before the wind. In 1898 tank
tests had been used in the design of Sir
Thomas Lipton's first challenger for the
America's Cup, but though angle of heel, and
also, it is believed, leeway, were taken into

account, a dynamometer able to measure the forces involved in the sailing action had not then been invented.

Angle of heel alone was not enough to account for the great increase in resistance occurring when sailing to windward compared with that experienced with the yacht moving in the direction of her own centreline. The crucial feature affecting windward performance was the angle of leeway, or yaw. The importance of this had long been appreciated but the magnitude of the resistance augmentation produced by yaw angle had not been recognized or the fact that it held the secret to good windward performance. The following figures broadly express the conditions for a 50-ft waterline yacht working to windward at a speed of $7\frac{1}{2}$ knots:

Total resistance at $5°$ yaw 548 lb (248.57 kg)
Total resistance at $7°$ yaw 716 lb (324.77 kg)
Total resistance at $0°$ yaw 377 lb (171 kg)

The additional resistance compared with the upright condition is about 45% for $5°$ of leeway and 90% for $7°$. Yaw angle, in fact, affects resistance appreciably more than any practicable variations in wetted surface or fore-and-aft distribution of the displacement. Means of reducing yaw angle were thus a key to good windward performance. This was revealed by tank testing, which also provided the experimental means of discovering the design features able to achieve the result. Davidson gave an account of his research up to that date in a paper, 'Some Experimental Studies of the Sailing Yacht', read before the Society of Naval Architects and Marine Engineers, New York, in 1936. In 1937 J-Class yacht *Ranger* defeated by a wide margin the challenger *Endeavour II*, herself an outstandingly fast yacht, in the *America*'s Cup races of 1937. The design of *Ranger*, initially known as Model 77-C, was selected by tank results from among several other designs of a less extreme type also tested, a tribute to the confidence felt in the tank technique and the reliability of the dynamometer evolved for the work by Davidson. The designer of the British yacht *Endeavour II*, Charles E. Nicholson, later said 'It is quite useless for us to hope to compete successfully in Anglo-American class racing before our designs can be properly tank tested.'

For sail, as for mechanical propulsion, the model-testing tank became an essential tool of design. Its value lay not only in the testing of individual designs but, as in general naval architecture, in the broader sphere of basic research. The tank played a considerable part in redirecting the approach to scientific design for sail, particularly in relation to the aspects of the hull-keel combination.

The role of the keel as a hydrofoil operating at various angles of attack (yaw angle) to the water and producing, as to the laws of hydro-

T.O.M. Sopwith's Endeavour II, *beaten so decisively by* Ranger *in the 1937* America's Cup

dynamics bound, lift and drag in the process, came under closer consideration. The difference between a good and an indifferent lift-drag ratio might be 25% in terms of resistance when sailing to windward; and in close class racing differences of speed in the order of a few seconds per mile may be critical. With such small differences the tank dynamometer has to cope. A new importance was assumed by aspects of keel design – the sectional and profile shapes – to keel-rudder interactions, and to those aspects of hull design that might contribute to a high lift-drag ratio. The yacht architect was transformed to realms where the trained aerodynamicist was more at home than he. The aerodynamicist had simply to change from dealing with one fluid, air, to another, water,

for which similar laws applied. A new vocabulary was necessary, unknown to former yacht architects. This approach to design had no place in the textbooks, from those of Dixon Kemp in the 1880s to Norman Skene in the 1930s. It represented considerable rethinking about the principles of sail propulsion; though it has always to be remembered that designers, working intuitively, had been making allowance for the leeway factor for generations; but their approach lacked the scientific support of numerical data and knowledge of the precise physical factors involved.

It was in the keels that the new approach to design showed itself most strikingly. It has been seen that as early as the *Dilemma* in the early 1890s, Herreshoff had produced a yacht with a fin-keel and independently hung rudder. In 1902 a scow sloop that was built, but not selected, for the defence of the *America*'s Cup, had been designed by William Gardner with a fin-keel and a separately hung rudder. The yacht was not a success, a fact not necessarily attributable to the keel configuration. She was 52 ft (15.85 m) on the waterline and 88 ft (26.82 m) overall. But the fin and independent rudder were almost wholly confined to smaller craft until the early 1950s. After this time, lateral planes composed of a narrow fin-keel providing most of the lateral area and carrying the ballast, associated with a rudder placed well aft and hung on its own, or having an area of skeg ahead of it, became familiar. This type of underwater profile was adapted to the larger craft and even those intended primarily for ocean-going rather than racing.

That there was enough area in these cut-away underwater profiles to generate the necessary water side force to hold the yaw angle down to an acceptable smallness may be attributed to (1) the efficiency of modern sail plans, which give a smaller lateral component of air force, this being partly attributable to the use of sailcloth of man-made fibre; (2) the high lift-drag ratio of the small keel area, resulting from its high aspect ratio and effective longitudinal sections. Assisting the latter may be a flap or tab forming the trailing area of the fin-keel. Setting this at an angle of weather helm increases the lift-drag ratio of the fin while simultaneously lowering the drag of the main rudder.

There has always been a tendency for cruising yachts to follow the design fashions of those produced primarily for racing, and this has led both to important technical improvements in the former and sometimes to irrational copying. The hydrodynamic advantages of the fin-keel and independent rudder when speed alone is primarily impor-

tant does not of necessity make the configuration ideal for the cruiser, when directional steadiness is an important quality; and the association of this form of underwater profile with unbalanced hull forms, which is a feature of the offshore racing yachts of the 1970s, is not desirable in most yachts. Such yachts demand particular skills for their handling, not appropriate to the cruising role.

The bustle stern, or unfair swelling of the hull lines aft immediately ahead of the waterline ending, is a hydrodynamic development in hull form that has not been influenced by the distorting demands of rating formulae. As such it may be regarded as an advance in design applicable to all yachts; though this may be questioned. The effect of the bustle is to produce lower wave-making resistance at the higher speeds. Such discontinuities in the smooth fairness of hull lines are a well-known feature of naval architecture. The bulbous bow has become familiar. The potentialities of the bulbous stern were recognized more than a quarter of a century ago, but no advantage could be taken of it in propeller-driven ships owing to its effect on the wake stream. This objection not applying under sail, the bustle became a feature of racing-yacht form during the 1960s. The theory of the bustle stern is not perfectly clear. A bustle appears to increase the effective length of a hull, thereby delaying the steep rise in wave-making resistance at the higher sailing speeds. Then a suitable bustle may reduce the total resistance by as much as 8%; but since at such speeds resistance is growing rapidly the increase in speed will be no more than 1–2%. This is an amount of interest in class racing. The bustle stern is not a feature of importance for most yachts, and it may produce erratic steering effects.

See also PERFORMANCE AND YACHT DESIGN; SAIL DESIGN AND MATERIALS

Deviation

A deflection of the magnetic compass due to the proximity of iron; it varies with the HEADING. *See also* MARINER'S COMPASS; NAVIGATION

Difference of latitude *see* D. LAT.

Differential Omega

A form of OMEGA in which propagation variations are measured at a shore station and broadcast to vessels using the system locally to give greater accuracy than a published table of predicted variations will allow. *See also* OMEGA

Dinghies and centreboard classes – origins

The word dinghy is derived from the Hindi word *dēngī* or *dīngī*. In the 1700s and before, rowing vessels fitted with a single sail in Bombay were called dingas, and dengis were a frequent sight on the river Hoogli carrying cargoes or rice and jute downstream to the old port of Calcutta.

Today the word dinghy is used of craft from beamy workboats to lightweight skiffs and even rubber inflatables. A dinghy is best described as a small unballasted open boat and most modern craft in the Western world owe much of their development to the old workboats and tenders that were used in centuries past. Most of these craft were of heavy wooden construction designed primarily for stability and durability; some, built to suit local conditions, were so successful that their lines are still copied faithfully today. The coble, the characteristic beach boat of the northeast coast of England, is one such design. Ranging in size from around 18 to 35 ft (5.5 to 10.5 m), these boats have fine bows and a deep forefoot to cut through waves, a great deal of sheer to heighten bow and stern clear of breaking waves, and are fitted with skids beneath to ease hauling up and down the beach. There are the pretty wineglass-shaped designs from Scandinavia built in pine with heavily flared bows to deflect the spray from the short choppy seas experienced in the fjords and lakes; and the Grand Banks dory, a type seen in Europe as well as North America, with its flat bottom and heavily flared topsides designed for carrying out to the fishing grounds stacked on the deck of the mother ship, is another craft built for special local conditions.

Reference must also be made to naval influence in the design of dinghies. This has supplied most nautical nomenclature and phraseology (much of it now irrelevant but tenaciously adhered to); it also led to small-boat and lifeboat designs with great sea-keeping qualities, narrow-beamed gigs capable of good speed under sail, and estuary dayboats for the sail training of cadets. Two of the working boats from which sailing dinghies have been developed are, in England, the Norfolk punt, and, in North America, the similar sneakbox. Both originated as flat-bottomed boats paddled or poled (quanted) through the reed beds, each carrying a sportsman in search of wildfowl. When approaching the birds, the fowler would lie prone in the bottom and use hand paddles to manoeuvre the punt to bring his guns within firing range. Historically, sail was never part of the essential equipment of such boats but was added for recreational purposes 'out of season' so successfully that local enthusiasts still race both types today.

Iceboats originated in northern Europe

during the 1700s, but it was the conversion of another wildfowling punt, the Barnegat Bay sneakbox, that helped to popularize this particular aspect of sailboat racing in North America. In fact one particular class of ice-boat, the Great South Bay Scooter as it became known, was developed out of necessity. The U.S. Lifesaving Service established sea watches every few miles along the entire south shore of Long Island, and getting to and fro over partly frozen bays was always a problem until an ingenious serviceman took a punt and fitted runners beneath. The boat was still able to sail across open water but when it reached ice, instead of coming to a halt, it simply scooted out and ran along at much higher speeds. Wildfowlers also saw the advantage of this conversion and when the shooting season was over, scooting over the ice became a competitive sport between hunting clubs, a recreation that continues in the area today.

As a single-hulled boat, the canoe in all its forms has spent more time being paddled than sailed. There has been the Polynesian war canoe, the Viking longship, the Eskimo kayak, and the American Indian open canoe, all designed to suit local conditions. However, one breed of canoe has been developed purely for sail racing and is epitomized in the International 10 (Square Metre) canoe, one of the most efficient sailing boats today, and one which has influenced design thinking in many other classes.

– the modern sailing dinghy
DEVELOPMENT AND EXPANSION

As a sport or recreation, small-boat sailing has only come into its own since the late 1940s. Before World War II international sailing could, with some truth, be called yachting; the particular thrills of hurtling across the water in a sailing dinghy, powered only by a suit of sails, and muscle, was known only to a few.

When the world emerged from war in 1945, the sport of sailing was just one of many to blossom. Among contributing factors were the new atmosphere of general relief and the fact that, compared with before the war, the international exchange of information had greatly improved. However, traditional materials, such as the boatbuilder's familiar Honduras and African mahoganies for planking hull shells and spruce for masts, were in short supply. The growing number of people interested in small-boat sailing and racing began to turn to the highly efficient synthetic resin glues and durable waterproof plywood

A modern development of the canoe, this International Sailing Canoe is noted for its speed and efficiency. The use of a sliding seat necessitates an extension to the tiller

that were among the technological gains of
wartime. Within a matter of a few years these
hull materials (*see also* HULLS: Construction
components) were augmented by the appearance of metal masts, nylon and other
synthetic fibres for sailcloth and cordage, and
efficient hardware for hulls and rigging made
from stainless steel and reinforced plastics (*see*
SAIL DESIGN AND MATERIALS; MASTS AND RIG-
GING). This new range of superior materials
and constructional techniques naturally had
a dramatic influence on small-boat design
and, later, marketing.

Before 1939 the only dinghy classes raced in
Great Britain on a national basis were the
National 12 and the International 14 classes.
It is a tribute to the sound thinking of those
early dinghy-racing enthusiasts that both
classes still flourish, having served as test beds
for a great many innovations that have allowed younger dinghy classes to develop to
the present high standard. In America similar
moves were being made to establish national
classes. By this time the hard-chine Star
keelboat, designed in 1911, had begun to
make an impact following its first appearance
at the Olympics in 1932. Certainly, its flat-
bottomed shape was to be an important
influence on other designs such as the Snipe,
Comet, and Lightning – all hard-chine
classes that continue to have flourishing
support today.

Back in Britain, an indication of what was to
come appeared in 1947: the 12-ft Firefly
based on, and very reminiscent of, the hull
shape produced by the British naval architect
Uffa Fox in the late 1930s for his highly
successful Uffa King design for the National
12 class. In the Firefly, however, the rise of
floor had been reduced in an attempt to
improve planing ability. The hull itself was
extremely clean and based on a hot-moulded
birch-ply (soon to be changed to agba) shell.
The technique of bonding veneers together
over a male mould under heat and pressure,
developed for manufacturing the nose sections of warplanes, was used here. It was in
this boat, too, that the first commercially
produced aluminium-alloy mast was used. At
its inception the Firefly was a very advanced
sailing dinghy, eminently suitable for club
racing. It did much to encourage dinghy
sailors and designers to be forward-looking
where the new materials were concerned. It

*The National 12 is a restricted class dinghy. It
may, therefore, consist of several designs provided
they fall within certain limits. The one illustrated is
a Cheshire Cat*

*A Firefly (opposite) taking part in the National
Championships. A racing dinghy for a crew of two,
the Firefly is decked forward and has built-in
buoyancy*

soon became firmly established and was the first true one-design to be sailed on a national basis.

Soon to follow was the Merlin, designed by Jack Holt; this 14-ft restricted-class dinghy was intended to provide the sort of high-speed racing hitherto enjoyed only by those who could afford an International 14. Next to appear from the drawing board of the same designer, and sponsored by *Yachting World* magazine, was the chunky little pram-bowed Cadet, intended for junior racing only; any one over eighteen became ineligible to sail the boats in class competition. It was designed to be easily built from materials readily to hand and by anyone with even a limited ability with woodworking tools. The boat's fittings were as simple as possible and also designed so that they could be made up by the amateur builder should he be unable to find a stock item in the local chandlery. The Cadet deserved to succeed – and did so on an international scale with a strong following in the Eastern bloc countries and Australia. There are many small-boat sailors of international repute who cut their dinghy-racing teeth in the hot competition provided by this class.

But whereas the Cadet has proved to be an ideal two-man trainer, it is the 7 ft 6 in Optimist that has done most to generate top single-handed sailors. Originating in Florida as the Clearwater Pram, Clark Mills' plans for this plywood-box trainer were taken to Denmark, from where the design, renamed the Optimist, spread through Europe and the rest of the world. Today numbers are claimed

Merlin-Rockets of the Arun Yacht Club. This dinghy is a development from Jack Holt's Merlin design and a similar product, the Rocket from

Wyche and Coppock. Belonging to a British National Class some latitude is allowed in hull shape and sail plan

International Cadets negotiating the first marker buoy at Burnham-on-Crouch, Essex, during the Ninth National Sailing Championship for this class

The single-handed Laser (opposite), noted for its planing, is widely sailed. Made of GRP, it has a centreboard and built-in buoyancy

to exceed 135 000 boats, increasing by 12 000 annually and available in various constructions from plywood, fibreglass, or ABS plastic to self-skinning polyurethane foam.

During the 1950s the sport of small-boat sailing and racing grew strongly throughout the world. For many years, however, Britain provided the true nursery for dinghy racing and many new designs began to appear: some faded almost as soon as they had been conceived; others, such as the Hornet, 5-0-5, Albacore, Wayfarer, Enterprise, and GP 14, flourished.

It was during this period too, that British designers, owners, and builders began to exploit the new materials and building techniques. These materials enabled builders to produce hulls that were both light and very strong. It was classes such as the Enterprise

and GP 14 – constructed from profiled-out plywood parts – that showed the most rapid growth. The reason was that in order to succeed commercially and satisfy an expanding market, the professional had to turn from boatbuilding as an expression of traditional woodworking skills to the production of kits of parts for his men to assemble 'off the shelf'; it was only a small step from there to making standard kits available to the owner-builder.

The standard of kits for home building improved rapidly and it was not long before boats were being put together in lofts, living rooms, and garages everywhere. The frenzy of home building provided a spectacular boom in dinghy sailing in Britain in the early 1960s and it was supported by several companies that set up to make suitable fittings, spars and sails. Elsewhere, however, there was not the same enthusiasm shown for home

building: neither America nor Australia was to experience the great expansion in dinghy sailing seen in the British Isles, and this was to leave them behind in both the development of equipment and sailing expertise.

During the early 1960s the novelty of fibreglass construction filtered down from the building of larger craft to the dinghy classes, where it had a mixed reception, not least from the class associations themselves who were a little nervous of the possible repercussions of adopting this new material. For a time fibreglass and timber boats flourished side by side. As builders using fibreglass became more understanding of the material, so quality of structure and finish improved. The suppliers of wood kits also improved their techniques, and then came the Jack Holt/Barry Bucknell Mirror dinghy, which in its first year sold 800 boats: an unheard-of

Marionette (opposite) *is typical of a highly successful modern ocean racer, whose form has been so influenced by the rating rules*

International Optimists (above) *taking part in a world championship for this class on the Silvaplanasee in Switzerland in 1974*

Very popular throughout the world, the Albacore (above) is a fast dinghy made of GRP or wood, designed by Uffa Fox

The parts of a kit dinghy

achievement at the time. The Mirror dinghy sold in large numbers: in the heyday of the class over 400 kits were leaving the factory each month. The rapid growth of this class soon had a beneficial effect on dinghy sailing in general because apart from becoming a very large class numerically, the Mirror was soon feeding contemporary racing classes. Although for a number of years a few professional and rather more amateur builders had experimented with glass-taping the joints of plywood hull panels and glassing-in the tank sides and bulkheads, it took the Mirror dinghy to give the technique respectability

*Shown here with its spinnaker, the Fireball was
purpose-designed for home construction in plywood.
Now it is also constructed in GRP*

and it was not long before this method of
construction became commonplace throughout the kit market.

CATAMARANS

While the orthodox racing dinghy was evolv-
ing rapidly in the 1950s, another breed – the
catamaran (*see also* HULLS; MULTIHULLS) – was
making its first rather faltering appearances.
As was to be expected, some of the early
designs showed that their creators had something yet to learn and the extravagant claims
of unheard-of speeds by early cat enthusiasts
were seldom borne out in practice. It was not
until the Prout brothers' Shearwater arrived
on the scene that a high-performance small
catamaran became readily available. The
faintly amused interest of some dinghy sailors
at the sometimes undignified progressions of
certain of the early cats slowly turned to
grudging, and then open, admiration of the
performance potential of well-designed examples of the breed. In a breeze, modern cats
such as the Tornado, Dart, and Unicorn are
capable of hurtling across the water at a
speed quite unattainable even by the fleetest
centreboarder. Without any doubt the greatest success in catamarans, both commercially
and as far as the enthusiastic owners are
concerned, must be the Hobie, built in 14-,
16-, and 18-ft versions and, by the late 1970s,
sailed almost as a cult all over the world.

The rising costs of building materials and
labour have combined to check the boom in
dinghy racing. Advances are still being made,
however, and occasional attempts are made
to start a new class, but the innovators are
often chastened to discover that enormous
sums of money have to be sunk in marketing
research, tooling, and advertising if their
projects are to have any chance of success.

SINGLE-HANDERS AND BOARDBOATS

In recent years two developments have taken
small-boat sailors by storm. The first was the
appearance in 1970 of Bruce Kirby's little
Laser one-design single-hander. Having
completely saturated its Canadian home
market, the Laser, which is light enough for
car-top transport, has now spread throughout
the world. Completely different, and expanding still faster, is the sport of sailboarding or
windsurfing. The boardboat used is powered
by a simple pivoting sail set on an unstayed
mast and yoke boom with the heel of the mast
attached to the board by a universal joint.
The sailor stands while holding the rig and
using his body weight to extract the drive. He
steers by leaning the rig forward or aft to alter
the relative positions of the CE (CENTRE OF
EFFORT) and the CLR (CENTRE OF LATERAL
RESISTANCE) of the board with its daggerboard and skeg. Many firms throughout
the world have foreseen a boom in this
branch of sailing, and everywhere board
sailors are taking to the water in increasing
numbers.

– evolution of equipment and technique

Until the early 1900s, the working boats of the day were both heavy and robust. Sailing was largely a sedate, gentleman's sport. Sitting out to balance the rig was limited in effect, and if winds blew hard, crews either reefed down or stayed ashore. Capsizing was generally frowned on: sailors who did were expected to sink. It was only when Uffa Fox and Tom Thornycroft developed their International 14 designs in the early 1930s to beat the acknowledged boats drawn by Morgan Giles that the first planing dinghies were evolved, and the search for lightness and sitting-out aids began.

Toestraps or bars in the bottom of the boat have long been an aid for the crew, though at first they were probably thought of as being there more to improve safety than increase performance; otherwise they would no doubt have been banned at a very early date. The established sailing fraternity both in Britain and elsewhere could see no reason for developments that made life easier afloat. They tended to abhor change and any ideas that improved performance, like the trapeze and self-draining cockpit, were resisted vehemently, an attitude that was to dog development for many years. The early planing dinghies, which still had heavy metal centreboards, were designed to meet minimum rather than maximum beam measurements, and in an effort to give the crew a better righting force Charles Currey, a keen International 14 sailor, developed the donkey or hiking bar. This was a vertical tube that hooked into the fairlead track on the gunwale and was swapped from one side to the other on each tack to give the crew a good handhold so that he could lean out. Although the idea was quite within the rules, such would have been the animosity from other crews if they had had a close look at it that the bar was clipped on after leaving the shore and always hidden in the bottom of a sailbag before returning after a race.

As heavy plates were gradually replaced by wooden centreboards without any ballasting function, later boat designs were built wider to compensate. But this did not stop further

The Shearwater's symmetrical hulls (opposite) *may be constructed of plywood or GRP. It is equipped with a sliding seat and a trapeze*

The Rodney March-designed Dart catamaran, shown above, with trapezes in use. A Dart was the winner of the International Catamaran Week held off the Isle of Sheppey, Kent in 1978

The asymmetrical hulls of the Hobie 16 catamaran are constructed of GRP sandwich. With foam flotation the hulls are unsinkable and the boat is easily righted

53

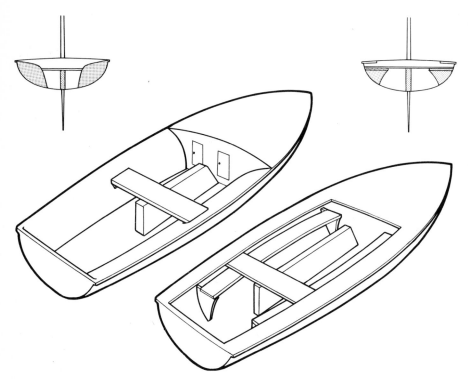

Fig. 1 *Rolled-in and bench layouts compared*

Fig. 2 *Buoyancy bags of two kinds strapped in position* (below)

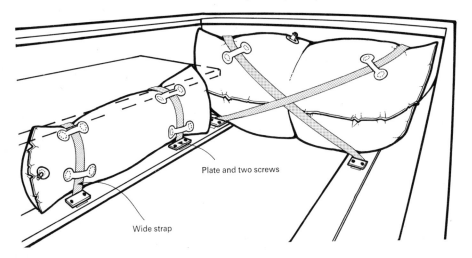

Plate and two screws

Wide strap

features. In 1934 *Alarm*, built for the British Olympic yachtsman Stewart Morris, was fitted with a tray in the bow to catch the spray and funnel it down and out through the centreboard case. It was the first semi-self-draining dinghy, but as many felt that it helped him to win the Prince of Wales Cup that year, the offending arrangement was removed and the idea barred. Undeterred, Morris in *Alarm* won the Prince of Wales Cup again in 1936 in far worse conditions, but this brought no change of view.

Jack Holt was one of the first to cut drainage holes through the transom of a dinghy, an action that quickly earned him disfavour: in those days it was the crew's job to bail out the boat during and after racing and few could see any reason for change. The Chinese developed the first self-bailer some 2000 years ago, using a hollow bamboo tube projected through the hull, but it was not until the 1950s that the idea was taken a step further by Jack Holt and Beecher Moore. This was a fixed scoop fitted in the bottom of their Hornet dinghy, with a large plug to seal it off and stop water from pouring back in when stationary. Again, ingenuity was rewarded with opprobrium; for years the rule had been that once the masthead pennant touched the water the yachtsman should retire. With the advent of self-bailers, and later transom flaps, the rule became irrelevant, but it took some time for the establishment to realize it.

Jack Holt was also one of the first to develop the sail luff groove cut into the mast, though it was expense rather than design that gave him the idea now used almost universally. When building his first boat, an 18-ft clinker design, he could not afford the costly brass track normally screwed to the after face of the mast in which the sail slides travelled up and down, so he cut a groove into the mast, made up from old flooring boards glued together, large enough to take the boltrope sewn to the luff of the sail.

Fashions in rig design are revolving constantly and have turned full circle more than once, moving away from stiff spars with little support to narrow affairs supported by all manner of wires. The first metal spars were developed from Reynolds aluminium-alloy sections for Uffa Fox's Firefly in 1947 and fitted with spruce tops to create a tapered shape above the hounds. Ian Proctor, who was working on similar ideas at the time, took the development a stage further, extruding purpose-made sections cut and tapered at the top to form a one-piece mast, and from this beginning his company quickly grew to become the world's largest manufacturer of spars for yachts of all sizes.

As the search for lighter boats continued the cast heavy gunmetal, galvanized, bronze or brass fittings used extensively during the early part of this century were superseded, by

ideas. A group of Canadian International 14 sailors devised a crew harness that held a cleat set in the middle of the wearer's chest to take the jib sheet, so that he could sit out further without undue strain. It was the beginnings of the trapeze – and banned immediately.

Crews swinging out from the weather side on the end of 'bell ropes' were a common sight on A-Raters based on the Thames during the early 1930s, an idea copied from boatmen off Colombo in Ceylon (Sri Lanka) who measured the wind strength as either a one-, two-, or three-man breeze depending on how many were hanging out; however,

these A-Raters raced to a set of rules different from other National classes emerging at the time. It was not until 1937 that Peter Scott surprised the yachting 'establishment' by lying outside his International 14 suspended in a harness attached by wire to the mast hounds. This was the first true trapeze, but like the sliding seat first developed by the American Paul Butler for his early 10 m² Canoes, it was quickly outlawed.

The establishment could see little point in self-draining cockpits or automatic bailers either, and consequently a number of ideas, commonplace enough today, were categorized as go-fast gadgets rather than safety

lighter equipment first fabricated from stainless steel and Tufnol, and then from alloy and plastic mouldings.

Clothing too has changed. At the turn of the century amateur sailors were sporting their weekend best, the more well-to-do wearing white flannels and jackets, together with an assortment of favourite headwear from flat caps to straw hats. Later when boats started to plane, crews needed more protection from the spray and they turned first to oiled woollen jumpers, canvas smocks, and oilskins, which gradually became lighter and more flexible. The 1950s brought neoprene-rubber wet suits, obscene garments to some, which required a quantity of talcum powder sprinkled inside in order to get them on. However, these suits, which trap a warm layer of water next to the skin and insulate the body, soon became fashionable; today nylon linings have dispensed with the need for the preliminary talc.

– the influence of materials
From the dugout canoe onwards, man has always built from materials ready to hand. Wood has been the natural choice in most parts of the world, but where this has been in short supply or found to be unsuitable, alternatives have influenced development. The reed boats of Egypt and Bolivia were built to a bulky design encapsulating air, very much like inflatable boats do today. The Irish curragh, the Welsh coracle, and the Eskimo kayak were skinned with hide over a flexible wood or whalebone framework, anticipating the canvas-sheathed craft of a later generation. In the Middle East seafarers relied on bamboo wickerwork covered with a hard-setting mixture of powdered resin and manure to produce a watertight shell.

Today the materials used for boatbuilding are no less diverse, the choice ranging from the traditional ones to metals, man-made fabrics, and compositions, all of which are utilized in an increasing number of composite constructions.
WOOD
Available in a multitude of densities, textures,

flexibility and strength properties, there is at least one species of wood ideally suited to any single boatbuilding need. Teak and its related varieties have long been accepted as one of the most durable hardwoods for hull planking and decks, but where a lighter construction is required, the mahoganies and even pine softwood have been used with success. Likewise, oak, elm, and ash were choices for framing, though in dinghies spruce has always been a favourite light-weight substitute. Wood composites such as marine plywood, developed during World War II, extended further the versatility of this natural resource. Indeed, it is the availability of high-grade plywood together with the development of modern fastenings and synthetic glues and resins that has had the most influence on present design thinking. Clinker or lapstrake construction (*see also* HULLS: Construction components) is a traditional method of building wooden boats in which longitudinal planks that overlap each other at the edges are bent over a framework of transverse moulds set up to form the shape of the boat. The planking is braced with ribs or frames set at short intervals along the whole length of the boat, and usually fastened with copper clench nails riveted over. The

joints only become fully watertight after immersion when the planking 'takes up' or swells to close the gaps. Today, the use of synthetic glues produces such strong joints that the framing, and overlapping of planking, and metal fastenings have been dispensed with in most dinghy designs, and using a thin plywood for skin planking a very light, strong shell can be built. Some dinghies were carvel built (*see also* HULLS: Construction components) to form a smooth exterior and reduce the 'wetted area' and thus drag. Instead of overlapping, the planks are butt-jointed at their ends before being clenched up against the ribs. Uffa Fox was a keen exponent of this form of construction for his pre-war International 14s, and even built a series of frameless hulls, side-fastening each plank to the next. Unfortunately, though very light, the boats tended to twist and move a great deal when sailing through waves and none has stood the test of time.
COLD MOULDING
The advent of modern synthetic glues, and more recently resins, has made it possible to produce very light, waterproof, and immensely strong moulded-veneer hulls. Narrow strips of thin wood veneer are laid diagonally over a building mould and held in place

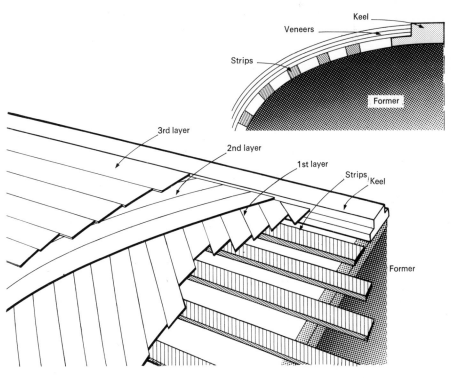

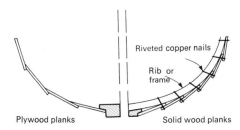

Fig. 3 Clinker (lapstrake) construction of a dinghy hull using two different materials

Fig. 4 A dinghy hull (bottom up) constructed with moulded veneers. The smaller diagram is a cross-section of the hull and the mould upon which it is constructed

with staples. A coating of glue is applied to the first layer of veneer before a second is laid diagonally across the first with the strips again stapled in place temporarily until the bond has cured. This process is repeated until the veneers together produce the required stiffness and strength, but there are normally never less than three plies to ensure that the laminate is in balance.

MARINE PLYWOOD

The influence this material has had on boat-building cannot be overstated. The method of building a hull with flat sides and bottom is a very old one, but not until the introduction of

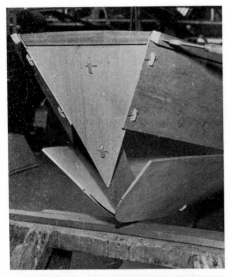

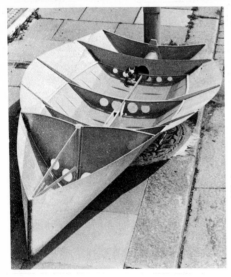

*Sheets of marine plywood (*top*) being used in the construction of a Miracle dinghy. Designed as a progression on the Mirror it has a Bermudian rig and a crew of two*

*The developed plywood (tortured) shapes of a Moth (*above*) – a single-handed, una-rigged dinghy having a daggerboard*

plywood was it so simplified. The pre-World War II building method was to construct a skeleton of closely set frames, then plank up sides and bottom with $\frac{5}{16}$-in (16-mm) mahogany or gaboon strakes, which were then held to the frames with metal fastenings and relied on cotton caulking and mastic between the joints for watertightness. Among the many classes of dinghies to be built in this way were the International Snipe, the Comet dinghy in America, and the German 10 m² monotype designs. The introduction of plywood to these classes, however, reduced the amount of framing required, saving weight and simplifying construction considerably for the panel had only to be fastened to the chine and other stringers.

The next development in the use of plywood was the 'stitch-and-glue' method of glass-taped construction, which led in turn to the development of tortured-ply hull shapes particularly suited to catamaran building but also used for monohulls. Here the curved shape of the hull is developed onto the flat sheet so that when cut out and the seams glass-taped together the plywood takes up the designed shape. However, their possible curvature is two-dimensional, rather than three-dimensional as for cold-moulded, planked, or fibreglass hulls.

REINFORCED PLASTICS

Although glassfibre has become the most common reinforcement in moulded plastic boats, it was the newspaper headlines moulded into a small dinghy at the London Boat Show in the early years of plastic boatbuilding that caught the public eye and showed that there are many other materials that can be used to increase the tensile strength of plastic. On their own, polyester and other suitable resins are too brittle for boatbuilding purposes and have to be combined with other materials so that they become resilient and tough enough to withstand the many knocks and scrapes that they receive afloat. The newspaper-reinforced dinghy was moulded for a publicity stunt and other materials such as stranded and woven glassfibre, Kevlar, and carbon-fibre filaments offer a far greater tensile strength, though the last two materials are very expensive and only used whenever particularly high tensile strength or an extremely light moulding is required.

Compared with wood, a glass-reinforced plastic (GRP) laminate is more flexible, but this can be countered at the design stage by reducing the flat unsupported areas to a minimum. A dinghy like the 5–0–5, designed specifically for GRP construction, has round bilges and flared topsides and relies on the curved shape rather than thickness of laminate for panel stiffness. However, comparable strength and stiffness can be achieved on flat chine sections by utilizing a sandwich construction of fibreglass laminated over

lightweight synthetic foam or squares of balsa wood cut across the end grain as an inner core, which has the added advantage of offering positive buoyancy. Local stiffening can also be added by moulding in lightweight GRP webs, sometimes over a paper-core rope, to improve rigidity; one class, the 470, in which sandwich construction was banned until after the 1980 Olympics, relied on this form of stiffening almost exclusively.

The chemical industries are constantly developing new materials and methods of construction, some of which can be applied in dinghy building. One of these is polypropylene, well known for its toughness and resistance to fatigue. Tooling costs are very high but once in production, injection-moulding machines can produce boats at seven-minute intervals and continue doing so day and night without the need for an army of craftsmen to put them together. One example of this production method is the British Topper boardboat which is injection-moulded in such large quantities that the manufacturers are able to sell to a worldwide market.

– dinghy rigs

In the early days of sail, rigs may not have been highly efficient but they were certainly simple and easy to handle. The standing lug-sail, once a common working rig, was carried on a yard or gaff that could be quickly hoisted or lowered on an unstayed mast. The tack was attached to the gunwale, and with the loose-footed sail sheeted to the stern, the working area in the boat remained uncluttered. A more refined version of the same rig is the balanced lugsail, which has both boom and gaff extended forward of the mast to carry extra sail to help balance the rig and prevent the peak of the mainsail from falling away to leeward.

A foresail or jib improves rig efficiency by creating a Venturi effect, speeding up the airstream across the leeward side of the mainsail. The gap or 'slot' between the two sails is critical: too wide and the Venturi is not formed; too narrow and the airflow becomes choked, backwinding the mainsail (*see* SAIL TRIM).

The Bermudian rig, so called because it was seen in the Bermudas at the turn of the century, and also known as the Marconi rig because the plethora of standing rigging recalled that inventor's early radio masts, did not find international favour in other parts of the world until the 1920s. Before that time, little thought had been given to windage and it was the gunter rig that was the accepted high-performance sailplan, with its gaff hauled nearly vertical to increase effective mast height without the need for a single tall spar and heavy rigging. Today the gunter or gaff rig is still chosen for some small 'cartoppers', such as the Optimist and the Mirror

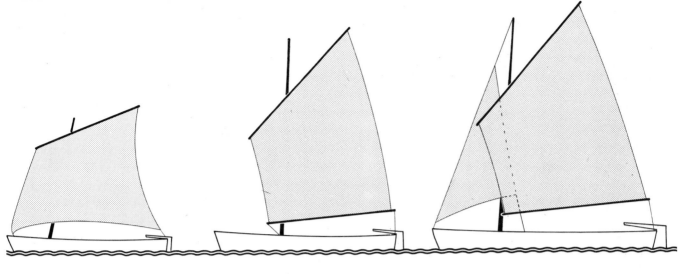

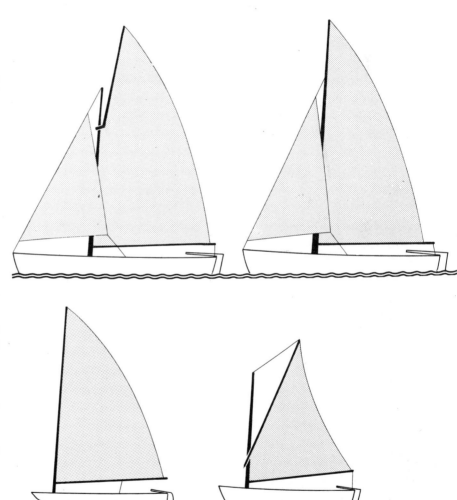

dinghy, because the spars are short enough to stow inside the boat. The Bermudian rig only really came into its own when advances in adhesive technology made it possible to produce hollow wooden masts of reduced weight, because at the time most dinghies were kept on moorings and too much top weight would have capsized them in strong conditions. The higher-aspect Bermudian sailplan is certainly a cleaner, more efficient rig than the gunter, and offers better control over the top section of the sail. One-piece masts were set up with all manner of rigging wires and spreaders to stiffen the spar as much as possible, but with the development of the una or cat rig in such single-handers as the Finn Olympic class dinghy, which has an unstayed flexible mast, sailors began to learn more about sail shape and the advantages a bendy rig has to offer. Hitherto it had always been necessary to have two or even three sails cut with varying degrees of fullness to get the best out of one rig in all conditions, but then the sailmakers began to develop more universal sails that relied on mast bend to control the degree of fullness. The adjustment of spar bend and sail shape is highly developed in certain high-performance dinghy classes today, and the two elements are conceived in interaction.

In the catamaran world, the una rig was taken a step further with the development of the rotating wing mast. One of the most successful early designs was that fitted to the C-Class catamaran *Lady Helmsman*, the successful Little America's Cup defender in 1966, '67 and '68. This was a very light structure utilizing polystyrene ribs covered with ⅛-in (3-mm) gaboon ply and weighing 159 lb (72 kg). This semi-rigid rig, with its mast taking up a third of the total area on which the wind acted, was designed by Austin

Fig. 5 Early dinghy lugsail rigs (top, from left to right): *dipping lugsail, balanced lugsail, and standing lugsail with foresail*

Fig. 6 Dinghy rigs (centre, from left to right): *gunter, Bermudian*

Fig. 7 Dinghy rigs (above, from left to right): *cat (una Bermudian), and spritsail*

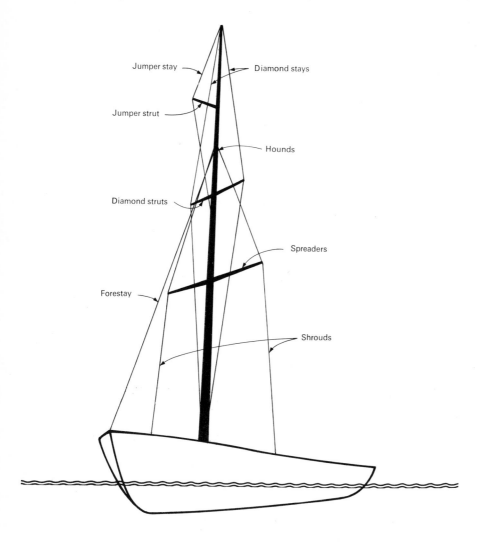

Fig. 8 *The early rig of an International 14 (proportions exaggerated for illustrative purposes)*

Labels on figure:
Jumper stay — Diamond stays
Jumper strut
Hounds
Diamond struts
Spreaders
Forestay
Shrouds

Farrar and carried a fully battened sail that set without any twist in it: i.e. the upper sections curved in the same way as the lower. This was achieved by designing the mast with a convex-shaped trailing edge to match the curved leech of the soft sail, so that when set at the correct angle to the wind, it produced both a constant curve and angle from top to bottom. Since that time, the Americans have developed the principle further, dispensing with the sail altogether and replacing it with articulating flaps to form a complete wing.

Fig. 9 *A diagrammatic representation* (bottom left) *of a dinghy's mainsail rolling equipment and reefing claw*

Fig. 10 *Two typical mainsheet systems:* below, *a four-part purchase from the centre and*, bottom, *a two-part purchase operating from the transom*

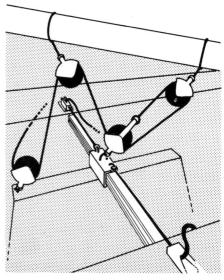

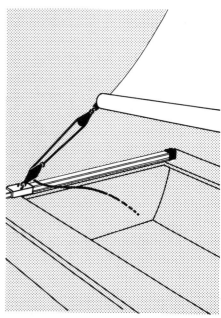

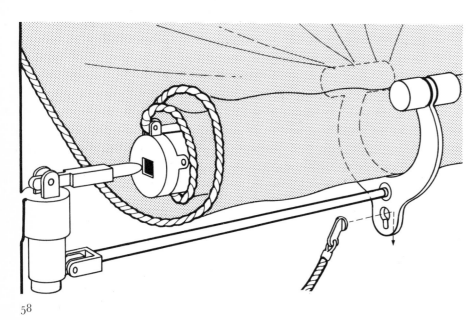

Dinghies

Fig. 11 The drawing shows the wing mast of the 1978 Little America's Cup defender, Patient Lady IV

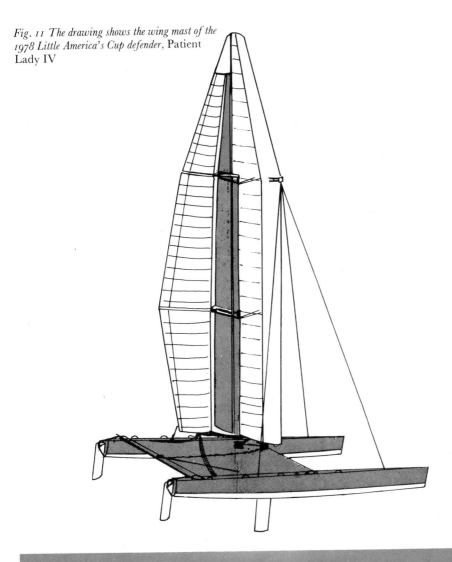

Dip (of the horizon)
The angle between the horizontal plane through the observer's eye and the direction of the horizon. *See also* HORIZON DISTANCE

Dipping lug *see* RIGS: Lateen and lug rigs

Displacement
The weight of a vessel.

Divergence *see* WIND AND WEATHER: Atmospheric pressure and weather systems

D. lat.
Difference of latitude: the north-south component of a RHUMB LINE, measured in NAUTICAL MILES.

DME
A secondary radar distance-measuring equipment, intended for aviation but with application to fleet operations such as whale catching. It can give an accurate knowledge of distance from a parent vessel up to 400 km.

Docking loads *see* HULLS: Scantlings

Dodger (weather cloth)
A protective screen, typically of canvas, to keep off sea and spray.

Dolphin striker
A short spar pointing downward fitted under the bowsprit in sailing vessels to act as a strut in staying the jib boom.

Double
To round, e.g. a cape, with a near reversal of course.

Double sheet bend *see* ROPEWORK: Bends and hitches

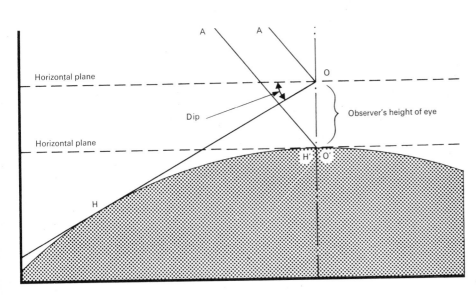

The dip of the horizon must be allowed for when observing the altitude of a heavenly body with a sextant. The diagram shows that if the observer's eye (O) were at sea level then the horizontal plane passing through his eye and the plane of the visible horizon (H) are the same. Thus no angle is formed and the altitude of the heavenly body (A') would be true (subject to refraction). However, as the observer's eye is never at sea level, an angle is formed between the horizontal plane passing through the observer's eye (O) and the horizon (H). This greater angle represents the observed altitude of the heavenly body (A). For the sake of simplicity it is reckoned that the heavenly body is far enough away for the line A'O' to be considered parallel to the line A'O'. The dip angle must be subtracted from the observed altitude (AOH) to obtain the correct altitude

Downhaul *see* MASTS AND RIGGING: Glossary

Draught, draft
The depth to which a vessel is submerged.

Draw
(1) To be submerged to a particular draught;
(2) a sail is said to draw when it is filled by the wind.

Drift
The effect of the movement of the water on a craft, or the amount made to leeward.

Drift angle *see* LEEWAY

Dutchman's log
An old way of judging the speed of a vessel. Something that will float is thrown into the sea from the bows and timed until it reaches the stern; in this time interval the vessel will have covered her own length. Before watches with a second hand were available the interval was measured by counting one's pulse or reciting some form of words, as for example the Lord's Prayer; the final syllable would indicate the vessel's speed – though hardly convertible into knots except from previous experience. The Dutchman's log method is still occasionally of value, as when the presence of weed or sea ice makes it inadvisable to stream a taffrail log. *See also* LOG

Ease
To slacken.

Ebb
The movement of a tide as it recedes from high water.

Eddy
A movement of water in a different or opposite direction from the tidal stream or current.

Electrics
The use of electricity on board a yacht fitted with an auxiliary engine will of necessity be limited by the size of generator and the number of running hours each day. Unless the engine is hand-started, which is not always convenient, about 15 min charge at full rate will be needed to replace energy drawn from the battery for starting. Additional time will be required to replace losses due to self-discharge in a lead-acid battery that has been idle for any length of time between trips. During warm weather the loss will be 2% per day. Provision for navigation lights and domestic comforts will have to be made by increasing the generating capacity, either by extending the engine running hours beyond those actually needed for leaving and entering harbour or by relying on shore supply for battery charging.

An electrical balance sheet may be made up showing estimated consumption against generating capacity over a 24-hour period. Details will be varied to suit individual requirements. The charging time will be proportionately increased if the rate of discharge remains constant and charging takes place at longer intervals. *See* table *below*.

The generating capacity of inboard engines may be increased by fitting an alternator in place of the conventional dynamo. Another method is to add a belt-driven alternator. The original generator is then retained to charge the start battery, leaving the alternator and a second battery to take care of all other loads. This arrangement is suited to some smaller engines that are fitted with Dynastart – a combined generator and start motor that cannot be replaced by an alternator.

The twin-battery system ensures that whatever may happen on the domestic side, the start battery should always be fit for duty. Also, two batteries of moderate size are easier to handle and stow than a single large one. Two batteries may be charged from a single source through a blocking diode unit. Here the charging current passes through two diodes, one for each battery, and back charging from one battery to the other is prevented by the diodes. The system is self-regulating so that the bulk of the available charging current will go to the battery most in need, gradually reducing as the difference in voltage between the two batteries becomes less. The batteries may be of different capacities, but must be of the same type, i.e. both lead-acid or both alkaline. A split charging relay used in conjunction with an alternator is cheaper than a diode unit and performs the same function.

Alternators have a high specific output, are easy to install, maintenance is minimal, and they can deliver a useful charging current over a wide speed range. Fig. 4 shows a typical speed output curve from which it will be seen that charging begins at 1200 rpm rising to 45 amps at 6000 rpm. The machine may safely be run at speeds up to 12 000 rpm, but the self-regulating character of the windings ensures that there is no increase in output at speeds in excess of 6000 rpm. Control of the charging rate is by a small solid-state unit that monitors battery voltage. Low battery voltage causes maximum field current to be applied, but this reduces as battery voltage rises, and the charging rate becomes a trickle when a state of full charge is reached.

By selecting suitable diameter pulleys for the alternator drive the safe operating speed of 12 000 rpm can be achieved at full engine speed. Thus, useful charging current will be

Generating capacity: estimated consumption during a 24-hour period

	NUMBER	CONSUMPTION PER HOUR	TIME IN USE	
Navigation lights	4	12 watts	1 hour	48 watt-hours
Interior lights	3	12 watts	4 hours	144 watt-hours
Anchor lights	1	6 watts	8 hours	48 watt-hours
Add: two starts, standby losses, etc. (say)				120 watt-hours
			Total	360 watt-hours

Generating capacity 120 watts (i.e. 10 amps at 12 volts)

Therefore running hours to break even $\dfrac{360}{120} = 3$ hours

Output current
(amperes)

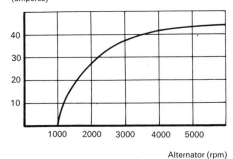

Alternator speed curve at 13.5v

available from a quarter to full engine speed.

A range of mounting brackets is available for adapting existing dynamo mountings to take an alternator. These may also be used to make up floor mountings when adding an alternator to the existing arrangement. Alternators may be driven in either direction so long as the fan blades are suited to the rotation. These are standard parts that can be exchanged without the use of any special tools.

Maintenance is relatively simple. Ventilation slots and air passages have to be kept clean. Cable connections must be clean and tight, especially the main output terminals where a poor connection can damage the machine or regulator. The bearings are self-lubricating but can be damaged by excessive belt tension. On the other hand, a slack belt or one so worn that it touches the bottom of the pulley grooves will seriously reduce output. Advice on this point should be in the engine manual. As a rough guide a 12-in (305-mm) length between pulleys should give $\frac{1}{2}$ to $\frac{3}{4}$ in (about 12 to 19 mm) from the direct line under the pressure of one finger. The two carbon brushes carrying field current have to be kept clean and free to move in their holders. These, together with the associated sliprings, need occasional service to remove carbon dust and oily deposits. There are no other moving parts or contacts requiring attention.

Diodes built into the machine rectify the alternating current (AC) to direct current (DC) for battery charging. These diodes are virtually everlasting, but certain precautions have to be observed. They are sensitive to reverse polarity and will be damaged if the battery is wrongly connected. Also, the circuits between alternator, battery, and control unit must not be broken while the machine is running. Particular attention should be paid to terminal connections. The push-on terminals in common use are not entirely proof against accidental disconnection, and cable ends close to terminal lugs should be watched for corrosion or signs of fracture caused by

vibration. Unless testing in accordance with makers' instructions, all main and control connections must be properly made before starting up. But a switch may be included in the field circuit if for any reason it is desired to control charging manually. A change-over switch for charging two batteries from a single alternator should be of the 'make before break' type, or care has to be taken to see that it is not operated when the machine is charging. A blocking diode unit or split charging relay is preferred for this duty. Alternators for marine use are given a special finish to resist damp and corrosion, but this cannot be expected to withstand water drawn in by the fan. The machine has to be shielded from the splash of bilge water and drips from above. Totally enclosed alternators are produced for road vehicles, but cost and weight are against their general use on small auxiliary engines.

Other means of catering for loads in excess of generating capacity are to take on board a battery that has been charged ashore, use a shore supply for charging, carry an auxiliary generator or harness the energy from a solid propeller that is free to rotate when sailing. The first method is often used on club yachts that will only be away from base for a week or ten days and are not expected to do much night work anyway. So long as the home base is in a regular yacht harbour the problem of transport to and from the charging station is not serious. Better still there may be a supply of shore electricity on the pontoon so that the battery may be charged onboard. To bring the same battery weighing 50 lb (22 kg) or more off in a dinghy and put it on board without getting acid on clothes or some other mishap is not easy. The battery box developed for camping and caravans is worth considering. This consists of an acid-proof carrying case with the necessary wiring and controls for connecting to the electrical system of a car. The box is carried in the boot and the battery is charged while the car is in motion, or it may be taken home and connected to a charging set in the garage. Petrol-engined generating sets with outputs of 300 watts at 12 volts and weighing under 15 lb or 7 kg are available. However good the silencing and anti-vibration mounting may be, the owner will have to decide whether this intrusion on the peace of a pleasant mooring will be objectionable to him or to his neighbours. For the larger cruising yacht, where some drag is acceptable, the propeller is allowed to motor when sailing and an alternator is belt-driven from the shaft. Under favourable conditions enough electricity can be generated to satisfy all simple needs. There are also a number of wind-driven generators on the market, many of them very effective and of particular use to boats without engines.

– batteries

Lead-acid batteries as fitted to the majority of road vehicles are normally used for storing electricity on yachts, mainly on account of low first cost. Alkaline (nickel-iron or nickel-cadmium) batteries may appear to be expensive, but very long life and the ability to stand up to difficult working conditions will justify the capital outlay. They will withstand high rates of charge and discharge, and may be left in a state of charge for quite a long time. The self-discharge rate is very low, so if left on board for several weeks an alkaline battery should be capable of starting the engine. Both types are made in various grades to suit differing rates of discharge. A heavy duty or premium grade should be used for engine starting, a lighter type will suffice for lighting and domestic loads.

SIZE OF BATTERY

This is expressed in ampere-hours (amp-hours) at a standard rate of discharge. For lead-acid cells this is the 20-hour rate; e.g., a 100 amp-hour battery should deliver 5 amps for 20 hours. The capacity of normal alkaline cells is expressed at the 5-hour rate and 2 hours is used for heavy-duty types. Higher rates are possible for all batteries, but a corresponding reduction in capacity has to be accepted, this can be as much as 40% for continuous discharge at maximum rate. Using the figures from fig. 3 the consumption for lighting is 240 Watt-hours in 24 hours. For a 12-volt system a battery of $\frac{240}{12} = 20$ amp-hours should suffice. To this must be added the engine makers' estimate of capacity needed for starting, and a margin of up to 20% for contingencies and loss of capacity due to age of battery.

– lead-acid batteries

The initial cost is relatively low but they need regular attention to make good losses by self-discharge of about 1% per day. State of charge is ascertained by measuring the specific gravity of the electrolyte with an hydrometer. The reading should be 1.270 to 1.290 for a fully charged cell, readings of 1.200 and below indicate the need for recharging. Rate of charge is normally 1/10th of the capacity in amp-hours, i.e. 10 amps for a 100 amp-hour cell. This may safely be increased so long as the cell temperature does not exceed 104°F (40°C). Modern control units allow a high rate of charge that tapers off as cell voltage rises. Prolonged charging at high rates is to be avoided. The time taken to re-charge will be about 1.4 times that for discharge at the same rate.

ESSENTIAL MAINTENANCE

This consists of keeping cell tops clean and dry, the terminals clean and tight and protected by a coating of Vaseline. Loss of electrolyte by evaporation has to be made good by topping up with distilled or purified water. Never add acid unless it is to make good loss by spillage. This type of battery should not be left in a state of low charge for any length of time. Recharging will be necessary at intervals of 2–3 months when not in use.

– alkaline batteries
This type is high in first cost but has a correspondingly long life, 15 years or more. They are extremely robust, will accept high rates of charge and discharge, are virtually immune to overcharging, and have a very low self-discharge rate.

CAPACITY
Capacity is expressed in ampere-hours (amp-hours) as for lead-acid cells. The 5-hour rate is used for normal cells and 2-hour for heavy-duty. Normal charge rate for all cells is 1/5th of the capacity in amp-hours, e.g. 20 amps for a 100 amp-hour cell. This may be increased by 50% or more so long as the electrolyte temperature does not exceed $104°F$ $(40°C)$. The charge-to-discharge ratio is 1.4:1.

ESSENTIAL MAINTENANCE
This differs from lead-acid cell maintenance in a number of respects. Electrolyte level is from $\frac{3}{4}$ in to $1\frac{1}{4}$ in above the plate tops according to size of cell. Topping up should be done with distilled or purified water as for acid cells. An alkaline solution may be used for making good spillage, but not for fortifying electrolyte weakened by age. Specific gravity does not indicate state of charge. This is taken once or twice a year to check the condition of the electrolyte, that deteriorates slowly with age so that the whole charge has to be renewed at intervals of 6 years or longer, and cannot be revived by adding fresh alkali. The state of charge is shown by cell voltage which is 1.3 volts when fully charged, and should not be allowed to fall below 1.1 volts before re-charging. Care must be taken to avoid contamination of the electrolyte by acid. Do not use any hydrometer or utensil that has been in contact with acid. The tops of cell cases and terminals should be coated with Komoline jelly and the sides protected with Celvar varnish, both obtainable from the battery makers. Vaseline may be used instead of Komoline. Insulating bushes and wood-cell crates must be kept clean and every attempt should be made to prevent electrolytic corrosion of the metal cell cases by leakage currents. Translucent polystyrene cell cases are available. They are less robust than steel but are impervious to corrosion, occupy less space, and electrolyte level may be checked without the use of a dip tube.

STOWAGE OF BATTERIES
It is essential that they be properly secured for sea to prevent damage to the cases and loss of electrolyte. The start battery should be sited as close to the motor as possible to minimize loss of power caused by voltage drop in the cables. Adequate ventilation of the battery compartment is necessary to disperse the hydrogen gas given off during charging. There should be enough headroom above the cell tops for taking hydrometer readings and topping up.

See also ELECTROLYSIS; MAINTENANCE

Electric steering gear *see* SELF-STEERING GEAR

Electrolysis
At the beginning of the nineteenth century the Royal Navy was experiencing trouble with the copper sheathing on wooden warships, the probable cause being patches of impurities that set up cells activated by seawater. The English scientist Sir Humphrey Davy (1778–1829) recommended the use of zinc plates to counteract this. The principle was sound but the plain zinc plates used were not entirely satisfactory. After a period of use impurities in the zinc led to the formation of a passive skin that stopped the electrolytic action and rendered the anode useless. The cast zincs in use today are made from an alloy that resists the formation of a skin and ensures that the anode remains efficient until it has wasted away.

With the coming of iron and steel ships corrosion was caused by a more obvious form of cell, formed by non-ferrous seacocks and propellers being in electrical contact with the hull. The principle is well-known: two dissimilar metals immersed in seawater form a primary cell. When they are connected electrically a minute current flows from one to the other through the connection and a stream of ions flows in the reverse direction through the water. The table shows some of the metals in common use and their relative potentials.

The electrical potentials of metals are relative to a standard calomel electrode when immersed in sea water at $77°F$ $(25°C)$. These figures will be increased as temperature, velocity of water, and degree of aeration rise, but the relative values remain the same.

Metals at the top of the table will waste away when they are part of an active cell with one lower down. Corrosion may be expected to begin when potential difference between the two exceeds 0.25 volts. The anodic or wasting metal of the two will in time form a passive skin that stops further electrolytic action. This cannot be depended upon for protection because any break in the skin will lead to intense local pitting in that area. Bituminous paints afford some measure of protection but cannot be depended on for the same reason. The practical remedy is to fix zinc anodes to, or in electrical contact with the metal to be protected. For example, anodes are fitted to the hull of a steel ship close to seacocks and propellers; some engines have anodes in the cooling water spaces.

The most obvious cell in a wood or glass-reinforced plastic yacht is formed by steel rudder fittings, propeller shaft, and a bronze propeller. Yet wasting of non-ferrous parts does occur and the cause is not always electrolytic. Non-ferrous pipework in circulating water systems is liable to severe attack that may appear to be electrolytic. The cause is more likely to be erosion brought about by a sudden change in the flow pattern set up by a flat on a badly formed bend, the step that occurs when a pipe is fitted inside a hose or at the junction of two flanges with different bores. A specialist firm must be consulted to ascertain the cause and advise on protection.

See also ELECTRICS; HULLS; MAINTENANCE

Engines, choice of *see* AUXILIARY ENGINES

Equation of time
The difference between mean time and apparent time.

Establishment of the port
The time interval between the transit of the moon across the local meridian and the next high tide. At any given place the interval is approximately the same throughout the year. The 'vulgar establishment' is the average luni-tidal interval on the days of full moon and new moon, or 'high water full and change' (HWF&C), and as such was formerly marked on charts and given in the pilot books as a means of estimating the state of the tide. The establishment for 14 ports in northern Europe is shown in the fourteenth-century *Catalan Atlas*.

To apply the method it was necessary to know the time of the moon's meridian passage for that day and this was determined from the 'age of the moon', the number of days since the new moon, by arithmetical rules similar to those given in the English Book of Common Prayer to find Easter Day.

Relative potentials of some metals

↑	– 1.6 Magnesium	↓
↑	– 1.1 Zinc	↓
↑	– 0.75 Aluminium	↓
↑	– 0.70 Mild steel	↓
↑	– 0.70 Cast iron	↓
↑	– 0.55 Lead	↓
↑	– 0.45 Tin	↓
↑	– 0.27 Bronze	↓
↑	– 0.26 Brass	↓
↑	– 0.25 Copper	↓
↑	– 0.20 Monel and stainless	↓
↑	– 0.15 Nickel	↓

↑ *Direction of current through connections from cathode to anode*

↓ *Flow of ions through water from anode to cathode*

F

These include the golden number, the sequence of the year in the metonic cycle of 19 years after which the phases of the Moon return to the same dates, and the epact, which is the age of the moon on 1 January.

However, neither the moon's motion nor the sequence of the tides is as regular as these arithmetical rules and even on coasts where there are two equal tides each day, the estimated time of high water may be out by one or two hours. The method has therefore been superseded by the publication of computed tide tables.

Eyes *see* MASTS AND RIGGING: Glossary

Eye splice *see* ROPEWORK: Splices

Fairlead *see* MASTS AND RIGGING: Glossary

Fair wind
A wind favourable to the course being steered. Generally on or abaft the beam. Also termed a leading wind, and sometimes a soldier's wind.

Fall off
To sag to leeward.

Fastnet race *see* YACHT RACING: Major races and series

Fathom
6 ft (1.83 m); used as a nautical measure of depth.

Fetch
(1) The distance waves travel without interference: the longer the fetch, in general, the higher the waves; (2) to reach the destination without tacking.

Fid *see* MASTS AND RIGGING: Glossary

Figure-of-eight *see* ROPEWORK: Bends and hitches

Fin keel
A short, comparatively deep keel fitted amidships in some sailing yachts that performs much the same function as a dinghy's centreboard or dagger plate.

Finn Dinghy Gold Cup *see* YACHT RACING: Dinghy racing

Fire-protection systems *see* HULLS: Hull and accommodation systems

First point of Aries *see* ARIES, FIRST POINT OF

Fisherman's bend *see* ROPEWORK: Bends and hitches

Fix
The position obtained by the intersection of two or more POSITION LINES.

Fixed, fixed-flashing lights *see* LIGHTS: Characteristics of lights

Flare
Outward curve of a vessel's bows.

Flashing light *see* LIGHTS: Characteristics of lights

Flat seizing *see* ROPEWORK: Splices

Flood
The movement of a tide as it rises from low water.

Flying Dutchman World Championship *see* YACHT RACING: Dinghy racing

Fog signals
These were practically unknown until the mid-nineteenth century. Bells and gongs were the first sound signals to be used, but they are the least efficient as far as the distance at which they can be heard is concerned. They are usually operated by compressed gas or electricity.

Explosive signals in the form of a small gun were used at many lighthouses and on light vessels, but at offshore stations where space is limited the gun cotton was usually exploded from a small jib on the lighthouse. Sometimes aluminium was combined with the explosive to give a brilliant flash as well. Automatic explosive fog signals are usually of the acetylene/air fog-gun type. In these a mixture of acetylene gas and air is exploded automatically and they can be started and stopped by radio.

Reed horns are operated by compressed air. Whistles are used in some countries, but they are extravagant with compressed air, and the sound they make can be confused with the whistles of vessels.

Sirens and diaphones are the most efficient sound signals; both types are operated by compressed air. The sound is caused by air passing through circumferential slots in a rotor or piston working inside a cylinder with similar slots. In the siren the sound is produced by the speed at which the rotor revolves. In the diaphone the sound depends upon the rate at which the piston moves with a reciprocating motion to cover and uncover the ports. The diaphone always gives a distinctive grunt at the end of each blast.

Nautophones produce a note of 300 cycles per second generated by an electrically vibrated diaphragm. Modern fog signals of this sort are usually of the multi-horn type with a number of emitters facing the directions over which the sound is to be heard.

Synchronized radio and sound signals are operated at a few stations, mainly in the United States, where a radio signal is transmitted simultaneously with the sound signal. This enables an approximate distance off to be obtained by noting the time in seconds between receiving the radio signal and hearing the sound signal.

Fore-and-aft line
The longitudinal axis of a craft.

Fore-and-aft rig *see* RIGS

Foregripe *see* HULLS: Construction components

Forepeak *see* HULLS: Hull accommodation

Fore-reach
To make headway when hove to.

Forestay *see* MASTS AND RIGGING: Glossary

Fore triangle
The triangle formed by the mast, the fore masthead stay, and deck level.

Forward
Towards the bows, or stem.

Foul
In the nautical sense, the opposite to clear, as in foul anchor, foul berth etc.; obstructed or otherwise unsatisfactory.

Frames *see* HULLS: Construction components

Free
Off the wind, or not close-hauled.

Freeboard
The height of a vessel's side above the water-line.

Front
The boundary between air masses of different temperatures. *See* WIND AND WEATHER

Full-and-by
Sailing close-hauled with the sails full (i.e. not shivering) and by the wind (rather than on the compass).

Furl
To roll or fold a sail.

Futtock band: *see* MASTS AND RIGGING: Glossary

Futtocks *see* HULLS: Construction components

Gaff *see* MASTS AND RIGGING: Glossary; RIGS: Fore-and-aft rigs

Gaffsail *see* RIGS: Fore-and-aft rigs

Garboard strake *see* hulls: Construction components

Gate *see* MASTS AND RIGGING: Glossary

Genoa
A large jib that fills the fore triangle and generally overlaps the mainsail. *See also* RIGS: Fore-and-aft rigs

GHA *see* GREENWICH HOUR ANGLE

Ghost
To make headway by a skilful handling of the sails in almost no wind.

Gimbals
Devices of pivoted rings that enable compasses and other objects to remain level whatever the movements of a craft under way.

Glénans, Centre Nautique des
A French sailing school, founded in 1947 by ex-members of the Resistance with long-term objectives that intentionally go somewhat beyond the teaching of navigation and seamanship. The original centre is on the Îles Glénans off the south Brittany coast. There are now also other centres, including the Golfe du Morbihan in the south of Brittany and Paimpol in the north, Marseillan on the French Mediterranean coast, and Corsica; Bryher in the Isles of Scilly; and Bere Island and Baltimore on the southeast and Clew Bay on the west coast of Ireland. In general courses are of two weeks and each course is required to be self-sufficient. Instruction provides for every stage from complete beginners to deep-sea cruising and ocean racing. The instructors are volunteers; some 300 craft from dinghies to ocean racers are owned by the organization.

GMT *see* GREENWICH MEAN TIME

Gnomonic chart
A chart on which great circles appear as straight lines.

Gooseneck *see* MASTS AND RIGGING: Glossary

Great circle
The intersection at the surface of a sphere of a plane passing through its centre. The great circle is the shortest way between any two points on a sphere; thus the great-circle distance is the shortest route when the earth is represented as a sphere.

Green flash
As the upper limit of the sun disappears below the horizon at sunset, or appears above the horizon at sunrise, a brilliant green 'flash' lasting one or two seconds may occasionally be observed. If conditions are favourable, with a clear atmosphere and a sharp distinct horizon, a careful observer may see this green flash on nearly half of the possible occasions;

Genoas in use at the start of an inshore race for the Admiral's Cup

at sunset care must be taken to avoid dazzle from the setting sun, and at sunrise sight must be directed at the point on the horizon at which the sun will rise.

The phenomenon is due to refraction in the lower, denser layers of the atmosphere – which, when enhanced by temperature inversion, leads to longer and more readily observable flashes. Sunlight is dispersed into the familiar spectrum ranging from red through green to blue and violet; typically the spread is about 10″ of arc. The longer (red) wavelengths are refracted less than the shorter wavelengths so that, at sunset, the red light is the first to disappear and the green, blue, and violet last (in that order). However, the short wavelengths of violet and blue light are scattered by the atmosphere (giving the sky its characteristic blue colour) and the green light is the last that is normally seen. Occasionally it is followed, at sunset, by a blue flash, and very rarely indeed by a hint of violet. The order is reversed at sunrise.

The duration of the green flash depends on the amount of refraction, the geometry of the dissection of setting or rising, and on conditions of visibility; it may be as short as 0.5 sec, though durations of up to 10 sec are on record.

Greenwich hour angle (GHA)
Hour angle measured westward from the Greenwich celestial meridian.

Greenwich mean time (GMT)
Time related to the hour angle of the mean sun at Greenwich.

Gripe
The tendency of a vessel to come up into the wind when close-hauled, and so carry excessive weather helm.

Grommet
A rope ring made by laying up a single strand three times; also an eye inside the boltrope.

Grounding load see HULLS: Scantlings

**Ground tackle
– anchors**
The earliest form of ground tackle probably consisted of no more than two sticks lashed together and a large stone, but marine archaeologists have brought up extremely ancient iron anchors and even bronze anchors, which would, of course, predate them. In its early form the anchor usually looked like the modern fisherman type, but with a wooden stock to ensure that one fluke dug into the bottom.

In former days, sailing vessels, whose windward qualities were poor, tended to carry the largest anchors they could to prevent them becoming embayed or drifting on to a lee

shore. The modern yacht is a more weatherly craft and is normally expected to be able to claw off a lee shore without help from the engine. Modern yachts, too, seldom anchor in exposed positions but tend to lie in sheltered creeks and anchorages. As a result the modern yachtsman tends to ask what is the smallest anchor that will hold his boat rather than what is the largest anchor he can handle given the size of his boat and his own physical capabilities. The tendency is thus to carry lighter gear than is seamanlike.

For vessels over 20 tons (Thames Measurement) the difficulties of getting an anchor on board and stowing it make auxiliary handling gear, whether hydraulic or electric, more or less essential and point to the advantage of self-stowing anchors.

The classical form of anchor, the principal

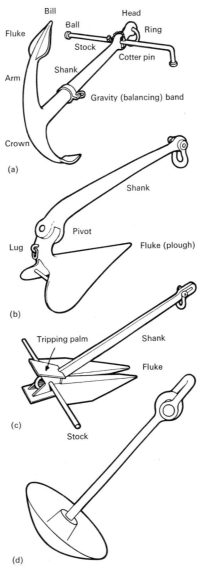

Anchors: (a) *fisherman's;* (b) *CQR;*
(c) *Danforth;* (d) *mushroom*

parts of which are illustrated, is variously known as a fisherman-type anchor, Admiralty-type anchor, or a yachtsman's anchor. It is perhaps the most adaptable of all anchors in that it can be used effectively on many types of bottom, but for its weight the holding power is only mediocre. It is not easy to stow on board and, perhaps more important, there is a danger that the anchor line or cable will get itself round the exposed fluke, generally at the turn of tide, and break the anchor out. Despite all these objections, it remains a standard form of anchor and far from obsolescent.

Various improvements in design have overcome one or other of the drawbacks of the fisherman anchor. In modern fisherman anchors a folding stock, held in by a metal pin when the anchor is in use, overcomes most of the stowage difficulty. Various improvements in the shape of the fluke (palm), notably in the Herreshoff and Nicholson versions, increase its holding power or make it more suitable for particular kinds of bottom. The Herreshoff version with its large triangular flukes is a good all-round anchor that has the additional advantage that on deep-sea passages it can be dismantled into three parts and stowed below in the bilges.

A number of anchors have been designed that overcome the disadvantages of the fisherman type of which the best known are the CQR (or plow), and the Danforth; the former is more popular in Europe, the latter in America. The CQR takes the form of a double ploughshare that can pivot within certain limits on the shank; it has no stock. When the anchor is lowered to the bottom it topples, the point facing gently downward, but as soon as the cable gives a horizontal pull the flukes begin to dig in and the anchor buries itself on an even keel. The efficiency factor of the CQR, which measures its performance in different kinds of bottom (mud, shingle, and clay), exceeds that of any other type and its holding power is approximately one-third more than that of the best fisherman type. It is important to distinguish the genuine CQR anchor from the various ploughshare anchors that resemble it: each may have certain advantages in some conditions but the overall performance is generally inferior.

The American-designed Danforth anchor has the advantage over the CQR that it can be stowed flat on deck, although its holding power is marginally less. Essentially it consists of two very large flukes with the shank in between and the stock lying across the crown.

The mushroom anchor is perhaps the most effective of all but it involves such stowage problems on board that it is generally used only for permanent moorings. A number of experimental anchors of totally new design have been developed in connection with the offshore-oil industry of which the Bruce type

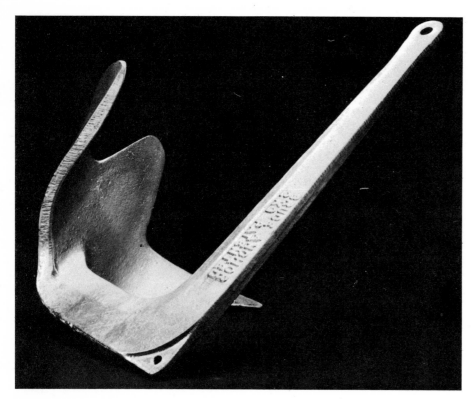

The Bruce anchor: the one illustrated weighs 4.4 lb (2 kg) and can be used for a sailing boat of 15 ft (4.8 m) LOA and 6.6 ft (2.0 m) beam

appears by far the most promising for small craft.

– anchor cable

Until the early part of the nineteenth century the anchor cable or warp was generally made of hemp, cable laid, that is to say made of three hawser-laid ropes of three strands, each laid up left-handed. The cable was generally too large to fit round the capstan and was thus fed direct into the chain locker. When the anchor was weighed by hand the cable was secured temporarily to a messenger that went round the capstan in an endless line.

Chain was introduced in the early 1800s and is now standard for all vessels except small yachts. Anchor chain is studded to prevent it kinking and its size is measured by the diameter of the metal of the link. Marine chain is sold in lengths of 15 fathoms (27 m), known as shackles, and at the end of each shackle is an oversize link. This may be joined to the next shackle by means of a joining shackle with an oval-shaped pin secured in place by a wooden peg. To break the shackle it is only necessary to put a punch to the end of the pin and knock it out, whereas a screw shackle might well cause difficulties. The BITTER END of the chain is secured inboard, preferably by a length of nylon line that can be cut in an emergency should it be required to slip the chain.

In European waters chain cable tends to be used more generally by yachts than in the United States, partly perhaps because American galvanized-steel chain has a poor reputation among the yachting community. An advantage of chain, or indeed wire, for anchoring over rope is that it will not chafe from friction on the bottom, or if the boat rides over its cable as can happen when the boat is WIND-RODE in a tideway. The weights of chain recommended for various yacht sizes with various types of anchor are given in Table 1.

The advantage of line over chain cable for anchoring lies mainly in the greater ease with which it can be handled, although it will not have the same catenary effect as chain. It is intensely strong for its weight and if about five metres of chain is used next to the anchor to ensure a horizontal pull and to prevent chafe on the bottom, it should provide a satisfactory anchor warp for most conditions. A further advantage of nylon rope, in addition to its great strength, is its stretch, which absorbs a lot of the loading when the boat snubs in rough weather. Triple-plait nylon provides the ideal anchor warp.

For deep-water anchoring, such as in Pacific atolls, something like a 15-fathom (27-m) length of chain used with a nylon warp is preferable to an all-chain cable, the weight of which would make it very difficult to recover.

A common mistake is to anchor with too little scope. The weight of the chain on the bottom has a considerable anchoring effect on its own, and with chain and a fisherman-type anchor three or four times the depth of water should suffice. With modern light-weight anchors with a rope anchor warp spliced on to a length of chain, five times the depth of water should be allowed.

When anchoring in small harbours where there is little room to swing, the boat should be moored between two anchors when she can be expected to swing in little more than her own length.

– riding gear

Boats that anchor with chain often have a chain pawl, which holds the chain link by link as it is brought in; when veering the pawl is simply turned back letting the chain run free. Ideally the pawl is fitted over the stem-head roller, but may be incorporated in the anchor windlass.

– capstan

A capstan is a winch with the barrel mounted in the vertical plane. The chain comes up over the barrel roller and after a turn round the capstan barrel is fed into the chain locker forward of the capstan. The advantage of a

Table 1: Recommended anchor weights and chain-cable sizes for cutter- and sloop-rigged yachts

THAMES TONNAGE	APPROX. ANCHOR WEIGHT						DIAMETER OF SHORT-LINK CHAIN	
	FISHERMAN		CQR		DANFORTH			
up to 5	40 lb	18 kg	35 lb	16 kg	30 lb	14 kg	$\frac{1}{4}$ in	6 mm
5–8	45	20	35	16	30	14	$\frac{5}{16}$	8
8–10	50	23	35	16	30	14	$\frac{3}{8}$	9.5
10–14	60	27	35	16	30	14	$\frac{3}{8}$	9.5
14–18	70	32	45	20	40	18	$\frac{7}{16}$	11
18–20	80	36	45	20	40	18	$\frac{7}{16}$	11
20–24	100	45	45	20	40	18	$\frac{1}{2}$	13
24–28	120	54	60	27	65	29	$\frac{1}{2}$	13
28–32	130	59	60	27	65	29	$\frac{9}{16}$	14

A modern capstan with a chain gypsy beneath a warping drum

A CQR bower anchor stowed in deck chocks with anchor windlass, whose chain gypsy and warping drum are carefully aligned with the twin bow rollers

capstan over a windlass is that a lead can be taken round the drum of the capstan from any direction without being led through blocks, with their consequent friction. The disadvantage is that in all but the largest craft the capstan must be worked by hand from the kneeling position. A windlass with the barrel in the horizontal plane, which can be cranked with a long handle, generally about waist high, is far more usual in yachts. Windlasses vary considerably in complexity and in the largest yachts are operated by electric or hydraulic power. On small boats with no foredeck anchor winch, capstan, or windlass, the anchor line can be led back to a cockpit winch, or a halyard winch.

Capstans and windlasses on small craft are most frequently electrically powered. In this case the motor is best housed down below and the capstan will have an advantage over the windlass in that it is more easily driven by a below-deck-mounted motor. In addition, electrically powered windlasses tend to need long, heavy cables running from the batteries and are not particularly powerful. There should be a good backup arrangement to guard against the eventuality of flat batteries and thus no power to start the engine and no anchor windlass. Hydraulically powered capstans and windlasses, which basically are operated by a hydraulic pump belted off the engine or generator, are more powerful and

more reliable than electrically driven ones.

– chain riding gear

The essential step to keep a boat from dragging, and the anchor from breaking out, is to remove the shock load from the chain. This can often be done by veering more chain; another method is to lower a weight such as a pig of lead on a U-shackle down the chain. Snubbing the anchor is not only likely to break it out, or even to break the cable, but also puts a considerable strain on the windlass or capstan shaft or the bitts. For this reason a stopper is often used, so that the strain is taken on the stopper rather than on any part of the boat. Various types of chain stopper are available, of which one of the best is a length of nylon rope whose elasticity absorbs the shock load. A metal claw can be used to grip the links.

A bow roller over the stemhead for line can be flat, but for use with chain it requires a groove in the centre slightly larger than the diameter of the chain, since each link is at right angles to the other. The friction of a chain on a flat roller can be massive since the boat seldom lies facing the anchor but tends to tack back and forth. It is essential that the rollers should have strong cheeks, splayed outwards so that a foul lead does not hook on to them. The cheeks should also extend upwards to keep the chain from jumping off when the bow plunges; a large removable pin

or bolt through them over the chain will provide further security. A large roller with well-splayed cheeks that reach well above the roller can be used to stow a CQR anchor on the roller itself, if the shape of the bow permits.

– stowage

Large yachts frequently have hawse pipes in which the anchor can be stowed; this gives a good lead to the anchor chain, but the possibility of a cracked hawse pipe, which in heavy weather could flood a vessel, must be watched.

As mentioned above, with a properly designed bow roller a plough anchor can be stowed directly on the roller itself without being touched by the hand. The Danforth can also be stowed in a well-designed hawse pipe but chocks should be placed to prevent the side of the boat being damaged by the flukes and head of the anchor. Danforths are frequently stowed on deck, in which case the stock should be allowed to drop into upright wooden blocks and the base plate rest against a wooden vertically mounted block to prevent sheets and lines fouling the anchor. A further alternative is to replace the stocks of the Danforth by pipe stocks that can be unscrewed when the anchor is stowed on deck.

Nylon rope is easily stowed because unlike manila or hemp, it does not rot when stowed wet. In fact, since ultraviolet is the greatest danger, it is best stowed down below rather than on deck. The simplest method of stowage is to make the rope up in a large coil, figure-eight it, and fold it back on itself, secured with a few sail ties. A plastic washing basket from which the water can drain out can also provide a useful stowage for nylon rope. Rollers can also be used, installed directly under the navel pipe and spring-mounted so that the line is automatically rolled on to it.

Chain is easy to stow because a large quantity will fit into a comparatively small space. An approximate idea of its stowage capacity is given in Table II. Since it is very heavy, chain should always be stowed as low down as possible in the boat. If the chain is to be self-stowing it should be stowed in a fairly tall, narrow locker with a free fall from the hawse pipe to the top of the piled-up chain of at least two or three feet; otherwise the chain will pick up kinks and turns in the course of time and jam in the navel pipe. The chain should never be allowed to lie up against the planking or floorboard or any bronze keel bolts which would rapidly cause electrolysis and produce weak links in the chain. For preference it should be stowed in a locker that is lined, with a free air flow between the chain and the planking, and with drain holes in the locker, so that the whole of the locker may be scrubbed out and drained periodically. The bitter end should be secured in the manner previously suggested.

Table II: Space required to stow one shackle (15 fathoms) in self-stowing chain locker

CHAIN DIAMETER		SPACE REQUIRED		APPROX. WT PER SHACKLE	
(in)	*(mm)*	*(ft³)*	*(dm³)*	*(lb)*	*(kg)*
$\frac{1}{4}$	6	0.9	26	70	32
$\frac{5}{16}$	8	1.3	37	102	46
$\frac{3}{8}$	9.5	1.8	51	148	67
$\frac{7}{16}$	11	2.4	68	202	92
$\frac{1}{2}$	13	3.1	88	257	117

Careful thought should be given to the placing of anchor gear on board since, with the windlass or capstan, the anchor and the chain, it adds up to a considerable weight. So far as practicable, the weight should be kept aft, both from the point of view of stability and keeping the weight near the centre of buoyancy. Everything possible should be done to keep weight out of the bows and on long passages when the anchor is unlikely to be used it will pay to stow it back aft and send the chain down below.

Groundwave
A radio signal constrained to follow the curvature of the earth but not discretely reflected from the ionosphere.

Group-flashing, group-occulting light *see* LIGHTS: Characteristics of lights

Gudgeon
A metal eye bolted to the sternpost or transom to take the rudder PINTLES. The latter may also be mounted pointing upwards on the hull to receive the gudgeons fastened to the rudder.

Gunter
A fore-and-aft rig for small craft in which the

The first successful gyrocompass, invented by the German, Hermann Anschütz-Kämpfe, was introduced in 1908. Three years later came the American Sperry compass. The compass illustrated, dating from c. 1916, was invented by the Englishman S. G. Brown

quadrilateral sail has a long LEECH and short LUFF (1), the yard lying almost parallel to the mast. *See also* RIGS: Fore-and-aft rigs

Gunwale *see* HULLS: Construction components

Guy *see* MASTS AND RIGGING: Glossary

Gybe (jibe)
To bring the wind from one quarter to the other when wearing ship so that the boom

swings over and the stern moves through the wind.

Gyrocompass

A gyroscope is a heavy rotor revolving at high speed and freely suspended so that its axis can turn in any direction. Once started, unless subject to any constraint, its axis will continue to point in the same direction in space and so will appear to wander and tilt as the earth rotates.

If a gyroscope is made so that when it tilts due to the rotation of the earth vertical pressure is introduced, its axis will oscillate about the meridian and about the horizontal. To make it into a compass that points north, it is necessary to make it settle by damping out this oscillation.

The motion of a ship over the surface of the earth causes the gyrocompass to be deflected in the direction of the port beam, by an amount that is dependent upon course and speed. Thus on alteration of course or speed the compass must move from one settling position to another. It has been found that if the period of undamped oscillation of the axis is made approximately 85 min, the compass will naturally precess from the old settling position to the new during the time of the alteration of course, thus avoiding a consequent wander.

The main advantages of the gyrocompass are its ability to be placed almost anywhere where space can be found, and the facility with which it can be made to operate repeaters. It is unaffected by magnetism, unless this is of such exceptional strength as to be rarely met with. Its disadvantage is that a power failure of even short duration can make it virtually useless until it has had several hours to resettle.

Hadley's quadrant

The forerunner of the modern marine SEXTANT and identical with it in principle. Reflecting instruments, though often with only one mirror on a movable arm, for measuring altitudes above the sea horizon or lunar distances, had been described or demonstrated to the Royal Society by Robert Hooke, Sir Isaac Newton, and Edmond Halley before 1700, but the first practical tests were made in the yacht *Chatham* in 1732 when John Hadley's quadrant was found to be extremely convenient for use at sea and capable of measuring altitudes with an accuracy of one or two minutes of arc. It very soon came into general use. A similar instrument had been made by Thomas Godfrey in America at about the same time.

The quadrant, which was much larger than a modern sextant, had a wooden frame, often of ebony with an inlaid ivory arc, and a plain pinhole sight instead of a telescope. In the earlier types the reflecting surfaces were of speculum metal rather than of silvered glass and the arc was read with a diagonal scale instead of a vernier.

Halyard, halliard *see* MASTS AND RIGGING: Glossary

Hand

To lower or take in a sail.

Handicap systems

Handicaps are imposed in yacht racing, as in various other forms of contest, to equalize the chances of competitors of differing size and potential.

– the need for handicapping

Much of yacht racing is carried out in one-design classes whose rules at least intend them to be very similar. In a racing fleet of such boats, the first across the line is the winner. The result ostensibly depends on the tactical ability of the crew and the preparation of the boat. Even if minor changes are allowed between boats – and this varies under the rules of each class – the designs of the hull, rig, weight of BALLAST KEEL, and other main factors are the same for each competitor.

Yet it is frequently necessary to depart from this satisfactory way of racing sailing boats and invoke some form of handicapping so that unlike boats can race together. Among other reasons for this, an owner may have a cruising vessel or general-purpose dinghy originally bought with no idea of racing, but he then finds that a local club runs weekend events in which his friends compete and he wishes to join in. Then again a racing man may have no taste for the particular one-designs of his area, which logically must be the choice of someone else. Another reason for difference in yachts is the simple matter of size: a big boat will invariably beat a small

one in a race, which, of course, is no sport. If some form of time allowance is applied between them, then it can be used to adjust the difference in finishing times giving three possibilities: a dead heat (which to some observers would mean the time allowance system was perfect, but in reality this is not necessarily the case), the big boat wins, or the small boat wins, her time allowance having been greater than the difference in recorded finishing times.

– difficulties in achieving a fair system

There are inherent difficulties in running a system of time allowances that can be said to be absolutely fair. Leading clubs are wise to be content with 'pleasing most of the owners most of the time'. The most basic objection to a time-allowance system between yachts of unequal size is that they do not have equal opportunity. In other words, in a one-design class, if the wind suddenly increases at a point on the race course, any of the class could have been at that position, if her crew had steered her there. Where yachts are of unequal size, the big yacht may be one mile ahead of the small yacht, even though the small yacht was being sailed with greater skill. If the advantageous breeze reaches the big yacht, she has an advantage that her opponent had no possible opportunity of obtaining. A more striking example is when larger yachts in a race reach the finishing line and the wind then drops completely leaving smaller craft with no chance of compensation by means of time allowance.

A second difficulty is that the many variables in yacht racing due to the ability of the crew, DISPLACEMENT, cleanliness of bottom, as well as actual hull lines and the efficiency or otherwise of the rig, make comparison between different sizes and types too complex to rationalize. As a result of this time allowances are either awarded somewhat arbitrarily or by using rating figures obtained from chosen measurements. The third main difficulty then arises when boats are built to such measured ratings or altered to fit them and thus gain an advantage in whatever system is current. In the upper echelons of yacht racing by time allowances rating is therefore the basis of any time-allowance system applied. It has its own application and history, discussed below.

Time allowances themselves, once decided or established, can be applied relatively easily by a race committee. It is usually only a matter of addition or subtraction to an elapsed time or its multiplication by a factor: a few seconds' work on a pocket calculator.

– the situation in modern yacht racing

Among the centreboard dinghy classes and open (day) keel boats, one-design classes predominate, although there are some restricted classes. This term implies limitations and maximum (or minimum) dimensions in which there are some design freedoms, but no time allowances are applied. Where there are 'menagerie' groups of dinghies in local areas, either arbitrary time allowances are applied or the Portsmouth Yardstick Scheme is used (*see below*). Among habitable sailing yachts handicapping predominates; only a very few one-design classes exist, although there have been proposals to revive the idea with new designs. The larger the class of vessel, the less likelihood there is of a one-design class. Habitable, or in other words, offshore boats, in international or national racing use the International Offshore Rule (IOR) of measurement and rating and with this various time allowance systems are applied. The most established time allowance system is that of the UNITED STATES YACHT RACING UNION (USYRU) which has tables for seconds per mile for all ratings under the IOR. In most other countries time-allowance methods as applied to the IOR are changed or adjusted after a few years. There are also other rules of rating and measurement. Most of these are in different regions of the United States and go by such names as The New England Rule, the Off Soundings Rule and the Midget Ocean Racing Club (MORC) rule. Some rules, such as the (British) Medway Clubs measurement, are simple self-measurement kinds that work because the boats concerned are known and raced only locally. Apart from the possible exception of the MORC, it is accurate to say that the only rating rule to which boats are systematically designed and built is the IOR. As a result the IOR is also used very widely for club and regional racing of all sorts. In September 1977 there were just over 10 000 yachts with valid IOR certificates throughout the world. Of these 2416 were in the United States, 1873 in the UK, 953 in Germany, 682 in Sweden, 607 in France, 595 in Holland, 434 in Australia, and the balance in a number of other countries throughout the world.

– how rating rules evolved

The IOR as used today is essentially evolutionary. This is important to know, because there are from time to time calls to 'scrap the rule and start again', usually on a 'scientific' basis. Such calls ignore the fact that yacht racing is a sport with various motivations and the decisions of owners are not always predictable; such factors as fashion and appearance are quite as important as the results of a tank test. The various rules have existed in the climate of a running battle between designers trying to exploit the rule and rule-makers plugging loopholes. A 'scientific' rule would only see the same process repeated, while existing yachts (designed to the current IOR) would be outdated on the introduction of such a rule. If the evolution of rating rules is understood, a number of errors in their future maintenance or, if necessary, creation can be avoided.

An IOR rating certificate, the result of a computer print-out

Early nineteenth-century yacht racing consisted of matches, boat against boat, and since the rule was 'first wins' and all knew that biggest wins, it is recorded in the history of the ROYAL YACHT SQUADRON that when two large cutters, *Lulworth* (127 tons), under Captain Joseph Weld, and *Louisa* (162 tons), under Lord Belfast, were launched in 1828, the owners 'were always ready to increase the size of their vessels by lengthening'. When, naturally, Weld was frequently beaten 'he was equally ready to meet them with a new

and larger vessel, as when he crowned the long struggle between his builders and theirs by launching *Alarm* of 193 tons in 1830.' Such an arms race in the building of huge yachts continued for many years: in 1851 *America* won her cup at the finish line at Cowes, IOW, without any time allowances being in force. If they had been, *Aurora*, who finished 8 minutes astern of *America*, and was only 47 tons to the schooner's 170, must have won. This does not however invalidate the conclusions about *America*'s speed because she was leading by a great deal at the Needles and *Aurora* had caught up in the light airs preceding the finish.

Meanwhile experiments in time allowances did begin. On 17 August 1838 the Queen's Cup at Cowes was held on time allowances devised by George Ackers, owner of the schooner *Dolphin*. The allowance was three minutes for every ten tons of difference. In 1843 Ackers further developed his 'graduated scale' basing it on tonnage and distance. It was a sliding scale, as are time-on-distance systems today. The point is that whatever the time scale, it was measured tonnage that it was based on, so in the early 1840s the problem of rating yachts fairly began. The tonnage rule of the time was based on the cargo carrying capacity for working craft and was calculated from: length × beam × depth of hold. Divided by 100 this gave a reasonable tonnage figure. Such figures had already been calculated by Customs officials. Trouble began almost immediately over the measurement of length *L*; if the keel base was used then owners could shorten the hull shape below the waterline (fig. 1); if length between stemhead and rudder post was used, it paid to bring the rudder post inboard and have a long counter.

A simpler method of measuring tonnage was to dispense with the tedious measurement of depth inside the hold and approximate this by substituting $\frac{1}{2}B$, which approximated to the depth. This meant that only length and BEAM appeared in the formula, and to lower the rating for a given length, the less value for *B*, the better. Thames measurement tonnage introduced as a rating formula by the ROYAL THAMES YACHT CLUB in 1855 was a rule of this type:

$$\text{Tonnage} = \frac{(L - B) \times B \times \frac{1}{2}B}{94}$$

The result of this tonnage rule was that yachts became narrower and still yet narrower so that the cutter yacht *Trident*, designed in 1879, had a waterline of 32 ft but a maximum beam of only 6 ft. Since there were no other rated factors the sail area of such cutters was large and the amount of outside ballast carried was considerable. This was the 'plank-on-edge' era (fig. 2). An attempt was made to correct this unsatisfactory trend by the newly formed Yacht Racing Association in 1882 by introducing the '1730 rule'. This was another narrow beam inducing rule and why it should have been thought that it would improve matters remains something of a mystery. It was:

$$\text{Tonnage} = \frac{(L + B)^2 \times B}{1730}$$

The result was that yachts became even

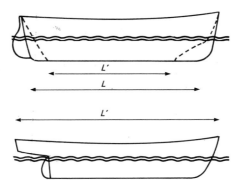

Fig. 1 Methods of shortening the length (L) in the early rating rules of the nineteenth century. When it was measured along the bottom of the keel the builders shortened the profile to L', and when measured from stem to rudder post a long counter produced the false length, L'

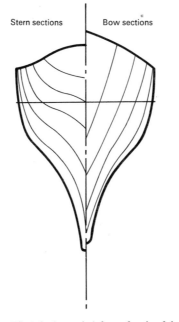

Stern sections | Bow sections

Fig. 2 The 'plank-on-edge' form of yacht of the late nineteenth century. Yachts of narrow beam were traditional in England for many years

Fig. 3 A section of a 'skimming disk', encouraged by the LWL rules, showing the long overhangs and low freeboard

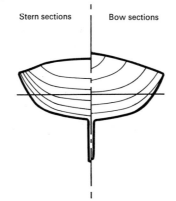

Stern sections | Bow sections

narrower. Dixon Kemp, editor of the British magazine *The Field* (then an influential force in yacht racing) had proposed a completely new approach in the issue dated 10 January 1880. This was to measure sail area and combine it with length on the waterline in the form:

$$\text{Rating} = \frac{L \times \text{sail area}}{6000}$$

The famous 'length and sail area' rule was finally adopted after much debate in 1887. The formula gave a 'linear rating' with figures from one half (a half rater) to boats of various ratings such as a 143-rater that might be a large cutter with a crew of 12. This rule put an end to the extremely narrow beam, but encouraged light displacement that could be driven by the rated area, low freeboard and in the smaller classes FIN KEELS. American yachtsmen had rating problems as well, but not those of tonnage. Their rules had measured actual depth resulting in a shallow hull, but sail area was not accounted for and they had developed the 'centreboard bugs' to rival the 'plank-on-edge' and 'cutter cranks'. A length and sail area rule was adopted in the United States in 1883, the famous Seawanakha Rule:

$$\text{Rating} = \frac{L + \sqrt{S}}{2}$$

The length and sail area rules had a limited life. Designers were soon developing flat boats with long overhangs and wide sterns, the boats thus becoming longer for the same rating (fig. 3). The America's Cup defender *Reliance*, designed by the American marine architect Nathanael Greene Herreshoff (1848–1938), had an LOA of 143 ft 8 in (43.8 m), but a waterline length of only 89 ft (27 m) and was the first boat to be known as a racing machine. As a result of these extremes, Herreshoff himself was asked to devise a better rule. His adopted proposal was the Universal Rule of 1904. This brought in displacement as well as length and sail area, so that very light boats were to some extent controlled. Length was measured at last with some subtlety, being taken slightly out from the fore-and-aft centreline and a little above the waterline plane: this had some control on the long flat overhangs. The Universal Rule gave a rating in feet as follows:

$$\text{Rating} = 0.2 \frac{L \times \sqrt{\text{sail area}}}{\sqrt[3]{\text{Displacement}}}$$

This rule was successful in the United States for many years. It was used to foster class boats (for instance the M and R classes), albeit under additional rule restrictions, and was used for the *America's* Cup races of 1920, 1930, 1934, and 1937. In the first of these time allowances were applied, but in the last three before World War II a fixed rating of

Endeavour and Velsheda, *two J-Class yachts that, with* Yankee, *raced in the 1935 season at the maximum of the Universal Rule*

76 ft under the Universal Rule was used: this was the rating of the J Class.

In England the length and sail area formula was in trouble and in 1896, the designer and scientist R. E. Froude suggested a rule that the YRA promptly adopted. It brought beam B back in and introduced a girth measurement G that followed the section of the yacht. The lighter the displacement it was reckoned, the bigger G and therefore the rating. The rule was:

$$\text{Rating} = \frac{L + B + 0.75G + 0.5S}{2}$$

Unfortunately this had little effect on light displacement, but in Scandinavia a rather similar rule was under experiment that utilized a measurement called d. This 'girth difference' was obtained by subtracting a girth taken tightly round the hull from the skin girth G and this really did seem to control displacement (fig. 4). The inventor of this factor was Alfred Benzon, a Danish chemist.

– the International Rule
A conference was organized in London in 1906 by Brooke Heckstall-Smith (1869–1944), a British yachting writer and secretary of the YRA. The object was twofold: to bring in international rules for racing and also for the rating of yachts. It succeeded in both and as a controlling body was needed, the sixteen nations concerned formed the

International Yacht Racing Union. Two American delegates were scheduled to leave for London, but just before they sailed 'the Atlantic Clubs Conference' was called and voted that they should not be sent. A letter was then sent to the London conference, but arrived after it had closed. It said that '... they could not take part in the movement for an international rule without serious injury to the sport here, because it would practically amount to reopening for our clubs, the whole question of measurement, that we have just succeeded after years of effort in settling.' In the event the Universal Rule continued to be used in the United States, but in 1921 the leading American clubs adopted the International Rule and the Universal Rule was used only for the 56-ft, 65-ft, and 76-ft J Classes. The North American Yacht Racing Union did not join the IYRU until 1949.

The International Rule of 1906 gave a rating in metres:

$$\text{Rating} = \frac{L + B + \frac{1}{2}G + 3d + \frac{1}{3}\sqrt{S} - F}{2}$$

It will be seen that F, FREEBOARD, has been introduced and this reversed the trend of the very low freeboards of the end of the nineteenth century. The International Rule of the IYRU was responsible for many years of fine racing in the 'metre boats'. These were

principally the 6-Metre, 8-Metre and 12-Metre classes. There were other Metre classes, but these three were to predominate after World War I. The 6-Metres particularly fostered international racing, including the British-American Cup. They were used in the Olympic Games from 1908 until 1952.

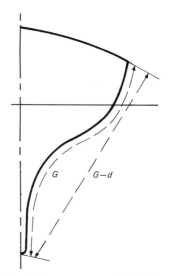

Fig. 4 The measurement of girth difference (d) solved the problem of excessive light displacement. This is still used to measure the 12-metre class

One weakness in the rule was that B was on the top line thus encouraging narrowness. In the 1919 version of the rule B disappeared so that each class had a minimum beam limit. In 1933 the rule was revised yet again and simplified to:

$$\text{Rating} = \frac{L + 2d + \sqrt{S} - F}{2.37}$$

This again was hedged about with numerous measuring provisos and maxima and minima on dimensions. This rule is used to rate the 12-Metre class today for the *America*'s Cup. There are still a handful of 6-Metres sailed in Seattle in the northwest United States and one or two Scandinavians have built 6-Metre boats in the 1970s. There is an Australian-American Cup in which single 6-Metre match races are sailed between clubs in Sydney and San Francisco.

It is ironic that this rule, at first shunned by American yachtsmen, should now be preserved by a few of them. As for the Universal rule, that died with the J Class, though there are some elderly one-design classes in the United States that were based on its formula when they were designed and it will be shown below that the Universal Rule ended up as part of the IOR as used today.

– Offshore Rules
All the rules discussed above were used for racing boats in sheltered waters and often

with professional crews. It will have been noticed too that the original object of time allowances had largely been lost and the boats were built to a required rating so that they could race level. The Bermuda race had been revived under new organization in 1923 and the Fastnet was started in 1925 so it now became necessary to find some basis for time allowances for such a diverse collection of rugged cruising yachts. When the Fastnet men came to look for a rating rule, the British authority on yacht-racing rules, Malden Heckstall-Smith, recommended that they should try a formula that had been adopted by the 'Boat Racing Association' in 1913 for rating miscellaneous inshore boats whose owners did not wish to use the International Rule. This gave a rating in feet:

$$\text{Rating} = \frac{1}{3}\left(\frac{L \times \sqrt{S}}{\sqrt[3]{\text{Displacement}}}\right) + 0.25L + 0.25\sqrt{S}$$

It will be seen that this was in effect a combination of the old Universal Rule and the Seawanakha Rule. It had never been used because of the onset of the war in 1914, but an 18-ft restricted class had been proposed and this idea had remained for many years. Indeed when a new inshore class was called for after 1945 to replace the 6-Metre class, Malden Heckstall-Smith and the British yacht designer and builder, Charles E. Nicholson (1868–1954), proposed a very slight variation of this rule for a 4.5-Metre and a 5.5-Metre class (which is about 18 ft). The first was never built, but the second had some support and was an Olympic class from 1956 to 1968. After that formula classes were removed from the Olympics in favour of one-designs. For a couple of years in the late 1920s, the Fastnet and Bermuda races were run under a common rule, which was a variation of the Universal Rule:

$$\text{Rating} = \frac{0.2L + \sqrt{S}}{\sqrt{(B \times D)}}$$

This short-lived rule was notable for combining beam B and the depth of hull measurement D to give a representation of displacement. Unlike the International Rule, B was on the bottom line and therefore, roughly speaking, the larger beam gave a better rating. At the time, however, the advantage of the beam was not appreciated because the

Eight-Metre yachts (top) *in Sydney Harbour, N.S.W. The leading boat's spinnaker is about to be broken out; that of the other boat is out of hand*

The 12-metre yacht Lionheart, *Great Britain's hope for the 1980* America's Cup *series*

73

influence of other rules still showed in the types of boat built. It was to be another 25 years before British owners finally threw off the ghost of the plank-on-edge boats.

The use of the common rule on both sides of the Atlantic did not last long. The CRUISING CLUB OF AMERICA (CCA), which ran the Bermuda race, decided on a quite different rule that can now be seen as being outside the mainstream of rule development. It was a 'base-boat' rule, where an ideal yacht was envisaged and factors for beam, sail area, draft, engine weight and so on added or subtracted to a measured length to give a theoretical sailing length, or rating in feet. Length was measured in a profile at 4% above the waterline plane. This made for wide sterns.

For its Fastnet races the ROYAL OCEAN RACING CLUB took length by means of girth stations at bow and stern. The beam was measured and a proportional girth slung fore and aft. Where these girths found themselves fixed the positions (with minor corrections) were established between whichever length was taken. This mitigated against full bows and sterns, which were considered a means of increasing sailing length when heeled. The rule itself came directly from the old BRA formula, but with $B \times D$ used instead of direct displacement. Eventually the CCA rule ended up by physically weighing boats.

Though the RORC rule had periodical minor amendments, its main formula was little changed up to 1970 when it was phased out in favour of the IOR. The RORC rule gave a rating in feet:

$$\text{Rating} = 0.15 \left\{ \frac{L \times \sqrt{S}}{\sqrt{(B \times D)}} \right\} + 0.2 \left(L + \sqrt{S} \right)$$

± stability allowance
− propeller allowance
+ draught penalty

All the factors in the rule ran into trouble at one time or another and some brief examples will show the year to year corrections from which rating rules suffer. For instance sail area took the triangulation of the mainsail but only measured the FORE TRIANGLE (the area bounded by the deck, mast, and fore-stay) at 85%. Sails were allowed to overlap by 20% and this resulted in increasing genoa jibs and smaller mainsails. In 1956 the rule was changed to rate the fore triangle at 100% and to penalize high aspect ratios, but because such features are speed inducing, the tall rig with large fore triangle has persisted, particularly in the IOR. The earlier rules on depth were torpedoed by *Myth of Malham* in 1948. The depth of hull was taken from deck to inside of the hull, but the *Myth*, owned by John Holden Illingworth (1903–), British

Offshore rules: the Brazilian Class I yacht Wa Wa Too *in the Fastnet race of 1971*

Fig. 5 In Myth of Malham, *the depth measurement was exploited by having a high freeboard. The RORC rule was later corrected (right) by subtracting freeboard to give immersed depth (solid line) only. This system remains in use to gauge depth in the IOR*

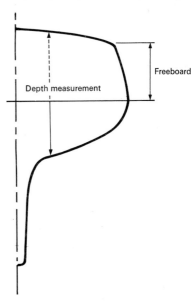

naval officer and yacht designer, took advantage of this by high freeboard. This of course had no bearing on the displacement that the depth was meant to reflect (fig. 5). As a result the rule was changed to include the measurement of 'immersed depth' by subtracting the freeboard component.

Yet a further example of the way rating rules can influence design was provided by this classic loophole. It was found in practice that the extra freeboard not only had no undue adverse effect on the sailing performance of this very successful boat, but additionally gave extra room below. Since that time freeboards have been markedly higher than those seen in the Metre boats. Seventy years before, the plank-on-edge with its outside ballast had shown the possibilities of exterior lead ballast, which eventually became a customary and safer (than inside ballast) arrangement for all yachts. The additional factors in the rule, stability and propeller, took into account such matters as weight of engine, type of screw, whether the ballast was lead or iron, and whether the mast was of wood or alloy.

The RORC rule of rating gave excellent racing to British yachtsmen from 1926 to 1970, and this was in a period of expanding offshore racing. The old ways of yacht racing in keel day boats were dying and amateurs now required habitable boats for weekend living and racing. The growth of offshore racing encouraged crews who expected to drive their boats hard in all weathers and this contributed immensely to the proven seagoing type of yacht seen from 1945 onwards. The RORC rule was evidently a sound basis for a time allowance system used when these yachts raced together. Not only was the rule used in the Fastnet race, but also in the many other RORC races in the English Channel and off the coasts of western Europe. It was used in transatlantic races and adopted by the main clubs in France, Italy, Sweden, and other European countries. It was also used in Australia (for the Sydney-Hobart race for instance) and in New Zealand. Only in the United States and a few places in South America was it not used for the first-class offshore racing.

The rule was not only used for ocean racing. It gradually came to be adopted for many cruiser races 'around the cans' and over short day courses. The fact that each boat had a ready RORC rating that could be used for such events was a boon to other clubs. The RORC therefore undertook, not only to measure boats eligible for its races, but almost any boat that was not actually a dinghy or a multihull. Only in its own races did it lay down eligibility and safety rules. In North America the CCA rule was most commonly used but there were also a number of other rules of measurement and handicapping in use in the American tradition.

– uniting the Offshore Rules

From 1960 there was an 'Offshore Rules Coordinating Committee' with British and American members and Continental representation. Its job was to try and bring the RORC and CCA rules together as far as possible. It managed to standardize some measurement methods and sail-area for-

mulae, but could really do little against two separate and strongly independent club committees. In 1966, at the IYRU annual meeting in London, it was resolved that a sixth Olympic class should be sought and that this should be an ocean racer of about 35 ft (10.7 m) length overall. To get such a class it seemed that a common rating rule was needed and King Constantine of Greece (who knew little about ocean racing) was asked to approach the International Olympic Committee (who knew even less).

Offshore rules: the Sydney-Hobart race 1978. On the left is the winner Kialoa, *and on the right* Phantom

Nothing came of what now seems an amazing proposal, except the aim of uniting the RORC and CCA rules by November 1968, primarily by means of a small committee of which the American naval architect, Olin J. Stephens Jr (1908–), was chairman.

This move was really a reflection of the spread of international contests in ocean racing, particularly of series that had a couple of ocean races and a few inshore races – a way of racing originated by the Admiral's Cup. This spread to the One Ton Cup, an old inshore trophy that had been out of use since the 6-Metres last sailed it in 1962. The Cercle de la Voile de Paris presented it in 1965 for RORC-rated boats at a fixed rating of 22 ft without time allowance. The contest, a new concept for an ocean-racing rule, attracted immediate interest among all yachting

nations. It was not really conceivable that American yachtsmen should adopt the RORC rule, but the One Ton Cup did mean that they started building a few boats to it. This was less necessary in the established Admiral's Cup where CCA type boats could be measured to the RORC rule.

The existing RORC and CCA rules were due for major revision and the logical step was to combine the best features of both rules. The end result was much closer to the RORC than to the CCA, both in basic formulae and in the method of measuring hulls with girth stations. The sail-area systems for both rules were already not too dissimilar, but one feature to disappear was the long RORC sail batten in favour of the very short CCA style.

Olin Stephens' committee that handled this was called the International Technical Committee, and had as serving members the American Dick Carter, who had twice won the Fastnet race with boats of his own design, the Swedish designer Gustav Plym, the Dutch designer Ricus van der Stadt, and David Fayle, the British RORC chief measurer and his understudy Robin Glover. Once the rule was established, Glover became permanent technical adviser to the committee, and this resulted in an unprecedented close monitoring of a rating rule and thus its remarkably effective maintenance.

It took three years to get a usable rule formulated and IOR Mark II was announced in January 1970. (Mark I had been announced to meet the deadline of November 1968, but was really a draught.) Some extra basic factors were later added, so that by 1977 the rule (IOR Mark III) looked like this:

$$\text{Rating} = 0.13 \times \left[\frac{L \times \sqrt{S}}{\sqrt{(B \times D)}} + 0.25L + 0.2\sqrt{S} + DC + FC \right] \times \\ \times EPF \times CGF \times MAF \times SMF \times DLF$$

In this formula L is the measured length, S the measured sail area, B the beam, D the depth, DC the draft correction, and FC the freeboard correction. The multipliers are EPF, the engine and propeller factor, CGF the centre of gravity factor, MAF the multiple appendage factor, SMF the spar materials factor, and DLF the displacement limit factor. All these factors are derived from submeasurements or preliminary calculations and the formulae and working is intended for computer operation. The official certificate in all countries is a computer print-out: if there is any change in minor formulae at any time, hundreds of certificates can be recomputed in minutes (fig. 6). By 1977 the rule filled an A4 size book with 55 pages of formulae and measurement details.

In North America IOR Mark II was used for the 1970 season and numerous yachts were soon measured to it. The CCA gave up control of the rule to the national authority, NAYRU (later USYRU) who had an establishment that could deal with the quantity of certificates and the computer operations as well as the nationwide measurement organization. In Europe only RORC races used the IOR in 1970, but the RORC rule was declared phased out in autumn 1970 and for 1971 all rated races used the IOR.

To control the rule on an international level, the old Offshore Rules Coordinating Committee became the Offshore Rating Council (ORC) (later OFFSHORE RACING COUNCIL), with the ITC answerable to it. Countries with measured yachts were represented on this body, which was independent of the International Yacht Racing Union. The ORC authorizes amendments to the IOR and systems of measurement and certification under it, thus ensuring worldwide uniformity.

At the end of 1971 a number of important revisions were made to the IOR, though the basic formula remained unaltered. These changes included the method of measuring the stern, the way depth was arrived at, and the establishment of a minimum CGF to prevent very tender boats taking advantage of this factor, which was in the rule to correct high ballast ratio and thus light and weak hulls. The rule then became IOR Mark III. Since then modifications to component parts of the rule have been made from time to time. Designers are continually trying to find what sort of boat it appears to favour.

– IOR influence on yacht design

It is not possible to separate clearly which features in a yacht are induced by the rule and which are purely speed-producing parts of the design: the two aspects are entwined. The history of rules described above does show that each rule produces a characteristic type, even though various different experiments are made. It is therefore possible to describe the IOR class yacht, though by no means all yachts, including successful ones racing to the IOR, will answer this description. One reason for the acute development of design is the One Ton Cup and similar level-rating series under the IOR. These races have shown small differences in characteristics more clearly than if time allowance were in force. Indeed the time allowance systems have become secondary in first class IOR racing, new boats (late 1970s) tending to polarize near the established level-rating figures: 32.0, 27.5, 24.5, 21.7, 18.0, and 16.0 ft.

HULLS

Fin keel and spade rudder or rudder with narrow SKEG are universal; displacement is carried well aft, and hull measurement points give an almost chine effect in some boats. The hull meets narrow fin keel at right angles. Ends are short with the stem a straight line and low sections flat. Freeboard is high, draft is controlled by DC in the rule. Beam is large by previous standards (e.g. for LWL of 30 ft, a beam of 11 ft would be normal). The beam is not carried over any great length fore and aft, the plan view of the boat showing the deck line moving in sharply. Rigidity in building materials is favoured including aluminium, moulded plywood (perhaps reinforced with carbon fibre), C-flex glass fibre, or foam or balsa sandwich. Glass-reinforced plastic (GRP) built in a female mould is used for production boats. No one material has prevailing advantage under the rule.

RIGS

Except in boats over about 55 ft, where sloop rig is used. Over this size a mizzen is often used to keep the size of sails manageable. Two-masted boats are always ketches, because the rudders are well aft. The yawl is therefore unknown in modern racing and very rare in modern yacht design. Masthead rig is most common but not universal – well-developed three-quarter rigs being successful, especially in smaller sizes. Mainsails are usually to minimum size under the rule, genoas with 50% overlap, and great emphasis on spinnakers and auxiliary downwind sails. The whole sailplan is controlled by variable geared, high speed, and powerful winches.

ACCOMMODATION

The shape of hull allows spacious accommodation, but this is not always installed to save weight when racing. It does mean that IOR boats can make excellent cruisers, for they are designed for offshore work in the first place.

DECK FEATURES

The ORC has extensive rules for safety and emergency equipment, that affect the design of the deck where space has to be found for life-line and pulpits, watertight cockpits, life rafts, and man overboard equipment. In

Section of a typical IOR class yacht (above) *with high freeboard, light displacement (taken well aft) and fin keel. (The hole in the transom takes a dan buoy for man-overboard equipment)*

IOR class boats with high freeboard and straight or convex stems (top right). *The spinnakers are comparatively large and the other sails on the decks indicate a multiplicity of headsails*

Sail plans as developed under the IOR feature tall masts and large overlapping headsails. In the yacht (right) *the genoa is in a groove (no hanks); the short battens in the mainsail were inherited from the CCA rule*

racing boats the emphasis is on speedy handling and minimum WINDAGE. This means that the 'submarine' effect is not always useful for cruising. The IOR has little to do with this, but it is IOR boats that receive the most attention in this way.

– criticisms of the IOR

The rule has come under heavy criticism during the whole of its life. This is partly because it is so widespread in use that more owners have grounds for one complaint or another. The intensity of competition in modern conditions is one of the reasons why the keenest owners and designers will go to great lengths to win with the latest boat to be designed under the rule. The fact is that they would do the same with any rule: yet the IOR has stood up remarkably well to this test, certainly in comparison with rating rules of the past. The type of boat designed to it has sailed in all sorts of weather, in all conditions, including races round the world, through the Roaring Forties and round Cape Horn. No other rule has undergone such a test. The greatest criticism has come from the United States: the old CCA boats were certainly not favoured under the new rule, whereas some old RORC boats did remain competitive. The tradition in the United States is not for a homogeneous rule as many areas still retain local measurement systems. In the mid-1970s however, certain elements in the CCA became aware that they had given up their 'Bermuda race rule' to national and international bodies and so reacted against this. But the Bermuda race was no longer the most important ocean race in the United States and the introduction of CCA alterations to the IOR for the 1976 race had no impact, as it might have done a decade earlier. Consequently there has been a continuing tug-of-war between European and American interests at the annual ORC meetings, with a number of investigations into alleged inequities in the IOR. The result of most of such inquiries has been negative. In 1976 the USYRU announced that it would create a new rating rule of its own for 'second-line' racing, but still intended to continue to administer the IOR within the United States for all who wished to use it.

Similar pressures have caused the introduction of a 'retrospective rule' within the IOR, known as IOR Mark IIIA. This alters part of the formula, but can only be given to boats built before a certain date. Therefore, although it is not possible to take advantage of the changes to design a new yacht, it can give a bonus to boats that are not of the latest type.

– time-allowance systems

These are operated by using the IOR, but laid down nationally or locally. The United States seemed destined to continue the time-on-distance system of the USYRU (seconds per mile) for many years despite discussion of possible new methods. The tables of the USYRU are based on the following formula, where R and r are the different ratings of two yachts.

$$\text{Allowance} = \frac{2160}{\sqrt{r}} - \frac{2160}{\sqrt{R}}$$

Many countries in Europe use the time-on-time system of the RORC (1977):

$$TMF = \frac{0.2424\ \sqrt{R}}{1\ +\ 0.0567\ \sqrt{R}}$$

The *TMF* (time multiplying factor) is used to multiply the elapsed time to give the corrected time: the yacht with the shortest corrected time in a race is the winner. R is the rating of the yacht. A slightly different formula is applied to yachts below 23.0-ft rating. Tables give *TMF* for every rating.

– other methods of handicapping
The use of other rules particularly in the United States was mentioned above. The point about such systems is that they work well for an existing fleet, but fail if a yacht is built to exploit the rule. Such building is rare because standard yachts are built to the IOR and owners who wish to race keenly would find a yacht built to a local rating rule useless to achieve success elsewhere.

Where measurement is not used, then the time allowances given will depend on performance. They will be allotted by a club handicapper – the more successful yachts carrying extra time (say seconds per mile) to compensate for the poorer performance of their opponents. The most widespread and systemized performance handicap method is the Portsmouth Yardstick Scheme, originated by S. Zillwood Milledge of London. Under this scheme, boats are given a number equal to the time taken over a theoretical but unspecified distance. The validity of the number is graded at local and national level for each class of yacht. Non-standard designs can be allotted a number by the club handicapper. Strictly standard well-known designs will already have a number confirmed at national level. Tables are available to convert numbers into corrected times over various course lengths. The Portsmouth Yardstick Scheme has spread from Britain to the United States and other countries. It is locally or nationally administered, though there is an informal international exchange of information. It is widely used for dinghies, and can accommodate larger boats.
See also YACHT RACING

Hand lead *see* LEAD AND LINE

Handy billy
A tackle used to give extra power on a rope.

Harden in
To flatten a sail by hauling on the sheet.

Head
(1) The top edge of a sail; (2) a ship's lavatory; (3) the wind is said to head a vessel that is close-hauled when it draws ahead causing her to pay off.

Headboard
A piece of wood or light metal built on (or riveted) to the head of a Bermudian sail to prevent twist and distribute the loading.

Heading
The instantaneous direction of the fore-and-aft axis of a craft, generally measured by the compass.

Headstay *see* MASTS AND RIGGING: Glossary

Headway
Forward movement through the water.

Headwind
A wind that compels a vessel to BEAT.

Heating systems *see* HULLS: Hull and accommodation systems

Heave to, lie to
To trim a vessel so that she remains virtually stationary with the seas on the weather bow. *See* HEAVY-WEATHER SAILING

Heaving line
A light line, generally weighted at one end, used to heave ashore when coming alongside so that a heavier line may be hauled over.

Heavy-weather sailing
Heavy weather may be said to arise when the force of the wind and the state of the sea become too high for a sailing vessel to con-. tinue on her course. She may then be obliged

A yacht reaching under a storm sail

to lie to, or bring to, which generally means coming close to the wind under reduced sail in a position with seas on her weather bow with a minimum of forward motion (hove to), or, in broader usage the term can include lying a-hull (*see below*).

Heaving to is the traditional way for a sailing vessel to ride out a gale at sea. The vessel forereaches as close to the wind as possible, easing through the rough seas with only sufficient forward way on her to enable a steady close-hauled course to be achieved. The conventional method for a fore-and-aft rigged sailing vessel is with the storm trysail or close-reefed mainsail sheeted hard in, the storm jib aback (to prevent her getting in irons) and the helm down. The older types of yachts with long keels heave to most readily, but most yachts with keels of only moderate length can do the same, if of well-balanced design. Success in heaving to is a matter of trial and error to suit the requirements of the individual boat and storm sail plan, and can sometimes be achieved under trysail alone with helm up, or storm jib alone with helm down. Modern offshore racing yachts with narrow fin keels and separate rudders on SKEGS are often difficult to heave to, as they are too lively in a seaway and may require a man at the helm the whole time. The term a-try or trying is sometimes used for lying to under storm trysail.

– lying a-hull
A sailing vessel is said to be lying a-hull or hulling when all sail has been furled and she is lying under bare poles finding her own natural position in the seas. The helm is usually lashed down so that if she begins to gather way downwind she will LUFF back to the normal position about broadside to wind and sea. Leeway is about $1\frac{1}{2}$ knots but may be considerably more in some yachts so adequate sea room is needed. Hulling is the easiest gale tactic and throws least strain on a small crew. Nevertheless, it is not recommended in

The Dutch catamaran Nacra *pitchpoling during the 1977 John Player World Sailing Speed Trials in Portland Harbour, Dorset. Undamaged, she sailed again, and achieved the fastest speed that day.*

severe gales with really big seas: a yacht is vulnerable to these when lying broadside to them.

– running off under bare poles
This is generally considered to be the safest tactic in severe gales or storms. A sufficient number and length of warps are streamed to reduce speed and hold the stern to the following seas, but retain sufficient speed to maintain good steering control. The method is not desirable for boats with open cockpits, and considerable sea room is required.

– knockdown
The picking up and throwing of a sailing vessel onto her beam ends into a horizontal position with her mast in, or nearly in, the sea. In a knockdown, stores and internal equipment may be thrown to the lee side, and superstructure or coamings on that side may be damaged by the violent impact with the water. A knockdown need not be disastrous in a yacht with a deep ballast keel, which should be sufficient to right her.

– capsize
The term applies when a sailing vessel has turned completely over with the keel above and the mast below the water. If continued through 360° it is often termed a complete roll-over. Such incidents are very rare, but have occasionally occurred in great storms on the ocean, usually with dismasting.

– pitchpoling
When a vessel is picked up by a following sea and turned over completely stern over bows this is termed pitchpoling. It very rarely occurs, and only with huge, high waves, but it has happened to a few yachts caught out running, even with warps streamed, in great ocean storms.

Heel
To lay over.

Heeling error
Deviation of the magnetic compass caused when a vessel heels and there is a change in the relative position of nearby ferrous material. *See* MARINER'S COMPASS

Height of eye *see* HORIZON DISTANCE

Helm
Tiller or wheel used for steering.

Hi-fix
A radio positioning system based on the DECCA NAVIGATOR.

High-focal-plane buoys *see* BUOY: Navigational buoy

High-speed sailing
The object of high-speed sailing is to achieve maximum speed under sail, with no restriction on the number of crew, or the size, shape or seaworthiness of the yacht. The

speed is averaged over a measured distance, greater than a stipulated minimum, and it is essential that the measurement arrangements should be both very accurate and impartial.

Despite this lack of restrictions, no high-speed-sailing records were attempted or claimed, at least as a regular activity, until commercial sponsorship began in 1972. Before that time almost all claims of high speed under sail lacked either the accuracy or the impartiality that would now be expected before any record is ratified. Nonetheless there are a handful of earlier claims to speeds of 25 knots or more. First the hydrofoil yachts *Monitor* (Baker, US Navy), *Flying Fish* (Don Nigg, United States), and *Flying Feline* (Apollonio, United States). Each of these three was independently developed in the 1950s and '60s. *Monitor* was a 30-ft, (9-m), two-man monohull with aircraft-configuration, variable-incidence ladder foils; her accurately paced speed of 30.4 knots in October 1956 remains the fastest measured speed claimed for any sailing hydrofoil. Although the record is not impartial by today's standards, *Monitor* was a US Navy project, and there was certainly a desire for accurate speed measurement, with ample facilities available. *Flying Fish* was the end-product of a single-handed canard-configuration foil development, also based on a monohull; the main foils have their upper surfaces shaped to the arc of a circle, lower surfaces flat, and are set at 45° dihedral. Each has an unsupported tip on which the boat rides at high speed. This design has been much used in subsequent craft. *Flying Feline* was a 15-ft (4.5-m) catamaran with a 'foil on each corner'; there are photographs of both these last-mentioned craft riding so high on the foils that simple calculations confirm the claims to speeds of over 20 knots.

As regards craft not borne on foils the American D-Class cat *Whirlwind* is likely to have exceeded 20 knots, as is the A-Class *Scow* also in the United States. The craft mentioned so far all sailed in sheltered waters, where speed measurement is easy. In the open sea accurate measurement is far more difficult; despite their size the square-rigged ships only claimed speeds of up to 20 knots, although it may be assumed that this speed was exceeded at times during a day's run at an average speed of 19½ knots, claimed by the four-masted *Champion of the Seas* running in the Southern Ocean in December 1854. Much more recently there are accounts of big ocean racing catamarans, such as *Manu Kai*, with speedometers recording 25 knots for minutes on end while running across the front of big waves on the Transpacific Race. A man with a hatchet apparently sits ready beside the spinnaker sheet and guy, able to effect a quick reduction in sail power if the boat starts to nose-dive! These non-hydrofoil craft could doubtless be matched by others of a similar type, before 1972. However, there was no response when a request for further claims was made in the British magazine *Yachting World* in December 1971.

There were two early attempts at accurate and impartial speed trials, both held in England. The first was organized off Cowes in 1954 and '55. The 1954 meeting was won by the naturalist and yachtsman Peter Scott in an Uffa Fox-designed Jollyboat, at 10.2 knots. In 1955 the winner was Ken Pearce in his 18-ft (5.5-m) catamaran *Endeavour* at a speed of 14.6 knots. Interest then lapsed until 1970 when the first success, in England, with sailing hydrofoils re-awakened the desire to measure speed accurately. Two meetings were organized in the estuary at Burnham-on-Crouch, Essex, by a team consisting of the AMATEUR YACHT RESEARCH SOCIETY, the editorial staff of the *Yachting World*, and the Grogono family. The distance of 500 yd (457.2 m) was measured to the highest accuracy by land surveyors' Tellurometers and radio communication were used to operate stopwatches. The 1970 meeting was won by Mike Day's standard Tornado catamaran, at 16.4 knots, considerably faster than James Grogono's hydrofoil-converted Tornado *Icarus*, which at that time had frail and unwieldy wooden foils. The 1971 meeting was marred by the lack of wind, but again won by a standard Tornado at 14.9 knots. Second place was taken by Philip Hansford's tiny hydrofoil catamaran, at 13.9 knots. The hydrofoil sailors were enthused, although defeated, but they lacked the organization and resources to run a bigger event. In 1969 Peter Scott and Bernard Hayman had discussed the need for a competition quite separate from yacht racing, so that sponsors could be given free rein. An informal speed sailing committee (John Fisk, James Grogono, Bernard Hayman, Bee Mackinnon, Don Robertson, and Peter Scott) met at the ROYAL THAMES YACHT CLUB, and outlined the conditions necessary for a competition. This committee agreed not to meet again unless a sponsor could be found. By good fortune the tobacco company John Player made an approach shortly afterwards, and its request to sponsor a speed-sailing competition was channelled through the ROYAL YACHTING ASSOCIATION. An RYA subcommittee was formed, under Peter Scott's chairmanship, and the John Player RYA High-Speed Sailing event was announced – and well publicized at the 1972 London Boat Show.

Each year, since 1972, has seen a competition, in two parts, run on broadly similar lines. The first part is a week-long open meeting held in October in Portland Harbour, Dorset, where all timing and accrediting is centrally organized, and would-be record breakers simply enter their boats. The second

part is open to any sailor anywhere in the world provided that his own national authority is prepared to verify the accuracy of measurement and have an observer present when the record is made. The RYA must be notified a month in advance, to send its own

observer should it so wish. For both parts of the competition there is a minimum distance of 500 m. There are certain other prohibitions such as power storage in control systems, agents reducing skin friction, pilotless craft, and ice yachts. It is also required that the

Icarus (below), the hydrofoil-converted Tornado that in 1972 achieved a speed of 25.4 knots

Hi Trott III (bottom), a Japanese B-Class entrant during the 1978 Speed Week in Portland Harbour

Crossbow I with Timothy Colman at the wheel during the 1975 Speed Week (right, above)

Colman's Crossbow II competing at Portland in 1977, when she achieved a record 33.8 knots (right, below)

craft should accelerate from rest by sail power alone. Nonetheless the essentially unrestricted nature has been preserved. Only one run, in any direction, is necessary for the record. It could thus be made by a sled towed downwind by a kite; or by a hydrofoil-supported frame, which could become foil-borne away from the course, and jettison spare equipment, crew members, and the initial flotation hulls before entering the measured section – the fate of the craft after completing its run is no part of the competition.

Speed Week in Portland Harbour has proved to be the highlight of the new sport. Each year has seen a variety of new designs, and almost every year records have been broken. After two years it became clear that overall size confers an advantage, and since 1974 there have been 'size prizes' related to the standard catamaran sail areas designated as C-, B-, and A- Class in descending order of size, with the addition of the 10-m² Class as the smallest size. The measured sail area includes the spars, to allow for wingsails and semi-solid rigs. Since 1974 there has been a small but inevitable amount of scrutineering of entrants, pleasantly absent from the first years of the competition.

The course in Portland Harbour consists of a clockface of buoys each moored to the nearest decimetre by accurately surveyed markers on the harbour floor. Each entrant chooses the optimum wind angle for the conditions of the day, and sails across the clockface on a chosen 'corridor' (for example, if entering the circle between two and three, then the exit must be made between eight and nine). Timing boats are stationed to sight across each end, and a committee boat, in radio contact with both timing boats, records the elapsed time on a battery of stopwatches. Time is saved if a group of boats all wish to use the same course, but inevitably some have a different optimum wind angle from others. The exact speed is calculated from the surveyors' calculation of the length of each corridor, which is slightly more than 500 m.

The main event has so far (1978) been dominated by the two *Crossbows* owned by Timothy Colman and designed by Roderick Macalpine Downie. *Crossbow I* was designed as a 'conservative' speed sailer, using only well-proven design features, such as a long, slender, lightweight hull, and large sailplan. The 60-ft (18-m) main hull is less than 2 ft (0.6 m) wide, and her 950 ft² (88 m²) of sail is balanced by the crew of four being carried in a 'gondola' held on an outrigger 30 ft (9 m) to windward. Initially the crew aimed to keep the gondola airborne (to reduce drag) by running to and fro on the outrigger. However, this made for difficulty in sail control, and the crew retired into foxholes in the windward hull, which was supported by a foil or planing skid to reduce drag if it happened

to touch down. *Crossbow I* created a new world record on each of her three appearances at Speed Week (see diagram) but her limitation to sailing one-way-only severely restricted her sailing time, and Colman opted for a more practical design. *Crossbow II* is an asymmetric catamaran 60 ft (18 m) long with the leeward hull well in front of the

windward one. Unlike *Crossbow I* she can sail without assistance on either tack, although she is only capable of high speeds on starboard tack. The rig consists of twin una-rigs with one mast on each hull, and an elaborate metal bracing to keep the masts apart. The sails are kept from twisting by a vang at 45° to the horizontal, and the single-part main sheets are linked into twin winches. In 1976 she was hardly completed and had major steering problems, but managed to beat *Crossbow I*'s record by a small margin. In 1977 she raised her own record to an impressive 33.8 knots, and chanced to split the leeward hull just as she completed the run. Not for the first time this team carried out a major repair in less than 24 hours, but suitable weather had run out for that year. Each year so far (1978) *Crossbow*'s top speed at Portland has also been the fastest anywhere and Colman has held the John Player World Sailing Speed Record since its inception in 1972.

By 1978 only five other craft had exceeded 22 knots in the stringent conditions laid down. The first was *Icarus*. In the first year of the competition the foil-borne version at last beat the standard Tornado – the speed was 21.6 knots. *Icarus* luckily won £1000, the same prize as *Crossbow*, since she was the only entrant to finish within 5 knots of *Crossbow*'s speed. *Icarus* improved her speed to 25.4 knots in an observed trial at Burnham-on-Crouch, and she finished that year less than a knot behind *Crossbow*. *Icarus* did not regain that speed after the introduction of size prizes, but her 1977 speed of 22.2 is narrowly sufficient to hold the B-Class World Record.

The second boat to exceed 22 knots, besides *Crossbow* was *British Oxygen*, the big offshore catamaran also designed by Roderick Mac-alpine Downie. She won the 1974 event at 24.3 knots in the only year when neither of the *Crossbow*'s entered. The third in this speed range was *Clifton Flasher*, a 27-ft (8-m) asymmetric catamaran with a solid multiplane rig consisting of five vertical wings. Her 1974 speed of 22.1 knots stood as the C-Class world record, although subsequently exceeded by both the smaller B- and A-Class records. The A-Class record was held by *Mayfly*, Philip Hansford's purpose-designed foil catamaran, perhaps the most successful small sailing hydrofoil ever. Her Portland speeds steadily improved (see diagram) and her measured best of 23.0 knots, in the hands of her third owner, Ben Wynne, was in 1978 by far the highest speed, size-for-size, that any sailing craft has ever achieved. She is a highly practical small sailing craft, equally fast on either tack, and by no means slow to windward, although her fastest speed is a 'right-angle' broad reach.

The fifth craft to exceed 22 knots was Professor Bradfield's *nf²*, a canard-configuration monohull with variable-incidence foils. She reached 22.5 knots as a B-Class entrant in a series of trials held in Long Island Sound in October 1977. At the time this was the fastest B-Class speed recorded since the size divisions were introduced in 1974, but was not the necessary 2% greater than *Icarus*'s record speed at Portland a month earlier. By coincidence, *Icarus*'s record had been ratified

The large, 70-ft (21.3-m) catamaran British Oxygen. *In 1974 she not only won the speed event but also the Round Britain Race*

the day before *nf²* made her record run, and the *Icarus* record thus stands.

The smallest division, the 10-m² Class, has always had a large entry at Portland since the small size enables the boat to be light, simple, and inexpensive. The record stood at only 15 knots, attained by Reg Bratt's foil-assisted catamaran *Boreas*, until 1977, when a large 10 sq. m entry of 20 was easily led by the Dutch board-sailor Dirk Thijs, who sailed *Windglider*, a German-made sailing surf-board, at an amazing 19.1 knots.

Although this account appears to centre the new sport of high-speed sailing on England, and a given week each October in Portland Harbour, interest has been shown from the West and East Coasts of the United States and also in Italy, the Netherlands, South Africa, and Australia.

High water full and change (HWF&C)
The mean interval at any place between the transit of the full or new moon and the following high water. *See* ESTABLISHMENT OF THE PORT

Hitches *see* ROPEWORK: Bends and hitches

Hog *see* HULLS: Construction components

Hogging *see* HULLS: Scantlings

Horizon distance
The geometrical distance to the visible *horizon*, assuming a spherical earth, from an observer at height H metres (h feet) above the surface of the sea, is approximately $1.92\sqrt{H}$ ($1.06\sqrt{h}$) nautical miles, the same as the DIP of the horizon in minutes of arc. The effect of

the refraction of light in the lower layers of the atmosphere is to increase the distance to about $2.08 \sqrt{H}$ ($0.97 \sqrt{h}$), on which values most tables are based. A conspicuous object, such as a light, can thus be seen by an observer at a distance equal to the sum of the two horizon distances appropriate to their heights above the sea. However, the effect of refraction varies greatly with atmospheric conditions, particularly the relative temperature of the sea and air, and its variation with height; these effects, of which there are many manifestations, are collectively known as mirage effects. In particular, objects normally well below the horizon may become visible in extreme conditions of temperature inversion, a phenomenon known as 'looming'; a light that is below the horizon may also be seen as a glow caused by its reflection in the solid particles in the air – this is often referred to as 'loom'. Opposite effects (leading to a reduction in the visible distance of the horizon) can also occur, so that navigators must use caution in interpreting distances based on tabular values, necessarily calculated for mean conditions. *See also* DIP

Horn timber *see* HULLS: Construction components

Horse *see* MASTS AND RIGGING: Glossary

Horse latitudes
Areas of calm on the poleward side of the trade-wind belts.

Hounds *see* MASTS AND RIGGING: Glossary

Hour angle
The angle in the plane of the celestial equator measured westward from a specified celestial meridian to a celestial body.

Hove down
Excessively heeled.

Clifton Flasher, *an asymmetric C-Class catamaran with solid multiplane rig, shown here during 1976*

Mayfly, *the A-Class record holder at speed during 1977* (bottom)

Hulls

The hull is the main body of a vessel, excluding masts, rigging, and any internal fittings and equipment.

– hull forms

RAFT

A raft is essentially formed from a collection of self-buoyant objects bound together to have sufficient combined buoyancy and stability to carry its crew and cargo on the surface of the water. It does not have to be watertight. It is propelled slowly by poling or paddling and does not need to have a form that gives it directional stability and of course is very subject to drifting with winds and currents. The stability of a raft is high until it heels to the point where some of the under surface lifts clear of the waters, when it very quickly reduces. Rafts therefore need to be of good size and preferably heavy to give them a good range of stability. Some rafts can be quite sophisticated with platforms, cabins, decking, and bulwarks to protect the crew and cargo. A measure of sailing performance is also possible if they are fitted with centreboards, rudders, and sails although in this manner they may be better designated as slow-speed craft. The raft is essentially cumbersome to handle and very wasteful in materials.

DUGOUT

The dugout is usually a single tree in which a deep hollow has been carved to act as a cockpit. The step from raft to dugout was in its way as momentous as the invention of the wheel because it transformed sea travel. Not only was the resulting craft sufficiently stable but the reduction of weight and the great improvement in hull form from the very much better proportions gave speed, which in turn allowed lengthy voyages to be made. The construction of the dugout form was still extremely laborious and very wasteful in materials, but the first minor improvements such as fitting washboards probably originated the whole science of shipbuilding.

HEAVY DISPLACEMENT

Boats developed according to the materials available for their construction and the facilities available in their home ports for handling them. Where good wood abounded and boats could be left afloat or on the beach during the course of a tide without danger from surf or rollers, it was natural to build stout and heavy craft for their durability. Wood rots and the more that wood was used for building heavy boats the thicker became the wood members employed to make allowance for the reduction in strength that was bound to occur from rot during the life of the craft. Also, the heavier the boat the more sail it required to drive it, and this in turn meant ballast to hold it up against the winds. The heavy-displacement boat therefore tended to develop into a distinct type, usually short and fat with the extra beam also helping with the stability. Such a vessel is of course ideal for load carrying, and it was the heavy-displacement type of vessel that dominated world exploration and trading right up to the introduction of the metal constructions.

LIGHT DISPLACEMENT

The light-displacement type was most often developed where the boat had to be plucked from the surf and lifted up the beach clear of the sea. To a certain extent this requirement overrode the difficulties of building materials. The light boat therefore very often had to be an excellent seaboat and the classic type has well-balanced ends, usually with a fine form, and a good sweeping sheer. Such a craft can be operated under oars and therefore is planned to use either sail or oars depending on the conditions. A light vessel needs only a modest sail plan to drive it and therefore little or no ballast. The main problem at sea is that of capsizing, and a very high order of seamanship is required in open water.

KEEL BOATS

The traditional problems of the sailing ship are working into the wind and being becalmed. For windward ability a fine hull of small resistance has to be combined with a form that acts as a sideways hydrofoil to stop undue drift. The need to get ballast lower to hold up exaggerated racing sail plans was probably the inspiration for curving the bottom of the hull down along the centreline. The inside ballast laid in the trough thus formed eventually gave way to bolted-on outside ballast. The improvement in windward performance of the deep keel this formed was noticeable, and in fact sail plans had to be improved to match up to the potential performance. However, this improved performance was essentially confined to pleasure sailing, for the world trade routes were well established for commercial sail, which would have found the deeper draught a barrier in penetrating to their established loading berths. The development this century has

A shallow-keeled boat

An aluminium yacht hull with a fin keel, under construction

been to match the keel size to the ever decreasing displacements of current sailing yachts until now the keel has an appearance, and indeed a construction, somewhat like the wing of a fast aircraft.

CATAMARANS AND PROAS
These are twin-hulled craft with immediate and exciting possibilities. The first is an enormous gain in initial stability both for crew on deck and for sailing in appropriate con-

ditions. The second is that the power of the sailplan is applied to two very slender hulls giving a very high speed potential. The problems for the sailor lie in the very sudden loss of stability once a hull lifts in a gust of wind. For the builder the problems lie in the very heavy structural stresses between the hulls and connecting beams. The solution cannot be heavy for this destroys the very power-to-weight ratio that gives the catamaran or the

proa its high performance. This characteristic light weight gives a catamaran very little momentum to take it through the eye of the wind when TACKING, and the proa is one answer to a feature which used to be a problem. On the proa the whole sail plan is turned end for end, driving the hull alternately in each direction. The proa is in fact very similar to the outrigger canoe but uses two full-sized, paired, hulls. *See also* MULTIHULLS

TRIMARANS
The trimaran is essentially an unballasted single-hull craft making use of twin floats port and starboard to give her stability. It has the essential difference from the catamaran that when pressed by a squall the lee float is pushed down as the weather float lifts, leaving a reasonable stability base that greatly extends the positive stability range. The builder is again faced with the structural problems of the connecting beams and also has to make the floats such that they tend to lift when driven forward and down, so as to stop the whole vessel from tripping. *See also* MULTIHULLS

TUNNEL
Now that wood planking is not the dominant feature in determining hull form a number of hulls are built on catamaran or trimaran principles, but as one continuous hull moulding. These perform very much as the catamaran or trimaran in light conditions, but in stronger breezes the shape and form of the tunnels have an effect on the performance, and not just in terms of stability. Such craft have to be extremely carefully designed to get the correct water flow in the tunnels and have to be very strong to cater for the very heavy hull loadings that can build up as the sea, scooped into the tunnel, is accelerated and slowed down. *See also* MULTIHULLS

– construction and materials

LOGS
The log is the largest basic material available to man that can be worked easily and that floats. The log by itself therefore is the very simplest kind of boat available and, when roughly trimmed by axe, may be used by itself or grouped and lashed into a raft for fairly elementary boating or seagoing. If a log is hollowed out to let the crew and load in general sit low enough to give a reasonable stability, the dugout becomes a very efficient boat in terms of speed for effort when paddling. Essentially the hollowing of logs was carried out by chopping and burning, although some modern dugouts are produced using machinery.

A normal sophistication of the process is to use fire and water in the hollowing process and make use of the steam produced to bend the 'topsides' into a better shape. Fire was also used to seal the wood. To make them more seaworthy many dugouts were, and still are, fitted with wooden coaming planks

Frygga of Cymru, *the 40.5-ft (12.4-m) ketch-rigged Polynesian-style catamaran* (top) *designed by James Wharram*

The American trimaran Rogue Wave *being sailed by Phil Weld and David Cooksey during a* Round Britain Race *(above)*

pegged into place. The log canoe is a very wasteful and labour-intensive method of boatbuilding and is limited by the size of trees available. The log cut into planks, however, was for many years the principal ingredient of boat- and shipbuilding, and the shapes that wood can be built into still influence the shape of ships.

BLADDERS

Animal skins were another easily available material for early boatbuilders. A skin sewn into the form of a bladder and inflated obviously made a very useful swimming aid, but in various regions between Arabia and Mongolia and also in Chile the bladders were tied together into groups of from three or four up to many hundreds. Over these was then tied a light framework that made the working deck. On the larger rafts the skins were placed with the orifices upwards so that they could be reflated on passage if necessary. The rafts used in Chile were made of twin seal-skins in a manner very similar to some of the rubber inflatable boats in use today. For some river rafts in India the bladders were replaced by sealed pottery jugs.

PAPYRUS

In many countries where suitable trees are not available boats are built of fascines made of stout stalks such as sedges, rushes, and papyrus. At their simplest these consisted of two or three bundles tied together with the ends tapered and pointed up clear of the water to reduce the penetration of moisture along the stalks from the cut ends. Boats of this kind were used principally in North and Central Africa and on the west coast of South America, where in fact they are still to be found at lake Titicaca. Other very similar craft were built of faggots of branches or even palm leaves, and in Tasmania they were built of bundles of tree bark.

BARK BOATS

Boats up to 40 ft (12 m) in length have been and still are being built using the cork-rich bark of some trees as a sheet skinning material. The traditional Canadian birch-bark canoe consists of a light skeleton framework covered athwartships from gunwale to gunwale with wide strips of bark. The skin is sewn together with fir-tree roots and the seams dressed watertight with gum from the balsam tree. Other craft, including the South American canoes, are made from one sheet of bark that might be 40 ft (12 m) in length. The centre section is braced with light THWARTS and then heat is used to curve the ends together until they can be sewn and dressed. A similar construction is employed for Australian canoes using gum bark, but these are only quite small.

BASKET BOATS

The simplest form of basket boat consists of a framework of withies of general basket form around which is stretched a skin of leather or

A clinker-built hull for a fishing boat being constructed on the south coast of England

close-woven fabric treated to make it waterproof. Sophisticated versions of this construction, however, produce very good lightweight seaboats up to the 60 ft (18 m) of the biggest Eskimo craft. The Irish curragh, for instance, is built upside down with a basic heavy gunwale framework onto which is set up a series of hoop frames that are in turn strapped with a close-spaced set of longitudinal stringers, the whole originally lashed together with leather thongs, but now often nailed. This completed and self-supporting structure is then covered with a skin of ox-hides or tarred canvas sewn together to the approximate shape of the hull and stretched with heavy thongs to the inside of the strong gunwale. This kind of construction is still used in many parts of the world. Bamboo and animal bones are also used for framing, and the skin might be hides of goats, cattle, bear, or seals. Tannin, tree resin, animal tallow, and tar are all used for a waterproofing dressing.

PLANKED HULL WITH WOOD STRAPPING

The wood-plank coamings pegged around the cockpit of the dugout canoe are perhaps historically the first steps towards the evolution of the intricate and delicate clenched-lap, clincher or clinker (lapstrake) planking method of construction. This reached something of a zenith with the Viking ships, but has remained an important method of building small boats and light ships right up until the middle of this century. Essentially it is a method of building a hull by fastening plank to plank with a lap joint until a big enough hull shell is achieved. For any but the crudest hulls this necessitates every plank being shaped independently and bevelled to meet

the next plank in a joint accurate enough to be watertight.

Some modern builders used moulds to guide the rise of planking, but many hulls up to 70 ft (21 m) or bigger were built with only the eye of the shipbuilder to achieve the required form. In the earlier constructions the planks were often fastened together with leather or rope thongs passed through holes in the plank and secured to CLEATS carved onto the inside of each plank. Treenails or trunnels (wooden pegs or nails) were also used and the ship (c. seventh century AD) excavated at Sutton Hoo in Suffolk, England, in 1939, for instance, was secured with iron rivets. In modern constructions copper is used with the nail riveted or clenched over a conical washer called a roove. A hull construction of this type depends heavily on the quality of timber, but even the best timber is not strong across the grain. The completed planked hull therefore was almost always reinforced with frames put in after planking. These took the form of sawn frames or, more commonly, wood-strap frames, bent into the hull and fastened to each plank either side of the lap joint. This form of construction was principally valued for its light weight.

FRAMED HULL WITH WOOD PLANKING

Ships built for carrying heavy loads of cargo or ballast for sailing were usually built as a framed structure that was then planked over to make it watertight. The essence of the construction was that the framing was itself strong enough to carry the sea and wind loadings and cargo stresses, leaving the planking in a secondary structural role. For this construction the keel member is laid on the building ways and stem and stern framing

The framed hull of a luxury yacht showing the ribbands and wales

British Steel *with Chay Blyth at the helm in August 1971 as she arrives in the Solent after her 'wrong-way-round-the-world' voyage*

added. Along the length of this centreline structure is set up a complete series of frames. At one time these were shaped by the eye of the shipbuilder, but in the last few hundred years they have been the result of careful plotting on the mould-loft floor of the lines of the ship. The frames are faired and secured together with temporary longitudinal members called ribbands. The main longitudinal members, or wales, are then added. These wales are stout planks that are securely bolted to the frames on the outside and, in addition, similar members called stringers are secured to the inside. This, together with the deck beams and a whole host of minor stiffening, completes the skeleton of the ship. The skin planking is then added, fitted edge to edge – a method termed carvel construction – to shutter in the spaces between the wales. In ancient times when iron was precious and bolt fastenings few, the planking would be secured in place with treenail pegs and caulked with oakum. Yachts built with fine craftsmanship did not use wales but relied on the bolt fastenings of each plank to the frames to stop the hull spreading apart under the wedging pressures of the caulking. The height of craftsmanship was to build such a hull 'close-seamed', that is with such perfect joints between the planks that only the swelling of the wood when immersed was necessary to make it watertight.

Composite hulls

Composite construction can cover a mixture of almost any building techniques to suit particular requirements. It is quite common, for instance, to reduce the number and weight of heavy sawn frames by fitting inter-mediate steamed-timber strap frames. The

mixing of iron and wood came about in the middle of the nineteenth century mostly in response to the heavy stresses put on hulls by the introduction of steam power. Iron framing gave hulls that were stronger and lighter and also with greater cargo capacity, advantages that were not ignored by the sailing-ship builders. For instance, the *Cutty Sark*, now preserved at Greenwich, London, was built in 1869 with an exceptionally fine set of iron frames planked in wood. As iron became cheaper as a result of the Industrial Revolution, ships in general were plated in iron and eventually built of steel. Smaller vessels, and especially yachts, continued, however, to be built with a composite con-struction until very recently. The advantages of strong and light steel frames compared with wood frames made from timber crooks (in increasingly short supply) became in-creasingly obvious until the introduction of laminating resins changed the whole picture.

Iron

Iron has good working properties including the ductility that allows it to be produced in good engineering sections and strongly con-nected together with rivets. This meant that the basic ship framing could be made stronger and lighter than with wood con-struction. In the same manner, iron plating, which was reliable in thickness and quality, could relatively easily be shaped to suit the curves of the vessel, and arrived at the ship-yard in large sheets, made a much more convenient skinning material than wood planking. The all-iron construction therefore established itself very quickly in the middle of the nineteenth century and was only really superseded by the improved qualities of steel

towards the end of the century. The relative pureness of iron makes it very durable. In fact the rate of erosion is similar to steel but is spread evenly over the iron, thus making for a very much longer life. Many iron-built ships are still afloat, several serving as sail museum ships in various countries.

Steel

Steel is now the standard construction ma-terial for ships and for most vessels over about 60–70 ft (18–20 m), but it is also used for small yachts down to about 30 ft (9 m) in length built at specialist yards. Riveted construction has given way almost com-pletely to welded construction, which is not only lighter but ensures a completely water-tight shell. Steel also offers some protection against fire and of course complete protection against the shipworm. The disadvantages lie principally in rusting, sweating, and a ten-dency to unsightly dents. Generally speaking the bad name that steel at one time had for small sailing vessels was due to poor-quality steels badly used. High strength and low corrosion steels such as Cor-ten are now sometimes employed. The modern protective coatings have also very much reduced rusting and the use of sprayed-on foam plastics inside can help eliminate condensation and make for a quieter hull at sea.

Aluminium

Aluminium has been used for small-boat building since the 1890s, but suffered very badly from electrolytic corrosion in seawater until the introduction of the salt-water resist-ing alloys in the 1930s, mostly as a result of the development of the seaplane. Riveted aluminium boats were then built in modest numbers but still with a reputation for

electrolytic problems and it was not until the advent of the new welding alloys that the picture changed. An aluminium hull weighs approximately half that of the equivalent steel hull and now aluminium is one of the most popular materials for building one-off racing boats over about 30 ft (9 m) long. Aluminium welding needs special equipment with inert gas shielding, but wise it is a very easily worked and clean material. The modern aluminium boat does not suffer appreciably from corrosion if treated with reasonable care, and in fact many do not even have any protective paint coatings. Some of the smallest boats are built by stretch-forming, where a sheet of material is pushed over a hull-shaped former to make a complete seam-free hull.

GLASS-REINFORCED PLASTICS (GRP)
The introduction of glass-strand reinforced plastics resins after World War II has transformed the small-boat-building industry and practically eliminated traditional wood construction in boats. Production glass-reinforced hulls are built up to about 100 ft (30 m) in length, but above this steel and aluminium are still preferred. The overwhelming advantage of glass-reinforced plastics lies in the construction of a hull and deckworks that are effectively one piece compared with the hundreds of separate components that make up a wood vessel. The standard production process involves the building of an initial plug incorporating all the detail required in the finished mouldings. In turn a mould is made from this plug and into it is laid up the actual hull moulding. An external colour and finish gel-coat is applied first followed by layer after layer of glass mat or heavy woven material called woven rovings, and occasionally a glass cloth. Each layer has to be carefully placed and rolled into the sprayed resin to be thoroughly impregnated without entrapping air bubbles.

An alternative and more highly skilled process is to spray the inside of the mould with a mix of glass fibres and resins, which of course has to be rolled down into a thoroughly homogeneous, impregnated, mix. Additional reinforcements, engine beds, tanks, bulkheads, etc. are then moulded into place with additional layers of mat and resin. Hull and deck can be moulded separately in several components but finish moulded together into one watertight unit with, compared with wooden hulls, very much reduced upkeep maintenance. Glass-reinforced plastics are strong, but tend to be flexible and therefore a hull may have to be built more heavily than an equivalent in wood if it does not use a sandwich construction to increase the rigidity. The most common sandwich materials used are PVC foam and end-grain balsawood blocks, fitted in place with about two thirds of the laminate thickness on the outside.

The aluminium ketch Pen Duick VI, *skippered by Frenchman Eric Tabarly* (top), *nearing the finish of the Rio de Janeiro-Portsmouth leg of the Atlantic Triangle Race in 1976.*

The GRP form of the popular Enterprise dinghy (above) *on the River Thames*

The costs of plug- and mould-making are only economic for a production run and several methods have been evolved for making one-off glass-reinforced plastics yachts. The most common involve the use of a core material, such as PVC foam, cedar strips, or glass rods, stretched over temporary wood formers. The completed core is then glass-laminated on the outside, the hull removed from the moulds and glass-laminated on the inside. All these methods require a very thorough and skilful fairing if an acceptable outside finish is to be achieved. Although glass is by far the most common reinforcement, other materials such as jute have been considered for low strength applications. Carbon and silica fibres are also increasingly used where high rigidity is required.

Thermoplastics

An increasing number of boats up to about 18 ft (5.5 m) in length are being manufactured from sheets of thermoplastic materials such as ABS, polyethelene or polycarbonate. Sheets of these materials, which soften and are malleable when heated, are clamped into frames, heated by a battery of independently programmed heaters to control the degree of softening, then blown into a bubble that is collapsed by vacuum over a boat-shaped former on which it cools and sets hard. Matched mouldings are usually used to make the interior and exterior skins, sometimes filled with foam plastics as an aid to buoyancy. The thermoplastics materials mould with fine detail, but are often on the soft side and prone to ultra-violet degradation and are therefore often protected with a thin acrylic skin moulded with the main skins. A number of small hulls are also formed by sinter moulding where plastic pellets or powder are heated in a hollow mould that is rotated in all directions in a heated chamber until the plastic is centrifugally formed on the inside of the mould.

Foam

The foam plastics are used throughout boating for buoyancy and for insulation, and also as a construction-core material. There have been several productions using foam plastics castings as the complete hull, although these have been rather vulnerable unless protected with an auxiliary covering. Now there are several self-skinning foams coming into use, for example, for cabin furnishing units, and it is likely that this development will carry through into the production of complete hulls with both internal and external details moulded in one operation.

Ferroconcrete or ferrocement

Concrete has been used for shipbuilding since World War I, but the current method is based on the work of Professor Luigi Nervi in Italy in the 1940s. It is a popular method of constructing one-off hulls of between 25 and 75 ft (7.5–23 m) in length, although both

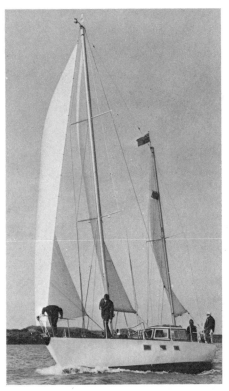

Ferroconcrete was used for the hull of this 40-ft (12-m) centreboard ketch

The cold-moulded method being used to construct the hull of Heath's Condor. *The finished yacht is illustrated on p. 281*

bigger and smaller have been constructed. A framework, usually of iron pipes or welded steel rods is built to the finished shape of the hull and this is covered inside and out with closely secured layers of fine wire mesh until the finished thickness of the hull, similar to that of the equivalent wooden hull, is achieved. This is then plastered with a fine cement pushed through the wire mesh from the outside. Normally this has to be completed by a large team in a single operation, including the final smoothing and fairing of the topsides, bottom, and interior surfaces. The concrete is then allowed to cure under carefully controlled conditions that normally include a continuous moisture spray for a period of at least two weeks. The method is very attractive to amateur builders who find all the materials readily available, and is also increasingly being used for commercial hulls.

Plywood

The introduction of the marine resin adhesives just after World War II transformed plywood practically overnight into a thoroughly practicable boatbuilding material. Although used very widely, its principal immediate advantage was as a skin sheeting material replacing the complication of planking. Plywood is made in a wide range of grades and materials, but all are factory made on flat presses as flat sheets capable of only simple bending. This limited its use

more or less to hulls of chine form and these became very popular. The simplicity of building in plywood led to the great postwar boom in 'build-it-yourself' boats and these are still popular, especially now that the internal wood members are often replaced with an application of glass-reinforced plastics. Plywood has now largely been replaced in production hull building by GRP, but there are very few boats in which it is not used for bulkheads or furnishings.

Moulded ply

Between the two world wars the builders of performance boats produced a method of planking hulls alternately in diagonal directions. Such a skin when firmly clenched together was light and strong and capable of taking some of the hull stresses. With the new marine glues these skins were able to be secured together much as in the production of plywood. This led to a refining of the technique with quite thin veneers being used in multiple skins to make very strong and light one-piece hull mouldings that were comparable to plywood in general characteristics, but built on a mould to the exact double-curvature shape required for the hull. Two principal techniques are used. The first uses heat and pressure in an autoclave to hold the laminations and set the glue. The other, the so-called cold-moulding process, uses a multitude of staples to hold each veneer in place until a cold-setting glue has cured. The former is limited by autoclave size to hulls of about 35 ft (10–11 m) or smaller, but cold moulding has been used for hulls up to 80 ft (24–25 m) and is often found in one-off fast racing sail and power boats.

– construction components

Any discussion of the components of the hulls of ships and boats must inevitably employ specialist terms. At first sight the terminology of this ancient art is quite as obscure as any of the specialist modern sciences. Unlike them, however, the boatbuilders' terms tend to roll easily off the tongue. This air of familiarity is because despite the 'quaintness' of some, they are largely drawn from everyday words used over the centuries for any kind of construction in wood. The following individual components are listed in the approximate order in which they would be assembled by the builder, but of course many variations are possible.

Keel   From the Middle English *kele* and the Old Norse *kjolr*; the keel is the principal backbone member of the hull and the first to be laid on the building stocks. The length of keel is an important factor in determining the size of the new ship and was often quoted rather than the overall length.

Hog   The keel was often reinforced with an upper member to which the planking was attached, but its principal function was to reduce the hogging or arch-backing of the ship when riding over the crest of a wave.

Stem   The front member of the ship, from the Old English *stemn, stefn*.

Apron   A timber attached to protect and reinforce the stem and take the plank fastenings.

Sternpost   The aftermost principal structural member, equivalent to the stem. The word stern is probably from Old Norse *stjórn* ('steering') and therefore refers to the aft end of the vessel where the steering oar, and later the rudder, were situated.

Foregripe (stem knee)   The kneelike member that secures or 'gripes' the stem to the keel.

Stern knee   The knee that secures the sternpost to the keel.

Deadwood   Wood in the centreline structure that is used for continuity rather than for any specific structural strength.

Horn timber   A light keel-like timber projecting aft from the sternpost to carry an extended or counter stern.

Transom   The principal transom is a transverse frame or bulkhead closing the stern of the vessel, although it has other minor applications.

Frames   The cross members that define the body shape of the hull.

Rungs   The lowest parts of the frames that cross the keel in a manner similar to the rungs of a single-string ladder commonly used in many yards at one time.

Sleepers   Fore-and-aft members that rest on the frames beside the keelson.

Floors   Reinforcing members used in conjunction with the frames in way of the centreline structure.

Keelson   A lesser keel-like member laid usually across the top of the frames for an additional reinforcement; also spelled kelson.

Futtocks   The kneelike members that join the relatively flat rung-frames to the rising topside frames. The term is a contraction of 'foot hooks'.

Sheer   The top curving line of the hull, derived from sheering or cutting.

Gunwale   The top fore-and-aft structural member laid around the frames from stem to stern. A wale is thicker than the planking beside it and therefore shows as a raised stripe or weal around the hull. The gunwale was the principal strength member placed immediately below the ports cut for the guns.

Stringers   Longitudinal members that run around the hull inside the frames and are secured to the stem and stern.

Shelf   The principal longitudinal members that run inside the frames just below deck level to carry the ends of the deck beams.

Breast hook   The hook or knee joining the forward ends of the shelves and stringers to the stem.

Invale   The name given to the shelf member of an open boat that does not have to carry deck beams.

Planking   The timber used for the outside skin of the vessel and probably connected with the French *planche*.

Strakes   A general name for the complete lengths of planking from stem to stern as opposed to the planking from which they are made, and which will not stretch the full length of the vessel.

Garboard strake   The important planking line immediately next to the keel that 'gathers' the various parts of this construction together.

Sheer strake   The uppermost strake that in fact defines the sheer line and is often made thicker than the normal planking to increase the hull strength against bending.

Clinker (lapstrake), clincher, clenched lap   A form of planking where each plank overlaps the plank below and is riveted or otherwise secured directly to it. This form of planking is usually used for small boats and light hulls. 'Clincher' comes from the clenching of the securing rivets. 'Clinker' is probably from the Dutch form *klinken* 'to rivet'.

Carvel   A form of planking where each plank is laid side by side and fastened only to the frames and inner structure. In fact most ships and larger craft are planked in this manner and the term carvel is only used in reference to lighter hulls and is a derivation from 'caravel', a small fast light ship of the late Middle Ages.

Caulking   In carvel planking a 'V' is worked into the plank seams into which a caulking material is hammered with special implements. Tarred oakum was the normal caulking material, but twisted cotton is often used for more delicate hulls. The word derives from French *cauquer*, 'to press'.

Knees   The wooden hull structure has to be extensively braced against twisting and wracking strains by means of brackets. These were usually wooden knees cut from tree crooks, but metal brackets were also extensively used.

Hanging knees   Knees fitted in the vertical plane between beams and frames were known as hanging knees.

Lodging knees   Knees fitted horizontally, usually between the various structural parts of the decks, were known as lodging knees.

Treenails, trunnels   Wooden pegs or nails often used to hold structural members together and even to secure the planking. 'Trunnel' is simply a corruption of 'treenail'.

Bilges   Although very often used to describe the lowest parts of the hull where water accumulates, the bilges are in fact the fat swellings or bulges of the hull between the bottom and topsides. 'Bulge' was sometimes used in place of 'bilge'.

Deck beams   The horizontal members laid across the hull to support the deck, usually spaced in conjunction with the frames to provide continuous structure.

Clamp   The deck beams were further secured inboard of the shelf by a secondary member, called a clamp, that locked them in position.

Bulkheads   Solid planked partitions between compartments of the vessel.

Bulwarks   A solid extension of the shipside planking and framing to form a protective half-height wall around the edge of the deck, derived possibly from the word for a defensive rampart of timber, a 'bole work'.

Carlings   The solid edging members fore and aft between beams at all deck openings.

Coamings   The raised planks around the deck openings and, later, the walls of deckhouses.

Covering boards   A wide deck plank fitted around the outer edge of the deck and covering the frame ends and other constructions.

King plank   The centre main plank of a deck.

Soles   The interior walking decks inside a hull are called soles to differentiate them from floors that are structural members. The word has the same derivation as the underside of the foot or shoe.

Ceilings   The interior linings of the hull and not necessarily the overhead linings. Probably derived from 'sealing' rather than from the household term.

Taffrail   The rail across the stern is often called the taffrail, but the name properly applies to the picture or decorative carving that used to be fitted at the stern of most vessels and is derived from the Dutch word for these – *tafereel*.

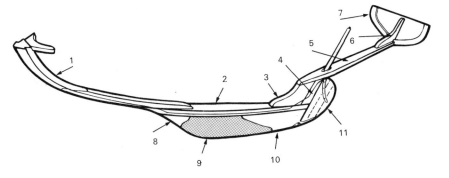

Centreline structures of a small yacht. 1 stem;
2 keel; 3 deadwood; 4 sternpost; 5 counter timber;
6 transom knee; 7 transom; 8 chock; 9 ballast
keel; 10 false keel; 11 rudder

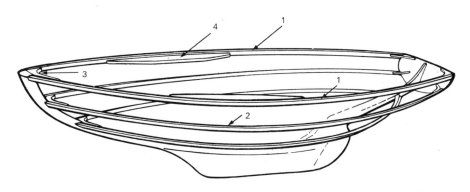

Fore-and-aft framing. 1 shelf or beam shelf;
2 stringer; 3 breast hook; 4 clamp

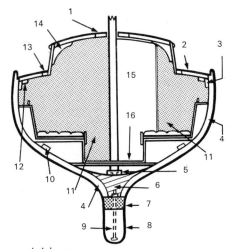

Cross section: 1 mast partners; 2 deck beam;
3 clamp; 4 rib or frame; 5 mast step; 6 floor timbers;
7 keel; 8 ballast keel; 9 keel bolt; 10 bilge stringer;
11 bulkhead; 12 deck shelf; 13 carlin; 14 hanging
knee; 15 doorway; 16 cabin sole

Cathead Short, strong, wooden members
projecting from the bow each side to act as
cranes for pulling the anchor clear of the
water and traditionally decorated with cat's
head carvings.

Knightheads Relatively large timbers that
come through the decks either side of the
stem to support the BOWSPRIT.

– hull scantlings

The term scantling means 'dimension' and
refers to the measured size of the members
used in construction of a ship. A fast sailing
ship endeavouring to make to windward in
bad weather and big seas is subject to wracking stresses that are not matched by any other
comparable man-made structure. Ships have
to be built strongly, not only to meet the
extent of the stresses involved, but also to
cater for the much more damaging cyclical
nature of the stressing that may be reversed
with each wave encountered. It is not unknown even in these days for hulls to be
wracked apart and sink in freak conditions.

The nature of the loadings for which ships
are designed varies very much with size as
well as with the trade or location. In relation
to its size, a big sailing ship, when compared
with a small one, is operated at comparatively low speeds, meets relatively small
debris, and is docked with care. The hull is
therefore predominantly designed to cater for
the bending loads from differing cargo loads
and sea support. A very small vessel, on the
other hand, is at sea in currents and winds
which are relatively strong compared with
her actual speed and is therefore comparatively more difficult to handle. The maximum loads to be catered for in a small boat
therefore may well turn out to be those of
possible impact when docking.

Wooden ships were designed by rule of
thumb and experience and the final products
were masterpieces of the structural arts,
catering for the excesses of stressing without a
single constructional member bigger than a
tree trunk. The introduction of iron, and later
steel, not only coincided with the great development of stress calculations among engineers, but the simplicity and reliability of
the materials in fact made it possible to start
calculating the strengths of hulls. Ships can
now be stressed as carefully as aircraft, although the very much more complex loadings on the ship are more difficult to predict.
The principal loadings to consider are:

Hydrostatic This is simply the pressure applied to the hull by virtue of the head of water
outside any specific area. It is usual to take
the maximum depth of immersion from some
arbitrary point to allow for the changing
attitude of the hull in the sea in bad weather.
For instance, it would not be unusual to
consider hydrostatic pressures as if the whole
vessel was submerged except for masts and
rigging.

Velocity loading An additional pressure is put on a hull as it moves forward. This is very small in most sailing ships, but becomes an increasingly important factor in fast craft. It is usually considered for calculation purposes as applying to the forward two thirds of the hull.

Slamming loading The forefoot of a hull pitching heavily can rise out of the sea and slam heavily back. The extent of the loading depends very much on the distribution of the weights inside the hull and the shape of the forefoot. For modern planing hulls pounding into successive waves, slamming can be the principal loading to be considered in the hull calculations. The amount to be allowed for is very much a matter of experience and is usually considered as being at a maximum at between 20 and 60% of the length of the hull from the bows.

Hogging When a ship is supported by a sizable wave somewhere amidships leaving the bow and stern practically in the air, she is said to be hogging and the ship's structure has to be assessed on cantilever principles. This is a major factor in ships, but is usually swamped by other factors in small-vessel design.

Sagging When a ship is supported at her ends by sizable waves leaving the centre body largely unsupported, she is said to be sagging and the ship's structure has to be assessed as if it were a beam or a bridge. This is a major factor in ships but only one of many other factors in small-vessel design.

Wracking Wracking or twisting loads can be set up when a ship is rolling, and also to an appreciable extent from the distribution of large loads such as tanks. These have to be allowed for by the design of bulkheads as structural diaphragms and by minor structural stiffening at keel, bilges, and deck edges, and the careful design stressing of all deck openings. Multihulls are particularly subject to wracking strains and have broken up in consequence.

Rigging loads In addition to providing local support for the chain plates and other attachment points for the rigging itself the hull builder has to consider the often heavy overall loading on the hull structure from the rig. For instance, a modern sailing boat will have very heavy upward loadings at the ends from the forestays and backstays and a corresponding downward thrust through the heel of the mast which is in fact supporting those rigging loads. The hull is therefore taking a rigging stress in a manner similar to an archer's bow.

Docking loads The forward shoulders of the vessel have to be checked for strength against the impact to be expected from unskilful docking. This is usually taken as coming at about $15°$ from the bow and may vary from very little indeed in big ships docked with great care and low speed by tugs to a very heavy proportional loading in small vessels,

perhaps without reverse and subject to occasional poor handling in proportionally stronger winds and tides.

Debris loading It is almost impossible to cater for all the possibilities of ships hitting semi-submerged debris when under way. All the shipbuilder can do is to choose some arbitrary situation and attempt to cater for it. This varies very much with the size of ship but, for instance, it would be considered that a moderate-sized plank, such as is often washed overboard from a timber ship, is the kind of debris that should not seriously injure a modern sailing-boat hull.

Grounding load Taking the ground may place very localized stresses on hull, keel and, perhaps, rudder. Some large ships are not designed at all for taking the ground except under the very carefully controlled conditions of the dry dock.

Launching loads The launching of a ship down the building ways puts quite unusual and never-repeated loads on a ship hull while it is partly supported on the building blocks and partly by water while travelling astern at some speed.

Classification societies Over the years, of course, a very great deal of empirical knowledge about construction techniques and scantlings has accumulated. The classification societies came into existence largely to assure the insurance companies that new construction was built to incorporate the best of the existing practice and of proper materials of such scantlings as to give the prospect of a reasonable life afloat for the vessel concerned. The societies, such as Lloyd's Register of Shipping, the American Bureau of Shipping, and the French Bureau Veritas, publish rules for the construction of ships and vessels to meet their classification requirements. These include very detailed information about scantlings and shipbuilding practice and they are backed up by an extensive series of surveys both during the building of the vessel and during her life.

– hull accommodation

The accommodation of a sailing vessel has to fulfil all the normal functions for living provided by a house ashore, but with two important fundamental differences. First, it is an essentially self-contained community without services brought to the door, with the possible exception of garbage and waste disposal. The second is that the whole accommodation is sometimes in lively motion and as often as not at a considerable angle of heel. The motion of the ship can mean that loose objects not stowed properly can be catapulted off shelves, for instance, and at the bows a pitching movement can alter gravity from double to nothing. The accommodation also has to be designed to resist drips and general dampness, although in modern vessels this is yearly becoming less of a problem.

The very first requirement of the accommodation is to protect the occupants against injury from the motion of the vessel. Alleyways have to be narrow and cabins planned so that a slip does not mean someone plunging out of control to do themselves or the ship's equipment any damage. To assist in this the accommodation has to be well-equipped with handrails and anything which might be grabbed in an emergency has to be strong enough to take the full weight of a man. The next requirement is that the crew shall be able to sleep and take reasonable meals in some comfort. Bunks have to be narrow to restrain the occupant when the ship is rolling heavily, and have to have leeboards to stop both occupant and bed-clothes from tumbling out. Tables have to be arranged to swing with the ship or to have deep fiddle leerails to hold cutlery and crockery securely. A pitching movement tends to chuck things towards the aft end of the boat and therefore such items as refrigerator and oven doors should be athwartships and open forward. Doors on board a sailing vessel are also best placed athwartships so that they can easily be opened with the ship heeled on either tack. Doors on shipboard are never left loose and therefore have to be arranged with securings for both the open and closed positions.

Overall the accommodation is likely to be cut up into sometimes inconvenient areas by the watertight bulkheads necesssary for collision, and by other bulkheads. Provision has also to be made for escape from each compartment should the main access be closed by accident.

On deck the same general principles apply, although it is generally considered that the crew is at once in greater general danger and on greater guard against it. The most basic protection is to fit good high bulwarks or liferails and stanchions all around the decks, and in fact all areas to which there is normal access. The companion entrances to the below-deck accommodation are, of course, fitted with closing hatches, but it is a normal requirement that they are also fitted with high permanent coamings to stop solid water, sweeping across the deck, making its way below. Vulnerable hatches on open decks are made watertight and other hatches arranged in protected areas with, if possible, provision for any water coming through them to drain away before it gets into the main accommodation areas.

The principal accommodation compartments can be identified as follows:

Forepeak A small compartment in the bows of the vessel often separated from the rest of the accommodation by the forward collision bulkhead. It is very commonly used as a store for combustible materials such as paints.

Chain locker One or two compartments low

in the hull, probably under the forepeak, for storing the main anchor chains, which are led from the compartments to the deck winches through navel pipes.

Forecastle Although originally meant to refer to the accommodation space under a raised section of deck at the bow, it is usually used nowadays to refer to a living compartment for junior crew members in the forward part of the ship. In a small boat it may be devoted to sail and gear stowage.

Saloon The principal cabin of the vessel used normally as a day cabin, but sometimes fitted with either permanent or convertible sleeping accommodation.

Galley The ship's kitchen, which may be arranged close to the crew accommodation when a professional cook is employed or, in a yacht, may be in the owner's accommodation so that the cooking may be done by one of the owner's party.

Heads A common term for the ship's lavatories, and dating back to the time when the beakheads of sailing warships were used for the crew's ablution areas.

Cuddy A name frequently given to a small storage cabin, often fitted below the saloon and used for the officers' special stores. Also used for a very small cabin of a small vessel.

Stateroom A name often used for a sleeping cabin that would typically be fitted with two berths, wardrobe, dressing table, and storage drawers and sometimes also with a wash-basin.

Cabin A general name for a major compartment, very often used for a sleeping room.

– hull and accommodation systems

Modern sailing vessels are increasingly reliable in terms of hull and rig and therefore the main factors that are likely to influence the life of either crew or those on board are increasingly the extent and reliability of the many systems fitted. Some are fitted to assist the normal daily life on board, others are fitted to improve the quality of that life, and others yet again because their existence on board is a reassurance. The systems are sometimes very simple, but those on a typical modern vessel are extensive and complex to the point where they require specialist attention for major maintenance and repair. The major systems referring to the hull and accommodation can be listed as follows:

Steering The steering system is essential to the operation of the ship and therefore of prime importance. In early times a wide-bladed oar was used over the side of the stern controlled by an athwartships tiller. When this developed into a centreline rudder it was controlled by the familiar fore-and-aft tiller and all subsequent steering systems relate to the application of additional power when the rudder is too large to be conveniently handled directly. Early systems used blocks and tackles, sometimes connected to a vertical WHIPSTAFF, and later to a drum controlled by one or more steering wheels.

Many modern yachts and small sailing vessels still operate a wire-and-drum system of this nature, using wire or even chain for the control lines. An increasing number, however, are now fitting mechanical shaft-drive systems using a series of gearboxes and universal joints to connect the shaft of the steering wheel directly to the tiller arm. Hydraulic systems are also becoming more widely used, especially in bigger vessels where power assistance can be more easily added to the system. The steering arrangements for a sailing vessel should be so connected that the helmsman can sense the outside loads on the rudder. There must also be some method of indicating the rudder angle as excess angle causes drag that might be eliminated by adjustments to the sails.

Ventilation A ship or boat hull is essentially a closed box whose contents are likely to grow stale unless there is an airflow right through it. In the days of wooden vessels a very good airflow was essential to keep the structural humidity below that which promoted rotting. The modern metal or fibreglass yacht does not require the same order of ventilation, but it is still essential to have a good through draught to reduce condensation, remove odours, and to stop the air getting stale. When most yachts lay on swinging moorings it was almost possible to guarantee a normal wind over them from ahead and a consequent through draught below decks from aft to forward. Now that yachts are moored fore and aft the flow may be in any direction and is more difficult to arrange. Power ventilation is increasingly being used and it is normal for air to be pumped into hot weather yachts and out of cold weather yachts. An engine compartment which is part of the main accommodation will usually be fitted with an exhaust fan to reduce the spread of engine smell. The galley, bilges, and toilet compartments may be similarly ventilated.

Heating Now that practically all vessels with accommodation are fitted with auxiliary engines it makes little sense to be cold. A wide range of heating systems are available, ranging from small flameless gas heaters to full central heating similar to that of houses ashore. Air heating is a very convenient method for some vessels and can be incorporated in the main ventilation arrangements using diesel or electrical heating units and electric fans for circulation.

Air conditioning Air conditioning is perhaps not fitted as often to sailing vessels as to power ones because of the outdoor nature of the rig. However, it is increasingly fitted, basically of course to improve the living conditions on board, but also for the protection it gives to complex electronic equipment. Air conditioning as fitted usually concentrates on the cooling and humidity aspects rather than on the filtration and heating of a full system. Both individual and central units are employed. The individual units are generally more economical in occasional use but involve a great deal of cooling pipe runs. The central unit is basically more economical in constant hot conditions but involves a great deal of insulated ducting to the cabin outlets that may be very wasteful in space. Most people find a temperature range of 68–71°F (20–22°C) and a humidity of 45–65% comfortable, and air-conditioning units are usually aimed at producing results of this order in the worst ambient conditions to be expected.

Heat insulation Wooden hulls give good insulation against heat as wood is a good insulation material in its own right. Most modern fibreglass or metal cruising vessels are fitted with some heat insulation on the underside of cabin tops and side decks and frequently down to the waterline as well. Still air makes an excellent heat insulation and most heat-insulating materials are based on the principle of providing a high proportion of void spaces where air is trapped by a light surrounding structure such as plastics or glass-wool. In hot climates it is necessary to keep radiated sunlight to a minimum and to keep a good ventilating airflow to remove the hot air that rises to the underside of the insulation. In cold climates, on the other hand, radiated sunlight should be encouraged and insulation arranged to keep heat inside the hull.

Sound insulation The materials generally used for yacht and ship construction are, unfortunately, excellent noise conductors and, in many ways worse, excellent sound reflectors. The noise from machinery, and even sea noise, will often be reflected around inside the hull and can build up to a higher level than would be found in the open air. Noise has to be insulated and absorbed either before it gets into the main conducting structure or after it leaves that structure and before it gets into the compartment to be insulated. High-frequency noise is best absorbed by porous materials that convert it to heat and low frequency noise is often best catered for by panels that absorb the energy in harmonic motion. Noise is an extremely insidious thing to cater for as it can be channelled through quite small paths such as fastenings or ductings. Heavy carpets, draperies, and upholstery are among the best general noise-absorption items that can be fitted.

Vibration insulation Any machinery and quite a lot of rigging can produce vibrations that can be spread easily through a hull by the ship's own structure. Vibrations should be insulated at their source if possible and vibrating machinery is often mounted on flexible vibration-absorbing mountings. Energy-absorbing features such as heavy carpeting also assist in the reduction of vibrations. The worst offenders are often panels in the accommodation joiner-work that sets up sympathetic vibrations. These have to be traced individually and the vibration period altered, usually by adding mass to the centre of the panel.

Water-supply system A fresh water supply is perhaps the most elementary system to be fitted. Beyond the simple tank and dipper or hand pump an increasing number of pressure systems are to be found even in small yachts. The simplest perhaps uses a foot pump to pressurize the tank itself. Rather bigger boats often use an electric pump, either directly or through a small auxiliary tank, which is controlled by a pressure switch in the line. The pump operates until the line is pressurized and starts again as soon as the turning on of a tap reduces the line pressure. Larger vessels usually make use of a header tank to pressurize the system with the header tank supplied automatically from the main supply. Hot-water systems usually make use of an oil-fired or electrically heated domestic boiler pressurized in the same manner.

WC systems (marine toilets) Sailing-vessel WCs can be divided roughly into three main types. On the smallest yachts they are likely to be hand-pumped and draw their flushing water and discharge their waste directly into the sea. An increasing number of harbour authorities are producing regulations on pollution control and the sea-water lavatories are increasingly being replaced with self-contained units that incorporate a holding tank and use chemical treatments to allow recirculation of the flushing water. These units are either taken ashore for periodic discharge into the shore system or pumped out when the yacht is at sea. In larger vessels a salt-water pressure flush toilet is more usual. This may often be pressurized by a header tank and the waste is likely to be discharged into a holding tank for chemical treatment and eventual discharge overboard at sea or, in harbour, into a dockside disposal unit.

Waste systems At one time all ship's waste was pumped overboard, either directly or by way of holding tanks. Nowadays domestic as well as WC waste is banned in many harbours and has to be accumulated on board until it can be discharged at sea or into the dockside system. Waste tanks are also necessary on board if the discharge is below waterline, but these can be fitted with automatic pump discharges.

Fire systems Fire afloat has been the dread of seamen since the beginning of shipping. Modern materials bring new fire hazards such as the dense smoke given off by some plastics, and modern fuels bring more combustible materials on board. To combat these, modern prevention techniques include the fireproofing of some of the materials and

very careful attention to details, such as the spark-proofing of electrical equipment. In addition more care is being taken to reduce the spread of a possible fire, by isolating valves on fuel systems, for instance, and gas bottles are now placed in special compartments so that gas leaks may drain overboard rather than into the hull. Fire-fighting materials have to be chosen with care for some will, for instance, melt the hull material of a fibreglass boat. Again boats' and ships' accommodations consist largely of small compartments and the extinguishants should not be of a toxic type. Yet again the equipment on board may well be urgently required minutes after the suppression of a fire and the extinguishant should not have put this out of action.

Two major types of fire have to be catered for. The first is that of inflammable liquids that need a strong smothering extinguishant such as dry powder or carbon dioxide or BCF that can be used in non-manned space. Other major fires occur among electrical equipment and for these a non-conducting extinguishant must be used, and not, for instance, water. Fire mains supplying water through hoses are quite commonly fitted in bigger vessels, but mostly to deal with large fires where electrical and other problems have become secondary.

Pump systems Most modern vessels take in comparatively little water and therefore the pumping system can be divided into two distinct types. The first is the everyday pumping out of water that may have accumulated in the bilges from minor leaks and spillages. These are usually dealt with by a hand pump or a low-powered electrical pump that may even have automatic operation. The second requirement is to cater for big problems that might occur from a pipe failure, grounding, or other damage. For this kind of disaster large-capacity pumps are required and these are quite commonly arranged for operation from the main or auxiliary engine. In small craft, manual pumps must be sited where they can be used when the vessel is flooded or at an angle of heel. All intakes must be fitted with strainer boxes to prevent blockage.

Deck-wash system For washing down the vessel with sea water it is usual to arrange for the pump system to include provision for drawing water through a seacock for discharge through a deck fitting to a hose. The essence of this sytem is that it should be arranged so that it is impossible for the seacock to be accidentally coupled to the bilge inlets. This is usually achieved by interlinked controls. The deck wash is sometimes combined with the emergency fire-hydrant supply.

Alarm systems In addition to the normal range of engine alarm systems and alarms to draw attention to the non-functioning of items of equipment, it is increasingly usual to

fit alarms that give notice of such things as bilge water or explosive gases building up in the bilges. Sadly, it is also becoming more necessary to fit intruder alarms now that yachts are moored in accessible berths such as in marinas.

See also DINGHIES AND CENTREBOARD CLASSES; MAINTENANCE; MASTS AND RIGGING; MULTI-HULLS

Hurricane *see* WIND AND WEATHER: Tropical cyclones

HWF&C *see* HIGH WATER FULL AND CHANGE

Hydrographic surveying

Before a navigational chart can be compiled some kind of survey must be made of the area of land and sea concerned. In the early days such a survey was little more than a record of the courses and distances sailed by one or more vessels, at different times, with here and there a depth sounding or a bearing of a headland or other recognizable land feature. Such coastal surveying developed during the great days of French and British exploration in the eighteenth century into a definite technique termed 'a running survey', which Captain Cook, in particular, first brought to a fine art during his discovery and laying down of the coasts of New Zealand and New South Wales in 1768–71.

Clearly Cook was developing for seagoing use the land surveyor's technique of plane-table mapping, first described by Jean Dominique Cassini, Louis XIV's cosmographer, in *Connaissance des Temps* as early as 1683. The plane table is a rectangular board on which is mounted or pinned a sheet of paper, the board itself being set up on a portable tripod. To lay down topography a number of stations are occupied by the surveyor, the relative distance between each being measured by pacing out, or some more exact method, and the direction from one station to another obtained by compass bearings, so that the stations may be plotted on the sheet of paper. At each station the alidade, a telescope mounted on a straight edge, is directed upon easily recognizable hilltops, conspicuous trees, buildings or other topographic features; in each case a pencil line is drawn on the paper along the straight edge of the alidade. As the survey progresses, and if the relative positions of the stations are correctly plotted, the intersecting rays from two or more stations will 'fix' the positions of each individual feature enabling the intervening topographic detail to be sketched in by eye.

To employ this technique for laying down a coastline from the poop of a ship sailing along offshore, the seaman found it necessary to record most accurately by log and line and sandglass the speed of his ship and hence the distance run between each alteration of course necessitated by the trend of the coastline or a shift in the wind's direction. It was also necessary to record compass bearings taken from the deck of the ship to prominent features on the shoreline, hilltops or distant peaks inland, and the estimated position of the ship on each such occasion, while coastal detail was sketched in. The secret of Cook's success in running surveys, and of those who followed him, was to plot the courses, the

intersecting bearings, and the resulting fixed positions of topographic features along the coast each night while the ship was in the offing and while all the details were fresh in the minds of the officers who had done the work during the day.

When the explorers found a natural haven or snug anchorage it was normal to make a plan of it showing depths related to the surrounding shoreline, and here a different technique was developed. The first thing was to establish some form of baseline, either by pacing out a straight piece of shore or adjacent terrain; or, failing that, sound could be used. It was found that an observer onshore could measure with fair accuracy his distance from the ship at anchor, up to 5 miles distant, by observing the number of swings of a pendulum – composed of a bullet on the end of a thread 11.24 in (284.5 mm) long – between the flash of a gun fired onboard and

Octant: an early navigational instrument used for measuring the altitude of heavenly bodies

the arrival of the sound; each swing of the pendulum recorded 1/10th of a geographical mile (0.16 km) of distance.

Once a baseline had been measured it was necessary to establish the location of one end on the earth's surface as well as the direction of the base itself before the survey built upon it could be positioned and orientated.

Finding the latitude of a terminal of the baseline onshore was achieved by the sea surveyor at the end of the eighteenth century by meaning the results of a number of meridian ALTITUDES of the sun using the octant devised by John Hadley (1682–1744) with an artificial horizon. The longitude was usually obtained from sets of observations of the distances of selected stars from the moon, the laborious calculations being made with the assistance of special lunar tables devised by Dr Nevil Maskelyne (1732–1811), the British Astronomer Royal. As chronometers became

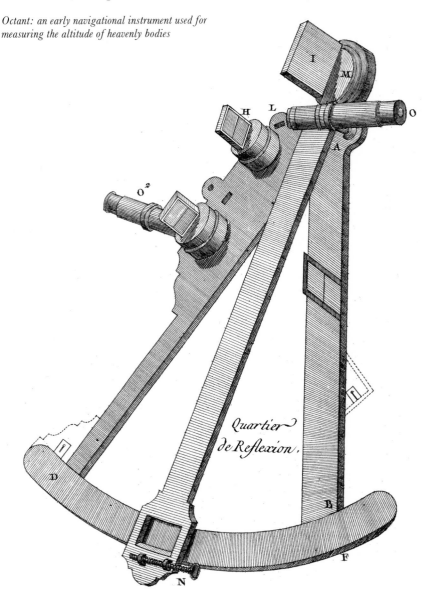

Quartier de Reflexion.

more readily available to the sea surveyor in the early nineteenth century chronometric methods of finding longitude took over.

Once the latitude and longitude of a terminal of a baseline were obtained the bearing of the other terminal could be determined by measuring the angle between the baseline and the sun at a low altitude by means of a theodolite.

With the baseline established, compass bearings or theodolite angles were taken from each terminal to numerous conspicuous natural or erected marks around the harbour to fix them by intersection. Subsequently these marks were used as stations, compass bearings of which could be taken from the ship's boats to fix the latter when employed in sounding or locating reefs or rocks.

Jacques Cassini succeeded his father at the Paris Observatory in 1712 and began a survey of the whole of France by extending a series of triangles from a baseline; this could be done by observing with a theodolite the three angles of each triangle, the apexes of which were situated on high points and marked with beacons. Closely in touch with Cassini was Colin Maclaurin, a mathematics professor at Edinburgh University who taught, among many subjects, the art of surveying and hence the new French methods of extending triangulation from a baseline.

When a land and sea survey of the Orkney Islands was proposed Maclaurin put forward the name of one of his pupils, Murdoch McKenzie, as having the mathematical qualifications necessary for making a 'geometrical' survey. Murdoch McKenzie started the Orkney survey in 1742. He measured a baseline on a frozen lake, using a 30-ft (9.14-m) pole, and from this baseline he then extended his triangulation to cover the islands. He particularly established triangulated stations along the coastline so that he could subsequently take compass bearings of them to fix the position of his boat when taking soundings. He sometimes marked the limits of shoal water with temporary buoys and then fixed them by intersecting 'rays' by theodolite from two of his triangulation stations, using a second triangulation station as a reference for measuring the angle to the buoy.

Murdoch McKenzie subsequently surveyed much of Britain's west coast, turning over the work, now paid for by the Admiralty, to his nephew of the same name in 1770. The McKenzies came to realize that a more accurate way of fixing a sounding boat than using compass bearings would be to observe the two angles between three triangulation stations using the Hadley sextant in a horizontal manner.

Such a 'resection' fix was laborious and time-consuming to plot graphically entailing the drawing of two circles, each of which required to pass through two of the triangulation stations, the boat's position lying at the intersection of the circles. What was needed was an instrument to plot the fix rapidly.

A number of persons were involved in developing the required instrument, and it is not clear to whom the invention of the STATION POINTERS may be attributed. However, by the end of the eighteenth century Edward Troughton, the London instrument maker, was supplying the Royal Navy with station pointers. The instrument consisted of a circle graduated in degrees and minutes with one fixed and two movable legs so that the two observed angles could be set between them. A fieldboard on which the positions of the triangulation stations were plotted was carried in the sounding boat enabling the station pointers to be manoeuvred upon it until each of the three legs passed through the position of the appropriate station. This was rapidly achieved and indicated the boat's position at the centre of the graduated circle of the station pointers, which could then be pricked onto the fieldboard.

Fixing by sextant and station pointers was a rapid and accurate process and could be regularly repeated as the ship or boat sailed along, always provided an accurate network of clearly marked stations had first been established on the adjacent land. Each fix was consecutively numbered both alongside its plotted position on the fieldboard and in a fieldbook where the sounding taken at the time of the fix, and those taken between fixes, were recorded. In the evening, when the ship anchored and her sounding boats returned, those who had been in charge of the work reduced the recorded soundings to low-water datum, according to the observations made at a tidegauge during the day, and 'inked in', as appropriate to the plotted fixes, on the fieldboard.

With the advent in the second half of the nineteenth century of steam propulsion the surveyor could accurately plan the ship's pattern of sounding lines, course being altered appropriately after each fix to keep the vessel on the line. In the early twentieth century power boats, often acting as ship's tenders, were similarly able systematically to sound out an area, running parallel lines of soundings much as a ploughman drives his furrows.

Surveys out of sight of land, but still in the comparatively shallow waters of the

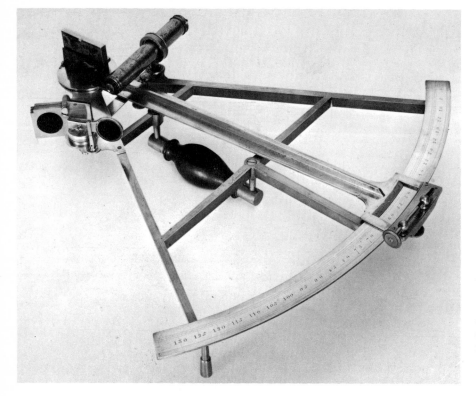

Sextant made in 1775 by the famous English instrument maker Jesse Ramsden

High-speed sailing (opposite) *is epitomized by such craft as* Crossbow I: *see also p. 80*

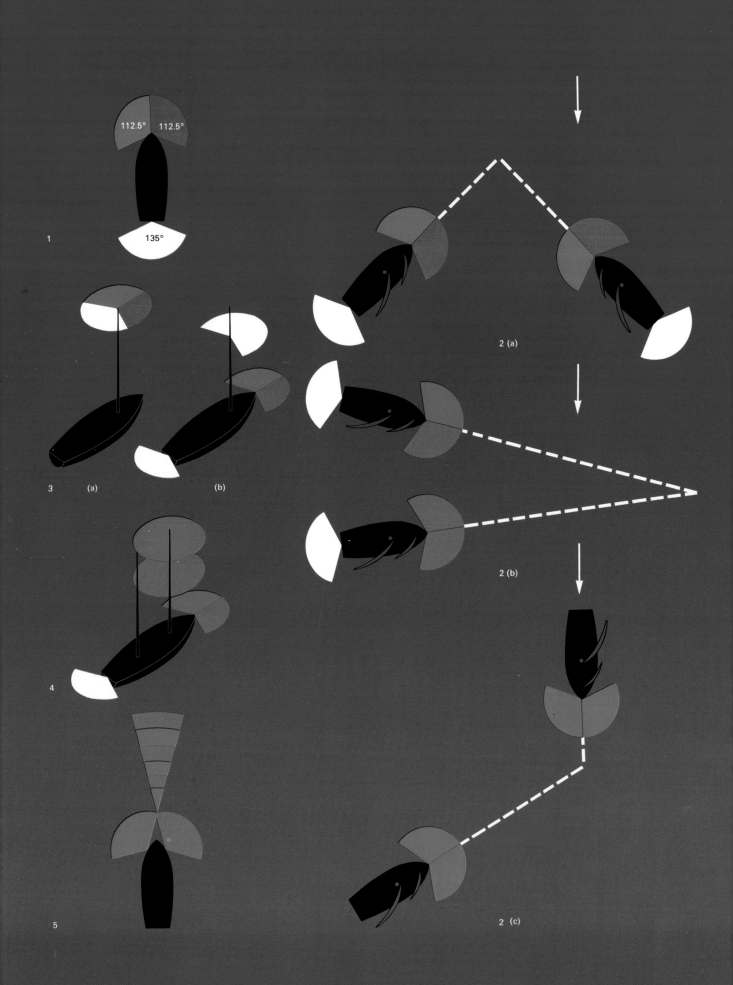

1

112.5° 112.5°

135°

3   (a)   (b)

4

5

2 (a)

2 (b)

2 (c)

continental shelf, were controlled by 'floating triangulations'. For this purpose floating beacons were used that could be assembled onboard and fitted with 30-ft (9.14-m) high bamboo masts carrying large flags. These were moored in positions such as to form a pattern of triangulation, the sides of the triangles each of about 5 miles in length. The first 'floating stations' might be moored within sight of shore triangulation stations from which they could be intersected and fixed by theodolite. Thereafter the angles of the floating triangulation were carefully observed with sextants from the bridge of the ship, stopped close to each moored beacon in turn, due account being taken of the 'false station', that is the distance and direction of the ship's bridge from the beacon at the time of observation.

It is difficult to overestimate the importance of the sextant and station-pointer fix and the role it played in the advancement of hydrographic surveying in the nineteenth and first half of the twentieth century in the coastal waters of every country in the world.

The method of sounding remained, until World War I, little changed over the centuries, carried out as it was with a lead weight on the end of a carefully marked line, the former 'armed' with tallow in a hollow in the base to retrieve a sample of the nature of the seabed at each cast. In the third quarter of the nineteenth century, largely as a result of the requirements for laying the international telegraph cables, a technique for sounding the deep ocean beyond the continental shelf was developed. At first such soundings had been taken by allowing a weight on the end of a long, regularly marked rope to run out freely from a reel; the time intervals between

each mark were noted and when these significantly increased it was assumed bottom had been reached, the length of rope run out indicating the depth. However, this was never a satisfactory method and was superseded by the Lucas wire-sounding machine. Developed by the British Telegraph Cable Company, it consisted of a weight that was allowed to fall to the ocean floor on the end of a wire, which passed from a storage reel over a measuring sheave on a spring-loaded gallows. When the weight reached the seabed the lightening of the load permitted the gallows to rise and automatically apply a hand brake to the wire reel. Depth was recorded on the measuring sheave and the wire and weight were reeled in by a small steam engine.

The 1920s and 1930s were significant in the development of hydrographic surveying, for during that period echo-sounding replaced the lead. As its name implies, the echo-sounder relies on recording the time between the emission of a sound source directed towards the seabed from the hull of a vessel until its return as an echo from the seabed; the speed of sound in sea water being known, the echo sounder may be designed to display the result of each double sonic journey as depth in fathoms, feet, or metres.

The use of this technique appeared in the United States, Britain, France, and Germany in the early postwar years; it was the direct result of efforts made during World War I to locate submarines by sonic methods. The simplicity of the first echo-sounder is typified by the German Behm depth indicator. The instrument consisted of a rifle, loaded with a detonator signal, two microphones fitted, below the waterline, to the side of the ship, and a recorder showing depth on the bridge.

Over the years between the two world wars the echo-sounder developed from instruments using audible sound sources to inaudible frequency transmissions, the latter including magneto-striction machines emitting signals at very frequent intervals. By the late 1930s such machines were displaying on the bridge a continuous graphical representation of the seabed beneath the ship's track, replacing the infrequent spot soundings obtainable with lead and line that often completely missed shallow depths as the ship passed over them.

In the twentieth century the increasing ability to receive accurate radio time signals with which to compare the chronometer, carried ashore in many remote locations, enabled the sea surveyor to adopt the theodolite for fixing a geographical position of his survey on the earth's surface. The true ZENITH DISTANCE of a heavenly body, when compared with the zenith distance calculated from an assured position, enables a position line to be plotted. If the altitudes of four different stars are observed during the night and the time of

each observation carefully recorded; and if the four stars are observed at roughly the same elevation and each in a direction about 90° apart; then four position lines may be worked out. These should give a final position having an accuracy on the earth's surface that should fall within the area covered by a tennis court.

The ability to receive radio signals improved also the accuracy of observing the AZIMUTH of the survey in comparison with the sun's true bearing; and the accuracy of base measurement itself improved with the introduction of calibrated steel tapes, the temperatures of which were recorded during measurement to allow for the coefficient of expansion.

Computing the surveys themselves in terms of geographical coordinates, which was a complicated business, was gradually superseded in hydrographic surveying, at least on medium and large scales, by working in terms of rectangular coordinates on a plane surface.

A rectangular grid is established on a plotting sheet with an origin usually outside the western and southern border. The X and Y rectangular coordinates of the triangulation stations are then worked out mathematically from the theodolite observations made in the field so that each may be plotted in its rightful place within the grid. Intersecting 'rays' observed from the triangulation stations to fix secondary marks, erected for coastlining and sounding purposes, are then plotted with station pointers. Fieldboards provided on the ship's bridge, in the sounding boats, and for the shore parties engaged in laying down the coastline, are simply copies of the appropriate part of the plotting sheet.

When it comes to putting the survey within the framework of a geographical grid so that the resulting chart may be compiled on the same, or more often smaller, scale, the geographical coordinates of the four corners of the chart may be converted by an appropriate formula to rectangular coordinates, so that they may be located on the plotting sheet and the geographical borders drawn in.

Today, with few parts of the world left without national triangulation networks, the sea surveyor may get a flying start by obtaining the rectangular coordinates of at least two established triangulation stations enabling him to use them as terminals of his baseline.

Just as echo-sounding resulted from wartime developments in World War I, so did an electronic method of fixing a surveying ship at sea result from technical developments in World War II.

During the war the Decca Record Company developed a method of fixing a ship at sea by electronic means that was first successfully used by the Allied navies when making their landfalls on the Normandy beaches on the morning of D Day. In this British system, one

master station and two slave stations, widely placed onshore in positions of known location, enabled a vessel with a receiver and recording decometers to fix her position as frequently as she wished. The system relied upon phase comparison between the signal transmitted by the master and that emitted by the two slave stations when triggered by the signal from the master station. The two phase comparisons read from the decometers on the ship's bridge were plotted on the navigational chart according to predrawn hyperbolae, the 'fix' being given by the intersection of the two appropriate hyperbolae (*see also* DECCA NAVIGATOR).

Once the war was over the sea surveyors decided that they required their own transportable Decca chain with two transportable slave stations that could be erected on triangulated stations onshore, while the master station would be carried onboard the surveying ship. By this means two direct electronic distances could be regularly and frequently measured between the ship and the two shore stations, and the position lines became easy to plot circles, rather than hyperbolae.

Such a system was developed by the Decca Company in the late 1940s, and a more sophisticated system, the Lambda, followed soon after.

The measurement of pulse-transit times, on which wartime radar was based, led to the development of a ranging system by the Radio Corporation of America for fixing aircraft during long-range bombing operations. This system also was adopted for hydrographic use after the war, a ship-fitted transmitter being used to transmit signals to accurately located active transponders onshore. An indicator on the ship's bridge measured the elapsed times between transmitted pulse and the receipt of the returning signal from two transponders to give a two-range fix. This system, much used in North America, was called Shoran.

Over the years since World War II the phase-comparison systems may be said to have largely led the field for use in hydrographic work. The introduction of solid-state components enabled more portable and simpler equipment to be made for the shore stations making the transport and establishing of the slave stations a simpler and quicker business. Today the hydrographic surveyors may use Decca Lambda, HI-FIX, Sea-Fix, Raydist, Hydrodist or MRB 201 among the phase-comparison systems or Motorola and Artemis among the short-range time-pulse systems, or LORAN for ocean surveying at long ranges from the shore stations.

So now, day or night, in clear or thick weather, the surveying ship may continue to fix herself far from land, yet in direct relationship to the shore triangulation, while she maintains her continuous lines of echo-sounding. A gap between the lines still exists where hidden dangers may pass undetected so that the sea surveyor now awaits developments in sidescan sonar (*see under* SONIC DEPTH-FINDING) to fill in the gaps between his lines as the next step in this now highly technical business of hydrographic surveying.

Hydrostatic pressure on hulls *see* HULLS: Scantlings

Hyperbolic fixing systems
Radio-navigation systems (such as DECCA, LORAN, OMEGA etc.) in which the position lines are determined by the measurement of phase or time difference between transmissions from linked stations. The position lines are hyperbolae.

IJK

IALA Maritime Buoyage System 'A' *see* BUOYAGE SYSTEMS

Inboard engines *see* AUXILIARY ENGINES

Index error
The error of a marine SEXTANT due to lack of parallelism between the horizon glass and index mirror at zero reading. A small residual index error after the other errors have been removed is generally allowed for in the calculations.

Insulation (heat, sound, vibration) *see* HULLS: Hull and accommodation systems

Intercept
The difference, measured in NAUTICAL MILES, between the altitude of a celestial body and the altitude calculated for an assumed or DEAD-RECKONING position. *See* ASTRONOMICAL NAVIGATION

International Offshore Rule (IOR); International Rule *see* HANDICAP SYSTEMS

International Yacht Racing Union
The IYRU was originally formed in 1906 at the instigation of Major Brooke Heckstall-Smith to devise an international rule for measurement of yachts that would be acceptable to all European yacht-racing nations. The original meeting was held in London, presided over by Augustus Manning, senior Vice-President of the Yacht Racing Association.

The original countries were: Britain, France, Germany, Norway, Sweden, Denmark, the Netherlands, Belgium, Italy, Switzerland, Austria-Hungary, Finland, and Spain. The committee adopted the International rule of 1906, and also decided that the yachts built under the rule should be registered with Lloyd's Register of British and Foreign Shipping, the Germanischer Lloyd, Berlin, or the Bureau Veritas, Paris.

Nowadays the object of the union is the promotion of the sport of amateur yacht racing through the world without discrimination on grounds of race, religion, or political affiliation. The union is the sole authority responsible for the establishment and amendment of rules for international yacht racing, and of all rules for classes it recognizes as International Yacht Classes. The organization of the union consists of the Officers (HM King Olav of Norway is President of Honour), a General Assembly, a Permanent Committee and Subcommittees of the Permanent Committee.

The authority controlling yacht racing in any country may apply for full membership. Yachtsmen interested in the sport of yacht racing may apply for individual membership.

The Permanent Committee consists of a President of the Union who is Chairman, 3 Vice-Presidents, and 20 nominated members who represent the following groups of countries:

United Kingdom, Ireland, and South Africa (includes Rhodesia) 2 members

Central Europe
Austria, Switzerland, West Germany, Yugoslavia 2 members

Eastern Europe
Bulgaria, Czechoslovakia, East Germany, Hungary, Poland, Romania 2 members

Southern Europe
France, Greece, Israel, Italy, Malta, Monaco, Turkey 2 members

Iberian Peninsula and North Africa
Algeria, Egypt, Portugal, Spain 1 member

Low Countries
Belgium, Netherlands, Luxemburg 1 member

North America
Bermuda, Canada, Mexico, United States 3 members

Scandinavia
Denmark, Finland, Iceland, Norway, Sweden 2 members

Southern and central South America
Argentina, Brazil, Chile, Ecuador, Peru, Uruguay 1 member

Union of Soviet Socialist Republics 1 member

Eastern Asia
Burma, Hong Kong, Indonesia, Japan, Korea, Malaysia, Republic of China (Taiwan), Singapore, Sri Lanka (Ceylon), Thailand 1 member

Southwest Pacific
Australia, New Zealand, Papua New Guinea 1 member

Northern South America, Central America, and the Caribbean
Bahamas, Barbados, Colombia, Costa Rica, Cuba, Dominica, Grand Cayman, Guatemala, Jamaica, Puerto Rica, Salvador, Trinidad and Tobago, Venezuela, Virgin Islands 1 member

The Subcommittees of the Permanent Committee consist of: the Keelboat Technical Committee; Centreboard Technical Committee; Constitutional Class Policy and Organization Committee; Multihull and Technical Committee; Measurement Committee; International Regulations Committee; Racing Rules Committee; and Youth Sailing Committee.

Interrupted quick-flashing light *see* LIGHTS: Characteristics

Inwale *see* HULLS: Construction components

Irons
A vessel is said to be in irons when she has been allowed to come up into the wind without sufficient headway to pay off on either tack.

Isogonic line
A line joining points with the same magnetic variation at any epoch.

Isolated danger marks *see* BUOYAGE SYSTEMS

Jackstay *see* MASTS AND RIGGING: Glossary

Jacob's ladder
Originally the rope ladder fitted on the after side of the topgallant mast where there are no ratlines (*see* MASTS AND RIGGING: Glossary). In naval parlance, the rope ladder that swings from the lower boom of a warship at anchor for ships' boats to make fast.

Jacob's staff *see* CROSS STAFF

Jamming cleat *see* MASTS AND RIGGING: Glossary

Jib *see* RIGS: Fore-and-aft rigs

Jibe *see* GYBE

Jib sheets *see* MASTS AND RIGGING: Glossary

Jockey pole *see* MASTS AND RIGGING: Glossary

Junk *see* CHINESE RIG

Katafront *see* WIND AND WEATHER: Fronts and frontal depressions

Kedge
A small anchor, generally used with a line instead of chain, for warping a vessel from one berth to another or hauling her off when she has gone aground.

Keel
The principal fore-and-aft member of a vessel on which the remainder of the construction is built. *See also* HULLS: Construction components

Keel bolts
Bolts that hold the ballast keel on to the keel.

Keelson *see* HULLS: Construction components

Ketch
A two-masted, fore-and-aft-rigged vessel with the mizzenmast stepped forward of the sternpost. *See also* RIGS: Fore-and-aft rigs

Kicking strap (boom vang) *see* MASTS AND RIGGING: Glossary

King plank *see* HULLS: Construction components

Knee; stern–; hanging–; lodging–; *see* HULLS: Construction components

Knightheads *see* HULLS: Construction components

Knockdown *see* HEAVY-WEATHER SAILING

Knot
A speed of one NAUTICAL MILE per hour.

L

Lanby *see* BUOY: Navigational buoys

Lanyard *see* MASTS AND RIGGING: Glossary

Lapstrake (clinker) *see* HULLS: Construction components

Larboard
(Obsolete) term for the port side of a vessel.

Lateen *see* RIGS: Lateen and lug rigs

Lateral system, marks *see* BUOYAGE SYSTEMS

Latitude, difference of *see* D. LAT.

Launching loads *see* HULLS: Scantlings

Law of storms
A law, originally formulated by the British meteorologist Henry Piddington (1797–1858), used to describe the course of revolving tropical storms at sea. In the northern hemisphere the wind rotates in an anti-clockwise direction around a centre of low pressure; in the southern hemisphere in a clockwise direction. On this phenomenon is based the rule for avoiding revolving storms. *See also* WIND AND WEATHER

Lay
(1) The direction in which the strands of a rope are entwined, generally right-handed; (2) a vessel is said to lay her course when, on the wind, she can sail to her destination without tacking.

Lead
A weight, generally of lead, on the end of a sounding line.

Lead and line
A leaded weight on a graduated line for sounding the depth of the water when navigating in shallows, making a landfall, or preparing to anchor. It is perhaps one of the oldest of navigating instruments and is mentioned by the Greek historian Herodotus (*c.* 500 BC).
When taking a sounding the leadsman in the bows casts well ahead so that the way of the ship will bring him vertically above the point at which the lead strikes the bottom. Repeated soundings show the slope of the sea bed, as an aid to avoiding shoals or judging one's position in poor visibility. To obtain a sample of the bottom ground as a further aid to judging position the lead is 'armed' with tallow.
'Swinging the lead' meant that the leadsman went through the motions and sang out a fictitious depth, without the repeated labour of casting and recovering.
The line traditionally has tags of white cotton, red bunting, blue serge, and leather, for the 2-, 3-, 5-, 7-, and 10-fathom 'marks', and so on up to 25 fathoms: the intervening fathoms are unmarked 'deeps'; The choice of materials for the tags is to enable the leadsman to distinguish them in the dark. The fathom of 6 ft (1.83 m) originally represented the stretch of a leadsman's arms when recovering the line. Modern charts show depths in metres, but no new standard marking of the line has yet been adopted.
The deep-sea lead, used before the invention of sounding machines, weighed about 30 lb (13.6 kg) and the line was held in bights (bends, loops) by sailors stationed along the ship's side, unless she was hove to for the sounding.

Leading edge
The luff of a sail.

Leading wind *see* FAIR WIND

Lee
The opposite side to that from which the wind is blowing.

Leeboard
An early form of drop keel in the shape of a board lowered on the lee side of a shallow-draughted vessel to prevent her sagging to leeward.

Lee, by the *see* BY THE LEE

Leech
The aftermost part of a sail.

Lee helm
A vessel is said to carry lee helm when she has a tendency to pay off and the helm must be kept to leeward to prevent her doing so.

Lee shore
A shore on to which the wind drives a vessel.

Leeward
Down wind.

Leeway
The angular deviation of a vessel from its HEADING due to DRIFT.

Leg *see* BOARD

Let fly
To let fly the sheets is to pay them out until the sails are shivering.

Level-rating racing *see* YACHT RACING

LHA *see* LOCAL HOUR ANGLE

Lie to *see* HEAVE TO

Lift *see* MASTS AND RIGGING: Glossary

Lighthouses and light vessels
These structures and craft exhibit a characteristic light to aid navigation at night and warn of danger at sea.

– lighthouse
The term lighthouse is usually only applied to substantial buildings housing important lights.
Early lighthouses were masonry towers in which beacon fires were maintained at night. One of the earliest of which there is some record is the Pharos of Alexandria in Egypt. This was a massive stone tower said to have been 600 ft (180 m) in height, built in 280 BC and reckoned one of the seven wonders of the ancient world. A wood fire was kept burning at the top. The tower was destroyed by an earthquake in the early fourteenth century AD.
Several lighthouses were constructed by the Romans, the most important of which were those at Ostia, Ravenna or Porto Corsini, Pozzuoli, and Messina. Also, to assist vessels crossing the English Channel after the conquest of Britain in AD 43, the Romans built the ancient pharos at Dover and Boulogne (later known as the Tour d'Ordre). Nothing remains of these towers now, but that at Boulogne lasted after some restoration until 1644, when it collapsed.
In medieval times a number of lighthouses are known to have been established in the Mediterranean. In Italy the Lanterna di Genova originally stood on the promontory of San Berrique. It was built in 1139 and first used as a lighthouse in 1326; it was rebuilt on its present site in 1643.
In Britain small local light towers are recorded as having been established at St Catherine's Point, Isle of Wight, and other places in the fourteenth and fifteenth centuries. The lighthouse at Cordouan on a rock off the mouth of the Gironde in France provides the earliest example still existing of a wave-swept tower. The first tower on this rock is supposed to have been built in AD 805, the second about 1360. The existing structure was started in 1584 and completed in 1611, but in the eighteenth century the upper part of this fine building was removed and replaced by a loftier round tower rising to about 207 ft (63 m) above the rock. The source of light until reconstruction was a log fire, then for many years afterwards it remained a coal fire. It now of course has a modern light apparatus.
In the seventeenth and eighteenth centuries numerous lighthouses were built around the coasts of Europe and in Britain. A tower was established on the Isle of May in 1636 and another at St Agnes, Isles of Scilly, in 1680; the latter is still maintained as a daymark.
The oldest lighthouse in the United States is on Little Brewster Island off Boston, Mass., and was established in 1716 using oil as an illuminant.

STRUCTURES

Lighthouses built on the coast, or on islands, present no particular structural problem and they vary from simple masonry towers to elaborate buildings; or, in modern times, they may be no more than a steel lattice tower.

Offshore lighthouses sited in exposed positions have to be built to withstand tremendous wave forces. Design considerations for modern offshore lighthouses usually allow for waves over 50 ft (15 m) in height and winds exceeding 120 knots.

One of the earliest offshore lighthouses to be built well away from the land is that on Eddystone Rocks, some 13 miles south of Plymouth, Devon. The first lighthouse on these rocks was built of timber and completed in 1698. It was a rather ornate affair and suffered storm damage during its first year of operation. It was enlarged and strengthened in 1700, but in November 1703 it was completely swept away by a severe storm and the designer, Henry Winstanley, and his men perished.

The second lighthouse on Eddystone Rocks, designed by John Rudyerd and built of oak and iron, was completed in 1708, but fire destroyed it in 1755. The third structure, nearly 80 ft (24 m) high, completed in 1759 by John Smeaton, was built entirely of stones each weighing about a ton and dovetailed into each other to give enormous strength. This method of interlocking stones became the standard practice for the construction of later wave-swept towers. In 1877 it was discovered that the rocks on which Smeaton's tower stood were being undermined by the sea and Trinity House, the venerable organization responsible for many aspects of maritime safety in British waters, decided that another lighthouse would have to be built on a different part of the rocks some 120 ft (37 m) south-southeast of the Smeaton tower. Work on this fourth Eddystone Lighthouse, about 138 ft (42 m) tall, was started in 1878 and completed in 1882. The upper two-thirds of the Smeaton lighthouse was then removed and re-erected on Plymouth Hoe as a memorial.

Modern lighthouses in offshore positions where there are no rocks to build on often take the form of large steel-lattice structures. These are fabricated ashore and then floated out to their positions where they are upended and then lowered under control to stand on the sea bed. The main legs of the structure are large-diameter pipes through which piles are then driven deep into the sea bed so as to hold it securely in position. Additional structure is then added to the lower framework to accommodate the crew and house the power supplies for the light, fog signal, and radio. Such structures also invariably include a flat deck for servicing helicopters to land on. A typical lighthouse

The lighthouse erected in 1854 on Fastnet, off the southwest coast of Ireland. The rock gives its name to the race organized by the RORC

of this kind is Buzzards Bay Light, Rhode Island, which stands in about 70 ft (21 m) of water and the helicopter platform is 75 ft (23 m) above the level of high water. The light has an elevation of 102 ft (31 m) and a power of 10 000 000 candela, the fog signal can be heard at 5 miles, and the radio-beacon has a range of 100 miles.

Another modern offshore lighthouse is the Royal Sovereign, which was built in 1967 to replace the *Royal Sovereign* light vessel stationed about 8 miles east-southeast of Beachy Head on the English south coast. It stands in a depth of about 33 ft (10 m), south of Royal Sovereign Shoal. The lighthouse consists of a reinforced-concrete base some 101 ft (31 m) square resting on the sea bed, from which a slender concrete tower rises about 92 ft (28 m) to support a box-type cabin. At one corner of the cabin superstructure there is a tower housing the control room, the main light, fog signal, radio, and radar aerials.

ILLUMINANTS

Wood or coal fires in braziers at the top of lighthouse towers were the usual form of illumination until well into the eighteenth century. Open fires were followed by tiers of candles. Smeaton's lighthouse on Eddystone Rocks had 24 candles in two tiers: the consumption rate was the equivalent of about

8 candles per hour. Oil lamps with wick burners for animal or vegetable oils came into use in the mid-eighteenth century. Towards the end of the nineteenth century multiple wick burners for mineral oil were used. Then, with the invention of incandescent mantles and oil-vaporizing burners early in the twentieth century, the intensity of lights was increased immensely over that available from multiple wicks.

Coal gas was used to some extent in the nineteenth century for lights where a mains supply was available. Liquefied petroleum gas was also used, but early in the twentieth century it was found that acetylene gas dissolved under pressure in acetone produced an excellent light. It could be used in open-flame burners or with incandescent mantles and has become a commonly used illuminant throughout the world for minor unattended lights.

Electricity for lighthouse illuminant was first used about 1860, but the arc lamps and the steam generating plant required a great deal of attention. Therefore it was not until the 1920s, when high-power gas-filled filament lamps became available, that lighthouses were in general converted from incandescent petroleum vapour to electricity.

OPTICAL SYSTEMS   The usual type of lens is based on catadioptric principles as propounded by Augustin Jean Fresnel, the nineteenth-century French physicist, in which the central lens or bull's eye is surrounded by a number of concentric rings of prisms to concentrate the rays of light. Several panels of these lenses and a reflecting prism mirror are mounted on a rotating platform that floats in a trough of mercury to give smooth and level movement round the light source. The number of panels and the rate of rotation dictate the characteristic of the light. Minor lights usually have a drum-type lens in which the central portion has rings of prisms above and below. This type of lens produces a fixed light unless the light source is made to flash.

– light vessel
A craft placed in a position where it is not possible to build a lighthouse, or where the dangers to be marked are constantly changing, such as the Goodwin Sands off the southeast coast of England.

The first light vessel was stationed at The Nore in the Thames Estuary in 1732. Early light vessels were usually small converted sailing craft, in which the light consisted of a number of candles in a lantern hoisted up the mast. A typical modern light vessel is built of steel and is from 115 to 150 ft (about 35–40 m) length and of 200 to 500 tons displacement. They usually have two masts with a framework structure amidships, on which the main light is mounted at an elevation of about 40 ft (12 m) above the waterline. It is

essential that light vessels remain in their assigned positions whatever the weather, and they are therefore securely moored to anchors of about 4 tons weight with heavy studded link cable of about $1\frac{1}{2}$ in (38 mm) diameter. In bad weather a light vessel may have 220 to 330 yd (about 200–300 m) of cable out, therefore her position may vary by about 2 cables depending on the tidal stream, strength of the wind and the depth of water.

Modern light vessels are equipped with four diesel generators, only one of which is needed to supply the light and domestic services, and two diesel air compressors to supply air for the fog signal. The crew usually number about 11, of whom seven are on board, for about a month at a time.

The main light and optical equipment are similar to those in lighthouses, but they are mounted on ball bearings instead of floating in a trough of mercury, and slung in a pendulum apparatus so as to counteract movement of the vessel and maintain a level light beam.

A powerful fog signal of the siren or diaphone type is fitted together with a radio-beacon or racon. There is also radio-telephone communication with the shore.

Most light vessels have to be towed to their stations as they have no propelling machinery. However, in the United States some light vessels are self-propelled and are fully equipped navigationally so that they can

take up their assigned positions accurately.

Because of the ever-increasing cost of maintaining light vessels they are being replaced at many stations either by Lanbys (Large Automatic Navigation Buoys) or by offshore towers.

See also BUOY; FOG SIGNALS; LIGHTS; SEAMARK

Lights
– characteristics
The characteristic of a light is the description of the intervals of light or darkness presented and includes the colour.
FIXED
Shows a continuous light. Usually restricted to minor harbour lights.
FLASHING
A single flash at regular intervals. The duration of light is less than that of darkness.
GROUP-FLASHING
Shows at regular intervals a group of two or more flashes.
OCCULTING
Steady light with sudden eclipses at regular intervals. The duration of darkness is less than that of light.
GROUP-OCCULTING
Steady light with a group of two or more eclipses at regular intervals.
FIXED-FLASHING
A fixed light with a regular single flash of relatively greater brilliance.
QUICK-FLASHING
A light flashing more than 60 times per minute.
VERY QUICK-FLASHING
A light flashing more than 120 times per minute.
INTERRUPTED QUICK-FLASHING
A light showing flashes of more than 60 per minute interrupted at regular intervals by an eclipse of relatively long duration.
MORSE CODE
A light that exhibits long and short flashes so as to reproduce letters or numerals of the Morse code. The total duration of darkness is longer than that of light in each period.
ALTERNATING
A light that changes colour on the same bearing. Alternating lights may also be flashing, group-flashing, occulting, group-occulting, and fixed-flashing.
– description
The following terms are used in describing lights:
PERIOD
The time taken to make one complete sequence of the characteristic.
LUMINOUS RANGE
The distance at which a light can be seen (at night) as determined by the intensity of the light measured in candelas and the meteorological visibility prevailing; it takes no account of elevation of the light, height of eye of the observer, or curvature of the earth.

The Varne Bank lightship, stationed in the busy Dover Strait, showing its helicopter landing deck

Lists of lights (*see below*) usually contain a diagram from which the luminous range can be found.

NOMINAL RANGE

The luminous range when the visibility is 10 NAUTICAL MILES.

GEOGRAPHICAL RANGE

The distance at which a light can be sighted as limited by the curvature of the earth, refraction of the atmosphere, the elevation of the light, and the height of eye of the observer.

SECTOR LIGHT

A light that presents a different characteristic over various arcs to cover navigational dangers or to indicate safe water.

LEADING LIGHTS

Two or more lights that if kept in line provide a lead for vessels to follow.

DIRECTION LIGHT

A light that shows a very narrow sector so as to provide a lead. This sector may be flanked by sectors of reduced intensity or different colour.

LISTS OF LIGHTS

Most hydrographic offices publish lists of lights in which the details of light characteristics, their sectors, elevations, type of structure, and FOG SIGNALS are given. Some countries include lighted buoys in their lists of lights.

France, the United States, and Britain are the only countries that publish lists of lights

covering the whole world. The numbers allocated to lights in the 12 volumes of the British Admiralty *List of Lights* are regarded as the International Number for the light.

Lights, navigation

In common with other types of vessel, the navigation lights of a yacht serve two quite distinct purposes: first, to tell the observer what type of vessel he is looking at; and second, to show which way she is heading. The new International Regulations for Preventing Collisions at Sea (IRPCAS: *see* COLLISION REGULATIONS), which came into force in July 1977, included several changes aimed at making it easier for yachts to be seen in the dark, and these new rules require an improved standard of lights fitted to yachts. In recent years there has been a considerable outcry from other users of the sea about the generally poor standard of navigation lights fitted to yachts and it was against this background that the new, more exacting regulations were framed, which have brought some problems for small yachts.

– general principles of navigation lights

The simplest form of illumination, and the easiest to see, is a plain white light. At sea, a white light on its own can indicate a variety of things: a buoy, the shore, a vessel at anchor, the stern of a vessel going away. The action to be taken is always the same: avoid it.

Because it tells the observer so little, a white

light is used only for that aspect of a vessel under way that represents the least danger – her stern.

Whenever a vessel under way is seen from any angle from right ahead to two points abaft the beam ($112\frac{1}{2}°$), it should always be possible to see either a red or a green light depending on whether the viewer is on her port or her starboard side. These three lights, red to port, green to starboard, and white astern, are the three basic 'running lights' that all vessels (with the exception of certain very small boats) have to display whenever they are under way in darkness or reduced visibility (fig. 1, facing p. 97). All other lights serve merely to show what kind of vessel it is.

It is important to realize the significance of these three basic lights in relation to the IRPCAS rules. Rule 13, Overtaking, states:
a. 'Notwithstanding anything contained in the Rules of this Section any vessel overtaking any other shall keep out of the way of the vessel being overtaken.'
b. 'A vessel shall be deemed to be overtaking when coming up with another vessel from a direction more than $22\frac{1}{2}°$ abaft her beam, that is, in such a position with reference to the vessel she is overtaking, that at night she would be able to see only the sternlight of that vessel but neither of her sidelights.'

Thus, the overtaking rule is an overriding one that makes no distinction between different types of vessel. This is unavoidable because, as has been pointed out, it is not possible to decide what type of vessel is involved when seen from astern.

As far as power-driven vessels are concerned, the 'crossing' situation is quite simple and governed by Rule 15, which says: 'When two power-driven vessels are crossing so as to involve risk of collision, the vessel which has the other on her own starboard side shall keep out of the way. . . .' In the words of the jingle that many mariners use to recall the rule, 'If to starboard *red* appear, 'tis your duty to keep clear.'

The situation for sailing vessels crossing each other at night is a little more complicated and is governed by Rule 12. The basic rule is that the vessel that has the wind on her port side (i.e. is on port tack) shall keep out of the way of the other. In addition, when two sailing vessels are on the same tack, the one that is to windward shall keep out of the way (fig. 2).

The problem at night is that it is not always possible to tell which tack a vessel approaching from windward is on, especially if she is running before the wind. A vessel close-hauled on port can thus find herself in the position of seeing a green light to windward that may belong to another sailing vessel that is on starboard gybe and thus the right-of-way vessel. Because of this, there is an important new clause in Rule 12 which says that in

The port and starboard navigation lights on the Venus, *positioned on the standing rigging of her mainmast*

these circumstances the port-tack vessel shall keep out of the way. In other words, the onus is placed on the close-hauled vessel to assume that she must give way.

– lights to be exhibited

VESSELS UNDER 7 M LENGTH OVERALL
Although vessels under 7 m LOA are urged to show the prescribed lights *if practicable*, they are technically exempted from showing anything other than a white, all-round light such as a lantern or torch. This applies to vessels under oars or sail, or power boats capable of less than 7 knots. It is intended as a let-out clause for dinghies, open boats, and small launches where it is very difficult to fit any kind of permanent lights. Nowadays, however, there are thousands of seagoing yachts of less than 7 metres LOA and some people take this clause as exempting them from the need to fit proper running lights. This is a most foolish and dangerous attitude and it would be most irresponsible for anyone to go to sea at night in a vessel that carries nothing other than a torch.

VESSELS UNDER SAIL OF LESS THAN 12 M LOA. Vessels under sail are required to show only sidelights and a stern light. In yachts under 12 m LOA these may be combined into one 'tri-colour' lantern, which must be mounted at or near the masthead 'where it may best be seen'. This is a new provision in the Rules, introduced in 1977, recognizing the great difficulty small sailing yachts have in either finding a good place to mount sidelights so that they can be seen, or in providing sufficient electric current to keep three separate lights shining brightly. By adopting the tri-colour light, a sailing yacht can have one, good, bright bulb mounted well up in the air so that it is not obscured by waves or the sails. There is no doubt that yachts fitted with tri-colour lights are much more easily visible at a distance. There are, however, certain problems with this system.

The first problem is that a tri-colour light may be difficult to spot at close quarters because the observer may not be looking high enough in the air. Experience with offshore racing has shown that a dangerous situation can occur when yachts converge in the dark, at a turning mark for instance. The lookout will be busy looking for and interpreting a number of sets of lights, all of which appear close to the water, and at the same time he may completely miss the lights of a yacht which is very close but whose tri-colour lantern is 50 or more feet up in the air. The same thing can also occur in a harbour or among moorings where the occupant of a small boat may simply not look up enough to spot an approaching sailing yacht.

The other problem with the tri-colour system becomes apparent when a sailing yacht is using its auxiliary motor. Under these circumstances, the yacht should exhibit the

A modern starboard navigation light, visible for 2 miles, suitable for vessels up to 65 ft (20 m) in length

lights of a powered vessel of the appropriate size. These will always consist of sidelights plus a white 'masthead' light *above* them. If the yacht is relying on her tri-colour lantern to provide the sidelights, she has no way of exhibiting a white light 1 m above them. Therefore, in order to exhibit the correct lights when motoring, a sailing yacht really needs to fit sidelights low down *as well* as the tri-colour lantern at the top of the mast (fig. 3). As the lanterns, plus their associated wiring and switchgear, are very expensive items, there has been a tendency for yachts with tri-colour lights to 'forget' to fit the lights required for motoring. In this instance, the introduction of the tri-colour lantern has actually been a retrograde step.

– optional lights for sailing vessels

Rule 25 says that sailing vessels may, *in addition* to their other lights, exhibit 'at or near the top of the mast, where they can best be seen, two all-round lights in a vertical line, the upper being red and the lower green.' These, however, may not be used in conjunction with a tri-colour lantern.

The purpose of these optional lights is to make quite clear that the vessel in question is *sailing* (fig. 4). Although not much used by yachts, this is a useful signal for large sailing vessels such as training ships, which are as big as small merchant ships, particularly on the radar screen. They need to use every possible means to alert the lookout of an approaching ship that they are under sail and have right of way under most circumstances.

– visibility

In vessels of less than 12 m LOA (which covers the vast majority of sailing yachts), all the white lights must be visible at a range of 2 miles and the red and green sidelights at 1 mile. If the vessel is between 12 and 50 m LOA, these figures are doubled.

– meeting the requirements

The small sailing yacht has a lot of difficulty in providing adequate lights. Firstly, she has a limited supply of electricity (no other method of lighting is really practicable on small yachts). The car-type batteries that are fitted to almost all yachts do not give a very good performance when they are running 'off-charge'. A nominally 12-V battery actually delivers about 10 V potential even when it is in good condition, and as it is increasingly discharged this voltage will drop still further.

Wiring of inadequate size, poor connections, corrosion, and dampness are all factors that conspire to reduce the flow of current to the lights, and spray and salt reduce the transparency of the glasses.

Big ships can use a lens system on their lights to concentrate the beam, but if this is done on a sailing yacht, it means that when she is heeled the lights will be either shining up into the air or down into the water. Therefore, a yacht's lights can only be 'wide-angle'. This is one reason why the very bright quartz-iodine bulbs used in car headlights cannot be used, as they need to be accurately focused to be seen.

For all these reasons, it is obviously worth having one bright bulb rather than several less bright ones and this is the appeal of the tri-colour lantern.

If the tri-colour lantern is fitted with the readily available 24-W festoon-filament bulb and a voltage of 10.5 V is assumed, something of the order of 2.4 candelas (cd) of luminous intensity outside the coloured part of the lamp should be achieved. As the Rule only calls for an intensity of 0.9 cd in order to achieve a visible range of 1 mile, there is plenty of light in hand to cope with misting of the lens and less than perfect visibility (the Rule assumes a 'clear, dark night'). The white sector will obviously be more than bright enough when it is realized that the coloured screens cut down luminous intensity by 85%.

If, on the other hand, a 12-W bulb is fitted, a system of very marginal performance will be obtained. With a well-charged battery, such a lamp will just attain the 0.9 cd called for outside the coloured screens but not if the voltage is down to the normal 10.5 V.

If instead of the masthead tri-colour lamp the yachtsman decides to fit a combined port and starboard lamp on the bow pulpit, he will, of course also need a separate stern light. Being white, this can be of less power, say 12 W instead of 24 at the bow. If to these two lights a compass light, a chart-table light plus some instruments and occasional cabin lights are now added, there could be a current drain of between 4 and 5 A. If all these lights are left on for 10 hours, this will flatten a 45-ampere-hour battery and this demonstrates the problem that small yachts are up against. If lights that meet the requirement with something in hand are fitted, a normal car battery will hardly suffice for two nights at sea without recharging.

Some sailing yachts still fit separate port and starboard running lights instead of a combined lantern but it is difficult to see why. Apart from needing twice as much electricity, separate lamps are far more likely to be obscured by sails or waves. In addition, the 'cut-off' between one colour or the other being visible is often very vague with separate lamps and yachts are often seen where both colours are visible at the same time over quite a wide arc (fig. 5). But for a combined lantern to comply with the required standard, the 'zone of confusion' where both colours can be seen must be no larger than 3°.

In conclusion, a properly designed combined port and starboard lamp of 24 W will easily give a visible range of 1 mile, even with less than perfect voltage and cleanness. A 12-W stern light easily gives 2 miles visibility. A 24-W tri-colour lamp easily meets both requirements but cannot legally be used in conjunction with a steaming light.

Limber holes
Holes in the floors to allow bilge water to run towards the pump inlet.

Line of position *see* POSITION LINE

Line squall
A severe squall occurring along a cold front, generally one of several accompanied by thunderstorms.

Link *see* MASTS AND RIGGING: Glossary

List
A long-term attitude about the fore-and-aft axis of a craft due to internal forces.

Little America's Cup *see* YACHT RACING: Major races and series

Local hour angle (LHA)
Hour angle measured from the observer's celestial meridian.

Lodestar, loadstar
A name for the Pole Star.

Log
An instrument used to measure the distance travelled by a vessel through the water. In one type, it is possible to measure the distance relative to the sea bed. The log may provide additional information such as the vessel's

speed and/or a pulse rate proportional to speed for feeding into a true motion radar.

In the first century BC, the Roman architect and engineer Vitruvius invented a paddle-wheel log that protruded through the side of the hull. The inboard end of its shaft was fitted with a box containing pebbles, so that as the paddle wheel revolved, pebbles fell into a container, thus measuring the distance travelled.

– common log
In the late sixteenth century, the common log or ship log came into use. This took the form of a triangular drogue held in each corner by three pieces of line, one of which was secured by a peg. The drogue was paid out over the stern, and assumed to remain stationary in the water, while forward motion of the vessel unwound the line from the user's hand-held spool. The length of line that passed while a sandglass ran out measured the speed in knots made in the line at set intervals.

– towed logs
Following the common log came the first successful towed log produced by Edward Massey and fitted to HMS *Donegal* in 1805. It consisted of a shallow rectangular box to hold the registering wheelwork. A float on its upper side carried three dials that displayed the distance run in fractions, units, and tens of miles. A rotator with fins set at an angle was towed behind the apparatus to activate it. To read the dials, it was necessary to haul in the mechanism and rotator each time. In 1807, the Vicomte de Vaux described what is now known as a Pitot log, afterwards improved by the English clergyman Edward Lyon Berthon while he was vicar of Fareham, near Portsmouth, and fitted to HMS *Dauntless* in 1850. In 1861 Thomas Walker introduced the Harpoon log. Based on the Massey log, it had its rotator and wheelwork made in one unit.

– taffrail logs
In 1870 W. F. Reynolds removed the wheelwork to the taffrail, and he was followed in this by Walker in 1876 with his Cherub log. Various improvements have been made over the years and even in the 1970s, merchant ships and small private craft still use these taffrail or patent logs.

– hull-fitted logs
Because of the relative inconvenience of towed logs, hull-fitted instruments were developed, with sensing devices projecting below the steel plating or skin. The Royal Navy used a Forbes log in which a small impeller was mounted inside a tube projecting downwards beneath the hull. Openings facing fore and aft at the bottom and top of the tube respectively allowed water to flow upwards, passing the impeller and causing it to rotate and operate electrical contacts. These were used to pulse distance indicators. After World War I, the Chernikeeff log,

which worked on the impeller principle, was produced. Here the water bore directly on the impeller mounted at the lower end of a support tube and, again, operated electrical contacts as in the Forbes type.

– pitometer logs
In the 1930s, Pitot logs became commercially available. In these a pitometer or Pitot tube projecting below the vessel has an aperture facing forward. This is subjected to a static pressure due to its vertical distance below the water level at any instant, together with a dynamic pressure caused by the forward movement of the vessel. On comparing the total pressure at this aperture with that due to the instantaneous draught a measure of the vessel's speed is obtained. This differential pressure is theoretically proportional to the square of the vessel's speed. Distance run is obtained, mechanically or electrically, by integration with respect to time. Such logs are in current use and are particularly suited to high speeds where the differential pressure is relatively large. Conversely, at low speeds they become insensitive and this, in conjunction with the practical effect of the deep draughts often encountered in the 1970s, has caused such logs to be replaced in many cases by the electromagnetic type.

– electromagnetic logs
An electromagnetic log is an inherently linear device, insensitive to draught and in a good design unaffected by changes in the salinity and temperature of the sea water. In principle, a log probe or sensor projects a magnetic field into the surrounding water. Considering the water under the influence of the magnetic field as an electrical conductor, it is seen that any movement of the water will result in the generation of a potential difference in that water. By sampling this potential difference, a basis for speed measurement is obtained, and hence distance run by integration. Although the principle is old, it was not until the 1960s and '70s that electronic techniques made such a log practical. By suitable design of the sensor, whether it be of the projecting type, or flush with the hull, a linear relationship between the vessel's speed and the generated potential difference can be obtained, thus producing a log that is both accurate, and at low speeds considerably more sensitive than other types.

All the logs referred to give speed or distance run through the water. By using ultrasonic techniques it is possible to reflect sound waves off the sea bed within certain limitations of depth. Employing the Doppler principle, the ultrasonic waves received after reflection differ in frequency from those transmitted, thus giving a measure of the vessel's speed over the sea bed. By counting the individual pulses of the beat or difference frequency a direct measure of the distance travelled over the sea bed is obtained.

Logbook

A written record of a vessel's movements and of other matters of navigational significance.

Longitude, discovery of

The concept of longitude is as old as the concept of a spherical earth with an axis about which the heavenly bodies appear to revolve in their daily motions. Meridians are GREAT CIRCLES passing through the poles and perpendicular to the plane of the equator; the longitude of any place relative to another place is the angle at the pole between the meridians passing through them, and therefore also the difference between the local times at their two places. Local time can be determined by the sun or stars; the Greeks recognized that differences in longitude could be measured if the local times of some external event were known. Hipparchus in about 160 BC suggested timing eclipses of the moon, but it would not appear that many such determinations were made. The longitudes on Ptolemy's world map in the second century AD were based on estimated distances east and west and on an estimate of the earth's circumference.

The problem of finding longitude differences continued to interest astronomers and geographers, but with long ocean voyages and the discovery of distant lands in the fifteenth and sixteenth centuries it became a matter of great practical importance to mariners. An eclipse of the moon was observed by Columbus in the West Indies in 1494. Eclipses of the moon are, however, rare events and difficult to time with any precision because the earth with its atmosphere casts a blurred shadow on the moon's surface. Nor could the instant of an eclipse then be predicted with any accuracy; Columbus was out by about 18°.

Estimates of the distance sailed eastwards or westwards continued to depend on DEAD RECKONING long after latitudes were observed by the altitude of the Pole Star or the sun at noon, but the longitude concept was still important to the mariner because of the convergence of the meridians and the related problem of plotting RHUMB LINES on a chart. Courses were sailed by compass and where the magnetic variation from the true north, as determined by the Pole Star, became apparent it was appreciated that a world chart of the variation and a knowledge of the latitude would provide an alternative method of position fixing. With the instruments and observational data then available the results were disappointing.

In 1598 Philip III of Spain offered a handsome reward for any accurate way of finding longitude at sea and similar rewards were later offered by the King of France and the Republic of Venice. The largest of all, £20 000 for a method reliable within half a degree, was authorized by an Act of Parliament in London in 1714. Such rewards encouraged a spate of suggestions, serious or fantastic, but the practical proposals resolve themselves into two categories: astronomical methods and the perfection of timepieces for use at sea.

As soon as Galileo discovered the satellites of Jupiter in 1609 he saw the possibility of predicting the time (at Rome) of their very frequent eclipses for comparison with the observed local time of these events. Accurate prediction was, however, impossible before the elaboration of a gravitational theory of their mutual perturbations, and a fairly large telescope is needed to observe them. He failed to win the Spanish prize. The difficulty of observing Jupiter's satellites at sea was never overcome although with improved eclipse tables, such as were included in the first NAUTICAL ALMANAC for 1767, the method was later of great value ashore. A 'marine chair' in gimbals for the observer with his long telescope did not prove a success.

All the other practical astronomical methods depend in one way or another on accurate predictions of the moon's orbital motion since its distance from a fixed star near the ecliptic changes by about half a degree in an hour. A measurement of the angular distance to within one minute of arc can therefore determine the Greenwich Time to within two minutes, or the longitude to half a degree. Unlike the eclipses of Jupiter's satellites or of the moon itself this LUNAR DISTANCE is not, however, a unique external event simultaneous for all observers, but because PARALLAX depends on the place of observation, and 'clearing the distance', to obtain the geocentric angle, requires an elaborate calculation. After the first publication of accurate predictions in the *Nautical Almanac* for 1767 and of the requisite tables, lunar distances became a standard method for finding longitude at sea. Ashore, where fixed telescopes can be used, two related observational methods capable of greater accuracy were formerly important. The occultation of a star, usually not a bright one, by the moon when it passes between the star and the earth serves to mark the time of 'zero distance', and the time of the moon's meridian passage can be compared with that of adjacent stars. Eclipses of the sun are in fact total or partial occultations, but they are infrequent.

The most obvious way of finding a ship's longitude is, of course, to carry a mechanical clock that has been set to keep the local time of some known place ashore. This was appreciated as soon as spring-driven clocks and watches became available, and the pendulum clock invented by the Dutch scientist Christiaan Huyghens was seriously tested at sea, but none were at all satisfactory until the English horologist John Harrison perfected his chronometers in the eighteenth century. By the beginning of the nineteenth century chronometers were coming into general use but lunar distances provided a valuable check on their performance until radio time signals superseded them early in the present century.

When chronometers and lunar distances provided a reliable means of finding a ship's longitude it became important to establish the longitudes of points ashore to at least the same degree of accuracy. Astronomical methods had been used extensively in the seventeenth and eighteenth centuries, principally the eclipses of Jupiter's satellites. Captain Cook made a very accurate determination in Newfoundland in 1766 from an eclipse of the sun corrected for parallax and subsequently compared with observations of the same eclipse made at Oxford. In the nineteenth century surveying ships carried batteries of chronometers for such longitude determinations: HMS *Beagle* in her circumnavigation of 1831–6, more famous for the presence on board of Charles Darwin as a naturalist, carried no fewer than 22 chronometers to establish a chain of longitudes around the world. The extension of overland and submarine telegraph lines made still more accurate determinations possible and European observatories like Greenwich and Paris were connected by geodetic triangulation. Time balls or noonday guns at places of well-determined longitude provided time checks for ships in port. It was not, however, until 1884 that the Greenwich meridian was adopted by international agreement as the standard reference for all longitudes, recognizing that most sea charts were based on that meridian and that astronomical observations at Greenwich had been maintained for more than 200 years. There had previously been many local standards defined by national observatories. An earlier standard inherited from Ptolemy was the island of Ferro in the Canaries, which he considered to be the western end of the world.

See also ASTRONOMICAL NAVIGATION; LUNAR DISTANCES; MARINE CHRONOMETER; NAVIGATION: Historical

Long splice *see* ROPEWORK: Splices

Loom, looming

The glow of a light that is below the horizon. See also HORIZON DISTANCE

Loran

A hyperbolic navigation system; it takes its name from *long-ra*nge *n*avigation.

– Loran A

This version of the system uses pulse transmission on a carrier frequency in the region of 2mHz. It has a GROUNDWAVE range of several hundred kilometres over sea and with SKY-WAVE propagation at night the range is extended to over 500 km. The use of pulses makes it possible to distinguish between groundwave and skywave, and there are no ambiguities as in phase-comparison systems. The time difference of arrival of signals from a pair of transmitters is read from a cathode-ray display or with an automatic receiver by locking on to the received pulses. Charts are overprinted with the hyperbolic pattern of numbered time differences.

Skywave operation requires considerable skill and experience from the operator to ensure that similar modes of propagation have been selected for both the signals of a pair. These signals often exhibit fading or splitting, which makes it difficult to achieve automatic tracking. Nevertheless a fix accuracy of 40 km should be obtained, compared with 2 km for groundwave operation.

By the end of World War II Loran A was a standard Allied long-range navigation system and covered all the theatres of war. It remains in Japanese, Hawaiian, and North American coastal areas, but in the long term it is expected to be replaced by Loran C and OMEGA.

– Loran C

A hyperbolic navigation system with pulse transmissions on a common carrier frequency in the band 90–110 kHz for all stations. Different pulse-repetition rates are used to avoid mutual interference. The low frequency and the high-power transmitters give a groundwave range of 1500 km. Phase comparison between master and slave carrier signals leads to an accuracy of 150 m at 500 km and using skywave signals the range may extend to 3000 km with an accuracy of the order of 20 km. Skywave signals require corrections that are printed on Loran C charts; their use depends on a skilful operator to distinguish between different modes of propagation.

It is possible to convert the incoming pulses to standard Loran (Loran A) frequencies and use them as Loran A signals, but these do not realize the potential performance of Loran C. Loran C receivers track a master and two slaves simultaneously and so provide a fix from two position lines. Within a pulse a specific cycle (the third) is selected for phase comparison either manually or automatically. The 'indexing' process compares the relative amplitudes of the cycles either side of the one to which the receiver is locked, this ratio being unique for the wanted cycle of the pulse. Transmissions are 'multipulse' in groups of eight pulses, which are synchronously detected to improve the signal/noise ratio and are coded to discriminate against certain types of interference.

The complexity of the transmitters and the receivers is considerably greater than for Loran A, which it is, however, displacing by virtue of its greater range and accuracy. Loran C first came into use in 1957 and now covers large areas of the northern hemisphere.

Low

An area of low atmospheric pressure. *See* WIND AND WEATHER

Loxodrome

A RHUMB LINE.

Lubber line

The vertical mark on the inner surface of the compass bowl that is lined up with the vessel's bow.

Luff

(1) The fore part of a sail; (2) to bring the vessel's head closer or into the wind.

Luff tackle

A purchase using a single and a double block. When rove to advantage, with the standing part rove to the strop of the single block, the power is increased four times. Originally used to tauten the luff of fore-and-aft-rigged vessels by hauling down the tack of the sail.

Lugger

A sailing vessel, normally two-masted, with a lug rig.

Lug rig *see* RIGS: Lateen and lug rigs

Lugsail

A four-sided fore-and-aft sail somewhat similar to a gaffsail, the yard of which projects forward of the mast. *See also* RIGS: Lateen and lug rigs

Lunar distance

The observed angle between the edge of the moon and a star or planet or the sun. The moon in its monthly rotation round the earth moves through 360° on the celestial sphere and its angular distance from any heavenly body on or near the ecliptic will vary by about 13° in a day or by 1′ of arc in 2 min of time. If the position of the moon relative to the stars at any instant of Greenwich Time can be predicted long in advance, a measurement of the lunar distance provides a method for determining Greenwich Time at sea, which is fundamental in determining a ship's longitude. The possibility of determining longitude in this way was suggested by Johann Werner of Nuremberg in 1514, but its practical application at sea required accurate predictions of the moon's position, accurate measurement of the angular distance, and some fairly simple method of making the necessary calculations.

The reduction of an observation to the geocentric angle between moon and star is laborious because of the perspective difference in the angle as measured at different positions on the earth's surface, the actual distance of the moon being only some thirty-six times the diameter of the earth. The reduction, 'clearing the distance', requires that the ALTITUDES of moon and star should be observed or calculated to determine the effects of refraction and PARALLAX in altitude. Allowance must also be made for the 'augmentation' of the moon's SEMI-DIAMETER, which is greater than it would be if measured geocentrically.

The moon's orbital motion is notoriously complex, 'the only problem that ever made my head ache' said Newton, and it was not until 1765 that sufficiently accurate predictions of the geocentric lunar distance from selected stars, planets and the sun, based on the lunar tables of the German mathematician Johann Tobias Mayer and nearly a hundred years of observation at Greenwich, were published by Nevil Maskelyne, then Astronomer Royal, together with an approximate method for clearing the distance and the requisite tables. The invention of HADLEY'S QUADRANT had provided sailors with an instrument for measuring the angle to within 1′ of arc. Although chronometers soon came into general use for the determination of longitude at sea, the lunar-distance method was very widely practised and long continued to provide the only absolute check on the chronometer itself. Many new methods for clearing the distance, rigorous or approximate, continued to be devised and the predicted distances were only omitted from the NAUTICAL ALMANAC early in the present century when wireless time signals had rendered the method obsolete.

As a method of finding longitude the accuracy of a lunar distance is necessarily limited. Whereas an error of 1′ of arc in measuring the altitude of the sun or a star above the sea horizon will introduce an error of 1 mile in the ship's position, the same error in measuring the angle between the moon and a star will introduce an error of up to 30 miles. Even with the greatest care and numerous repeated observations, the use of such refined instruments as the reflecting circle and by rigorous calculation, the error in longitude might well be as much as 20 miles. *See also* LONGITUDE, DISCOVERY OF; MARINE CHRONOMETER; NAVIGATION: Historical

Lying a-hull *see* HEAVY-WEATHER SAILING

Scrubbing off the bottom. This is frequently undertaken by boatyards using a high-pressure water spray and is generally done as soon as the boat is slipped or lifted out of the water

season. Some boatyards want to do other work as well, such as re-antifouling, but most owners these days do as much of the necessary work on their boats as they can, finding pleasure and satisfaction in a good job done. Maintenance, however, is not simply a winter scheme of work to be carried out either at laying-up time or during the spring fit-out, rather it should be a continuing process throughout the whole season, designed to prevent the need for any major repair work to return the boat to a truly seaworthy condition.

Every part of a boat and her equipment requires some maintenance at some time. The following entries concentrate on the main items and problems, and also consider a number of points that are frequently forgotten. For the most part the entries are presented directly as instructions to the person carrying out the work.

ANODES (ZINC)
Before the boat is launched for the season, inspect all anodes fitted to the hull and clean off heavy white deposits with a wire brush. If the anode is wasted away more than about 50% it is time to renew it. This must be done before the anode is 80% wasted.

CHAFE
This is the most persistent and insidious of all enemies to a boat at sea. It is impossible to take too much trouble over protection against chafe. Anything that moves can chafe and so will anything that is rubbed against.

Sails are perhaps the most obvious items affected by chafe, whether it manifests itself as a dirty mark where the cloth has lain against a shroud or as a hole needing patching. Protect crosstree (spreader) ends with split tennis balls or some of the plastic clip-on protectors sold in chandlers. Plastic tube rollers on the shrouds help reduce chafe on both sheets and headsails. All split pins (cotter pins) must be taped over and the wiring on bottle screws (turnbuckles) needs covering too, either with tape or some of the plastic 'boots' now available.

BAGGYWRINKLE is not as extensively used on rigging to protect sails as it used to be, but it is still very effective, even if it does increase WINDAGE somewhat. Quite a lot is needed for full protection.

Radar reflectors hung in the rigging often cut through sails that rub on them. Tape over all corners after filing down rough spots. Movement can wear through the metal of the supporting shackles or the reflector itself, and it will certainly chafe through the halyard on which it is hoisted. Any damage that alters the reflecting angles from 90° will seriously affect performance, as will display in any attitude other than the correct 'catch water' position.

Where a headsail rubs on the lifeline terminals at the pulpit is a very common

Mainsail
The principal sail: in fore-and-aft-rigged vessels set on the after side of the mainmast; on square-rigged vessels on the lower part of the mainmast. *See also* RIGS

Maintenance
Maintenance, as opposed to repair work, restoration, or alteration, is carried out in order to maintain a boat in a seaworthy condition rather than to raise or return her to such a condition. Boats are maintained in order to keep them looking trim, to extend their useful life, to keep up their value, and above all to ensure safety at sea.

Any work done by a boatyard is expensive, but yards are increasingly insisting on doing basic work like scrubbing off the bottom when the boat is hauled out at the end of the

place for chafe. Again tape is usually the answer.

Sheets and guys (preventers) tend to chafe on lifelines. If you are likely to be on one point of sailing for some time and either of these is chafing wrap a rag round the wire or apply a spirally cut plastic tube.

Mooring WARPS can be passed through short lengths of plastic tube at the FAIRLEADS to reduce chafe, although a good fairlead should not chafe the rope much itself. The same tubing can be used to good effect where a warp has to run over the edge of a quay or pontoon or if slipped over an eye it will reduce the chafe at a BOLLARD.

Ensure a fairlead from mast SHEAVES for all halyards. Having a large-diameter sheave so as to avoid crippling the rope, but then leading it off so that it rubs against the side of the sheave box doesn't make any sense. In the same way make sure that sheets have a fair lead to winches or CLEATS and do not chafe against coamings or stanchions.

Electric cables, fuel and gas pipes all need protecting against chafe. The final length of rubber hose to a gimballed gas cooker is often chafed as the stove swings to and fro. The loss of a grommet where an electric cable comes out of the mast can go unnoticed until the wire chafes through. Fuel lines rubbing as the engine vibrates could perforate and spill fuel, possibly causing a fire. Cooling water pipes are equally vulnerable; wear could cause engine damage or hull flooding.

You must keep a constant vigil against chafe. It happens in the unlikeliest places as well as in the obvious ones and it can happen very fast indeed.

COMPASS

Every time the compass is removed and replaced, or whenever a large ferrous metal object is moved, or some new wiring or electrical instruments are put in, the compass must be swung and a new deviation card drawn up. A continuous check should be kept on the free movement of the gimbals (applying oil regularly), the correct operation of compass lighting (including dimmer if fitted), and on the liquid in the bowl for bubbles. If any bubbles appear, return the compass to an instrument repairer for refilling. Older compasses can be topped up with an alcohol-and-water mix, but modern ones frequently use special oils and it is best not to meddle with them. (*See also* GYROCOMPASS; MARINER'S COMPASS.)

DECKS (canvas)

Careful inspection must be made for any cracks due to paint drying along deck seams. Where this happens the canvas will also crack and a leak will occur, possibly resulting in rot. If the covering is still intact then a coat or two of ordinary deck paint may be applied. Where there is cracking and leaking, it may be necessary to remove an area of canvas and

recanvas the deck. This is not the easiest of jobs and it would be worth considering coating the whole deck with a brush-on plastic sheathing such as Dekaplex. This compound remains flexible when dry and is thus less likely to crack in the same way as a canvased deck will – it's also much easier to apply than new canvas.

DECKS (fibreglass)

Fibreglass decks with a moulded-in non-slip tread, normally a diamond pattern, need no real maintenance beyond scrubbing to clean any trapped mud or sand from the diamond pattern. In time they may need painting (as with the hull) to restore appearance, and at that time a normal non-slip deck paint can be applied over a suitable primer. Any cracks or crazing that may appear must be repaired in the same way as for any other fibreglass surface.

DECKS (laid-teak)

Frequent buckets of seawater and plenty of scrubbing keep laid-teak decks in good shape. After a few years they will become grey, but the original warm colour can be recovered either by scraping or with the use of a proprietary brand of teak restorer. In very dry weather it is particularly important to wet the decks often in order to avoid drying and splitting. If leaks occur and can be located it will be necessary to rout out the seams in the area of the leak and then re-pay them using a flexible sealer.

DECKS (painted)

Decks of whatever material, which are painted with a non-slip deck paint will require repainting every couple of years. Scrub the surface with a stiff brush and water to remove any dirt, rinse off, and apply two coats of paint to the dried surface. The paint is thick and goes on quite easily, but be sure to work it in hard so that adhesion is complete.

DECKS (Trakmark)

Like fibre-glass decks with a moulded non-slip pattern, Trakmark only really needs scrubbing clean each season. A careful inspection should be made of all joints and seams for any signs of lifting. Where the Trakmark has begun to lift, it may be possible to inject glue under the material and press it down, excluding all the air in the process, but if the lifting or blistering is serious and has stretched the material, it will be necessary to remove a section and fit in a new piece. Old worn areas can be slippery.

DECKS (Treadmaster M)

This material is similar to Trakmark in that it is applied in sheets and has a raised diamond pattern, but the Treadmaster is a far heavier material with a larger pattern, and is generally applied in patches on the deck rather than as a complete covering. This patch system has the advantage of allowing a better check to be made for lifting and blistering besides making application of new or extra

pieces easier. Maintenance is generally the same as for Trakmark with a good scrub and clean being the usual extent of the job.

DINGHIES

A dinghy should be treated in the same way as the vessel to which she is the tender. Rigid dinghies will therefore be repainted and generally maintained according to the advice given for larger craft of their material; inflatables must be treated as follows. The whole dinghy should be washed and cleaned then examined for chafe and damage. Any known punctures will of course need repairing with the kit provided by the manufacturer. Inflation valves may need dismantling and cleaning, otherwise simply check that non-return valves are not jammed open by sand or grit. Chafe is the greatest cause of deterioration, produced by grit trapped in the folds between sides, floorboards, and bottom, or careless handling. Whereas worn places can be recoated with the makers' repair kits, general wear cannot. As a safety measure, inflatables are divided into separate compartments, with diaphragms between, and these should be checked for integrity by testing each section separately.

On all dinghies check the security of the painter attachment point and examine the painter for chafe. Renew if necessary. Oars must be revarnished (leaving the handles bare) and the leathers will need an application of neatsfoot oil. If the runners on the bottom of a rigid dinghy are badly damaged these should be renewed. (*See also* DINGHIES AND CENTRE-BOARD CLASSES)

ELECTRICS AND ELECTRONICS

Saltwater, a damp atmosphere, and electrical installations do not mix well. One of the prime aims in maintaining an electrical system on a boat must be to protect it from damp and saltwater. This involves coating all connections with petroleum jelly, using watertight connectors on deck (and coating them as well to be sure), and particularly installing the batteries in a place where no water can get at them. When laying a boat up it is as well to remove the batteries and store them in a dry place ashore, preferably running them partly down and recharging with a trickle charger. Always maintain the correct level of electrolyte in the batteries and make sure they cannot spill in rough weather. If a battery does not hold its charge get it checked by a garage to see if any of the cells are dead.

If a masthead tricolour light is fitted consider renewing the bulb at the beginning of the season before the mast is stepped – it might save you a trip aloft later on. Clean all light-bulb sockets and spray with a damp inhibitor or a circuit promoter such as Electrolube or WD40; do the same for switches and fuse boxes. Battery terminals must be cleaned of any corrosion and coated with petroleum jelly.

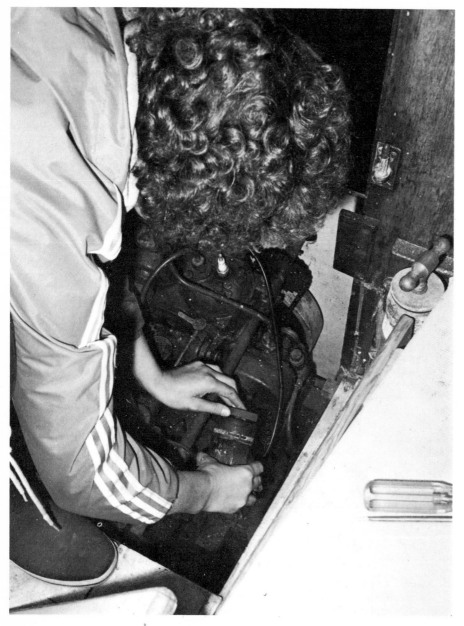

If the auxiliary is fitted with a magneto it should be removed during the winter season and stored ashore in a warm dry place

Winches should be stripped and serviced in accordance with their makers' instructions. (*See also* Electrolysis)

GAS INSTALLATIONS

Regular inspections of the piping, both copper and rubber, are necessary to spot any deterioration before it allows gas to leak. Check all unions and wherever a nut has to be tightened use Calortite or similar compound to ensure a good seal. If hose has to be replaced use only trade-approved gas hose. Keep burners clean at all times and check that any drain holes in the gas-bottle locker are clear.

If an automatic gas detector alarm is fitted, it should be tested periodically and carefully maintained according to the makers' directions, otherwise it may give a false sense of security. Even with an alarm fitted, always turn the gas off at the bottle when it's not in use, and when leaving the boat for any length of time turn off at the bottle (source) with the gas lit so that the pipe is emptied.

GROUND TACKLE AND MOORING GEAR

Remove all anchor cable from the locker and untwist it as it is almost certain to have twisted up during the season. Check the lashing at the BITTER END and renew if necessary. Examine cable markings and repaint or mark as required; an aerosol car-retouching paint can be used for this. Clean the locker and its limber holes.

Rope to chain splices need inspection, particularly with regard to chafe of the rope where it works against the chain links. If the rope does show signs of wear cut the end off and re-splice it.

Check all shackles and grease the pins, then put new mousings on, using (for preference) monel metal wire.

If by any chance the anchor is bent – shank or stock are the most likely parts – straighten out, but if serious consider renewing anchor and carrying old one as a spare.

Mooring WARPS (lines) must be checked for wear and washed in fresh water to remove salt and dirt. Pay particular attention to removal of oil deposits. This applies also to fenders, which will certainly transfer any oil left on them to the boat's topsides. Renew chafed fender ropes.

HEADS

Whatever type of head is fitted it should be cleaned regularly with disinfectant, but check makers' instructions regarding chemicals to be used or avoided. Seacocks need stripping and their packing checked each season. Every few years the unsavoury job of taking the head out and renewing hoses and gaskets is necessary. Pumps too should be stripped down and valves and seatings checked. Tighten any loose jubilee clips (hose clamps) and put a spanner on retaining bolts. Inspect wooden base and hull underneath for rot due to persistent dampness.

Make sure that none of the wiring has chafed through, particularly where it passes through retaining clips. Check that the wire is held tightly and in good contact at all connectors, terminals, and switches.

Electronic instruments and navigation aids must be treated according to makers' instructions, but if they run off internal dry batteries, these should be removed at the end of the season and renewed at the beginning of the next. Clean any corrosion from the battery terminals and particularly any deposits if the battery has leaked. (*See also* ELECTRICS)

FITTINGS (hull and deck hardware)
All hull and deck fittings such as cleats, tracks, stanchion bases, skin fittings, and bullseyes must be checked for security. Where these fittings are on wood the wood must be examined for any signs of rot. Loose fittings must be removed, rebedded on mastic and refastened.

Skin fittings should be dismantled and repacked if necessary to ensure watertightness and ease of operation. Check carefully for any signs of electrolysis on all through-hull fittings, or attached piping and clamps.

HULLS (aluminium, ferro-cement, steel)
These hulls are really all treated in exactly the same way as a wooden hull provided the old paint is basically sound. It is only when starting from bare materials that the different procedures described in the section on painting need be used. It is important to remember that before painting any surface it must be rubbed down well so that the new paint will key in properly, otherwise your efforts and paint will be wasted.

HULLS (fibreglass)
Until such time as they need painting, which certainly won't be for 8–10 years, a fibre-glass hull only needs cleaning and polishing each season to maintain its glossy appearance. Inevitably there will be some small scratches and possibly a few larger gouges on the top-sides and these must be attended to. The smallest scratches can be removed with a mild abrasive rubbing compound; deeper scores can be filled with an epoxy filler with colour pigment added to match the rest of the surface. Avoid silicone waxes, as they can prevent adhesion of future paint coats.

Waterline staining from fuel and other substances in the water slowly builds up and eventually it may be this as much as anything that makes the owner decide to paint, but painting can be delayed if the stains are tackled regularly and their build-up kept to a minimum. Use detergents and mild abrasives then polish. If really necessary a light sanding with fine sandpaper will remove stains, but this of course quickly destroys the surface if used too often.

The patching of actual holes does not come into the realm of maintenance so much as repair, but if the hole is in an accessible place surprisingly good results can be obtained without very great difficulty. The technique is to trim back to solid material, dry, and relaminate around and over the hole (the method is simply described in the repair kits). Dryness and complete freedom from oily contamination are essential for good results.

If the hull shows signs of extensive blistering it is worth calling in a surveyor to examine it in case the cause of the trouble is osmosis. If it is, and the damage is not yet too serious, the hull can be dried out completely, the blistered areas cut right back, built up with epoxy fillers and the bottom then painted. If the trouble is widespread it might be necessary to grind off the whole of the gel coat on the bottom and build up with many layers of paint. If caught early, osmosis can be cured without too much trouble, it's only in its later stages that it becomes a really major problem.

HULLS (wood)
Annual maintenance when no complete paint removal is necessary should simply entail a thorough sanding to produce a smooth, totally mat surface, filling dents and gouges, then a couple of coats of enamel. Any areas that have been scarred and are down to bare wood must of course be primed and undercoated before enamelling.

ANTIFOULING must be rubbed down with wet and dry paper used wet. Never dry-sand antifouling as the dust may be toxic. Once it is sanded and all loose material removed, a couple of coats of antifouling can be applied. Rust should be removed from external iron keels and the surface primed before antifouling.

PAINTING (aluminium)
An aluminium hull is treated very similarly to a steel one. If the paint is to be removed completely it can be burned off and the hull then coated with a self-etch primer and a special primer for alloy. After that painting proceeds as for a steel hull. (*See also* HULLS)

PAINTING (brushes)
For a high gloss 'yacht' finish it is essential to use good-quality brushes, and as these are not cheap it is also worth looking after them and making them last. A cheap brush will shed hairs and quickly lose its bristle shape, whereas a better quality brush, although there may be an initial 'moulting' period, will soon settle down to give good clean results.

Never try to use a paint brush for varnish or antifouling work, or a varnish brush for paint, or any other permutation – buy a good brush for each kind of finish and keep it for that purpose. It is also very unwise to try cleaning a brush used for a dark-coloured paint and then to use it for a light colour; the reverse should also be avoided if possible.

A new brush of whatever size will contain a few loose hairs and some dust. To remove all this the brush should first be 'knocked out' on a table edge or some other firm object; if nothing else is available use the palm of your hand. After the brush has been knocked out it can be worked back and forth on a piece of paper or cardboard to supple up the bristles, and it is then ready for painting. Do not dip the brush too far into the paint – about half-way up the bristles is quite far enough – and try to avoid wiping excess paint off on the side of the tin where a deposit of part-dried paint will build up. Bits of this will transfer to the brush or fall into the paint and ruin the finish on the surface being painted. A much better method is to stretch a piece of cord or wire across the open mouth of the paint can and wipe the excess paint off on that. When it looks as though paint is building up on it, remove the cord or wire and either clean the paint off or replace it with a new piece.

Brushes should not be left with any paint or varnish on them for more than about 10 minutes, particularly in hot sunshine, because the paint will harden, destroying the suppleness of the bristles, and its removal then becomes a problem. If the brush is to be left for a while, say during a lunch break, leave it suspended in a jar of White Spirit or paint thinners. At the end of the job the brush should be completely cleaned out immediately, following the paint manufacturers' brush-cleaning instructions. Normally this will be done using some thinners, White Spirit, or a proprietory brand of paint-brush cleaner. Work the cleaning fluid well into the bristles, paying particular attention to any paint that has worked its way up to the roots of the bristles, but be careful not to splash the thinners in your face or to get it into cuts on your hands. Use a hard nailbrush to remove stubborn paint, but only brush parallel to the hairs from the roots to their ends. When the brush is mostly clean work it vigorously in a solution of liquid detergent before giving it a complete rinse in fresh water. Finally, when the brush is completely clean, shake the water out and wrap the bristles in either lint-free rag or shiny (glazed) paper and secure it with an elastic band. This helps to keep the bristles clean and in good shape. Alternatively you can store the brush wet by suspending it in a jar of cleaning fluid with the top of the jar sealed against dust.

When leaving a brush either temporarily or permanently in a jar of some liquid, never stand it on its bristles. Drill a hole through the handle near the metal band and push through either a long nail or a piece of wire, then lay that across the mouth of the jar to hold the brush up clear of the bottom.

PAINTING (ferro-cement)
If the boat has only just been plastered it must be allowed a full month to cure before painting is attempted. At the end of that time the hull is painted with two coats of special ferro-cement primer, the surface being rubbed down and faced up where necessary between coats.

Once that has been done the hull can be given a first coat of undercoat for enamel. Any irregularities that remain are faced up with the epoxy filler, remembering to leave it proud to facilitate rubbing down. This is done with a medium grit, wet and dry paper used wet. When the surface has dried thoroughly it is dusted and cleaned before a second coat of undercoat is applied. Where a polyurethane paint is to be used this second coat of undercoat can be omitted and a first coat of the polyurethane put on instead.

With the hull now undercoated and all irregularities filled and smoothed off, the painting is carried out in exactly the same way as for a wooden hull.

PAINTING (fibreglass)
Eventually, even the best-maintained fibre-glass hull begins to look shabby with stains along the waterline and scuffed and faded topsides. A hard rub down all over and careful polishing will restore the surface temporarily, but in the end the hull will have to be painted with a polyurethane or epoxy paint.

producing a surface similar to (but not the same as) the gel coat of the hull. This is the same process as is used for the restoration of a hull that has suffered from osmotic blistering, though in the case of a badly blistered hull it may be necessary to grind the gel coat off, while for normal painting this is far from being the case.

It is essential to comply in every way with the paint manufacturers' instructions for its application, and if at all possible the work should be carried out under cover. If the painting has to be done in the open then you must wait for a prolonged dry spell; you must not risk a break in the weather before everything is finished.

Any polish you have put on the hull in previous years must be removed, particularly if you have unwisely used a silicone polish, with the recommended cleaners. Well-ingrained dirt and oil stains will need to be removed by rubbing down well with wet and dry paper. The waterline and boot top too will need to be cleaned up as they will be painted over and then repainted in their own colours. Once all the polish and the stains have been removed it is likely that the hull will look better than it has for years, but don't be tempted to leave it like that and put off painting as the effect will not last very long.

The next stage is to de-grease the whole of the area to be painted by using the recommended de-greasing fluid, and once that has been done, be very careful not to put your hands on the surface or you will immediately begin to put a layer of grease back on.

It is possible to achieve a satisfactory paint job by next rubbing down thoroughly with wet and dry paper to produce a completely dull keying surface for the polyurethane or epoxy paint, but otherwise follow instructions and apply the recommended primer. This chemically softens and prepares the gel coat to form a chemical bond with the overlying paint. The primer must be put onto the hull quickly without any of the usual painting procedures of working it in or laying it off; it is much better simply to 'slap it on' regardless of appearance, but at the same time ensuring complete coverage of the surface.

The primer dries very quickly, but a period of between 6 and 24 hours is recommended before attempting to paint over it. As it is essential to work in really dry conditions it is likely that you won't have started till late morning, and as it is inadvisable to paint after late afternoon an overnight wait is probably the better plan.

Paint and hardener must be mixed together immediately prior to application, normally 1 litre at a time, but if the weather looks like being very hot mix only a half litre to avoid any problems with its going off prematurely. In any event, it must be mixed completely. Normal application is by brush, but the paint

can also be put on with a roller (lambswool or mohair), or by spraying – the method usually used only by professionals. Do not use a foam-plastic roller as it is possible for the paint to react with the plastic and for the whole job to go wrong. Whether using a brush or a roller it must be cleaned thoroughly between coats.

Even more than with conventional paints it is essential to keep a wet edge going with fibre-glass paints, and to do this a strange technique may be employed in which the paint is applied in vertical strips down the hull from deck to waterline, each strip being one or possibly two brush strokes wide. Any more than this and the wet edge will be lost with consequent ridges and 'drag' lines where the wet paint pulls on the tacky areas. Once started the whole hull must be painted in one go. For bigger boats it may be as well to rope in another person to take over when you tire and so work in relay.

It is likely that brush marks will be left in the paint, and although these should be kept to a minimum they can be dealt with after the paint has dried by burnishing the surface. After the first coat has stood overnight all irregularities, including any bad brush marks, are filled with a compatible epoxy filler and left a little proud so that when they are hard the whole hull can be sanded down hard with medium grit, wet and dry paper used wet. Getting the surface really smooth now is most important for good final results.

When the hull has quite dried off after this sanding it is rubbed over with the recommended thinners before a second coat of paint is applied. If any bad rough patches still appear after this coat they too must be faced up with filler, sanded down and washed with thinners before the third coat is applied. This coat and the final one should be put on at intervals of 24 hours, but they can if time is short be applied sooner; however, 6 hours must elapse between coats.

The final coat is allowed to cure thoroughly for some weeks before the surface is burnished with a very fine cutting compound to remove any lingering brush marks.

PAINTING (preparation)
The prime purpose of paint is to protect the surface it is applied to; and to do this it must be put on properly. The basis of any good paint finish is preparation on which lots of time must be spent in carefully producing a surface to which the paint will 'key'. Of all the time spent on a paint job, well over half will be taken up with the preparation of the surface.

If the old paint surface is flaking, peeling, blistered or generally patched up, it will be necessary to get right back to bare wood by either burning the old paint off or using a paint stripper. Under no circumstances should any attempt be made to burn paint off a fibre-glass hull, nor should a stripper be used. For removing varnish it is probably better to use a stripper than to burn it off as

Antifouling that has blistered and lifted should be scraped back to the bare hull, the surface primed and repainted

Hobie 14 catamarans (opposite) *taking part in the 1977 World Championships off Lanzarote, one of the Canary Islands*

any scorch marks will show through the new varnish, but for paint removal burning off is the easiest and probably cheapest method. Use a gas blowlamp connected either by hose to a large gas cylinder, or attached directly to a small cannister that can be held in the hand. A flat flame nozzle is better than a round jet, as the flat flame will give a better spread over the paint surface. Work with the hottest flame possible and scrape with a wide-bladed scraper, always working away from yourself, and always moving in the direction of the grain. Hold the flame over one patch long enough to blister the paint and thus make it easy to lift off, but not so long as to scorch the wood underneath.

Usually the paint can be burned down to the wood in one go, but occasionally it is necessary to go over the surface a second time. After the paint has mainly been re-moved, take off any remaining patches with a very sharp scraper. Scrape only in the direc-tion of the wood grain, do not be tempted to draw the blade across it even though the paint may be removed more easily by doing so, as any scratches will be awkward to hide afterwards.

With the whole surface now bare, inspect it for any areas of soft wood that will require the attention of a shipwright, and any places that need filling or patching. Attend to any seams that need filling or recaulking and then work over the surface with a medium grit sand-

paper. Clean the surface of all dust using a piece of rag and White Spirit, or better a 'tack' rag, and then either sand down again using a finer grade paper until the surface is really smooth (feeling almost like silk), or if you are at the end of your day's work time, apply a coat of bare wood primer. Try not to allow a bare wood hull to stand overnight as any dampness in the air will be absorbed into the wood and will have to be allowed time to dry out again before work can proceed.

The first primer coat will show up any irregularities in the surface and these must now either be rubbed down if they stand proud of the general level of the surface, or be filled if they are cracks or hollows. Where an area has to be sanded down the job will be made easier if a power sander is used, but only an orbital sander is recommended; a rotary sander will score the wood badly, particularly on a curved surface. Where there are deep scars as the result of unfortunate contact with quays or other hard objects, or where some butt joint or seam has opened up, a flexible (non-shrink) 'stopper' must be used. For shallower scratches or areas of proud grain, a non-shrinking 'filler' should be used. The stopper is altogether a heavier substance than the filler. Sand these filled areas down, dust off with either a tack rag or one dampened with White Spirit and all is set for the second primer coat. This coat is allowed to dry, and is gently sanded down, then the surface is

again cleaned and all is ready for the first undercoat. If you are really dedicated you would in fact keep on rubbing down and priming until no bare wood showed when sanded, thus ensuring a totally smooth sur-face on which to build a superb gloss finish.

So much for building up a paint finish from bare wood. If the old paint is sound it need not be taken right off; in this situation all that needs to be done is to rub it down very thor-oughly with wet and dry paper to remove all shine from the surface, if possible taking off at least one complete paint layer. When that has been done a top coat can be put on and all should be well.

Where there are irregularities in the surface these must of course be filled and sanded as before, and any loose paint must be taken off with a scraper until a sound surface is found. Feather the edges of a scraped area and either fill it or apply undercoat until it comes up to the level of the surrounding area. Then paint along with the rest of the surface.

PAINTING (steel)
First of all the surface must be freed from all signs of rust. If this means a complete removal of paint it can best be achieved by shot blast-ing, but as an alternative the paint may be burnt off in the same way as for a wooden hull. Paint strippers are not recommended as they may react with the steel. Once the paint is off the surface must be wire-brushed thor-oughly to remove any remaining rust patches, and the whole area cleaned.

Before there is any time for rust to start forming again (and that happens very quickly with bare metal) a coat of bare-plate primer is applied followed by two coats of undercoat for enamel, or one coat of under-coat and a first coat of polyurethane if that paint is to be used finally.

Rub down between undercoats using a fairly fine grade of wet and dry paper, used wet to avoid scratching, but it is not advisable to use more than a minimum of filler on a steel hull to take out irregularities in the surface. If too much is used it is possible for it to fall off when the boat works in a SEAWAY or receives a severe knock.

After the undercoats have been applied the painting is done in the same way as for a wooden hull.

Shot-blasting and subsequent zinc-spraying or other professionally applied treatment may be worthwhile.

PAINTING (technique)
Dust is probably the greatest enemy of a gloss finish and to combat it small areas should be gone over with a tack rag immediately before the paint is applied. Try to choose a day when there is little or no wind and not too much sun as you don't want the paint or varnish going off before you have had time to lay it out nicely.

If a non-polyurethane enamel is being used

Ian Proctor-designed Tempests (opposite) competing in an Olympic Week event at Weymouth

Hull sanding with an electric sander powered by a portable mini-generator

a coat of undercoat will show up unsuspected irregularities in the surface and these must be filled and sanded then re-undercoated until all have gone and the surface is perfectly smooth. A general dust-off is then performed and the first coat of enamel applied, dusting each area again immediately before applying the paint. Where a polyurethane paint is used it is often advised that no undercoat should be applied, but instead several layers of the actual finish paint. Follow paint manufacturers' recommendations on this point, but be prepared to apply up to half a dozen coats of polyurethane paint and be sure to use the recommended primer or undercoat.

With ordinary enamel the surface should be rubbed down very lightly with the finest grade of paper (used wet) after the first coat has dried, and again remove the dust immediately before applying the finish coat (after the surface has dried thoroughly). This finish coat should be 'flowed' on leaving a completely smooth surface without brush marks, but don't be too generous or you will create unsightly runs and curtains.

Early coats of primer should be applied with a slightly scrubbing motion of the brush if necessary to work the paint right into the grain of the wood, but thereafter all paint should be put on first at right angles to the grain, then it should be worked diagonally across the grain, and finally it must be laid off parallel to the grain. This laying off is done with very light strokes, holding the brush fairly gently, thus allowing it to adopt its own attitude to the surface. Always try to keep a 'wet edge' going otherwise new paint will make an unsightly 'drag' line over the part-dried paint.

Several fairly thin coats of paint are always better than one thick one. A thick coat is likely to produce runs and curtaining that will have to be sanded right off after the paint has dried. Only the finish coat should be applied with any liberality, and even then it should only be sufficiently thick to produce a smooth surface without brush marks. Don't forget, if you are not happy with the finish coat you can always rub it down and put another on.

Do not try to paint too early or too late in the day, either before the dew has dried away or after it has begun to form.

PUMPS

All bilge, fresh- and salt-water pumps should be stripped down annually and new washers and valves fitted as required. Check security of holding bolts for the whole pump unit.

RUNNING RIGGING

Where all-rope running rigging is used it is possible to prolong its life by turning it end-for-end when early signs of wear are noticed, for instance where a halyard passes over a masthead SHEAVE. An alternative method of freshening the nip on a halyard is to start off

with overlength ones and each season or two cut off a length from the end that attaches to the head of the sail and then re-splice or re-attach it.

At the end of each season, running rigging should be washed in fresh water to remove as much of the salt as possible from the rope, and particular care should be taken to clean off any oil deposits. Inspect laid rope for any signs of its becoming 'long jawed', thus indicating some maltreatment in its usage. Make sure all whippings are still secure, otherwise remove and replace them.

Wire running rigging should have a long life provided that the sheaves it runs through are of sufficiently large diameter (at least 12:1); however, regular checks for crippling and broken strands are essential. The serving from

a rope-to-wire splice should be removed every two seasons to allow examination of the splice and it should then be renewed. If there is any damage to either the rope fall or the wire it should be renewed.

Running rigging is often damaged by having to run in worn blocks or ones with damaged sheaves and pins. These should all be checked over regularly, in particular sheaves that carry wire rope. Oil the pins and check shackles for signs of wear.

Where separate headsail sheets are used they may be turned end-for-end in the same way as halyards, but if a continuous sheet is used and it wears badly it will all need replacing. *See also* MASTS AND RIGGING

SAFETY GEAR

Much of the safety gear carried on a boat is

This auxiliary-engined cruising yacht is dried out alongside the scrubbing posts for bottom painting. Careful use must be made of lines to prevent the boat from slipping, or even falling over

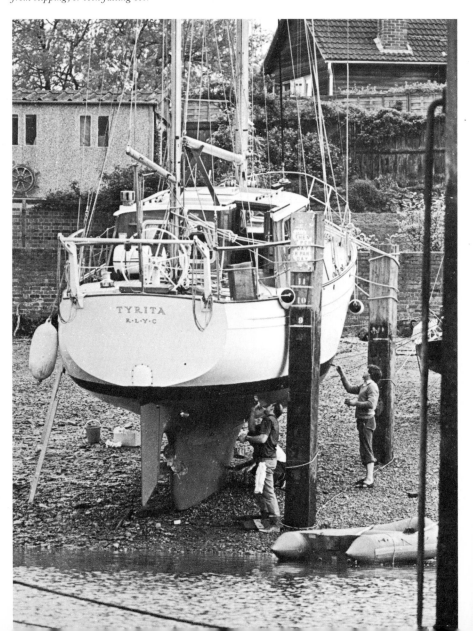

often ignored until required, at which time it may fail, simply because it has been ignored. Think safety and look after this equipment – it could save your life.

Life rafts must be serviced at the end of each season. It is better to send them off straight away to avoid delay at the beginning of the season and to minimize damage to the raft by such things as burst water cans or corroded inflation valves. If these are left over winter they may damage other parts of the raft, increasing the cost of putting things right.

Flares must be checked for damp and that they are still in date. The life of a flare is generally 3 years, after which it must be replaced. An out-of-date flare can be dangerous and at the very least will function with much-reduced efficiency.

Fire extinguishers can be weighed to check they have not leaked, and a visual inspection must be made for corrosion or denting. Serious denting of the case may indicate a loss of pressure and therefore effectiveness. If in doubt, replace.

Wash the salt off lifejackets and buoyancy aids, check inflation and every two years replace inflation cannisters. Make sure fastenings are still in good condition, and examine all seams. If inflatable, check that they retain air satisfactorily.

Life harnesses must be checked visually for signs of wear and chafe. Oil the carbine hooks and make sure the buckle is operating properly. Wash the webbing and line to remove salt.

Lifebuoys also must be washed in freshwater, but beyond that there is little to do. If there is a zip on the cover check the zip, examine the attachment of line and flashing light, and if the colour is faded, consider repainting the buoy with Dayglo paint.

Dan buoys are also passive safety aids and do not require much attention beyond cleaning and examination for the breakage of any part.

First-aid kits must be inspected and replenished as necessary. Do not hang on to old drugs, they must be replaced with fresh ones. *See also* SAFETY EQUIPMENT.

SPARS

The majority of aluminium spars are anodized to protect them against corrosion and the only maintenance required is a wash to get any dirt off. The LUFF groove on masts and the foot track on booms must be checked for smoothness and if necessary rubbed with wire wool. A very thin coat of Anhydrous Lanolin will help the smooth running of sails and slides in these grooves. Where external tracks are screwed on, check the tightness of all screws.

All mast wiring must be checked as far as possible for chafe at inlet and exit holes, and blocks and sheaves must be examined and oiled.

Wooden spars must be rubbed down and varnished or painted after careful examination for soft wood at all fittings, any lateral cracks, serious shakes (longitudinal cracks) and opening up of seams. Where seams have opened up they must obviously be re-glued if possible. Shakes can be filled with a flexible mastic. Any rot must be cut out and new wood scarfed in or a graving piece fitted.

Again check security of luff and foot tracks besides all fittings. Apply neatsfoot oil to the leather on gaff and boom jaws.

Roller reefing gear should be oiled and if possible the ratchet or worm gear inspected for wear. Gooseneck and boom-end fittings too need oiling and checking.

STANDING RIGGING

The majority of boats today use stainless steel standing rigging. It needs very careful and frequent inspection as it is not uncommon for stainless steel to give way when suffering from unsuspected fatigue. If any broken strands are found the stay should be renewed immediately as the remaining strands are not to be trusted. If any form of rigid end fittings are used (such as swaged terminals or Norseman or Sta-Lok terminals) the wire should be checked just above the fitting for any broken strands. The swaged terminals should be polished and checked for hairline cracks – if there are any the terminal should be condemned. Where wire rope is spliced round a thimble (either hand-spliced or by the Talurit or Nicopress systems) the wire should be inspected at the bottom of the thimble, as this is again the likeliest place for strands to break. Apart from these visual checks stainless steel standing rigging only requires washing down to remove dirt that will mark sails.

In the case of galvanized wire rigging the same visual check for parted strands should be made, and every two years the servings on hand splices should be removed, the tucks of the splice checked and the servings renewed. The wire itself is best coated with Anhydrous Lanolin to protect it against rust. This substance (available from chemists and chandlers) is like jelly and is best applied with the bare hand, but a cloth can be used. Alternatively coat the wire with a mixture of boiled linseed oil and paraffin.

Bottle screws (or open turnbuckles) should be kept well greased and any lock-nuts checked for tightness – a touch of Loctite will help. Even if there are lock nuts fitted (and not all have them), the bottle screws must be wired so that they cannot undo. Tape over any sharp ends of wire to avoid snagging on clothing, sails, and lines. *See also* MASTS AND RIGGING

TANKS (fuel)

Fuel tanks need cleaning out each season, and if they are fitted with proper water traps and a sump drain plug at the lowest point this is not too difficult. The water trap should be

emptied regularly and the drain plug removed once a season for cleaning. A small tank can be removed entirely and cleaned out by shaking it with the fuel in, then emptying. Keep the breather pipe clear at all times. When laid up the tanks should either be filled right up to avoid condensation or emptied and sealed with a bag of silica gel suspended inside. The latter method may be preferred to avoid fire hazard, but of course can only be used if the engine is being totally immobilized.

TANKS (water)

It is all too common to find boats with built-in fibre-glass water tanks that have no large inspection hatches. It is well worth cutting such a hatch and fitting a removable cover. Once a season the tanks can then be emptied

When laying up, the rigging should be labelled and removed from the mast along with the spreaders. Galvanized-wire rigging should be soaked in boiled linseed oil in order to protect it

and washed out with a solution of sodium bicarbonate. If individual plastic jerrycans are used they too can be cleaned with the solution by part filling and then shaking vigorously.

Galvanized tanks should be painted inside with a special paint for water tanks or coated with a cement wash.

Make sure that breather pipes are clear otherwise filling the tanks will be difficult.

VARNISHING

It is not particularly difficult to achieve a high-gloss finish with varnish if great care is taken over the preparation of the surface and a windless day is chosen for working. Because of its clarity, varnish will show up all imperfections of the wood beneath it, so any dark patches will have to be bleached, fillers must be chosen to match the rest of the surface when varnished, and only very fine sandpaper must be used.

Should the whole surface have to be stripped off it is better not to use a blowlamp as any scorched wood will show up strongly afterwards. It is better to use either a chemical stripper or a good deal of elbow grease and a very sharp scraper. If scraping is chosen it must only be carried out in the direction of the grain as any strokes against or across it will immediately roughen it up. On the other hand, if a chemical stripper is employed care must be taken not to spill it on other paintwork or on fibreglass, and to neutralize the surface when it is clean. When the old surface is still sound you will simply have to sand it until it is flat with no shiny areas and then varnish over it.

Use only very fine sandpaper on wood that is to be varnished as a coarse paper will leave scores on the surface of either bare wood or old (sound) varnish. For the same reason always sand parallel to the grain, never across it. If you want to use a power sander use an orbital one or a belt sander, not a circular rotary one as that too will leave indelible scars.

Any dark areas of wood should be bleached or scraped away, and any cracks that need filling should be attended to. Fillers tend to darken when varnished over so choose one whose shade is slightly on the light side.

Dust the whole surface and apply the first coat of varnish. If preferred this one may be thinned (according to manufacturers instructions) and used as a sealing coat. When it is dry rub it down with fine sandpaper and dust again before applying the next coat. Thereafter sand gently with fine paper between coats and dust carefully immediately before varnishing an area. Flow on the top coat with some liberality but be careful not to create runs or curtaining. Dust is the enemy of a good deep gloss so wait for a dry day with little or no wind. Don't start until the morning is dry and stop for the day before it gets damp in the evening. The old British adage is that you should not varnish after tea (late afternoon) if you want a good finish.

Make fast
To secure a rope.

Map and chart projections
A map projection is the representation on a plane of the curved surface of the earth. Some distortion of shapes, and of angles or of distance as measured on the sphere and on the map, is inevitable and many different methods of projection have been devised to minimize these distortions or to preserve some mathematical property. Many are of great antiquity: the projections used by Ptolemy (*c.* AD 130) for the maps in his *Geography* were applied to the mapping of the great sixteenth-century voyages of discovery; and the stereographic projection (attributed to the Greek astronomer Hipparchus, *c.* 150 BC) was a feature of the astronomer's astrolabe and used for solving spherical triangles.

These projections were ill adapted to the use of mariners, however, who in plotting their daily progress across the ocean needed to allow for the convergence of meridians towards the poles and for the differing length of a degree of longitude in different latitudes. For an area no larger than the Mediterranean the discrepancies of the 'plain chart' had not been important, and the network of RHUMB LINES and WIND ROSES allowed a simple geometry of distances and bearings. In Portugal in 1537 the mathematician Pedro Nunes, or Nunez, tackled the problem by considering the spiral line on a sphere, the loxodrome, which could be traced by a ship's course cutting all the meridians at the same angle. He showed that this would approximate to the rhumb line between two points on the plain chart if allowance was made for the convergence of the meridians at some middle latitude.

For his world map of 1569, the Flemish

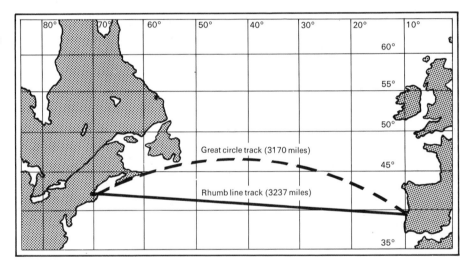

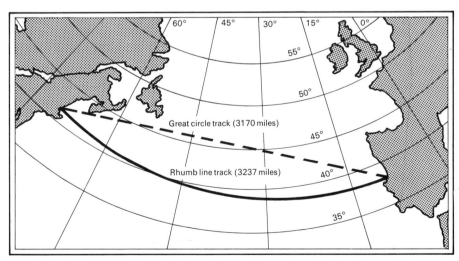

Mercator and gnomonic projections compared. For navigators, the great advantage of the former (top) is that rhumb lines appear as straight lines. In the latter (above) they are projected as curves, but the gnomonic chart is useful for plotting great-circle courses

geographer Gerardus Mercator (Gerhard Kremer), probably by using some graphical approximation, increased the scale of the map away from the equator by just enough to make the separation of the meridians always the same (*see also* MERCATOR PROJECTION). This restores both the parallel and straight meridians of the plain chart and the straight rhumb line that represents a loxodrome. In England the mathematicians Thomas Harriot, or Hariot, and Edward Wright drew up tables of MERIDIONAL PARTS (the distance on a Mercator projection of any parallel of latitude from the equator) in about 1590 by adding together the secants of successive small increments of latitude. In about 1645 Henry Bond noted that a table of meridional parts is identical with a table of logarithm tangents. It is in fact the integral:

$$M = \int_{0}^{\varphi} \sec \varphi \, d\varphi = \log_e \tan \left(\tfrac{\pi}{4} + \tfrac{1}{2}\,\varphi\right)$$

This is the basis of modern tables either for the sphere or, with some modification, for the spheroidal earth. The Mercator projection is conformal: angles measured on the surface of the sphere are truly represented and the scale of the map is the same in all directions at that point. A table of meridional parts provides the navigator with the scale factor he requires in using his chart.

At sea no other map projection is of comparable importance, but because of the distortion of land shapes away from the equator, conical projections are generally preferred for weather maps. The gnomonic projection, described before 600 BC, and in which the surface of the sphere is projected from its centre onto a tangent plane, is also still of interest. Any GREAT CIRCLE between two points is represented by a straight line, so that a chart on this projection is useful for plotting great-circle courses. It has also been used for harbour plans.

See also NAVIGATION

Mare's tails *see* WIND AND WEATHER: Clouds and their formation (Cirrus)

Marine chronometer

A marine chronometer or box chronometer is no more than a small portable clock designed specifically to produce a constantly accurate performance irrespective of changes in temperature or the movements of a ship at sea. It records Greenwich Mean Time and thereby enables a navigator to calculate the longitude of his ship.

As early as 1530 the use of a timekeeper to determine the longitude at sea was proposed by Rainer Gemma Frisius, the Flemish astronomer, but clocks and watches at that period were undeveloped, crude and highly inefficient. In 1660 Christiaan Huyghens made the first attempt to produce a timekeeper

specifically for use afloat, but when it was tested practically it proved hopelessly unsuited for use at sea. Even during the next 60 years the mechanical difficulties of constructing an efficient instrument appeared to be insuperable even to such notables as Sir Isaac Newton, Sir Christopher Wren, and Baron Leibniz, as well as to George Graham, Julien Le Roy and other leading clockmakers of the day. The need for a solution to the problem became so urgent that in 1714 the British Government offered up to £20 000 for any practical method accurate enough to determine the longitude of a ship at sea.

A Yorkshire village carpenter, John Harrison (1693–1776), devoted his life to the problem and was eventually successful in its solution and in winning nearly the whole of the £20 000. Working initially with wooden clocks, he approached the problem by devising a satisfactory method of compensating for errors in timekeeping that result from variations in temperature, something that no one else had been able to do. He also took great trouble to eliminate friction, including that caused by thickening of lubricating oil due to ageing. By 1728 he had made two very accurate longcase or grandfather clocks, and he then spent the next 30 years constructing three largely portable timekeepers or sea clocks as he called them. Finally, in 1760 he produced a large watch some 6 in (152 mm) in diameter that was revolutionary in design and phenomenally successful as a timekeeper. This watch, which is known as H4 (Harrison's fourth), was tested officially in 1761 and again in 1764 for the Board of Longitude on two voyages to the West Indies, and on each occasion it proved to be fully capable of determining the longitude. A facsimile of H4 was taken by Captain Cook on his second and third great voyages, when its extraordinary accuracy used in conjunction with LUNAR DISTANCES caused Cook to make several entries in his log giving high praise to the watch.

John Harrison's success in making his precision timekeepers inspired others to join his pioneering efforts, and in a short time the Englishmen Thomas Mudge (1715–94), John Arnold (1736–99) and Thomas Earnshaw (1749–1829) improved on Harrison's ideas, so much so that by 1770 the cost of some marine chronometers had been reduced from Harrison's figure of £450 to about £70. In the meantime, two eminent French clockmakers, Pierre Le Roy (1717–85) and Ferdinand Berthoud (1729–1807), proved themselves to be successful and progressive designers of early marine timekeepers. Le Roy was particularly outstanding, and his *montre marine* A (*ancienne*) of 1766 included two features that in a developed form are still used in all modern chronometers: he arranged that his device for temperature compensation was

fitted as an integral part of the balance, and he also invented a prototype of the chronometer detent escapement. This escapement was subsequently developed by Arnold and Earnshaw and is today used, universally, in all marine chronometers. From about 1840 onwards, the design of the marine chronometer became largely stabilized, and except for the development of special devices (middle-temperature error) and, later still, the use of modern alloys (invar), the modern marine chronometer has not altered fundamentally during the past 140 years.

The working parts of a box chronometer are contained in a brass bowl-shaped case with a screwed-on glass lid, the bowl being slung in gimbals so as to ensure that the timekeeper always remains level with its dial uppermost. The gimbals are fitted into a wooden guard box provided with a glazed lid. The dial is calibrated for 12 hours and it has two small

A marine chronometer, boxed and gimballed in the traditional manner

subsidiary dials: one shows seconds; the other is marked Up – Down and indicates the number of hours that have elapsed since the last winding. Some chronometers are designed to run for 54 hours and others go for 8 days between windings, but in either case it is the practice to wind chronometers every 24 hours so as to obtain as uniform a force as possible from the mainspring, the power of which lessens as it uncoils (fusée). Winding is carried out with a key; the brass case is turned bottom side up so as to expose the winding hole, which is normally covered by a spring shutter.

The mechanism of a marine chronometer is robust and is given a high degree of finish so as to eliminate friction. To this end jewelled bearings are used for some pivots, the latter being polished with special care. The balance wheel, the balance spring, and the escapement are the vital parts by which a good rate of consistency in timekeeping is obtained. It is essential, however, that the balance and its spring should be provided with some form of compensation to allow for errors resulting from changes in temperature. In the case of the balance this is accomplished by constructing the rim in the form of two bi-metallic strips joined to a central arm. An alternative arrangement used successfully in the American Hamilton chronometer is to construct the balance from an alloy, such as invar, which is almost unaffected by heat or cold. Special alloys are also used for making the cylindrical (helical) balance spring of the modern chronometer, thus eliminating the vagaries in timekeeping known as middle-temperature error, which affects chronometers fitted with the old-type steel balance springs. Formerly, special devices known as 'affixes' had to be used to provide auxiliary compensation to eliminate this error. All balances are carefully poised or put in balance in their axis of rotation, this being accomplished by moving small balance screws set in the periphery of the balance rim.

The escapement used in all chronometers is the type known as a chronometer spring detent, which has the double virtue of causing the minimum of interference to the free swing of the balance while requiring no lubrication. The actual spring-detent component of this escapement is small and delicate and, nowadays, is entirely machine made, but in the fine instruments constructed before World War II, the making of the spring detent was the hand-made speciality of a few workmen possessing the necessary exceptional skill.

The mainspring of any clock gives out a gradually decreasing force as it uncoils, and to avoid the errors that this causes, all marine chronometers are fitted with an age old device known as a fusée. This is a spirally grooved brass cone that is connected to the mainspring barrel by a small bicycle-type chain, and thus the progressively increasing diameters of the cone automatically compensate for the lessening force delivered by the mainspring as it unwinds. The base of the fusée also contains an auxiliary spring known as the maintaining power, a device invented by John Harrison to prevent a chronometer losing time while it is being wound.

A marine chronometer can be expected to have an average error(rate) of 0.1 to 0.2 sec per day over a wide range of temperatures. In the United Kingdom a Certificate of Examination covering test periods of at least a month is issued by the National Physical Laboratory, Teddington, for marine chronometers submitted there. In recent years standard marine chronometers at sea have been increasingly replaced by electronically driven clocks using a quartz crystal or tuning-fork timekeeper.

See also ASTRONOMICAL NAVIGATION; LONGITUDE, DISCOVERY OF; NAVIGATION: Historical

Mariner's astrolabe

The mariner's astrolabe, in general use in the fifteenth, sixteenth, and seventeenth centuries, particularly in Spain and Portugal, was a heavy graduated circle with sights on a movable arm pivoted at its centre. It was suspended by a ring at the top of the circle to measure the ALTITUDE of the sun or a star.

This instrument was a simplification of the atronomer's astrolabe which was generally larger and of lighter construction, having the graduated circle and sight on one face and on the other a 'planisphere', a stereographic projection of the celestial sphere engraved with a graticule of altitudes and AZIMUTHS for the latitude of the place of observation. Concentric with this was a movable fretted disk, the 'rete', incorporating the ecliptic and with the points of the fretted pattern corresponding to the positions of selected stars. It was used in the same way as the ARMILLARY SPHERE to determine azimuth and HOUR ANGLE from an observed altitude. Invented by Hipparchus (c. 150 BC) or perhaps by Apollonius of Perga (c. 250 BC), such astrolabes were used by the Greek and Arab astronomers and many fine examples survive. In England, Geoffrey Chaucer wrote a treatise on its use for his son in 1352.

The simpler marine type was adapted by the German navigator Martin Behaim or Böheim for Portuguese seamen and used in their discovery of the sea route to India in the fifteenth century; in earlier forms the circle was not graduated in degrees but marked to show the height of the Pole Star at Lisbon and at known places on the African coast. Nearer to the equator the Pole Star was too low for observation and a graduated circle became necessary to measure the altitude of the sun and allow for its DECLINATION.

Mariner's compass

The earth is a magnet, whose poles do not correspond with the geographical ones. The mariner's compass is an instrument that detects the direction of the earth's magnetic field and by indicating magnetic north enables a ship to shape her course, or to determine her position relative to objects ashore.

The existence of magnetic compasses was first recorded in China in about AD 1100, in Europe about 1187. These records refer to periods at which compasses were already in use at sea and not to dates of invention. Given the difficulties of communication in those times, it is impossible to find in these dates any indication of the country in which the compass first appeared; it is probable that invention occurred independently in two or more localities.

The earliest compass was a piece of iron wire that had been magnetized by rubbing it on a lodestone (a naturally magnetic ore). The wire was thrust through a piece of cork or wood to form a cross and floated in a bowl of water. This compass was not used to steer by, but was consulted occasionally to check the direction of the wind by which the course was set.

The floating element tended to drift into the side of the bowl and become immobilized. By about the end of the thirteenth century a new design was being evolved in which the liquid was abandoned and the compass needle was supported on a pivot. It was necessary to make the arrangement slightly pendulous and the expedient was adopted of having two needles one on each side of the pivot. These were carried on a card that had a central cap to rest on the pivot. The card was marked with the 32 compass points (originally wind directions) into which the horizon was divided. When smaller divisions were needed, half and quarter points were added and later the whole circumference was divided into 360°, numbered from zero at N and S to 90° at E and W. In comparatively modern times it has been found easier to number it clockwise from zero at N to 360° at N again. The two needles were originally curved inwards to meet at N and S, but by about 1600 it was usual to bend them into the form of a diamond.

Compass bowls were originally of wood, but these were too fragile and by 1700 metal bowls were becoming common, although wood persisted for another century.

In 1745 the British scientist Dr Gowin Knight perfected a method of magnetization that enabled him to replace the old wire needles by a larger and harder steel bar. Since this retained its magnetism it was no longer necessary to carry a lodestone to sea. The use of a single-bar needle had a disadvantage whose cause was not understood for nearly a century. If the weight of the needle and card is not equally distributed about the N–S and E–W axes the needle tends, when a ship is rolling, to try to set itself in the plane of the roll. The early cruciform floating compasses and those with diamond-shaped needles met the requirement to some extent, but Knight's single needles did not. The problem was resolved by reverting to a plurality of needles at distances apart that follow certain laws.

A compass mounted on the starboard side deck of a Flying Dutchman. The illustration also shows the sheeting arrangement for the jib and toe holds

North

compass magnetic true

Westerly deviation
Westerly variation

True course

Magnetic course

Compass course

Ship's heading

(a)

North

magnetic compass true

Easterly variation
Easterly deviation

True course

Compass course

Magnetic course

Ship's heading

(b)

Compass variation and deviation jointly produce an error. The diagrams show (a) *westerly, and* (b) *easterly error*

– variation

Since before the time of Columbus it had been known that the compass needle did not point true N, but had an error that was not the same all over the world. This error became known as the variation. Compasses for use in restricted localities often had their needles mounted askew on the card so that the N point of the latter showed the true N. In 1635 it was found that the variation was not constant in any locality, but was subject to an annual change.

– deviation

As early as 1538 it was noticed that a compass might be caused to deviate by the magnetic attraction of a ship's iron guns, but it was the 1790s before it became generally accepted that neighbouring iron could give trouble. Previously, badly made compasses were blamed for compass errors. In 1801, during a voyage to Australia, Captain Matthew Flinders showed how one cause of compass deviation could be corrected by placing a vertical soft iron bar of suitable dimensions near the compass. In 1820 the English mathematician and optician Peter Barlow proposed to use an iron plate placed in the vertical plane beside the compass to correct it.

Increasing use of iron in shipbuilding made it essential that something should be done and in 1838 Sir George Biddell Airy, the Astronomer Royal, made experiments that showed that a ship's magnetism could be considered under four headings. First, a ship while building acquires magnetism that is reasonably permanent and, if the compass position has been well chosen, this can be

corrected by placing near the compass a permanent magnet, or two groups of magnets arranged respectively fore-and-aft and athwartships. Second, a ship becomes temporarily magnetized according to the course steered and to her position on the earth's surface. Known as the soft-iron effect, this can be corrected by the use of soft iron, usually spheres placed on each side of the compass. Third, vertical soft iron produces a magnetic pole before or abaft the compass and this can be corrected by a Flinder's bar. Fourth, magnetism below the compass produces a changing error as the ship rolls, correctable by a vertical magnet below the compass.

Compass correction was little practised until in the 1870s Sir William Thomson, later Lord Kelvin, designed a compass outfit that included a binnacle embodying all the COR-RECTORS suggested by Airey, after which compass correction came into its own. Thomson used a properly designed, very light card that practically eliminated friction on the pivot, thus producing a very accurate compass. Unfortunately increasing engine power caused hull vibration and this was liable to disturb the light card, but its popularity delayed the ultimate solution, a liquid-filled bowl and a needle system in which most of the weight was taken off the pivot by a float attached to the card. With little pivot friction the compass remains accurate, while the liquid damps out any tendency of the card to oscillate due to vibration.

Liquid compasses had been suggested by Francis Crow in 1813, but for many years there were manufacturing difficulties.

The strong needles of liquid compasses

induce magnetism in the spheres, helping to correct the compass so that smaller spheres can be used, but this has the disadvantage that the correction is no longer true for all latitudes. It has given rise to two schools of thought. If the strength of the needles is reasonably low and a good compass position has been provided so that initial errors are small, the change of deviation on change of latitude can be kept within acceptable limits. This is usual in Britain, but in some others compass errors are allowed to start too large. Much stronger compass needles are used and the spheres can then be replaced by small pieces of soft iron attached to the compass bowl. The elimination of the cumbersome spheres and the possibility of correcting a compass in a magnetically atrocious position is very attractive, but the soft-iron pieces do not provide a worldwide correction: large changes of deviation can occur as a ship changes magnetic latitude.

During the present century a number of systems have been perfected by which repeaters can be made to indicate the direction taken by the compass card. Only one good compass position need be found and the helmsman sees the same ship's heading as the conning officer.

See also BINNACLE; BOXING THE COMPASS; COMPASS CARD; CONN; WIND ROSE

Marine sextant *see* SEXTANT

Marline hitch; marlinespike hitch *see* ROPEWORK: Bends and hitches

Mast coat (gaiter); – heel; – partner;

– pot; – step; – tenon *see* MASTS AND RIGGING: Glossary

Masts and rigging

The function of a mast and its rigging is to hold up the sails and to transfer the driving force created by the sails to the hull and thus move it through the water. The earliest vessels moved by this means ran before the wind: the sail merely added to the wind resistance of the hull and crew, and increased the craft's speed downwind.

It was soon evident that the natural lateral resistance of the hull, being greater than the fore-and-aft resistance, made it possible to sail not only dead downwind but, at low angles of deviation, across it. A logical next step was to increase the lateral resistance, and probably the sail area, which meant a taller mast and something to hold it up – a rope to windward from the masthead to the hull. The process continued, from a taller mast with one rope on to several ropes, and from a taller and a stronger mast to several masts and more rigging.

As efficiency improved and angles of course across the wind provided greater scope, so lateral rigging became necessary, to the point where increased hull efficiency and rigging forward of the mast allowed a vessel to sail towards the wind. Square rig (*see* RIGS) developed elements of fore-and-aft rig; lighter hulls of improved shape provided lower forward resistance and greater lateral resistance, which was coupled with better sails and rig; new materials and building techniques furnished spars and rigging that were increasingly lighter, smaller, and therefore stronger – all of which has brought the sailing boat to the stage where it can sail fast on all points of sailing up to 30° into the wind.

The driving force of the sail and its shape, and the material from which it is made, are now so well understood that the modern mast is built and rigged to bend in the plane of the sail so as to flatten it on certain points and wind strengths, and to induce fullness on others to improve boat performance. Speeds under sail in extreme cases have exceeded 30 knots (*see* HIGH-SPEED SAILING) and will no doubt continue to improve as new materials develop: lighter and stronger for masts and rigging; more stable and controllable for sailmaking, and so on.

– masts

Early masts were extended beyond the natural length of available materials by adding a second, third, fourth, and fifth spar. This had the advantage of making masts easier to erect or step. More important, it allowed the mast to be reduced in height when it became necessary to reduce sail area (reef) as wind strength grew. The highest section was lowered (struck) as the wind speed increased.

A mast is a spar or pole, the bottom of which

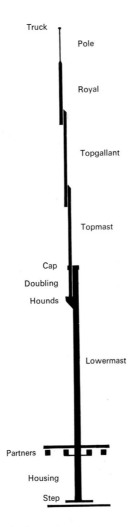

Fig. 1 Parts of a mast

is called the heel (there is a glossary of terms at the end of this article). The top, the head and masts, made up of several lengths, are defined (starting at the heel) as the lower mast, topmast, topgallant, royal, and pole. The overlap area is called the doubling; the lower part of this is termed the hounds, and the top the cap. The top of the pole has a wooden disk called the truck in which there is a SHEAVE that allows a flag or sail to be hoisted on a rope or halyard (from 'haul yard'; sometimes spelled halliard). The yard is a spar across the mast from which is hung or set a squaresail, or a gaff, which supports a fore-and-aft sail and pivots at one end against the mast.

The old solid-timber lower mast had its greatest girth at deck level where it passed through the partners. It tapered downwards to the heel where a tenon located it fore and aft in the step. It also tapered above deck to the cap. The hounds had wooden cheeks applied each side with crosstrees (usually termed spreaders on modern vessels), lateral

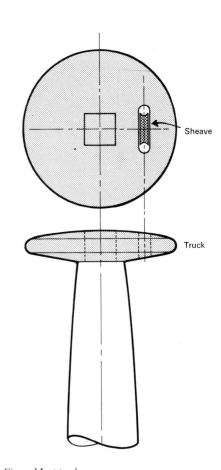

Fig. 2 Mast truck

timbers to spread the upper rigging and to provide a square to locate the lower end or heel of the topmast. This had a lateral sheave to raise or lower it and a lateral pin, or fid as it was properly called, to hold it in place under load.

These principles were perpetuated up the mast at each doubling. Lower masts were wedged at the deck with fitted wedges tapered over their length with a shoulder at the top like a tent peg and tapered in section towards the centre of the mast like the staves of a barrel. A coaming was fastened about the mast hole through the deck. The mast was wedged into the coaming and a mast coat (or gaiter) was seized round the mast and coaming, and painted to make a watertight seal about the mast where it entered the deck. Current practice differs little, but it allows controllable movement of the mast at deck level as rubber is generally used in place of wooden wedges, and butyl rubber for the mast coat in place of the old canvas.

Masts may be stepped on the keel, or on

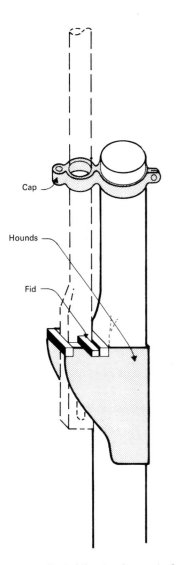

Cap

Hounds

Fid

Fig. 3 The doubling (overlap area) of a mast

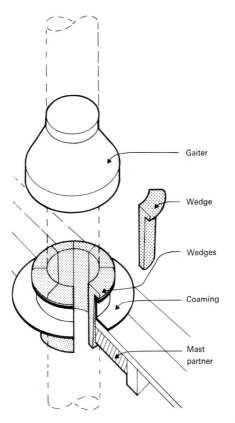

Gaiter

Wedge

Wedges

Coaming

Mast partner

Fig. 4 Mast components at deck level

Fig. 5 Mast pot

Fig. 7 Scarph joint

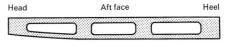

Head   Aft face   Heel

Taper   Solids

Fig. 8 Longitudinal and cross section of a hollow spar

Fig. 9 Cross section of a hollow spar of rolled, laminated spruce

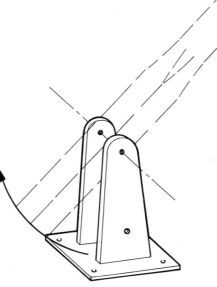

Fig. 6 Tabernacle

deck in a mast pot, or on a rigid fitting, or, in the case of masts that have to be lowered, above the deck in a tabernacle.

MATERIALS

Solid timber spars were usually made of pitch pine, a very good durable timber, but rather heavy; Oregon pine came in as pitch became less easily available and also Columbian pine, which was lighter; later Sitka or silver spruce was used as saving weight aloft became more important. Solid spars developed and, as glues became more reliable, timber was quartered and end-for-ended before being glued up, so that one part was in opposition to another. As spars mature, the natural solid spar can go out of shape, whereas the two parts of a cut and glued spar oppose one another and stay in shape. Efficient glue also allowed timber to be joined on end to build up a very much longer spar than nature could provide. The parts were scarphed together and the joins shifted out of adjacency with other joins. These advanced techniques allow taller pole-mast rigs, which are more

efficient and provide a good mast for the Bermudian rig.

As rigs continue to increase in height so size and weight reduction becomes more important. Hollow spars are built of many lengths of silver spruce, with solid parts for shroud attachments and spreaders. One of the lightest and strongest methods of building a hollow spruce spar, rolling out of cut laminates and gluing up, was developed by McGruer and Co. of Clynder in Scotland (fig. 9).

Masts and spars can be built up of steel, from rolled plate riveted or welded. Such masts have served many of the world's fastest clipper ships and 'J' Class yachts. A very much better material now used for the majority of yacht masts is seawater-resisting aluminium alloy. It is extruded to the required sectional shape, incorporates sail tracks or grooves, and is produced with the exact requirements of strength and weight per unit length. This material is one-third the weight of mild steel strength for strength; in a sailing yacht, up to 30% weight saving over the hollow spruce spar can be achieved with aluminium.

The extruded aluminium spar, unsurpassed during the last 30 years, continues to be the most universally accepted spar. Its qualities are superb and equally welcome to the naval architect, boatbuilder, repairer, marina operator, owner, and billpayer. Its contribution to the improved efficiency of the modern sailing yacht has been considerable.

Aluminium, produced from bauxite, has been developed during the last 170 years into the most-used non-ferrous metal. In its pure form, it is soft and not particularly strong, but its corrosion resistance is high and its specific gravity low – approximately one-third that of the usual structural metals. Alloyed with other metals, its strength can be greatly increased, and with heat and precipitation treatment this can be increased still further to form an extremely useful, light, high-tensile material. Alloyed with copper, the strength is high but its anticorrosive properties are low. Alloyed with manganese and magnesium, however, corrosion resistance is high enough to be suitable for marine application.

Aluminium can be rolled, formed, cast, extruded, and drawn. Drawing increases the strength a little and early aluminium spars were made very successfully from shaped drawn tube with extruded tracks applied. Increased production costs and the necessity for an ever-competitive product coupled with the development of improved heat-treatment techniques produced a stronger extrusion and eliminated the drawing operation.

Most mast sections are now extruded with the sail track or groove as an integral part and the material is heat and precipitation treated to give a theoretical tensile strength of from 19 to 21 tons per square inch. In practice, random tests of material from the best extruders seldom yield less than 22 tons per square inch. This material is known as HE 30; manufacturers have their own identification symbols, i.e. B51STF from Alcan, and 6061T6 its American equivalent, supplied also by the best European extruders. Mastmakers need to be aware of air-quenched alloys, which seldom exceed 17 tons per square inch. Many extruders produce this material; it makes good masts but they have to be larger and heavier to produce the required strength. This quality aluminium will anodize better and this facet alone may alert the maker to its weaker mechanical properties.

Extrusions are delivered in maximum average lengths of 40 ft (12 m) – some extruders can do better – and masts in excess of this length are made up of two or more sections. Most are joined with a riveted butt joint on an internal sleeve made of the same section with a longitudinal slice removed from it and

Fig. 10 Aluminium mast construction details: (a) *sleeved butt join and CSK pop rivet;* (b) *integral sail truck;* (c) *welded scarph joint in a mast with an integral luff rope groove;* (d) *mast taper*

closed to fit tightly inside. Smaller masts are riveted at the butts with cadmium-plated monel metal 'pop' hollow blind rivets, closed from the outside by withdrawing the mandrel upon which each rivet is pre-assembled. Butts in larger masts are fastened with countersunk stainless-steel screws.

The best racing masts demanding the maximum weight-saving and 100% fairness of bend are not butted on sleeves but are joined by a welded scarph: this eliminates the sleeve, saving the weight of some 3 ft of mast section per join and ensures a uniform bend throughout the length of the mast.

The upper end of most masts is tapered by removing a 'V' from each side, closing up and welding each seam. A mast taper is parabolic and the aft side of the mast remains straight with all the taper taking place on the forward face and each side.

Because of the nature of the alloy used both in aluminium masts and in the stainless-steel fittings applied, it is necessary to eliminate the introduction of oxygen while both metals are in a molten state, otherwise they will oxidize and ruin the fine properties necessary

to good sparmaking. Thus welding has to be carried out in a totally inert atmosphere of argon gas. The electric welding torch has a shield about the electrode into which is introduced a controlled flow of argon. This system of argon arc welding is widely and successfully used in manual, semi-automatic, and fully automatic applications.

The uniform bend of the sleeveless aluminium mast on Marionette, *the successful 1977 Admiral's Cup contender*

Plates profiled from aluminium sheet or plate are cut into and welded in place for masthead fittings drilled to take the clevis pins for forestay and backstay shroud attachments. Slots are cut at various places throughout the length of the mast section to take internal shrouds, and to act as internal halyard exits. Sail entry apertures are cut into the groove or track and the whole is mechanically polished, chemically etched, and anodized before final assembly, when polished stainless-steel shroud tangs are applied, and spreader sockets, halyard sheaves, spinnaker tracks, winch pads, cleats and goosenecks. Also fitted at this stage are: internal foamed polystyrene to deaden sound or lower the amplification potential of an aluminium tube when struck by a wire halyard; electric wiring in conduits for navigation and deck floodlights; electronic masthead devices, to measure wind speed and direction; and VHF radio antennae etc.

Internal halyards for raising and lowering sails, lifts for controlling booms and poles, all have to be installed. Mast-heel castings are applied and the aluminium mast of today is

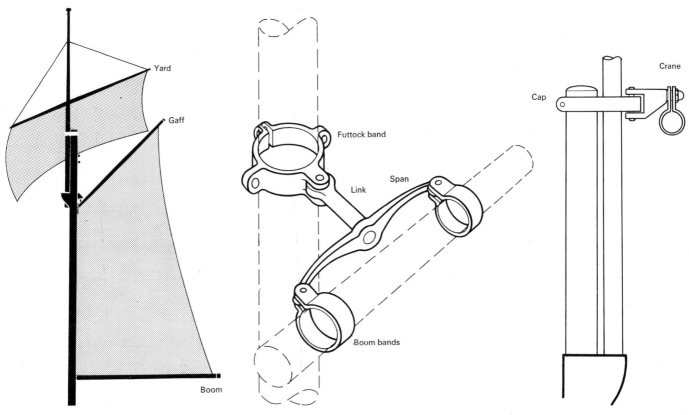

Fig. 11 Spars   *Fig. 12 Lower yard attachment*   *Fig. 13 Lower topsail attachment*

complete – and weighs much less than it would if it were built of any other known material offering similar ease of manufacture.

Fibreglass masts have been built to some effect in America and in Sweden, but because of the low strength-to-weight ratio of this material compared to aluminium alloy they have not proved a success in the racing field, and are now disappearing from the cruising scene.

YARDS

Yards are horizontal spars set laterally for carrying square sails. They are attached to masts in several orthodox ways, evolved through the ages to meet their complicated function of supporting a sail capable of being squared away (angled to the fore-and-aft centreline of ship as far as possible to allow the ship to sail closer to the wind) and at the same time clear the abundant lateral and fore-and-aft rigging.

A lower yard has to be held away from the mast to clear the lower mast stays or shrouds when squared away; it is also necessary for a lower yard to be set low enough below the forestay to clear it when squared away. In

addition, the overall width of the ship must be reduced when loading or discharging cargo when the yards would otherwise foul the wharf at low tide, and the dockside warehouses at all states of the tide. Thus the yards must be able to be tilted vertically (cock-billed), to increase the clearance beneath the forestay and above the shrouds to allow a greater angling of the yard and a consequent reduction in overall width of the rig. This calls for a yard-to-mast attachment special to each yard: the rigging configuration and its problems differ at each yard.

The lower yard attachment has a mast or futtock band, a link, a spar, and two yard bands all supported by a lift allowing universal movement in the limited arc required to clear all rigging and meet the various requirements.

The lower topsail yard carries a smaller sail, is shorter and less highly loaded and can therefore do away with the lift but it requires a crane, which again provides the required movement within the acceptable limits. Higher yards carry less sail, are shorter, and the loads are decreased further. These yards

are easily lowered or raised and are attached to sections of the mast that can be struck; thus they seldom have more than a band encircling the mast and attached to the yard allowing it to perform its own functions.

GAFFS

These are yards set fore-and-aft to carry fore-and-aft sails. They are pivoted against the mast with gaff jaws and parrel balls to hold them in place. The jaws are wishbone shape. The gaff is raised and lowered by two halyards, a throat halyard at the jaw end and a peak halyard at the outer end. The gaff can be squared away and the halyards adjusted to allow a good set to the sail. The peak can be dropped to spill wind to slow down or lessen the strain on gear.

BOOMS

Booms are fore-and-aft yards at the bottom of the sail, they are attached to the mast by a gooseneck, fixed on the mast to bands about it, or sliding up and down on a gooseneck track to allow tensioning of the luff and better adjustment to the shape of the sail. This gooseneck, whether fixed or sliding, allows universal movement of the boom so that the outer end can be raised or lowered and squared away to port or starboard when reaching or running, and hauled in taut when beating. All booms, particularly in larger vessels, should be allowed by the gooseneck to swivel about a horizontal axis. This is because the sail on the top of the boom and the opposing sheet at the bottom creates torque in the boom that varies on different points of the wind. To resist such torque would require an unnecessarily strong and heavy gooseneck fitting, so it is simpler to design into it freedom of movement and allow a smaller fitting.

Current sail trimming techniques demand close vertical control of the boom so a kicking strap (boom vang) is fitted from the forward one-third of the boom to the mast at deck level, or directly to a deck track or fitting, and the luff and leech of the mainsail are controlled by tensioning lines through reinforced holes in the sail called Cunningham holes (after the inventor of this technique of flattening or giving fullness to the sail as required on different points and strengths of wind). Full-width or simicircular tracks allow greater vertical control via the mainsheet.

Bendy booms intended to bend in the plane of the sail, thus controlling sail shape for differing wind strengths are used with good effect across the board in competitive sailing.

The sectional shape of masts to give the best aerodynamic results is a constant controversy and goes the full circle through the ages for reasons that seem plausible at the time.

SAIL ATTACHMENT AND CONTROL

Sails were attached to early masts with hoops of wood which were seized to the sail, and later by wooden parrel balls. Tracks and sliders appeared later: first, a galvanized-iron or brass track (fig. 15a) with a C-slider; then a C-track (fig. 15b) with a solid all-brass slider, later of anodized aluminium. Tracks were usually centre-fastened at first but as loads increased and tracks tended to be pulled off, they were side-fastened (fig. 15c).

Such tracks are used today but sliders are usually nylon injection mouldings or, in the larger, highly loaded examples, nylon-coated stainless steel. This form of attachment allows a mainsail to be raised or lowered easily with the minimum of effort and has the advantage of holding the sail captive to the mast when lowered or stowed. An alternative, said to be more aerodynamically efficient, is the BOLT ROPE-in-groove method. The rope sewn to the luff and foot of the mainsail slides in a slot shaped in the spar known as the luff or bolt-rope groove (fig. 15d).

Terylene (Dacron) sails have diminutive bolt ropes of low-friction high-strength man-made materials that slide in the modern groove of an extruded-aluminium spar. In a 12-Metre yacht, where the mainsail luff is about 85 ft (2.6 m) long, the rope diameter can be as little as 8 mm and the slot width

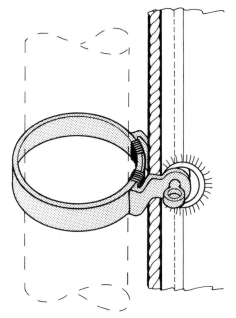
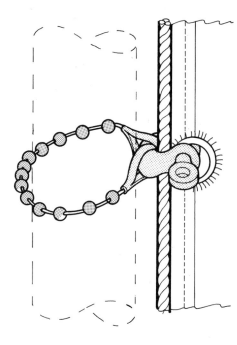

Fig. 14 Two early methods of bending sails to the mast; above, a wooden hoop and, right, parrel balls

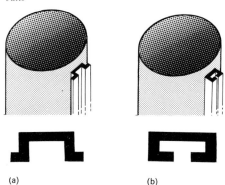

(a)   (b)   (c)   (d)

Fig. 15 Tracks and slides: (a) track for a C-slider: (b) C-track; (c) side-fastened track; (d) luff or bolt-rope groove

Fig. 16 (right) Groove attachment in a modern extruded aluminium mast

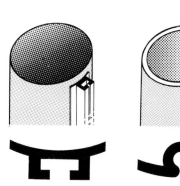
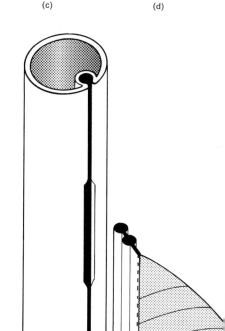

4 mm. This is very efficient under way but restrictive when lowering because the sail cannot bunch up or 'flake' on the boom and still be attached to the mast under control. Instead, it has to be hauled out of the groove and bagged or flaked on deck, which requires a large crew, particularly in the case of large yachts. This system therefore, works well for racing crews, but cruising boats tend to stick to tracks and slides.

To sum up, sails are set on booms and gaffs in one of the following ways:
1. loose footed, i.e. attached at forward and after ends of the boom only;
2. laced to the boom with hambro line through eyelets along the foot of the sail;
3. on a track attached to the top of the boom

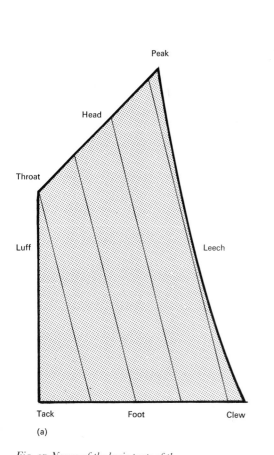

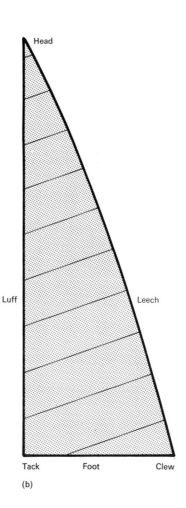

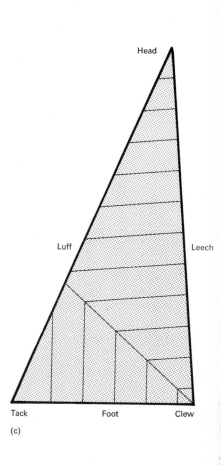

(a)
(b)
(c)

Fig. 17 Names of the basic parts of three common sails: (a) *gaff mainsail;* (b) *Bermudian mainsail;* (c) *jib*

and slides attached to eyelets in the sail; 4. in a groove on top of the boom where the foot rope on the sail slides into the groove.

Headstays are set usually on a stay with piston hanks – or set 'flying' without a stay for downwind or crosswind sailing, viz. spinnakers, tall boys, bloopers etc. Current racing practice demands high-speed sail changing and to this end the grooved headstay having two grooves has been developed; the stainless steel C-stay with single groove, the aluminium stay with two grooves at 180°, both types taking the full tensional loads, have been used with great success. Following these there have been a wide range of aluminium or plastic, double-grooved extrusions that embrace the standard wire or rod headstay, which takes the full tensional load. All have their merits and all speed up sail changing and, in some cases, help the flow of air across the sail.

All mainsails, mizzens, and the like set on masts and booms have to be firmly attached at the tack, usually in a fork on top of the vertical gooseneck bolt or pin by a horizontal

pin called the tack pin. This passes through the tack cringle, an eye reinforced into the sail at this point. A shackle or lashing may also be used.

The foot of the sail has to be tensioned – stretched out towards the CLEW – and this is achieved in several ways. Usually the clew has a slider in a track called the outhaul slide, and a wire or rope span over an outhaul sheave in the boom end, and forward to a PURCHASE outside or inside the boom; to a winch on the boom; or to a winch on deck by passing over a sheave or pulley at the forward end of the boom through a lead block at the mast-to-deck connection and back aft to a winch.

An alternative to this is the screw outhaul, usually reserved for roller-reefing booms. This has an outhaul carriage and track into which the claw cringle is pinned, as would be the case above, but the carriage is tensioned with a strong screw thread by a handle operated through the after face of the boom and, as a refinement in a smart racing yacht, also remotely from a second position at the for-

ward end of boom where the handle can be shipped to operate the outhaul through a set of internal bevel gears and a countershaft. This allows the sail to be adjusted while the boom is squared away and the outer end is beyond reach.

REEFING GEAR

Reefing or shortening sail to compensate for increased wind velocity and strength is a necessary facility for every vessel (*see also* SAIL TRIM). Different wind strengths call for different sail areas. Mariners in the days of square rig were able, as mentioned earlier, to shorten their masts. They reduced the sail areas for heavy weather, and as the wind strengths decreased they reset more sails and added sail area by attaching another piece of canvas, a 'bonnet', to the already set sail.

Headsails, jibs, and spinnakers are carried in a variety of weights and areas and are handed (lowered), and reset (raised) to suit the various wind strengths and conditions. Over the normal range of wind strengths, sails set on spars are made large and are set for light airs and reduced in area (reefed) as the wind increases. This is achieved in two basic ways, both of which have been in existence for very many years.

Points reefing, slab reefing, and jiffy reefing, depending on which century you live in, consist of hauling down a section of the sail from luff to leech parallel to the foot. This area might be a sixth or less of the total area of that sail. It is called the first reef. There is then a second, usually a third, and occasionally also a fourth reef. There is a reinforced cringle or eye at the luff and a similar one on the leech of the sail at each reef point. These have to be hauled down, usually on to a hook at the gooseneck and with a pennant or rope at the leech which is positioned to allow the sail to be pulled out taut as well as down, thus flattening the sail and doing the job of the outhaul. The bunt (middle portion) of the sail is then folded in on top of the boom and laced through eyelets provided in the sail for this purpose and under the footrope between the sail slides, making a neat parcel.

Modern racing techniques do not allow such a slow operation, so two contra-laced lines previously rove through these eyelets provide BIGHTS of line on each side of the sail to be hauled down and hooked over small clips fastened to the boom and open at the bottom – this is known as jiffy reefing.

Each reef has to be accommodated while the luff continues to be hauled down one eye upon the other on alternate sides, and the clew works forward on subsequent reefs due to the taper of the sail.

Early slab reefing was achieved with hemp reef pennants, a rope made fast to an eyebolt in the boom just aft of the position where the leech cringles would meet the boom. The pennant would be rove through the leech cringle and down through a wooden eye or bee block on the opposite side of the boom forming a fairlead and led forward to a purchase. Thus, as the halyard was slackened, the luff was hauled down and secured to the gooseneck, and the reef cringle pulled down to the boom and out to tension the new foot. Modern methods have speeded up and improved this system but the principle remains the same.

Roller reefing This system requires for preference a round boom, a clew outhaul at the after end in the normal way, and a swivelling end fitting to take the topping lift and the only sheet attachment allowable by the system and, usually, eyes port and starboard for attaching the boom foreguy (preventer) when required.

At the forward end is a gooseneck that performs the normal functions and is also able to rotate the boom around its fore-and-aft axis. This is normally geared, usually by a worm gear providing the maximum mechanical advantage with a non-return arrangement. Earlier gears perfected by Turner and

called after him had a ratchet and lever with a pawl; these were efficient but less easy and safe to use, particularly when shaking out a reef. In all cases the sail is attached to the boom in the normal way, but here the tack is attached to the boom and not the vertical bolt of the gooseneck as it has to revolve with the boom.

The operation is simple. The halyard is slacked away and the roller-reefing gear turned, the boom revolves, the sail is wound on, luff tension being applied by the careful control of the halyard (or winding of boom up the gooseneck track in the case of a sliding gooseneck). In this arrangement there is no provision for the leech to be hauled out and the sail flattened. The sail shape tends to be baggy and not so efficient when set.

Through-mast reefing is a development of roller reefing. The boom is revolved by a handle on the foreside of the mast *via* a shaft through the mast and a universal joint to the boom. In small vessels this can be a direct drive.

The claw ring used in roller reefing is a horseshoe-shaped fitting with rollers at the points and a sheave or block in the 'bight', which is located on the boom, suspended on its rollers. It provides an attachment for a

sheet lead or a boom vang along the boom where it can function at all times, allowing the sail to be furled onto the boom within the space between boom and fitting.

Because of the force induced into the claw ring by the angle of the sheet it is necessary to locate the ring along the boom by means of a light line to the gooseneck or outer-end swivel, or both, depending on the direction of this force.

There is today a popular headsail-reefing system that has a grooved aluminium extrusion revolving about the standard wire or rod forestay and a drum at the lower end on which there is a rope or wire led back to the cockpit. This is hauled in by a winch, thus reefing or completely furling the sail. By releasing this and hauling on the sheet, the sail can be partly or fully reset. This is a development of the old, well-tried system known as the Wykeham Martin gear.

Modern materials and techniques have improved this system and now it is not only available with electric control, but it has been used since the mid-1960s with great effect here and on the luff of the mainsail. Push-button headsail and mainsail control is available (with mechanical back-up in case of failure): ideal for short-handed yachtsmen.

Fig. 18 (a) *Standing rigging: sloop rig with single spreaders*

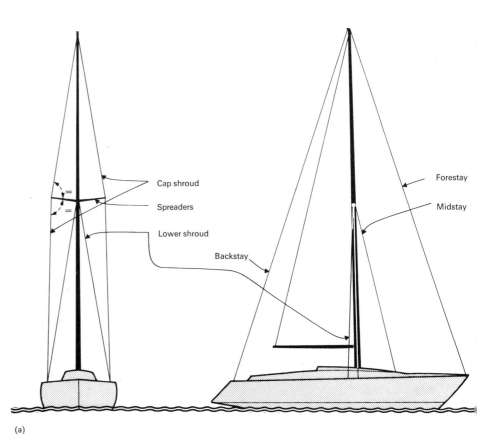

(a)

CROSSTREES OR SPREADERS

Crosstrees, now usually called spreaders, are struts that project outwards from a mast to the lateral rigging. Their outer ends are higher than the inner ends. Their function is to 'spread' the shrouds to increase the angle between the shroud and the mast at its attachment point and thus reduce the tension in the shroud and the compression in the mast it causes while increasing the effective staying angle. The spreader is thus under compression and its correct angle to the mast (dihedral) is governed by the change of angle at the shroud. The spreader must properly bisect this angle. In the modern yacht the usual shroud angles will demand a spreader dihedral of $5° - 6°$ above the horizontal or $84° - 85°$ to the mast. Spreaders can be round in section, or oval or streamlined aerofoils. To achieve ultimate efficiency they should present the minimum frontal area to the (head) wind and should therefore be a thin aerofoil. Because of the upward direction of the wind off the water, their major axis should be canted down about $16°$ (light tapes attached along a spreader will serve to confirm this angle).

The attachment of spreaders to mast should always allow some fore-and-aft movement.

Fig. 18 (b) *Standing rigging: cutter rig with double spreaders*

Rigidly attached spreaders have to be very strong, large, and heavy to oppose the shock loadings imposed by a gybing mainsail, or the weight and acceleration of slack lee rigging going to windward in a short steep sea, which a large yacht will show instantly. There are many methods of attaching spreaders to mast and shrouds to spreaders; some are good, many are bad. In general positive attachment at the mast allowing limited universal movement, and rigid attachment to shrouds allowing no movement, is a good and well-tried method.

– rigging

Rigging falls into two categories, referred to by self-explanatory terms: standing rigging is relatively rigid and holds up the mast and other fixed spars; running rigging is the flexible moving gear.

STANDING RIGGING

The components of fore-and-aft rigging are called stays: headstay, forestay, backstay and, in the case of the vessel with a bowsprit, bobstay, and in the modern yacht, midstay or baby stay, an innermost and low forestay.

The components of lateral rigging are called shrouds: cap shrouds, intermediate shrouds, lower shrouds, and main shrouds. The odd

man out is the portable stay called the running backstay or runner, a useful component for steadying the mast in a fore-and-aft manner when need arises; it has to be portable as its location prevents full movement of boom and sail out from the centreline.

Stay attachment, originally in rope, later in wire, was by a soft spliced eye served for protection and placed over the mast to embrace it completely and bear on a bolster or shoulder. Shroud attachment was similar, except that there was no spliced eye; a seized bight in each pair of shrouds would simply be placed over the mast and located on cheeks, and all rigging would be attached in a particular order which was common the world over.

Current practice differs in that spliced eyes or swaged terminals are located in a toggle, which provides the necessary universal movement in all headstays, forestays, and any stay with a sail set on it. The toggle is located between two lugs with a clevis pin passed through all three parts. Shroud attachments are similar.

Outside attachment was in galvanized steel bands or straps on early wooden masts and is in stainless steel on modern spruce masts; galvanized steel was used on early aluminium masts and stainless steel on later ones.

Shroud attachments are called tangs. Spade tangs are for fork terminals, forked tangs for eye terminals; the latter are more widely used at present. More sophisticated racing boats now have internal shroud attachments to reduce turbulence and the wind resistance of the rig as a whole. Thus the shroud disappears into the mast and is positively attached internally; the methods favoured vary with different sparmakers.

The quest of riggers and designers through the ages has been to reduce the stretch, weight, and wind resistance – in that order – of rigging materials. The early stays and shrouds were reed, later hemp, and the early very effective method of tensioning was with a rope purchase made up of lanyards and deadeyes. The best deadeyes were made from lignum vitae, greenheart, or hornbeam. Each had three holes allowing a six-part purchase to be achieved – this was multiplied by the parts of the additional whips and tackles used to set up the lanyards.

Because of the amount of stretch expected from hemp shrouds, there was no sense in splicing in the upper deadeye to the shroud, as in no time at all the purchase would be 'two blocks' or block on block owing to shroud stretch. The standard procedure, therefore, was to seize the shroud end about the upper deadeye. Three seizings were found to be sufficient and when the shrouds stretched these could be removed, the purchase overhauled to the full extent of the lanyard, and the deadeye reseized higher up the shroud.

Cap shroud
Upper spreaders
Intermediate shroud
Lower spreaders
Main shroud
Lower shroud
Runners

Headstay
Forestay
Midstay
Backstay

(b)

This process would be repeated throughout the life of the shroud.

There was, however, a risk that seizings might fail for one reason or another, and so as a precaution, which became accepted by seamen the world over, these three seizings were painted white and it was the duty of the watch officer to check every shroud at regular intervals. A failed seizing would be noticed immediately, and the possible disaster of a shroud failure and consequent dismasting averted.

To their credit, mariners in the early days of sail learned from their mistakes and those of others, agreed remedies, and put them into practice to the general benefit.

A long time after the lanyard and deadeye came the bottle screw or rigging screw (turn-buckle), which has continued in different metals and forms up to the present day. Shrouds tensioned with early forms of screw developed, and as loads increased, four rather than three seizings became usual but they were still painted white and treated with the same respect.

A major component in the support of any mast is the lower attachment of stay or shroud. It is highly loaded and its design and construction are every bit as important as any part of the mast.

Headstays, forestays, and backstays are secured on the stemhead fitting or some stout fitting on deck, usually through rods or bars bolted to the underdeck that transfer their great loads to the main frame, stem, keel, or horn timber, enabling these loads to be properly distributed throughout the hull. The shrouds are attached to shroud plates, or chain plates, bolted or welded to structural members or moulded into the hull shell. In the early days of sail they were often offset on bolsters away from the ship's side. These channels as they were termed (from 'chain-wales') were a very practical device that increased the staying base of shrouds, reduced the tension in the shroud and the corresponding compression in the mast, and made more effective the staying of the mast with the limited materials then available for shrouds. Channels were particularly important on the faster ships, such as tea clippers, which were by definition narrower in beam with more highly stressed rigging. Their purpose was much the same as that of the spreader. They held off a steel-bar chain plate: a bar, bolted through the planking, and doublers, bolted through the channel and gunwale, capable of taking the whole load of the shroud.

Chain plates or shroud plates to this day do the same job but are not led over wales to increase their staying base. On the contrary, high-strength rigging allows shrouds to be set inside the full width of – admittedly, wide-beam – boats. The resulting low shroud angles are exploited to permit highly efficient overlapping sails to be set flatter and closer to enable the yacht to sail closer to the wind. More highly stressed rigging and lower shroud angles make the shroud plate just as important as ever it was and its proper design, construction, and attachment to strong members of the hull remain just as necessary.

Iron-wire rigging developed into steel rigging. Construction and lay have become progressively more scientific. High-grade galvanized-steel (plough) 7×7 rigging remains the best of the non-stainless standing rigging. For some years 1×37 stainless-steel rigging was used in racing yachts, but now the universal norm is 1×19 stainless steel with rotary-hammer-swaged terminals. (Swaging properly done is excellent and should be left to the accredited experts. A bad swage is as dangerous as a broken seizing but impossible for anyone but an expert to recognize.) A more advanced standing rigging, used in racing yachts, is available; this is rod rigging whose construction is solid, of one single rod, and has minimal stretch for maximum strength and minimal size and windage. However, because of its lower ductility it

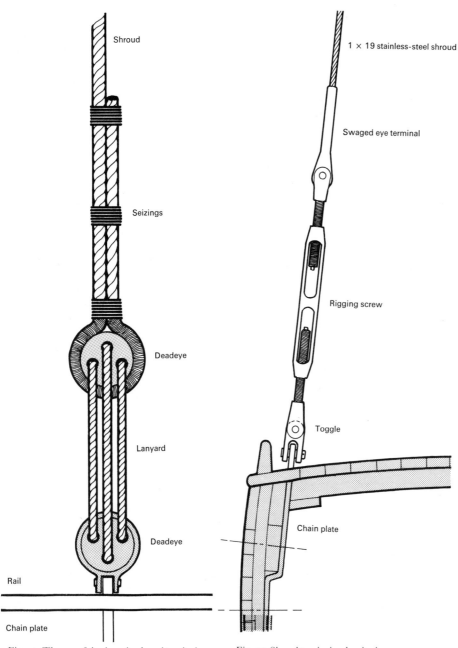

Fig. 19 The use of deadeyes in shroud tensioning

Fig. 20 Shroud tensioning by rigging screw

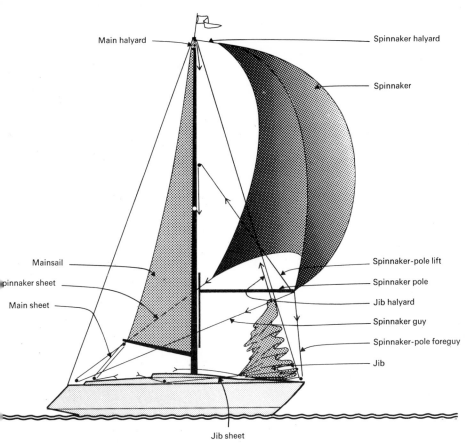

Main halyard

Spinnaker halyard

Spinnaker

Mainsail

Spinnaker sheet

Main sheet

Spinnaker-pole lift

Spinnaker pole

Jib halyard

Spinnaker guy

Spinnaker-pole foreguy

Jib

Jib sheet

Fig. 21 Running rigging of a sailing yacht – the basic components

is more prone to fatigue than other forms of standing rigging and is not recommended for long passages. These rods are threaded and used with screwed terminals or rotary-hammer-swaged terminals and can be excellent.

Swaged, formed, or screwed terminals cover the whole range of alternatives to solid-rod rigging, but besides splicing (possible, but not very practical in 1×19) there are other methods of terminating wire rigging. There is the pressed ferrule (Talurit is the trade name in Europe, Nicopress in the United States), which is a metal collar embracing both parts of wire round a thimble, i.e. the standing part and the spent part. This is clamped together in a hydraulic press and develops about 60% of the breaking strain of the wire per ferrule. There is also the 'swageless' screwed terminal, produced by various manufacturers. This is also very good.

Tuning the standing rigging system, usually learned by experience, is very logical and can be achieved with thought and a little practice. Some masts require more care than others, depending on their strength and the corresponding amount of rigging required to support them. Here again fashion changes with the passing of time. The late 1970s have brought the return of the flimsy spar with its

accompanying mass of rigging, requiring careful adjustment to produce an advantageous shape. A momentary lack of attention can result in disaster when the whole system goes overboard.

For a time streamlined rod rigging, sometimes called lenticular, was considered superior to the ordinary kind. But it fluttered at certain wind speeds, and eventually fatigued and failed. It has a small following now.

The continuing search for greater efficiency will demand reduction in windage and weight, increase in stress and, therefore, strength. New materials and techniques will doubtless come into use for rigging and for spars. The next breakthrough will almost certainly be achieved by the carbon-fibre mast and spars. Carbon fibre is an excellent unidirectional material of great stiffness and light weight. It can produce a spar 40% smaller than an aluminium spar of the same weight, 40% lighter than an aluminium spar of the same size – and 40% stronger for equal size and weight. It has a great future once it becomes economical and techniques for making good masts of it have been developed.

RUNNING RIGGING

The components of running rigging, the halyards to raise and lower sails, lifts to raise and lower booms and poles, sheets to handle

sails, guys to control booms and poles, are handled variously as size and loads differ.

In the sailing dinghy most gear can be worked by hand. In any larger craft such gear was handled with purchases or tackles in the early days; later with the early capstan, windlass, or winch; and today, with highly developed winches into which the power of several men can be introduced. There are also hydraulic rams, windlasses, and electric winches used in various ways.

The average modern cruising yacht has drum or reel winches on the mast to handle halyards and two, three, or more drum winches in the cockpit to handle sheets. External halyards are led straight to the mast winches; internal halyards are led over exit sheaves or, currently, through slots and over stainless-steel anti-chafe strips to the winch drum and on to a cleat.

The racing yacht of the last few years has no winches on the mast so as to reduce the above-deck weight and windage of the winch and of its operator – a considerable factor in any size of boat going to windward. Instead the halyards are led through lead blocks at the mast-to-deck intersection to deck winches where their weight is lower, their wind resistance less, and their crews, in many cases, down in crew cockpits where their strength is more effectively applied and their weight and windage less of a penalty.

Cleverly designed and well-engineered systems of shafts and bevel gearboxes are now available that enable one or more men to insert a handle into a deck socket, or several deck sockets, connected by shafts and gearing into a remote winch barrel. Thus the power of several men can be introduced into the winch barrel to handle a highly loaded halyard or sheet, from positions where they are: not impairing each other's efficiency; not necessarily creating unnecessary windage; and if properly managed, are in such positions as to be aiding the correct ballasting of the yacht.

All this improves the efficiency of the modern sailing yacht and contributes to the increased loadings that are applied to masts and rigging, and of which the mast designer and builder must take account.

Belaying pins. Halyards and sheets in the early days of sail were made fast or belayed to vertical wooden or iron pins called belaying pins. These were like a handle on top with a flange or shoulder that prevented them from dropping through the hole in the supporting rail. They were a loose fit in the rail and, depending on the size of vessel, they were usually of such a length as to allow 6 or 7 in (152 or 178 mm) above the rail and the same amount below. A halyard or sheet would be belayed by forming a figure of eight about the pin. The excess rope would be coiled and the bight of the last coil would be passed round the coil and through it to form a 'gasket' and the bight passed over the head of the pin, thus supporting the whole coil. The whole point of this excellent arrangement, not bettered since, was that in the event of any emergency, or normal course of action requiring the instant release of the sheet or halyard, it was necessary only to withdraw the pin from the rail and the complete gasket collapsed, allowing the belayed halyard instant freedom for its whole length. A highly loaded belaying pin could still be removed by taking a maul (heavy hammer) to it.

Today the cleat, a useful fitting, seems to have superseded the belaying pin. The halyard is still coiled the same way and the gasket still used by the informed, but the release cannot be so instant as it is necessary to unlay the halyard from the cleat before release is possible.

Jamming cleats are a refinement that allows one turn of the cleat to reduce the load in sheet or halyard and then the part is jammed beneath the inclined plane of one end of the cleat. Release is instant by reversing the process. The reliability of this cleat is not as positive as the belaying pin, so jamming cleats, although good, are seldom used on heavily loaded rigging.

Cam jammers are used widely today, particularly in the racing yacht where instant and positive locking of a sheet or halyard is required, and the process can be quickly reversed. The cam jammer is a serrated-edged cam, mounted horizontally or vertically in a channel on a strong bolt. The channel wall facing the serrated edge of the cam is also serrated, and the rope passes between. Moving in one direction, the rope opens the cam and can therefore pass freely, but when the direction is reversed, the cam tightens onto the rope jamming it against the non-moving serrations of the channel. The tighter the rope is pulled, the tighter the jamming effect. Instant release is possible by reversing the load in the rope and releasing the cam.

Such cams mounted in train between block and winch can be of enormous help by allowing several sheets or halyards to be led to one winch. As the task of hauling one halyard with the winch is completed, the load can be held by the cam and the fall thrown off the winch, which is now available for the next task, i.e. handling a sheet or lift etc.

Cam jammers and cam cleats have the disadvantage that they cause more wear to lines, and do not permit a line under tension to be eased gradually through while still under control. The one-horned jam cleat and the conventional two-horned cleat give complete control even against great tension or a flogging line.

– glossary

Babystay The stay from the lower spreader to foredeck on modern sailing yachts.

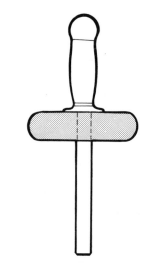

Fig. 22 Belaying pin in its supporting rail

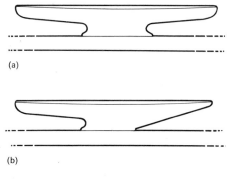

(a)

(b)

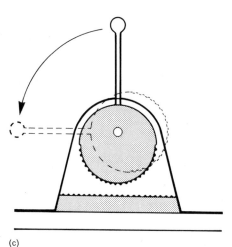

(c)

Fig. 23 Cleats: (a) *standard:* (b) *jamming:* (c) *section through a cam jammer*

Backstay The stay from the masthead to counter or transom.

Bail Strong eye on boom for attachment of sheet.

Bee block A wooden fairlead on the side of boom to pass reef pennant.

Belaying pins Stout pins through the rail for securing halyards and sheets.

Bobstay The stay holding down the bowsprit or bumpkin from the outer end to the lower part of the stem; generally a rod or chain.

Boom Horizontal yard at the foot of a fore-and-aft sail.

Boom-end reef sheaves Pulleys in the end of a boom to take reefing pennants.

Cam jambers Cams to jamb ropes in spars or on deck.

Cap A band encircling the head of the lower mast in early multipart masts; the head of a modern mast.

Cap shroud Rope, wire, or rod standing rigging from masthead to deck or linked at the spreader end.

Chain plate A metal strap, formerly of iron or bronze, to which the lower ends of the shrouds are secured on either side of the vessel.

Claw ring Horseshoe-shaped fitting to support a sheet block at mid-length of a roller-reefing boom.

Cleat A T-shaped unit bolted to spars or decks to secure halyards or sheets without taking a hitch.

Clevis pins Pins of galvanized or stainless steel with head and split pin for attaching shrouds and stays to tangs, heads etc.

Coaming A raised flange about the mast hole through the deck on which the mast coat is secured (also the raised lip around other deck openings).

Crane A metal bracket between the cap and yard.

Downhaul A line for hauling down a sail.

Eyes Eyeplates of stainless or galvanized steel attached to spars for running rigging.

Fairlead A fitting radiused to locate and allow free passage of rope or wire with minimum chafe.

Fid A wedge through the lower end of topmasts, topgallant masts, and royal masts to secure them and take the whole thrust.

Forestay The stay from the upper spreader to the foredeck.

Futtock band A metal band about the lower masthead to take a yard crane.

Gaff A spar to which the head of a quadrilateral sail is bent; it is usually set fore-and-aft.

Gate Controllable entry of sail track for sail slides.

Gooseneck A hinge unit providing universal movement at boom-to-mast or boom-to-pedestal attachment.

Guy Line used for controlling the lateral movement of booms and poles.

Halyard, halliard Line of hemp, sisal, galvanized steel wire, stainless-steel wire, nylon, Terylene (Dacron), or polypropylene that raises and lowers sails, signals, flags etc.

Headstay The stay from masthead to the bow.

Horse A bar on which the sheets can travel laterally, as with a self-tacking staysail.

Hounds Supports on a mast for the shrouds and lower rigging.

Intermediate shroud Rope, wire, or rod rigging span from the inner end of the upper spreader to the outer end of the lower spreader.

Jackstay A wire or rope pendant used as a support.

Jambing cleat A quick-action jambing version of the cleat.

Jib sheets The lines from the clew of the jib used for controlling the jib etc.

Jockey pole (reaching strut) The pole used from the side of the mast to push the spinnaker guy away from the mast, opening the angle of guy to the pole end when the spinnaker is carried shy and the pole end is on, or nearly on, the forestay. The opening of this angle allows the pole still to be controlled from aft by the guy.

Kicking strap (boom vang) A wire or hydraulic span between boom and deck at mast to check vertical movement of boom.

Lanyard A short length of rope, used generally for setting up the rigging.

Lift Lines, of rope, wire, nylon, Terylene (Dacron), or polypropylene, that support and control the hoisting or lowering of booms and poles.

Link A metal universal toggle between futtock band and span.

Lower shroud Rope, wire or rod rigging span from inner end of lower spreader to deck.

Lug Strong plate eye in spar for attachment of rigging.

Main halyard The hemp, nylon, Terylene (Dacron), polypropylene or flexible wire rope that runs from the head of the mainsail over a sheave in the masthead and down to a winch and cleat to haul the mainsail aloft. There are also jib, mizzen, spinnaker, and staysail halyards.

Mainsheet The line used for controlling the mainsail boom or main boom.

Main shroud Rigging span from the outer end of the lower spreader to the deck where upper rigging terminates at the outer end of the lower spreader.

Mast The vertical spar in a vessel that carries sails, signals, lights, or aerials, or a combination of all of these.

Mast coat (gaiter) A canvas or butyl-rubber coat about the mast at deck to effect a watertight seal.

Two types of kicking strap: top, *the more conventional kind;* right, *a hydraulic kicking strap*

Masthead The top of the lower mast in early multipart masts; the top of the pole mast in modern sailing vessels.

Mast heel The bottom or butt of the mast.

Mast partner A strengthening chock beneath the deck planking between the main deck beams through which the mast passes.

Mast pot A metal plate and flange in which a deck-stepped mast is stepped.

Mast step The strengthened part in a vessel into which the mast heel fits. It takes the whole compression of the mast.

Mast tenon The fore-and-aft third of the mast heel that locates and directs the mast in the step.

Outhaul Tackle or screw for hauling the clew of a sail out to the boom end and tensioning the foot of the sail.

Outhaul purchase Purchase or tackle to haul sail to extreme end of the boom.

Parrel A rope or fitting to hold a spar to the mast. The jaws of a gaff and the yards of a square-rigged ship are held to the mast by parrels in a manner that allows them freedom of movement.

Parrel balls Small wooden balls with holes for a lanyard used for attaching sails to spars.

Partner(s) – see **Mast partner**.

Pendant A hanging line, such as the reef pendant by means of which the cringle is hauled down.

Ratlines Steps formed by seizing lengths of rope to the outer shrouds of a sailing vessel to provide a ladder in the rigging.

Remote screw outhaul A gearbox and shaft to control screw outhaul from forward end of the boom.

Rigging – see **Running rigging; Standing rigging**.

Rigging screw (turnbuckle or bottle screw) A metal body with a fork or eye threaded into each end, one with a lefthand and the other with a righthand thread, so that the action of rotating the body results in contracting or extending the distance between the two forks or eyes. With fine threads and high-tensile material, this unit is capable of great power, and its purpose is to set up and tension rigging.

Roller-reefing gear Mechanical equipment to revolve the boom to reef sail.

Runner A portable rigging span from the spreader root to the deck giving fore-and-aft support.

Running rigging The ropes or wires, called halyards, lifts, and sheets, by means of which the sails are handled and set.

Screw outhaul Screwed gear to haul sail to extreme end of the boom.

Sheet Line of rope, wire, nylon, Terylene (Dacron), or polypropylene used for the control of sails and booms.

Shoulder The remaining port and starboard thirds of the mast heel at the top of the mast tenon.

Shroud Rigging that gives a mast lateral support.

Socketed terminal A conical socket formed into an eye or fork into which a wire end is reeved, and the parts of the wire are unlayed for a short distance and turned into the centre through $150°$, thus doubling the girth and forming a cone pulled into the neck of the conical socket, and held in place by pouring hot zinc, or other molten metal, into the cone.

Span A metal yoke attaching a link to yard bands.

Spinnaker guy The line from the spinnaker boom and spinnaker tack or weather clew used for controlling the spinnaker boom.

Spinnaker pole downhaul The rope used for hauling down the outboard end of the spinnaker pole.

Spinnaker pole heel downhaul The rope, wire, or chain used for lowering the inboard end of the spinnaker pole on track slider.

Spinnaker pole heel lift The rope, wire, or chain used for raising the inboard end of the spinnaker pole on a track slider.

Spinnaker pole lift The wire or rope used to raise or lower the outer end of the spinnaker pole.

Spinnaker sheet The line from the clew of the spinnaker used for trimming or controlling the spinnaker.

Spliced eye An eye worked into the end of a line by interlacing the parts of the rope or wire through the parent material.

Spreaders (crosstrees) The compression struts that hold the shrouds away from the mast to increase the angle of shroud to mast and make the whole system more effective.

Spreader sockets Sockets of galvanized or stainless steel or aluminium that hold the spreaders to the mast.

Standing rigging The ropes, wires, or rods that hold up the mast and distribute the driving force of the sails to the vessel.

Stay Standing rigging that supports the mast in the fore-and-aft direction.

Swaged eye A steel eye terminal, usually of stainless steel, whose hollow shank is placed over the end of a wire and compressed uniformly into the lay of the wire by a rotary hammer or press to form an eye of great strength.

Swaged fork A fork produced in the same manner as a swaged eye.

Swageless terminal A screwed eye or fork terminal made to slip onto the wire and grip the lay about a conical wedge forced into the heart of the wire and screwed tightly into place.

Tabernacle A deck fitting in which a lowering deck-stepped mast is stepped.

Tack downhaul Tackle for hauling the inboard end of the main boom down its track (booms on sliding goosenecks only), thus tensioning the mainsail luff.

Talurit or Nicro pressed eye An eye in the end of a wire formed, usually around a thimble, and clamped to its parent part with an aluminium or copper ferrule, which is pressed into the lay of the wire with a hydraulic press.

Tang Highly stressed fitting, usually of galvanized or stainless steel, sometimes aluminium alloy, for attaching shrouds to the mast.

Toggles Used at the head and foot of all stays on which a sail is set and on all shrouds between the rigging screw (turnbuckle) and shroud plate. This component provides universal movement and takes the bending load out of all rigging so equipped – essential in any well-found vessel.

Topping lift A rope or flexible wire that takes the weight of a spar while it is being hoisted or lowered. In yachts the topping lift supports the outboard end of the boom or spinnaker pole.

Tracks Used for sail slides on masts and booms, goosenecks, spinnaker sliders, genoa lead blocks, mainsheet blocks etc; it can be internal or external.

Traveller A ring or similar fitting by means of which the tack of a sail is hauled out along a spar, as with a bowsprit, or a sail is hoisted, as with a lugsail.

Truck The wooden cap at the masthead with a sheave or holes for the burgee halyard.

Truss A metal yoke unit for attaching a yard to the mast.

Vang A line leading to the outer end of a gaff or sprit to steady it and prevent it sagging to leeward when on the wind. *See also* KICKING STRAP

Winch pad The base on which a halyard or sheet winch is mounted.

Yard A spar for carrying sails, usually set laterally.

Yard bands Metal bands about a yard for attaching a spar.

Match racing, match-racing rules *see* YACHT RACING

Mean sea level

This is generally understood to refer to the level of the sea in the absence of tidal variations. Mean sea level is perturbed by meteorological phenomena, notably barometric pressure and wind stress, variations in water density, dynamic effects arising from marine currents, and long-term geophysical phenomena associated with tectonic movements of the solid earth and changes in volume of the world ocean. Thus it is highly variable in both time and space and has no meaning unless associated with a particular location and a particular period. It is customary to refer to mean sea level appropriate to a certain day, month or year, and related to a precise coastal station. In common parlance heights of terrestrial features are sometimes related to mean sea level. This arises especially where a national survey levelling network is referred to a mean-sea-level datum. For example, land surveys in Great Britain are referred to Ordnance Datum, Newlyn. This datum is defined as mean sea level at Newlyn, in Cornwall, calculated from a six-year tide-gauge record between 1915 and 1921 and established physically by reference to a local fixed mark. By 1960 mean sea level at Newlyn had in fact risen more than 100 mm above Ordnance Datum.

Basic data usually takes the form of a continuous record of sea level referred to a local survey bench mark. Removal of the effect of tidal oscillations demands care. The simple mean of successive high- and low-water heights can be deceptive, especially where there are shallow-water distortions of the tidal profile. Greater success is achieved by taking the arithmetic mean of sets of successive hourly elevations over a period of 25 hours. In most modern work, mean sea level is computed by the successive application of a numerical tidal filter. A low-pass filter with a cut-off on the low-frequency side of the diurnal tidal band would achieve this result. In practice the method most commonly used is a simple filter devised by A. T. Doodson that can be applied to a span of 38 hours of data. This filter has a complex response function that is approximately zero at each tidal frequency band. Using this filter the tide-free level at time t is calculated by taking $\frac{1}{30}$ of the sum of 30 elevations of the tide before and after time t at the following intervals in solar hours:

19, 17, 14, 12, 11, 2(9), 7, 6, 2(4), 3, 2, 2(1)

i.e.

$$\frac{1}{30}\left[E_{(t+19)} + E_{(t-19)} + \ldots\ldots 2 \times E_{(t+9)} + \right.$$
$$\left. + 2 \times E_{(t-9)} + \ldots\ldots 2 \times E_{(t+1)} + 2 \times E_{(t-1)} \right]$$

where $E_{(t+19)}$ represents the observed elevation at time $t+19$ hours.

Values of mean sea level for each day may be achieved by successive overlapping applications of the filter at intervals of 24 hours in t.

Values of mean sea level for each month are calculated as the simple arithmetic mean of daily values within the calendar month. The variation in the number of days in the month is commonly ignored. Since at this stage it is not possible to eliminate long period tidal effects, values of mean sea level contain a contribution from small amplitude tides of fortnightly and monthly period.

There is a pronounced and complex oscillation revealed within a year's span of monthly values. This contains small tidal effects with periods of a solar year and of six months, although usually these tides are submerged beneath seasonal meteorological effects. The

seasonal variations in mean sea level are of the order of 20 cm in range in the United Kingdom with a maximum level in November and a minimum in April/May. The range can be much greater elsewhere, particularly in regions affected by the monsoons: at Calcutta the range is 1.4 m with a maximum in September and a minimum in January.

Yearly values of mean sea level contain a contribution of the order of a few millimetres from the lunar nodal tide with a period of 19 years.

Of considerable interest is the evidence, afforded by studies of mean sea level, of long-term movements of sea level with respect to land. It has been established that near the head of the Gulf of Bothnia the land is rising with respect to the sea at a rate of 9 mm per year, whereas in southeast England the opposite is happening, at a rate of approximately 2 mm per year. Not all this motion is in the solid earth since the world ocean level seems to be rising at a rate of approximately 1 mm per year.

Studies of the topography of the mean sea level surface at a particular epoch, the use of mean sea level as a connection between separate survey levelling networks, and the comparison of survey levels along coastlines with levels derived from oceanographic considerations comprise the discipline of coastal geodesy.

Under the international sponsorship of the Federation of Astronomical and Geophysical Services, a Permanent Service for Mean Sea Level collates and publishes mean-sea-level data from every accessible recording station around the world.

Mean time
Time based on the rotation of the earth relative to the mean sun.

Mercator projection
A conformal cylindrical projection, used for most marine charts, in which the earth's surface is conceived as developed on a cylinder tangent at the equator. Its convenience for navigation stems from the fact that all RHUMB LINES on the projection cut the meridians at the same angle. Its defects are a scale that varies with latitude and the fact that the nearer the poles, the greater the degree of distortion. Named after Gerardus Mercator (Gerhard Kremer), the Flemish geographer (1512–94). *See also* MAP AND CHART PROJECTIONS

Meridian
A semi-GREAT CIRCLE joining the two poles.

Meridian altitude *see* NOON SIGHT

Meridional parts
The distance on a Mercator chart along a

projected meridian from the equator to any parallel of latitude, measured in minutes of arc on the constant longitude scale allowing for the ellipticity of the earth.

Midshipman's hitch *see* ROPEWORK: Bends and hitches

Miss stays
A vessel is said to miss stays when she fails to tack and has to fall back on the original tack.

Mitre
The seam in a sail joining cloths the weaves of which run in different directions.

Mizzen, mizen
A fore-and-aft sail set on the mizzenmast (the aftermost mast on two- and three-masted vessels, the third on craft with four or more masts). In yachts mizzen generally refers to the sail. *See also* RIGS

Monitoring sailing performance
The ability to measure quantitatively the performance of a yacht under various conditions of wind and sea and on various points of sailing is valuable for several reasons. Firstly, standards of performance can be established against which the effects of changes of sail design, ballasting, etc. can be tested. Secondly, the yacht can be trimmed when racing to achieve the highest performance without the need to test the effects of trim and heading changes against other similar craft in the vicinity. Thirdly, having established the best heading in relation to the apparent wind direction, the instruments can be used to assist the helmsman to maintain that heading.

Absolute accuracy of measurement is not necessary: the important requirement in the design of instruments is that the consistency, or repeatability, of their readings over a long period of time is of a high order.

– performance calculation
The measurements that are required to enable the performance to be estimated are:
1. The speed of the hull through the water
2. The apparent wind direction in relation to the fore-and-aft axis of the yacht
3. The apparent wind speed
4. The leeway angle (i.e. the angle between the fore-and-aft axis of the yacht and her direction of motion through the water)

The term 'apparent wind' is used to distinguish between the true wind, as felt by a stationary observer, and the wind that is felt on board a moving vessel. The vessel's motion in effect generates a wind equal and opposite to her velocity and this compounds with the true wind, as shown in the 'triangle of velocities' in fig. 1, to produce the resultant vector V_a (i.e. the velocity of the apparent wind). If it were not for the effect of leeway the apparent wind angle β, would be that

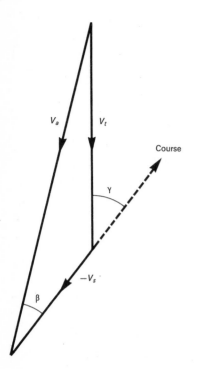

Fig. 1 *The true wind velocity is represented by the vector V_t, the self-generated wind due to the yacht's velocity by $-V_s$ and the apparent wind velocity by V_a; β is the apparent wind angle and γ the true wind angle*

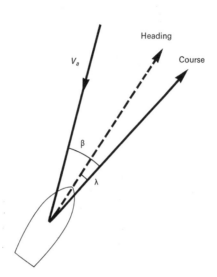

Fig. 2 *Due to the effect of leeway, the fore-and-aft line of the yacht is inclined by the angle λ to the course vector, V_s. The burgee or wind-vane angle is therefore $(\beta-\lambda)$*

shown by the burgee or wind vane (fig. 2).

The leeway angle, which is the angle between the course that the yacht makes good through the water and the fore-and-aft line, is negligible except when sailing CLOSE-HAULED. The close-hauled leeway angle of a modern racing yacht is typically $5°$ in light to moderate wind strengths. Therefore if, for example, the wind-vane angle is $28°$, then β is $33°$. The corresponding value of the true wind angle γ can be calculated from the following trigonometrical equation containing the measured quantities V_s, V_a and β.

$$\sin \gamma = \frac{\sin \beta}{\sqrt{\left[1 + \left(\dfrac{V_s}{V_a}\right)^2 - 2\dfrac{V_s}{V_a}\cos \beta\right]}} \qquad (1)$$

– the windward performance criterion

It is generally agreed that the point of sailing that is of most importance to the yachtsman is when the boat is close-hauled. Most races are won or lost on the windward leg and the safety of a yacht when caught out near a LEE shore will often depend upon her efficiency in sailing to windward. For any given value of wind speed this efficiency is measured by the 'speed made good to windward', generally

abbreviated to V_{mg}. V_{mg} is the boat's velocity resolved into the direction of the true wind: i.e.

$$V_{mg} = V_s \cos \gamma \qquad (2)$$

(fig. 3). γ is obtained from equation (1).

To help in understanding the concept of V_{mg} a motorboat may be imagined proceeding in company with a windward-going yacht but steering dead into the eye of the wind. If its speed is adjusted such that the yacht remains always ABEAM (relative bearing $090°$) then that speed is equal to the yacht's V_{mg}. If the yacht TACKS it will approach the motorboat from abeam on a collision course and, if the racing mark is dead to windward, the two vessels will reach it simultaneously. Clearly, the larger the V_{mg} the shorter will be the elapsed time on the windward leg. Even though the windward leg may not lie exactly parallel with the wind direction it still follows that, regardless of which may be the more favourable tack, the golden rule still holds good i.e. the yacht is trimmed for maximum V_{mg} on both tacks. The motorboat will then have the windward mark dead abeam at the instant when the yacht reaches it and the elapsed time is still a minimum. The golden rule ceases to apply only when the mark is so far from the windward RHUMB line that the

yacht may go for it without tacking. She must then simply be trimmed for maximum speed through the water.

The object of the crew when sailing to windward is at all times to keep V_{mg} at its maximum value. In bearing away from the wind V_s increases but $\cos \gamma$ decreases. In hauling closer to the wind V_s decreases but $\cos \gamma$ increases. The art of windward sailing lies in seeking the compromise that gives the product its highest value. In monitoring the windward performance one compares the peak V_{mg} value for a given wind speed with a previously attained standard. The computation of V_{mg} from equations (1) and (2) is obviously too lengthy and tedious to be carried out at sea. Books of V_{mg} tables and a graphical V_{mg} calculator 'Hawk' have been prepared by Brookes & Gatehouse Ltd of Lymington that cut the time of computation down to a few seconds. The 'Hawk' enables also the true wind angle γ to be obtained. An electronic computer, 'Horatio' (manufactured by the same firm), is available which automatically accepts the V_s, V_a and β electrical signals and indicates V_{mg}/V_t. The leeway angle λ is set in by hand.

The advantage of using the V_{mg}/V_t ratio over using V_{mg} alone is that the value of this term is practically independent of the wind speed over quite a wide range of wind speeds. Therefore, when the crew is trimming for best performance the results of their actions are not seriously invalidated by the changes in V_{mg} that occur through changes in wind strength. Nevertheless, large and random variations in V_{mg}/V_t do arise in all except steady, light-wind conditions due to wave action on the hull and to rapid wind shifts. In the electronic computer these are partially averaged out by 'smoothing' circuits. In manual computation it is advisable to take several readings of V_s, V_a, and β and to calculate their mean values. This work can be done in a matter of seconds on a pocket calculator.

For those who may wish to make their own performance calculator or computer program the relevant equation is:

$$\frac{V_{mg}}{V_t} = \frac{\dfrac{V_s}{V_a}\cos \beta - \left(\dfrac{V_s}{V_a}\right)^2}{\sqrt{\left[1 + \left(\dfrac{V_s}{V_a}\right)^2 - 2\dfrac{V_s}{V_a}\cos \beta\right]}} \qquad (3)$$

Messrs Hewlett Packard of the United States manufacture a programmable pocket computer on which the V_{mg} equation may be solved.

Since the 'Horatio' computer gives a direct read-out of V_{mg}/V_t, optimization can be continuously carried out by making slight changes in course angle and holding that angle which gave the highest meter reading.

– the reaching performance criterion

When sailing with the wind free, sheets are

trimmed simply to attain the highest value of V_s. The efficiency of the yacht is assessed in terms of the ratio V_s/V_t. For practical purposes, for example in determining the effects of sail changes, sufficient accuracy is achieved by calculating the ratio V_s/V_t, 'Horatio' provides a direct read-out of this quantity.

– the running performance criterion
The down-wind leg is not necessarily sailed in the shortest time by steering straight for the LEEWARD mark. In light winds, particularly, it may pay to sail a zig-zag course as some yachts sail faster with the wind over the quarter than when it is dead astern. As with windward sailing, speed through the water is traded off against extra distance to sail such that the speed made good in the direction of the true wind attains a maximum value. The

vector diagram for down-wind sailing is shown in fig. 3(b). The performance tables and calculator mentioned include downwind V_{mg} data.

– the performance chart
If the optimum value of V_s for a given wind speed on each course angle γ to the true wind is plotted on polar graph paper, it is possible to see the complete performace figure at a glance (fig. 4). Data may be accumulated over a period of time to produce a family of curves for different wind speeds. These are useful when racing for such purposes as:
1. Estimating whether a spinnaker should be prepared for the next leg of a course
2. Determining the correct downwind tacking angle
3. Monitoring the boat's speed for any

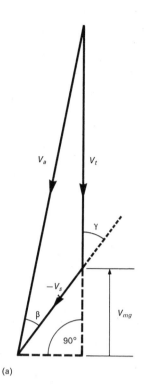

(a)

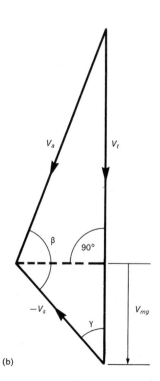

(b)

Fig. 3 Two examples of how speed made good (V_{mg}) is found from velocity triangles: (a) *to windward* (b) *to leeward*

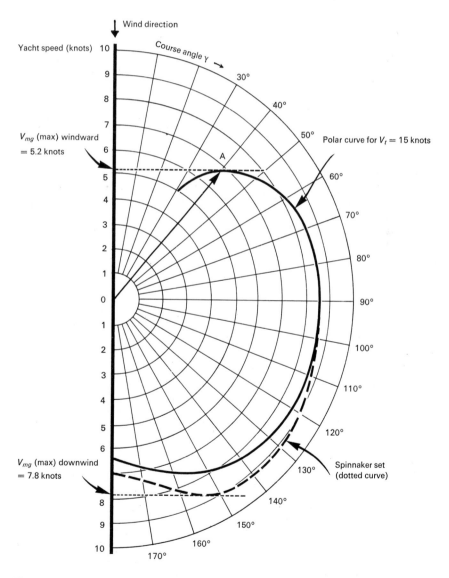

Fig. 4 Polar performance diagram for one particular value of true wind speed. The distance *from the centre O to any point on the curve represents the speed (V_s) of the boat in that direction*

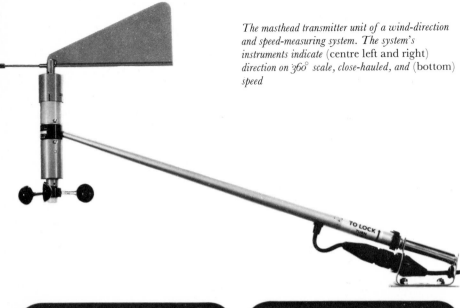

The masthead transmitter unit of a wind-direction and speed-measuring system. The system's instruments indicate (centre left and right) direction on 360° scale, close-hauled, and (bottom) speed

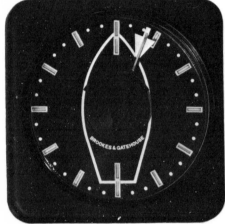

entirely negligible at that point, particularly with masthead rigs. Errors of up to 3° have been measured when sailing to windward. The strut would have to be several feet long if sail-deflection errors are to be avoided. However, they appear to be reasonably consistent and although they lead to errors in the calculation of V_{mg}, at least they do not affect the accuracy with which one can seek and sustain peak windward performance.

Three indicators are normally provided (fig. 6). These indicate:

1. The wind direction on a 360° scale, for REACHING and RUNNING.

2. The wind direction on a 15°–45° scale, for close-hauled sailing. The requirement for accuracy in course-holding to windward is higher than can be achieved by means of a 360° scale. This 'magnified' indicator is read easily to within 1° at a distance of several feet.

3. Wind speed: normally 0–60 knots with a logarithmic scale.

YACHT SPEED

The miniature through-hull magnetically coupled impeller, developed in 1962, has stood the test of time (fig. 7). Operating on the end of a fin below the turbulent boundary layer adjacent to the hull the impeller provides standards of accuracy and consistency comparable with those of the towed, or 'taffrail' log. The liability of early designs to become clogged by weed has been overcome by the use of the novel form of deflector fin shown in fig. 7. The impeller in its two forms of propeller and paddlewheel is the most commonly used type of sensor for yacht speedometers and logs.

Several firms have developed for small craft the so-called electromagnetic system of speed measurement that has been used in naval and merchant ships for many years. There is no rotor or other moving part. The flush-mounted transducer contains an electro-magnet and has two metallic probes on its lower surface that are in contact with the water. The interaction of the magnetic field and the moving water generates a small electric potential that is sensed by the probes. This potential is proportional to the speed of flow. It is amplified by transistors and rectified, and is then applied to the speed meter. This system is becoming increasingly popular in the smaller racing yachts because of its low water drag, but suffers from errors due to its operation within the boundary layer. Regular cleaning of the transducer face is essential in the interest of consistency of speed indication.

In order that very small changes in speed may be observed, many makes of yacht speedometer have provision for displaying a 'magnified' reading. A typical magnification factor is 5, giving the effect of increasing fivefold the length of the speedometer scale. A control knob is provided to enable the pointer

particular course angle against previous performance

In fig. 4 the distance from the centre *o* to any point on the curve represents the speed of the boat V_s in that direction. Dropping a perpendicular from that point on to the vertical axis enables V_{mg} to be read on that axis. When the perpendicular is tangential to the curve, as at *A*, V_{mg} is at a maximum (5.2 knots) and V_s is 6.8 knots. The true wind angle is 40° and the yacht will therefore tack through 80°.

– **sailing instrumentation**

WIND DIRECTION AND WIND SPEED

The transmitters, or sensors, of nearly all makes of windgauge for yachts use a weather-cock vane fixed to the shaft of an electrical potentiometer for wind direction and a rotary cup-type anemometer driving either a small generator or a reed switch type of make-and-break contactor. The electrical circuits required to convert the outputs of the sensors into meter readings are simple. Nevertheless the prices of most windgauges are high owing to the need for excellence in mechanical design to ensure operation without failure for

long periods of use in all weather conditions.

The two sensors are normally combined in a single assembly that is mounted on a strut projecting above and ahead of the mast cap where it is clear of turbulence created by the mast and is not fouled by the burgee (fig. 5). The effect of the sails on the direction and speed of the wind is unfortunately not

The 'Hermes' impeller-type boat-speed sensor and its deflector fin (below) *and* (beneath) *a digital speed indicator*

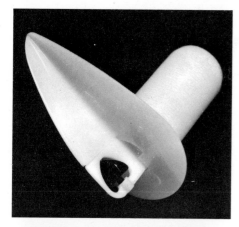

to be brought back on to scale when the limits are exceeded. When this facility is switched on the meter serves as a variation indicator only and the actual speed can no longer be observed. However, in some makes a separate meter is provided for the magnified display. Several firms are now manufacturing digital speed indicators (fig. 8) that overcome the problem of reading the true speed while simultaneously seeing small changes in a single display. The last digit represents one-hundredth of a knot.

LEEWAY ANGLE
No means has yet been devised for measuring leeway satisfactorily. Articles have appeared in journals on the design of instruments that depend upon the use of a towed drogue and the measurement of the angle between the drogue line and the yacht's fore-and-aft axis. This angle is not equal to the leeway angle since the water in the wake of the yacht has a lateral motion due to side force on the hull and keel. Also, the towed line is deflected by the wind. The value of λ used in calculating V_{mg} is generally taken from the yacht designer's data.

The unavoidable errors in the measurement of β and λ, both due to flow distortion, mean that performance monitoring cannot be treated as an exact science. It is, however, a very considerable aid to the evaluation of changes of sailing efficiency and to the optimization of trim etc. when racing.

ADVANCES IN COMPUTERIZATION
The digital computer has not, with one exception, been used on board yachts for the automatic monitoring of sailing performance, mainly because most clubs forbid its use when racing. However, no such ban exists in the racing rules for the *America*'s Cup: in the 1977 campaign the three American and one Swedish 12-Metre yachts contending for selection were fitted with digital computer systems. These accepted data continuously from the electronic sensors, which measured water speed, wind speed, and wind direction.

These computers were designed to perform three main tasks:
1. To record the data from the sensors continuously during the trials and working-up period for subsequent analysis by larger, shore-based computers. This analysed data was stored on magnetic tape for reference and comparison purposes.
2. To calculate and display continuously performance and tactical data (e.g. V_{mg}/V_t true wind direction, apparent wind direction, and speed on next leg of course.
3. To calculate and display continuously the position of the yacht in relation to the next mark of the course using data from the electronic log and an electronic compass.

The development of the microprocessor has made it economically worth while to manufacture custom-built digital computers for many applications where hitherto computerization has been out of the question. It is therefore likely that yacht-instrument manufacturers will soon offer automation in quite a wide range of navigational functions at prices that most yachtsmen will be able to afford.

See also HULLS; NAVIGATION: Under sail; PERFORMANCE AND YACHT DESIGN; SAIL TRIM

Moor
To anchor a vessel with two anchors so that she lies between them; also to make fast a vessel head and stern between two buoys or piles, or alongside.

Mooring buoys *see* BUOY

Multihulls
A multihull has two or three parallel hulls joined together with a connecting structure. The wide overall beam gives the stability to carry sail. The hulls, which are relatively long and narrow and light, give a potential speed advantage over ballasted craft. The Pacific Islands were settled over 2000 years

ago by people who originated in Southeast Asia and voyaged in simple double- and triple-hulled craft made and rigged without any metal tools or fittings. When Europeans reached the Pacific they were surprised to find the islanders' multihulls sailing over twice as fast as the ballasted European craft.

There are three distinct types of multihull. The catamaran (from the Tamil *kattu*, 'to tie', and *maram*, 'wood') now describes a double-hulled vessel with equal-sized hulls. The name trimaran, coined by Victor Tchetchet in the 1930s in New York, refers to a triple-hulled vessel with the central hull larger than the two outrigger hulls. Proa (from the Malay *prāū* or *prāhū*) today means a craft with two unequal-sized hulls symmetrical about amidships and so rigged that it can be sailed in either direction, always keeping the smaller outrigger hull (Polynesian: *ama*) to windward. A recent variation of the proa, sometimes referred to as an Atlantic proa, has relatively equal-sized hulls, but keeps the *ama* to leeward and the heavier main hull to windward where its weight contributes most to stability.

Europeans designed and built a few multihulls based on descriptions by the early European explorers, but none of these were close enough copies to realize the potential of the native multihull types. Nathanael Greene Herreshoff (1848–1938), the brilliant Rhode Island yacht designer and builder, made several catamarans about 30 ft (9 m) long in the 1870s. One of these was successful enough to beat the entire NEW YORK YACHT CLUB racing fleet in 1876, for which the reward was banishment from all further club races. In 1937 Eric De Bischop sailed *Kaimiloa*, a catamaran he designed and built on the beach at Waikiki, from Hawaii to France with Joseph Tatiboet.

Development of reliable waterproof glue and marine-grade plywood during World War II encouraged a postwar wave of multihull interest. While the former British Olympic canoeists Francis and Roland Prout were perfecting their 17-ft (5-m) Shearwater catamaran (250 of one model were built the first year) and subsequent larger cruising catamarans in Canvey Island, Essex. Woody Brown and Alfred Kumalae in Honolulu designed and built *Manu Kai*, a 38-ft (11-m) catamaran that was soon being used to take tourists sailing off Waikiki Beach. At the same time Victor Tchetchet was experimenting with trimarans on Long Island Sound, New York. A few Frenchmen made long ocean passages in catamarans, inspired by De Bischop's example.

These early pioneers soon had competition from many other designers, builders, and experimentors. Dr John Morwood in Hythe, Kent, England founded the AMATEUR YACHT RESEARCH SOCIETY, which helped early efforts (and continues to help) by publishing data on new developments throughout the world. Louis Macouillard and Arthur Piver started independently to design, build, and sail multihulls on San Francisco Bay in the mid-1950s. Piver sailed his 30-ft (9-m) *Nimble* trimaran transatlantic, wrote the first of three books and was then off on a design and sales spree that got hundreds of sailors afloat in their own home-built triple-hulled vessels. Early claims for multihulls could not always be backed by facts, and this turned away many experienced seamen reared in the tradition of ballasted craft. Design progress has since enabled catamarans and trimarans to live up to their proponents' enthusiastic claims. Based on the success of the early Hawaiian catamarans, Rudy Choy, Warren Seaman, and Alfred Kumalae (CSK) combined to design and build catamarans that dominated the southern California and Transpac race scene in the 1950s and 1960s. Bob Harris's 17-ft (5-m) *Tigercat* won *Yachting* magazine's One of a Kind Regatta in 1959 and was put into production. In England, Rod Macalpine Downie's designs dominated early racing, which started in 1960, for the 'Little America's Cup' in C-Class catamarans – 25 ft (7.6 m) maximum length; 300 ft² (28 m²) maximum sail area. In recent years Denmark, Australia, and the United States have won this match-racing series in this most sophisticated of all racers. Lack of the kind of rule restrictions that often hamper development in monohull classes has encouraged innovative thinking on the multihull frontier, best exemplified by George Patterson's introduction of the pivoting wing mast that has now evolved into solid wing sails with elaborate camber control to give superior windward performance, achieving excellent lift/drag ratios.

The Macalpine Downie-designed proa *Crossbow II* holds the speed sailing record of 31.8 knots for 0.5 km. Designer-builder Lock Crowther's catamarans and trimarans have been popular in Australia and New Zealand and range the world. Commodious cruising catamarans and trimarans from many designers have found favour with coastwise and transocean voyagers. Some are appreciated for their non-heeling and shallow-draught characteristics rather than ultimate performance.

Designed and built by American Richard Newick, the 34-ft (10.5-m) experimental wood/epoxy PRO$_a$ *(top) has its outrigger carried to the windward in the Pacific Island style*

Manureva, *the trimaran in which Alain Colas and Eric Tabarly achieved so many sailing feats. Alain Colas and his boat were lost at sea during the first Route du Rhum race (St-Malo, France, to Pointe-à-Pitre, Guadeloupe), in 1978*

The first multihull to sail around the world was Colin Mudie's 40-ft (12-m) design *Rehu Moana*, in the able hands of Dr David Lewis who raced her in the 1964 *Observer* Single-handed Transatlantic Race (OSTAR) and was then joined by his family for the rest of the voyage. The solo Atlantic race and the two-man Round Britain race (RBR) are rare in that all types of craft are accepted to race together with a minimum of restriction other than the number of crew. Such intense competition has encouraged comparison and evaluation of new developments that would be almost impossible otherwise. These races were inspired by H. G. 'Blondie' Hasler and are run by the ROYAL WESTERN YACHT CLUB of Plymouth, Devon, England with sponsorship help from the London *Observer* newspaper. Derek Kelsall raced a Piver trimaran in the 1964 OSTAR and won the 1966 RBR in his 42-ft (13-m) trimaran design *Toria*, which pioneered glass/foam sandwich-hull construction in England. André Allegre designed and built for Eric Tabarly, the aluminium trimaran *Pen Duick IV*, later renamed *Manureva*, by Alain Colas, who won the 1972 OSTAR in 20 days, 13 hours, 15 min, and then sailed solo around the world in the incredible time of 167 days with only one stop, averaging 175 miles a day, a single-handed record that bettered Sir Francis Chichester's time by 63 days and may stand for a long time to come.

It is unlikely that ballasted craft of similar size or cost will ever again be able to consistently do well racing against multihulls. Not having to carry non-structural weight, cats, tris, and proas can be lighter and shallower, giving them access to cruising areas inaccessible to deeper, heavier vessels. Drying out between tides offers multis no problems, so that they depend less on shipyard facilities for maintenance and repairs. However, their inevitable wide beam is a disadvantage in marina slips, adding to berthing expense or forcing the use of moorings. Folding and variable-beam designs such as John Westell's 30-ft (9-m) *Ocean Bird* trimarans have successfully addressed this problem. Many sailors appreciate the comparatively upright sailing angle of a multihull. Life aboard can be more pleasant at the usual 10° maximum heel compared to 20° or 30° in ballasted craft. The trade-off here is a livelier motion in a SEAWAY due to light weight and wider beam. With proper hull shape this need not be excessive. Payload is generally less for multihulls than for monohulls of comparable size, except where performance is not important.

Initial stability of multihulls is comparatively greater, but in extreme conditions, the ultimate stability of a ballasted vessel at 90° of heel permits those with strong decks and hatches (properly closed) to regain an upright position from even a 180° capsize posi-

tion. Until now, such a capsize in a seagoing cat or tri required outside assistance to right. At the 1976 Toronto Multihull Symposium Carlos 'Jim' Ruiz of San Salvador proved with a scale model that seagoing self-righting multihulls can be made using selectively floodable watertight compartments, boomed-out water ballast bags and inflatable buoyancy, all to induce re-capsize over the bow instead of sideways as the means by which small day-sailing catamarans are righted. At about the same time, Nicholas Clifton, working with designer Derek Kelsall, installed a similar system on Clifton's 1976 OSTAR entry *Azulao*, a 32-ft (9.75-m) trimaran. The breaking of two watertight hatches after a capsize during a later cruise caused this particular system to malfunction.

Many offshore catamarans and trimarans are now being built incorporating these self-rescue principles. The capsizing of large vessels is rare, but none is completely safe from the devastating chance combination of a sharp squall and an extra steep sea. Given these improvements, crews of properly designed offshore multihulls have as good a chance of sailing into port after a capsize as the crews of ballasted craft. Living aboard a capsized vessel until the weather moderates enough to permit righting is not so much of a problem as the sinking of a ballasted craft might be.

Lightweight vessels need materials with good strength to weight ratios. Sheet plywood and cold moulded veneer were most common in early multis. Fibreglass, almost universal now, is fine for small craft, but in sizes over about 26 ft (8 m) it becomes too heavy for many hull and deck applications unless it is used as the outer skins of a 'sandwich' with a lightweight core such as end-grain balsa or polyvinyl chloride foam. Aluminium is practical for larger hulls and is almost universal for the connecting structure in multihulls under 20 ft (6 m) long. Carbon fibres and epoxy will be seen more as volume production lowers the prices. Several types of unidirectional fibres can be used effectively in highly stressed areas such as boards, rudders, trunks, mast steps, and connecting structures.

Below water, hull cross sections vary considerably. The minimum wetted surface semicircle is most common for small craft used in sheltered waters. Offshore vessels generally have deeper sections with narrower waterlines for an easier movement through the waves. Keel rocker is more acceptable in narrow fast hulls than it is in fast single-hulled vessels. High speed potential makes full-ended shapes with a high prismatic coefficient desirable so long as sharp bows are maintained. Light multihulls may tack slowly due to lack of inertia so optimum rudder size and keel rocker are important design considerations. Asymmetry, with the flatter side

away from the vessel's centreline, can develop useful resistance to leeway. Hobie 14 and 16 hulls, and the early CSK catamarans, are good examples of this type, that save the expense and bother of centreboards. For maximum windward performance, however, boards are valuable. Hydrofoils, which can add to stability, are occasionally used to 'fly' the whole craft. The overall beam for racing catamarans and trimarans has slowly increased over the past 30 years as intense competition has encouraged lighter weight. Sail-carrying power is a function of weight and overall beam, so a given sail area requires more beam as weight decreases. Other important considerations for high performance multihulls are minimum hull waterline beam, low WINDAGE, and adequate clearance over the water for the connecting structure.

Sailing technique for light craft differs from that used in ballasted vessels. REEFing is required sooner and quick reaction time is important in squally weather when acceleration on the face of a sea can surprise sailors used to more sedate craft. Bearing away in a squall rather than LUFFing up is the best practice on some courses. Greater speeds accentuate the difference between real and apparent wind, which is drawn ahead. Waves, square running, or close hauled sailing slow any sailing craft unless it is light enough to surf on waves from astern.

Major offshore races in which multihulls participate are the annual Crystal Trophy race from Cowes to Plymouth via Cherbourg and Wolf Rock (305 miles), the annual Round the Isle of Wight race (60 miles), the semi-annual Newport to Bermuda race (640 miles), the Los Angeles to Hawaii race (2225 miles), and the Ensenada race (125 miles) from Newport Beach, Cal., to Ensenada, Mexico. The *Observer* Singlehanded Transatlantic Race from Plymouth, Devon to Newport, Rhode Island (2900 miles), and the Round Britain race starting and finishing in Plymouth (2000 miles) are held every four years. The annual Brisbane to Gladstone race (309 miles) is the principal event in the Antipodes. In the Caribbean there is the annual St Maarten Tradewinds race (755 miles); and the Azores and back and MOCRA Azores races from Falmouth to Punta Delgada, and from Portsmouth to Horta (approximately 1200 miles each way), and the Route du Rhum (4000 miles) from St-Malo, France, to Guadeloupe, French West Indies, have recently been started.

Whereas in the offshore classes, opinion continues to be sharply divided as to the relative merits of two or three hulls, in the smaller, day-sailing classes catamarans predominate.

The development of fast, day-sailing catamarans, or 'cats' as they are universally

Olympic class Tornado catamarans (above), *at the start of a trial. Their two symmetrical hulls, connected with aluminium, may be of wood, wood and GRP, or GRP sandwich*

The single-handed Hobie 14 catamaran (right) *is simple to sail and so has become deservedly popular. The GRP-sandwich hulls are asymmetrical, there are no centreboards, and the rudders are of the kick-up type*

known, has taken place entirely since World War II. Britain and the United States have been the leaders in development, followed by Australia, Denmark, and Sweden and, to a surprising degree, the USSR.

In Britain, experimenters such as Don Robertson, P. V. Mackinnon, and Ken Pearce led the way in the early postwar years, but it was the Prout brothers (*see above*) who first succeeded in producing a commercially successful catamaran, the Shearwater. The Mk III version of this design became a national class and is still built and keenly raced today. By present standards it seems a some-what heavy and chubby boat, but because the design of the rig has always been left open in class rules, a great deal of useful development of streamlined rotating masts and fully battened sails has taken place.

The Shearwater, and other designs such as the Macalpine Downie-designed Thai, established a basic 'English' style of catamaran with approximately semicircular sectioned hulls, and centreboards or daggerboards, but it was not until the mid-1960s that a Post Office engineer, Rodney March, produced the classic of this *genre*, the Tornado.

Compared to earlier designs, the 20-ft (5.5-mm) Tornado catamaran sloop is exceptionally slim-bowed and fine-lined, a shape that is only practical if the boat can be kept very light. This is achieved by a special type of construction generally referred to as 'tortured ply' in which two sheets of plywood are first joined along the keel line with GRP tape and then forced into shape in a jig. This method produces a stressed-skin hull of exceptional stiffness and lightness and, when powered by the Tornado's very efficient, high aspect-ratio sailplan, produces a boat of enormous speed potential. There are now, in addition, competitive Tornados built in GRP, but the original form of construction still appears to be the best.

In a series of trials organized by the INTERNATIONAL YACHT RACING UNION to find a B-Class catamaran suitable for international competition, the Tornado proved to be the outstanding design. Acceptance by the IYRU was the first step along the road to the Tornado's becoming the first catamaran to sail in the Olympics: in 1976 at Kingston, Ont.

Attempts by the IYRU to produce a range of sizes of catamaran for international competition proved much less successful. The single-handed Australis cat has failed to achieve any wide popularity, and most people who are interested in this type of sailing seem happier with the Unicorn.

Although development of catamarans in the United States originally proceeded along similar lines to Britain, things changed quite dramatically with the appearance of the Hobie cat. This was designed by Hobie Alter, an American West Coast surfing enthusiast, who arrived at the shape of the Hobie more by trial and error than any academic process of design. What emerged was a boat well adapted to the open beaches and big swells of the West Coast. Centreboards were eliminated by giving the centre part of the boat a deep, narrow section, and this makes the Hobie simple, strong, and cheap to build. With its very high ends and deep centre section, the Hobie has a pronounced 'banana' shape, which gives it both a remarkable ability to survive in big waves and a marked tendency to capsize end-over-end if mishandled.

The single-handed Hobie 14 and two-man 16 have been an enormous commercial success and are by now by far the most numerous multihull class in the world, and one of the most numerous of any small boat (there are over 30 000 of the 16 sailing and actively racing worldwide). In spite of their slightly cranky sailing characteristics, the Hobies are fast, very exciting, and above all simple to sail and maintain. This is in fairly sharp contrast to a boat such as the Tornado, which requires a good deal of skilled and careful looking after.

The recently introduced 18-ft (5.5-m) Dart class represents an interesting attempt to combine the advantages of the Hobie and the Tornado in the same boat. Designed by Rodney March, it is like the Hobie in having no centreboards, and like the Tornado in having long, slim bows, a straight sheer, and basically semicircular section hulls. Lateral resistance is provided by an ingenious streamlined SKEG. The Dart can be sailed by either one or two persons, with or without a jib.

Racing a high-performance catamaran is intriguingly different from racing a normal dinghy: particularly downwind. In fact, catamaran racing has been described as dinghy racing 'inside out' because the running leg seems to have the tactical character of the beating leg in a dinghy race.

This is because catamarans normally 'tack downwind' in a series of fast broad reaches that get them to the leeward mark much more quickly than running straight downwind. For the same reason, spinnakers are not normally found worth while on cats.

Although all small-boat sails are a compromise between the varying requirements of different wind speeds, catamarans can afford to concentrate more on the higher apparent wind speeds that their performance so often creates. For this reason, fully battened sails and streamlined, rotating masts are found to be an advantage. In a tall rig of high aspect ratio such as the Tornado's, mainsail twist is at once all important and it is quite common to see a wire running down from the head of the sail, down through the end of each batten in turn to a winch on the end of the boom.

Mainsheets have to be very powerful to control these sails and multi-part tackles are fitted in order to give the helmsman sufficient power. Because of their greater beam, catamarans have a much greater range of possible sheeting angles and it is normal to run mainsheet blocks on full-width tracks so that the sail can be sheeted hard down but well off the centreline when reaching.

It often used to be said against catamarans that they would not tack or, alternatively, that they would not point high on the wind. Although this view may have been at least partly justified in the case of some of the early, experimental boats, it certainly is not true of any of the well-known modern designs. However, because of their light weight in comparison to their size, cats do tend to tack slowly and 'tacking battles' of the kind that are familiar in dinghy racing are hardly ever seen in catamaran events.

Craft with more than one hull have become accepted by experienced yachtsmen only slowly. Some have objected to the different appearance, others have required more assurance of safety and carrying capacity. Sophisticated design, building, and sailing techniques have answered most objections so that today there are dozens of small multihull classes. There are, however, many clubs that still prefer not to have multihulls because of the extra space they require ashore and afloat and the fact that the great disparities in speeds mean that they cannot share the same courses as dinghies. But catamaran sailing has a very special appeal because of its great speed and excitement and thus the sisters of ancient Polynesian, Micronesian, and Melanesian vessels now cruise all of the world's seas in increasing numbers.

See also DESIGN; DINGHIES: Catamarans; HULLS; YACHT RACING: Major races and series (Little America's Cup)

N

Nautical almanacs

Almost every maritime country publishes an almanac designed solely to facilitate the practice of ASTRONOMICAL NAVIGATION at sea. Its principal contents consist of the positions of the sun, moon, planets, and stars in a form suitable for its purpose; additional material, with the exception of lists of 'standard times', is limited to that necessary for use with the tables of astronomical data. However, many other publications with similar titles (e.g. *Brown's Nautical Almanac, Reed's Nautical Almanac*) combine other ephemeral and constant material with the astronomical data – for example, tidal predictions, traverse tables, sight-reduction tables, as well as general data and information on navigational matters.

In all publications the astronomical data are basically the same, although there are a few (principally the Japanese almanacs) in which they are presented in a different form. Otherwise the GREENWICH-HOUR-ANGLE (GHA) method is used; many countries (Brazil, Denmark, Greece, India, Indonesia, Korea, Mexico, Norway, and Sweden, as well as the United States) have adopted identical presentations (reproduced by photolithography) of the tabulations in the (British) *Nautical Almanac* to which this article will specifically refer.

The Nautical Almanac was first issued in 1766 for the year 1767. Although it was not the earliest publication to give astronomical data for navigational purposes (the *Connaissance des Temps*, issued in France for 1679, is easily the oldest of the national almanacs) it was the first to provide the essential data for the practical determination of longitude at sea. It was planned, designed and prepared by the fifth Astronomer Royal, Nevil Maskelyne, who had successfully practised the method of LUNAR DISTANCES at sea, using the position of the moon deduced from the tables of the German astronomer Johann Tobias Mayer. Its publication, 250 years after the method of lunar distances had been suggested, represented a theoretical and practical triumph that was to provide the seaman with the means to find his position, without reference to other aids or even to time, for nearly 150 years.

With the increasing availability of GMT, originally through mechanical timepieces and now by radio time signals, supplemented when necessary by highly precise crystal and atomic clocks, the need for lunar distances gradually declined and has now completely vanished. *The Nautical Almanac* is thus designed on the assumption that GMT is immediately available to the navigator to an adequate precision, generally of about 1 sec; those few navigators who may occasionally require GMT more precisely must be prepared to apply corrections (up to ±0.9 sec)

to the broadcast time signals, which are now based on International Atomic Time rather than on the rotation of the earth.

The Nautical Almanac tabulates the positions – specifically the two coordinates of direction, DECLINATION and GHA – of the sun, moon, and planets (Venus, Mars, Jupiter, and Saturn) to a precision of 0'.1 at a tabular interval of 1 hr of GMT; provision is made for direct interpolation to 1 sec. For the stars GHA Aries is similarly tabulated for each hour: declination and sidereal hour angle (SHA), both of which change slowly, are given at intervals of 3 days; GHA of a star is obtained simply by adding its SHA to GHA Aries. 'Aries', more strictly the first point of Aries, is the vernal equinox; but it is used here solely as the zero point from which SHA is measured. The *Almanac* thus provides a simple means of determining the true direction, as would be seen from the centre of the earth, of any object at the time of observation. This may be converted, by direct calculation or by the aid of sight-reduction tables, to direction (in the form of calculated ALTITUDE and AZIMUTH) relative to the *latitude* and ZENITH of the observer. Auxiliary tabulations and tables enable corrections to be applied, usually to the observed altitude, for PARALLAX (arising from the distances between the observer and the centre of the earth) and for atmospheric refraction, SEMI-DIAMETER, and phase (when the centre of the object is not directly observed), as well as for the DIP of the horizon. Comparison of the corrected observed altitude with that calculated from the data in *The Nautical Almanac* for the time of observation provides an INTERCEPT from which a POSITION LINE can be drawn (*see* ASTRONOMICAL NAVIGATION).

The only additional material included in the *Almanac* is that designed to assist in the planning of observations: times of sunrise, sunset, twilight, moonrise and moonset; notes on the availability and suitability of the planets for observations: star charts and lists of selected stars.

Nautical astronomy *see* ASTRONOMICAL NAVIGATION

Nautical mile

The unit of distance commonly used at sea. The International Nautical Mile, proposed by the International Hydrographic Bureau in 1929, and subsequently adopted by most of the maritime world, is 1852 m long. It is very nearly equal to one minute of latitude, or of any other GREAT CIRCLE of the earth.

Originally, the length of the mile was not associated with the size of the earth. The ancient Roman mile (from Latin *mille*, 'thousand') was 1000 paces or 5000 Roman feet (4856.6 ft or 1480.3 m) in length. During the fifteenth century, when long voyages of

discovery became popular, charts came into wider use. The number of miles to a degree of latitude varied with the accepted size of the earth. The first relationship of 60 miles to 1° (60') of latitude appeared on a chart of Asia in the 1466 edition of Ptolemy's *Almagest*.

With the introduction of the mariner's LOG, first mentioned by William Bourne, or Bourn, in his *Regiment of the Sea* (London 1574), the need for a standard length of the mile increased. By this time it was generally recognized that 1° of latitude is longer than 60 Roman miles. Either the number of miles to a degree, or the length of the mile, needed to be increased. On land, where there was little need to relate the unit of distance to the size of the earth, the shorter mile, later lengthened in England to 5280 ft (1609.34 m), generally predominated. Seamen adopted the proposal of the English surveyor Richard Norwood in 1637 that mariners should use a longer mile, which he put at 6120 ft (1865 m), but later shortened to 6000 ft (1829 m). The name nautical mile first appeared in 1730.

The length of the nautical mile used at various times by different countries has varied in accordance with different determinations of the size and shape of the earth and differences in definition. The value of 1852 m proposed in 1929 was near the average of the various lengths in use at that time. Further, it recognized the need for one standard unit of length (the metre), which is no longer defined in terms of the size of the earth, thus giving stability to the length of the unit.

Although 1 nautical mile does not equal exactly 1' of latitude (which varies from 6046 ft or 1843 m at the equator to 6108 ft or 1862 m at the poles), the relationship is close enough for practical navigation. This relationship makes a mile scale of any latitude scale, and simplifies great-circle sailing and computations in astronomical navigation.

Nautical triangle *see* ASTRONOMICAL TRIANGLE; ASTRONOMICAL NAVIGATION

Nautophone

A foghorn with an electrically activated diaphragm.

Naval architecture *see* DESIGN: Historical introduction

Navigation

The process of conducting a craft as it moves about its ways. Navigation involves position, direction, distance, and time.

– historical

Geography, climate, economic needs, and technology have played decisive roles in the development of navigation. The retreat of the last icecap some 30 000 years ago gave rise to uniquely propitious conditions for the development of civilization, as for example the settled city communities of *c*.9000 BC in the fertile crescent between the valleys of Egypt and Mesopotamia and flanking the island-studded eastern Mediterranean. It was here that the first proto-Neolithic communities appeared. By 7000 BC, with the invention of pottery, the practicability of food production and conservation was firmly established and trading developed by land and sea. The Neolithic culture had reached Cyprus by 6000 BC and Crete by 4000 BC; in Egypt and Mesopotamia the production of the first metals, copper and bronze, by *c*.3500 BC heralded the construction of bigger and better boats.

By 3000 BC the square sail, efficient on a following wind, had appeared, direct trade between Egypt and Crete flourished, and the Megalithic monument builders of the western Mediterranean were spreading northwards along the Atlantic coasts of Europe to Britain. By *c*.1800 BC iron weapons and tools, which were to enable ships of great structural complexity to be built, first began to be manufactured in Anatolia in Turkey but the use of iron, like that of copper, spread slowly so that iron did not reach India until the ninth century BC and China later still. When the English naval explorer, Captain James Cook (1728–79), discovered Oceania, which had been populated between *c*.1500 BC and AD 1300 by peoples from Southeast Asia, the cultures were still at a Neolithic stage of development. Allowing for factors of geography (terrain and latitude), meteorology (prevailing wind patterns and cloud cover), and culture (literacy and numeracy) the navigational techniques of the Pacific islanders comprehended those of all Neolithic navigators and all navigators in the Indian Ocean, the China seas, the Mediterranean and the northern seas of Europe down to the Vikings of the tenth century and their Norman successors in the eleventh century. Even today, in emergency, the navigator reverts to them. They used the sun's rays and diurnal positions, a sidereal compass of horizon stars, a wind compass, 'moving' reference islands, swell orientation, wave-refraction patterns, land loom, cloud lore, ice glare, homing birds, sea marks, and zenith stars.

During the period *c*. 1400 to 400 BC the Phoenicians were the great trader-colonizers of the Mediterranean and first originated the script that became the ancestor of the modern Western alphabets, but it was the Greeks succeeding them who first wrote down sailing directions in the fourth-century BC, using eight characteristic winds to define direction and giving distances in linear terms (miles) as well as in temporal (days' sailing) terms. They measured the depth of water with a sounding lead and line in fathoms. Later they became the sea carriers of the Roman and Byzantine Empires.

From *c*. AD 50 to *c*. AD 250 merchants from the Mediterranean traded to India and Indo-China by way of the Red Sea, Indian Ocean, and South China Sea. But between 50 BC and AD 50, instead of sailing around the coasts of the Indian Ocean, sailing across it on the monsoons was pioneered, probably by Persian, or perhaps by Arab pilots. At the same time monsoon sailing also enabled the Indonesians to colonize the island of Madagascar at the southern limit of the monsoons.

The long east–west tropical ocean passages were helped by brilliant horizon stars with little or no change of AZIMUTH and made practical by the development of fore-and-aft rigs that were efficient with winds such as the northeast–southwest monsoons (*see* RIGS). Certainly by *c*. AD 650, when the Arabs set forth in conquest, monsoon sailing was further aided by stellar altitude navigation, evolved from observation of the change of the meridional altitude of polar stars at ports on the predominantly north–south coastlines of these seas. By sailing down to the known meridional altitude of a star then east or west, while keeping it at that altitude, the pilot was assured of reaching his destination; altitudes were measured by finger's breadths at arm's length (1 *isba'* = 1° 37').

By the fourteenth century Arab and Chinese pilots were using an instrument made of wood and cord called the *kamal* (Arabic word for 'guide') to measure *isba'*, together with tables of latitudes and distances to sail to raise or lay one *isba'*. But by about AD 1100 the Chinese, who sailed more often under cloudier skies, had invented a north-pointing sea compass – a piece of iron magnetized by a lodestone and floated on water in a bowl – to help determine direction under overcast skies. This was known to the Arabs by the mid-thirteenth century and adopted by them, but neither they nor the Chinese developed it into a precision instrument, and Arab pilots, unlike the Chinese, continued to rely chiefly upon their 32-point star compass. The Chinese used it to define 24 points and sailed by it (*see also* MARINER'S COMPASS; WIND ROSE).

In the West, meanwhile, Christianized

An early Chinese compass showing 24 points

Norsemen, who used the same four cardinal points as the Anglo-Saxons and Frisians (north, south, east, and west), had made conquests and settlements in northwest Europe and penetrated into the Mediterranean, bringing with them rudimentary written SAILING DIRECTIONS and encountering the dominant sea traders from the Italian city states of Amalfi, Genoa, and Venice, and also those in the eastern Mediterranean from the Byzantine Empire and Islam.

Within 30 years of the Norman conquest of England (AD 1066) the first Crusade had been launched by land against Islam in the Levant. Following the capture of the Holy Places in Jerusalem and the adjoining coastlands the continuing opposition of Islam made the land route so hazardous that it became a question of unprecedented support by sea from the West, demanding 1000-mile voyages out of sight of land in all weathers and, if practicable, in all seasons. Italian shipping gave support and at the same time developed trade with Islamic countries, the profitability of which depended also upon reliable and regular voyaging. Since earliest times all shipping had been confined to port during the winter months partly because overcast skies made navigation too uncertain a risk. Probably by the sailing of the second Crusade in AD 1147, and certainly by AD 1187, a liquid magnetic sea compass for finding the direction of north under overcast skies had been invented, independently of the Chinese.

The fourth Crusade was diverted to the capture of Constantinople in AD 1204 and this may have yielded written sailing directions dating back to the Greeks. It may also have stimulated the radical developments in navigation that over the next 50 years stemmed from the magnetic compass and resulted in a progressive lengthening of the sea-trading season. By the end of the century sailing all the year round was established and Italian ships were trading far beyond the Mediterranean to ports in the Low Countries and England. Voyages facilitated by the adoption of the centreline rudder developed at the end of the twelfth century in northern waters. By 1254 a dry sea compass, which continuously indicated direction all round the horizon to within $3°$, was being used by Italian pilots. Also a sandglass enabled the pilot to measure equal intervals of time and thus estimate closely the distance sailed in miles. Arabic numerals were used to calculate progress that was plotted on a portolan chart geometrically constructed from magnetic bearings and estimated distances between places. This was further aided by a *tavoleta di marteloio* that enabled the pilot to calculate course and distance to be sailed to maintain his track when winds were adverse, and a portolano or book of organized sailing directions

giving distances between places in miles and their compass bearings to within $3° - 5°$ within the Mediterranean and the Black Sea. This was the beginning of mathematical navigation and was highly efficient within the enclosed Mediterranean.

In 1415 the Portuguese captured Ceuta on the north coast of Morocco and in 1420, under the inspiration of Prince Henry of Portugal (1394–1460), known as the Navigator, began to seek by sea the source of the cargoes of the trans-Saharan caravans. They

mastered the Mediterranean art of navigation with the aid of Italian and Catalan pilots and hydrographers but, when they started sailing down the coast of Africa, they were forced by the prevailing north–northeast winds to sail out into the Atlantic to find favourable winds to return. Here their reckoning was thrown out by unknown currents, and by changes in magnetic variation. By this time they were also using the clockwise circulation of the winds in the North Atlantic to return to Portugal and,

A portolano chart incorporating discoveries up to the time of Fernão Gomes' voyages (1470–75)

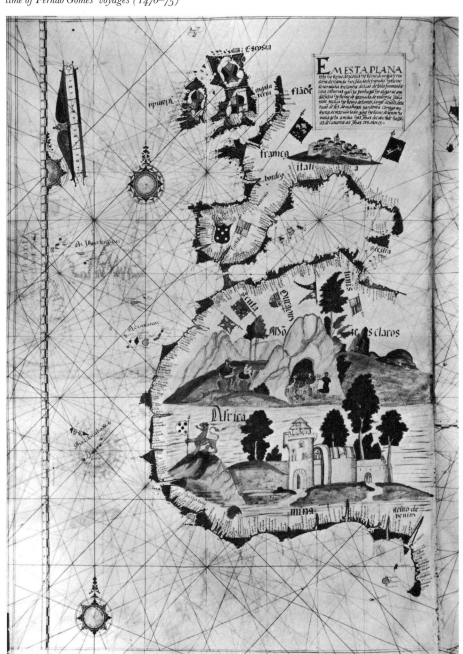

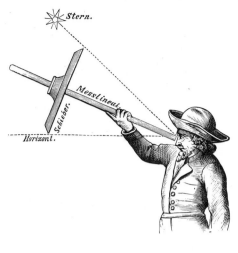

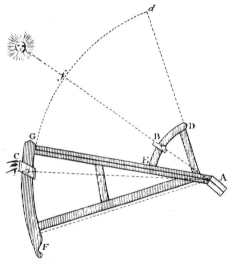

as their courses lay chiefly north – south, they developed altitude navigation to check their reckonings. They used the altitude of the Pole Star at Lisbon as a datum and converted the difference in the star's altitude, as measured by a quadrant, into linear distance on the basis of 16 leagues (later 17½ leagues) to a degree. To make a landfall they sailed to its 'height' (altitude of the Pole Star) then 'ran down' the land until it was sighted.

By the 1470s it was necessary when approaching the Equator, first crossed in 1471, to use the meridian altitude of the sun because the Pole Star became invisible and the new stars were uncharted. The sun's daily change of DECLINATION soon made altitude navigation impracticable and so the more complicated latitude navigation had to be used whereby the sun's noon altitude, corrected with the aid of tables of declination according to rules based on the observer's shadow, were converted to angular distance north or south of the Equator. The navigator now ran down the latitude of his destination aided by a table to raise or lay 1° of latitude. By 1482 the MARINER'S ASTROLABE, scaled for altitudes and/or zenith distances, was being used, and by 1500 a latitude scale was being added to Portuguese portolano charts. Soon nautical almanacs and manuals of navigation were being printed as sailing directions had been from 1490. A hydrographic office was established in the Casa de Contratación, Seville, in 1508 and here standard charts were compiled, for the Spaniards quickly acquired the Portuguese art of navigation. Following the voyage of the Portuguese navigator Vasco da Gama (c. 1460–1524) to and from India by way of the Cape of Good Hope between 1497 and 1499, the Portuguese developed the CROSS STAFF, perhaps from the *kamal*, and also instruments to measure magnetic variation.

The errors of the plane sea chart studied by the Portuguese geographer Pedro Nunes, or Nunez (1492–1577) in 1537 led to the terrestrial globe being improved for navigators by the addition of RHUMB LINES in 1541 by the Flemish geographer Gerardus Mercator (1512–94) who also constructed the first so-called Mercator chart in 1569. The meridional parts, devised independently by Thomas Hariot, the English mathematician and astronomer, and the English mathematician Edward Wright (1558–1615) in the 1590s, made commercial production of Mercator charts practicable in the seventeenth century; the BACKSTAFF, invented in 1594 by the English navigator John Davis (c. 1550–1605), greatly improved the accuracy of the noon sights.

During the first quarter of the seventeenth century certain improvements were made in the calculation of a ship's position for plotting on a Mercator chart. In 1614 Handson published the trigonometrical formulae for the

Top, a German illustration of an early cross staff used for measuring the altitude of heavenly bodies

A backstaff (above) from an engraving in Chambers's Encyclopaedia *(1786). This instrument replaced the cross staff and was so named because the observer had the sun behind him*

solution of the nautical triangle involving course and distance sailed, and difference of a latitude and departure; the Scottish mathematician John Napier (1550–1617) published his treatise on logarithms in 1614 and in 1615 Wright published a special edition for seamen; Henry Briggs (1561–1630), the English mathematician, published common logarithms to the base 10 for numbers in 1617, and in 1623 the English mathematician Edmund Gunter (1581–1626) did the same for the trigonometrical functions with the inclusion of logarithms on his scale for the mechanical solution of the nautical triangle; straight, circular, and cylindrical slide rules followed within the next 10 years. Gunter popularized the use of the English log chip and log line, first described in 1574 by the English mathematician and writer on naval

subjects William Bourne, by explaining in 1623 the use of knots in the line to facilitate measurement of speed and also the use of the Dutchman's log. In 1633 the English mathematician and astronomer Henry Gellibrand (1597–1636) identified secular change of variation and introduced tables of amplitude for measuring compass error. Edmond Halley (1656–1742), the English astronomer, published the first ISOGONIC chart of magnetic variation in 1701 and the first chart of tidal streams in 1702.

A ship's longitude and the velocity of ocean currents, however, could still not be measured. To measure longitude it was necessary to measure the ship's 'local' time and the time at a prime meridian accurately enough to find the difference and hence the ship's longitude. In 1514 Werner had suggested the use of LUNAR DISTANCE for determining the time at prime meridian, and later in 1530 the Flemish astronomer, Rainer Gemma Frisius, had proposed carrying it on board ship by means of a chronometer. But practical solutions themselves were in turn dependent upon other factors such as the means to measure angles of and between celestial bodies far more precisely than was possible with the unaided eye, the means for the precise measurement of time (timekeeping), and the exact determination of the length of a degree. By the end of the century, however, longitude determination on land was made practicable by the work of the Italian scientist and astronomer Galileo Galilei (1564–1642) who discovered the isochronism of the pendulum in *c.* 1580, invented the astronomical telescope in 1609, and discovered the satellites of the planet Jupiter in 1610. Following the foundation of the Académie Royale de Paris in 1667 the exact length of a degree was measured by Jean Picard (1620–1682), the French astronomer, in 1669 using optical instruments and pendulum controlled regulators derived from the pendulum clock commercialized in 1657 by the Dutch astronomer and physicist Christiaan Huyghens (1629–95). When, however, Huyghens' marine pendulum clocks were tested at sea they proved unreliable, but his invention of the isochronous balance spring watch (*c.* 1673) made accurate portable timekeepers practicable. Also, the publication of *La Connaissance des Temps* (from 1679) made longitude determination on land by the use of Jupiter's satellites internationally available.

Attempts to find ways of determining longitude at sea followed closely in 1675 the foundation of the Royal Observatory at Greenwich, London, and were encouraged by the Longitude Act of 1714 that offered prizes of up to £20 000.00 for practical solutions. The invention of the reflecting quadrant in 1731 by the English mathematician John Hadley (1682–1744) made it possible for angular measurements to be taken from a ship at sea with sufficient precision (to within 1′) to enable local time to be determined accurately by altitude observations of celestial bodies and for angles of lunar distance to be measured with similar accuracy to calculate time on a prime meridian. Using the manuscript of lunar tables compiled in 1753 by the German mathematician and astronomer Johann Tobias Mayer (1723–62), the English astronomer Nevil Maskelyne (1732–1811) demonstrated in 1761 the practicability of the lunar distance method of determining longitude at sea to within 15–30 miles on a voyage to the island of St Helena off the west coast of Africa. With the publication of his *Tables Requisite* in 1766 and his first annual *Nautical Almanack* for 1767 the method became universally available.

With the commercial production of MARINE CHRONOMETERS from the 1780s the method became increasingly widespread. The age of scientific navigation when a ship's position could be confidently expressed in terms of latitude and longitude had now arrived.

The invention of artificially magnetized steel compass needles in 1745 by the English scientist Gowin Knight (1713–72) initiated a steady improvement in the sea compass and made the lodestone obsolete. Scientific navigation was reinforced in 1795 by the establishment of the Admiralty Hydrographic Office in London. Magnetic variation and deviation were now systematically studied, charts were constructed on the basis of triangulation and from the 1820s sold to seamen of all nations, reliable tide tables based upon mechanical tide gauges (1830) were published from 1833, and a series of Admiralty pilot books soon provided reliable sailing directions for all the seas of the world.

By the 1880s the majority of seamen were using British Admiralty charts and the NAUTICAL ALMANACS. As a consequence the meridian of the Royal Observatory at Greenwich in London was internationally recognized in 1883 as the prime meridian of the world and the basis of the world time zone system. This greatly facilitated navigational accuracy. Meanwhile the 'position-line' method of fixing a ship's position, devised by the American navigator Captain Thomas H. Sumner and published in 1837, greatly improved the accuracy and frequency with which the position of a ship could be obtained and avoided the necessity of noon sights. In 1873 and 1875 Admiral Marcq St Hilaire of the French navy developed a simpler way of obtaining a position line that is still today the basis of most methods of sight reduction.

– the practice

As the preceding section shows, navigation in past ages was a highly developed art, and the successful navigators were those who had the ability to observe carefully and interpret

correctly their observations. The history of navigation has consisted essentially of orderly transition from art to science. Although skill in observation and accuracy in interpretation continue to be essentials of successful navigation, the modern mariner has numerous instruments, visual and electronic aids, charts, publications, information sources, computers, and even satellites to help him guide his craft safely to its destination. The prudent navigator acquaints himself with the means at his disposal, develops judgment and skill through constant use of these means, seeks independent confirmation of his data whenever practicable, and maintains constant vigilance.

The equipment available for navigation, and the procedures used, vary considerably with the craft and its purpose. Large seagoing passenger ships and tankers, hydrographic or geophysical survey vessels, fishing craft, sailing vessels, harbour tugs, small yachts that remain close to shore, transocean single-handed boats, underwater craft, warships, hydrofoils, hovercraft, lifeboats, and vessels operating in high latitudes all have individual requirements reflected in differences in equipment, organization, and methods, but all of these craft utilize the same basic principles, adapted appropriately to their needs.

The position of a vessel is generally stated in terms of geodetic latitude and longitude, but in restricted waters its position relative to land, an aid to navigation, or some danger may be of greater interest.

Two fundamentally different methods of position determination are used. One is by applying the distance and direction travelled from a known position, allowance being made for the disturbing effects of wind and current. This method is called dead reckoning. It is sometimes considered the primary method of position determination because it is always available in some form, providing continuous position information for any time, past, present, or future. However, it is subject to error because of possible inaccuracy of the 'known' position and imperfections in determining the direction and distance travelled. The uncertainty increases with time and distance travelled.

The second method of determining position is by reference to something external to the craft, such as lighthouses, celestial bodies, electronic transmitters, or soundings. This method is called position fixing.

In the common practice of navigation, dead reckoning is maintained until a fix is obtained, when the fix constitutes a new 'known position' for the start of a new dead-reckoning plot.

Dead reckoning is most commonly performed by plotting on a chart or plotting sheet, the latter being a blank chart showing only the latitude and longitude graticule,

sometimes with one or more compass roses for measurement of direction without the need for a protractor. Plotting equipment consists of a straight edge, dividers, compasses for drawing arcs of circles, pencils, and erasers. The straight edge may be in the form of PARALLEL RULES, a device for transferring a line parallel to itself; some form of plotter combining a protractor with the straight edge; or a more sophisticated drafting machine.

Dead reckoning may also be performed by computation, the various methods of doing so being called SAILINGS. The principal differences among the various sailings relate to the direction of motion, whether the earth is considered a plane or a sphere (or spheroid), and whether a RHUMB LINE or GREAT CIRCLE is involved. Mechanical or electronic devices may be used to perform the computation, and sometimes to trace the dead-reckoning plot on paper.

Several directions are involved in the progress of a vessel. The forward direction along the longitudinal axis of the craft at any moment is its HEADING. This term is also applied to the average direction over a period of time. Because of a cross current, resulting in a lateral *set* of the vessel, or a cross wind, producing leeway, the craft's direction of motion, called the course, may differ from the heading. The direction from one fix to a later one is called the course made good. The path followed by a craft in moving from one point to another is called its track, which may involve one or a number of courses.

The heading of a craft is determined by a compass. This instrument senses a reference direction, usually north. Heading of the craft is indicated by a mark, called a lubber line, in the bowl holding the sensing element. This bowl is fixed with respect to the craft, and the lubber line is aligned with the longitudinal axis of the craft. A COMPASS CARD, a sort of circular protractor graduated in degrees (and sometimes, also, in 32 compass points) around its periphery is attached to the sensing element. The graduation on this compass card opposite the lubber line is the heading of the craft.

Two principal kinds of compass are in common use at sea. The magnetic compass has a sensing element that aligns itself with the horizontal component of the lines of force of the earth's magnetic field, called magnetic meridians. Magnetic north, along the magnetic meridian through any point, seldom coincides with true north along the geographic meridian through the same point. The difference, called variation, varies with location and is shown on nautical charts. The direction north indicated by a magnetic compass may differ from both magnetic north and true north because of local magnetic influences within the craft. The difference

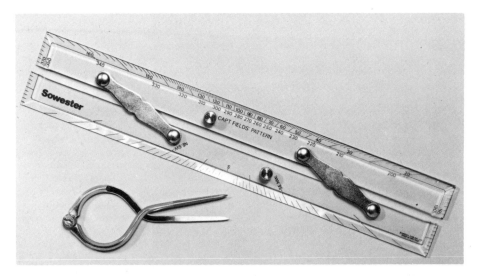

Parallel rules and chart dividers (top) *are two of the simple instruments required for plotting. The grid compass* (above) *can be used for determining the heading of small vessels, but its chief function is to enable the helmsman to steer the course more easily*

between compass north and magnetic north is called deviation, which varies with the heading of the vessel. Most of the deviation is eliminated by establishing compensating magnetic forces, a process called compass adjustment. A small amount of residual deviation generally remains. The values on various headings are determined by comparing the magnetic and compass headings, and these values are recorded on a correction card, usually attached to the binnacle, in which the compass is housed, for ready reference. Both variation and deviation are expressed in degrees east (plus) or west (minus) indicating the direction of deflection of the north (zero) graduation of the compass card. The algebraic sum of variation and deviation is called compass error. A magnetic compass is unreliable near the magnetic poles of the earth, where the directive force is weak because the magnetic lines of force of the earth are essentially vertical.

A second kind of compass, widely used in all but small craft, depends for its directive force upon the properties of one or more gyroscopes mounted so as to remain horizontal and seek true north. Variation and deviation are not involved. This GYROCOMPASS, is, however, subject to several errors related principally to the latitude and motion of the vessel. Compensation for these errors is made either automatically or manually. A small residual gyro error may remain. It is constant in all directions and places, like the error of a watch that is fast or slow. Like variation and deviation, gyro error is designated east (plus) or west (minus) to indicate the direction of deflection of the north graduation of the compass card. A gyrocompass is unreliable in high latitudes, where the directive force is weak because of the large angle between the horizontal and the axis of rotation of the earth.

Speed or distance travelled is determined by some form of LOG. A primitive log generally consisted of an object, with a line attached, thrown overboard, and a sandglass to indicate a time interval during which the length of line paid out was measured, usually by means of a number of knots at specified intervals in the line. This is the origin of the term knot as a unit of speed, one knot being equal to one international NAUTICAL MILE (1852 m, very nearly the length of one minute of latitude) per hour. In time, this chip log gave way to a mechanical device with a rotor and indicator. This taffrail log was so designated because it was attached to the taffrail, at the stern of the vessel.

Modern logs are attached to the hull of a vessel and generally measure speed (1) by comparison of the dynamic and static water pressures at a tube with its open end (for determination of dynamic pressure) in the forward direction (a Pitot-static log); (2) by measurement of an electric current generated by a small propeller rotated by passage of the craft through the water (an impeller-type log); or (3) by measurement of the voltage of an electromagnetic sensing element that develops a voltage directly proportional to the speed through the water (an electro-magnetic log). The engine revolution counter also provides an indication of speed, but this method is generally less accurate than the indications of a modern log.

Time aboard ship is measured by means of a MARINE CHRONOMETER, a timepiece with a nearly uniform rate. The chronometer is not reset at sea because this might disturb its rate. Its error is determined from time to time by means of radio time signals, and between comparisons by means of its rate. The various clocks and hack watches used throughout the vessel are set by comparison with the chron-ometer. Traditionally, three chronometers were carried aboard ship so that the identity of the errant instrument could be established if one of them became unreliable. With radio time signals available nearly everywhere now, the need for three chronometers has lessened, and this number is often reduced. Before this era, the daily winding of the chron-ometers was a ceremonial occasion of con-siderable importance because of the essential need of accurate time for determining longi-tude from astronomical observations.

The navigator's chart is a map giving pref-erence to navigational information. Latitude and longitude graticules, positions of useful landmarks and aids to navigation, and sound-ings are displayed prominently, and other useful information such as ice limits, characteristics of navigational lights, mag-netic variation, and currents is indicated by symbols or notes. Chart corrections are pub-lished periodically to permit the navigator to keep his charts accurate.

Charts, like other maps, are prepared on some form of map projection, usually called chart projection by navigators. For ordinary purposes of navigation, the Mercator pro-jection is used almost universally by mariners. Two properties are primarily responsible for this popularity. One is orthomorphism; that is, angles about a point are represented cor-rectly, so that directions can be measured directly on the chart. The second is its por-trayal of RHUMB LINES (loxodromes on the surface of the earth) as straight lines. The means of navigation of a vessel constrain its motion to that along a loxodrome, or nearly so. Long voyages generally consist of a series of loxodromic sections, called legs. Pro-jections other than the Mercator are some-times used for special purposes, such as great-circle voyage planning (*see also* MAP AND CHART PROJECTIONS; MERCATOR PROJECTION).

Position fixing is generally accomplished by visual PILOTAGE, use of electronic aids, or by

ASTRONOMICAL NAVIGATION, often referred to as astronavigation but sometimes called celestial navigation or nautical astronomy.

Visual PILOTAGE or piloting consists of determination of the position of a craft by reference to identifiable landmarks, both natural and man-made, and aids to navigation such as lighthouses, light vessels, beacons, and buoys. The positions of these landmarks and aids are shown on nautical charts, and some are listed in certain navigational publi-cations.

During passage through a channel marked by buoys, it is generally sufficient to proceed from buoy to buoy, identifying each one as it is passed. Elsewhere in pilot waters, position is usually determined by means of POSITION LINES, on some point of which the craft is presumed to be located. Thus, if the direction to a landmark is measured, the craft must be somewhere on a line extending in that direc-tion and passing through the landmark, if the measurement is accurate. Such a direction, called a bearing, is measured by means of a compass, compass repeater, or a pelorus. The last is a device resembling a compass but lacking a directive element. It is set manually to the heading of the vessel or to zero. In the latter case the measured direction is called a relative bearing. Measurement of distance from an object provides a circular position line. The intersection of two simultaneous position lines establishes a fix. A third posi-tion line provides a check on the accuracy of the observations and plotting.

If position-line observations are not made simultaneously, the lines are adjusted to a common time, to provide a RUNNING FIX. Generally, an earlier line is advanced (moved parallel to itself in the direction of motion of the vessel) for a distance equal to the run between the time of observation of this line and the time of the last one observed. Because any error in the course or speed of the vessel is reflected in the position of the advanced position line, fixes are preferred over running fixes, and when the latter are used, the time interval between observations is kept to a minimum consistent with other con-siderations. The cut (crossing angle) between position lines also affects the accuracy of a fix or running fix. For two lines the ideal is $90°$; for three it is $60°$.

Sometimes two objects are seen in line, one beyond the other. In this case the position line, called a transit (range), is shown by drawing a line through the positions of the objects and extending it to the vicinity of the vessel's position. In some cases transits are established in line with channels to provide a steering guide for vessels traversing them. Of course, the navigator must know when to change course to stay in navigable waters.

Another method of fixing the position of a vessel is by means of horizontal angles,

usually measured with a marine sextant, between three identifiable objects. These angles are then set on a STATION POINTER (a protractor with one fixed and two adjustable arms) and the device is placed on the chart so that the three arms are directly over the three objects. The common intersection of the three arms indicates the position of the vessel, unless the positions of the three objects and the vessel are all on a circle, when only a circular position line, not a fix, is established.

A position line or fix can also be established by means of soundings, depth of water meas-ured by a hand lead or echo sounder (sonic depth finder). A given sounding establishes a position line along the depth contour so identified. A series of soundings establishes a fix. Allowance for the state of the tide may be needed. The accuracy of this method depends upon the uniqueness of the bottom topogra-phy as well as upon the accuracy and detail of its portrayal and the accuracy of depth measurement. Under suitable conditions this method can be very useful in keeping the vessel in safe water, particularly in poor visibility. It can also be used as an inde-pendent check on other methods.

Electronic aids, in general, provide a means of extending visual piloting techniques to greater distances from shore and into periods of poor visibility. The distances at which they are useful depend upon the frequency used, geometry, and propagation conditions. Special equipment is needed for most elec-tronic aids.

In pilotage waters radar can be used to measure both direction and distance, or the entire radar paint can be compared with the chart. Bearings can also be measured by a radio direction finder. If the distance from the transmitter is more than the visual range in clear weather, as a general rule, a cor-rection may be needed for plotting on a Mercator chart to allow for the fact that the radio signal follows a great circle, while a rhumb line is plotted.

Another commonly used electronic tech-nique is to measure the difference in arrival time of synchronized signals from two or more transmitters. A position line represent-ing a time difference between arrival times of signals from two transmitters is a hyperbola. Because a hyperbola consists of two sym-metrical parts, some means is needed for determining which of the two parts is the applicable position line. The distance difference determination is made either by direct measurement of the elapsed time, in microseconds, between reception of synchron-ized pulsed signals from the two transmit-ters, or indirectly by comparing the difference in phase of continuous-wave sig-nals from the two sources. In the latter case, any given phase relationship is repeated systematically at intervals related to the

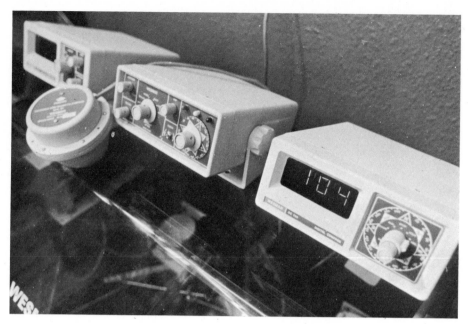

This selection of electronic navigational aids includes (from left to right) *a digital echo sounder, auto-pilot and a digital compass with built-in clock and bearing-hold switches*

frequency and position in the coverage pattern, requiring a means of identifying the applicable position line. This process is called lane identification, a lane being the area encompassing all possible phase relationships.

A widely used phase comparison system utilizing harmonically related low frequencies useful to a distance of about 200 nautical miles from the transmitters, is the DECCA NAVIGATOR system. Farther from shore, the LORAN (long-range navigation) systems are available. Loran A is a medium-frequency time-difference system; Loran C is a low-frequency combination time-difference and phase-comparison system of somewhat longer range, extending to about 1500 nautical miles. OMEGA is a very-low frequency phase-comparison system providing global coverage with only eight transmitting stations.

Another system, based upon phase comparison, is known as CONSOL. The navigator merely counts a series of dots and dashes transmitted in a rotating pattern during a period known as 'keying cycle', and, by reference to a table or special chart, establishes a hyperbolic position line of such short base line (the line connecting the three synchronized transmitters) that the position line can be considered a bearing at distances over some 25 miles from the transmitters.

Other uses of electronics for navigation include radio time signals, broadcast of weather information and urgent warnings of dangers, harbour surveillance, and aircraft radio ranges that are sometimes useful to mariners.

Astronavigation utilizes the apparent positions of celestial bodies to establish position lines. Its use requires visibility of the bodies and a horizontal reference, usually the horizon. Although these limitations restrict its use, astronavigation provides usefully accurate position fixes with relatively inexpensive equipment, global coverage, and is not subject to many of the restrictions of electronic navigation. Although some skill is involved in making astronavigation observations, the good navigator prides himself upon his ability to perform this operation. (The traditional significance of astronavigation is reflected in the fact that the marine sextant is commonly used as a symbol of navigation.)

Predicted apparent positions of celestial bodies used for navigation are tabulated at hourly intervals of GMT in the *Nautical Almanac*, using declination and GREENWICH HOUR ANGLE, coordinates similar to latitude and longitude except that GHA is reckoned westward through 360°.

The navigator measures the ALTITUDE (elevation angle) of the body by means of a sextant, noting carefully the time of observation. Time is involved because of rotation of the earth, resulting in continuous apparent motion of the body. An error of one second of time can introduce an error in the position of the craft of as much as one fourth of a nautical mile. Certain corrections are applied to the measured sextant altitude to compensate for errors introduced by such things as atmospheric refraction, depression or DIP of the

horizon because of the observer's height above the surface, SEMI-DIAMETER of the sun or moon when one of its limbs (edges) is observed, PARALLAX in altitude of bodies close to the earth, and index error of the sextant.

By addition or subtraction of longitude, the GHA is converted to LOCAL HOUR ANGLE at an assumed position, which may be either the dead-reckoning position or another position nearby, selected to reduce interpolation later. Declination and LHA are then converted, by solution of the spherical navigational triangle (usually by precomputed sight-reduction tables), to altitude and AZIMUTH (coordinates of the horizon system similar to latitude and longitude). This calculated altitude is then compared with the observed altitude (the corrected sextant altitude) to obtain the intercept (altitude difference). This entire process is called sight reduction.

The final step is to plot the astronavigation position line. The calculated and observed altitude each defines a circle on the earth, centred at the geographical position of the body observed (the point on the earth having the body in its ZENITH) and having a radius equal to the zenith distance (co-altitude). The intercept, in minutes of arc, is the difference between the radii of the two circles, in nautical miles. A distance equal to the intercept is measured along the azimuth line from the assumed position, toward the geographical position if the observed altitude is greater and away if the calculated altitude is greater. At the point thus established, a line is drawn perpendicular to the azimuth line. This perpendicular, considered a part of the circle of position through the point, is the position line.

Three bodies are generally observed, the position lines being adjusted to a common time, to establish a fix (not called a running fix if the entire period of observation is not more than a few minutes). The observations, sight reduction, and plotting are seldom of sufficient accuracy to produce a common intersection of all three position lines at a point. More commonly, a small triangle, called a COCKED HAT, is formed. The centre of this triangle, equidistant from the three position lines, is commonly taken as the fix.

If only one body is available for observation, as frequently occurs during daylight hours, an estimated position can be obtained by dropping a perpendicular from the best determination of position before the observation was made to the position line; or a running fix can be obtained by taking two observations separated in time sufficiently to allow for an adequate change in azimuth.

The process of sight reduction can be simplified somewhat if Polaris or a body on the celestial meridian is observed.

Recent years have witnessed the addition of

advanced techniques to the more classical procedures that have been described. Among the advances have been wider use of electronic computers, development of inertial navigators that measure and integrate accelerations of the craft in a highly sophisticated dead-reckoning system, adaptation of Doppler sonar to provide an acoustic dead-reckoning system, perfection of automatic star trackers, introduction of a highly accurate system using Doppler measurement of signals from navigational satellites, and the combination of various aids to form complex composite systems using some form of filtering to provide a single indication of position. These are expensive systems of limited application.

Some future advances under development or consideration include the use of night-vision techniques for astronavigation, low light level television, lasers, infrared, and better gyroscopes for greater accuracy.

The successful navigator is the one who acquires excellent knowledge of the basic principles of navigation, appreciation of the requirements and limitations of his situation, thorough acquaintance with the equipment available to him, and who keeps constantly alert, assumes nothing that cannot be verified, and uses every opportunity to develop judgement and skill through continual study and practice.

– under sail

The principal constraint in navigating under sail arises from the fact that a sailing vessel will only point to within a certain angle of the APPARENT WIND: for a square-rigger this angle might be as large as 75°, for a close-winded yacht as small as 35°. In making good a course to windward, therefore, a sailing vessel will have to TACK or make a series of BOARDS. Where there is a choice it is generally accepted that the most favourable tack will be that which looks up best for the destination, i.e. the master tack.

In principle it does not matter whether the immediate destination to windward, or windward mark, is made in two boards of equal or different lengths according to the circumstances, or in a series, since the distance sailed will be the same. When the immediate destination is dead to windward, however, it is sounder to tack either side of the mean course, say when each tack becomes the unfavourable one by about 5°. In this way the mark is kept more or less to windward so that any shift of wind will be favourable in the sense that it will free the boat on either one tack or the other.

On the other hand if a shift of wind can be forecast, then these tactics will be biased in the direction from which the new wind is expected to blow. Thus the boat might be tacked when she is 15° to the right of the direct windward course if the wind is

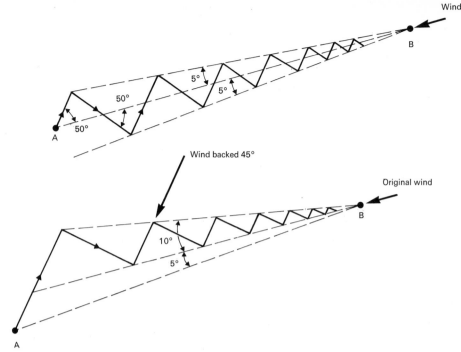

Fig. 1 Tacking with the mark dead to windward (top). *Assuming the boat makes good 50° to the wind, the boat will be tacked when the mark bears 5° on either bow*

   A = starting point; B = mark

Fig. 2 (above) *When the navigator wishes to take into account the possibility of a wind shift, the boat will be tacked so as to stand further in the direction of the new wind and so minimize the chance of overstanding*

expected to VEER and to the left if it is expected to BACK. In this way she will be in a position to take advantage of the wind freeing without the danger of OVERSTANDING.

Under sail there is always some duality of purpose, especially on the wind, between the requirements of keeping the boat moving fast and keeping her headed in the right direction. In general terms it has always been accepted that when close-fetching at a considerable distance from the mark little will be lost by sailing the boat a point FREE in order to gain speed. How close it will pay to sail will depend on the distance to the mark, the boat's sailing qualities and the likelihood of a wind shift, and perhaps other imponderables such as tidal stream etc. If the mark is a long way off – say 250 miles rather than 50 – then a wind shift is more probable and the broad objective will be to get as near to the mark as possible before the wind shifts.

When sailing off the wind it will generally be possible to steer direct for the destination. However, with fore-and-aft rigs sailing dead downwind is an uncomfortable and inefficient point of sailing, so that it is usual to put the wind a few degrees on either quarter in order to gain speed, especially in light weather (*see* RIGS). The extra distance to be sailed will vary as the secant of the angle between the courses and if the destination is distant this is generally negligible; to justify steering 20° off the direct course downward, for example, it will only be necessary to

increase the speed by one sixteenth.

Sailing performance in ocean racers is nowadays derived for the most part electronically from measurements of hull speed and apparent wind velocity (*see* MONITORING SAILING PERFORMANCE). In both windward and downwind sailing the criterion is hull speed resolved in the direction of the true wind, and the yacht will be sailing at her best advantage when this factor, termed velocity made good (V_{mg}), is at a maximum. V_{mg} can be obtained for both windward and downwind sailing from yacht performance tables, or curves, or by a sailing performance computer that indicates when V_{mg} has reached its maximum value for the existing strength of wind. The sensors used are a masthead wind-velocity indicator, the electronic log, and a compass.

Bearing in mind these considerations it is evident that a major part of the navigator's task under sail offshore is to keep an up-to-date dead-reckoning position from a record of the courses steered and distances run (*see* DEAD RECKONING). One of the difficulties, especially in ocean racing, is that whatever the course ordered the course steered is likely to vary from moment to moment to take advantage of temporary wind shifts because the helmsman is likely to be watching the sails rather than the compass, only occasionally pausing to check his course. In ocean races therefore it is customary to log the course steered and distance run quite frequently; it can be as often as every quarter of an hour in some circumstances.

The most common way of measuring speed or distance under sail is still perhaps by towed LOG that records on an instrument mounted inboard, in terms of mileage and/or speed, the rotation of an impeller towed astern. In conventional merchant and naval vessels bottom logs of one kind and another are in general use. These work on an electronic principle and have either a pitot tube or an impeller mounted in a tube through the hull. In racing yachts, where the drag of the line of towed logs is considered unacceptable, an electronic log using a very small fixed impeller is generally integrated with the other sensors that indicate sailing performance. Speed changes as low as 0.01 knots can be detected and these can be useful when trimming sails in light weather. There is also an electromagnetic log that senses the flow of water past its face and has the advantages of no drag and no possibility of fouling up.

All logs except those whose measurements relate to a fixed frame of reference such as the sea bed or the earth's magnetic field, measure the rate of passage through the water, which may itself be moving in relation to the earth. Their readings must thus be corrected for the effect of tidal stream or current (*see* LOG).

Although gyrocompasses, which indicate true as opposed to magnetic north, are almost universally used in commercial and naval vessels, their weight, power consumption, and probably expense have prevented their adoption in sailing yachts where the magnetic compass remains the standard HEADING reference. Magnetic compass readings, whether of bearings or courses, need to be corrected first of all for deviation – the amount the compass needle is deflected by components of the ship's own magnetism, and which varies with the heading; and then for variation – the angle at any position between the North Pole and the North Magnetic Pole. The former quantity is taken from a deviation card that gives for each heading the residual error left when the compass was last corrected; the latter quantity may be read off the chart.

A convenient type of magnetic compass for yachts is the spherical compass, which magnifies the readings of a very small card so that they can be read several feet away. Two such compasses mounted one on either side of the cockpit prevent parallax when the helmsman is to one side, as he generally will be on the wind.

Compass correction is generally carried out by a qualified compass adjuster. Using an established true bearing, from a transit or a distant object, or a timed azimuth of the sun, the ship is placed on successive magnetic headings to obtain, in the first place, a deviation curve. Magnets are then placed to counteract the error on each of the main

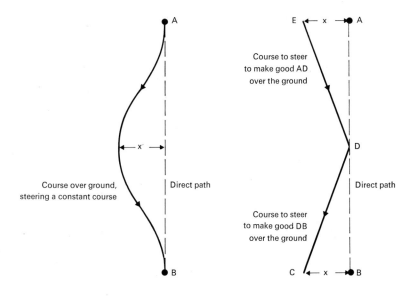

Fig. 3 In a passage over a single tide the yacht in the left-hand diagram travels a greater distance over the ground by steering a constant heading but less through the water than the yacht in the right-hand *diagram, which corrects for both ebb and flow so as to keep to the direct path. It will be evident that the sum of the two corrected courses, ED and DC, is greater than the direct distance AB*

headings and the ship is finally reswung to establish the residual errors on each heading, as recorded on the deviation card. Because they spend prolonged periods on one tack or the other sailing vessels are particularly vulnerable to the effect of the horizontal component of vertical magnetic force that comes into play when the vessel is heeled. In yachts this HEELING ERROR, which is removed by the use of vertical magnets, is generally due to the engine or an iron ballast keel.

Although bearings can be taken from the standard or steering compass on board, a hand-bearing compass is generally more convenient and can be used from a position where it is known to be free from error (*see* MARINER'S COMPASS).

The ship's position, whether derived from dead reckoning (the estimate from the course steered and distance run) or from a fix (the position determined by position lines, whether visual, radio, or astronomical) is usually plotted on the navigation chart.

Unless they are for special purposes, such as measuring great circles or for use in very high latitudes where the meridians converge, charts for use at sea are constructed on a Mercator projection on which RHUMB LINES cut all the meridians at the same angle. In moderate latitudes, which is where most sea navigation is carried on, this greatly simplifies the navigator's task even though the rhumb line that appears on the Mercator projection as a straight line is in fact, on the globe, a

curve spiralling towards the Poles, and not thus the shortest distance between any two points. In high latitudes the distortion of the latitude scale to compensate for the convergence of the meridians, which on the globe all meet at the Poles, becomes too great and other projections such as the polar stereographic or GNOMONIC will be used (*see* MERCATOR PROJECTION).

The standard charts for navigation are published by the hydrographic departments of the various maritime nations, although there are a number of private chart-publishing companies; their data, however, is usually taken from the same source. Charts and sailing directions intended specifically for small craft are for the most part produced by private companies or associations.

Although tidal-stream information is given on most of the standard coastal charts, a better general picture is obtained from tidal-stream atlases, which show what the stream is doing at various states of the tide, generally given for a standard port (Dover, for example). Under power it is customary to allow for the effect of tidal stream by making a correction to the course so that the ship follows a straight line over the sea bed (*see* TIDES AND TIDAL STREAMS). However, although the ship will thus travel a shorter distance over the earth's surface she will in fact travel further through the water and in ocean racing, for example, as much of the tide as possible is allowed to cancel out and a correction of course made only for the residual set.

When going to windward under sail the tidal stream should, whenever possible, be placed under the lee bow so that the tide pushes the boat up to windward; this will both increase the apparent wind strength and make the boat sail faster and closer to the true wind.

Because the imponderables in dead reckoning build up from inexact knowledge of the course steered, the distance run and the set and drift, the ship's position should be fixed whenever possible and the dead reckoning updated. When land is visible and not too distant, visual bearings of recognized points of land or landmarks should be taken on the compass and laid off on the chart. Two such bearings, if the angle is not too acute, will in principle fix the position of the ship. However, a third bearing is taken, whenever possible, to increase the reliability of the fix. Because these bearings will not be completely accurate they generally intersect to form a triangle. In principle the ship's position will generally be in the centre of the triangle, but it is usual to adopt a position nearest to the land, since that will be navigationally the most dangerous direction.

When out of sight of land the position may be fixed by the sun, moon, planets, or stars if both they and the horizon are visible, or by a variety of electronic methods that require special equipment.

The principles of astronomical navigation are described elsewhere (*see* ASTRONOMICAL NAVIGATION). Here it will suffice to discuss the use to which they are put in small craft. The overwhelming advantage of astronavigation (as it may be termed) is that its coverage is worldwide and it is completely free. The major disadvantage is that it is not always available due to cloud cover or, for example, a hazy horizon. The accuracy of an astronomical fix will depend on a number of considerations that will include the skill of the observer, the conditions of observation, the method of reduction used, and certain variables such as the accuracy to which dip and refraction are known. It is thus impossible to give a figure that will cover the general case but as a guide one might say that a good observer in favourable conditions will probably expect to obtain a position within a mile or so of the true position.

Statistical theory tells us that the random error of the mean of a number of observations is reduced as the square root of the number. Averaging a series of observations of, say, the sun does not necessarily reduce the error by this factor because the errors will not always be random. Nevertheless because of the difficulties of taking sextant observations at sea, especially in small vessels with a low height of eye and rapid acceleration, it is general practice to make a series of observations and then take the mean of the altitudes and the times at which they were taken.

Almanacs and tables intended for marine navigation are tabulated to an accuracy of $0'.1$ of altitude and $0°.1$ of azimuth. It can be shown, however, that where there is an inescapable error, in this case that of observation, little will be gained by reducing other sources of error beyond a certain point and many will maintain that the air almanac and tables such as the combined British and American *Sight Reduction Tables for Air Navigation*, which tabulate altitude to $1'$ and azimuth to $1°$, suffice for all practical purposes at sea.

There is a wide variety of method for solving the astronomical triangle and the choice will to some extent be an individual one. Nevertheless it seems likely that tabular methods will predominate for the present because of their simplicity and cheapness, and that of these the direct-entry tables giving altitude and azimuth for arguments LHA and declination will, at least until some radical new developments, continue to be the most popular. As they become cheaper and are manufactured specifically for a marine environment, hand-held calculators designed to solve the astronomical triangle are rapidly supplanting tables.

It has been said that the mark of a good navigator is not so much his ability to obtain accurate information as his ability to evaluate and interpret correctly the information available to him. With astronavigation this means assessing the likely error of each position line and so interpreting the plot. There are various methods of analysing the plot, of which perhaps the most practical is to bisect the external angle between the azimuth lines and take the intersection of the bisectors rather than the position lines as the fix. This method will be independent of systematic errors such as dip and, within certain limits, will average random errors as well.

For further discussion of other aspects of navigation, including recent developments, *see* ASTRONOMICAL NAVIGATION; DECCA NAVIGATOR; DISCOVERY OF LONGITUDE; GYRO-COMPASS; HYDROGRAPHIC SURVEYING; MAP AND CHART PROJECTIONS; MARINER'S COMPASS; PILOTAGE; SATELLITE NAVIGATION; TIDES AND TIDAL STREAMS; WIND AND WEATHER

Navigational buoys *see* BUOY

Navigational triangle *see* ASTRONOMICAL TRIANGLE; ASTRONOMICAL NAVIGATION

Navigation lights *see* LIGHTS, NAVIGATION

Neaped, beneaped
A vessel is said to be neaped when she grounds at high water and the following tide is not high enough to float her off.

Neap tides
Tides that occur near the times of the moon's first and third quarter when the range tends to decrease.

Newport-Bermuda *see* YACHT RACING: Offshore racing, Major races and series

New York Yacht Club
The New York Yacht Club was formed by John C. Stevens on board his schooner *Gimcrack* in 1844. Although this club was not the first in the United States, it was for many years the mouthpiece of American yachting. It certainly must have been one of the first to hold races for amateurs only. Also there is a category of Lady Associate Members.

The model room at the clubhouse in New York has the world's finest collection of yacht models. It includes all the *America*'s Cup challengers and defenders, exhibited side by side. (One of the rules requires a member, if asked by the Model Committee, to give a model of any yacht entered for a club race, with the bow to the right, and so the club is full of half models.)

It was Commodore Stevens and others who took the schooner *America* to Cowes, to come away with the ROYAL YACHT SQUADRON'S £100 Cup, which adorns the trophy room and is now known as the *America*'s Cup (*see* YACHT RACING: Major races and series). The trophy room also includes the Sovereign's Cup, presented by the reigning British monarch of the day. This is raced for during the annual NYYC Cruise, a highlight of the American yachting scene, at least on the Eastern seaboard. The New York Yacht Club Cup is one of the most treasured and sought-after cups sailed for during Cowes Week.

Nip
Pressure on a rope where it passes through a fairlead or over a sheave; a sharp bend in a rope.

Noon sight
Taking the altitude of the sun at APPARENT NOON, generally to determine latitude.

North
The GREAT-CIRCLE direction from any point to the (true) North Pole. Magnetic north is

O

the direction of that part of the horizontal component of the earth's magnetic field that runs towards the North Magnetic Pole.

North American Yacht Racing Union *see* UNITED STATES YACHT RACING UNION

Notice to Mariners
A (normally) weekly publication issued by hydrographic departments throughout the world giving information about changes in aids to navigation that affect mariner's charts and publications.

Nun buoy
(American) conical buoy.

Occlusion
The overtaking of one front by another. *See* WIND AND WEATHER

Occulting light
A navigational light the characteristic of which provides a period of light longer than the period of darkness. *See* LIGHTS

ODAS buoys *see* BUOY: Navigational buoys

Offing
The part of the visible sea at a distance from the shore.

Offsets
Measurements supplied to the boatbuilder so that he can lay down a vessel's lines in the loft.

Offshore racing *see* YACHT RACING

Offshore Racing Council (ORC)
The INTERNATIONAL YACHT RACING UNION recognizes the ORC (formerly the Offshore Rating Council) as the sole body to administer the International Offshore Rule and the correlated special regulations, measurement, classes, and time allowances (*see* HANDICAP SYSTEMS).

Council members are nominated by the national authorities of countries taking part in offshore racing and represent areas as follows: Australasia; Benelux; France/Spain; Greece/Italy/Turkey/Yugoslavia; Japan; North America; Scandinavia; South America; United Kingdom/Irish Republic; West Germany. There are two delegates from IYRU. The ORC is the international authority for the level-rating classes of the IOR.

Committees comprise: Executive; International Technical; Measurement; Small

Yacht; Level Rating; Special Regulations; Time Allowances.

Offshore rules *see* YACHT RACING; HANDICAP SYSTEMS

Offshore wind *see* BREEZE, LAND

Offshore yachts *see* YACHT RACING: Offshore racing, Ocean and cruiser racing

Off the wind
Sailing free.

Olympic Games
Sailing has been an Olympic sport ever since the Paris Games in 1900. There was a break for the St Louis Games, but since then there have been sailing races at each Olympiad. In the early years very few nations competed. The biggest Olympic regatta so far was at Kiel in 1972, where 48 nations were represented by 165 boats.

The classes to be sailed are decided by the INTERNATIONAL YACHT RACING UNION (IYRU) at the next annual meeting after each Olympiad. Classes for 1980 are Soling, Star, Tornado, Flying Dutchman, 470 and Finn. The events are to be held at Tallinn, capital of Estonia. The Olympic Games Course is shown on p.262.

At present only one boat per nation is allowed to race in each class. The Olympic series consists of seven races of which the yacht's six best races are counted for her total points (the 1977 International Yacht Racing Rules, Appendix 5, set out the scoring system).

The medal record for Olympic yachtsmen is held by Paul Elvstrøm of Denmark, who won the gold medal for the single-handed dinghy in 1948, 1952, 1956, and 1960.

Tempests sailing during the 1976 Olympiad at Kingston, Ontario. Designed by Ian Proctor, this two-man GRP racing dinghy has a retractable keel and built-in buoyancy

– Olympic games yachting results

		CLASS	COUNTRY	YACHT	OWNER/CREW
1900	PARIS. YACHTING EVENTS AT MEULAN AND LE HAVRE; 6 NATIONS	0.5 ton	1. France	*Quand-Même*	Texier
			2. France	*Baby*	P. Gervais
			3. France	*Sarcelle*	H. Monnot
		0.5–1 ton	1. Great Britain	*Scotia*	L. C. Currie, J. H. Gretton, L. Hope
			2. France	*Crabe II*	J. Bandrier, J. Lebret, W. Martin, Marcotte, Valton
			3. France	*Scramasaxe*	E. and F. Michelet
		1–2 ton	1. Germany	*Aschenbrödel*	M. Wiesner, H. Peters, O. Weise, G. Naue
			2. Switzerland	*Lérina*	Comte Hermann de Pourtalès
			3. France	*Marthe*	Vilamitjana
		2–3 ton	1. Great Britain	*Ollé*	E. Shaw
			2. France	*Favorite*	Susse
			3. France	*Mignon*	Donny
		3–10	1. United States	*Bona Fide*	H. Taylor
			2. France	*Gitana*	M. Gufflet
			3. United States	*Frimousse*	MacHenry
		10–20 Le Havre	1. France	*Estérel*	E. Billard, P. Perquer
			2. France	*Quand-Même*	Duc Decazes
			3. Great Britain	*Laurea*	E. Hore
		Open	1. Great Britain	*Scotia*	L. C. Currie, J. H. Gretton, L. Hope
			2. Germany	*Aschenbrödel*	M. Wiesner, H. Peters, O. Weise, G. Naue
			3. France	*Turquoise*	E. and F. Michelet

1904	ST LOUIS. NO YACHTING				

		CLASS	COUNTRY	YACHT	OWNER/CREW
1908	LONDON. YACHTING EVENTS AT RYDE, ISLE OF WIGHT, 12-METRES ON CLYDE; 5 NATIONS	6-Metre	1. Great Britain	*Dormy*	G. Laws, T. McMeekin, C. Crichton
			2. Belgium	*Zut*	Léon and Louis Huybrechts, H. Weewauters
			3. France	*Guyoni*	H. Arthus, L. Potheau, P. Rabot
		7-Metre	1. Great Britain (Walkover)	*Heroine*	C. Rivett-Carnac, N. Bingley, R. T. Dixon, F. Clytie
		8-Metre	1. Great Britain	*Cobweb*	B. Cochrane, A. Wood, H. Sutton, J. E. Rhodes, C. R. Campbell
			2. Sweden	*Vinga*	C. Hellström, E. Thormåhlen, E. Wallerius, E. Sandberg, H. Wallin
			3. Great Britain	*Sorais*	Duchess of Westminster, R. Himloke, C. Hughes, F. St John Hughes, G. Ratsey
		12-Metre	1. Great Britain	*Hera*	T. Glen-Coats, J. Buchanan, J. Bunten, A. Downes, J. H. Downes (helmsman), D. Dunlop, J. Mackenzie, A. Martin, G. Tait, J. Aspin
			2. Great Britain	*Mouchette*	Charles MacIver, J. Baxter, W. P. Davidson, J. Jellico, J. Adam, C. R. McIver, J. Kenion, T. Littledale, C. McLeod-Robertson, J. Spence
		15-Metre	No entries		

NOTES Glen-Coats and Downes in *Hera* received Gold medals, the crew Silver. MacIver in *Mouchette* received Silver and crew Bronze. Cochrane in *Cobweb* received Gold medal and his crew Silver. Hellström in *Vinga* received Silver and crew Bronze. Rivett-Carnac received a gilded Silver medal and his crew Silver.

1912 STOCKHOLM. YACHTING EVENTS AT NYNÄSHAMN; 6 NATIONS

CLASS	COUNTRY	YACHT	OWNER/CREW
6-Metre	1. France	*Mac Miche*	G. A. and J. Thube
	2. Denmark	*Nurdug II*	H. Meulengracht-Madsen, S. Herschend, S. Thomsen
	3. Sweden	*Kerstin*	H. and E. Sandberg, O. Aust
8-Metre	1. Norway	*Taifun*	T. Glad, T. Aas, A. Brecke, T. Corneliussen, C. Jebe
	2. Sweden	*Sans Atout*	B. Heyman, E. Henriques, H. and N. Westermark, A. Thiel
	3. Finland	*Lucky Girl*	B. and G. Tallberg, A. Ahnger, E. Lindh, G. Westling
10-Metre	1. Sweden	*Kitty*	C. Hellström, E. and H. Wallerius, H. Lundén, H. Nyberg, H. Rosenswärd, P. Isberg and F. Ericsson
	2. Finland	*Nina*	H. Wahl, W. Björksten, J. Björnström, B. Brenner, A. Franck, E. Lindh, A. Pekkalainen
	3. Russia	*Gallia II*	E. Belvselvsky, Brashe, Pushnitsky, A. Rodionov, I. Shomaker, Shtraukh
12-Metre	1. Norway	*Magda IX*	J. Anker, A. Larsen, N. Bertelsen, H. Hansen, M. Konow, P. Larsen, E. Lund, F. Staib, A. Heje, G. Thaulow
	2. Sweden	*Erna Signe*	N. Persson, H. Clason, R. Sällström, N. Lamby, K. and D. Bergström, C. Lindqvist, P. Bergman, S. Kander, F. Johnson
	3. Finland	*Heatherbell*	E. Krogius, M. Alfthan, E. Hartvall, J. Hulldén, S. Juslén, E. Sandelin, J. Silén

NOTES The only Olympic regatta in which Tsarist Russian yachts took part; an 8-Metre also competed. Ferenc Mezö's *Olimpiad Kalauz* (Budapest 1936) states that Aleksandr Vishnegradsky was helmsman of the Russian 10-Metre.

1920 ANTWERP. YACHTING EVENTS AT OSTEND; 6 NATIONS, 24 BOATS IN 14 CLASSES

12-ft dinghy 1919	1. Holland	*Beatrijs III*	J. and F. Hin
	2. Holland	*Boreas*	A. E. van der Biesen, P. B. Beukers
19-ft dinghy	1. Great Britain	*Brat*	F. A. Richards
30-sq. m	1. Sweden	*Kullan*	G. Lundqvist, R. Steffenburg, G. Bengtsson, A. Calvert
40-sq. m	1. Sweden	*Sif*	T. and Y. Holm, A. Rydin, G. Tengvall
	2. Sweden	*Elsie*	G. Svensson, R. O. Swensson, P. Almstedt, E. Mellbin
6-Metre old type 1906	1. Belgium	*Edelweis*	E. and F. Cornellie, F. Bruynseels
	2. Norway	*Marmi II*	E. Torgersen, A. Knudsen, L. Ericksen
	3. Norway	*Stella*	H. Agersborg, T. Pedersen, E. Berntsen
6-Metre new type 1919	1. Norway	*Jo*	A. Brecke, P. Kaasen, I. Rød
	2. Belgium	*Tan-Fe-Pah*	L. Huybrechts, C. van den Bussche, J. Klotz
6.5-Metre new type 1919	1. Holland	*Oranje*	J. and B. Carp, P. Wernink
	2. France	*Rose Pompon*	A. Weil, F. Picon, R. Monier
7-Metre old type 1906	1. Great Britain	*Ancora*	C. Macey Wright, D. Wright, R. Coleman, W. Maddison
8-Metre old type 1906	1. Norway	*Ierne*	A. Ringvold, T. Holbye, T. Wagle, K. Olsen, A. Jacobsen
	2. Norway	*Fornebo*	N. Nielsen, J. Faye, C. Dick, S. Abel

	CLASS	COUNTRY	YACHT	OWNER/CREW
1920 *continued*	8-Metre new type 1919	1. Norway	*Sildra*	M. Konow, R. Marthiniussen, R. Vig, T. Christoffersen
		2. Norway	*Lyn II*	J. Salvesen, L. Schmidt, F. Schiander, N. Thomas, R. Tschudi
		3. Belgium	*Antwerpia V*	A. Grisar, W. de l'Arbre, L. Standaert, H. Weewauters
	10-Metre old type 1906	1. Norway	*Eleda*	E. Herseth, S. Holter, I. Nielsen, O. Sørensen, P. and G. Jamvold, C. Juell
	10-Metre new type 1919	1. Norway	*Mosk II*	W. Gilbert, A. Arentz, R. Gjertsen, A. Sejersted, H. and T. Schjøtt, O. Falkenberg
	12-Metre old type 1906	1. Norway	*Atlanta*	H., J., and O. Østervold, Hans Mæss, L. Christiansen, H. Møgster, R. and H. Birkeland, K. Østervold
	12-Metre new type 1919	1. Norway	*Heira II*	J. Friele, O. Ørvig, A. Allers, C. Wiese, M. Borthen, E. Reimers, K. Hassel, T. and E. Ørvig
1924 PARIS. YACHTING EVENTS AT MEULAN AND LE HAVRE; 19 NATIONS, 31 BOATS	12-ft dinghy 17 boats	1. Belgium 2. Norway 3. Finland		L. Huybrechts H. Robert H. Dittmar
	6-Metre 9 boats	1. Norway 2. Denmark 3. Holland	*Elisabeth V* *Bonzo* *Willem IV*	E. Lunde, C. Dahl, A. Lundgren W. Vett, K. Degn, C. Nielsen J. Carp, J. Guépin, J. Vreede
	8-Metre 5 boats	1. Norway	*Bera*	A. Ringvold sen., R. Bockelie, H. Hagen, I. Nielsen, A. Ringvold jr
		2. Great Britain	*Emily*	E. Jacob, T. and W. Riggs, E. Roney, G. Fowler
		3. France	*Namoussa*	L. Bréguet, P. Ganthier, R. Girardet, A. Guerrier, G. Mollard
1928 AMSTERDAM. YACHTING EVENTS ON ZUIDER ZEE (NOW IJSSELMEER); 23 NATIONS, 43 BOATS	12-ft dinghy 20 boats	1. Sweden 2. Norway 3. Finland		S. Thorell H. Robert B. Broman
	6-Metre 13 boats	1. Norway	*Norna*	J. Anker, Crown Prince Olav, E. Anker, H. Bryhn
		2. Denmark	*Hihi*	N. Otto Møller, A. Høj-Petersen, P. Schlütter and S. Linck
		3. Estonia	*Tutti*	N. Wekschin, W. von Wirén, E. Vogdt, A. and G. Fählmann
	8-Metre 8 boats	1. France	*L'Aile VI*	D. Bouché, V. Hériot, A. Lesauvage, J. Lesieur, C. de la Saplière, A. Derrien
		2. Holland	*Hollandia*	J. van Hoolwerff, L. Doedes, M. de Wit, G. de Vries-Lentsch, H. Kersken, C. van Staveren
		3. Sweden	*Sylvia*	J., P., and C. Sandblom, Tore Holm, C. Hamar, W. Thörsleff

	CLASS	COUNTRY	YACHT	OWNER/CREW
1932 LOS ANGELES. 11 NATIONS, 23 BOATS	Snowbird 11 boats	1. France 2. Holland 3. Spain		J. Lebrun A. Maas S. Cansino
	Star 7 boats	1. United States 2. Great Britain 3. Sweden	*Jupiter* *Joy* *Swedish Star*	G. Gray, A. Libano jr C. Ratsey, P. Jaffe G. Asther, D. Sundén-Cullberg
	6-Metre 3 boats	1. Sweden	*Bissbi*	T. Holm, M. Hindorff, O. Åkerlund, Å. Bergqvist
		2. United States	*Gallant*	F. Conant, R. Carlson, T. Ashbrook, C. Smith
		3. Canada	*Caprice*	P. Rogers, G. Wilson, G. Boultbee, K. Glass
	8-Metre	1. United States	*Angelita*	O. P. Churchill, J. Biby jr, W. Cooper, K. Dorsey, R. Sutton, A. Morgan
		2. Canada	*Santa Maria*	R. Maitland, E. Cribb, H. Jones, P. Gordon, H. Wallace, G. Gyles
1936 BERLIN. YACHTING EVENTS AT KIEL; 26 NATIONS, 59 BOATS	Olympia-jolle 25 boats	1. Holland 2. Germany 3. Great Britain		D. Kagchelland W. Krogmann P. Scott
	Star 12 boats	1. Germany 2. Sweden 3. Holland	*Wannsee* *Sunshine* *Bem II*	P. Bischoff, H. Weise A. Laurin, U. Wallentin W. de Vries-Lentsch, A. Maas
	6-Metre 12 boats	1. Great Britain	*Lalage*	C. Boardman, M. Bellville, R. Harmer, C. Leaf, L. Martin
		2. Norway	*Lully II*	M. and K. Konow, F. Meyer, V. Nyqvist, A. Tveten
		3. Sweden	*May be*	S. Salén, L. Ekdahl, M. Hindorff, T. Lord, D. Salén
	8-Metre 10 boats	1. Italy	*Italia*	G. Reggio, B. Bianchi, L. de Manincor, D. Mordini, L. and E. Poggi
		2. Norway	*Silja*	O. and J. Ditlev-Simonsen, H. Struknæs, L. Schmidt, N. Wallem, J. Thams
		3. Germany	*Germania*	H. Howaldt, A. Krupp von Bohlen und Halbach, F. Scheder-Bieschin, E. Mohr, F. Bischoff
1948 LONDON. YACHTING EVENTS AT TORBAY; 23 NATIONS, 75 BOATS	Firefly 21 boats	1. Denmark 2. United States 3. Holland		P. Elvstrøm R. Evans jr J. de Jong
	Swallow 14 boats	1. Great Britain 2. Portugal 3. United States	*Swift* *Symphony* *Margaret*	S. Morris, D. Bond D. and F. Bello L. Pirie, O. Torry jr
	Star 17 boats	1. United States 2. Cuba 3. Holland	*Hilarius* *Kurush III* *Starita*	H. and P. Smart C. de Cardenas sen., C. de Cardenas jr A. Maas, E. Stutterheim
	Dragon 12 boats	1. Norway 2. Sweden s. Denmark	*Pan* *Slaghöken* *Snap*	T. Thorvaldsen, S. Lie, H. Barfod F. Bohlin, H. Johnson, G. Brodin W. and O. Berntsen, K. Bæss
	6-Metre 11 boats	1. United States	*Llanoria*	H. Whiton, A. Loomis, J. Weekes, M. Mooney, J. Smith
		2. Argentina	*Dijinn*	E. Sieburger, E. Homps, R. de la Torre, R. Rivademar, J. Sieburger
		3. Sweden	*Ali Baba II*	T. Holm, T. Lord, M. Hindorff, K. Amelin, G. Salén

	CLASS	COUNTRY	YACHT	OWNER/CREW
1952 HELSINKI. YACHTING EVENTS AT HARMAJA; 19 NATIONS, 93 BOATS	Finn 28 boats	1. Denmark 2. Great Britain 3. Sweden		P. Elvstrøm C. Currey R. Sarby
	Star 21 boats	1. Italy 2. United States 3. Portugal	*Merope I* *Comanche* *Espadarte*	A. Straulino, N. Rode J. Price, J. Reid J. Fiuza, F. Andrade
	Dragon 17 boats	1. Norway 2. Sweden 3. W. Germany	*Pan* *Tornado* *Gustel X*	T. Thorvaldsen, S. Lie, H. Barfod P. Gedda, L. Boldt-Christmas, E. Almkvist T. Thomsen, E. Natusch, G. Nowka
	5.5-Metre 16 boats	1. United States 2. Norway 3. Sweden	*Complex II* *Encore* *Hojwa*	B. Chance, S. White, E. White P. and V. Lunde, B. Flakum-Hansen F. and M. Wassén, C. Ohlson
	6-Metre 11 boats	1. United States 2. Norway 3. Finland	*Llanoria* *Elisabeth X* *Ralia*	H. Whiton, J. Roosevelt, J. Morgan, E. Endt, E. Ridder, E. Whiton F. and J. Ferner, C. Mortensen, E. Heiberg, T. Arneberg E. Westerlund, P. Sjöberg, R. Jansson, A. Konto, R. Turrka
1956 MELBOURNE. YACHTING EVENTS AT PORT PHILLIP; 28 NATIONS, 71 BOATS	Finn 20 boats	1. Denmark 2. Belgium 3. United States		P. Elvstrøm A. Nelis J. Marvin
	12-sq. m Sharpie 13 boats	1. Holland 2. Australia 3. Great Britain	*Jest* *Falcon IV* *Chuckles*	P. Mander, J. Cropp R. Tasker, J. Scott J. Blackall, T. Smith
	Star 12 boats	1. United States 2. Italy 3. Bahamas	*Kathleen* *Merope III* *Gem IV*	H. Williams, L. Low A. Straulino, N. Rode D. Knowles, S. Farrington
	Dragon 16 boats	1. Sweden 2. Denmark 3. Great Britain	*Slaghöken* *Tip* *Bluebottle*	F. Bohlin, L. Wikström, B. Palmquist O. Berntsen, C. Andresen, C. von Bülow G. Mann, R. Backus, J. Janson
	5.5-Metre 10 boats	1. Sweden 2. Great Britain 3. Australia	*Rush V* *Vision* *Buraddoo*	L. Thörn, H. Karlsson, S. Stork R. Perry, N. Cochran-Patrick, J. Dillon, D. Bowker A. Sturrock, D. Mytton, D. Buxton
1960 ROME. YACHTING EVENTS AT NAPLES; 46 NATIONS, 128 BOATS	Finn 35 boats	1. Denmark 2. USSR 3. Belgium		P. Elvstrøm A. Chuchelov A. Nelis
	Flying Dutchman 31 boats	1. Norway 2. Denmark 3. Germany	*Sirene* *Skum* *Macky VI*	P. Lunde jr, B. Bergvall H. Fogh, O. Petersen R. Mulka, I. von Bredow
	Star 26 boats	1. USSR 2. Portugal 3. United States	*Tornado* *Ma Lindo* *Shrew*	T. Pinegin, F. Shutkov J. and M. Quina W. Parks, R. Halperin
	Dragon 27 boats	1. Greece 2. Argentine 3. Italy	*Nirefs* *Tango* *Venilia*	Crown Prince Constantin, O. Eskidjoglou, G. Zaimis J. Salas-Chaves, H. Calegaris, J. del Rio A. Cosentino, A. Ciciliano, G. de Stefano
	5.5-Metre 19 boats	1. United States 2. Denmark 3. Switzerland	*Minotaur* *Webb II* *Ballerina IV*	G. O'Day, J. Hunt, D. Smith W. Berntsen, S. Christensen, S. Hancke H. Copponex, P. Girard, M. Metzger

	CLASS	COUNTRY	YACHT	OWNER/CREW
1964 TOKYO. YACHTING EVENTS AT ENOSHIMA; 40 NATIONS, 109 BOATS	Finn 33 boats	1. Germany 2. United States 3. Denmark		W. Kuhweide P. Barrett H. Wind
	Flying Dutchman 21 boats	1. New Zealand 2. Great Britain 3. United States	*Pandora* *Land C* *Widgeon*	H. Pedersen, E. Wells K. Musto, Arthur Morgan H. Melges, W. Bentsen
	Star 17 boats	1. Bahamas 2. United States 3. Sweden	*Gem* *Glider* *Humbug V*	D. Knowles, C. Cooke R. Stearns, L. Williams P. Pettersson, H. Sundström
	Dragon 23 boats	1. Denmark 2. Germany 3. United States	*White Lady* *Mutafo* *Aphrodite*	O. Berntsen, C. von Bülow, O. Poulsen P. Ahrendt, W. Lorenz, U. Mense L. North, C. Rogers, R. Deaver
	5.5-Metre 15 boats	1. Australia 2. Sweden 3. United States	*Barrenjoey* *Rush VII* *Bingo*	W. Northam, P. O'Donnell, J. Sargeant L. Thörn, S. Stock, A. Karlsson J. McNamara, F. Scully, J. Batchelder
1968 MEXICO CITY. YACHTING EVENTS AT ACAPULCO; 41 NATIONS, 123 BOATS	Finn 36 boats	1. USSR 2. Austria 3. Italy		V. Mankin H. Raudaschl F. Albarelli
	Flying Dutchman 30 boats	1. Great Britain 2. W. Germany 3. Brazil	*Super* *Leda* *Mach*	R. Pattison, I. McDonald-Smith U. Libor, P. Naumann R. Conrad, B. Cordes
	Star 20 boats	1. United States 2. Norway 3. Italy	*North Star* *Sirene* *Romance*	L. North, P. Barrett P. Lunde jr, P. Wiken F. Cavallo, C. Gargano
	Dragon 23 boats	1. United States 2. Denmark 3. E. Germany	*Williwawe* *Chok* *Mutafo*	G. Friedrichs, B. Jahncke, G. Schreck A. Birch, P. Lindemark, N. Markussen P. Borowski, K. Thun, K. Weichert
	5.5-Metre 14 boats	1. Sweden 2. Switzerland 3. Great Britain	*Wasa IV* *Le Toucan IX* *Yeoman*	U., J., and P. Sundelin L. Noverraz, M. Stern, B. Dunand R. Aisher, A. Jardine, P. Anderson
1972 MUNICH. YACHTING EVENTS AT KIEL; 48 NATIONS, 165 BOATS	Finn 35 boats	1. France 2. Greece 3. USSR		S. Maury I. Hatzipavlis V. Popatov
	Flying Dutchman 29 boats	1. Great Britain 2. France 3. W. Germany		R. Pattisson, C. Davies Y. and M. Pajot U. Libor, P. Naumann
	Tempest 22 boats	1. USSR 2. Great Britain 3. United States		V. Mankin, V. Dirdyra A. Warren, D. Hunt G. Foster, J. Hamber
	Star 23 boats	1. Australia 2. Sweden 3. W. Germany		D. Forbes, J. Anderson P. Petterson, S. Westerdahl W. Kuhweide, K. Meyer
	Soling 29 boats	1. United States 2. Sweden 3. Canada		H. Melgnes, W. Allen, W. Bentsen S. Wennerström, S. Kröök, B. Knape D. Miller, J. Eckels, P. Cote
	Dragon 27 boats	1. Australia 2. E. Germany 3. United States		J. Cuneo, T. Anderson, J. Shaw P. Borowski, K. Thun, K. Weichert D. Cohan, C. Horter, J. Marshal

	CLASS	COUNTRY	YACHT	OWNER/CREW
1976 MONTREAL. YACHTING EVENTS AT KINGSTON, ONT.; 39 NATIONS, 130 BOATS	Finn 28 boats	1. E. Germany 2. USSR 3. Australia		J. Schumann A. Balashov J. Bestraud
	470 28 boats	1. W. Germany 2. Spain 3. Australia		F. Hübner, A. Bode A. Gorostegui, P. Millet I. Brown, I. Ruff
	Flying Dutchman 20 boats	1. W. Germany 2. Great Britain 3. Brazil		J. and E. Diesch R. Pattisson, J. Brooke-Houghton R. Conrad, P. Ficher
	Tornado 14 boats	1. Great Britain 2. United States 3. Germany		R. White, J. Osborn D. McFaull, M. Rothwell J. Spengler, J. Schmall
	Tempest 16 boats	1. Sweden 2. USSR 3. United States		J. Albrechtsen and I. Hanson V. Mankin, V. Akimenko D. Conner, C. Findlay
	Soling 24 boats	1. Denmark 2. United States 3. E. Germany		P. Jensen, V. Bandelowski, E. Hansen J. Kolius, W. Glasgow and R. Hoepfner D. Below, M. Zachries, O. Engelhardt

The three-man Olympic-class Soling is an exciting boat to race. Designed by Jan Linge of Norway in 1966, its first appearance in the Olympic Games was in 1972. A keelboat of GRP construction, with an LOA of 26 ft 9 in (8.15 m), it is sailed without a trapeze (see also p. 262)

Omega

A very-low-frequency (VLF) radio aid to navigation using phase comparison of continuous-wave transmissions to obtain hyperbolic lines of position. The frequencies chosen provide economical global coverage and stable propagation conditions. The geometry of the system calls for only eight stations and the very long ranges available usually give the navigator the choice of more than the minimum two lines of position needed for a fix. Signals at VLF can be received by completely submerged submarines: Omega is the only radio aid with this capability.

The basic frequency of 10.2 kHz corresponds to a phase pattern repeating every 15 km. Each station radiates two further frequencies (13.6 kHz and 11.33 kHz) from which phase differences corresponding to the beat frequencies (3.4 kHz and 1.13 kHz) give coarser hyperbolic patterns of 45-km and 133-km lane width to resolve the ambiguities. These frequencies are transmitted on a time-sharing basis from all eight stations, with a total cycle time of 10 sec.

The shipboard receiver includes a highly stable oscillator to provide a reference wave since the signals to be compared in phase are not present simultaneously. The phase measurement is made in intervals of one-hundredth of a cycle, called a 'cec', or in 'centilanes' (1.8° of phase), and is displayed on numerical counters for plotting on a chart carrying the Omega lattice.

These charts assume no diurnal or seasonal changes in propagation over the path between transmitter and receiving station although such changes do occur, particularly between day and night conditions. They are, however, very stable and detailed correction tables, giving predicted variations, are used that assume a knowledge of location within 10° of latitude and longitude, approximate time and date, and the pair of stations being observed. With these corrections the accuracy of Omega is 2–6 km throughout the coverage. *See also* COMPOSITE OMEGA; DIFFERENTIAL OMEGA

One-design *see* YACHT RACING: Inshore racing

Onion patch *see* YACHT RACING: Major races and series

Onshore wind *see* BREEZE, SEA

On soundings

An area in which soundings can be obtained by the lead and line, generally assumed to be less than 100 fathoms (183 m).

On the wind

Sailing close-hauled.

OSTAR *see* YACHT RACING: Major races and series

Outboard engines *see* AUXILIARY ENGINES

Outhaul *see* MASTS AND RIGGING: Glossary

Overfalls

Turbulence caused by a tidal stream or current passing over a shoal or obstruction.

Overhand knot *see* ROPEWORK: Bends and hitches

Overhang

The parts of a vessel that extend beyond her waterline length.

Overstand

To sail (or stand on) too far before tacking for the mark.

P

Painter

A line attached forward in a dinghy to make her fast.

Paints and painting *see* MAINTENANCE

Parallax (in ALTITUDE)

The angle between the lines from a celestial body to an observer on the earth's surface and to the centre of the earth.

Parallel rules

Two rules of wood or metal joined by shorter swinging arms so that when separated they remain parallel. Parallel rules are used to transfer a given bearing from the WIND ROSE printed on a chart to any other point, or to transfer a POSITION LINE to take into account the distance sailed between two observations.

Parallel rules do not seem to have been used in navigation until late in the sixteenth century. Courses were laid down from the network of RHUMB LINES on the older portolan charts with a pair of dividers, to find two points on the course equally distant from the selected rhumb and therefore parallel to it. A modern modification of the parallel rule has rollers instead of swinging arms. Captain Field's rule is graduated round its edges as a protractor so that bearings can be transferred from the chart meridians.

Parcel

To bind canvas around a rope as a protection.

Parrel *see* MASTS AND RIGGING: Glossary

Partner(s) *see* MASTS AND RIGGING: Glossary (Mast partner)

Patent (taffrail) log *see* LOG

Pay off

A vessel is said to pay off when her head falls away to leeward.

Peak

The upper end of a gaff; the upper after corner of a gaffsail.

Pendant *see* MASTS AND RIGGING: Glossary

Performance and yacht design *see overleaf*

A Chinese junk in the Strait of Malacca. It is likely that the balanced lugsail of the West was derived from an early Chinese form. Today, similar rigs, with modern materials, are being used on a number of yachts (see, for example, illustrations on pp. 28, 29, 194, and the plate facing p. 32)

Performance and yacht design

Why does one boat sail faster than another?
What is the best course to windward? How
much does the crew contribute to yacht
performance? How close to windward can a
given boat sail? How can boat performance
be measured or predicted?

To inquire meaningfully into questions like
these it is necessary to acquire some understanding of the basic principles governing
yacht motion and the forces involved.

– resistance and performance

At first sight a sailing boat appears to bear a
close family resemblance to a ship. It is a
characteristic of all hulls, which are supported by water-buoyancy force – discovered
by Archimedes some 22 centuries ago – that
their resistance takes a sharp upturn as soon
as the so-called relative speed $V_S/\sqrt{L}$ exceeds
only a little more than unity. This effect,
due to rapid increase in the wave-making
resistance, puts an effective brake on the
maximum speed, which in the case of displacement craft rarely exceeds $1.4\sqrt{L}$. It has
long been understood that designers cannot hope to continue indefinitely the speed
improvement of these monohull yachts by
increasing thrust, i.e. sail power, alone.
However, it may be argued, that 'to really
improve a boat's performance, one must be
able to reduce resistance'. This obvious,
commonsense inference, apparently well-
substantiated by fig. 1, and accepted as an
axiom in ship science, is not applicable without qualification to sailing craft, except in the
case of a yacht sailing upright and downwind.

In the early 1930s K. S. M. Davidson
proved, in his now well-known paper 'Some
experimental studies of the sailing yacht'
(*Techn.Mem.* No 130, Stevens Institute of
Technology, Hoboken, N.J.), an almost
paradoxical point: overall boat performance
can be improved when hull resistance is
increased. Fig. 2a and 2b illustrate the point.
The measured resistance curves of the two 6-
metre boats given in fig. 2a indicate that the
yacht *Jack* had lower resistance when sailing
upright in the range of useful speeds than the
older *Jill*. As might be expected, *Jack*'s racing records in running conditions were better
than that of the rival boat, but she proved to
be distinctly inferior to *Jill* in close-hauled
ability. It was generally agreed that the
failure of the newer boat *Jack* could not be
attributed to faulty sails or to incompetent
handling; a number of different sails had
been tried and various experienced sailors
had raced her.

Subsequent calculation of close-hauled
speeds in terms of speed made good to windward – based on model tests in the towing
tank and shown in fig. 2b – confirmed the
observed performance differences of the full-
scale yachts, which were quite conspicuous.

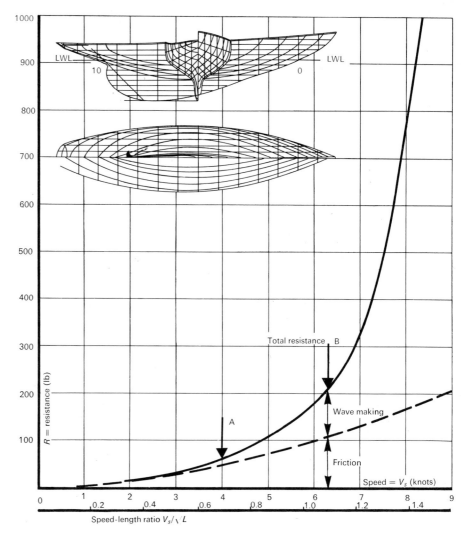

Thus, these tests seem to dispose of any idea
that the upright resistances could be regarded
as a sufficient indication of the overall performance of a yacht hull under sail. When the
poorer performer of two boats, Davidson
argued, has slightly more sail area (as in the
case of *Jack*) and appreciably lower upright
resistance over much of the useful speed
range, it is evident that other factors must be
at least as important as the upright resistances: the differences must lie in the hulls.
But where, in the first place, should these
differences be sought?

– sailing-yacht mechanics

The answer to the question just posed was
given, many years before Davidson's paper
was written, by F. W. Lanchester. In his book
Aerodynamics, vol. 1 (London 1907), he made
an outstanding contribution, by his contem-
poraries' standard, to understanding the mechanics of windward sailing. According to
him, '. . . the problem of sailing-yacht mechanics resolves itself into an aerofoil combination
in which the aerofoil acting in the air (a sail)

and that acting under water (a keel, fin, or
dagger plate) mutually supply each other's
reaction.

'The result of this supposition is evidently
that the minimum angle at which the boat
can shape its course relative to the wind is the
sum of the under and above water gliding
angles.'

Introducing contemporary sailing terminology, 'the gliding angles' are equivalent to the
so-called aerodynamic and hydrodynamic
angles ε_A and ε_H, defined in fig. 3, which
presents Lanchester's concept in diagram-
matic form. The problem is usually simplified
by looking down from above the boat and
considering separately:

1. the aerodynamic forces (3a);
2. the hydrodynamic forces (3b);
3. the equilibrium of sail and hull forces (3c).

Fig. 3 shows a dinghy sailing upright (or
nearly upright) to windward and driven by a
single sail. The forces on a boat come from
two sources: apparent wind V_A action on the
sail, and hydrodynamic action resulting from

Fig. 1 (opposite) *Resistance characteristics of a heavy displacement keelboat, sailing upright in smooth sea:* New York 32 LOA 45.50 ft (13.87 m) LWL (L) 32.26 ft (9.83 m), beam 10.58 ft (3.22 m), draught 6.56 ft (1.99 m), displacement

11.38 tons (25 000 lb or 11 567 kg). It is seen that, in order to obtain maximum speed V_S close to $1.4\sqrt{L}$ (where speed V_S is in knots and the hull length L in feet), sails must provide driving force = resistance of about 800 lb

Fig. 2 (below) *Comparison of the 6-Metre boats* Jack *and* Jill : (a) *upright resistance;* (b) *calculated close-hauled speeds in terms of* V_{mg} *and* V_s *(for a definition of these terms see fig. 7)*

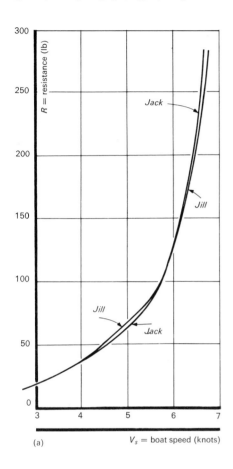

(a) V_s = boat speed (knots)

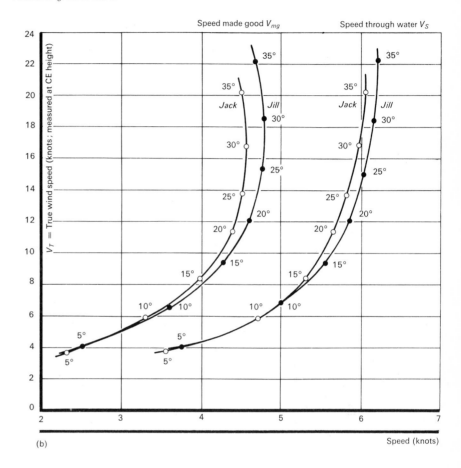

(b)   Speed (knots)

Fig. 3 Sailing-yacht mechanics: (a) *aerodynamic forces on sail;* (b) *hydrodynamic forces on hull* (c) *equilibrium of sail and hull forces.* CE = *centre of effort;* CL = *centreline;* D = *drag;* ε_A = *aerodynamic angle;* ε_H = *hydrodynamic angle;*

F_H = *heeling force;* F_R = *driving force;* F_S = *hydrodynamic side force;* F_T = *total aerodynamic force;* L = *lift;* λ = *angle of leeway;* R = *resistance;* R_T = *total hydrodynamic force;* V_A = *apparent wind;* V_S = *course sailed*

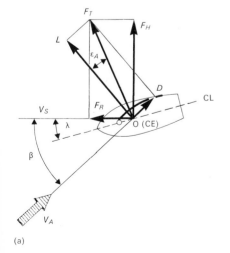

(a)

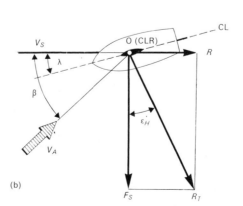

(b)

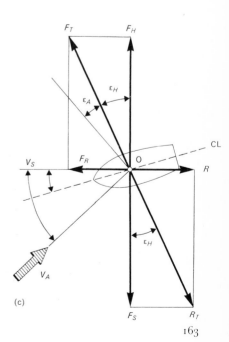

(c)

the hull speed V_S through the water.

The total aerodynamic force F_T may be considered to act solely through the CENTRE OF EFFORT (CE). The magnitude of F_T and its direction of action can be established by measuring the two components of F_T, namely lift L and drag D by, say, wind-tunnel tests; the drag D is measured in the same direction as the apparent wind V_A and lift L at right angles to it. The two other components, in which every sailor is directly interested, labelled driving force F_R and heeling force F_H

respectively, can also be considered as the equivalent of the same single total force F_T. The driving force F_R, shown in the direction of the course sailed, propels the boat. The heeling force F_H, at right angles to the former, causes drift of the hull and also heel.

When estimating the merits of the sail as an aerofoil, or a lift-generating device, drag D may be regarded as a price paid for the lift L. The drag angle ε_A, distinguished by Lanchester as the angle between the lift L and the total aerodynamic force F_T, may serve as an index of the aerodynamic efficiency of the sail. This angle specifies the direction of F_T, and if the drag could be made smaller without altering the lift magnitude, the sail would be more efficient in windward work. Clearly, the total aerodynamic force F_T would then be inclined more towards the bow, therefore the driving force F_R would be a larger fraction of the undesirable heeling force F_H that the hull must somehow cope with.

The underwater part of the hull together with attached centreboard, fin, and rudder – operating as a combined hydrofoil – is shown in fig. 3b. At some angle of leeway λ it must produce a hydrodynamic force F_S equal and opposite to the aerodynamic force F_H. This function is mainly performed by the fin; the hull contribution in this respect is relatively small. It is self-evident that this fin action should incur the smallest possible penalty in terms of resistance to forward motion. However, when a yacht is driven hard to windward the cost of the required side force may well be 20–30% of the total resistance. Thus the resistance R, as indicated on fig. 3b, consists of two parts: resistance of the hull proper and an additional resistance due to the action of hull appendages.

The two hydrodynamic force components F_S and R can be measured in the towing tank in order to find the total or resultant force. It is represented in fig. 3b by a vector labelled R_T that goes through the CENTRE OF LATERAL RESISTANCE (CLR) of the hull.

In a similar manner as in the case of the sail, the hydrodynamic drag angle ε_H specifies the hydrodynamic characteristics of the hull in generating the side force F_S. It is evident that the efficiency of the underwater part of the hull lies in its ability to produce the necessary side force F_S at the least resistance R. Thus, an increase in the F_S/R ratio, either by increasing F_S or by decreasing R through the range of practical leeway angles λ, is equivalent to a decrement in ε_H angle. As a result, the potential ability of sailing craft when close-hauled is improved.

– effects of sail and hull efficiency on performance

The above conclusions are incorporated in Lanchester's theorem, called by some the 'course theorem'. It states that on any heading, the angle β between the apparent wind

A one-quarter scale model of a Dragon class yacht being tested in a wind tunnel. The object of this test was to measure the forces on sails and the changes they made to sail shape. A wind tunnel will not provide all the answers, but when properly used it does assist in establishing the 'how and why of sails'

direction V_A and the course sailed, as presented in fig. 3c, is equal to the sum of the two drag angles ε_A and ε_H i.e.

$$\beta = \varepsilon_A + \varepsilon_H$$

The relationship between the drag angle ε_A and the L/D ratio is given by:

$$\cot \varepsilon_A = L/D$$

which is equivalent to the statement: ε_A is the angle whose cotangent is L/D. Similarly:

$$\cot \varepsilon_H = F_S/R$$

This theorem refers to steady sailing conditions. That is to say, when the relevant sail and hull forces are equal and opposite, so no acceleration takes place, the boat is in equilibrium and steady motion. If the wind velocity increases the aerodynamic forces also increase and the boat will accelerate. Conversely, if the wind velocity decreases the boat will decelerate until a new steady-state motion is again established.

From what has been said it may be inferred that, in searching for better performance, the sailing boat should be regarded as an aircraft-ship hybrid rather than a ship. If so, it would be right to assume that some of the aerodynamic theories, developed for low-speed flying machines, are if wisely interpreted applicable to sailing craft too. For instance, the aspect ratio (AR) of sail planform has, for many years, been considered as an important factor by which the efficiency of different rigs may be judged. Concurrently, the theory was supported by experiments, first on wings and then on sails. Gradually it became common knowledge that for the same given area sails with a higher AR are better in windward work. This is because their L/D ratio is higher.

Figure 4 illustrates the trend towards higher-aspect-ratio sails, and keel planform too, observed during the last 65 years and particularly noticeable in racer design. It appears that publication by the celebrated French engineer Gustave Eiffel of some of his wind-tunnel results on aerofoils in 1910 stimulated yacht designers. According to A. E. Reynolds Brown ('How the Sail Plans Changed', *Yachts and Yachting*, 5 August 1955) '. . . there was no doubt that something happened to sail plans in 1912. Mr Charles Nicholson brought out *Istria* [fig. 4] with a taller sail plan than anything before, also a topmast long enough to make a topsail yard unnecessary, the topsail luff setting on a track, like a modern Bermudian rig. The mast was thought to look like a wireless mast, and in derision it was called the Marconi rig. But it stood through the windiest summer in memory and she collected 35 prizes in 36 starts, 25 of them first.' Indeed *Istria*'s mast was cleaner aerodynamically than most contemporary rigs: the air flow around the most sensitive leading edge of the mainsail was no longer disturbed, as it was in the presence of the topsail yard and topmast junction.

Besides, a reduction of the weight of the spars aloft certainly contributed towards greater stability.

Figure 5, applicable to any sailing craft, demonstrates the effect of improvement of either L/D ratio (sails) or F_S/R ratio (hull) on the windward ability. For example, let it be assumed that, at a certain speed to windward, the attainable L/D ratio of the rig (adjusted at its optimum) is 5.5 and the F_S/R ratio of the hull is 3.5.

It can be determined from the graph that the minimum angle that could be sailed relative to the apparent wind would then be just above 26°.

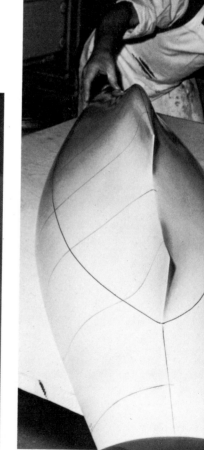

One of the principal factors determining the performance of a sailing yacht is the efficiency of the underwater part of its hull in generating hydrodynamic side force. Towing-tank tests have helped designers to develop better hull forms; the illustration shows a model hull in the tank at MIT. The model is attached to dynamometers that measure the resistance and side force developed at a given angle of heel and leeway

The underwater part of an embryo America's Cup challenger being prepared at Southampton University for testing the effect of the 'bustle' arrangement

Fig. 4 Evolution of sailplan and the shape of underwater part of hull leading towards higher-aspect-ratio foils. Left to right: Tara 1833, LWL 65 ft (19.8 m); Istria 1912, LWL 50 ft *(15.2 m); J-Class Endeavour 1934, LWL 83.3 ft (25.4 m); racer 1977, LWL 27 ft (8.2 m). (Drawings not to scale)*

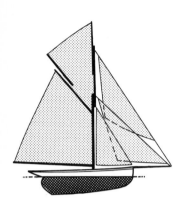
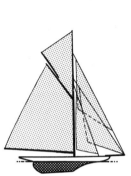

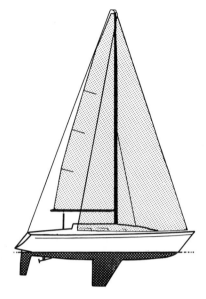

– relative importance of sails and hull in performance

Some practical questions can be answered with the help of fig. 5: for instance, which is more important from the viewpoint of yacht performance, sails or hull? The answer is that both parts are important because the sailing craft must be considered as a complex system consisting of two interdependent parts, aerodynamic and hydrodynamic. Each part is therefore the cause and effect of the other, so there is no reason to assume or believe that one of the parts is more important than the other. The only difference from, say, the crew point of view is that the sail efficiency is somewhat accessible to intervention, through the tuning or adjusting process, whereas the hydrodynamic properties of the hull, once predetermined on the designer's drawing board, depend very little on crew efforts – except, perhaps, in keeping the hull surface smooth!

Another question that can be answered is: if a development or modification of a given boat is considered, which part is likely to give more conspicuous gain in terms of windward performance, sails or hull? The answer is the part that is poorer aerodynamically or hydrodynamically deserves more attention, i.e. the part that in average sailing conditions produces a lower L/D or F_S/R ratio. In other words, there is relatively little to be gained by improving efficiency of an already good rig that drives an inefficient hull.

Let us consider this problem numerically assuming that the underwater part of the hull – its shape, labelled 'original design', is given in fig. 6 – develops in average conditions an F_S/R ratio in the order of 2.9. The boat is driven by a sloop-type rig producing an L/D ratio in the order of 6.0, which is an average value applicable to this type of rig. If these numbers are entered on the graph in fig. 5 it is found that the minimum pointing angle β would be about 29°. An improvement of rig efficiency, say, from $L/D = 6$ to 7 (not necessarily easy to achieve, for reasons that will be given later) would result in a reduction of the β angle from 29° to 28°, i.e. 1° only. In contrast, improving the keel efficiency by the same step from 2.9 to 3.9 would result in a β reduction from 29° to 24°, i.e. 5°.

A difference of one degree in windward ability means 90 to 180 ft (27 to 55 m) more made good to windward for every nautical mile sailed. The smaller gain value is applicable to already sophisticated racers, such as 12-Metres; the larger benefit can be expected by improving vessels of less efficient aero-hydrodynamic forms, such as those represented in the photograph opposite and in fig.5. Thus, 5° reduction in β angle could mean about 900 ft (270 m) more made good to windward per nautical mile sailed.

In the context of fig. 6 it should perhaps be noticed that shallow draught does not entirely preclude the possibility of reasonably efficient side-force generation. Certain modification of the initial design, leading to a slightly swept bottom of the keel, demonstrates that relatively small changes in keel planform may greatly improve the windward ability of the vessel in question (I. Howlett, 'Considerations Relating to the Performance of Large Sailing Vessels', Royal Institution of Naval Architects paper).

These examples, together with the implication of fig. 5, clearly show that spectacular

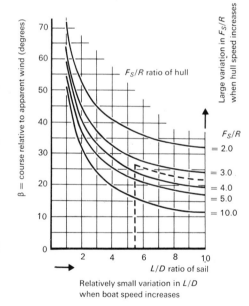

Fig. 5 The effect of changes in L/D ratio of sail and F_S/R ratio of hull on windward ability of any sailing craft. $L = lift$; $D = drag$; $F_s =$ hydrodynamic side force; $R = resistance$

improvements in windward ability can only be achieved if the craft in question is inefficient in terms of the L/D and F_S/R ratios. But when these ratios are already high, as in the case of modern 12-Metre boats, further progress towards higher performance becomes painfully slow, and no dramatic breakthrough can possibly be expected in these or similar racing machines.

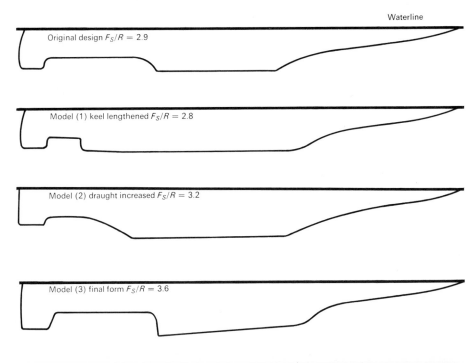

Waterline

Original design $F_S/R = 2.9$

Model (1) keel lengthened $F_S/R = 2.8$

Model (2) draught increased $F_S/R = 3.2$

Model (3) final form $F_S/R = 3.6$

– measuring sailing performance to windward

Although the potential windward ability of sailing craft, as measured by β, can be regarded as the most critical test of the aerodynamic and hydrodynamic efficiency of rig and keel, it is not used as a criterion of yacht performance. In fact, the windward performance of a sailing craft is ultimately measured by the distance she has travelled directly to windward in a given time. As drawn, fig. 7 could represent a boat sailing close-hauled. The direction of the true wind is indicated by the arrow, and the symbol V_T is used to represent the magnitude of the true wind speed. The boat sailing at speed marked by V_S is following course γ relative to the true wind V_T. The apparent wind speed is V_A in magnitude, making an angle β degrees to the direction of boat speed V_S. The V_S direction

This model (above) of a 1000-ton displacement sailing vessel was tested in a wind tunnel (illustrated) and a towing tank. The question asked was: Is the rig efficient enough to drive the vessel with predetermined speed at a given wind velocity? Some of the results are given in Fig. 6

Fig. 6 Keel development guided by the towing-tank tests may yield substantial gains in terms of overall

boat performance. The diagram (top) shows the planform of the underwater part of the vessel depicted in the photograph. Both wind-tunnel and towing-tank tests were conducted by the Wolfson Marine Unit, Southampton University, and the results are published here by kind permission of Laurent Giles and Partners Ltd, Lymington, Hampshire, and Southampton University. $F_S =$ hydrodynamic side force; $R =$ resistance

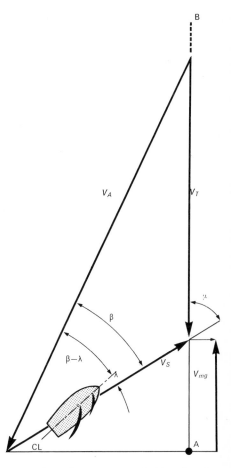

Fig. 7 The sailing triangle – a definition of speed made good to windward (V_{mg})

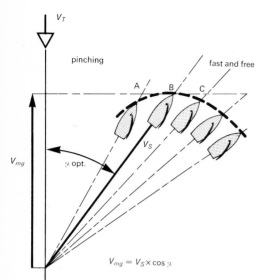

Fig. 8 *The sailing triangle – showing that pinching does not produce higher V_{mg}*

does not coincide with the centreline of the hull because it includes the angle of leeway λ.

Since the objective of close-hauled work is to progress as effectively as possible in the direction A to B, i.e. towards a destination point lying ahead and along the true wind direction V_T, it is the speed component represented by the arrow labelled V_{mg} that is of particular interest. This is usually referred to as the 'speed made good to windward'; and if the yachtsman is to get to windward as quickly as possible, he must choose a course γ so that the resulting boat speed V_S is such that V_{mg} is the maximum that can be achieved in a given wind strength V_T. This maximum value of V_{mg}, shown in fig. 8, is referred to as the 'optimum value'. Skill in sailing to windward therefore comes down to the ability of a crew to judge correctly whether or not the optimum conditions have been reached at a given moment.

Noteworthy is the simple mathematical formula:

$$V_{mg} = V_S \times \cos \gamma$$

which indicates that V_{mg} is a composite product of the boat's speed V_S and the true sailing course γ. From fig. 8b it may be inferred that merely pointing high (pinching) is not a merit in itself.

Although boat A sails closer to the wind than boat B, her speed V_{mg} is lower than that of boat B. A similar argument applies to boat C, which sails fast but free.

See also MONITORING SAILING PERFORMANCE

– what determines the best course to windward?

Selection of the best of a range of γ courses, each with its own best sheeting angles for the rig, is not an easy task and it seems that no two helmsmen would ever agree about this. And there is no simple way of determining

which judgement is at fault, except after the event.

In a number of papers ('The Physics of Sailing', *Physics Bulletin*, March 1964; 'The Factors Governing the Best Course to Windward', Private communication; 'The Behaviour of the Sailing Yacht', Royal Institution of Naval Architects paper March 1960) H. Barkla greatly contributed to the understanding of the factors governing the best course to windward. He has shown that the γ angle, V_{mg}, and rig and hull efficiency factors ε_A and ε_H are mutually related through the following expression:

$$\frac{V_{mg}}{V_T} = \frac{\cot \gamma}{\cot (\gamma - \varepsilon_A - \varepsilon_H) - \cot \gamma}$$

This formula, which may appear complicated at first, is straightforward in interpretation, provided caution is exercised when giving numerical values to the sail and hull drag angles ε_A and ε_H respectively. They are not constant but depend to a greater or lesser extent on wind speed V_T and the resulting boat speed V_S. The formula demonstrates, in yet another way, that the rig and hull efficiency determine decisively the attainable V_{mg}/V_T ratio. The value of this ratio obtainable by an ordinary yacht is about 0.6 and it falls as the wind V_T increases. Famous J-Class *America*'s Cup challengers of the 1930s, the fastest all-round vessels ever built, reached a V_{mg} of 0.62 times the true wind speed V_T.

Barkla proved that the optimum course γ largely depends on how fast the hull resistance builds up with speed. That is to say, how quickly the ε_H value deteriorates when the hull moves faster, and the side force F_S is increasing in proportion to $V_S{}^2$, while the resistance is increasing at a much higher rate.

Fig. 9 shows an approximate relation between the resistance, expressed per unit displacement $R/_\Delta$, and the speed-length ratio $V_S/\sqrt{L}$, for several hulls of different displacement-length ratios $\Delta/(\frac{L}{100})^3$ ranging from 400 to 25. It reflects the resistance characteristics of a variety of contemporary sailing craft – from a heavy-displacement form with $\Delta/(\frac{L}{100})^3$ ratio in the order of 400, to extremely light planing forms of $\Delta/(\frac{L}{100})^3$ approaching 25. To make the comparison of resistance of hulls of different lengths possible, the boat speed is expressed in terms of speed-length ratio $V_S/\sqrt{L}$.

It can be seen from fig. 9 that the resistance increases in proportion to the displacement-length ratio, and that for heavy-displacement forms the resistance curves shoot upward very steeply, while for light-displacement forms the rise in resistance is more gradual.

The effect of these differences in resistance behaviour on the optimum course γ to windward is shown in fig. 10: first, the γ is greater in light winds than in moderate breezes, and second, it is wider for light-displacement

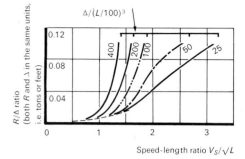

Fig. 9 *The displacement-length ratio, $\Delta/(\frac{L}{100}{}^3)$, which is commonly used to describe how heavy a given boat is in relation to her given waterline length L, determines how quickly the resistance R builds up with speed. Displacement-length ratio is calculated by dividing the boat displacement Δ (expressed in long tons: 1 ton = 2240 lb) by the cube of one hundredth the waterline length L (in feet)*

Fig. 10 (below) *Optimum true course angles γ for best V_{mg} in calm water*

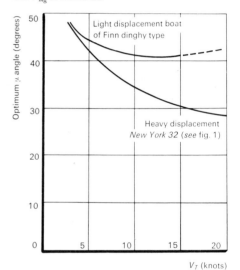

forms, such as the Finn dinghy type, than for heavy-displacement forms like the New York 32 shown in fig. 1.

These indicative trends are simply due to the fact that, in stronger winds, the resistance of heavy-displacement forms increases so rapidly that it does not pay to generate more driving force on sails by sailing free. The eventual gain in speed will not offset the losses incurred by sailing at larger γ. However, in the case of light-displacement forms, which generate much less resistance at higher speed, sailing freer and faster is advantageous from the standpoint of performance measured in terms of V_{mg}.

Experienced racing sailors have a knowledge of what seems to be the optimum sailing course γ for each type of boat. And they are well aware of the fact that a boat will not perform in the same manner to windward when sailed similarly to another boat of a different displacement: length ratio.

The data in fig. 10 apply to sailing in smooth water, i.e. when the progress of a yacht sailing to windward is not impeded by waves. The effect of the waves is to cause an increase in resistance of the yacht referred to as the 'added resistance'. Measurements on models and observations on full-size yachts indicate that waves have a harmful effect on speed to windward by forcing the crew to sail at a wider angle than the optimum γ angle for a smooth sea. Thus, for example, sailing experience teaches that in a 20-knot wind and corresponding rough sea, a 12-Metre class yacht will sail at an angle γ of about $40°$, which otherwise, in calm water, would be in the order of $35°$. Five degrees' loss in optimum angle γ means, for this particular class of yacht, about 450 ft (137 m) less made good to windward for every nautical mile sailed.

– effect of stability on performance
There are several reasons why the aspect ratio of the rig, and also that of keel or fin keel, cannot be much increased beyond present-day proportions, which are the result of experience acquired by trial-and-error routine, model testing, and theory. Thus, for instance, the optimum aspect ratio of modern rigs turns out to be not far from 3; i.e. a rig height of roughly 3 times the foot length.

The stability requirement is one of the most important limiting factors precluding the taller rig and deeper keels that might, for purely aerodynamic and hydrodynamic reasons, produce better windward performance. Unfortunately, the taller the rig and deeper the keel, the higher the centre of effort (CE) of the sail and the lower the centre of lateral resistance (CLR), and so, the greater the angle of heel of a yacht for the same heeling force. Examination of fig. 11 will show that the sail-carrying ability of any monohull form – no matter whether the stability is due to hull form and the crew sitting out, or to hull form and keel ballast – is strictly limited. As the ballasted yacht heels under the action of the heeling force F_H – which increases in proportion to wind velocity squared – the righting arm RA of the stability forces gradually increases until the heeling and righting moments balance each other, and no further heel occurs. Sooner or later, depending on wind strength and the sail area carried, the losses due to heel more than counterbalance the advantages gained in terms of sail driving force. This is because when the yacht heels the sail driving force decreases and the hull resistance increases, at first slowly and then more rapidly.

Figure 12 shows a typical set of resistance curves for the keelboat *Jill* (see fig. 2), as derived from towing-tank tests. It can be seen that when the angle of heel reaches $30°$, the hull resistance increases by about 30%;

therefore quite a high penalty must be incurred in the form of decreased hydrodynamic efficiency of the hull, i.e. greater hull drag angle ε_H. This example, although brief in interpretation, may serve as sufficient evidence that boat stability is an important performance factor. In fact, lack of sufficient stability can nullify the effects of otherwise splendid aerodynamic and hydrodynamic efficiencies of rig and hull.

Since the amount of sail that can be carried without suffering a large heel is strictly determined by the hull stability, this hull property can rightly be called the power to carry sail effectively. Taking stability into account, the performance equation, implicitly incorporated in fig. 3, can crudely be written as follows:

Performance to windward =
    hull efficiency (ε_H) + sail efficiency (ε_A) + stability

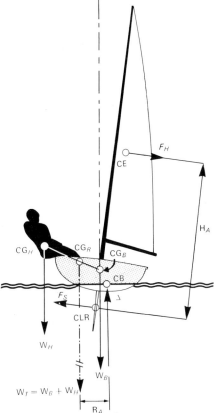

Fig. 11 Sail-carrying ability is a function of hull stability due to form and ballast. F_H = heeling force; F_s = hydrodynamic side force; CB = centre of buoyancy; CE = centre of effort (sail); CLR = centre of lateral resistance (hull); CG_B = centre of gravity of boat; CG_H = centre of gravity of helmsman; CG_R = resulting centre of gravity; W_B = weight of boat; W_H = weight of helmsman; W_T = total weight; Δ = displacement Δ = W_T; RA = righting arm; HA = heeling arm

– all-round performance: progress made
It is now pertinent to consider how much the windward ability contributes towards what might be called the all-round performance, in which the boat speed on other points of sailing is taken into account.

It is generally agreed that the windward performance is of primary importance. Although the speed on off-the-wind courses can affect the outcome of a race, it is the speed a sailing yacht makes good directly against the wind that is the most important factor in determining the chances of racing success. This is particularly so on a triangular course where the windward leg is the most time-consuming part. The reason for using V_{mg} as a measure of achievement of a sailing-craft design can be clarified by considering the V_{mg} effect on the average speed attained over the whole range of points of sailing relative to wind direction.

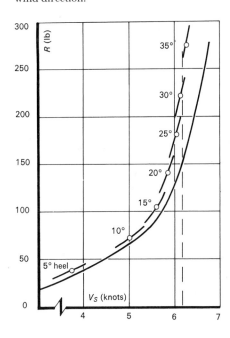

Fig. 12 Heeled resistances of 6-Metre yacht Jill *as predicted from model tests with leeway*

It is clear that the average speed directly against the wind for any sailing craft will be slower than the average speed in any other direction. Thus, over a series of trips round the WIND ROSE, a sailing craft's performance directly against the wind is bound to become the deciding factor in determining her success not only in sport but in trade too.

Figure 13 and the table, based on K. S. M. Davidson's findings ('The Mechanics of

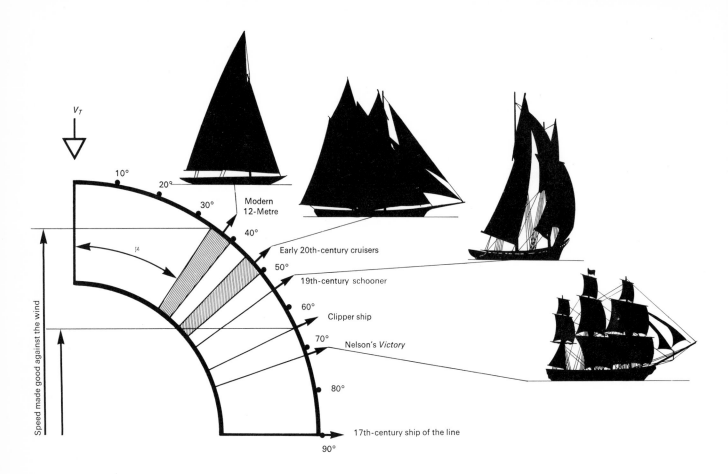

Fig. 13 Relationship between the weatherliness of sailing craft as measured by the course γ, and the potential speed made good to windward

Average sailing speeds

I	2	3 AVERAGE ACTUAL SPEED V_S (knots)	4 LENGTH OVERALL L (ft)	5 AVERAGE RELATIVE SPEED $V_S/\sqrt{L}$	6
DATE	TYPE ETC.				REMARKS
	SQUARE-RIGGED SHIP				
1492	Columbus	$3\frac{3}{4}$	70	0.45	Good passage
1837	Sumner [1]	$6\frac{1}{2}$	200	0.44	Good passage
1850	Clipper ship	6	250	0.38 [2]	Mean figure
1902	*Preussen* [3]	7	410	0.35	Mean figure
	FORE-AND-AFT RIGGED YACHTS				
1935	*Stormy Weather*	$6\frac{1}{2}$	53	0.90	Good passage
1935	6-Metre boats	$5\frac{3}{4}$	36	0.97	Mean figure
1935	J-Class boat	$9\frac{3}{4}$	135	0.87	Mean figure
1950	*Bolero*, Bermuda Race			0.83	Mean figure
1954	*Bolero*, Bermuda Race			0.83	Mean figure

[1] Thomas H. Sumner was the American ship's captain who devised the POSITION-LINE method now used in ASTRONOMICAL NAVIGATION.

[2] According to an analysis of 420 voyages of the wool clippers (AMATEUR YACHT RESEARCH SOCIETY) the average speed of these ships sailing from Australia to England was $6\frac{1}{2}$ knots (*see* D. Phillips-Birt, 'The Triumph of the Fore-and-Aft Rig', *Yachting World Annual*, 1958). This gives an average relative speed $V_S/\sqrt{L} = 0.41$.

[3] Largest sailing ship ever built (1902); belonged to the famous P Line, Bremen, Germany

Sailing Ships and Yachts', privately published, 1956), illustrate the point.

The data sampled in column 5 give the relative average speed for a variety of sailing craft, expressed in terms of speed-length ratio $V_S/\sqrt{L}$, where L is the overall length of the hull. This facilitates comparison of sailing performance of craft of such widely different lengths on a size-for-size basis. 'Size for size' refers to the well-known law, established by the nineteenth-century English naval architect and mathematician William Froude, that mere increase in size, with no change in design, will increase speed roughly in proportion to the square root of the increase of the hull length. Thus in comparing the sailing performances, it is not speed alone that counts but speed in relation to size of the craft i.e. the relative speed $V_S/\sqrt{L}$.

A glance at the table reveals: first, there is a striking uniformity of actually achieved relative speeds for square-rigged ships and fore-and-aft rigged yachts respectively; second, the mean value of speed-length ratio for yachts is roughly twice as big as that for ships. From fig. 13 it can be inferred that the key to this superiority of fore-and-aft rigged yachts lies in their ability to sail closer to the wind, a quality never attained by sailing craft of the days of commercial sail.

In the table we find that the clippers, when compared size for size, were not faster than Columbus's *Santa Maria*, which sailed some 350 years before. The data also suggest that there was not much real improvement in relative performance between the sailing ship of Columbus's time and the biggest sailing ships ever built, four centuries later, represented by *Preussen*.

A surprising comparison is that of the performance achievement of *Stormy Weather*, a 53-ft-long (16-m) cruiser-racer, with that of the clipper, five times longer, and *Preussen*, eight times longer. Their average speeds are roughly the same, in spite of the fact that in the most favourable reaching conditions the much larger clipper could attain $15\frac{1}{2}$ knots (even $16\frac{1}{2}$ knots were claimed).

Once again referring to fig 4 and 13, it becomes evident that the progressive improvement in the windward ability of sailing craft can be attributed mainly to the remarkable development in rigs and the underwater part of the hulls. This led to much lower drag ratios ε_A and ε_H, on which, as has been seen, performance of any sailing craft directly depends.

The relatively low average speeds of the square riggers were primarily due to the low aerodynamic efficiency of their sails, which although good in reaching and downwind sailing conditions, were hopelessly poor in the close-hauled attitude when compared with fore-and-aft rigs. It can be seen in fig. 13, for instance, that the difference in windward ability of a modern racer and a clipper is in the order of 30°. This is a great step. However, further, spectacular improvement along the same line of development should not be expected. The evolution of monohulled sailing craft, of inherently limited stability, has already reached its limit. There is evidence that the exceptionally high speed-performance figures achieved by some of the modern racers have been dearly paid for in terms of their deficiency in course-keeping ability, reduced seaworthiness, poor steering abilities: i.e., at the expense of the essential virtues of a good sailing boat that were prized by past generations.

If in the future sailing craft return as an alternative to power-driven merchant vessels, the sailing yacht may well serve as a pointer to the development of wind-driven ships. The relative speeds of cargo ships in service today range from 0.6 to 1.0 $V_S/\sqrt{L}$: just about the same as those of modern sailing yachts.

– theoretical prediction of a boat's performance

From the viewpoint of both the yacht designer and the crew it is important to know the potential speed performance of an existing or projected sailing-boat design. This is

the object of performance prediction, and yacht researchers attempt to provide information and methods by which theoretical curves of performance can be established, so that the comparable performance potential of a design can be estimated.

The subject of practical performance prediction, dealing with steady motion of a sailing yacht in calm water, was introduced

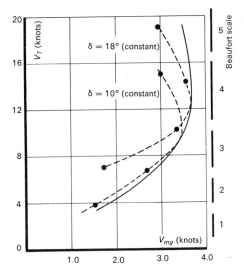

Fig. 14. Predicted performance curves of a Finn dinghy. One of the methods of presentation of windward performance is to show how V_{mg} changes with the true wind speed (V_T); δ = sheeting angle

in 1936 by Davidson ('Some Experimental Studies of the Sailing Yacht'). Since then, the technique of prediction has been advanced by others. However, all of them have used the same basic idea – that a yacht proceeds steadily through the water when the aerodynamic forces and heeling moment, acting upon the rig, are balanced by those due to hydrodynamic, hydrostatic, and gravitational effects, as shown in fig. 3 and 11. To find the conditions of equilibrium of aerodynamic and hydrodynamic forces and moments involved, at various courses, winds, and boat speeds, it is necessary to know how the sail forces vary with apparent speed V_A and sail setting; and also how the corresponding hull forces vary with boat speed V_S, heel angle, and leeway. These forces and moments cannot, as yet, be obtained through the mathematical expressions that incorporate the design parameters of a given yacht. However, they can be established through model tests, such as those illustrated in these pages, and the performance of a boat, with a known combination of sails and hull, can be predicted. Once the values of V_A, V_S, and β angle are known – from calculations of the equilibrium condition of sail and hull forces – the

remaining important quantities, namely V_T and V_{mg}, can be found via the sailing triangle relation given in fig. 7. Hence, the curve giving the variation of V_{mg} with V_T can be obtained.

The thick, continuous curve in fig. 14, illustrates such a theoretically predicted windward performance for a Finn dinghy sailed in calm water. This performance curve was established on the assumption that the helmsman of given weight, when sitting out as a 'live ballast' (fig. 11), is capable of balancing a certain amount of heeling force or heeling moment. Above a certain critical wind speed the sail must be spilled in order to keep the heeling force down to a tolerable magnitude; and since, in such a condition, the sail does not work effectively, the boat performance begins to deteriorate. This trend is clearly reflected in fig. 14. It can be seen that, up to a wind speed V_T in the order of 14 knots (force 4 on the BEAUFORT WIND SCALE), the attainable V_{mg} increases. However, when the wind speed V_T exceeds the critical 14 knots – and the potential sail power cannot be fully exploited, because of lack of stability – the V_{mg} curve bends to the left, towards smaller V_{mg} values. Thus, in stronger winds, in which the highest speeds might be attained, stability becomes the supreme merit of the boat.

This pattern of performance behaviour is not peculiar to sailing dinghies but is characteristic of any sailing craft. Fig. 15, which depicts the windward performance curves of several keelboats, clearly reveals the same trend: the gradually diminishing rate of V_{mg} increase with true wind speed V_T, finally leading to more or less rapid fall in V_{mg} value.

– determination of boat performance through full-scale tests

As already mentioned, the theoretical performance curves, illustrated in fig. 14 and 15, were derived on the principle that yacht speeds can be predicted if the sail and hull forces are known. In principle, yacht performance can also be established without prior knowledge of these aerodynamic and hydrodynamic forces actually developed on a boat. This can be done by making some basic measurements while sailing a full-size yacht with the assistance of instruments. The following information is needed:

apparent wind speed V_A (knots)
yacht speed V_S (knots)
course sailed β relative to V_A which includes leeway (*see* fig. 7).

These three variables are sufficient to find:
true wind speed V_T (knots)
yacht course γ relative to V_T and finally speed made good to windward V_{mg} (knots). In other words, with known values of V_A, V_S and β it is possible to find the remaining quantities in the sailing triangle shown in fig. 7.

The solution can be found graphically, by

means of compass and protractor; or mathematically, with the help of a hand-held calculator, solving the three following, relatively simple, equations:

1. $V_T = \sqrt{(V_A{}^2 + V_S{}^2 - 2V_A V_S \cos\beta)}$

2. $\sin\gamma = \dfrac{\sin\beta}{V_T} V_A$

and lastly the already known equation:

3. $V_{mg} = V_S \cos\gamma$

The result of the calculation can be plotted in terms of V_{mg} versus V_T. The large number of circular dots in fig. 15 illustrate such results obtained in close-hauled conditions, while sailing a full-scale 5.5-Metre boat. The measurements were taken in a variety of wind and sea conditions, on two different waters, as indicated.

The object of these particular full-scale trials was to establish the degree of correlation between the theoretically derived performance curve (the thick continuous line) based on model tests, and the performance actually achieved by helmsmen attempting to reach the best performance in given conditions.

It is evident from the scattered points of performance measurements that a yacht can rarely be sailed at optimum except momentarily and by chance. In fact on a few occasions only the actually measured performance figures coincide with the theoretical curve; which, it should not be forgotten, applies to smooth-water conditions. This thick continuous line curve, enveloping the measured points that lie within or to the left of the curve, can be regarded as an ultimate yardstick – very difficult to match in practice.

In fact, it is not easy to establish the optimum performance curve from full-scale trials. It takes a long time, and a large number of test runs must be recorded, to gather enough data to plot such a curve with a reasonable degree of accuracy. The whole idea of full-scale measurements which appears to be simple in principle, is difficult in realization. It requires a great deal of skill, on the part of experimenters, to execute the tests and interpret the results correctly. There are many reasons for the difficulties usually encountered, which are clearly reflected in the scattered test data of 5.5-Metre boats in fig. 15. Continual variations of wind and water flow greatly affect the air and water sensors and this in turn complicates the measurements (*see* photograph). Because of these changes in apparent wind speed V_A and its direction, the helmsman is not able to distinguish immediately and exactly enough what changes have occurred in the true wind. Recorded variations of wind speed V_T alone, in the order of 10 ft/sec – 50% of the mean speed of about 20 ft/sec – are fairly common

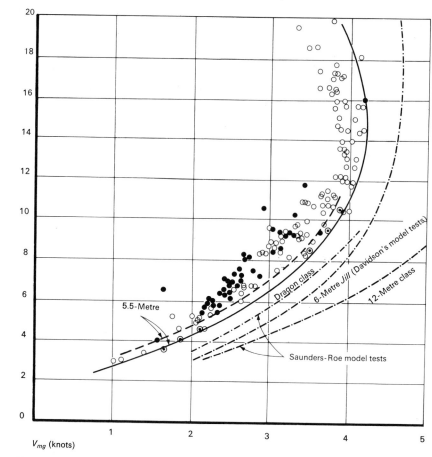

Fig. 15 Close-hauled results for some racing keelboats. (The open circles and the solid curve are the results of full-scale trials in Southampton Water; the solid circles and dashed curve are the results of full-scale trials in the King George VI Reservoir; the crosses are results based on model tests in the National Physical Laboratory, Teddington, Middlesex)

Because sails develop lift, the airflow in their proximity is distorted and thus to avoid unreliable readings, wind sensors must be positioned with some care. To reduce the effect of the distorted airflow the sensors are placed at a distance from the sails, although some desirable positions are precluded *because of their interference with boat handling (as in the photograph (below), where a Dragon is being tested by Southampton University). Similar problems arise when testing the hull with water-speed sensors that are operating close to it or its appendages*

over intervals of 2 minutes. This being so, the sail forces must also be subject to large fluctuations, and sheeting angles may not be matched correctly to the best performance requirements. The hull speed responds more or less slowly to these varying wind forces transmitted through the rig, depending on the weight (mass) of the hull. The time response of the measuring instruments, together with the helmsman's response to their pointers or merit indicators, is also an important factor. It is therefore highly unlikely that a yacht can be kept moving consistently well, 'on target', in such a variable environment. Some degree of departure from the optimum is inevitable.

– ways of presenting boat performance

The question of the sensitivity of performance to departures from, say, optimum sheeting angle δ, defined in fig. 16, now becomes relevant. To show its significance, the simple example of the Finn-type dinghy, driven by a single sail, has been chosen. (Obviously, the more sails there are to be considered, the more difficult the tuning problem becomes.)

Fig. 16 shows that over the lower wind-speed range, up to 2–3 on the Beaufort scale, the optimum sheeting angle δ remains fairly constant and at a relatively low value; but as the wind speed V_T increases so does the sheeting angle, quite sharply. The two thin, broken-line curves in fig. 14 may help to answer another practical question: how much boat performance deteriorates when the helmsman does not pay enough attention to the variation in wind strength and maintains the sheeting angle constant, regardless. These two curves, which just touch the optimum

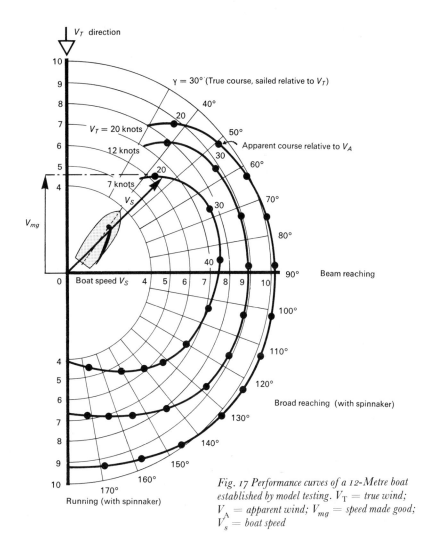

Fig. 17 Performance curves of a 12-Metre boat established by model testing. V_T = *true wind;* V_A = *apparent wind;* V_{mg} = *speed made good;* V_s = *boat speed*

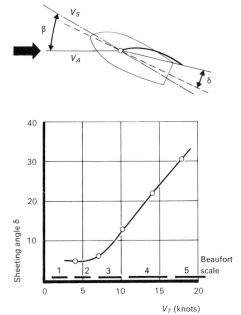

Fig. 16 Finn-type dinghy (left). *Optimum course sailed* β *and optimum sheeting angle* δ *for one particular kicking strap (boom vang) tension (Marchaj,* Aerohydrodynamics of Sailing). *Note: the sheeting angle* δ *is measured between the boom and the centreline of the hull.*

V_{mg} (thick continuous-line) curve twice along its length, give the attainable V_{mg}, assuming in one case the sheeting angle $\delta = 10°$ constant, and in the other $\delta = 18°$ constant. It can now be appreciated that in both cases the potential sail efficiency is fully exploited in only a small range of wind speed V_T. Below and above that particular wind strength, at which the thin curves coincide with the optimum curve, the V_{mg} speed increasingly deteriorates. Correct sail adjustment to suit the variety of wind conditions appears, therefore, to offer a dramatic degree of performance improvement.

Performance calculations, whether the data originates from model tests or full-scale trials,

can be presented in a variety of ways, depending on their intended use – by the yacht designer, racing crew, or a yacht-research establishment. Fig. 17, for instance, gives an overall picture of the performance of a ballasted racing yacht of 12-Metre class, sailing in calm water on courses ranging from close-hauled to running, and in true wind speeds $V_T = 7$, 12, and 20 knots. The three performance curves plotted were built up by drawing the boat speed vectors V_S from the origin o, at each relevant γ angle and wind speed V_T for which the calculations were made. As an example, only one such V_S vector is shown in fig. 17. It indicates that, at wind velocity $V_T = 7$ knots, the optimum boat speed V_s is 6.5

knots, and this results in $V_{mg} = 4.5$ knots. The optimum course β in this condition is about $22°$.

The performance curves shown (sometimes called speed polar diagrams) are in reasonable agreement with observations of actual 12-Metre performance in the wind conditions indicated. However, since full-scale observations and theoretical predictions from model tests are both subject to errors, these curves should not be regarded as representing the *absolute performance* of the boat for which they were calculated.

The effects of various design modifications can readily be assessed numerically by comparing the speed polar diagrams appropriate to them. However, diagrams of the form shown in fig. 17 provide no clear indication of the specific requirements for the optimum performance, such as optimum sheeting, in which the racing crew is directly interested. This need can be met by replotting the performance data in the manner given in fig. 14. When the data is presented in this form it is easy to estimate the improvement in performance that it is possible to obtain by refined helmsmanship.

Pilotage
Navigation by reference to objects or points external to the craft. Pilotage, sometimes called piloting, generally refers to determination of position or safety of a vessel along coasts and in estuaries by reference to identifiable landmarks and seamarks, both natural and man-made, shown on the nautical chart. Areas where pilotage is the primary method of navigation are called pilotage waters, often shortened to pilot water. With the establishment of various electronic aids, the techniques of pilotage have been extended far from shore.

Although the position of a vessel is generally stated in terms of latitude and longitude, the primary concern in pilotage is the safety of the craft. Accordingly, geographical position is often of secondary interest to location relative to the landmarks or seamarks used as references.

When a vessel is traversing an adequately marked channel, pilotage may consist essentially of checking off each buoy as it is passed. Offshore, a vessel might be kept in safe water by means of a danger bearing, the limiting direction of safe water relative to a landmark or seamark. Similarly, the limiting vertical angle between the top and bottom of a structure or vertical shoreline, or the limiting

horizontal angle between two identifiable objects, can be used for safe navigation without establishing position of the craft. Such a maximum or minimum angle is called a vertical or horizontal danger angle. A danger sounding, where appropriate, can likewise serve as a warning that a vessel is approaching shoal water.

The usual practice of pilotage, however, is to determine position of the craft by means of POSITION LINES, on some point of which the craft is presumed to be located. The intersection of two or more simultaneous position lines establishes the position of the craft at the time of observation. This position is called a fix.

A common method of establishing a fix is by means of bearings. If a lighthouse is due E of a vessel, the bearing is E, or $090°$. If the bearing measurement was accurate, the vessel must be due W, or $270°$, from the lighthouse. A line drawn on the chart in direction $270°$ from the lighthouse represents the position at the time of observation. If, at the same time, a tower is due N, or $000°$, from the vessel, a line drawn from the tower in direction $180°$ represents a second position line. If the vessel is on both position lines at the same time, it can only be at their point of intersection. Of course, the objects might be in any direction, usually measured to an accuracy of $1°$ or better.

Direction position lines can sometimes be established without measurement. If two objects are in line, one beyond the other, the position line, called a transit (range), is simply the line through the two objects. Transits are established in line with some channels to guide vessels traversing them. It is essential, of course, that the navigator should know when to change course to stay in safe water.

A circular position line can be established by measurement of the distance to an object, by some form of rangefinder or by radar. If both distance and direction of the same object can be observed, the one object suffices for establishing a fix.

Because of the always-present possibility of an error in identification, measurement, plotting, or the chart, a third object is generally observed when a suitable one is available. If the three lines do not intersect at a point, or nearly so, the navigator is alerted to the possibility of error.

In the selection of objects for observation, the cut (crossing angle) of the position lines is an important consideration. An error in lines crossing at a small angle is magnified in the fix. The ideal cut for two position lines is $90°$; for three it is $60°$. Another consideration is the distance of the object. The linear error resulting from error in bearing measurement increases with distance from the object.

When simultaneous observations are not

possible, a RUNNING FIX is obtained. If the observations are made in quick succession, the movement of the vessel between observations may be negligible. But sometimes the interval is appreciable, as when an offshore lighthouse may be the only object available for observation. In this case, the position lines are adjusted to a common time, usually the time of the last observation. This is done by advancing an earlier line, assuming it moves forward at the speed and in the direction of motion of the craft. Any error in the course or speed of the vessel is reflected in the position of the advanced line. For this reason, fixes are preferred over running fixes where there is a choice and other conditions, such as the cut, are favourable.

Sometimes the position of a vessel relative to an object is determined without plotting, by considering the geometrical relationship involved in two bearings and the course. A commonly used example is 'doubling the angle on the bow'. If the difference in direction between the vessel's course and the line of sight to the object, the relative bearing, doubles between observations, the distance from the object at the time of the second bearing is equal to the distance run between observations, assuming accuracy of measurement of bearings, course, and speed.

Another method of establishing position is by means of horizontal angles between three objects, measured by a marine SEXTANT.

Soundings offer still another means of establishing the position of a vessel. For accurate results, distinctive submarine relief, adequately portrayed on the chart, is needed. One technique is to draw a straight line on a transparency and mark off, to the scale of the chart, distances corresponding to the run in a short interval of time. Soundings taken at these intervals, and adjusted for the state of the tide, are recorded alongside the marks, and the transparency is placed over the chart so as to coincide with the depths of water shown on the chart. Each mark indicates the position of the vessel at the time of that sounding. If continuous soundings are taken, as by an echo sounder (sonic depth finder), the time of crossing any depth contour shown on the chart can be noted, and that contour used as any other position line.

Pilotage is used extensively, and because of the nearness of the vessel to obstructions, high accuracy, frequent fixing, and constant alertness are needed. *See also* LIGHTHOUSES AND LIGHT VESSELS; NAVIGATION; SEAMARK

Pilot books *see* SAILING DIRECTIONS

Pinch
To sail too close to the wind.

Pinrail
A rack in which belaying pins are housed.

Pintle
A metal pin that fits into the GUDGEON to provide a pivoting support for the rudder.

Pitch
Rotation about the transverse axis of a craft.

Pitchpoling *see* HEAVY-WEATHER SAILING

Plain (plane) sailing
A method of solving the problem of representing a spherical earth on a flat surface by assuming, for navigational purposes, that the earth may, over limited distances, be treated as a plane. Plain (or plane) charts were superseded by charts constructed on the MERCATOR PROJECTION.

Plain sail *see* ALL PLAIN SAIL

Point
A sailing vessel is said to point high, or well, when she is able to sail close to the wind.

Point (of the compass)
One 32nd of a circle, or $11\frac{1}{4}°$; obtained by successively halving and rehalving the circle.

Point of sailing
The HEADING of a sailing vessel in relation to the wind: thus, CLOSE-HAULED etc.

Poop
(1) The aftermost deck, generally raised above the quarterdeck, of a large sailing vessel; (2) a craft is said to be pooped when a following sea breaks over her stern.

Port
The left side of a craft looking forward, denoted by red.

Portolano, portulan *see* NAVIGATION: Historical; SAILING DIRECTIONS

Port tack
A vessel is on the port tack when she is sailing with the wind on her port side.

Position fixing *see* NAVIGATION: The practice

Position line
A line along which the craft lies. Two such lines fix the position. *See also* NAVIGATION: The practice

Prince of Wales Cup *see* YACHT RACING: Major races and series

Proa *see* MULTIHULLS

Projections *see* MAP AND CHART PROJECTIONS

Pump systems *see* HULLS: Hull and accommodation systems

Purchase
In its marine context the word purchase applies to the use of blocks or pulleys to gain power when lifting or hauling. The power gained will be proportional to the number of sheaves in the moving block, less a factor for friction.

When more than one block is used the combination is termed a tackle (the nautical pronunciation is *taykel*) and the blocks are identified as the standing block and the running (or moving) block. The rope rove through the blocks is known as the fall and is divided into three parts, the standing part, the running part, and the hauling part. Since the power gained varies as the number of parts at the moving block, a tackle can either be rove to advantage, when the power gained will be maximum, or to disadvantage. It is rove to advantage when the hauling part of the fall leads from the moving block, to disadvantage when it leads from the standing block. When the two blocks have a different number of sheaves, the tackle will be rove to advantage when the block with the greater number is used as the moving block. It is, of course, not always possible to REEVE a tackle to advantage.

There are many combinations of blocks and tackles used at sea; only those in general use are described here.

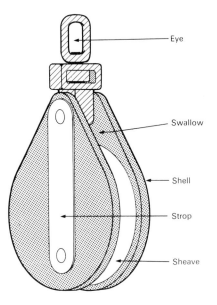

A modern metal-strapped plastic block; its parts have the same names and functions as those of the traditional rope-strapped wooden block illustrated on the next page. The eye may swivel, as shown in the diagram, be fixed in line, or across (turned through 90°)

– single whip
No power is gained by this use of a single block, generally to hoist objects or to alter the direction of a lead.

– runner
When a single whip is used to apply purchase to the end of a line so that the block moves, it is known as a runner. The standing part is made fast to something like an eyebolt, the fall rove through the block and taken to a belaying point such as a cleat. Runners are widely used to tauten the weather backstay in yachts (power gained × 2).

– whip and runner
This is really a double whip in which the running part of the upper whip is made fast to another single block instead of a belaying point. Since the hauling part must come from the standing block, a double whip cannot be rigged to advantage. This tackle was widely used on the halyards of single topsails and topgallants (power gained × 2).

– gun (or gin) tackle
A gun tackle consists of two single blocks, the fall being made fast to the heel of the upper block, rove through the lower and up through the upper block and belayed as required (power gained when rove to advantage × 3, to disadvantage × 2).

– handy billy or jigger
Jigger is rather a loose term, applied variously to a luff tackle with smaller rope, or a general-use tackle consisting of a double

The points of sailing shown are: (a) *running;* (b) *broad reaching;* (c) *beam reaching;* (d) *fetching (close reaching);* (e) *beating (close-hauled)*

Wind

(a)   (b)   (c)   (d)   (e)

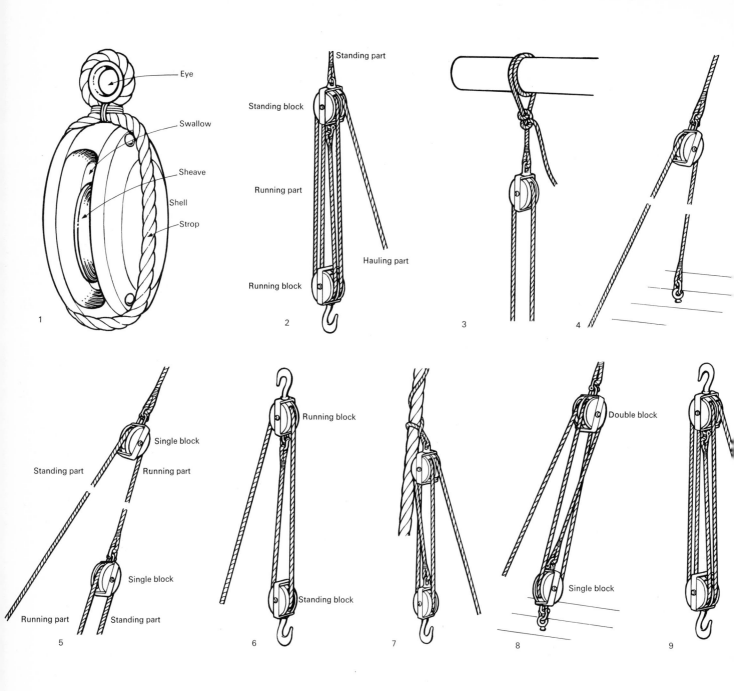

Eye

Swallow

Sheave

Shell

Strop

1

Standing part

Standing block

Running part

Running block

Hauling part

2

3

4

Single block

Standing part

Running part

Single block

Running part

Standing part

5

Running block

Standing block

6

7

Double block

Single block

8

9

block with a tail and a single block with a hook (power gained × 4 to advantage, × 3 to disadvantage).

– luff tackle
The standing part of the fall on a luff tackle is made fast to a single block, rove through one sheave on a double block, down through the single, back through the double to its belaying point (rove to advantage, gain × 4, to disadvantage × 3).

– twofold purchase
This is really a double luff, the fall being spliced to the heel of one of the two double blocks and rove through each of the blocks in turn until all the sheaves are in use, and so to

the belaying point (power gained when rove to advantage × 5, to disadvantage × 4).
THREE-, FOUR-, AND FIVEFOLD PURCHASES
These are used for heavy work, such as hoisting boats etc. It should be remembered that the number of sheaves increases the friction and so diminishes the power gained; large-diameter sheaves, however, lessen friction.

Fig. 1 The parts of a single block. The shell may be of wood or metal, and there may be two or more sheaves (hence double and threefold block, etc.). The strop may be of rope, wire, or a metal strap. Fig. 2 Twofold purchase rove to disadvantage. Fig. 3 Single whip. Fig. 4 Runner. Fig. 5 Whip and runner. Fig. 6 Gun tackle. Fig. 7 Handy billy. Fig. 8 Luff tackle. Fig. 9 Twofold purchase

The Krusenstern *(formerly* Padua*), a Russian training ship, is one of the finest tall ships afloat. A four-masted barque of 3064 tons, she was built in 1926 at Bremerhaven, West Germany. She is seen here during the* Tall Ships Parade of Sail in 1974

Q

Quadrant
The seaman's quadrant was a flat quarter-circle of wood or metal with sights along one edge and a plumb line to mark the vertical at the instant of observing the ALTITUDE of the sun or a star. It appears to have been the earliest instrument used by European sailors to determine latitude, although observations with a plumb line must have been difficult in any but the calmest weather.

Very large quadrants had long been used by astronomers, but the earliest mention of the use of a quadrant at sea is in 1456–7 by Portuguese discoverers along the west coast of Africa. At first the quarter-circle was not graduated in degrees but marked to show the height of the Pole Star at Lisbon, for example, and at the capes and islands visited on a voyage.

The name 'quadrant' was later applied to a very different instrument, HADLEY'S QUADRANT. The BACKSTAFF was also known outside England as the 'English quadrant'.

Quadrantal deviation
Deviation of the compass which changes its sign for every 90° change of HEADING.

Quarter
The point, on either side of a vessel, at 45° from the stern; generally taken to be the whole area from amidships on either side to the stern.

Quick-flashing light *see* LIGHTS: Characteristics

R

Rabbet, rebate
A groove cut to receive the edge of a plank, as in the keel, stem etc.

Race
A fast-flowing tidal stream or current produced by constriction, uneven bottom, or tidal streams crossing.

Racking seizing *see* ROPEWORK: Splices

Radar
A way of using radio waves reflected (primary radar) or retransmitted (secondary radar) to get the bearing and distance of distant objects.

Radar reflectors
When the beam of power transmitted from a radar aerial encounters an obstruction, it is scattered in all directions. A tiny fraction of the power goes back in the right direction to re-enter the radar aerial. This is amplified and presented so as to mark the position of that obstruction, forming a display like the one illustrated, which shows the channel leading to the Port of London. The radar on the end of the pier jutting out one mile from the Essex coast shows both coastlines, the ships, and the buoys, to a range of 6 miles.

Four small rings encircle the positions of the first four buoys in Sea Reach, No. 1 being on the right and to the east; No. 4 at 1.4 miles and No. 3 at 2.9 miles are seen displayed inside the rings, but No. 2 at 4.3 miles is so far from the radar that the amount of power it can scatter back is too small to be detected. The four buoys are alike, yet No. 1 is clearly seen although it is further away than No. 2, which is not seen. No. 1 is fitted with a radar reflector, a device that does not scatter the power coming from the radar aerial, but 'retro-reflects' it, i.e. reflects nearly all of it directly back to the radar aerial. On the radar display the appearance is of a larger object, that can be detected at greater ranges than the buoy alone.

The device is equally effective when fitted to a small boat. It is passive (i.e. it needs no power supply) and its WINDAGE and top weight do not present serious penalties. Many national authorities encourage the fitting of radar reflectors in the interest of safety at sea. This is because the radar can find it difficult or even impossible to detect a small vessel near the ship in winds of force 3 or above, which will cause waves whose radar signals ('sea clutter' seen within one mile of the pier in the display) can hide the small vessel.

Two types of radar reflector are suitable for

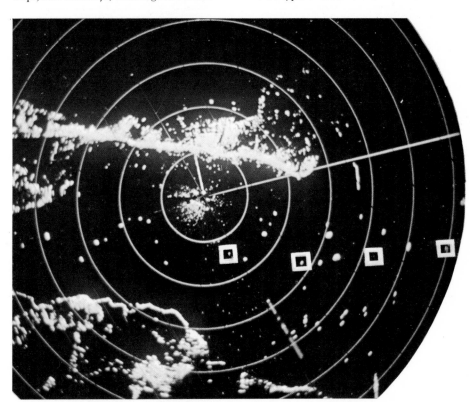

Alec Rose (later knighted) entering Plymouth harbour at the end of his circumnavigation on 4 July 1968 in Lively Lady. *A heavy cruising yacht, she was built of teak between the wars*

This radar display shows the sea reach at the entrance to the Port of London from the end of Southend Pier. Four identical buoys are marked, the two nearest are 'seen' but the third is too far away

for it to show on the screen. Buoy No. 1 on the 6-mile ring, shows up clearly because it is fitted with a radar reflector

small-boat fitting, the 'Luneberg lens' and the cluster of 'corner reflectors'. The Lune-berg principle is exploited by a reflector manufactured from foamed polystyrene spheres one inside the other, with densities carefully graded to a maximum in the middle. There is a metal reflecting band round the 'equator' and the whole is weather-proofed in a tough plastic skin and provided with a mounting bracket. It acts as a lens to focus any incoming beam of power to the opposite side, inside the reflecting band. After being reflected symmetrically the power emerges as a beam directed back to the radar aerial, retro-reflected not scattered. The device is very efficient. A 360-mm (14-in) diameter model reflects as much power into the radar aerial as would be scattered into the same aerial by a 3.5-m (11.5-ft) diameter metal sphere. Its effective reflecting area – its apparent cross-section to the radar beam – is 10 m², and is roughly equivalent to a 120-ft wooden fishing vessel.

The Luneberg lens is symmetrical, so a nearly uniform response is produced all round the horizon. The width of the reflect-ing band has to be a compromise – too wide and it scatters a large part of the incoming power before it can enter the lens, but too narrow and the permissible tilt is restricted. Efficient operation can be obtained up to about ±15° of tilt, so while it can be service-able on a motor cruiser, the Luneberg lens, if rigidly mounted, cannot be recommended for a sailing craft that spends a lot of sea time heeled to more than 15°.

A flat metal plate will not scatter the power. It will reflect it nearly all in one direction,

but like a heliograph mirror it has to be aimed. Three flat plates mutually at right angles (like one corner inside a tin box) form a trihedral corner which gives a strong retro-reflection in any direction within 20° of the axis of symmetry of the corner. Reflection takes place once at each of the three surfaces, but for directions more than 20° from the axis of symmetry smaller and smaller sections of the plates can achieve the necessary reflection into each other. At more than 35° off, the retro-reflection becomes negligible.

To operate all round the horizon an as-sembly of a number of corners is needed and the design of such a cluster needs care. If two or more corners retro-reflect in the same direction, their reflections will add together only so long as the corners are at nearly the same distance from the radar aerial, within a small fraction of the 3-cm wavelength, say 2 or 3 mm or $\frac{7}{16}$ in. Clearly if the assembly is tilted, a larger difference will result, and the reflections get out of step with each other until one completely cancels the other, and the assembly becomes 'invisible' to the radar. In exactly the same way a bloomed photo-graphic lens looks dark, because a second surface (the 'bloom') has been added to the lens' surfaces, spaced off just enough so that its reflection cancels the first.

Some assemblies of about a dozen small reflectors are available, claimed to be con-venient to hoist in the rigging of a small craft; this appears to be their only good quality. Independent tests indicate that they have a very small effective reflecting area, perhaps less than the craft carrying them.

A cluster of corners can be effective if the

angular coverage of one only overlaps the next by a small margin, and any one alone provides sufficient reflection. Some buoyage authorities use a 'pentagonal' cluster on some buoys, in which five separate corners face the horizon at 72° intervals, each covering its own sector and no other. Where two sectors meet, there is an arc of about 20° in which the response is slightly weaker, but the range performance is only reduced from 10 to about 7 miles. When scaled down in size and weight sufficiently to suit a small vessel, however, the reflection is insufficient.

An assembly more suited to small craft is the 'octahedral' cluster of eight corners, formed by three square plates of at least 340-mm (13-in) sides, each of which appears to cut through the other two at right angles. The points of the square plates may be cut back or rounded off with no loss of performance. Each corner is surrounded by three other corners that face directions 70° away. The eight directions are symmetrically distributed in space, all at 70° apart, so it is not possible to mount this reflector so that all corners face the horizon. It is commonly seen mounted with one point up – unfortunately some mounting brackets or holes seem to en-courage this. This is quite the worst way to mount it, since four corners (say, N, S, E, and W) face 35° up into the sky, and the other four (also N, S, E, and W) face 35° down into the sea. Coverage of the horizon is very poor, and instead of the 5-mile range which is achieved in the best attitude by one corner of an octahedron made from 340-mm (13-in) square plates, the maximum is no more than $3\frac{1}{2}$ miles, and this only in four narrow lobes as

Fig. 1 Octahedral reflector, point up; range of detection: poor

Fig. 2 Octahedral reflector, face up; range of detection: good

Fig. 3 Octahedral reflector, edge up; range of detection: not as good as when its attitude is face up, but at 35° heel the reflector's attitude would change to that position (see fig.2)

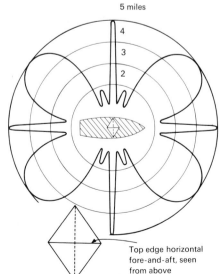

seen in fig. 1, falling to less than 2 miles over at least half the horizon. True, when a sailing craft heels, some improvement may occur abeam, but not ahead or astern. Over much of the horizon a ship's radar will be unable to detect this reflector in sea states that occur frequently.

The most efficient mounting attitude is shown in fig. 2 in which one corner faces upwards – it might help detection by a search-and-rescue aircraft – but the opposite one faces uselessly down. The other 6 face alternately 20° above and below the horizon at 60° intervals. Over at least half the horizon the range of detection exceeds 4 miles, and in no direction does it fall below 2.5 miles.

To maintain the reflector in this attitude for all conditions of sailing, an adjustable harness would be required, with the necessity for handling at each change of course or wind. To avoid this, a different non-adjusted attitude is suggested. The slight reduction in performance that it entails may be considered a fair price to pay for the work reduction. Fig. 3 shows that if two opposite points are aligned athwartships so that the square plate between them has its top edge horizontal and fore and aft, when the craft is on an even keel four corners face out directly to the horizon, giving four broad lobes of detection up to 5 miles. Only over about one third of the horizon does the range fall below 2.5 miles, in narrow sectors where the craft itself provides its best radar echo, and which would often be moved off an approaching ship's bearing by slight YAWING of the sailing craft.

The advantage is that the other four corners face up and down abeam, and as the craft heels the upper one to LEEWARD and the lower one to windward tilt to face the horizon. If the craft heels to 35°, the reflector is in the most efficient attitude of fig. 2. There is thus excellent performance at any angle of heel from 15 to 55°, and good performance within ±15°, without the tedious necessity for adjustment of the reflector attitude.

Mounting between twin triatic backstays is very practical, with a tie to keep the top edge horizontal. Alternatively a position between the mast and a side stay may be convenient. An error of a few degrees in the attitude will cause little reduction of performance.

The height of the reflector above the sea is important. This is because the signal received by the radar from an object at long range consists of two parts, one coming directly and the other by reflection at the sea surface. The difference in the distances they have to travel causes them to get out of step, and one can cancel the other, wholly or partly. The higher the reflector (and the radar aerial) the less harmful is the effect of this sea reflection.

On a 3-cm radar an octahedral cluster with 13-in (340-mm) sides appears to have an effective reflecting area of 10 m² when one

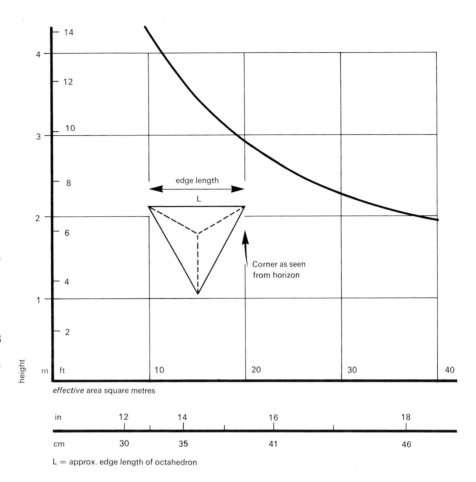

Fig. 4 Graph to show the size of reflector required to achieve a maximum range of 5 miles (8 km)

corner directly faces the radar. In free space a typical marine radar would detect this at 7 miles. Assuming the radar is on a deep-sea trawler of 700 grt (gross registered tons), its aerial will be at a height of about 15 ft. The same radar reflector at 12 ft above the sea will be detected at up to 5 miles, but at half this height (6 ft) it will not be detected much above 3 miles. This range can, of course, be increased by fitting a larger reflector. Fig. 4 shows the size of reflector required to achieve 5 miles maximum range, according to the height it is fitted above the sea. The advantage of height is clear.

Larger octahedral clusters than the 13-in size are available, but the disadvantage is the increased weight and windage, and the difficulty of handling and avoiding chafe if a permanent mount is not used. Perforation of the metal to ease this problem is not a satisfactory answer, since holes of about 1 cm (⅜ in) are the largest that will not reduce the reflection properties. These holes will effect some weight reduction but will hardly change the windage. Some advantage is

offered by the use of weatherproofed metallized nylon mesh instead of sheet metal. This is light and does not offer too much wind resistance, even though the cluster has to be more than doubled in size to maintain at least 10 m² reflecting area. It has the further advantage of folding into a compact form, which facilitates its use as emergency life-raft equipment.

In conclusion, the Intergovernmental Maritime Consultative Organization's (IMCO) Resolution A 277 (VIII) recommended that a radar reflector should be carried by all ships of less than 100 grt, and by all ships constructed of non-ferrous material. The IMCO document NAV XIX/W.P.11 of 16 February 1977 says that the 'recommendation' should now be replaced by a 'requirement', i.e. carriage of a radar reflector will become compulsory on small vessels. A specification for the operational performance to be achieved by such a radar reflector was issued by IMCO in 1976.

See also PILOTAGE; NAVIGATION: The practice

Radio aids to navigation *see* COMPOSITE OMEGA; CONSOL; DECCA NAVIGATOR; DECTRA; DME; HI-FIX; HYPERBOLIC FIXING SYSTEMS; LORAN; OMEGA; RADAR; RADIO DIRECTION-FINDING

Radiobeacon *see* RADIO DIRECTION-FINDING

Radio direction-finding

Measurement of the direction in which a transmitter lies requires a special antenna system, a receiver, and a display to give the bearing. The antenna must have a response that varies with the direction of arrival of the signal and the simplest example of this is the loop. If a loop is rotated about its vertical axis until its radio frequency voltage output is a minimum, the operator knows that the wave is travelling along the line AB of the polar diagram (left). Headphones connected to the receiver will serve as a signal indicator.

To determine the sense, whether from A to B or B to A, the loop diagram must be modified by adding a constant term from an omni-directional vertical wire. The combined pattern is a cardioid with only one minimum (right). This is less sharp than the loop minima, and the correct phase and amplitude relationships between the two antenna voltages are difficult to maintain, so that in practice the loop signal alone is used for the bearing measurement with an approximate cardioid to resolve the ambiguity.

To obtain adequate signal voltages, particularly at the lower frequencies, large antennas are needed which are difficult to rotate. The Bellini-Tosi system uses two fixed loops mounted fore and aft and athwartships and combines their signals in a radiogoniometer. This consists of two coils at right angles on a common axis and a third (search) coil rotatable about the same axis. The field set up by the fixed coils reproduces the bearing of the incident wave and the search coil is like a small rotating loop antenna that determines this bearing.

In the spinning goniometer the search coil is continuously rotated so that its output is modulated as a function of the bearing and can be used to derive a pointer or a cathode ray display on a 360° scale. A visual presentation is also given by showing the position of a loop antenna or radiogoniometer search coil that has been rotated to a signal null by a servo system. These methods are used in automatic direction finders (ADF).

All systems are subject to errors from radio propagation effects. A wave front is polarized in the direction of its electric field vector relative to the earth's surface and if this direction is not vertical the antenna response will change and lead to different bearing indications. The direction finder may also receive two or more waves that have travelled from the transmitter by different paths and their combination can produce a wave front with a direction different from the true bearing of the transmitter.

Passage through the ionosphere in several modes due to reflection from different, possibly tilted, layers changes both polarization and direction of arrival, and objects near the direction finder can also produce significant reflections in arbitrary directions. The siting of the antennas is thus important. Currents induced in the main structure of the ship give an error that has a maximum once in each quadrant and of opposite sign in alternate quadrants. This quadrantal error (QE) is greatly reduced by fitting one loop with a compensating circuit adjusted for a particular ship installation.

All this leads to a wide variation in accuracy: better than 1° in the best conditions, but with no upper limit, although signals over 5° in error are generally weak or unstable.

Raffee

A light-weather square sail.

Rake

The angle a mast, sternpost etc. makes with the perpendicular.

Ramark

A continuously transmitting radio beacon that will display a radial line of bearing on a radar set operating in the same frequency band.

Range *see* TRANSIT (2)

Range of tide

The difference at any place between the heights of high and low water. *See* TIDES AND TIDAL STREAMS

Ratlines *see* MASTS AND RIGGING: Glossary

Reach

A point of sailing with the apparent wind on or near the beam.

Ready about

A cautionary order to the crew on deck before a vessel tacks.

Reef

To shorten, i.e. reduce, sail by furling, rolling up, or other means.

Reefing gear *see* MASTS AND RIGGING

Reef knot *see* ROPEWORK: Bends and hitches

Reeve

To pass a line through a block, fairlead etc.

Reference station *see* TIDES AND TIDAL STREAMS

Reflecting circle

An elaboration of the marine SEXTANT in which verniers on two diametrically opposite index arms are read against the graduations of a complete circle. Besides enabling angles as large as 160° to be measured, the advantage of the complete circle was in reducing the errors due to any slight eccentricity of the axis of the index mirror or irregularities in the graduation of the arc. The reflecting circle was used to measure LUNAR DISTANCES, for which the greatest accuracy is essential, and was invented for this purpose by the German astronomer Johann Tobias Mayer, whose lunar tables were published in 1753.

A further refinement published by the French nautical astronomer Jean Charles de Borda in 1787 was the 'repeating circle'. With this instrument the distance is first measured in the usual way by rotating the index mirror; then a second measurement is made by rotating the telescope and horizon mirror while the index mirror remains clamped to the circle. The difference between the circle readings is then the sum of the measured distances; it is only necessary to read the verniers at the beginning and end of a series of observations, so that the effects of any irregularity in the divisions of the arc are reduced.

Radio direction-finding: how the loop diagram is modified to produce a cardioid

loop
(a)

+

vertical
(b)

=

cardioid
(c)

Refraction
The change in direction of a ray of light as it passes obliquely from one medium to another in which the speed of propagation is different. A correction for astronomical or atmospheric refraction is made to the sextant altitude of bodies observed in astronomical navigation. *See* ASTRONOMICAL NAVIGATION

Refraction, atmospheric *see* HORIZON DISTANCE

Relative bearing *see* BEARING

Remote screw outhaul *see* MASTS AND RIGGING: Glossary

Repairs *see* MAINTENANCE; SAIL CARE

Repeating circle *see* REFLECTING CIRCLE

Rhumb line
A line that cuts all the meridians at the same angle. *See also* NAVIGATION: The practice

Ribs
Transverse frames or timbers of a vessel.

Riding light
An all-round white light hung in the fore part of a vessel to show she is at anchor.

Rigging *see* MASTS AND RIGGING

Rigging loads *see* HULLS: Scantlings

Rigging screw (turnbuckle) *see* MASTS AND RIGGING: Glossary

Square rigs

A square sail has a rectangular outline; is hung from a yard at the head, which is suspended at its mid-point on the fore side of the mast; it sometimes has a boom also; and always receives the wind on the same side – the aft side – when driving the ship. (For comparisons, *see* Fore-and-aft rigs; Lateen and lug rigs *below*).

The terms 'sail' and 'rigs' have to be differentiated. A rig is an arrangement of one or more sails and masts and may be composite, including both square and fore-and-aft sails, but is described according to the character of the chief sails carried. Thus all the later square-rigged ships had some fore-and-aft sails; and some rigs described as fore-and-aft incorporated square sails, as on top-sail schooners.

Caution is needed over nomenclature, particularly concerning rig, where it has always been in a state of flux: terms have changed their meaning totally over the years, or in any given period may have had different meanings according to locality.

– the earliest sailing craft
A clay model of *c.* 3500 BC, found in a grave at Eridu, southern Mesopotamia, may be the oldest known evidence of a sailing boat. A small cylindrical socket in the bottom slightly forward of amidships, and a hole in either

A modern model of a ship of Pharaoh Sahure. When not in use the bipod mast could be lowered to rest on the stand near the vessel's stern

gunwale a little abaft this, may represent a mast step and the means of securing rigging. It is generally assumed that the model represents a skin-covered coracle; and although the above features look temptingly like fittings for sail, there can be no certainty.

An indisputable sailing craft, and the earliest known picture of one, appears on a small vase from southern Egypt, now in the British Museum, London. The hull swings up high either end and a single square sail is set on a mast without rigging stepped well forward. This vase is now considered to date from *c.* 3000 BC. Other possible representations of sailing craft are to be found on pottery dated 3200 BC, but interpretation is difficult. Numerous graffiti from southern Egypt show craft with a single square sail stepped near or forward of amidships. In the present state of knowledge, all that can be said with certainty is that in craft of skin and reed, rudimentary sail was used in Mesopotamia and Egypt during the fourth millennium BC and that it was in these areas of the Fertile Crescent, and not in the Far East, that sail was first hoisted.

– ancient Egyptian seagoing ships
The earliest evidence of sail in seagoing ships of any size comes from Egyptian bas-reliefs. The most important of these, though widely spaced in time, show considerable detail. The famous reliefs of Pharoah Sahure's ships,

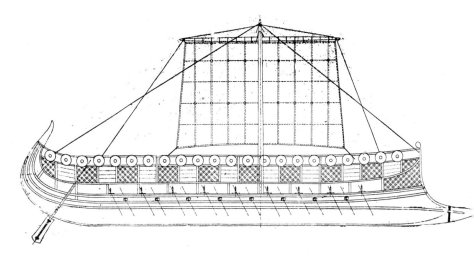

c. 2600 BC, show vessels about 60 ft (18 m) in length carrying a single tall, narrow square sail, its proportions approximately 3:1, on a mast some one-third of the length from the bow. The mast is a bipod stepped athwartships. It is not certain, but probable, that the sail had a boom, like those of Egyptian ships for centuries to come.

The first masts of which there are extant pictures were single poles stepped centrally on the bottom, the form into which they subsequently reverted and remained in all but primitive craft. But for a long period the bipod mast became the usual type. It is believed to have been an Egyptian invention, the best solution for setting sail in reed boats. A single mast entailed stepping the compressive load on the reed bundles of the bottom, the weakest part of a weak hull. It was sound engineering to make the mast double with the two legs pivoted on the side bundles. The retention of the bipod in wooden craft, such as those of Sahure's fleet, indicates the weakness of the hull construction pending the development of adequate internal framing.

A thousand years later the no less famous Egyptian reliefs commemorating the trading voyage to Punt instigated by Queen Hatshepsut, *c* 1600 BC, show some developments in sail propulsion. Most importantly in pointing the way to the future, the mast has become a single spar and is stepped near amidships. The single mast reveals improved hull structure. From its position it might be inferred that efforts were being made to sail with the wind a little further forward of dead astern. The sail has become shallow and very wide: an aspect ratio so much lower than on sails of a millennium earlier might appear curious if a better sailing performance was being sought; but such craft would not have sailed with the wind much further forward than 40° of dead astern, when aspect ratio would not be of material advantage. On the other hand, the reduced stresses in the lower rig would have been important when materials were so weak.

– sail in the Classical world
The elimination of the boom from the square sail of the Mediterranean, a process beginning by 1200 BC, was an important development in western rig. Thenceforward, through the Phoenician, Greek, and Roman eras, the principal sail used was the boomless square sail slung from a yard on a single mast; and it may possibly have been due to Phoenician and Roman influence that this kind of sail, and never, so far as is known, one with a boom, took root in northern Europe. Ships equipped with one pole mast and a boomless square sail, in galley as well as merchantman, had a means of sail propulsion whose basic form was to change little until the later Classical days when a topsail, and sometimes two or even three masts, were fitted in some

A drawing of a Phoenician galley, based on bas-reliefs from Sennaherib's palace, Nineveh, showing its single mast stepped on the rowing deck and boomless square sail

ships. Centuries of development lay primarily not in the proportions and fundamental character of the essentially simple single-masted square rig, but in the improvement of sail and rigging materials and of rigging leads able to raise its performance and reliability.

The topsail carried in the larger ships of the Roman empire period was the only superimposed sail known to the ancient world. Its use may have preceded the empire. Characteristic of this period in the Mediterranean was the artemon, a square sail set on a steeply angled bowsprit. This sail apparently disappeared from the usages of seamanship until its reappearance in the medieval three-masted ship, and any connection between the Mediterranean artemon of about AD 200 and the northern bowsprit sail of about AD 1500 is uncertain.

Caesar wrote of the Gallic Veneti of the Brittany coast and their sails of 'skins and leather, either for lack of flax and ignorance of its use or (as more likely) because sails of canvas were not considered able to support such force of wind and drive such heavy ships.'

– sail in the North
Although there is a theory that the northern square sail was a legacy of the Phoenicians who voyaged to southwest Britain for tin, it would seem at least as likely that the northern peoples may have devised a square sail of their own, as did the prehistoric peoples of the Fertile Crescent. Sail came late to the further north. Roman power in Britain and Gaul was a memory when the Norsemen first set a little canvas above their native hulls, whose clinker (lapstrake) construction (*see* HULLS: Construction components) already had a long tradition behind it. So long as the Norsemen

confined themselves to their fjords and coasts, the greater convenience and manoeuvrability that oar power offered in lightly built galleys may have deterred them from developing sail. Once the craft became heavier load carriers, and wider seas their highway, Viking sail was evolved.

Less is perhaps known about it than some published accounts suggest. The remains of the galleys show how they were constructed, but rigging is perishable and only a few stones depict Viking ships under the sails described in the saga of the eleventh-century St Olaf as 'white as snow with stripes of red and blue'. A Gotland stone of the eighth century AD indicates that sail and rigging were still primitive: the sail is criss-crossed by lines that may be strengthening bands for a weak fabric, and along the foot of the sail is a multiple sheet, presumably also to spread the load over fragile cloth. The Vikings must have learned quickly during the expansion period. The Gokstad galley, *c*. 850, indicates the serious use of sail, shown in the mast step, a heavy, well-devised structural member obviously intended for a mast bearing heavy loads; and in the wooden blocks to carry the heel of the *beitáss*, a wooden spar for holding steady the luff of the sail when the yard was trimmed forward. The spar, resting in the block near the mast, had its outer end engaged in the luff and served the same vital purpose as bowlines later. The excellent mechanics of the side rudder, replacing the cruder steering oar of a few centuries earlier, was another feature that improved sailing performance. The area of sail was small, and the galleys were open boats primarily for rowing; but in favourable conditions they could probably sail with the wind on or a little ahead of the beam.

– medieval single-masted square-riggers

The Viking rig set the precedent for north European sail until the two- and three-masted ship appeared in the fifteenth century. The medieval trade of northern Europe, in the English Channel and North Sea, reaching up to the Baltic and south to Biscay, was conducted in single-masted, square-sailed double-ended, clinker-built craft. Various names were applied to types that cannot now be accurately distinguished. Their important features were that in general they were beamy, high-sided load carriers, with a few oars used only for harbour work and emergency, primarily dependent on their single square sails. It is possible that the later Vikings used bowlines instead of the *beitáss*. In the medieval cargo carriers the bowline became a crucial piece of rigging, necessary to confer such weatherliness as they possessed. A bridle was rigged between cringles over the middle length of the fore leech of the sail and the bowline itself led to a point forward where it might be hauled taut. The reeving of bowlines became more elaborate with time as efforts were made to improve weatherliness. The bowsprit, which appeared in the course of the twelfth and thirteenth centuries, almost certainly was primarily designed to give a more effective lead to the bowlines, further forward. It apparently carried no sail before the later fifteenth century, although it was subsequently to become a more and more heavily loaded sail carrier.

– the three-masted square-rigger

What Professor Arnold Toynbee was to call the master tool of Western civilization, the three-masted square-rigged ship that was to conquer the oceans of the world, appeared quite suddenly in the course of the fifteenth century. There was a brief interregnum in the north of unsatisfactory two-masted ships. The position of the main single mast was sacrosanct by long usage and any major change in its location near amidships was not to be considered. Satisfactory hull and sail balance could not then be achieved with two masts, whether the second was placed forward or aft of the main: both positions appear to have been tried. Balance could be achieved with three masts, and with the three-master came a merging of the Mediterranean and northern rigs. The three-masted ship emerged with a square sail on the fore and main masts, a Mediterranean lateen (*see* Lateen and lug rigs *below*) on the mizzen. To whom credit should be given for this mighty invention is unknown; it is sometimes believed to have been due to Biscayan seamen, placed midway between Mediterranean and northern influences.

By 1450 the rig was increasing in numbers, the social compulsion behind it being the need for more and larger ships; and the earlier invention of the centreline rudder brought greater power of control for bigger hulls and more complex rigs. With the mainmast dominating the habits of seamanship, at first both fore- and mizzenmasts were tiny in comparison. The fact, however, that the mizzen carried a lateen marked the beginning of the combination of square with fore-and-aft sail, the composite rig, which was to give the later so-called square-rigged ship its ocean-going ability. The initial steps towards this type of vessel lay in increasing the size and sail-carrying capacity of the fore- and mizzenmasts, the addition of topsails, and of a square sail under the bowsprit, which may be termed a bowspritsail to distinguish it from the fore-and-aft spritsail. These changes converted the foresail and lateen mizzen

A modern model of the Santa Maria *(1492). Such three-masted ships with their combination of sails on fore- and mainmasts, and lateen on the mizzen masts, played a major role in the opening up of the world*

into driving as well as manoeuvring and balancing sails.

By 1450 three-masters appear to have been fairly common and main topsails may sometimes have been carried, the first example of superimposed sails since the topsails of the largest Roman ships. Like the first foresails and mizzens, the first maintopsails were tiny. They were increased in area; and the small square-rigged ship thus produced, of which the *Santa Maria* was an example, was the finest ocean-going machine yet devised, a giant's stride beyond the medieval trader with a single sail. Shortly a topsail was added also above the foresail (or fore course) and the smaller merchantmen retained this basic rig of six sails, five of them square and a lateen, for a long period. The *Mayflower* of 1620,

some 130 years after the *Santa Maria*, was so rigged. Records of the pedestrian little merchant vessels are sparse, but as late as 1704 the *Papers of Thomas Bowery* (Hakluyt Society 1927) give specifications for a merchantman of similar size to the *Mayflower* and identically rigged.

– the sixteenth century

For a brief period during the sixteenth century there was a fashion for prestige ships and additional masts. The French *Grand François* of 1527 had five masts; a fourth mast, the bonaventure mizzen, abaft the mizzen and also carrying a lateen, was carried in many galleons. A draught of a galleon, dated about 1586, by the English shipwright Matthew Baker, shows the further addition of topgallantsails on fore and main, but no topsails above the mizzen and bonaventure. Smaller vessels continued to have three masts, and in the later course of improving sailing and manoeuvring qualities in larger ships, experience proved three masts to be the best arrangement; this became standard with the mizzenmast a substantial spar and heavy sail carrier. (The largest naval ships of the line retained three masts to the end.)

– the seventeenth and eighteenth centuries

During the seventeenth century, many improvements were made in the three-masted square-rigged ship. A square topsail was set above the lateen mizzen, which added little to the driving power but much to manoeuvrability. Topsails were improved by enlarging them, particularly increasing their depth. A print of the English *Sovereign of the Seas* (1637), the biggest ship in the world of her day and three-masted, showed yards for yet another topsail above the topgallants, royals on both fore- and mainmasts, a detail at one time distrusted in view of the date, but now believed to be accurate; and she carried a square sail above the lateen mizzen. Towards the end of the eighteenth century royals became usual in larger ships, and further growth in size following the Napoleonic wars led to the occasional adoption of a further topsail, the skysail, though this was never widely used, and then mainly by clippers during the mid-nineteenth century.

Meanwhile, at the other end of the scale of size, during the sixteenth, seventeenth, and early eighteenth centuries, the two- and three-masted square-rigged herring busses continued riding to their nets in the North Sea; the latter carried four sails, a square mizzen, main and topsail, and foresail which was steadied on the wind with a spar descended from the Viking *beitáss*. These were

An engraving by J. Payne of Charles I's warship Sovereign of the Seas. *Her massive rig included a large spritsail*

one of the classes of craft that adopted the lug rig in the course of the eighteenth century (*see* Fore-and-aft rigs *below*).

Triangular fore-and-aft sails set on stays had been used in the smaller craft for many years before they appeared in larger ships as an important adjunct to the square sails. The tremendous accession of sailing ability gained by combining fore-and-aft with square sails in one rig had been latent since the three-masted square-rigged ship had emerged carrying the lateen of the Mediterranean on the mizzenmast. Before the adoption of tri-angular headsails, the canvas set ahead of the foremast was confined to the spritsail carried beneath the bowsprit, augmented in an unsatisfactory way in larger vessels by a spritsail topsail precariously set on a small and poorly stayed mast perched on top of the bowsprit. The setting of triangular sails on the forestays provided head canvas of much greater value, also more secure and easily handled. A third triangular headsail was later added beyond these, another jib for the set-ting of which the bowsprit was extended by an additional spar, the jib boom. This oc-curred in the early eighteenth century. There followed the addition of another jib, a flying jib, carried on a further extension of the bowsprit, a flying jib boom.

With these developments the medieval bowsprit, which was not used for carrying sail, had become a heavily loaded sail-carrying spar requiring ever stronger rigging to support it. The gammoning, holding the inboard end of the bowsprit down against the wind forces in staysails and jibs trying to tear it upwards, became a crucial element in this rigging. The bowsprit gathered an array of rigging about it – martingale stays, and for lateral support shrouds and jib-boom guys. Triangular headsails brought new powers of manoeuvrability and weatherliness, par-ticularly the latter. During the eighteenth century, staysails were added to the stays between the masts; and with this the essen-tials of the ultimate square-rigged ship, com-plex descendant of all those vessels that had been propelled by a single square sail since a thousand years and more before the Christian era, began its brief reign over the oceans before being ousted by steam.

A change was made in the sail set on the mizzenmast. Until about the middle of the eighteenth century the lateen continued to display this unaltered Mediterranean contri-bution to the square-rigged ship. The fore part of the sail ahead of the mast was then eliminated, making what remained essen-tially a gaff sail. Smaller craft, including such as naval frigates, were soon given a true northern gaff sail; but in the larger the for-ward bare half of the lateen yard was re-tained until the end of the century with the object apparently that it might be useful to

replace other yards in the event of damage. The gaff mizzen became known as the span-ker or driver.

The conventionally named square-rigged ship had become a composite-rigged ship, an arrangement of many square and fore-and-aft sails working in a unison that was the out-come of long experience and experiment. The further end of this line of development is illustrated in two draughts by Steel of the sails of a 20-gun ship of 1797. One plate shows the square sails, 13 in number excluding stun-sails; another shows the fore-and-aft sails, set on the stays between the masts and on the forestays, and including the spanker, a total of 11. Although this proportion of square to fore-and-aft sails gives a general picture of the later square-riggers' sail plans, it has to be appreciated that the area of the former type greatly surpassed that of the latter; and in the

the schooner – two cases of the square rig giving way to the fore-and-aft in vessels that spent much of their time in coastal waters. Rigs in which the principal sails carried, apart from jibs and staysails, combined both square and fore-and-aft were evolved for par-ticular purposes. Brigantine became the name of a separate type carrying square sails on the foremast and fore-and-aft sails on the main-mast. Various forms of brig were evolved. The hermaphrodite brig went half way to-wards the brigantine by having a gaff mainsail but square topsail above it; the snow, a rig confined to Europe, was a brig with a light trysail mast stepped almost against the aft side of the mainmast and sup-ported at the head by the main top, to carry a trysail that was bigger in area than the brig's spanker. In the jackass barque, a nineteenth-century type evolved for the nitrate trade

A wash drawing by Charles Brooking (1723–59) of a British man-of-war brigantine with fore-and-aft sail on its main mast

free winds of the trade-wind belts, the square sails were much the more effective area for area.

– brig, brigantine

During the last centuries of sail the rig ini-tially known as the brigantine, two-masted, square-rigged on both and with a spanker, was one of the most usual of smaller vessels. The name became shortened to brig; and just as the square-rigged buss gave way to the lugger, the brig was later largely replaced by

with Chile round the Horn, square and fore-and-aft rigged masts were mixed in equal proportions as in the brigantine, but it was four-masted: square-rigged on the two fore-most, fore-and-aft on the two after masts.

– barque (bark)

The basic law of naval architecture, that greater size improves economy of operation, led to a growth that affected rigs, particularly when iron and steel construction opened the way to large hulls of adequate strength. The

This Finnish three-masted barque, Fred, *built in 1920, was one of the last large wooden square-rigged vessels constructed*

barque, in which the aftermast of the ship was replaced by one carrying only fore-and-aft sails, improved manoeuvrability (the barquentine or barkentine was a variant with the foremast square-rigged, the two aftermasts fore-and-aft-rigged). During the course of the nineteenth-century barques grew from three-masters of about 2000 tons to five-masters of 5000 tons and more. Four- and five-masted fully rigged ships were built, but the barque rig was more usually favoured when masts exceeded three. Steel masts and spars and wire rigging, the latter coming into use by the mid-nineteenth century, and chain for parts of rigging, enabled rigs to be produced strong enough to drive large steel hulls. Increase in the total sail area of rigs led to further sub-division of the sail plan, and in the mid-nineteenth century it became the practice in larger ships to divide the topsails into two, a lower and upper; by the last quarter of the century the topgallants were also divided. The sails on a single mast were then the course, lower topsail, upper topsail, lower topgallantsail, upper topgallantsail, royal,

with a skysail above this in a few heavy sail carriers. (Clippers of the latter part of the century may have been rigged for skysails on both fore and mainmast.)

The last stages of the struggle to maintain the place of ocean sail against encroaching steam produced relatively coarse-lined, many-masted ships, mainly of steel in hull and rig. This final stage of development was epitomized in the German five-masted *Preussen* (1902), with masts of almost equal height each carrying six square sails; she also set 12 fore-and-aft sails, 8 between the masts, 4 ahead of the foremast, and a spanker – 43 sails in all.

– clipper

Clipper ships won a popular appeal out of proportion to their importance in the scheme of ocean-carrying trade. The term clipper was applied vaguely to fast cargo ships in which capacity was sacrificed to the fine lines demanded by speed, the pursuit of which enthusiasm sometimes led to a not over-close regard for operating costs. As the last days of ocean sail were running out, there appeared

during the 1840s one further refinement to add to the many evolved over the ages to improve the sailing ability of the square rig. Yards, instead of being hung in chain slings, were fitted in metal bracket trusses, which held them well forward of the mast; these enabled the lower yards to be braced further round without fouling the shrouds, making the ships closer winded.

Fore-and-aft rigs

Fore-and-aft sails, unlike square, receive the wind on alternate sides when driving the ship, depending on the course in relation to the wind. H. Patterson in the *Nautical Dictionary* (New York 1891) stated that fore-and-aft sails are those 'set upon gaffs and booms and stays'. For convenience, only fore-and-aft sails that conform to this definition will be discussed here: for lateen and lugsails *see* Lateen and lug rigs *below*.

Although large fore-and-aft-rigged vessels have been built, notably in the schooner class, the rig was primarily that of craft sailing in coastal waters. Here manoeuvrability was important, and the power to sail close to the wind vital when a lee shore threatened. A nineteenth-century gaff-rigged pilot cutter might have been expected to sail 10° closer to the wind than the best-trimmed clipper.

– spritsail

This is the simplest of all fore-and-aft sails, and now believed to have been the first: a four-sided sail with the luff laced to the mast, spread aloft by a diagonal spar engaging with the peak of the sail, and having the heel held to the mast at about deck level by a fitting that became known as a snotter.

In the mid-1950s, an American professor of classical studies, Lionel Casson, showed that the spritsail had been in use in the Mediterranean during Roman times. A sarcophagus from Ostia, the port of Rome, a relief on a tombstone from the site of Troy, and three other carvings on gravestones, gave evidence not hitherto recognized of boats with spritsails dating between the first and third centuries AD. The origin of the spritsail is therefore now placed in the eastern Mediterranean some time perhaps before the Christian era. How extensively the sail was used, and whether it was set in the larger cargo vessels is as yet uncertain.

Yet more lately efforts have been made to thrust further back and further east the origins of the spritsail. Richard Lebaron Bowen has sought its origins in the Indian Ocean and Indonesia, and possibly as early as the fourth century BC. The Indonesian spritsail is not the same as the Mediterranean: it has two sprits and no mast, the former being set up with ropes and lashings. The argument has no supporting archaeological evidence. It is certain, however, that the spritsail was known in the Mediterranean in the first century of

A contemporary engraving of two of the clippers, Taeping *(1863) and* Ariel *(1865), specially built for the tea trade by Robert Steele of Greenock, Scotland, taking part in the 1866 tea-clipper race*

from Foochow, China, to London. Taeping *arrived half an hour before* Ariel, *both having sailed 16 000 miles in 99 days*

our era, perhaps a few centuries earlier; and it may have been a sophisticated adaptation of a simpler eastern kind of spritsail, the idea for which was brought home by Graeco-Roman sailors.

The sail then disappears from history's small field of view, to reappear in Dutch waters in the fifteenth century. A manuscript *Heures de Turin* of 1420 shows a small boat in Dutch waters clearly sprit-rigged and running before the wind. The rigging details of the sheet and vang are clear, and the sprit itself is shown on the starboard side of the sail, as it has been rigged ever since. During the sixteenth century evidence of the rig increases. In Britain and Holland its use spread to larger craft, which entailed more gear to control the increasingly cumbersome sprits, by means of masthead tackles and vangs. The spritsail was brought to America by the colonists, but here was used only in small craft.

– leg-of-mutton sail

Early in the seventeenth century another type of fore-and-aft sail appeared in Holland. At this time, when northern fore-and-aft sails

and rigs were proliferating, exact dating is impossible; but it may be accepted that the triangular, or leg-of-mutton, sail was not used in the North Sea until more than a century after the spritsail. ('Leg-of-mutton', the original English name, will be used here; 'Bermudian' will be confined to the later yacht sail.)

Present archaeological knowledge indicates that the triangular sail, like the spritsail, may have appeared in Holland as a result of diffusion rather than independent invention. Sails of a related type were known to exist in the Pacific, and a Peruvian triangular sail was illustrated in, for example, the Latin edition (Leiden 1619) of a book by Joris van Spilberghen, who commanded a Dutch expedition to the Pacific that entered Peruvian waters. The accuracy of the drawing is questioned, but Professor G. F. Carter has said that there is a literary record of the Incas trading with people who came out of the Pacific under triangular sails. It has also been supposed that a leg-of-mutton sail might have been produced by eliminating the mast of a

lateener and stepping the yard directly into the bottom of the boat – a step taken by a practical North Sea sailor trying to make the lateen rig more suitable for stormy tidal waters. Whether the triangular sail travelled half round the world from the Pacific islands to Peru and thence to Holland, or whether a Dutchman one day thought of making a mast out of a lateen yard, must remain uncertain.

– shoulder-of-mutton sail

At some time not much later a variant on the leg-of-mutton sail appeared, one with a very short gaff at the peak, sometimes known as a shoulder-of-mutton sail. This kind of short gaff became a permanent and characteristic feature of certain Dutch sails. In time the gaff was given a curve, an equally distinctive style in Dutch rigs. One reason may be given for the short gaff, though the relationship between it and the leg- and shoulder-of-mutton sails is obscure. Initially the short gaff was little more than a head stick to an essentially jib-headed or triangular sail that still retained a single halyard. At first it was probably devised simply as a means of securing the halyard of the sail, analogous to the head-board of the modern yacht's Bermudian mainsail. Later the Dutch used short spars for this purpose at the head of jibs and staysails. The short gaff persisted in several smaller types of boat in Britain, and very much more prominently in America, during the eighteenth and nineteenth centuries.

– staysail and jib

The triangular sail set on a stay (staysail) or on its own halyard and luff rope (jib) was one of the most important inventions in the history of wind propulsion. (The terms staysail and jib are indeterminate, most vaguely used, and often employed as synonyms; and fore-sail, in one of its meanings, may be applied to such sails.)

This efficient, versatile sail lacked an ancestry: there are no records of it during all the ages of Mediterranean seafaring, and the most enthusiastic diffusionist cannot find traces of it further east. It made its remarkably late appearance no earlier than the sixteenth, or possibly the fifteenth century in the North Sea and English Channel, an original invention of the Dutch that can have been inspired by no former sail. Although of the fore-and-aft family, it was to play a most important role in predominantly square-rigged ships, giving them a degree of weatherliness and manoeuvrability not attainable under square canvas alone (*see* Square rigs *above*). In fore-and-aft rigged vessels its importance grew with the years from small beginnings.

There was clearly a need for some form of headsail in boats carrying spritsails, leg-of-muttons or gaffsails to assist in bringing round the head of the boat when tacking or manoeuvring. That the sail was aerodynamically efficient and helped a boat sailing to windward to a degree out of proportion to its area would have been an early lesson from experience. To fit the space available ahead of the mast the sail had to be triangular. To claim that the idea of lacing it to the forestay was one of genius may appear excessive, but in the course of millenia it had not been thought of before.

– gaffsail

The long gaff, which gave rise to that great northern invention, the gaffsail, is to be considered as a spar quite separate in origin from the short gaff set at the head of a shoulder-of-mutton sail – though it may be tempting to regard it as no more than the latter somewhat lengthened. Its origin appears to have been the sprit, which relates the northern gaffsail to the spritsails of the east and Oceania, albeit tenuously.

The gaff can be seen as a successful means of eliminating the unwieldy and often dangerous length and weight of the sprit. There were sprits in small craft whose heel was raised up the mast, producing a shorter spar;

these then had to be hoisted with the sail. Raising it further brought the spar to the head of the sail and shortened it further: that this was known as a half-sprit indicates its origin, as does the fact that early gaffs remained aloft and had the sail brailed up to them and into the mast in the spritsail style. To achieve the true gaff it was necessary to lace the head of the sail to the spar and to

A gaff-rigged yacht – the peak halyard above the spar is silhouetted against the sky

provide throat and peak halyards; also jaws on which the heel of the spar might ride up and down the mast. The short gaff suggested the jaws but had only one halyard. Early gaffsails were flat-headed, the gaff very long, the leech of the sail nearly vertical. The gaff became more highly angled and in most rigs slightly shortened; this represented something like a merging of the long and short gaffs. In competition with the cumbersome sprit the gaff established itself and remained the basic feature of a high proportion of fore-and-aft rigs until working craft discarded sail. There is evidence of the gaff, in an early form, by the first half of the sixteenth century, but the gaffsail was not to be common for more than a hundred years.

– boomed sails

Early in the seventeenth century, and for the first time in northern craft, use began to be made of the boom. It may have been introduced because of difficulties in sheeting a loose-footed leg-of-mutton sail. Initially it was no more than a temporary bearing-out spar; a gooseneck made it into a permanent fitting. It has been suggested that the idea of a boom came from the east, where most of the sails had one. It is at least possible, however, that the common bearing-out spar, for which the seaman had many uses, was put to this new one without inspiration from elsewhere. That the foot of the sail should be laced to the boom was a later development that became a common but far from general practice. Some working craft retained boomed but loose-footed sails to their last days.

– ketch

The ketch was an early two-masted rig for smaller craft that has persisted, in its yachting form, until the present day. It demonstrates clearly the importance of differentiating between sail and rig. Early ketches, to which for many years the names hooker and galleot were also given, were square-rigged on the mainmast and with a lateen mizzen; this was their form in the first quarter of the seventeenth century. The ketch characteristic lay in having the taller mainmast forward of the short mizzen. Earlier the ketch rig had been latent in two-masted spritsail boats with the smaller sail aft and no staysail.

In his *Architectura Navalis Mercatoria* of 1768 (*see* DESIGN: Historical introduction), the Swedish naval architect Fredrik Henrik af Chapman illustrates a variety of ketches ranging from one with square course, topsail and topgallant on the main, a jib and a lateen mizzen, to one with gaffsails on main- and mizzenmasts, a square main topsail and topgallant, and a staysail together with inner and outer jibs on a bowsprit. Records show that during nearly two centuries the ketch rig was subject to numerous experiments, like the schooner later; many combinations of square and fore-and-aft sails were tried, until it reached the form with only the latter.

– schooner

American fore-and-aft rigs were all derived from the Old World types and shared their origins; thereafter they followed markedly different courses of development. The ketch fell totally out of favour on the emergence of the schooner, whereas in Britain and Europe it replaced the lugger for many purposes

during the nineteenth century (*see* Lateen and lug rigs *below*). The ketch, often under the name of 'dandy', became one of the most familiar rigs in the fishing fleets and also appeared among coastal traders.

The schooner, as it evolved during the eighteenth and nineteenth centuries, was North America's most individual contribution to the techniques of sail propulsion; it

H.F.Bolt – a ketch built in 1876 at Bideford, Devon, for coastal trading

was in this rig that sail, in a working seagoing capacity, reached furthest into the steamship age. The origins of the name and of the characteristically American type are equally obscure. That both came into being simultaneously at Gloucester, Massachusetts, in 1713 depends on an unreliable story.

Essentially the American schooner was a derivative of the earlier Dutch rig that had leg- or shoulder-of-mutton sails, or spritsails, set on two masts with the smaller of them stepped far forward. The British and North American shallop preceded the schooner and persisted alongside it until well into the nineteenth century. The American schooner was produced by adding a jib on a long bowsprit; the sails on the two masts were gaffsails. The rig spread first over the American Atlantic seaboard; then to Europe; then over the world. Early American schooners had masts

not markedly different in height, each setting a gaffsail, with a boom on the mainsail, and sometimes on the foresail, and one or two jibs. The gaff was initially short but was later lengthened. There came to be associated with the American schooner a fine-lined, sharp type of hull, and the best of them could reasonably claim a performance superior to that of any comparable-sized craft in Europe.

In Britain there is pictorial evidence of the schooner as early as 1708; the rig consisted of foresail and mainsail with short gaffs, the mainmast near amidships, the slightly shorter foremast set well back from the stemhead, and a jib on a bowsprit. Early in the second half of the century the composite schooner with square topsails was developed. It had a square topsail and often topgallant above the foresail, and sometimes square topsails above the main also. The square sails were probably added to improve performance when running down wind: this rig suffered particularly under such conditions owing to the blanketing of the canvas ahead of the mainmast when squared off – with main and foresail trimmed wing-and-wing the head canvas was starved of wind. It is now considered likely that the first topsail schooners were brigantines with the fore course suppressed in favour

Indra, *a beautiful example of an American schooner yacht*

of a gaffsail, a development that might have followed admiration for the relatively new schooner rig. Without killing the ketch rig, as in America, the topsail schooner became the most numerous type among British coastal traders and packets, some of which also went deep sea. In America the purely fore-and-aft schooner was most favoured.

In the last days of sail trading it was believed briefly that the large multi-masted schooners fully equipped with winches for sail hoisting and trimming, and relatively lightly manned, might be able to compete economically with the steamer. Schooners appeared with four, five and six masts, with as a final extreme the American *Thomas W. Lawson* (1902) with seven identical masts each consisting of a steel lower mast and pine topmast. All sails were fore-and-aft.

– modern yacht rigs

Modern yachting may be considered to have had its beginning in the mid-nineteenth century, and it was to lead to remarkable developments in the fore-and-aft rigs. Many of these may have had origins traceable back through the long history of these rigs; but essentially the changes produced by yachting were of a different kind from those slower processes of working-boat evolution advancing gradually from their roots in the earliest of sails. Yachting produced 'designers'' rigs, born on the drawing board from the union of wealth with the new scientific knowledge of the period; the indebtedness of such rigs to those of the past is not always clear. Yachting inherited the gaffsail with its topsail, staysails and jibs, and the square sail set, in early days, in cutters and on the foremast of schooners for

running; the inheritance in rigs was mainly in the cutter, schooner, ketch, and yawl. The outstanding revolution achieved by yachting was the revival of the almost defunct leg-of-mutton sail.

– Bermudian sloop

The Dutch sixteenth-century leg-of-mutton sail was carried to Bermuda and there began a separate course of development. It was adapted to sloops that had, for no certain reason, a mast with extreme rake. The triangular mainsail was spread not by an ordinary boom but by a horizontal sprit from the clew of the sail to the mast. The tack of the sail was secured to the mast some distance below the inner end of the sprit, and its foot had a deep roach. The Bermudian sloop carried a large jib. In later Bermudian sloops the sprit was replaced by an ordinary boom.

Visitors to the islands took away with them a high opinion of the speed and weatherliness of Bermuda sloops; but the adoption of the triangular leg-of-mutton sail, at first in racing yachts, more slowly in cruising yachts, beginning in the years immediately before World War I, and proceeding more widely during the interwar years, may be attributed to a growing knowledge of aerodynamic science

yard still hung free of the mast and very slightly forward of it, but the area of sail ahead of the mast was negligible. The mechanical step of fitting a jaws on the heel of the yard and the means, such as a parrel, of holding this to the mast, virtually converted the yard into a gaff. Since the sail when fitted in yachts invariably had a boom, and a jib was also carried, the gunter-lug sloop as

line of the mast. Finally the lower part of the yard, which was then simply doubling the mast, was discarded; a triangular sail on a single mast emerged. It may be doubted whether this development, despite claims made, influenced the adoption of the triangular sail for yachts; or whether this was much affected by memories of the Dutch leg-of-mutton sail or the Bermudian sloop. The

A painting, dated 1807, depicts the large jib and mast rake of a West Indies sloop

rather than enthusiasm for the Bermudian sloops or a conscious imitation of the leg-of-mutton sail, by this time only rarely seen in a few small work boats.

– gunter lug

In the last years of the nineteenth century and the early ones of the twentieth a new style of mainsail was appearing in small and medium-sized racing yachts. Known as the gunter lug, or as sometimes the Ratsey lug after the famous British sailmaker, it might have been regarded as a descendant of the standing lug (*see* Lateen and lug rigs *below*), but it has claims to be regarded as a designers' sail. By inclining the yard of the standing lug more and more steeply the point was reached when it became virtually a continuation of the mast. In the earlier yacht rigs with this arrangement the heel of the

finally evolved lost all relationship to a lug-sail.

In 1910, in the office of the American yacht architect William Gardner, the original rig of the still-famous and active Star class was produced, and it was of this type. The step beyond these rigs to one with a triangular sail set on a one-piece mast was a mechanical one, involving a change in the methods of sail hoisting and staying, not in the type of sail. The step was duly taken, and the rig that received the names 'Marconi' and 'Bermudian' became standard in racing yachts during the 1920s thanks to its proved aerodynamic superiority.

In the Mediterranean the lateen sail in certain working craft underwent a similar process of change. The lateen yard was peaked higher until it virtually continued the

yachtsman's leg-of-mutton sail was an independent outcome of the mechanics of rigging and the revelations of aerodynamics as they appeared in the early twentieth century.

– genoa

The other chief effect of yachting upon fore-and-aft sail has lain in the transformation of the jib and staysail. Aerodynamic theory combined with the purely artificial influence of methods of measuring sail area for racing encouraged growth in the ratio of headsail area to mainsail area. In even the biggest yachts it was becoming the practice by the later 1930s to carry a very large single headsail, this sail overlapping the mainsail by as much as the measurement rule allowed. Such sails (genoas) might have appeared to belong to the old family of reaching jibs set in some work boats – sails of light canvas for use in reaching winds. They were in fact a totally new conception, headsails of heavy cloth designed to be sheeted hard in for sailing to windward.

This kind of headsail, the latest development of the small jibs that had first appeared in the fifteenth–sixteenth centuries, producing great stresses upon rig and hull, owed their effectiveness to modern sailcloth, rigging materials, especially wire rope, and the use of winches to handle them. But although they were luxury products of yachting, they represented also a considerable technological advance in the art of sailing to windward – one of the fundamental objects of the fore-and-aft rigs.

Lateen and lug rigs
Lateens and lugsails are set from yards. In this they differ from the sails discussed in Fore-and-aft rigs *above*. Other differences are that they are not pivoted or hinged at their leading edge on a mast or stay; and standing lugs (*see below*) and Arab lateens cannot be tacked through the wind. By some definitions they do not therefore belong to the fore-and-aft family; according to others they do, since they receive the wind on alternate sides depending on the tack the craft is sailing.

– lateen
This is a triangular or four-sided sail with a yard slung so that a considerable part of the sail area is ahead of the mast. At rest the yard crosses the mast at approximately 45° and lies in the fore-and-aft plane; but a characteristic of the lateen rig is the agility of the yard and the great variety of positions it may be made to assume when handled with experience.

A species of the lateen is the settee, which in shape lies between the lateen and dipping lug (*see below*), the lower forward portion of the former being cut off to form a quadrilateral sail with a short luff. The settee shades off into the lateen as its luff becomes shorter. (The settee, with its greater resemblance to the square sail, may have preceded the pure lateen). The length of the settee's luff varies and has sometimes been half the length of the LEECH. Both forms of lateen have their yards in two – sometimes more – pieces lashed together in the middle, giving considerable whip to the tapered ends of the spars, in which respect they differ from the yards of northern lugs; and these are also shorter in proportion to the length of the boat.

All forms of lateen and lug are now considered to have had their origin in the square sail, whose yard was tilted, the sail recut and, the rigging leads adjusted, with the object of improving weatherliness. For the triangular lateen this may not appear an easy transition; when the settee lateen and dipping lug are considered it becomes readily acceptable, and this is no less so for the balance lug,

A triangular lateen sail on a dahabiyah *in the Gulf of Suez near the entrance to the canal*

despite the profound modifications of the square sail found in the Chinese balanced lug. The lateens and lugs form a single great family of sails derived from the square sail and never discarding some of its characteristics.

It is now considered possible that the lateen was being used in the Mediterranean of the early Christian era. A tomb relief of a fisherman at Elusis, about AD 150, shows what appears to be a settee lateen, but is believed by some to be a simple square sail badly represented. A graffito, which could be as early as the Hellenistic age and as late as Byzantine, shows what is certainly a triangular lateen. At present it has to be accepted that the lateen made its appearance at some time between the 2nd and 8th centuries AD.

From *c*. AD 700 onwards the lateen was carried over the Mediterranean by the Arabs, where it became the dominant sail; it spread eastward, in the settee form, across the Indian Ocean; it spread northward up the Biscay coast, remaining in these areas the most characteristic feature of seascapes until modern times. The North Sea ports knew it from visiting Spanish and Mediterranean vessels during the sixteenth century and later. But for northerners, even in the earliest days of fore-and-aft rigs in their area, the lateen found little place. It was sometimes carried in the larger rowing and sailing boats of men-of-war, but no records exist of its being used to any extent in fishing craft and coasters. When these turned from the square sail it was towards combinations of spritsail and jib (*see* Fore-and-aft rigs *above*); later, in the course of the eighteenth century, wholeheartedly towards that close relation of the Arab lateen, the dipping lug. In North America from the colonial days onwards neither lateen nor dipping lug became important sails.

Into the modern age the lateen continued to

typify Mediterranean sail. But while the enormous lateen yards, doubled in the middle and flexing at the ends, may have hardly changed in perhaps 2000 years, the rigs in which they were incorporated had become hybridized. Highly steeved bowsprits carried forestaysails and jibs, and set on a light topmast might be a thimble-headed topsail above the part of the lateen yard lying abaft the mast; and so, disguised as northern cutters, the last lateeners sailed over a Mediterranean where an increasing number of rigs were of north European origin.

– dipping lug

This is a lugsail that has to be lowered a little way down the mast when the craft is going about so that yard and tack can be passed round the mast and then rehoisted and set again for the new tack.

The late appearance in any numbers of the dipping, and later standing, lugs in north European waters is as striking as the extent to which it was adopted during the eighteenth century. Knowledge of the lateen may have encouraged northern seamen to produce a kind of lug out of the square sail more suitable for their seagoing conditions. To convert a square sail with its bowline into a lug entailed vital changes more easily appreciated in retrospect than initiated without precedent. Whereas the yard of a square sail is slung at its centre, that of a lug hangs from a point about one third of its length from the fore end, and the yard is angled upwards, its outer end peaked. The point at which the yard was hung and the degree at which it was angled differed greatly in the many types of lug during the sail's history.

These alterations of the square sail were geometrical. The fundamental change was that the leading edge of the sail then became always the leading edge, the luff, and like the lateen, the sail presented alternate surfaces to the wind according to the wind's direction. There was another crucial difference from the method of setting a square sail: the yard was inside the shrouds or any other rigging supporting the mast athwartships, thus allowing the sail to be sheeted hard in to attain weatherliness.

Drawings of vessels carrying lugs embellish a chart in *Speculum Nauticum* (1585), by the Dutchman Lucas Waghenaer. There is also a record of a lug in an English mid-seventeenth-century manuscript, but the sail was little used then, or for the next hundred years. William Falconer, the Scottish seaman and poet, makes no mention of it in his *Universal Marine Dictionary* (1769) – nor did it appear in the 1771 edition. However, in *Architectura Navalis Mercatoria* (1768), af Chapman gives drawings of a single-masted Stockholm pilot boat and a two-masted Breton fishing boat, both lug-rigged; the latter craft looks little different from the

A model of a Zulu (produced during the war of that name), a fishing vessel used off the northeast coasts of Scotland. Its foresail was a dipping lug, whereas the mizzen mast carried a standing lug

luggers that were numerous until lately in the ports of Brittany.

In the English Channel and North Sea, the lug rig spread rapidly during the latter half of the eighteenth century. Here the square-rigged herring busses had persisted until this time; the smaller inshore boats carried the spritsail with forestaysail. Then the change was made to three-masted lugger for the larger craft, and in the early nineteenth century the smaller boats were often rigged with two masts, having a lug mainsail and spritsail mizzen. Generally, the craft of two coastlines not more than about 200 miles apart will influence one another. The whole-hearted adoption of the lug rig along the British coast may have been inspired from the northern French ports, which served as a link between the North Sea and the Mediterranean, the home of the lateen lug.

– standing lug

This is a rig in which the forward end of a lugsail yard lies close along the mast, so that there is no need to lower the sail and dip it round the mast when the craft goes about.

The standing lug appeared later than the dipping: it was a step further removed from the square sail. To convert the second into the first was a matter of moving the tack of the sail back to the mast, leaving only a triangle of sail ahead of it. A higher angling of the yard and perhaps slinging it nearer its fore end produced a sail approaching in character that of the gaffsail; while a little of the yard still projected forward of the mast, it was no longer necessary to dip the yard when going about, though the sail would set better when the yard stood to leeward.

The standing lug may have been carried to Europe from the East when mariners were trading on the coasts of India and Asia. It is also possible that the changes converting a dipping into a standing lug were the outcome of simple experiments aimed at producing a more easily handled sail. Smaller craft were often rigged with one or two standing lugs, and the sails were occasionally fitted with a boom, which might indicate an eastern origin; most commonly they were used in combination with dipping lugs as the mizzen of two- and three-masted luggers.

The archetype of French luggers, the *chasse-marée*, was tremendously canvased; one with three masts might carry two topsails above the fore and main standing lugs and one above the mizzen. To ameliorate the disability when yards were to windward these were slung on alternate sides of the masts.

The north European lugsail appeared in a great variety of shapes and rig arrangements. Some lugs were cut broad and shallow; others tall and narrow. Jibs were set in some types on a long bowsprit. A standing-lug mizzen might be sheeted over a sheave at the end of a stern outrigger of more than half the length of the hull. There were luggers in which the combined length of bowsprit and stern outrigger exceeded the length of the hull. A boat's rig could be varied with the season and occasion: winter rig; summer rig; and, for craft in localities where there was enthusiasm for racing, regatta rig. In many rigs the lug was tacked down to the stem, or beyond it on a short downward-inclined metal bowsprit (bumpkin). In other rigs the tack of the sail was far enough aft for a bowline to be rigged. In a few types a descendant of the Viking *beitáss* (*see* Square rigs *above*) was used, a bearing-out spar latterly known as a foregirt. Sometimes a spritsail was used as a mizzen; sometimes a leg-of-mutton sail.

– balanced lug
This is a lugsail with its foot laced to a boom. Both boom and yard project forward of the mast, to which neither is secured, when the sail is hoisted. It is in fact a dipping lug to which a boom has been fitted; but this was never done in Europe outside the Mediterranean, where it was fairly usual in the Adriatic and Aegean. It was the rig of the Italian fishing lugger and the coasting-trade *trabacola*, often in preference to the lateen. The *trabacola* had two masts and a triangular headsail, or jib, set from a long bowsprit. The Greek lugger was generally similar in character.

Whereas the jib was clearly imported into the Mediterranean from northwest Europe, there can be little doubt that the balanced lug came from the East: directly from the Chinese junks, according to a suggestion made by Dr Joseph Needham in his *Science and Civilisation in China*, vol. 4 (London and New York 1962).

The Chinese form of the balanced lug, with yard and boom and numerous closely spaced battens, is assumed, though no evidence can be offered, to be the descendant of a tall, narrow, battenless square sail, which, in the

Galway Blazer II, *a modern two-masted Chinese-rigged yacht which, with Bill King, completed a single-handed circumnavigation in 1972.*

Eastern manner, would have had a boom. The sail would then have become a balanced lug of the Mediterranean kind. The unique contribution of the Chinese to sail techniques was to attach a series of battens across the sail, a remarkable invention stiffening the sail and bringing exceptional qualities not only aerodynamically but, thanks to a style of rigging evolved nowhere else, particular advantages in handling (*see* CHINESE RIG). Adapted for modern materials, the Chinese type of lug is being used by a number of experienced modern yachtsmen, in preference to the Bermudian mainsail and jib: a tribute to the rig's innate qualities.

See also CHINESE RIG; MASTS AND RIGGING; PERFORMANCE AND YACHT DESIGN; YACHT RACING

Rising

A fore-and-aft strake supporting the thwarts in a small boat.

Roach

The outward curve in the side or foot of a sail.

Rolling hitch *see* ROPEWORK: Bends and hitches

Ropework

The term is used comprehensively here to include rope itself, and bends, hitches, and splices.

– rope

For a long time rope was measured by its circumference in inches or its diameter in millimetres. Nowadays the latter is all but universal. Technically the term rope denotes cordage greater than 2 in (51 mm) in circumference. Cordage smaller than this is referred to as small stuff. Cordage is manufactured from natural fibres such as manila, sisal, hemp, and cotton, or man-made fibres such as nylon, polythene, and polyester (Terylene, Dacron, Tergal).

The strength of a rope of natural fibre is due entirely to the friction between the relatively short fibres when the rope is stressed. In contrast, that of a man-made-fibre rope comes from the inherent strength of the material of which it is made, each filament extending throughout the length of the rope. These facts produce the significant difference in the manner in which different types of rope part when overstressed. The broken ends of a natural-fibre rope fall dead when the rope parts; those of a man-made-fibre rope behave like the broken ends of a taut spring that breaks under excessive tension. Special

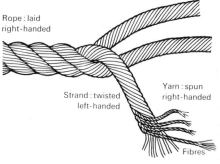

Rope: laid right-handed

Strand: twisted left-handed

Yarn: spun right-handed

Fibres

Hawser-laid rope

care, therefore, is needed when handling man-made-fibre ropes liable to part under tension.

The traditional construction of a rope involves twisting a sliver of fibres, usually right-handed, to form a rope yarn; twisting a number of rope yarns in the opposite sense to form a rope strand; and twisting a number of strands (usually three) in the same sense as

that of the fibres to form the rope. The alternate twisting of fibres, yarns, and strands ensures that the form of the rope is preserved. Three-stranded right-handed rope is called hawser-laid rope. Man-made-fibre rope is quite often plaited, a form designed to prevent twists, reduce kinkage, and to prevent accidents should such a rope part when under tension.

Fibre rope is usually supplied in coils. When breaking out a new coil, and indeed when handling rope at all times, care is necessary to avoid forcing out kinks such that the rope may become permanently distorted and weakened. The best method is to sling the coil clear of the deck or ground on a swivel and to uncoil from the outer end of the rope. Any leads through which a rope may pass should be smooth and the angle of lead, that is the angle between the standing and hauling parts of the rope, should be as near 180° as possible. If the angle of lead is less than about 50° a bad nip results and this may distort and weaken the rope permanently. If practicable the part of a stressed rope lying in a fairlead should be parcelled with burlap or similar material, to prevent damage from chafing. When a rope is rove through a sheave it is important that the sheave is sufficiently large to ensure that the rope is not unduly distorted. A good practical rule is to use a sheave at least nine times the diameter of the rope rove through it; for example, a rope of 1-in (25 mm) diameter should not be used in a sheave of less than 9 in (229 mm) in diameter.

All ropes should be protected from saltwater and dust. Crystals of salt or particles of grit lodged between the fibres of a rope may cause damage by abrasion when the rope is subsequently under stress. Dampness and heat are damaging to natural-fibre ropes so that rope lockers should be well ventilated, and such ropes should be dry before stowing for a long period. Ropes of man-made fibre do not deteriorate through dampness and they are not affected by mildew as are natural-fibre ropes. Neither do they absorb moisture or lose their strength. They can, however, harden and become brittle through prolonged exposure to sunlight.

A rope should always be coiled in the same direction as that in which the strands are laid. A right-handed rope (in which the lay runs from right to left, when held vertically) should, therefore, be coiled clockwise when looking down on the coil. When coiling a rope that is secured to a cleat or bitts, the coil should be started from the part of the rope secured in order to prevent kinks forming.

The tension in a rope at the point of parting is known as the breaking stress. This depends upon the size, material, and condition of the rope. For example, in manila rope the breaking stress B, in tonnes, is given by the formula:

$$B = \frac{2D^2}{300}$$

where D is the diameter of the rope in millimetres.

The British Standards Institution recommends a factor of safety of not less than 6 when using new natural-fibre ropes for lifting purposes. The factor of safety is the ratio between the breaking stress and the safe working load. Using this recommendation a manila rope of diameter 20 mm (the breaking stress of which is taken as 2 tonnes) should not be used to lift a weight exceeding one-third of a tonne. Nylon and polyester ropes can be used to 90 per cent of their breaking stress, although this should not be repeated too often, especially where a splice is involved. Knotting has a marked effect on the strength of a synthetic-fibre ropes – a bowline, for example, can reduce the strength by as much as 40 per cent. The comparative strengths of similar ropes made of various synthetic and natural fibres are given in Table I. Synthetic fibre ropes, because of their strength and durability, have almost entirely replaced those made of natural fibres in yachts for running rigging and warps. Table II illustrates the reduction in rope strength due to wetting; the strengths of a range of synthetic-fibre ropes are listed in Table III (pp.198–9).

Table I: Comparative strengths (kg) of 3-stranded, 24-mm diameter ropes

Nylon	12 000
Polyester (high-tension)	9 140
Polypropylene	7 600
Manila	4 570
Hemp	4 277
Sisal	4 060

Table II: Dry and wet impact strengths of 10-mm diameter cordage

MATERIAL	WEIGHT (kg)	
	DRY	WET
Nylon	223	182
Hemp	73	55
Sisal	55	36
Manila	50	32

Rope is often vitally important to safety; it is also an expensive item of equipment, and it should be used intelligently. Rope should be examined frequently to ensure that there are no abrasions: it is unwise to take undue risk with faulty cordage. The end of a rope should be prevented from unlaying by means of a whipping, or, with synthetics, heat-sealing. A cut end will very quickly unravel if the rope is treated roughly, and it is quite likely that it will be impossible to lay up the unravelled strands neatly and strongly, an eventuality that may necessitate cutting off the unlayed part and so wasting a rather expensive article.

A common whipping is made from roping twine, of flax, cotton, or polyester. The method of passing a whipping is illustrated in fig. 1. The end of the twine is laid along the rope and about half a dozen turns are made working towards the cut end of the rope. The working end of the twine is then laid along the rope facing away from the rope's end. Another few turns of twine are passed, still working towards the cut end of the rope, but this time covering the free end of the twine, which is finally pulled taut through these turns and cut off neatly.

See also WIRE ROPE

– bends and hitches
The more commonly used bends and hitches are shown in the accompanying illustration. The *overhand knot* (fig. 2) and *figure-of-eight* (fig. 3) are used in the end of a rope to prevent it from passing through a block. The *bowline* (fig. 4) is used for making a temporary eye in the end of a rope. It may also be employed for bending two lines together. Other useful hitches that may be used in the end of a rope are the *midshipman's hitch* (fig. 5) and the *Blackwall hitch* (fig. 6), either of which serves to secure a rope to a hook, one part of the rope being jammed against the other.

The *reef or square knot* (fig. 7), which takes its name from its use for tying reef points in a reefed sail, is employed whenever a common tie is required. For bending a small line to a large line a *sheet becket bend* (fig. 8) or *double sheet bend* (fig. 9) is required. The *carrick bend* (fig. 10) is used for bending two hawsers together.

For securing a rope to a spar a *round turn and two half hitches* (fig. 11) or a *fisherman's bend* (fig. 12) may be used. A *clove hitch* (fig. 13) hitches a small rope to a larger one, or to a spar, but when a sideways pull is required a *rolling hitch* (fig. 14) is used. For temporarily shortening a rope a *sheepshank* (fig. 15) is applied, and for shortening a strop a *catspaw* (fig. 16) is useful. A *marlinespike hitch* (fig. 17) is used for getting a purchase when passing a lashing or for heaving taut the turns of a seizing (*see* Splices below). The *marline hitch* (fig. 18) is used for such purposes as lashing a sail to a spar.

– splices
The two basic knots made with the strands of a rope are the *crown* (fig. 19) and the *wall* (fig. 20). The crown knot is formed by unlaying the end of a rope and laying the strands uniformly along the rope. The end of each strand is then passed over the adjacent strand, working with the lay, and through the

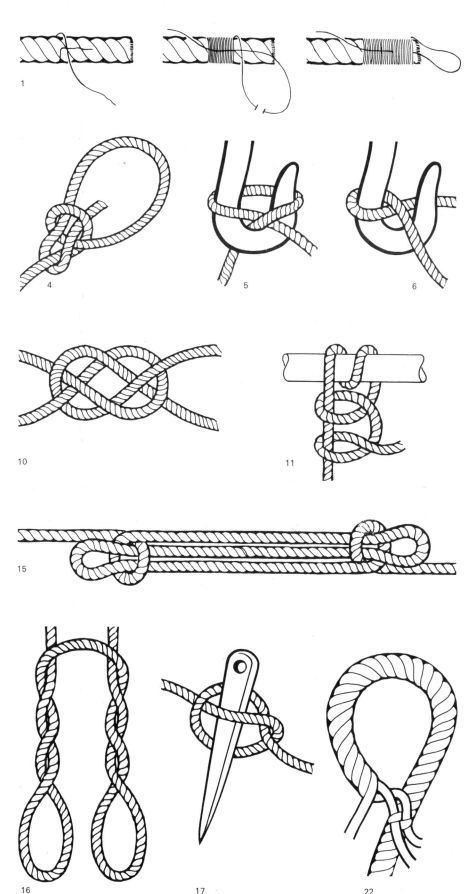

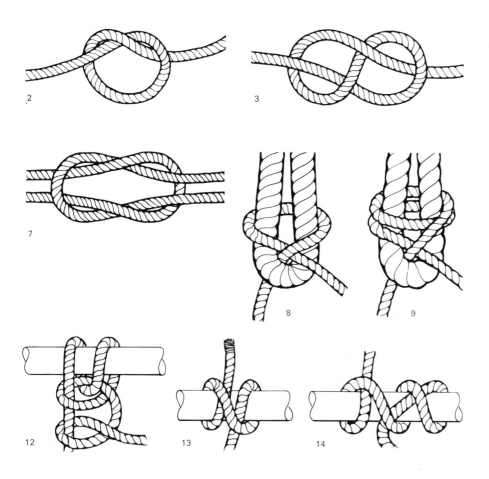

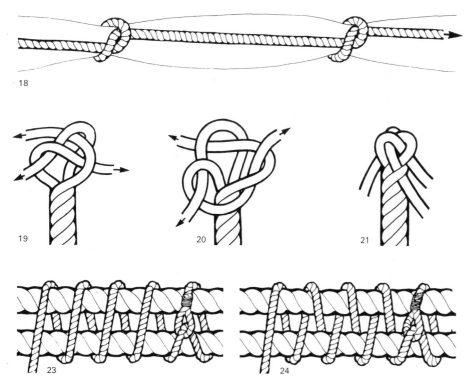

Fig. 1 Common whipping

BENDS AND HITCHES
Fig. 2 Overhand knot
Fig. 3 Figure-of-eight knot
Fig. 4 Bowline
Fig. 5 Midshipman's hitch
Fig. 6 Blackwall hitch
Fig. 7 Reef knot
Fig. 8 Sheet bend
Fig. 9 Double sheet bend
Fig. 10 Carrick bend
Fig. 11 Round turn and two half hitches
Fig. 12 Fisherman's bend
Fig. 13 Clove hitch
Fig. 14 Rolling hitch
Fig. 15 Sheepshank
Fig. 16 Catspaw
Fig. 17 Marlinespike hitch
Fig. 18 Marline hitch

SPLICES
Fig. 19 Crown knot
Fig. 20 Wall knot
Fig. 21 Back splice (showing first strand tucked, following the formation of a crown knot)
Fig. 22 Start of eye splice
Fig. 23 Flat seizing
Fig. 24 Racking seizing

loop formed by the next strand. The wall knot is formed by unlaying the strands, forming a loop with each and passing the adjacent strand upwards through the loop. When formed the strands lead away from the rope in contrast to the crown knot in which the strands lie along the rope itself.

The crown knot is the basis of the *back splice* (fig. 21) used to finish off the end of a rope in a more substantial way than when a whipping is used. To make a back splice, the rope is unlaid and a crown knot worked. The end of each strand is then tucked, against the lay, under the next but one strand. It is usual to make three or four tucks with each strand, after which the ends are cut off neatly close to the rope.

An *eye splice* (fig. 22) is worked into the end of a rope to form a permanent eye. The rope is unlaid to provide the working ends of the strands. A loop of appropriate size is then formed with the unlaid strands. The end of each working strand is tucked against the lay of the rope and at least three tucks are made to prevent the splice from drawing should it be stressed. Five tucks should be made with synthetic-fibre ropes.

To join two ropes a *short splice* may be used, but if the joined rope is required to pass through a block a *long splice* is necessary. The short splice is made by first unlaying the ends of each rope and interlacing or marrying the strands before tucking. After marrying, the strands are tucked against the lay. A short splice will reduce the strength of a rope by about one eighth. The long splice is made as follows: the ropes to be joined are unlaid for a distance equal to about 12 times the circumference of the rope. They are then married. One strand of the first rope is then unlaid, and the corresponding strand of the second rope is laid up in its place. The same is done with a second pair of strands. To complete the splice the ends are tucked, after first halving each strand, in the same way as in the short splice, but with instead of against the lay, so that successive tucks are made around the same strand. When it is necessary to secure the parts of two ropes, if a stress exists in either or both ropes, a *seizing* is used. A *flat seizing* (fig. 23) is the simplest form, but when the stresses in the two ropes to be seized are unequal, a *racking seizing* (fig. 24) in which figure-of-eight turns are made with the seizing stuff, should be used.

See also MASTS AND RIGGING; WIRE ROPE

Round-the-world races *see* YACHT RACING: Major races and series

Round turn and two half hitches *see* ROPEWORK: Bends and hitches

Round up
To bring a vessel head to wind.

Table III: Strengths of synthetic-fibre ropes

		TERYLENE/DACRON POLYESTER								
		3-STRAND				8-PLAIT			16-PLAIT	
DIAMETER		STANDARD		PRE-STRETCHED		PRE-STRETCHED		MATT FINISH		MATT FINISH
in	mm	lb	kg	lb	kg	lb	kg	lb	kg	lb	kg
$\frac{1}{16}$	1.5	—	—	—	—	143	65	—	—	—	—
$\frac{3}{32}$	2	308	140	—	—	165	75	—	—	—	—
$\frac{1}{8}$	3	506	230	506	230	363	165	—	—	—	—
$\frac{3}{16}$	4	649	295	649	295	649	295	449	204	—	—
$\frac{7}{32}$	5	880	400	880	400	671	400	671	305	—	—
$\frac{1}{4}$	6	1 243	565	1 243	565	1 243	565	1 034	470	—	—
$\frac{9}{32}$	7	1 694	770	1 694	770	1 694	770	—	—	—	—
$\frac{5}{16}$	8	2 233	1 015	2 233	1 015	2 233	1 015	1 232	560	2 464	1 120
$\frac{3}{8}$	9	—	—	2 794	1 270	—	—	2 068	940	—	—
$\frac{7}{16}$	10	3 498	1 590	3 498	1 590	3 498	1 590	2 233	1 015	4 400	2 000
$\frac{1}{2}$	12	4 994	2 270	4 994	2 270	4 994	2 270	3 498	1 590	6 600	3 000
$\frac{9}{16}$	14	6 996	3 180	6 996	3 180	—	—	—	—	7 260	3 300
$\frac{5}{8}$	16	8 932	4 060	—	—	—	—	—	—	7 700	3 500
$\frac{3}{4}$	18	10 054	4 570	—	—	—	—	—	—	8 470	3 850
$\frac{7}{8}$	20	12 276	5 580	—	—	—	—	—	—	12 276	5 580
1	24	17 886	8 130	—	—	—	—	—	—	17 886	8 130

Royal Cork Yacht Club
This Irish club is probably the oldest yacht club in the world. The Water Club of Cork harbour was formed in 1720. It consisted of not more than 25 members, who appear to have contented themselves with manoeuvring in company offshore and convivial living. The club was very active until 1765, but then interest seems to have been lost until 1806, when an attempt was made to revive it. As so often happens another club in the locality, the Little Monkstown, was formed by the survivors of the old Water Club to form the Cork Yacht Club – now the Royal Cork Yacht Club.

In the early 1960s the Royal Cork was in grave danger of extinction but in the season on 1966 it was amalgamated with the flourishing Royal Munster Yacht Club at Crosshaven, so that during the seasons of 1969–70 it was able to celebrate its 250th anniversary. The celebration in 1969 included a transatlantic race, followed by a cruise in company along the southwest coast of Ireland with yachts of the Cruising Club of America, the Royal Cruising Club, the Clyde Cruising Club, and the Irish Cruising Club.

Royal Cruising Club
Founded as the Cruising Club in 1880 by Sir Arthur Underhill at a time when there was no organization for cruising yachtsmen. In 1902 King Edward VII directed that henceforth it should be known as the Royal Cruising Club. Membership is now restricted to 400 ordinary members, most of whom are boat owners, and its principal object is to foster cruising under sail '. . . in accordance with the highest traditions of the sea'. The club offers a number of annual awards – for seamanship, exploration, and services to cruising – and publishes a yearly journal of cruising logs.

Royal Ocean Racing Club
The RORC was founded in 1925, and owes much in its origin to the author Weston Martyr. He was living in New York in the early 1920s and took part in three Bermuda races. When he returned to England in 1924 he was shocked to find that British yachtsmen had hardly ever heard of an ocean race.

He wrote several articles for British yachting magazines explaining what a great sport ocean racing was, and as a result Lt Cdr E. George Martin and Malden Heckstall-Smith, editor of *Yachting Monthly*, became interested. They met and discussed the possibility of arranging an ocean race in 1925. Martin and Heckstall-Smith approached some of the

Table III: Strengths of synthetic-fibre ropes

DIAMETER		NYLON				POLYPROPYLENE				POLYETHYLENE	
		3-STRAND		BRAIDED				8-PLAIT			
in	mm	lb	kg	lb	kg	lb	kg	lb	kg	lb	kg
1/16	1.5	—	—	—	—	—	—	—	—	—	—
3/32	2	—	—	—	—	—	—	—	—	—	—
1/8	3	—	—	—	—	—	—	—	—	—	—
3/16	4	704	320	—	—	—	—	—	—	396	180
7/32	5	1 210	550	—	—	—	—	704	320	—	—
1/4	6	1 650	750	—	—	1 210	550	1 100	500	792	360
9/32	7	2 310	1 050	—	—	—	—	—	—	—	—
5/16	8	2 970	1 350	—	—	2 112	960	2 002	910	1 386	630
3/8	9	3 300	1 500	—	—	—	—	—	—	—	—
7/16	10	4 576	2 080	—	—	3 135	1 425	2 992	1 360	2 156	980
1/2	12	6 600	3 000	—	—	4 466	2 030	—	—	3 049	1 386
9/16	14	9 020	4 100	—	—	6 138	2 790	—	—	4 136	1 880
5/8	16	11 660	5 300	11 660	5 300	7 700	3 500	—	—	5 522	2 510
3/4	18	14 740	6 700	14 740	6 700	9 790	4 450	—	—	—	—
7/8	20	18 260	8 300	18 260	8 300	11 814	5 370	—	—	—	—
1	24	26 400	12 000	26 400	12 000	16 720	7 600	—	—	—	—

leaders of British yachting, including Sir Philip Hunloke (King George V's sailing master) and Sir Ralph Gore, among others, to come to a meeting. At this it was agreed that the trio of pioneers, with the blessing of the Yacht Racing Association (now the Royal Yachting Association) should organize a race during August 1925 round the Fastnet Rock, finishing at Plymouth, Devon. The Royal Victoria Yacht Club, then at Ryde, Isle of Wight, agreed to start the race, and the Royal Western Yacht Club took on the finish at Plymouth.

That first Fastnet race attracted only seven entries, but at a meeting after the finish, which was attended by most of the crews of the competing yachts, it was decided to form a club to be called the Ocean Racing Club and to hold a Fastnet race each year. Membership was to be limited to those completing a Fastnet race. It was also decided that the club would make its own rating rules; it was under RORC rating rules that ocean racers were rated, on the eastern side of the Atlantic, until the adoption of the International Offshore Rule.

The number of races has been gradually increased, so that there were a couple of dozen offshore races on the 1976 programme. These included not only the old domestic favourites such as the Channel Race, but also the China Sea Race from Hong Kong to Corregidor Island in the Philippines, and the Skaw Race north of Denmark.

See also YACHT RACING: Major races and series

Royal Thames Yacht Club

In 1775 the Cumberland Society was formed under the royal patronage of Henry Frederick, Duke of Cumberland. By then there were a large number of small craft sailing on the Thames. In 1749 there had been a race from Greenwich to the Nore and back for the plate presented by the Prince of Wales, but it was Cumberland and the men he patronized who really began British yachting as it is known today.

Winthrop Aldrich, U.S. Ambassador, once remarked at a welcoming dinner at the Royal Thames Yacht Club, successor to the Cumberland Society, 'I find that the Royal Thames Yacht Club is older than the United States.'

According to *Memorials of the Royal Yacht Squadron*, 'The primitive sport of yachting on the Thames was no sport of millionaires, like that of Cowes today [1903] but the relaxation of the professional man, who when his day's work was done, stepped into his little cutter at the Temple Stairs, and of the retired city merchant with his country house at Chelsea or Marylebone and his boat on the river as the chief solace of his leisure.'

Much of the early racing took place between Blackfriars and Putney, and after it was over the competitors repaired to Mr Smith's Tea Gardens, at Vauxhall. Mr Smith was the first Commodore of the Cumberland Fleet; many of the early cups can be seen in the hall of the RTYC, together with a set of the Cumberland Fleet flags. Thomas Taylor, Commodore of the Cumberland Society from 1780 until 1816, owned the centreboard cutter *Cumberland*. RTYC has a model of her; it gives an idea of the type of boat in use at the time.

In 1823 the name of the society was changed to HM Coronation Sailing Society, to mark the coronation of King George IV. The Society was split in two over a protest in the very first race held under the new name. A number of members left to form the Thames Yacht Club. This became the Royal Thames Yacht Club in 1830, and the following year it absorbed the original society.

Sailing activities gradually extended below the bridges of the Thames; the regattas were held in the Estuary until the outbreak of World War II. As early as 1844 the club held a race at Cowes. Then, ten years later, it introduced 'Thames measurement', a tonnage that is still in use today.

In 1866 the first of the club's annual races from the Nore to Dover were held. In 1870 the club backed James Ashbury in this, the first challenge for the *America*'s Cup with his schooner *Cambria*. The club was not to challenge again until it backed Anthony Boyden's *Sovereign*, which was defeated in 1964.

In 1887, Queen Victoria's Jubilee, the club ran a race of 1520 miles round the British Isles for a first prize of 1000 guineas (£1050). Eleven yachts started; the winner was the famous *Genesta*, with *Sleuthhound* second.

After using the Tea Gardens at Vauxhall and various coffee houses as headquarters, RTYC established a clubhouse in St James's Street in 1857. It moved to Albemarle Street in 1860, where it remained for fifty years. Subsequently, until 1923, it was in Piccadilly. Now it is in a modern building at 60 Knightsbridge.

Between the world wars, the club's sailing base on the Solent was at Ryde. The RTYC and the Royal Victoria held Ryde Week, which preceded Cowes Week. In 1946 a base was established at Shore House, Warsash, on the river Hamble, from which the club has run races from committee boats in the Solent, or from either the Royal London Yacht Club or the RYS at Cowes.

Royal Western Yacht Club of England

Established in 1827 and known at that time

as the Port of Plymouth Royal Clarence Regatta Club. In 1833 it became the Royal Western Yacht Club.

In 1963 the club merged with the Royal South Western Yacht Club. The impressive clubhouse on the Hoe was sold and the club moved into the premises of the RSWYC at the water's edge. This had originally been built as a public bath house and was used mainly as a boat house before it was refurbished to be officially opened by HRH Prince Philip in 1965.

The club is internationally known as a joint organizer of the Fastnet Race since 1925. It is the organizing club of the Round Britain Race and also of the Royal Western *Observer* Single-handed Transatlantic Race.

Royal Yachting Association

The national authority for yacht racing in the United Kingdom was originally founded on 17 November 1875 at Willis' Rooms, St James's, London, with the Marquis of Exeter, then commodore of the Royal Victoria Yacht Club at Ryde, Isle of Wight, in the chair. Thirty-five eminent yachtsmen, representatives of many of the leading clubs, were present. It was named the Yacht Racing Association (YRA).

Lord Exeter was elected as the first president, a committee was formed and Dixon Kemp, the naval architect and writer, was made the secretary. The committee's first action was to draft a provisional code of Sailing Rules, which were presented to a general meeting of the association held at the Langham Hotel, London, on 22 February 1876. The rules were accepted as well as a scale of time allowances. These were immediately adopted by 12 royal and 5 other clubs. The new racing rules were based upon ancient customs and usages of the sea and were in agreement with the basic principles of the Board of Trade Rules, as far as they could be applied.

At first many leading clubs refused to join the association or accept its rules, and others only accepted them in part. However, gradually the YRA increased its authority, until in 1881, all the main yacht clubs in the United Kingdom were affiliated with the exception of the Royal Thames Yacht Club. At that time the Prince of Wales, afterwards King Edward VII, was both president of the YRA and commodore of the Royal Thames. In 1882 he succeeded the Earl of Wilton as commodore of the YRA. It is not hard to see how he influenced the RTYC to join.

On 24 January 1919, a public meeting of yachtsmen was held to restart yacht racing after World War I. On 27 March, the Prince of Wales, afterwards Edward VIII, was elected president.

In 1920 the National 14-ft class was accepted. Three years later the AGM approved

12-ft and 14-ft dinghy classes. It was claimed that it was still possible to build dinghies at £4 per ft: when the National 12-ft dinghy was adopted in 1935 the price limit was £45 complete. This was increased to £50, ex-sails, two years later. The most expensive suit of sails for these boats cost £6 6s in 1939.

As the 1948 Olympic Games were held in London, with sailing at Torquay, Devon, the YRA lost no time in putting forward the following classes: Firefly (as a singlehander) Swordfish, Swallow, International One-Design and 6-Metre. However, the IYRU in 1946 decided to put the Star class in, in place of the Swordfish, and the Dragon instead of the IOD.

This period brought the start of the great dinghy surge with the appearance through *Yachting World* of the Cadet (1948) and GP 14 (1949); and in 1950 National status was granted to the merged Merlin and Rocket classes.

In 1952, HM King George VI presented the Britannia Cup to the YRA, which was to be raced for on the Tuesday of Cowes Week by yachts of 30 to 60 ft (9.14–18.28 m). It was in this year that the YRA, because of its increased scope, changed its name at the AGM to the Yachting Association. It was granted royal status the following year.

Because of the mediocre British performance at the 1952 Olympic Games, with only one silver medal won by Charles Currey in the Finn class, the council determined on greater efforts and more facilities to be made available to enable likely helmsmen and crews to train up to Olympic standard.

HRH Prince Philip was elected President in 1956, and the Olympic training effort was rewarded when Britain won one silver and two bronze medals at the Melbourne Olympiad. It was in that year that the *News Chronicle* newspaper caught on to the dinghy boom and introduced the Enterprise dinghy.

In 1969, the first RYA National Team Racing Championship was held. Prince Philip was succeeded as President by Owen Aisher in 1970; Nigel Hacking became Secretary General.

The work of the RYA is varied. There is an elected council; some members are elected by regions and others directly. Besides the President there is a Chairman and Deputy Chairman of the Council. Below this body there are a number of Divisional Committees: Central Management, Central Finance, Development, Training, General Purposes, Yacht Racing, and Power Boats. The Development Committee has the Membership Subcommittee below it; the Yacht Racing Division has no fewer than eleven subcommittees, which may report to it. The Power-boat Divisional Committee has six subcommittees, reporting on all aspects of competitive boating.

The work of the competitive sailing and power-boat committees is readily imaginable, but many do not realize that much of the RYA's work concerns dealings with government and other bodies. For instance, in a recent 12-month period the secretariat dealt with 38 Parliamentary bills, 57 harbour revision orders, more than 200 Coast Protection Act matters.

Royal Yacht Squadron

In 1815 a number of gentlemen, who had sailed at Cowes, Isle of Wight, met at the Thatched House Tavern, St James's Street, London, to form the Yacht Club. Lord Grantham presided. The club was to consist only of men who were interested in the sailing of yachts in salt water. There were 42 original members, and the old minute books are still preserved at the RYS castle, at Cowes.

The qualification for a gentleman to become a member was the ownership of a vessel not under 10 tons; indeed, no vessel of under 10 tons belonging to a member was entitled to a number on the list. Members were to be balloted for at a general meeting of not fewer than 10 members, the candidates to be proposed and seconded by two members of the club, with two blackballs to exclude.

The rule concerning ownership of a yacht of more than 10 tons was in force until quite recently. It is said that the Squadron, as it is known, made a reasonable amount of money on the brokerage of a hulk that was sold and resold among candidates. The blackballing still continues and is followed with interest after the General Meetings.

'A taste for sea bathing among English people of condition' is said to have attracted many of them to Cowes, where there was a fine beach with bathing machines west of the castle. The men began to take an interest in the local craft – fishermen's and smugglers' boats, Revenue cutters – and this led eventually to the formation of the Yacht Club. In 1818 the Prince Regent, later King George IV, joined the club, which became the Royal Yacht Club in 1820. The first meeting places were the Vine and the Medina, at East Cowes, and later at the Gloster Hotel, West Cowes.

The club's original ensign was a white flag with the Union Jack in the corner. In 1829 the Admiralty issued a warrant allowing members of the club to wear the White Ensign of the Royal Navy, which they have done ever since. In 1833 the club's name was changed to Royal Yacht Squadron. It bought the lease of Cowes Castle, a fort built in Henry VIII's time, in 1856 and this has been its headquarters ever since, although much modified.

The Squadron has always been characterized by the large and powerful yachts owned by its members. However, it was not until

1853 that rules prohibiting steam yachts were rescinded.

The royal patronage begun by George IV was continued; it was Queen Victoria's liking for Osborne House nearby that kept the Squadron at the top of the social scale. Cowes Week became part of the 'season', sandwiched as it was between Goodwood race week and the start of the grouse-shooting season on 12 August.

In 1851 the Squadron presented a £100 cup, which the schooner *America* won in a race around the Isle of Wight, sailing against 15 British yachts. This cup became the *America*'s Cup and reposes in the trophy room of the NEW YORK YACHT CLUB. The RYS has backed six challenges by members to try to recapture it (*see* YACHT RACING: Major races and series).

The RYS continues to dominate the Cowes scene. Its starting line and famous 'platform' are used for many regattas, and by several of the clubs that organize yachting events at Cowes.

Rudder stock
The part of the rudder next to the sternpost.

Rule of the road at sea *see* COLLISION REGULATIONS

Run
To sail before the wind.

Rungs *see* HULLS: Construction components

Runner *see* MASTS AND RIGGING: Glossary

Running fix
A fix in which POSITION LINES obtained in succession are adjusted to a common time.

Running off under bare poles *see* HEAVY-WEATHER SAILING

Running rigging *see* MASTS AND RIGGING: Glossary

Rutter *see* SAILING DIRECTIONS

Sacrificial plate *see* CORROSION, ELECTROLYTIC

Safety equipment
In the great days of yacht cruising, in the early part of this century, safety recommendations consisted largely of advice on preparing the boat so that she should be safe in any weather. The idea of abandoning ship into a dinghy was unthinkable. Nowadays, and largely under the influence of deep-sea racing, codes of practice have become much more uniform and govern a wide range of equipment from guard rails to life jackets and apply to all manner of seagoing craft. The international rules for ocean racing in particular lay down minimum requirements of a very high standard.

– safety harnesses
Originally, the seaman's safety harness was simply a bowline fixed around his middle. The more practical equipment in general use today is based largely on a design by Peter Haward, a well-known yacht-delivery skipper, who led the campaign in favour of safety harnesses, following the loss of a crew member overboard in a gale in the early 1950s. The harness was simple and strong, and has been copied by most manufacturers. Difficulties in the first Round-the-World Race, when three men were lost overboard and not retrieved, led to a demand for a higher specification in safety harnesses. More recently the British Standards Institution published a standard governing the strength of hooks, lifelines, eyes, etc. The standard is of course extremely high, and indeed it might be questioned whether weekend sailors who

A safety harness in use on a small catamaran. In this position a tiller extension is necessary

are unlikely to fall overboard at speeds greater than six or seven knots require equipment strength of this kind.

– flotation gear
The early yachtsman's standard life jacket was a massive affair of cork blocks covered with canvas; it was difficult to stow, impossible to wear effectively on deck and, although the wearer floated in an upright position, his arms were so restricted that it was almost impossible to swim. Later versions used kapok enclosed in plastic envelopes and were a great improvement. Both were life jackets in the strict sense of the word, for use when the boat was actually sinking. Nowadays there is a variety of flotation equipment that can be worn on deck while handling sails. One of the most popular is the 'float coat', which will keep the wearer afloat the right way up, but is unfortunately only water-repellant rather than waterproof. In very wet conditions these garments become water-soaked and all but impossible to dry. Soft flotation vests, such as are worn by dinghy sailors, with a foul-weather jacket, provide enough flotation for a man who is a moderately good swimmer to stay afloat long enough to increase his chances of being picked up. The disadvantage of both these types of equipment is that movement is restricted, and some people prefer in such circumstances to wear inflatable life jackets.

The time it takes to put on, in succession, normal sailing gear, foul-weather gear, a flotation vest, and then a safety harness has led to the development of foul-weather jackets with a built-in safety harness and, inside the jacket, a blow-up flotation device.

– lifebuoys (rings)

Until about 1955 the classic round, white, lifebuoy, or ring, with the name of the boat on it was carried on all offshore cruising boats hanging from a bracket on the lifeline, generally so stowed that it was within reach of the helmsman to be thrown to anyone who went over the side. It had two major disadvantages: its weight was such that, if badly thrown, it could knock out the man overboard; and, secondly, the difficulty of getting into the ring – for a tired man would not find it easy to hang on to the outside for very long. In the 1950s the soft horseshoe ring was developed. It was not heavy enough to hurt the man overboard, and to get into it he had only to unclip a lanyard across the limbs and then clip it closed again. In heavy weather these light rings tend to go off to leeward faster than a man could swim and they are nowadays generally fitted with a drogue.

– man-overboard light

Naval ships carried man-overboard lights during World War II that consisted of a four-cell, waterproof torchlight designed to float and weighted so that it would float in an upright position. They were stored upside down and the light was activated by a mercury switch when the equipment was upright. The seals on the light were not entirely waterproof and for that reason the equipment does not seem to have been really efficient.

In 1960 the American firm Guest Products marketed what was probably the first man-overboard strobe light. Nowadays (perhaps following a dramatic rescue during a Bermuda race) all ocean racers in the Western hemisphere are required to use strobe man-overboard lights. They are now considered standard equipment aboard cruising yachts as well, although in Europe an improved version of the World War II man-overboard light is still used.

– man-overboard pole

The man-overboard pole, which is a type of dan buoy, came into use between the late 1950s and early 1960s. Basically, it is a long bamboo pole pushed through some fishing floats with a lead weight on the bottom and a flag at the top. Nowadays the poles tend to be fibreglass or plastic.

The original forms were usually stowed vertically, parallel to the backstay, although in some boats they were stowed horizontally on the lifeline. Today, ocean racers tend to have an excellent installation of two tubes, one either side of the boat, from which the equipment can be launched like a torpedo from the stern. When the horseshoe lifebuoy with its drogue, all of which is attached to the man-overboard pole, is heaved overboard it provides the drag necessary to pull the man-overboard pole out of its tube. Since it takes some time to heave all this equipment into the water during an emergency, trials are being carried out with man-overboard poles with a strobe light at the top. The next step would be a totally integrated unit of strobe light, horseshoe lifebuoy, and pole.

– life raft

Inflatable life rafts were developed during World War II for aircraft. They are now the standard form of lifeboat for yachts and many other small craft, and the more heavily built types can withstand prolonged periods at sea. To be effective life rafts must be double-tubed, in case of puncture, have a canopy for protection from the weather, an efficient method of keeping it topped up with air, and for bailing out. Standard equipment for life rafts includes a drogue or sea anchor to prevent it drifting far from the position in which the yacht was abandoned and which might have been broadcast.

– distress signals

The Very pistol, for long standard equipment in yachts, will fire flares, white, red or green, of various candlepower, according to the manufacturer, about 300 ft (90 m) in the air with a burning time of some 7 seconds. The flares are visible for a considerable distance. The pistol will also fire a parachute flare – to roughly the same height, but it takes much longer to reach the water and so increases the chance of being seen. There are nowadays self-contained parachute rockets that require no launcher and rise to a height of 1000 ft (300 m) giving some 40 seconds burning time. These are clearly superior to other forms of rocket but their cost is high. There are also several types of small rocket that do not require a launcher and are small enough to be carried in the pocket. They will rise to some 300 ft (90 m) and show a light of 20 000 candlepower. Smoke flares for daylight use give off coloured smoke, but in a strong breeze this is blown away along the surface of the water and only visible at close range.

– radio

In the days of double-sideband radio, all vessels at sea were required to maintain a listening watch on 2182 MHz, so that a distress message broadcast on this frequency stood a fairly good chance of being heard, particularly in coastal waters. The frequency bands have now become so congested, however, that in America practically no boats are licensed to have the double-sideband set at 2182 MHz so that it is not widely monitored and therefore not particularly effective as an emergency frequency. In Europe, however, until 1982, yachts and fishing vessels will be allowed double-sideband sets and ships and trawlers that are going over to single-sideband (SSB) are still required to listen in on 2182 MHz. Further, in the near future, all trawlers in northern Europe will be required to have a listening alarm system that will be triggered on 2182 MHz so that even if no one is listening on that frequency the alarm will attract attention.

Because of restrictions on amplitude-modulation frequencies, the overlapping of frequencies, atmospheric conditions, and changes in licensing laws, commercial vessels have now turned almost exclusively to very high frequency (VHF) for short-range communications. Medium-wave (MF) radio transmitters are or will be required to be SSB, at very much greater cost than for DSB equipment. Yachts are largely turning to VHF in consequence, and in acknowledgment that most only require a short-range capability. Inshore, the standard distress and contact frequency is channel 16 and most merchant vessels, even when offshore, will leave their radios on channel 16 to talk to passing shipping so that it is fairly easy to raise a ship on this channel even in the middle of the Atlantic.

Emergency radio sets that cover all the necessary frequencies are available on the market, but there is no set that covers each one. The type of set to purchase therefore is best decided in the light of the emergency frequency most likely to be monitored in the sailing area in which the sailing vessel is likely to be.

Safe-water marks see BUOYAGE SYSTEMS

Sag
To drift to leeward.

Sagging see HULLS: Scantlings

Sail care
Sail maintenance starts with proper care during use. Many faults stem from misuse and harsh treatment, not only afloat but also ashore. Correct handling, stowing, cleaning, and storing will keep them in shape and ensure a long life; early fault spotting will mean that repair work will be reduced.

– handling
The entry SAIL DESIGN AND MATERIALS shows how sailcloth distorts on the bias; prolonged stretching in one direction will cause permanent damage and ruin the set of a sail for all time. LEECHES in particular are vulnerable because they do not have a boltrope, wire, or webbing tape to reinforce the unsupported edge. The entry SAIL TRIM gives advice on how to support the main boom when hoisting sail so as to avoid stretching the leech, and it is worth repeating here.

LOWERING SAIL

One of the most frequent errors with sails is to pull them down by the leech. This is committed every day by owners and crewmen of every standing and experience, by those who are beginners, by those who ought to know better and, regrettably, sometimes by professional seamen. Always pull a sail down by

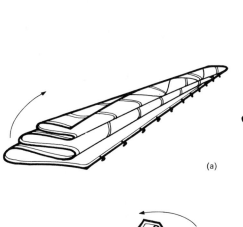

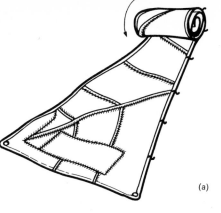

(a)

(a)

(b)

(b)

Fig. 1 Folding a mainsail. The sail should be flaked back and forth either vertically (a) or horizontally (b), after which it is rolled neatly and stowed in a sailbag

Fig. 2 Folding a jib. Such a sail should be rolled from head to tack down the luff wire or rope (a), and the tube so formed rolled from luff to leech (b). If present, a window should be positioned carefully to avoid heavy creasing

its supported edge. This is almost invariably the LUFF, but a spinnaker's leech is usually as well supported as its luff; in fact they are normally interchangeable.

– stowing and storing

Once down, the sail should be stowed out of the way. This will not only keep it clear of jagged edges in the boat and see that it does not get dirty, but it will also help to avoid point loading. If a sail is trodden on as it is lying over the engine controls in the cockpit, or over the centreboard casing in a dinghy, localized stretching can result. Sailbags should be plenty big enough so that the contents are not crushed too tightly, and small sails are best folded so that the leech is not creased. It is no good having big sailbags if they are then crammed into too small a sail bin with heavy gear laid on top (fig. 1).

BOOM STOWAGE

Sails that are stowed on the boom should be folded or flaked neatly with the cloth pulled well aft in the process. A loose-fitting cover will protect the cloth from being weakened by the ultra-violet rays of the sun or industrial smoke (a year's constant exposure can reduce synthetic sailcloth almost to the consistency of paper); it will also help to keep them free from stains (fig. 2).

WINTER STORAGE

When synthetic sails are put away for any length of time they should ideally be loosely flaked in a dry storage room; a weatherproof attic is as good as anywhere provided the sails are not forgotten. They should be turned over once or twice during the winter and checked to see that the attic is indeed dry (mildew can form on wet synthetics where dirt is also present) and that they have not been gnawed

by vermin. Where a good airy space is not available for spreading out, the sails may be hung up. Roll the mainsail round its boom if possible and hang it over the rafters in a garage; the jib can hang down against the wall supported by the head and TACK, and with the CLEW hanging free.

– cleaning

Sails give better service and look better if they are kept clean. A daily hose down with fresh water is part of the dinghy sailor's routine, and there is no reason why the man on a marina berth should not do the same to sails that have been soaked by sea water. This washes out the salt crystals that would otherwise work into the weave and saw away at the threads. Stains should be tackled according to their origin, and the quicker the better. The following treatments are suggested for polyester (Terylene; Dacron) and, to a lesser extent, nylon sails; they are offered in good faith, but neither the publishers nor the writer can accept responsibility for any damage whatsoever that may result from using them.

While many of the processes are harmless enough, it is wise to treat all chemicals with respect. Ensure plenty of fresh air and avoid fire risks (some of the chemicals can give off poisonous fumes when their vapour is drawn through a lighted cigarette).

WASHING

Many stains, such as mud and soot, can be washed away by using hot water 120°F (50°C) and liquid detergent. Small sails up to about 130–140 ft² can be washed in the bath; anything larger will either need a special container or else should be washed spread out on a clean concrete surface in the open air. In any case a hard scrub is the most effective

treatment, any stubborn stains being treated overnight in neat detergent or else left to soak in a bath full of water to which has been added 5–6 oz (not more) of caustic soda.

ADHESIVE NUMBERS

To remove all traces of the glue often used with adhesive numbers, soak overnight in one of the biological soap powders and then scrub. If this fails, brush on a solvent/detergent mixture such as Polyclens or Mr Clean, leave to soak for half an hour, and then wash off.

BLOOD STAINS

Biological soap powders will shift most blood stains, particularly if they are tackled early.

MILDEW

Remove as much surface mildew as possible by brushing in a dry state. Then tackle by soaking in a 10:1 solution of water and domestic bleach; this solution is best not used on nylon because it tends to accelerate degradation of the fabric by the sun's rays. Rinse well after treatment.

PETRO-CHEMICAL STAINS

Small oil-based stains can usually be removed with carbon tetrachloride (proprietory stain removers such as Thawpit, Dabitoff, Renuzit, or Energine are suitable). Hand-cleansing gels such as Swarfega, Palmit the American Flash, or 745 are also very good at dissolving pitch, tar, wax, or grease. Rinse.

RUST

Rust, and other metallic particles which are sometimes left behind by oil stains, should be immersed in hot water to which has been added ½ lb of oxalic acid per gallon (50 gm litre). Do not let galvanized iron, bronze, or copper get into the solution; rinse hands and sail thoroughly after treatment.

PAINT AND VARNISH

Turpentine substitute or White Spirits will usually be successful with paint and varnish marks providing they are fairly fresh. Liquid chloroform will work on most older stains unless they are left by shellac varnish, when methylated spirits (pure alcohol) should be used. Rinse well.

– drying

Sails should always be hung to dry so that the weight is taken on an edge supported by rope, tape, or wire; this is so that they will not stretch out of shape. The practical effect of this is that a sail should be hoisted by the head and/or tack.

In a garden, the head of the sail can be tied to one tree and the tack to another so that the clew hangs clear of the ground; two sails may be joined head to tack and a prop used to hold them clear of the ground (fig. 3). When drying sails on a boat it is usually best to hoist by the tack so that the largest area is aloft. Fit a retaining line to the head to hold the sail down, and make sure that it blows well clear so as not to chafe on the standing rigging or, indeed, the halyard.

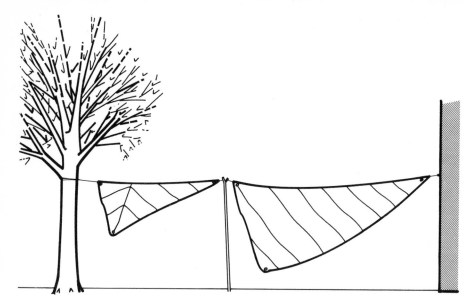

Fig. 3 When drying sails their weight must be taken on the luff by hoisting from the head and tack

– fault spotting

Any fault or damage should be acted upon as soon as it is noticed; in any event, sails should be thoroughly inspected before they are put away at the end of the season. Faults, as opposed to damage (which usually consists of chafe or tears and breakages), can be generally categorized as due to creases or wrong fullness.

Creases in a sail are nearly always wrong, and they should receive immediate attention, either with their extent being marked on the sail, or the position and extent noted in a book kept on board. The whole scope of the problem is so wide and complex that it is not possible in a small compass to categorize properly the origin and cure for even those creases that occur most commonly (fig. 4). But a general knowledge of how they arise will help an understanding of how broadly to set about avoiding the worst of them.

POOR SET

Apart from sailmaking faults, there are other problems that are more within the immediate control of the owner. These are principally problems that concern the shape of the sail as it is set and trimmed. A mast that is allowed to bend more than the sail is cut to accept will start a crease from the point of maximum bend to the clew; a mainsail tack that is forced further aft than it was made to accommodate (usually because a roller gear requires a stand-off of several inches, but the sailmaker was not given the vital dimension) will cause creases at this point; a jib tack that is too far aft of the point where the forestay meets the deck will similarly cause creases; a mainsail whose clew is not lashed down to the boom so that it rises above the line of the rest of the foot, will crease at the clew; a main halyard that does not lead fair to the headboard but pulls over towards the mast will crease at the head; battens that are too long for their pockets or which are too stiff will produce a hard area all down the leech; a halyard that is not pulled tight enough will crease the leech through lack of tension, and one that is too tight will crease the luff. These problems can usually be cured by the owner through proper attention to how the sail is bent on and hoisted.

LOADING

If loading on a sail is heavy or recurrent, it will deform the cloth to the point where it will eventually not recover its original shape. The degree or period of loading needed to do this will depend on both the weight and quality of the cloth; obviously a light material will stretch more readily, as will one that is not woven very tightly. Chemical fillers can improve resistance to stretch until they break down and are forced out of the weave (a process that is accelerated by repeated loading or flogging). A stretched cloth will go slack in the affected area and will not therefore support the stresses that are normally present in the sail. Thus a leech that has been pulled on repeatedly to lower the sail will elongate, but the reinforcement afforded by the tabling will not stretch quite so much, so a slack area will appear just forward of the tabling. Similarly a light genoa that is sheeted too hard in an effort to keep it flat as the wind gets up beyond the range for which it was built, will stretch along both foot and leech under the pull of the sheet; both edges will go slack and eventually vibrate. Vicious point loadings, such as occur when a spinnaker pole takes charge and attempts to spear the mainsail, or when a genoa foot is pulled too hard over the lifeline, will cause localized stretching and further creases.

POOR SAILMAKING

Sailmaking gives rise to creases if the workmanship is poor or misguided. Polyester cloth is a relatively hard material (particularly when compared with cotton) and even too much tension on the stitches can start creases. Panels that are overlapped too much will pull against each other to form hard spots, a ROACH that is too big for the length of the battens will turn the whole leech into a slab that hinges at the forward end of the battens like a barn door; too great a bias angle at an unsupported edge such as the leech will cause that edge to go slack and crease along its length. Also in poor sailmaking must be included bad cloth, because selection of canvas is normally the responsibility of the sailmaker. This may give rise to creases practically anywhere where loadings are

Fig. 4 Quick sketches and notes of faults, made while sailing, are invaluable for rectifying the faults when ashore

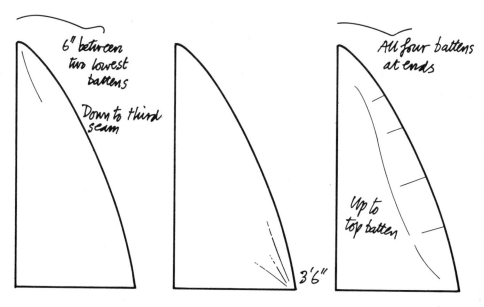

heavy, together with too much draught, bellied leeches, and generally poor set.

– cures

There are many cures that may be affected by the owner, and these can sometimes be swift and dramatic; the problem usually lies in isolating the reasons that are at the root of a particular fault. Often the broad experience of a sailmaker is needed because creases or wrong fullness can have the most unlikely origins.

CREASES

Creases due to poor set are the ones that the owner can most usually cure (*see above*). Similarly, excessive loadings should be avoided if the sailcloth is not to be pulled out of shape. The owner, of course, can do little about poor sailmaking (except to go to another loft next time he buys a new sail), but we have just seen that variation in the overlap of cloths can cause localized creases; this is because tension between the two panels concerned is changed at the point in question. It is therefore evident that proper application of this can be used to cure creases induced through other reasons. If a sail has gone slack at a particular place, judicious tightening of the appropriate seams can often effect a cure; if an area is tight, then seams must be eased instead of tightened. The decision as to which seams need attention, and by how much, is one that is often based on long experience.

WRONG FULLNESS

Fortunately it is easier to cure a sail that is too full than one that is too flat; the former, in one manifestation or the other, is the more common. The most usual forms of overfullness are a correctly shaped sail that has too much general draught, one that has too much

The creases in the sail of this OK-class dinghy have been caused by insufficient luff to cope with the amount of mast bend

belly in the aft part of the sail (i.e. near the leech), or one that is made to look overfull because another sail is BACKWINDING it.

TOO MUCH DRAUGHT

Whether it is a mainsail or a jib, a sail that has too much draught can be flattened quickly, cheaply, and effectively by pleating; what is more, the pleat can be easily removed if it does not cure the problem. The effect of a pleat is to remove surface area, thus reducing the round that has been added to the luff; there is then not so much cloth to form a belly, so the sail becomes flatter. If a sail needs flattening by pleating, this is therefore usually done about 4–8 in behind the luff. The general area of fullness has to be gauged so that the length of the pleat can be decided; then an assessment must be made as to how much round needs to be taken out, so that the width of the pleat can be fixed – this is usually somewhere between $\frac{1}{2}$–3 in, depending on the size of the sail and the amount it has to be flattened. The pleat is reckoned as the total amount of cloth that has to be taken out, which is twice the width of the final pleat when it is folded over on itself and sewn; thus a $\frac{1}{2}$-in pleat will finish by being $\frac{1}{4}$-inch wide when sewn, and this is about as small as can be reasonably controlled under the sewing machine. Pleats should be gradually tapered to zero at the top and bottom.

TOO FULL AFT

The first point to look at in control luff sails (all mainsails and those headsails with a roped or taped luff that is adjustable) is whether the luff can be stretched further. Extra tension on the halyard or Cunningham (*see* SAIL TRIM) adjuster will draw cloth towards the luff, produce flow forward instead of aft, and flatten the leech. If a sail is genuinely too full aft and it cannot be handled this way, it is usually the result of using it in winds too strong for it. If the cloth was slackly woven in the first place, the most ordinary breeze can blow it out of shape for all time – chemical fillers may help it hold its shape for a short while, but it will quickly go as soon as these break down; equally, even a well-woven light cloth will not stand up to prolonged use in strong winds. Broadly speaking, light genoas are being punished unfairly if they are being used in wind strengths of the same Beaufort number (or higher) as their cloth weight in ounces; thus a 3-oz genoa should not be exposed to force 3 winds for any length of time, nor a 4-oz sail to force 4. If they are, the flow will be blown towards the leech, where it will settle into an unsightly and inefficient belly.

TOO FLAT

It is not easy to cure a sail that is genuinely too flat; it has to be partly dismantled and extra cloth added to give more draught in the right place. Often, however, a headsail can be eased at the sheet to give the required

flow, and even a mainsail can have the OUTHAUL and halyard eased. A cure through sailmaking is normally beyond the average amateur. Control luff sails can be given a semblance of fullness by tightening the halyard or Cunningham adjuster as mentioned above, but this cannot in itself produce extra draft if the cloth is not there to provide it.

BACKWINDING

If a mainsail is constantly backwinded, it does not necessarily follow that it is too full in the luff. The jib leech should be looked at critically, and it is quite likely that it has too much belly or is too close to the mainsail, or possibly both. The slot must be wide enough for the wind strength in question, and adjustable jib sheet FAIRLEADS should be moved outboard as the wind rises. A control luff headsail should be pulled harder on the halyard in order to draw the flow forward (*see* Too full aft *above*), and only when this has failed should the jib leech be considered for flattening. Finally, if the jib and slot are both all right, then the luff of the mainsail may be flattened by pleating.

SLACK LEECH

A slack leech can often be helped by tightening a few seams for the appropriate amount. Experience is necessary when assessing how many seams to tighten by how much: an average dinghy mainsail may only need two seams adjusted by $\frac{1}{8}$ in each, into the sail for about 6–8 in; a cruising boat's mainsail, on the other hand, may need several seams tightened by $\frac{1}{4}$ in or more over a distance of 3–4 ft to the inner ends of the battens (fig. 5). It all depends on how slack the leech is and how far this extends; often only alternate seams will need attention, and those that come on batten pockets should be avoided if the work is to be kept to a minimum.

– inspection for damage

When sails are put away at the end of the season, they should be thoroughly inspected for damage in the form of chafe, tears, or loose fittings. Spread them on the ground and go over them methodically, picking at suspect stitching (which is always the first to show signs of chafe) and paying particular attention to leeches and other parts that are liable to rub against shrouds, spreaders, and lifelines; look carefully at all eyes for distortion, slides and hanks for slack seizings, batten pockets for chafe, and seams for loose stitching. Have a needle and thread of contrasting colour handy so that places can be marked for attention later. Spinnakers are best examined for small holes held up to the light, with the head tied about 6–8 ft above the ground and the clews pulled out to one side.

CHAFE

One of the main problems with synthetic sails is the way in which the cloth in general and the stitching in particular are liable to chafe. Wherever a sail bears constantly against

Fig. 5 A slack leech is cured by tightening the seams at the leech, either in to the battens if the whole leech is slack – like the one in the diagram – or only the outer 4–6 in (100–150 mm) if the affected area is limited to that amount. The amount by which each seam is tightened will vary between $\frac{1}{8}$ in (3 mm) for minor troubles in a dinghy sail to $\frac{3}{4}$ in (19 mm) for the sail of a large keelboat with greater problems. The number of seams to be tightened depends upon the nature of the problem

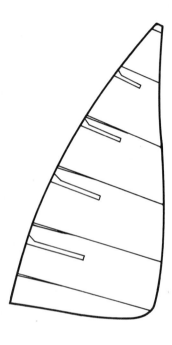

Anti-chafe pads fitted to the spreader ends of Sayula II *before she competed in the 1973/4 Round-the-World Race*

standing or running rigging, spars, or upperworks, or even another sail, movement of the boat and its gear will cause chafe; damage can quickly become important. A mainsail is open to the ravages of lee runners that have not been tied forward, a topping lift that has not been unhooked and carried up to the mast, and spreaders and shrouds when sailing downwind; battens can chafe both ends of the pockets; slide attachments can eat away at the boltrope or tape; a grooved spar can wear the sail just inside the rope. A jib can chafe on the lifeline and the shrouds; it can rub on the spreaders; and it can snag on the mast while tacking. A spinnaker will rub on the forestay if it is trimmed too tightly, and the swivel will chafe the head as it works from side to side in light winds. Above all, it is the stitching, sitting proud on the cloth, that will go first, especially if it has been weakened by ultra-violet rays from the sun over a considerable period of time. The effects of chafe can often be avoided by re-reeving or correct trimming, the use of shock cord to tie off offending rigging, or fitting of anti-chafe measures such as split tennis balls (or proprietory fittings) at the spreader ends, BAGGY-WRINKLE for the deep-sea cruising man, or protectors for the ends of full-length batten pockets. Weak points should, in fact, be written down as soon as they are noticed at sea, and either the sail itself marked in pencil or else reference points identified.

– repair equipment

Tears and ripped seams should be attended to as soon as they are noticed, or the damage will spread until it becomes a matter for the sailmaker (never was the adage more true that a 'stitch in time saves nine'). Even a piece of tape from the first-aid box or tool kit will act as a stopgap until the needle and thread can be got out.

The basic equipment required for the average home repair to sails comprises needles, pre-waxed twine, sewing palm, and the usual accessories for the sails in question (mainly slides and hanks of the correct size, but also some cloth for patches). An electric soldering iron will be useful for heat sealing if anything more than replacement of a few stitches is to be attempted, and an assortment of brass rings and liners together with the appropriate punch and die will enable eyes to be replaced or fitted. Adhesive tape in one form or another will find many uses in the repair kit.

NEEDLES

Sailmakers' needles can usually be bought in small quantity from a sailmaker. They are not rustproof and should thus be kept wrapped in a lightly oiled rag in a tin. The average owner will get by on most occasions with sizes 13, 16, and 18, plus a domestic needle for use on spinnakers. The following table represents a fairly comprehensive kit. Duplicate and extra palms allow for breakage

and mean that more than one person can be sewing at a time.

QTY	SIZE	USE
2	9	Whipping and seizing with heavy twine
2	11	As above, on a smaller scale
2	13 or 14	Roping or working eyes on cruiser sails
2	15 or 16	As above, for dinghies or dayboats
6	16 or 17	Sewing sailcloth 6–10 oz
6	17 or 18	Sewing sailcloth 3–6 oz
2	19 or domestic	Sewing spinnaker nylon or light reaching sails up to $2\frac{1}{2}$ oz

TWINE

The best twine for hand-sewing synthetic cloth is Terylene or Dacron and should be of the pre-waxed variety for better convenience; this protects it and holds it together during sewing (it is normally used doubled or even quadrupled, and the parts tend to tangle if not treated). If pre-waxed twine is not available, a piece of beeswax should be obtained from a sailmaker so that the twine can be drawn across it three or four times before use; in an emergency a candle will do as a substitute and even soap will hold the two parts together while sewing. Domestic thread should be used on sails up to $2\frac{1}{2}$ oz; a light seaming twine (2 or 4 lb, or No 1 or 2) for general sewing on dinghy sails and light headsails up to $4\frac{1}{2}$-oz cloth, and a medium weight (4 or 6 lb, or No 3) for working canvas up to 6–8 oz. Twine should be heavier for roping or working eyes through several thicknesses of cloth (or else quadrupled instead of the usual doubled), and this will normally involve using a size larger needle.

SAILMAKER'S PALM

Practice will soon show that elementary skill with a palm is not difficult to acquire; it is expertise that takes time.

ACCESSORIES

The right size slides, hanks, and shackles are important, and some offcuts of the right weight of cloth will avoid the need for a trip to the sailmaker each time a repair job is started.

SOLDERING IRON

A fine-pointed electric soldering iron will cut and seal synthetic rope or cloth. This will save much time and often make the job easier and neater, so it is a worthwhile investment

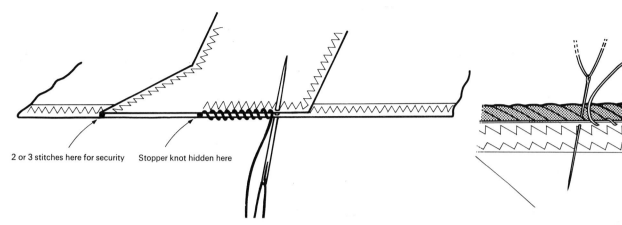

Fig. 6 The round stitch – the basis of all stitching
– is used when access to both sides of the sail is
convenient (above), as at this batten pocket
reinforcement

Fig. 7 Tabling stitch (below). Sail cloths should
be overlapped away from the worker. Progress is
from right to left, the needle being pushed down
through and back up in one movement, aiming
towards the left shoulder

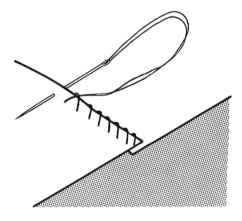

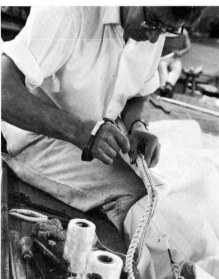

for anyone who is going to do more than ten
minutes' sailmaking at a time.

RINGS

If eyelets are to be worked, a ring must either
be sewn into the sail or else, if the strain on
the eyelet is not likely to be great, it may be
punched in. In either case, specialist equipment is needed to press the protecting liner
into the eye (either over the sewn ring or
straight into the cloth). Cheap versions that
merely punch the eyelet and liner together
without the hand-sewn ring inside can be
obtained from shops specializing in camping
gear (the Hipkiss eyelet kit is an example);
the more robust sailmaking job is a specialist
supply.

ADHESIVE TAPE

Plastic adhesive tape is useful for serving the
ends of ropes or to put over rigging screws
(turnbuckles) as an anti-chafe measure.
Double-sided, sticky-back tape is available
for holding two cloths together while they are
being sewn. Repair tape in spinnaker nylon
will put a temporary patch on light sails that
will often last the rest of the season (Sta-Put
or Rip-Stop varieties are available).

– hand work

A few basic stitches should be practised on a
piece of old sailcloth before the amateur
embarks on serious repairs.

USE OF THE PALM

With the thumb through the hole and the
needle guard snugly in the middle of the
palm of the hand, the needle is grasped between thumb and first finger so that the eye
rests against the guard. When the point is
pushed into the cloth, the hold is released and
pressure applied to the eye by the guard. As
the point comes out the other side, it should
be grasped between the thumb and forefinger
again and pulled through. With practice this
becomes almost one continuous movement.

ROUND STITCH

This is used where the needle can go in one
side of the work and come out of the other,
such as at the very edge of a sail. The needle
is pushed through the cloth, brought out on
the other side and carried back over the top
towards the worker. It is then pushed through
from the near side again in an over and over
action, working from left to right (fig. 6).

TABLING OR FLAT SEAMING STITCH

Where a seam or patch has to be sewn in the
middle of a sail, it will not be possible to push
the needle through from side to side without
turning the whole sail over at each stitch.
This means that it must be pushed down
through and then up again, all in one movement. The usual way is to work from right to
left, pushing the needle from the far side back
towards the body, angled slightly towards the
left shoulder (fig. 7).

ROPING

The average amateur will not need to do
much hand roping beyond re-sewing a short
length that has come undone; even if the rope
was originally put on by machine, a short
length of a few inches is best replaced by

Fig. 8 (top) The needle should be passed between
the lay of the rope and up through the sail, it is then
brought back towards the worker, pulled tight, and
the following stitch made between the next two
strands of the rope

The sailmaker (above) has put a needle through
the rope and sail ahead of his stitching. This acts as
a marker and as an anchor point for the bench hook
that has been fixed to his right to steady the work

hand (largely because machining requires
special heavy equipment to punch the needle
right through the rope). Replacement of a
rope that is sleeved in a tape is more a matter
of replacing the tape (and perhaps putting in
a few stitches to hold the rope in place). It is
therefore assumed that the rope is already
attached to the sail for most of its length so
that the loose end lies naturally in position.
The edge of the sail should be towards the
worker with the rope just underneath; it
will then be possible to turn the work up at

right angles for convenience of sewing (fig. 8).
Starting at the left end, the needle is passed
under one strand of the rope and then
through the sail in what is virtually the same
movement as the round stitch. The twine is
pulled tight and the needle brought back
over the top towards the worker and the
process repeated. It is important not to sew
through a strand of the rope, thus weakening
it and causing irregularities in the lay, and it
is convenient to dull the point of any needle
used for roping. Rope has a tendency to
shorten up during hand-sewing so, if any
length is involved, it should be pulled out
under tension alongside the sail and match
marks put on both rope and canvas at intervals of about a foot. A conscious effort then
has to be made to use up all the sail before
each set of match-marks is reached, by advancing the needle slightly in the sail after it
has passed through the lay of the rope at each
stitch.

SAILMAKER'S DARN

This stitch is useful for gathering the two sides
of a tear, and it is the same as the domestic
herring-bone stitch. Work is from left to right
and the start is made by pushing upwards
through the far side of the tear. The needle is
then brought back over the tear and passed
down through the near side, to be brought
up on the left side of the stitch thus formed
(fig. 9). Each stitch should not be pulled
tighter than is necessary to hold the two sides
of the tear together.

SAILMAKER'S WHIPPING

This is put on with a needle threaded with
doubled twine. The rope is whipped in the
usual way (against the lay) so that the two
parts of twine lie evenly side by side and close
up against the previous turn. The needle is
then passed between the strands of rope at the
end, the twine carried back along the lay of
the rope and sewn between the strands at the
other end; this is repeated twice so that three
holding turns have been made, and then
finished off securely (fig. 10).

WORKED EYE

The position for the eye is marked on the sail
by drawing round the outside of the brass
ring with a pencil. A small cruciform cut is
made in the centre and the ring laid on the
cut-out. The needle is passed down through
the canvas at any point on the pencilled
circle, and is brought up through the cut-
out and ring, pulled tight and passed down
through the canvas slightly along the circle
from the previous stitch; this is repeated until
the ring is completely sewn in (fig. 11). The
liner is then punched in with the correct size
punch and die to protect the stitching against
chafe by shackles etc.

PATCH

The tear should be pulled temporarily together with the sailmaker's darn or with adhesive tape; the outline of the patch is then

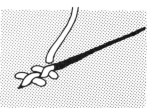
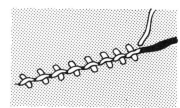

Fig. 9 The sailmaker's darn is the same as the ordinary herring-bone stitch

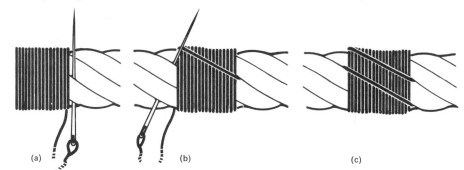

Fig. 10 A sailmaker's whipping lasts much longer than ordinary whipping because of the holding turns made before finishing off. This operation prevents the whipping from coming undone

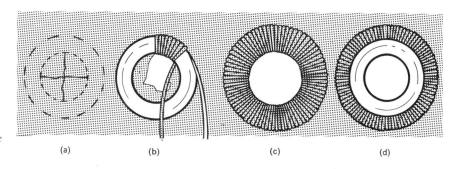

Fig. 11 Hand-worked eye. (a) The circumference of the ring marked on the sail, and the cruciform cut; (b) starting to sew the ring onto the cloth – the flaps of cloth from the cruciform cut are sewn in for added strength; the completely sewn-in ring (c) – the final stitch is made by sewing once up and down through the sail cloth; (d) the brass liner in position

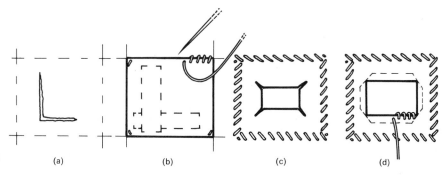

Fig. 12 Making a patch. The area to be patched marked out in line with the warp and weft (a); the edges of the tear joined together with sticky tape, the patch lined up, and the first few tabling stitches (b); the work turned over, with the tear trimmed to a rectangle with mitred corners (c); the flaps so made are turned under and sewn round (d)

drawn in pencil on the sail, lining up the sides with the warp and weft. A piece of similar weight cloth should be heat sealed along its edges to fit the pencil outline, again lining up the warp and weft. This patch is sewn to the pencil line using the tabling stitch; if it is at all big it should either be temporarily attached with pins, tacking stitches, or double-sided sticky-tape, or else struck up with match marks (the former are easier). The work is now turned over and the old sailcloth cut away to trim off to a neat rectangle; the edges may either be heat sealed (taking care not to burn through the patch as well), or else turned under (fig. 12). In any case, the cloth is sewn to the patch from the reverse side, again using the tabling stitch.

IRONING

Although ironing synthetic sails is not advised, it can sometimes be successful in removing small creases such as those at the leech that cause fluttering in what is known as 'motorboating', so precautionary advice is in order. Care must be taken not to overheat isolated patches of the sail, or localized melting of the yarns will occur, which will fuse together to distort the cloth into hard spots that can never be cured; even a low heat of $160°$ F ($70°$ C) will cause uneven shrinkage. A heat-controllable iron should be used on its coolest setting, and it should not be allowed to remain in contact with the same part of the sail for more than one or two seconds.

REPROOFING

The chemicals that are put into some synthetic sailcloths will eventually work their way out of the weave, and the sail will be the worse for it. As these fillers have been forced into the material straight from the loom, under pressure between heated rollers, they cannot be put back again once the cloth has been cut and sewn into a sail. There is nothing, therefore, that anyone – professional or amateur – can do to restore resin filling permanently and successfully to a synthetic sail.

See also MAINTENANCE; MASTS AND RIGGING; SAIL DESIGN AND MATERIALS; SAIL TRIM

Sail design and materials – sailplan design

It is the task of the naval architect to design a sailplan that will harmonize with the hull he has drawn, in the light of the use to which the boat will be put – be it racing to a handicap rule, cruising in offshore waters, or dinghy racing inland. If he has produced a TENDER hull that will react to the slightest puff of wind, he cannot afford a lofty mast and a high CENTRE OF EFFORT; if he has a beamy boat with plenty of power for offshore work, then he must see that she has enough canvas to move reasonably well in light weather, relying on REEFing or changing to smaller headsails in the stronger winds. In handicap classes, he will have to compromise here and

there so that, if he wants to keep the same rating, improvement in ballast ratio may have to be paid for in the sailplan; a gain in sail area for better light-weather performance may, for example, be at the expense of a compensating loss in the beam.

In assessing the power of a given sailplan the naval architect must work on the assumption that the sails will be reasonably cut and set to good advantage. This, of course, will not always be so, and can be the reason for the sometimes inexplicable shortfall in a boat's actual performance as compared with her predicted abilities.

If the sailplan design is the responsibility of the naval architect, the cut of the sails – flow design – is achieved in the sail loft, and trim is very much the sphere of the owner or skipper. Once the sailplan has been decided, therefore, the proper cut and flow of the sails become the responsibility of the sailmaker. He has to shape the sails so that they take up the most efficient aerodynamic profile. To determine this, he has to know how sailcloth will behave under differing conditions (and why), something of the characteristics of the boat in question and her equipment, the conditions of sea and wind in which she is going to do most of her sailing, and ideally something of the owner and what he wants from his boat: speed, reliability, windward performance, or trade-wind sailing. The sailmaker can then select his cloth, decide how flat or full the sails should be, and what degree of control over flow will be needed.

– sailcloth

Sails started to evolve from the moment man first realized that a palm frond, a bush, or a bulky cargo helped to propel a boat if the wind was astern; it was then a short step to making a sail specially for the task. Square sails were in use in the eastern Mediterranean and on the rivers of Egypt from about 2500 BC onwards, but it took over 3000 more years to develop the lateen fore-and-aft sail in the Middle East, thus opening the way towards progress into the wind.

Because the sails required to drive a boat to windward function on an aerodynamic basis, the material from which they are made assumes considerable importance, and no matter how much care goes into making a particular sail, it will never be much good if it is made from poor fabric.

FLAX

Flax (Old English *fleax*) was originally the name of a plant whose fibres were used to produce linen, from which all sails were made in Europe and North America from the Middle Ages until the nineteenth century. The staples produced when the tissues of the stem are separated in a process called retting are tough, fibrous, and fairly long, which makes them difficult to spin very fine. The material is about 20% stronger when wet than

dry, and the resulting cloth is coarse and particularly suited to hard use, but it stretches a good deal. In light winds, crews of old used to throw water on their sails to close the weave by shrinkage, and thus reduce porosity. To this day flax is sometimes used for storm sails, not only because of its strength, but also because it remains soft and easy to handle when wet. It is seriously affected by mildew, which will form readily on flaxen sails that are allowed to remain damp.

COTTON

In the middle of the nineteenth century the United States pioneered the use of cotton (Arabic *qutun*) for sails (part of the reason for the resounding victory of the schooner *America* in British waters in 1851 was her flat cotton sails). The staple formed by separating the lint from the seed in the ginning process is shorter and finer than flax and produces a more uniform cloth. Being finer, cotton can be woven more closely than flax, thus reducing stretch and allowing flatter sails. Cotton is as badly affected by mildew as is flax.

OTHER MATERIALS

Of various other materials used for sailmaking, silk and rayon were tried in the 1930s for light headsails and spinnakers; both cloths stretched too much for headsails and were too porous for spinnakers. With the increase in use of man-made fibres after World War II, a number of materials such as Acrilan were tried but they all stretched too much. In later years the search has gone on but, although some of the new cloths have advantages, they usually fail in at least one important area such as modulus of extensibility (like Melinex) or flexing fatigue (like Kevlar or Fiber B, which incorporated carbon fibres in the weave). Unwoven cloth like polythene suffers from the disadvantage of tearing once it is punctured, and attempts to mix it with a weave have not so far succeeded.

NYLON

Nylon is the generic name for the synthetic polyamide fibre that was produced from coal at the end of a long series of experiments started by the American chemist Wallace H. Carothers and his associates in 1932, but was not used for sails until just after World War II. The woven cloth has a certain inherent elasticity and is particularly suitable for spinnakers and light downwind headsails; it also absorbs water and thus can become mildewed, but this does not directly harm the material. It is, however, degraded by the ultra-violet rays of the sun, so the light cloth into which it is woven can quickly become weakened; acids accelerate this effect.

POLYESTER

In 1941 J. R. Whinfield and J. T. Dickson of the Calico Printers' Association of Lancashire, England, invented polyethylene terephthalate, whose generic name is polyester. It is a condensation product of terephthalic acid and ethylene glycol (familiar as anti-freeze), both of which are derived by chemical synthesis from products of mineral-oil cracking. Polyester is known differently throughout the world according to the trade name under which it is made: Terylene (Britain), Dacron (USA), Tergal (France), Trevira (Germany), Teteron (Japan), Terital (Italy), and Lavsan (USSR); regardless of where it is produced the raw material is all made to the same chemical formula, any difference in the finished sailcloth lying in the way it is woven and treated. Licences started expiring in 1967 and, from that date onwards, a free market has developed so that more than one trade name has appeared in some countries (Fortrel in the United States is an example). Polyester is virtually immune from most domestic chemicals, but can degrade if left exposed to ultra-violet rays for prolonged periods; alkalis can accelerate this effect.

– weaving polyester sailcloth

The polyester yarn filament is formed by one long extrusion, and threads are then made up of several filaments twisted together. Thus a particular thread may be formed by many thin filaments or fewer thicker ones. The thickness of a particular synthetic thread used to be denoted by its denier, the higher the denier the thicker the thread; now the metric system uses the decitex, (D'tex) count.

Polyester sailcloth is made by arranging a number of threads, or ends, on the beam of a loom to establish the warp, and then passing a shuttle back and forth under and over alternate warp threads to form the weft or picks – also known in the United States as the fill. This must be done at great tension to form a close-knit weave that is further tightened by beating up the picks as they build up so that they lie very closely together. The density of weave of a particular cloth, as achieved by the closeness of the ends on the beam and the amount which the weave is tightened by beating up the picks or weft as just described, is expressed as the cover factor. The highest theoretical cover factor that can be achieved for either warp or weft is 28, which represents threads placed so close together that there is no gap between them. A higher value than 28 can, in fact, be reached by beating up the weft so hard that the warp threads are crimped, or made to undulate, and the picks overlap slightly on top of one another; sailcloth with a cover factor of 32 has been recorded (fig. 1).

A given weight of cloth can thus be achieved by a small number of thick threads (of a high denier or a high D'tex number), or a larger number of thinner threads at possibly a higher cover factor. In either case the closeness of the individual threads forming the warp and weft, together with the degree of tension under which they are woven, will

affect the porosity and stability of the fabric.

There was one significant change in cloth construction in the 1970s. Doweave Inc of the USA patented a process of weaving tri-axial cloth, and this was taken up by North Sails Inc. There are two sets of weft, or fill, yarns interlaced at 60 degrees to the warp in a pattern which resembles basketweave (fig. 2). The idea is to produce a material with increased resistance to tear and with uniform stretch characteristics in all directions. It is expensive but, because it can be used over a wider wind range, the material enables an owner to have fewer sails.

A similar object lies behind the use of ply-cloth. First tried without success in the 1960s, the process of using two thicknesses of light cloth is now a proven success; for instance two 4 oz materials have better characteristics than one of 8 oz. At first it was thought that the cloths should be stuck together with adhesive, but this gave rise to problems of flexibility and adhesion; the cloths are now left free except where they are joined at the selvedges (and thus the seams), with resulting improvement in handling, porosity and stretch qualities.

When the cloth has been woven it is scoured and dried to clean it of impurities and lubricating agents, and is then heat relaxed at a temperature of about 200°C to shrink and settle the weave so that it locks tightly together. At this stage resin fillers may be added to improve smoothness and make the cloth more stable. While they can improve a slackly woven material for a time, these chemicals will eventually break down and detach from the cloth, which will then show typical marble crazing as the resins crack to powder or wash away as a milky-looking solution if rain or spray is also present.

The final process is to pass the finished

(a)

(b)

Fig. 1 The warp threads, or ends (black), tend to crimp when the weft (white sections), or picks, are beaten up during the weaving process, causing them to lie closely together (a). Tension on the warp will straighten out the threads (b) and slightly open out the weave as shown here

material through heated rollers under pressure in a treatment known as calendering; this puts a final polish on the material.

– requirements of sailcloth

The principal requirements of good sailcloth may be summarized as follows:
1. High modulus of extensibility
2. Good stability
3. High tensile strength
4. Low porosity
5. Restricted water absorption
6. Smoothness
7. Low reaction to chemicals
8. Easy handling

MODULUS OF EXTENSIBILITY

The readiness with which a material stretches elastically, as opposed to the degree of stretch, is indicated by its modulus of extensibility. In sailcloth this should be high so that the fabric does not stretch easily at low loads.

STABILITY

The single most important factor in sailcloth is stretch; there are three principal forms. First, the threads have been made up of two or more filaments twisted together, and these can untwist under tension, causing slight elongation; but this is minimal with modern synthetics and may be virtually discounted. Secondly, warp crimp, caused when the weft is beaten up until one pick is driven up on another, tends to straighten if loading is applied along the warp. Thirdly, and most important as far as sails are concerned, the weave itself can distort when tension is applied on the bias. Thus, when a well-woven material is subjected to tension along the line of the thread, either warp or weft, it will not change shape very much (fig. 3). But as soon as this tension is applied across the threadline (i.e. on the bias), the little squares formed by the weave will be distorted into little diamonds; the cloth thus lengthens in the direction of the pull. But the sail does not get any bigger, for it gains its extra length by shortening across the line of tension. A cloth that stretches in this manner should recover its original shape as soon as the tension is relaxed. In practical terms, as tension is applied to the LUFF of a sail (where the cloth is usually on the bias) flow is drawn forward and shows as a fold up the luff, while the ROACH is reduced and the LEECH flattened. This can be demonstrated with a handkerchief (fig. 4).

TENSILE STRENGTH

Individual yarns should have the highest tenacity consistent with a reasonable extension at break point; they will thus not only stand up to the shock loads inherent in close weaving under high tension on modern looms, but also form a cloth able to withstand harsh use. Alkalis lower the modulus of expensibility of polyester; acids do the same for nylon.

POROSITY

Porous sailcloth allows air to permeate from

one side of the sail to the other, thereby tending to equalize the pressure distribution to the detriment of thrust. Spinnaker nylon, being particularly thin, suffers more from porosity than the thicker polyester cloth used for fore-and-aft sails.

WATER ABSORPTION

Water harbours dirt, and the combination encourages the growth of mildew. This does not harm polyester or nylon cloth itself, but it is unsightly and difficult to remove, so a good sailcloth should not absorb water either through a porous weave or into the threads themselves. In addition, water in a sail adds to weight aloft and thus serves to promote inefficiency.

SMOOTHNESS

A rough surface breaks up the even flow of air, disturbs the boundary layer, and causes friction drag. The surface of a sail should therefore be smooth and free from ridges and creases.

CHEMICAL REACTION

Mildew, industrial smoke, ultra-violet rays from the sun, heat and cold can all affect synthetic sailcloth to a greater or lesser ex-

folded or stored in bags, without damage such as crazing or creasing to chemical fillers; the cloth should be soft and convenient to handle wet or dry.

– cloth weight

There are so many different types of sail and so many different sizes of boat that it is difficult to lay down a hard and fast rule to cover everything. The most important sails are the mainsail and working headsail, be it genoa or one-design jib. The table gives cloth weights for these (plus some other genoas) as a function of the waterline length of the boat concerned; the recommended weights can be increased slightly for a heavy cruising boat with plenty of beam, and they may be reduced where the boat will only sail on sheltered waters. For those who want to keep some sort of figure in mind, the waterline length (LWL) in feet should be divided by three and 10% subtracted to give a cloth weight in ounces per square yard (the British system of measuring cloth). For the American system of ounces per yard length of cloth only $28\frac{1}{2}$ in wide, the sum of the overall length of the boat (LOA) plus the height of the

mainsail luff in feet should be divided by ten. Thus:

British $$\frac{LWL}{3} - 10\% = oz/yd^2$$

American $$\frac{LOA + P}{10} = oz/yd \times 28\frac{1}{2}\,in$$

where LWL and LOA are measured in feet and P is the length of the mainsail luff in feet.

– flow design

Once the cloth has been selected, the sailmaker must then decide how much flow or draught to give the individual sail under consideration. Apart from the conditions of wind and sea that are mentioned above, he must also know something of the spars or stay on which the sail will be used: whether they are straight or flexible and, if the latter, how much they bend or sag. Other points of interest are the power of any winches used to sheet in the genoa, and the degree of purchase available when hoisting control luff headsails.

Having established the conditions of use, there are four principal ways open to the sailmaker in which a sail can have its flow designed or controlled.

1. Round to the luff and foot
2. Tapering the cloths or panels
3. Tension on the cloth
4. Lay of the cloth

ROUND TO THE LUFF AND FOOT

If the luff and foot of a mainsail are cut in a convex curve and are set on straight spars, the extra cloth will be pushed back into the sail where it will manifest itself as flow (fig. 5). This will lie close to the mast or boom, there being no control over its precise location unless other measures are also taken. A mast that bends will absorb this extra cloth as it bows forward so that the sail flattens; if extra fullness is required, it follows that sufficient round must be built into the luff to allow for mast bend, with further round for extra fullness on top of that (fig. 6).

A headsail receives similar treatment up its luff, only in this case it has to be cut with a basic concave hollow to it in order to allow for the sag of the forestay; round can then be put back for fullness. This usually results in a sail that has round in the lower luff and hollow near the head as in fig. 7.

TAPERING THE CLOTHS OR PANELS

In the same way that a dressmaker puts gussets in the seams of a garment to give it shape, a sailmaker can taper the panels of a sail. This will not in itself result in fullness, but will put the flow that has been given by round to the luff and foot into a predetermined place in the sail; the overall flow will have its point of maximum draft, or powerpoint, along the line where the inner end of the taper ceases (fig. 8).

This tapering of cloths is called broad seam,

Fig. 2 The basketweave pattern of tri-axial cloth, which has two weft yarns that are each interlaced at 60° to the warp

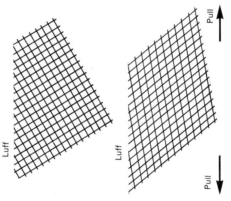

Fig. 3 The change of shape but not of size of a piece of cloth due to the pulling of threads at an angle

tent, in addition to the effects that ordinary chemicals such as fuels, detergents, and bleaches may have if they are accidentally or deliberately brought into contact with the fabric. Polyester suffers particularly from industrial smoke and sunlight, either of which can reduce its strength to the point where it will tear like paper if constantly exposed for a year or so. The material is, however, virtually immune to most normal domestic chemicals such as carbon tetrachloride cleaners or detergents, particularly if it is well rinsed with fresh water after such treatment.

HANDLING

Sails should be capable of being repeatedly

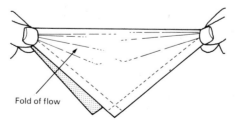

Fig. 4 When a handkerchief is pulled from corner to corner, a fold of 'flow' appears along the line of tension, and the two free corners rise as the cloth contracts across this line. A similar pull along one of the sides, in line with the warp or weft, produces little change in shape

although it may be given different names by different sailmakers: seam, nips, darts, and pies being examples.

An edge with panels running parallel to its length will not have any seams that can be tapered. If, therefore, such a sail needs broad seam at that particular edge, it must be incorporated through special darts cut into the cloth.

The leech can also be shaped by means of these tapered seams. In this area, however, it is not flow or draft that is required, but flatness to allow the wind to run off. So we can expect to find these particular seams eased rather than tightened, especially near the head and CLEW, to help free the leech where it has to curve back to windward somewhat to rejoin the mast and boom.

TENSION ON THE CLOTH

The section on Requirements of sailcloth *above* explains what happens when woven material is subjected to tension on the bias and in particular how flow is induced along a line of tension. This quality is used by the sailmaker to impart flow in addition to adding round to the luff and foot. A sail is made deliberately short on the luff so that, when it is pulled out to its marks, a fold of flow appears up the luff; the same holds good to a lesser extent for the foot of any sail set on a boom.

A sail with a rope luff will stretch with its rope and is controllable on the boat; one with a wire luff is made shorter than the wire and then either stretched in the sail loft and seized under tension permanently to the wire, or else there are two controls on the boat: a halyard to haul the wire up the stay until it is taut, and a control line to tension the luff of the sail that is sleeved over the wire (fig. 9).

LAY OF THE CLOTH

Because woven cloth distorts more readily when it is subjected to tension on the bias rather than along the threadline, the lay of the cloth plays an important part in sail shape. Panels that strike the leech of a sail exactly at right angles will not stretch unduly, whereas those that are as little as 5% off the threadline will distort. Where a sail has a fairly stout tabling, or doubled hem, along the leech, the tendency will be to restrict the natural deployment of the fabric; to counteract this a very slight amount of bias will allow both cloth and tabling to give a little, so that the effect of the extra thickness can be overcome – but here we are only talking about an angle of one or two per cent. If this small amount of tabling bias is not allowed, the leech will be liable to hook as the tabling stays fast and the cloth just forward of the leech distorts just enough to go into the familiar cupped or 'question mark' shape.

On the other hand, where it is desired to induce flow by means of tension on the cloth, it is best to lay the panels so that the line of tension comes well on the bias. This is why seams usually strike the luff of most sails at an appreciable angle; in this way the pull of the halyard can be made to produce a good fold of flow near the boltrope, that will then be blown aft into the sail by the action of the wind.

– types of cut

There are many types of cut for fore-and-aft

sails but, as has been indicated above, the most successful are likely to have their panels striking the leech at right angles (so that there is no stretch), and the luff at an angle that will ideally be the same all the way up the sail (so that stretch characteristics will be constant).

HORIZONTAL CUT

This is the most usual cut for mainsails, with panels running at 90° away from the leech and meeting the luff at the ideal constant angle, the amount of which varies directly with the aspect ratio of the sail – the higher the aspect ratio, the nearer to a right angle this will be. The cut allows as much or as little roach as required, with the weight and downward pull of the boom being easily carried by the weft pulling across the cloths. In addition, the seams arrive at the luff conveniently for the introduction of broad seam.

Headsails, for long made with a mitre seam, have also been using the horizontal cut successfully for some time. Once again, the cloths leave the leech at right angles and, since they remain parallel to each other, the angle at the boltrope is constant all the way; this means that stretch will be uniform as the halyard or Cunningham puts on the tension.

MITRE CUT

If the horizontal cut was the most usual for mainsails for a long time, so the majority of headsails used the mitre cut, at least until the introduction of the control luff jib. The importance of having panels that run at right angles or parallel to an unsupported edge (leech and foot in the case of headsails) was fully appreciated in the days of cotton. The earlier reverse mitre, or Scotch, cut had panels parallel to the leech and foot, but this did not allow the leech to be hollowed without incurring appreciable bias angle. This was followed by the conventional mitre cut that allows various seams to be tightened or eased to control tension of the free edges, besides enabling the weft threadline to be tripped round the curve of the hollow; it can also have the mitre itself adjusted if the sail needs to be shaped in this area. A development which arrived with the higher modulus of extensibility of synthetic cloth was to lay the foot cloths slightly off the right angle so that some stretch could develop in this area and allow the clew to draw aft and flatten the leech. The drawback is that the panels strike the luff at different angles above and below the mitre, thereby causing varying stretch characteristics at the luff. The cut has been used successfully with mainsails, although the arguments of restricted bias angle at the foot are weaker than those in the case of headsails, unless the mainsail is also loose-footed.

VERTICAL CUT

Gaff mainsails profited in the days of cotton from vertically laid panels, as the stresses

*Recommended cloth weights**

YACHT	MAINSAIL AND WORKING HEADSAIL	GENOA	INTERMEDIATE GENOA	LIGHT GENOA
DINGHIES				
Small	$3\frac{1}{2}$– $4\frac{1}{2}$	—	—	—
Stout	5 – 6	5 – 6	—	—
KEELBOATS				
Small	6 – $7\frac{1}{2}$	$5\frac{1}{2}$– $7\frac{1}{2}$	—	—
Larger (Dragon, Soling)	7 – $8\frac{1}{2}$	$5\frac{1}{2}$– $8\frac{1}{2}$	—	4 –5
LWL (ft)				
20	$5\frac{1}{2}$– 7	5 – 8	—	4 –5
21–25	7 – 8	6 – $9\frac{1}{2}$	7 – $9\frac{1}{2}$	$4\frac{1}{2}$–$5\frac{1}{2}$
26–30	8 – 9	6 –$10\frac{1}{2}$	$8\frac{1}{2}$–$10\frac{1}{2}$	$4\frac{1}{2}$–$5\frac{1}{2}$
31–35	9 –$10\frac{1}{2}$	$7\frac{1}{2}$–12	$9\frac{1}{2}$–12	5 –6
36–40	$10\frac{1}{2}$–12	8 –13	11 –13	5 –6
41–45	12 – $13\frac{1}{2}$	$9\frac{1}{2}$–$14\frac{1}{2}$	12 –$14\frac{1}{2}$	$5\frac{1}{2}$–$6\frac{1}{2}$
46–50	$13\frac{1}{2}$–$14\frac{1}{2}$			
51–60	$14\frac{1}{2}$–16	} require individual assessment		
61–70	16 –18			

*Weights are expressed in oz/yd². To convert to oz/yd × $28\frac{1}{2}$ in (the US system), multiply by 0.8; to convert to g/m², divide by 0.03.

(a) (b)

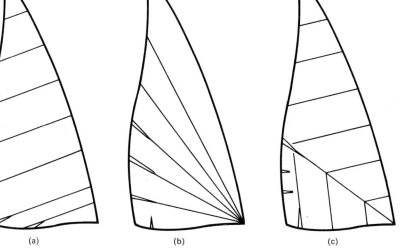

(a) (b) (c)

between the spars then ran along the warp, without distorting the sail across the cloths; synthetic cloth is strong enough to bear the weight on the weft. Roach cannot safely be put on a vertical mainsail, however, because

Fig. 5 (far left) *A mainsail with luff and foot round* (a). *When such mainsails are set on straight spars, the extra cloth moves into the sail to form fullness* (b)

Fig. 6 (centre left) *When the mast bends, it bows forward and takes up the round built into the luff, thus flattening the sail*

Fig. 7 (left) *The upper luff of a jib needs to be flat, and because all forestays sag, it is cut hollow to follow the line of sag. Round is built into the lower half to give draught low down (the drawing is exaggerated)*

Fig. 8 (left) *The horizontal cut* (a) *presents convenient seams for shaping at luff and foot; if there is no seam at the foot, the bottom panel may be split in half. The radial or sunray cut* (b) *varies its bias up the luff, and needs a dart if broad seam is required along the foot. The mitre cut* (c) *lacks bias at the lower luff, where it needs darts for broad seam, and has the cloth offset to provide bias along the foot*

Fig. 9 (below) *A controllable luff headsail can be made to slide over the luff wire so that it stops short of the tack by a few inches when slack* (a); *pulling down further will increase the tension* (b). *Another method is for the sail to be made full size and seized to the tack, with little tension in the cloth* (c), *and a Cunningham hole is used for adjusting the tension* (d). *Such a sail can be made with a rope luff, with or without a Cunningham hole*

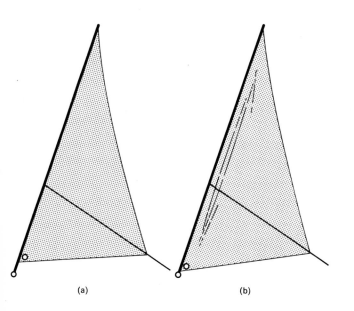
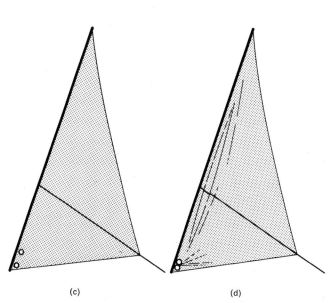

(a) (b) (c) (d)

this would immediately cause the leech to be on the bias with all the attendant problems of stretching. Headsails can also use this cut if they do not want leech hollow, and if the clew angle is such that bias along the foot will not be excessive; this virtually restricts its usefulness to jibs for dinghies (that are then usually remarkably free from leech problems).

SPIDER-WEB CUT

Also known as the multi-mitre cut, the idea behind the spider-web cut is to reduce the size of each panel in a large headsail. In this way the unbroken area of cloth subjected to the sometimes heavy stresses in a headsail is kept down in size so that the sail shall not distort too readily. The strength of modern sailcloth, however, means that such a cut is only really needed for very large headsails used in the upper wind ranges; this is fortunate, because it is an expensive way to make a sail, and one that offers many conflicting bias angles and plenty of opportunity for sailmaking errors.

RADIAL CUT

The radial, or sunray, cut differs from the spider-web in that, while it has several seams radiating from the clew, there are none also running at right angles to the mitres. The fact that there are panels running the length of the leech and foot means that these cannot have much hollow or round without giving rise to bias at the edge concerned. In addition, the angle of the threadline at the luff is one that varies with each panel, so stretch characteristics are constantly changing up the sail. Success with this cut is difficult, and it often incorporates seams running across the leech and foot panels (borrowed from the spider-web) so that seams are available for adjustment as necessary, and also the threadlines can then be tripped round at right angles to the free edges.

SPINNAKERS

Factors similar to those at play in mainsails and headsails also apply to spinnakers, with the added complication that the sail has all three edges free rather than the single loose edge of the mainsail (leech), or the two of the headsail (leech and foot). The ideal is therefore to have the threadline parallel or at right angles to all three sides of the sail, and this has given rise to a variety of cuts over the years, the most popular of which are the star cut (with panels radiating from the head and each clew) and one of the variations of the horizontal cut (with panels basically running parallel to the foot, with or without a centre seam). There are many other cuts that seek to exploit particular cloth characteristics or even fashions, and their number is legion. Being sails that can tolerate rather more draft than mainsails and headsails, spinnakers can accept lightweight nylon for their cloth, as opposed to the rather less elastic nature of polyester fabric; cloth weights are seldom heavier than 2 oz/yd² (70 gm/m²) unless it is a question of a storm spinnaker for a boat longer than about 60 ft overall.

It will be seen that the underlying reason for varying the lay of panels in a sail is a desire to reduce unwanted cloth stretch in a particular area, while at the same time allowing a controlled amount of give where this is desirable. Those parts of a sail where a stretch is not wanted include mainsail and headsail leeches, the foot of headsails, and the belly of spinnakers (particularly those used for close reaching). There is naturally an optimum cut for each type of sail, and the test of time has usually shown what this is, but fashion also takes a hand from time to time. A particular sailmaker may adopt a seemingly outrageous cut for a certain sail, with little reasoning behind it; but the owner wins races, so the cut gains a reputation not necessarily based on its own aerodynamic qualities. This is especially true with spinnakers where, as mentioned above, there are three unsupported edges all of which need restricted stretch; the belly of the sail should also be relatively flat. The use of light nylon cloth, however, means that there will be plenty of stretch if steps are not taken to prevent it. This encourages inventiveness in cutting up the panels and laying them at novel angles, but about the only durable new designs that have emerged since the horizontal and spherical patterns, are variations which distribute the load through panels running radially from one or more of the three corners: the star-cut, radial head or tri-radial cut.

See also DESIGN; PERFORMANCE AND YACHT DESIGN; RIGS; SAIL CARE; SAIL TRIM

Sailing directions

Long before charts were made, handwritten instructions resulting from the experience of mariners were set down as seamen's guides. In 500 BC 'The Periplus of Scylax of Caryanda' gave directions for coastal navigation, which included details of safe anchorages, currents to be expected, and headlands to be cleared as a ship proceeded clockwise around the shores of the Mediterranean.

The *periplus*, 'a sailing around', gave way to the Italian *portolano*, or 'port book'; in the sixteenth century these *portolani* were extended to cover waters beyond the Mediterranean, as far as northwest Europe, whence Mediterranean vessels were by now trading.

As the northern mariners had traditionally relied upon mental or written notes, handed down from one generation of seamen to the next, as guides to navigation they were more impressed at first by the *portolani* than the portulan charts the Mediterranean sailors brought with them. So with the advent of printing in the early sixteenth century the Germans, the Dutch, and the French began to publish the *Seebuch*, the *leeskaart* (reading chart), and the *routier* respectively.

Pierre Garcie, himself a pilot from the west coast of France, added to his own extensive experience that of other seagoing acquaintances in order to compile and publish in 1502 *Le Routier de la Mer*, to be superseded by his much larger *Le Grand Routier* in 1520, which appeared in many editions over the next hundred years. These *routiers* included details of courses to be steered, methods of estimating the ship's position by sounding and sampling the seabed, positions of safe anchorages to be found and dangerous shoals to be avoided and, a new innovation, crude woodcuts giving views from seaward of headlands and other land features to be used for recognition by the navigator. The *routiers* worked systematically around the coasts of northwest Europe, the British Isles and southward along the shores of the Bay of Biscay and the Iberian peninsula to the Strait of Gibraltar.

In 1528 an English edition of *Le Routier de la Mer* was published by Robert Copland, to be followed in mid-century by 'The Rutter of the North' compiled by Richard Proude. Thus did 'rutter' become the English word for sailing directions, which played an important part in navigation throughout the seventeenth and eighteenth centuries.

As modern sea charts developed in the nineteenth and twentieth centuries sailing directions, or 'pilots' as they came to be called, were increasingly used to carry a wealth of information for which no room could be found on the charts. The prudent navigator is expected to read the 'pilot' in concert with his charts when preparing for a voyage, and the major hydrographic authorities publish both.

Recognition views of the coastline, which have advanced from simple woodcuts to fine engravings and finally photographs, have increasingly found their place in the sailing directions. A culmination of this development is to be found in the oblique aerial photographs of ports taken from seaward that some hydrographic offices now include in sailing directions to give the navigator a clear picture of the harbour layout before he enters.

The British Hydrographic Department, which publishes over 70 volumes of sailing directions in support of its world cover of charts, was among a number of offices that in recent years have carried out a major study of sailing directions. The aim is to reduce the considerable amount of duplication that has developed over the years of material that may be read from the charts. In many cases useful port information, including facilities for taking on supplies and repairs, has been increased.

Whereas the British Hydrographic Office brings its Pilots up to date by Supplements, with a complete new edition of each volume

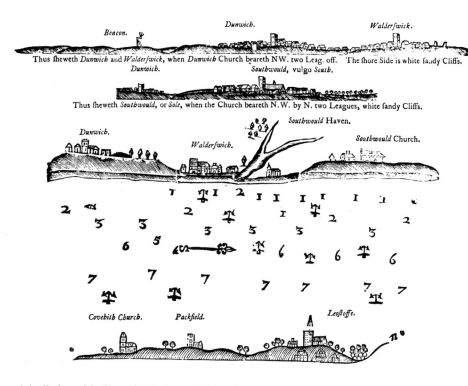

A detail of one of the illustrations in the 1758 edition of
The English Pilot for the Southern
Navigation describing the Sea-coasts . . .

about every ten years, the United States and
Canada have recently adopted computer
typesetting for their volumes of sailing directions so that updating may be easily included
in frequent new editions.

Although primarily for the use of mariners,
the many volumes of sailing directions now
maintained by the hydrographic services of
many nations provide useful reference books
on the coasts and seaports of the world.

See also HYDROGRAPHIC SURVEYING; NAVI-
GATION: Historical

Sailings, the
The sailings comprise the methods used for
finding: (1) the course and distance from one
position to another; (2) the position of arrival
after sailing on a given course for a given
distance from a known position.

Treating the earth as a sphere, it can be
shown that the length of an arc of any
parallel of latitude between two meridians is
proportional to the cosine of the latitude of
the parallel and to the difference of longitude
between the two meridians – a principle
known as parallel sailing. In sailing due east
(or due west) it is easy to solve either of the
sailing problems using parallel sailing. But
when sailing obliquely across meridians on a
constant course, the ship traces out an equi-
angular spiral known as a RHUMB LINE; and,
because the earth is a sphere, the oblique
sailing problem is relatively difficult. The
rhumb-line sailing problem was effectively
solved with the introduction of the Mercator

chart in the late sixteenth century. The essential feature of this chart is that all rhumb lines
are projected as straight lines.

In rhumb-line sailing the relationships
between northing (or southing), easting (or
westing), oblique distance, and course angle
form the plane-sailing formulae, so-called
because the three distances involved can be
accurately represented by the sides of a plane
right-angled triangle, and the sailing problems thus solved by plane trigonometry.

The rhumb-line track, although ordinarily
used in navigation, suffers the disadvantage
of not representing the shortest distance,
which is desirable for many ocean passages.
To follow this requires frequent course
alterations in order to maintain the GREAT-
CIRCLE arc connecting the places of departure
and destination.

Sailing-ship routes
The route chosen for a sailing vessel is one in
which she is most likely to be assisted by
leading winds and by favourable currents;
and distance is generally of secondary consideration.

In the Mediterranean, one of the cradles
of maritime trade, voyaging in classical
times was usually confined to the summer
months and advantage was taken of seasonal
winds (of which there is a great variety within
that sea) to acilitate navigation. It is of interest to note that directions were given, even
before the advent of the magnetic compass in

the twelfth century AD, in terms of the
names of local winds. In the Arabian Sea,
where the winds for about six consecutive
months are northeasterly and for the rest of
the year southwesterly, the name *monsoon* –
derived from an Arabic word meaning
'season' – was used. An ancient pilot named
Hippalus is supposed to have discovered the
open-sea route between Arabia and India,
and to have taken advantage of the local
seasonal winds, and the southwest monsoon of
the Arabian Sea was named Hippalus in his
honour. The term monsoon is now applied to
many parts of the ocean in additon to the
Arabian Sea, where winds are persistant in
direction at definite seasons of the year. Monsoons are in some respects similar to land and
sea breezes, but have a period of a year instead of a day, and affect vast areas instead of
limited coastal stretches as do land and sea
breezes. They are most prominent near the
northern and southern tropics, and represent
a departure from the so-called general atmospheric circulation. Sailing and steamship
routes between Europe and the Far East
were greatly influenced by the monsoon
variations.

When ocean navigation began during the
early phase of oceanic discovery in the fourteenth century, knowledge of the planetary
wind systems, especially of the Atlantic,
accrued quickly. Prominent among the major
wind systems of the globe are the trade winds,
which are northeasterly in the northern, and
southeasterly in the southern hemisphere.
The discovery of the Atlantic northeast trades
is usually attributed to Columbus, who is
supposed to have made the discovery during
his first transatlantic voyage of 1492. But
there is evidence that the regularity of the
northeast trades, and the variability of the
winds in the region immediately to the north
of the tradewind belt of the North Atlantic,
were known to Portuguese seamen much
earlier in the fifteenth century. By the end of
that century the Portuguese had verified the
symmetry of the wind pattern in the Atlantic
to the northward and southward of the equatorial region of calms, and the common name
ventos gerais was applied to the Atlantic trade
winds of both hemispheres. A. Teixeira da
Mota points out (in 'Atlantic Winds and
Currents in Portuguese Documents', *Proceedings of the Royal Society of Edinburgh*, Vol. 73,
1972) that considerable details of winds and
currents in the open ocean were rapidly
assembled during the early period of Portuguese maritime expansion. In an early
ocean *roteiro* (itinerary), dated *c.* 1550, wind
and current data are given in minute detail:

'. . . be careful, [the mariner is warned],
even if the wind is favourable, not to get close
to Cape Palmas, because if you are caught by
calms you will be carried on by the waters

that run from there to Mina Coast, and so you will not make good navigation. . . . When you have passed the equinoctial line and reached the 'ventos gerais' south east, you ought to go with them while it is possible: they will be going on the quarter little by little and you will increase in latitude till you are at 30°. And from there go on, because the winds will be turning to west, west-south-west, south-south-west, and with them you will reach the Cape of Good Hope . . .'

Da Mota also points out that Luiz Teixeira, author of the most ancient *roteiro* of the Brazilian coast, *c.* 1575, indicated that between latitudes 8° and 19° S there is a regiment of monsoon winds; and that Vicente Rodrigues, in his *Carreiro da India* (1577), remarked that in the crossing to Brazil the waters run into the Antilles. It is remarkable that this information was available at such an early date, and it is evident that the collective experience of the early Portuguese navigators was eagerly sought and carefully assembled by the compilers of the early ocean *roteiros*. So important was knowledge of winds and currents and their seasonal changes, that pilots were examined in their knowledge of these particulars before being allowed to take charge of the navigation of vessels in the Indies trade.

Not only the Portuguese but the Spanish also realized the importance of knowledge of winds and currents of the oceans. Their galleons utlized the northeast trades of the Pacific in their voyages of the fifteenth and sixteenth centuries in that ocean.

Edmond Halley, the eminent English Astronomer Royal, studied oceanic winds during a stay on St Helena from 1676 to 1678. This led to the publication of his paper of 1686 in which he attributed the cause of the trade winds to the warmth of the equatorial belt and the consequent ascension of equatorial air and its subsequent replacement by the equatorward surface flow of air from higher latitudes. But it was the scientific writer George Hadley who in 1735 explained the easterly component of the trade winds by bringing the earth's rotation into the account. In more recent times the trade winds are explained in relation to the oceanic anticyclones and to the wider air-pressure distribution on the surface of the globe.

Credit for systematizing maritime meteorology and climatology on a global basis belongs to Matthew Fontaine Maury of the United States Navy. Maury, in the mid-nineteenth century, analysed logbook records of oceanic winds, and his deductions led to the publication by the United States Government of *Wind and Current Charts*. These were distributed freely to all ship's masters who were willing to send copies of their weather logs to the Hydrographic Office at Washington to be used by Maury for improving

knowledge of maritime meteorology and for correcting or amplifying the information on the *Wind and Current Charts*. By following Maury's *Sailing Directions*, which were published with the charts, the passage times of sailing vessels on many ocean routes appear to have been reduced drastically. Today Pilot Charts (or Routing Charts) giving similar information are published for both Atlantic and Pacific Oceans.

The global wind systems are described as either cyclonic, having low surface air pressure at the centre, or anticyclonic, having high surface air pressure at the centre. In general, winds have an easterly component in tropical regions and a westerly component in temperate zones. The permanent cyclonic systems of the equatorial belt form, over the oceans, the calms known as the doldrums. The wind systems of the tropical zones, the trades, are separated from those of the temperate zones by the so-called calms of Cancer and Capricorn – those in the North Atlantic being associated with the 'horse latitudes', named from the practice in the eighteenth century of casting overboard the corpses of horses who had died through lack of water when voyages were prolonged by calms.

Polewards of the calms of Cancer and Capricorn, between the parallels of about 35° and 60°, are the belts known as the 'westerlies', where prevailing winds have a westerly component in both hemispheres.

Because the wind systems are linked with the atmospheric pressure systems of the globe, and because the plane of the earth's rotation is inclined to the plane of her orbit around the sun, the wind belts migrate latitudinally with the changing declination of the sun. Moreover, because of the greater ratio between the areas of sea and land in the southern hemisphere compared with the northern hemisphere, corresponding wind belts have different latitudinal extents in the two hemispheres: the zone of the southeast trades, for example, is broader than that of the northeast trades.

The trade winds are strongest when the sun is in the opposite hemisphere and when its DECLINATION is greatest. They then blow from a more northerly (or southerly) direction than when the sun is in the same hemisphere. The doldrums in the Atlantic are narrowest in February and broadest in August, but throughout the year the width diminishes towards the west. The most favourable time for crossing the doldrums of the Atlantic in a sailing vessel is between December and June, when, sometimes, the northeast and southeast trades meet somewhere between the meridians of 28° and 35° W, and where a sailing vessel may pass, in a single squall, from one trade to another.

In the Pacific the southeast trade blows from about 250 miles from the South American

coast to the east coast of Australia; but it blows with constancy in the southwest Pacific only from June to October, being prevalent off the northeast coast of Australia only between the months of April and September. Its limits here are ill-defined due to the influence of the Indian Ocean monsoons.

The northeast trades of the Pacific extend from the North American coast to the meridian of about 148° E, where they are interrupted by the monsoons of the western Pacific. Their average limits are about 7° N and 27° N, whereas those of the southeast trades of the Pacific are 5° N and 27° S, the axis of the doldrums being located northwards of the equator at all times of the year.

For sailing vessels bound from the Atlantic to the Indian Ocean the best time of year is between April and October when westerly winds prevail. For the remaining part of the year winds generally are southeasterly, although westerly winds are not infrequent. The passage westwards round Cape Horn is hampered by westerly winds, which prevail throughout the greater part of the year, and gale follows gale in quick succession. Easterly winds are most frequent in the period April to June.

The westerly winds of the southern hemisphere blow with considerable force and regularity compared with those of the northern hemisphere. It is not without good reason that sailors refer to the winds of the zone between the parallels of 40° and 50° S as the 'roaring forties': Maury described them vividly in *Physical Geography of the Sea*, 1855.

The Indian Ocean has often been described as having been made for sailing vessels. The southwest and northeast monsoons of the Indian Ocean are so well known as to demand but brief comment. But the monsoon regime extends beyond the Indian Ocean from about 20° S in the Mozambique Channel, northwards along the east coast of Africa, over the north Indian Ocean (including the Gulf of Aden, Arabian Sea, and the Bay of Bengal) into the seas of the west Pacific to beyond the Marianas and northwards to the islands of Japan. The southwest monsoon, which occurs in northern summer, is strongest in the Indian Ocean; the northeast monsoon, which occurs in northern winter, is strongest in the Pacific.

The surface currents of the ocean are of less importance in choosing a sailing-ship route than are the winds. Nevertheless, the prudent navigator, by his knowledge of ocean currents and their seasonal variations, was often able to facilitate his voyages from their careful consideration. The planetary system of ocean currents corresponds in large measure to that of the planetary wind system, but the former is related to the latter in a relatively complex manner. In general the surface currents of the ocean are strongest on the western sides of ocean basins. The Florida Current and Gulf Stream in the North Atlantic, the Brazil Current in the South Atlantic, the Kuroshio or Japan Current in the North Pacific, and the East Australian Current in the South Pacific, are examples of such currents, all of which flow polewards and have speeds that may amount to as much as a hundred or more miles per day. Currents off oceanic shores on western sides of continents, particularly in the Atlantic and Pacific Oceans, tend to flow equatorwards relatively slowly.

The northerly and southerly limbs of the principal oceanic current systems of the Atlantic, Pacific and South Indian Oceans are linked by equatorial currents and by drift currents, the latter lying in the zones of the westerlies.

There is a continuous belt of sea around the continent of Antarctica. Within this belt westerly winds are strong and persistent, and the surface currents tend also to be strong. At the restricted Drake Passage, between Cape Horn and the northerly tip of the Grahamland peninsula of Antarctica, the strong hydraulic current played a significant role, no less than the adverse winds, in the practice of doubling Cape Horn westbound from the Atlantic.

The planning of an ocean route for a sailing vessel involved consideration of the time of year in relation to the seasonal changes of winds and currents to be encountered during the voyage; the expected duration of the voyage in relation to supplies of food and water and the locations of suitable ports of call for replenishment of supplies; as well as consideration of matters of secondary importance such as the utilization of GREAT-CIRCLE sailing; the avoidance of icefields and icebergs; and the avoidance of tropical storms characteristic of certain localities at certain seasons, and which are related to the tropical wind systems. Successful weather routing in days of sail required considerable knowledge of maritime meteorology as well as consummate skill in seamanship. *See also* WIND AND WEATHER

Sailmaker's whipping *see* SAIL CARE: Hand work

Sail Training Association

This British body has organized the popular Tall Ships Races since they began in 1956. It also owns the two sail training ships *Sir Winston Churchill* and *Malcolm Miller*, which were built in 1966 and 1967 respectively. These ships have strenuous programmes that introduce young men and women to sailing in comparatively large vessels.

Sail trim

Tune, as opposed to trim, is the passive preparation of a boat so that she is capable of giving her optimum performance if all other factors are correct. It includes such points as mast position, rigging tension (slack or tight), adjustable shrouds and backstay, headsail leads, and the hundred and one small items that can be attended to before the boat starts to move. These make a difference to the ability to POINT high when on the wind, to sail faster through reduction in wetted area or weather helm, and generally to get more power from the rig. This subject is covered in MASTS AND RIGGING, but a reference to the effect of mast bend and rake on the balance of the sail plan would be useful here.

The entry SAIL DESIGN AND MATERIALS shows how round built into the luff of a mainsail will make for fullness. If the mast bends, the sail must bow forward in the middle, thus surrendering some of its luff round; this flattens the sail. If, on the other hand, the mast can be raked forward or aft by means of adjusting the fore- and backstays simultaneously, the CENTRE OF EFFORT (CE) will be moved. This will affect weather helm and the CE is moved nearer to or further away from the CENTRE OF LATERAL RESISTANCE (CLR), thus reducing or increasing the turning moment. Control over spars has been enhanced by use of hydraulic pumps. Great power can be switched from point to point, so that one crew member can control the tension on the boom vang, backstay, forestay, inner stay, baby stay and, indeed, a variety of other stays wherever the designer deems it useful. This movement of the whole rig is not a particularly seamanlike operation, and the IOR only permits adjustment of either the forestay or the backstay, not both.

Sail trim is different from tune in that it is the fine adjustment of the various sail controls to achieve optimum thrust – and thus boat speed – under different conditions of wind and water. It starts with choice of which sails to set, how to bend them to the spars or stays, and how to hoist them. Only then can sheets and other controls be adjusted.

– choice of sails

Owners of dinghies or keelboat one-designs may have two or three mainsails and twice that number of jibs. These will be flat or full, small or big, and heavy or light according to whether they are designed for heavy or light weather respectively; which mainsail to use must normally be decided before starting the day's sail jibs are easier to change.

Different mainsails to suit light, medium, and heavy weather are really one too many; the choice should be limited to two sails at most, otherwise the worry of a wrong selection will haunt the owner for the whole race. With modern controls such as bendy masts, zippers, and jiffy REEFing, two sails should be quite enough, and one can usually be made to cover most likely conditions.

The cruising or offshore-racing man, on the

The Norwegian three-masted barque, Christian Radich, *is an example of the many large sailing vessels used by the maritime nations for training. She is seen here at the start of the 1976 Tall Ships Race, at Plymouth*

other hand, carries his problem of sail selection afloat with him. He will usually only have one mainsail, but there will be a variety of headsails (and indeed spinnakers) in the sail locker. If he is caught out in strengthening or dying winds he can switch headsails accordingly, and often have storm canvas to put on instead of the mainsail if it gets really rough. A specific point to watch for is the natural tendency to hold onto a light genoa as the wind increases beyond the range for which the sail was designed. This is often because the sail is setting nicely and pulling the boat along well at the lower wind speeds, so the skipper does not want to lose time by changing to a heavier sail that might not set so well; this reluctance gives an excuse for any laziness in the crew. There are circumstances where this may be accepted, such as the end of a leg to windward where the turning mark is only a quarter of a mile away, but the owner must be prepared for the particular sail to have its flow blown aft and to stretch out of shape for all time.

It has already been seen that the IOR has something to say about adjustment of stays. In addition various other racing or handicapping rules often have sections on sails. The

IYRU goes into the size and positioning of sail numbers and sailmakers' marks; level rating regulations limit the number of sails which may be carried while racing; the RORC has requirements regarding storm canvas; specific race instructions may add to or relax these regulations.

Once the choice of sails has been made (and the owner who only possesses one mainsail and one all-purpose headsail is sometimes to be envied, because he is relieved of the problem of selection and the indecision that can accompany it), the time comes to bend and hoist them.

– bending on
Sails should be bent to their spars or stays so that they lie naturally when hoisted. The skipper should check that unnecessary wrinkles are not being caused due to careless adjustment or to ill-fitting gear that ought to be changed, and he should see that LEECH lines, if fitted, are slack (leech lines are really a sailmaker's confession of failure, because a vibrating leech ought to be rectified in the sail loft and not by means of tightening the drawstring, which will only steady the noise and also give a hook to the sail just where it will do the most harm).

MAINSAILS
The halyard should lead fair to the head eye; the most common fault is for the mast SHEAVE to be too small in diameter, so that the wire or rope pulls the headboard over towards the mast (fig. 1). The tack fitting should allow the boltrope plenty of room to take up a normal line; the fault here is usually that the sailmaker has not been told the distance between the tack pin and the aft face of the mast, so that the sail can be cut back to accommodate a roller reefing gear. The CLEW should lie in the same line as the rest of the foot; if it is allowed to rise because it has no slide, or perhaps no lashing round the boom, creases will result (a lashing round the boom at the clew is also useful on a sail that runs in a groove, because it will stop any tendency to pull out of the groove) (fig. 2). If slides are fitted, they should all be at an even distance from the boltrope; one slide which has a slack lashing or a longer shackle will cause the LUFF to lie out of true at that point, with resulting wrinkles. Battens should be the correct length for their pockets and not too stiff; an overlong batten will chafe the pocket ends and force the sail into creases, and a stiff one will cause the whole leech to lie at an awkward angle.

HEADSAILS
The same remarks apply to the headsail halyard as to the mainsail; if the halyard does not run from the correct point just under the stay, the head of the sail will be pulled out of line (usually aft) unless a hank is fitted to the head eye itself. Similarly the TACK should be close up to the stay, or creases will run from the bottom hank unless one is fitted at the

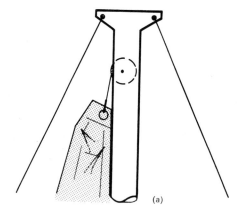

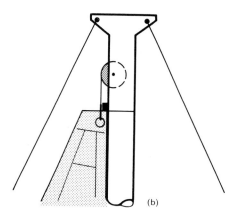

Fig. 1 Head creases are caused by the headboard being pulled over towards the mast. Two solutions are shown: either a large-diameter sheave (a) or a spacer (b) to act as both stop and fairlead for the halyard

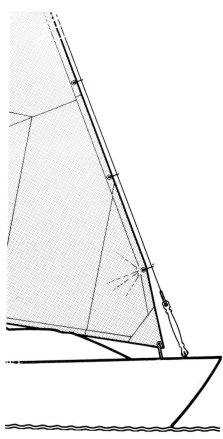

Fig. 3 The tack creases shown would disappear if the tack fitting were nearer the forestay, so that the luff formed a continuous straight line

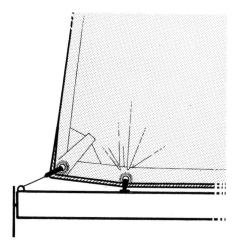

Fig. 2 Clew creases can be prevented by fitting a slide at the clew to stop it rising. A lashing round the boom will do the same job, and is also useful on a grooved boom to stop the boltrope pulling out at the clew

tack – often not possible owing to a bulky rigging screw (turnbuckle) at the bottom of the stay. The sheet fairlead should ensure that tension of the sheet is correctly shared between the leech and foot, so that the sail lifts evenly all along the luff as the boat is pointed into wind (fig. 3).

– hoisting sail
The entry SAIL DESIGN AND MATERIALS shows how shape is built into a sail by adding round to the luff and foot and by tapering the panels. We also know that draught can be drawn to different places by the application of tension at appropriate points; the halyard is thus an important control in sail shape.

HALYARD
Black measurement bands are painted on the spars of many boats, including those that seldom if ever race. There is no need to become a slave to these marks, and the intelligent owner watches the shape of the mainsail as he hoists the last few inches. In light weather, little tension is needed on halyard and outhaul because the sail will

take up the shape the sailmaker has built into it, and the wind will not be strong enough to blow it out of position; this may well call for the sail to be anything up to 8 or 9 in short of the upper black band, and 2 or 3 in short at the clew, depending on the size of sail and the way it has been made. In medium winds there should be enough tension for a small fold to appear up the luff and along the foot. This will probably require nearly full stretch on most sails, and the wind will soon blow the fold into the required shape. In heavy weather cruising boats can pull beyond the marks if there is room for the sail to travel on the spar, but the racing man is required by the rules to keep within the black bands. Strong winds will push the flow well aft so maximum tension is needed in order to draw it forward again, and it may be that a Cunningham hole is needed; pulled hard down, this allows extra tension to be applied to the luff, yet the sail remains as set up by the halyard within the measurement marks.

While the sail is being hoisted, remember to take the weight of the boom, either by holding it up by hand or by an hydraulic ram kicking strap (boom vang) if fitted, or else by taking up the slack on the topping lift.

CLEW OUTHAUL
The mainsail clew outhaul acts in a similar way on the foot, as the halyard does on the luff. Light tension will leave plenty of flow for light airs, and a strong pull will flatten the foot area for strong winds.

TWIST
Once the mainsail has been properly hoisted, it must not be allowed to develop too much twist so that the top of the sail is angled further off the centreline of the boat than the foot. If it is, and the head is not to be caught aback by the wind getting behind it, the boom of a twisted sail has to be trimmed nearer the centreline than would otherwise be necessary; this means that the lower half will be pushing sideways rather than forward – an inefficient state of affairs (fig. 4). The cure lies in straightening the leech by pulling down on the boom, which may then be eased; this can be achieved by means of a kicking strap. The problem is aggravated somewhat if the mainsheet is attached to a point on the centreline of the boat, so that the boom rises as well as moves sideways when the sheet is eased; a full-width mainsheet TRAVELLER ensures that the pull is straight down until the attachment point on the boom moves outboard, beyond the end of the traveller.

A certain amount of twist can be accepted, and even encouraged, in light winds, and it seems that dinghies may not profit quite so much from a full-width traveller as was at one time thought; this is partly because it tends to make the slot too narrow unless the jib fairlead can also be moved outboard. Instead of

easing the sheet in brisk conditions, a dinghy is pointed high into the wind so that the head of the sail 'feathers' and so reduces the forces acting at the top of the mast; under these conditions a small amount of twist can even be beneficial.

HEADSAILS
The same generalizations about halyard tensions hold good for headsails fitted with a rope luff. Those with a wire up the luff, be they fixed or with the luff sleeved over the wire so that it may be controlled, should have the wire set up as tight as possible in the pursuit of the straight luff that is so important for windward work.

A control luff headsail should have its flow adjusted by varying the tension on the luff of the sail: pull hard on the halyard or downhaul to draw the flow forward in strong winds, ease it as the wind eases. In almost all cases, a rope luff genoa should be hoisted harder after about an hour even if the wind has not become stronger, because there will have been a small amount of elasticity in the system which will need taking up. With large variations (and a genoa with a luff of 50 ft [15 m] may need to be stretched up to 4 or 5 ft [c. 1.5 m] on the luff in a stiff breeze), the sheeting angle will also have to be changed to suit the new clew height.

Headsails are often made for a groove, just like a mainsail, only the groove is either incorporated in a rod forestay or is formed

by an extrusion which fits round the forestay wire. Twin grooves make for much easier drills, because one man can feed the luff into the groove opening and then hoist without having to clip individual hanks or snap hooks round the stay. This can be done alongside a headsail that is already set, whereupon the old sail can be subsequently as easily lowered and stowed; the boat is thus not left bald-headed during any part of the change.

One final advantage which a grooved forestay shares with rod rigging: its surface is so much smoother than wire that spinnakers tend to slide off it rather than wrap themselves round it.

– the slot
The interrelation of the mainsail and headsail is important on any sailing boat. Most sailing people know that the total thrust of a correctly trimmed mainsail and genoa combined is greater than the sum of the two thrusts from each sail acting on its own. A comparison may be drawn with a low-speed aerofoil, such as is presented by a sailplane when coming in to land at a high angle of incidence (fig. 5). Air is passing across a cambered surface that by its shape is turning this action into thrust (lift in the case of a sailplane). Wind-tunnel tests have shown that the introduction of a slot into the aerofoil cleans up the airflow to leeward as it passes over the section. The task of the headsail in this arrangement is twofold:

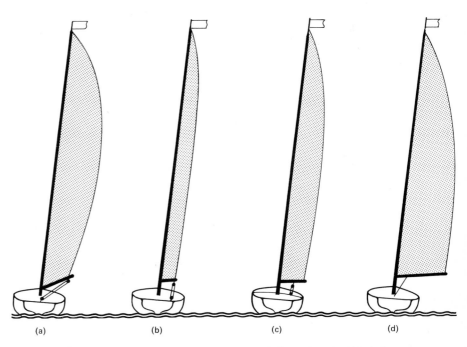

(a)   (b)   (c)   (d)

Fig. 4 A centreline mainsheet attachment (a) *allows the boom to rise and twist the leech as the sail is eased. A transom traveller* (b) *enables the leech to be tensioned while the boom end is over the travel of the sheet slider; while a centre-boom traveller* (c) extends the arc through which the boom can move before it lifts. The kicking strap or boom vang (d) holds the boom down at all angles off, so that the leech is evenly tensioned and the whole sail is at a fairly constant angle to the wind

The centre-boom mainsheet attachment of this Jeremy Rogers Contessa 32 does not even require the full width of the short traveller, forward of the main hatch, to keep a firm downward pull on the well- *eased reefed mainsail; the result is almost no twist. The spinnaker is beautifully trimmed so that pull is well forward. The boat must be doing about 7 knots, her theoretical top speed*

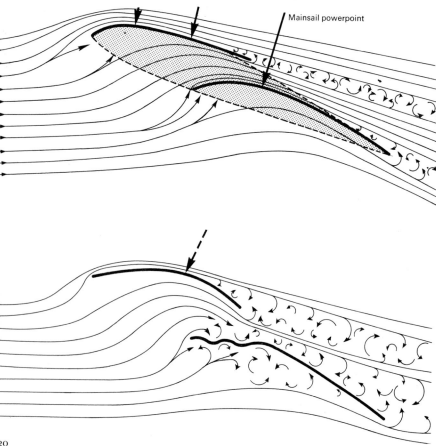

1. To produce an efficient slot with the mainsail.

2. By virtue of the fact that it forms the leading edge of the combined aerofoil, to carry the main driving force generated by the two sails acting together.

TOO NARROW

If the slot is not large enough, or has a large obstruction in it, air will not be able to pass through freely and it will become turbulent and inefficient. This can be caused by a number of factors.

1. The headsail is too close to the mainsail, making the slot opening too small. This sometimes occurs on a twin-head cutter rig, though it is not a common problem (but see the remarks on full-width dinghy mainsheet travellers above).

2. A genoa has too great an overlap, so that its leech is too close to the position of maximum camber, or powerpoint, of the mainsail; the slot is thus too narrow. Wind-tunnel tests have shown that greatest efficiency is obtained where the genoa leech is level with the mainsail's powerpoint. In strong winds, when more air is trying to get through the slot, a heavy-weather genoa should have its leech well hollowed to allow for this.

3. The headsail has its flow too far aft (so that the leech is bellied); wind is thus directed into the lee side of the mainsail, causing it to lift (fig. 6). A backwinded mainsail can often be cured by hauling harder on a control luff genoa's halyard or downhaul, which draws the headsail's flow forward again and flattens its leech.

4. The headsail leech is tight, with a curl or hook to windward causing disturbance to the airflow at the exit to the slot, just where it most needs to be smooth. This is the source of one of the most common sail faults and is among the most important to get right.

TOO WIDE

Equally, but not so damaging, too wide a slot is wrong. If the mainsail and headsail are too far apart, the beneficial effect of the latter will be largely dissipated. The wind will come off the leech in turbulent fashion, without

Fig. 5 (left above) *The mainsail and jib must be imagined as one combined aerofoil with a slot through the middle, not as two independent aerofoils. The Venturi effect of the slot ensures that the air flow sticks to the lee side of the mainsail well past its power point, and it also draws the air along the lee side of the jib so that the flow stays smooth past the jib power point, turbulence not occurring until past the power point of the whole (combined) aerofoil*

Fig. 6 Backwinding. The flow in this genoa has been pushed aft, causing the airflow to be directed into the lee side of the mainsail, producing turbulence and blockage. A hooked genoa leech would have the same, but smaller, effect

being drawn cleanly away by the action of the air passing round and over the lee side of the mainsail luff. This is not a particularly common fault and only really occurs when a small headsail is set at a wide sheeting angle in light winds; in brisker conditions a large slot is needed and a small jib will exert its influence properly.

CUTTERS AND TWIN-MASTED RIGS

The same principles apply to a cutter rig as to a sloop, except that there are two slots to watch for instead of one. Normally the jib and the staysail will be fairly close together, but the two sails should have been designed so as not to interfere with each other (usually by cutting the clew of the jib fairly high, to reduce any tendency to blockage in the slot). The slot between the staysail and the mainsail does not normally present any problem, because the former is relatively small.

The schooner carries the problem to the gap between her two masts, but this is usually so large that the effect is one of two sails operating independently rather than that of a second slot; unless the boat is a staysail schooner, when there are two masts, two staysails and two slots, and the combination which is set from the mainmast has to operate in the dirty wind created by that which is set from the foremast, so it has to be sheeted slightly harder. Virtually the same applies to yawls and ketches, where we can generalize to the effect that the mizzen (or jigger) provides little thrust on its own account. It operates in the dirty wind of the mainsail except when the wind is aft, so cannot expect to be particularly efficient. Its advantages lie principally in the extra bite that strapping it in can give to the helm when going to windward; the large area incorporated in the mizzen staysail for reaching purposes, which can be most useful when cruising and is not usually highly handicapped when racing; and the ability to snug down quickly to a workmanlike storm rig by dropping the mainsail completely and continuing under jib and mizzen.

LESS COMMON SAILS

It is worth mentioning here one or two of the less common sails that may be met from time to time.

The Yankee jib is a high-clewed jib, which sets in front of a staysail on a cutter (incidentally, it is not known by any special name in America). It is cut high in the clew in order not to cause blockage in the slot by too much overlap, and its sheet should bisect the angle at the clew – which usually means taking it to the counter.

The ghoster is a full-sized headsail, made of cloth weight no heavier than 2 oz, designed to take advantage of the lightest wind. It may well have no piston hanks or snap hooks, both to save weight and to make it easier to take in when the wind gets up beyond force 1. Also

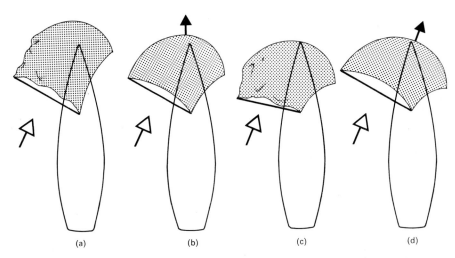

Fig. 7 The object of spinnaker-sheet adjustment is to ensure that the sail pulls forwards and not sideways. If the sheet is eased too much the luff will fall in and the whole sail will collapse (a). Correct trim on a broad reach would enable the sail to pull forward efficiently (b) but if, with the sheet trimmed correctly, the pole is then squared too far aft, the sail will collapse again (c). The most common fault in spinnaker trim is to sheet the sail too hard (d); even though the pole is correctly square to the wind, the drive of the sail is partly sideways, resulting in loss of speed

known as the drifter, the sail needs lightweight sheets and a very gentle touch when trimming so that it takes up a nice curve to accept the lightest air.

The reaching jib is a genoa-sized sail, usually with a fairly high clew, designed for reaching purposes. The canvas is half way in weight between the ghoster and the genoa. There are several special names for this kind of sail, as sailmakers try to popularize their own particular cut: blast reacher, flanker, beamer, compensator etc. The sheeting angle is well aft, which gives some twist to the sail and allows the wind to escape easily.

The quadrilateral jib is a light genoa, with a second clew (and thus a second sheet) above the first, designed to gain area within the old RORC headsail limitations. It is now banned by the IOR, largely because it is unseamanlike and confers only a slight advantage in light weather out of all proportion to the extra cost, so it was a rich man's sail.

The trysail is a triangular sail which is attached to the (main) mast for use in storm conditions; its area is about one third of the unreefed mainsail. If it is attached by slides, it should either have its own track (in case the main track is torn away) or else use parrel beads, preferably both. The foot is loose, so the sail sets without having to use the main boom which can be housed in a crutch and the trysail sheets taken over the top and to each side of it. It is not particularly close winded, but will take the boat to windward slowly.

The Swedish mainsail is another storm mainsail, which sets on both mast and boom, and is thus closer winded than the conventional trysail. Its area is about two fifths that of the unreefed mainsail, with a luff and

foot about 75 per cent of the larger sail. It loses a lot of area by virtue of having its leech cut very hollow, which also does away with the need for battens; it has a stout ring at the top instead of a vulnerable headboard. The main drawback is that it uses the boom, which can slam about in heavy weather and, indeed, may have been broken by the very circumstances that call for the use of a storm mainsail.

The fisherman staysail is a quadrilateral sail set between the two masts of a staysail schooner, and used largely for reaching because in a close-hauled condition it would be in a hopelessly dirty wind.

The mule, or back staysail, is a triangular-shaped sail which is hanked to the standing backstay of a yawl or ketch, and is sheeted to the top of the mizzen or jigger mast. It is designed to fill the gap that otherwise exists aft of the mainsail leech, but is not a very efficient sail and not really worth the bother or expense.

The mizzen staysail is a lightweight sail of 1–2 oz nylon set from the top of the mizzen or jigger mast to the heel of the mainmast, and often sheeted to the mizzen boom end. It confers considerable extra area on a broad reach and is lightly taxed by most rating rules.

– forward thrust

REACHING

When sailing off the wind the object of sail trim is to produce as much forward thrust as possible. A broad generalization can therefore be made that all sheets should be eased until the sail lifts, and then hardened slightly again. There are exceptions such as when a fully eased mainsail would be heavily BACKWINDED this is often the result of too much twist), or when a slight hardening of the mainsheet can help to reduce rhythmic rolling downwind, but the principle is correct.

TELLTALES

Most helmsmen are used to feeling a boat to windward as the wind shifts slightly when sailing CLOSE-HAULED. The wind does not cease to move about as soon as the boat starts REACHing, and constant sheet trimming is needed if full advantage is to be taken of every free puff; telltales will help in this task. These are small tufts or streamers of dark thread, about 6–8 in long, sewn at quarter, half, and three-quarter height about 10 in aft of the luff. When the airflow is smooth along both sides of the sail, in what is known as laminar flow, the telltales will stream aft on both sides of the sail; when this smooth airflow is disturbed for any reason, the telltales will start to behave erratically. Laminar flow breaks down first on the side opposite that from which the wind is striking the sail most directly. In other words, a leeward telltale will lift when the sail is sheeted too tightly and the wind is thus blowing too directly onto the weather side of the luff; a windward one will lift when the sail is eased too much so that the wind has been allowed to get too much round the lee side of the sail. The golden rule is to sheet towards a lifting telltale: ease sheets if the lee streamer is lifting, harden them if the windward ones are not streaming aft.

CLOSE-HAULED

The principle of forward thrust also applies when a boat is closehauled, but there are other factors. When reaching, a boat can maintain a steady course and play her sheets; when BEATing, the sheets are made fast and it is the tiller that is played, as the helmsman seeks to take advantage of wind shifts in order to work his boat to windward. Under these circumstances it can sometimes pay to trim sails well inboard, even up to windward, in an attempt to point high without losing too much speed; this pays best when the sea is smooth and the wind not more than force 3. Outside these conditions the sheeting base should be gradually eased and the boat sailed slightly more free so that she powers her way through the waves. Telltales are doubly useful to windward, in this case to tell the helmsman when he is pointing correctly. He should try to maintain laminar flow, and therefore needs to turn his craft so that the wind can be made to blow more freely on an erratic streamer in order to clean up the flow: luff if the leeward telltale lifts, BEAR AWAY if the windward one misbehaves. The quick memory check for streamers is 'tastes': *t*urn *a*way from or *s*heet *t*owards *e*rratic *s*treamers.

– the spinnaker

TRIM

Of all the sails the spinnaker is the most important to keep in proper trim; because it has such a large area acting from the masthead, any unnecessary side force will cause the boat to heel unduly, thus slowing her down when it should be pushing her forward. The sail is always operating when the boat is sailing free, so it is through altering the angle of the pole and tension on the sheet that advantage must be taken of wind shifts; coarse adjustment is effected through the guy and pole downhaul, while fine trim comes from the sheet. The sail is thus brought into basic trim through shifting the tack at the end of the pole, and also through keeping the two clews approximately level with the horizon so that the sail is symmetrical; the object is to ensure that the sail is open to the airflow, and this is broadly achieved by having the spinnaker pole at 90° to the apparent wind (fig. 7). More delicate trim then comes from the sheet.

Under most conditions wind flows across a spinnaker from luff to leech just as it does across a genoa, but the spinnaker does not have the advantage of the latter's straight luff and flat leech. Trim has to be careful and constant if the sail's sagging luff is not to collapse or the full-bellied leech to backwind the mainsail. The sail should be kept so that the luff is just on the point of falling in; in this way the sheet will be well-eased and the sail angled nicely forward, which in turn means that thrust will be as much forward and as little sideways as possible. If the sheet is not able to keep the spinnaker full on its own (because it cannot pull it flat enough), the guy has to be eased off in order to bring the sail back into a basic attitude where the sheet can regain fine control.

SPINNAKER SELECTION

A general-purpose spinnaker will respond to most uses where the wind is on or aft of the beam; the flat-cut reaching spinnaker comes into its own as the apparent wind freshens and moves forward of the beam. The danger, however, is that the sail will have too much belly which will lay the boat on her side on a brisk reach, throw a lot of water about but, apart from looking dramatic, will give less speed than an efficient genoa. This is particularly true in the higher wind ranges (above force 3). A rule of thumb can be stated that a reasonably flat general purpose spinnaker can be carried with advantage in a force 3 apparent wind, 5° forward of the beam for each amount by which the spinnaker is larger than the headsail that would replace it. Thus, if the ratio is 6 or 7:1 (for instance on a Soling, which is as large a difference as is usually met), the larger sail would pay with the apparent wind up to 35° forward of the beam; a ratio of about 3:1, as is common on offshore racers, brings this angle down to 15° (i.e. an apparent wind angle of 75°). Special flat-cut reaching tri-radials (variously called star-cut

sails, gennikers or spankers) can reduce this apparent wind angle to 55° for the offshore racer, and can also be more efficient under these close reaching conditions on the one-design keelboats and dinghies. Really light (ghosting) winds and anything over force 4 are, however, unsuitable for this knife-edge situation, where skilled trimming is of paramount importance.

SUBORDINATE SAILS

There are several sails that can be used with the spinnaker, the most popular of which is the big boy or blooper. This is an adaptation of a light genoa, which is set flying from the masthead on the opposite side of the boat to the spinnaker itself. The object is to fill the gap in the foretriangle, and thereby capture untapped windpower. To do this, the sail has a very deep skirt to its foot, which almost drags in the water, and a marked hollow to the luff so as to get the sail well out to leeward (some bloopers are made with a positive notch in the luff). Its halyard is

Fig. 8 Broaching. The shaded area of the hull (a) shows leeward wetted area when a boat is beating to windward. When reaching under spinnaker, the wetted area is enlarged forward (b), thus moving the CLR forward. This increases the turning arm of the force couple which has to be countered by the rudder (c) and (d). If the effect of movement of the CE to leeward under the influence of heel is also added, the forces become too much for the rudder, and the boat broaches

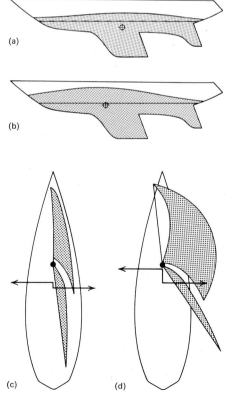

(a)

(b)

(c)   (d)

usually not hoisted all the way, once again to encourage the sail to sag off to leeward in the hope of catching wind round the leech of the mainsail. This sail only sets properly when the wind is over 8 or 9 knots and is within 30° of dead astern. When it is re-membered that a boat is not particularly efficient with the wind less than 15° off the dead aft position, it will be realized that the right conditions for the big boy are fairly limited. Even then it does not so much add to speed by direct thrust, as through the steady-ing effect it has on any tendency to roll. A side effect is that it makes the helmsman virtually blind forward.

The tallboy is another sail sometimes used with the spinnaker. Its object is to form a slot at the leading edge of the mainsail in order to clean up the airflow. To this end it is tall and narrow, and siting of the tack and clew is critical: the sail should form a forward exten-sion to the mainsail, so its tack comes aft and to windward as the wind goes astern, while the clew goes forward and to leeward, until the moment when the mainsail is eased right off and the tallboy is set athwartships.

The traditional spinnaker staysail can take various forms, from a low-cut light nylon sail hoisted from half-way up the mast and with a clew that droops until the wind lifts it clear of the deck, to a number 1 or 2 genoa set full height on the forestay. Sometimes a full hoist sail used in this manner has reef eyes some 6–10 ft (2–3 m) up the luff and leech, so that it can still be used when the wind rises to force 4 and beyond. There are boats which set a full genoa *and* an inner staysail under the spin-naker when the wind is on the quarter, but the correct interplay of halyards, sheets and guys is a delicate art, with the danger that the sail that really does the pulling (the spin-naker) will be trimmed away from its op-timum purely so that the subordinate sails can be made to set better. This is particularly true of the blooper, which is a popular sail with the average crew, because it is easily set and doused, looks dramatic, and provides an extra interest downwind; but its proper trim should not be at the expense of that of the spinnaker.

– broaching
Broaching is a manifestation of imbalance in terms of directional moments that are out of trim. It frequently occurs as a result of rhyth-mic rolling when a short-keeled boat is being sailed under spinnaker in a brisk wind, and is caused by the forces acting on the sails and the hull getting out of balance. When a boat heels under spinnaker the pull from the mast-head tends to bury the bows, which increases the wetted area of the front part of the hull and moves the centre of lateral re-sistance (CLR) forward. At the same time the centre of effort (CE) moves to leeward with the heel of the boat, so that the force

couple has a turning moment that is trying to push the bows up to windward (fig. 8). The result is a BROACH. Preventive measures open to the crew include shifting weight aft and to windward in order to raise the bows (and thus bring the CLR aft again) and reduce heel; pull hard down on main halyard and/or Cunningham hole to draw the flow, and thus the CE, forward; ease the mainsail to reduce heel still further; and finally collapse the spinnaker.

The broaching problem has been made worse by the advent of a number of light-weight centreboard offshore racing boats. These craft plane under spinnaker, but they suffer badly from broaching, to the point where they knock-down until the top of the mast touches the water. Such critical designs need to be sailed to fine tolerances, usually with one hand on the kicking strap or boom vang, so that it can be let run at the first sign of a broach. This allows the boom to sky, thus dumping wind upwards from the mainsail and easing pressure on the turning moment. A second hand must be ready on the spin-naker sheet, to collapse that as well in case dumping the mainsail should not prove enough. Even so, some of these boats can broach as often as every ten minutes, spinning completely on their sides and coming to a stop in the water; they can still average 15–20 knots for distances of 50 miles or more when the wind is right. Raking the whole rig can do much to control the balance of forces, so that CE and CLR are kept near enough to each other to enable the rudder to maintain course, unless the boat is allowed to heel excessively, thus taking the rudder partly out of the water and also offsetting the CE to leeward, thereby opening up the force couple again. Many fin and skeg boats adopt a twin headsail rig of genoa and inner staysail when the wind goes forward of the beam and above force 3; this reduces heel, thereby lessening the chance of broaching.

– checking trim
The object of proper trim is to improve boat speed. The best check of this is another boat alongside, against whom you have not gained or lost a yard for 5 minutes. The next best is an expanded scale to the speedlog, to give extra-sensitive indication of changes in speed.
HOW TO CHECK TRIM
Apart from telltales, which give a permanent indication of the airflow at the point in ques-tion, checks should be made on the sails themselves. Firstly make sure that the mast is straight on both tacks, that there is no ex-cessive forestay sag, and then that leech lines and topping lift are slack, or you will never get a true picture. Now try easing and hardening halyard or downhaul and Cun-ningham while you watch the camber in the sail (and the speed indicator or the boat you are trying to pass). Go forward and look at

each sail from leeward, sight up the genoa luff for a straight stay and draft well forward, and have a general look at the slot (par-ticularly the genoa leech for belly, curl, or hook). Ease or harden sheets, try moving fairleads, experiment with tension on the backstay. Above all, only try one change at a time and put it back if it does not improve things, or you will not know what precisely has helped if the boat picks up speed after two or three adjustments.

– trim tips
Apart from the bigger items of trim already discussed, there are other trim tips that can sometimes improve boat speed.
TRAVELLER
In light winds and smooth water haul the mainsheet traveller up to windward so that you can point the boat really high; the jib sheet fairlead should be similarly hauled inboard. When conditions are the reverse – heavy weather with choppy water – ease travellers right down to leeward and power the boat through the water.
KICKING STRAP (BOOM VANG)
It is important in all but light winds not to let the mainsail develop too much twist; firm tension on the kicking strap will stop this.
HALYARD
Always watch the shape of the sail when hoisting, and not necessarily the black measurement bands; pull a halyard hard in hard winds, and lightly in light winds. A wire luff jib should always be set up with full tension on the wire.
OUTHAUL AND DOWNHAUL
These obey the same broad rules as the hal-yard: hard in hard winds, light in light winds.
FORESTAY
No boat will go properly to windward with an unduly sagging forestay.
BACKSTAY
On most boats the backstay should be tight when going to windward (to help keep the forestay straight); it may be eased downwind.
CUNNINGHAM HOLE
One of the cheapest and most effective items of go-fast gear, the Cunningham hole should have its control line permanently rove with plenty of purchase for ease of operation (pul-leys or winch).
BARBER HAULER
Named after the two American dentist brothers, Manning and Merritt Barber, who pioneered its use on their International Lightning in 1963, this is a device for altering three-dimensionally the jib sheet lead. In its most basic form it is an eye or thimble free to run along the sheet between the fairlead and the jib clew that can be pulled downwards by a line running through the deck a short dis-tance forward of the fixed fairlead. Variations can include use of pulleys, travelling fair-leads, and adjustment inboard and outboard as well as fore and aft. Inboard trim will help

the boat point high in light winds; angling the lead more forward will give more camber low down on a reach; angling it aft will increase twist and open the slot at the head.

TELLTALES OR STREAMERS

Telltales should be attached to the luff of the sail so that they cannot catch on hanks, snap hooks, or even seams. Action to maintain laminar flow is to turn away from a streamer that is behaving erratically (luff if a leeward one is lifting and bear away vice versa), or to ease or harden sheets respectively.

JIFFY REEFING

A mainsail or genoa can be quickly reefed by lowering the sail until the reef eye at the luff can be hooked to the tack. The reef eye at the leech of a mainsail should have a line permanently rove so that it can be pulled down to the boom; a genoa needs new sheets attached at this point. The result in both cases leaves the reefed section of sail lying loose at the foot; this may be cleaned up by tying off with reef points if desired.

LOWERING SPINNAKER

Use of a spinnaker chute is limited to sails with a maximum area of 500–600 ft^2 (boats about 27 ft LOA); beyond this the loadings become too high. Lowering drill for larger sails can be speeded up by having a grab line attached to the middle of the sail; both tack and clew are allowed to fly and the sail collapses to be pulled in by the grab line as the halyard is eased.

SHEET TENSION

Sheets are often too tight. Where two boats have been sailing neck and neck for some time, with neither gaining the advantage, it may be worth easing sheets marginally in an attempt to get more forward thrust and less heeling moment. This generalization also holds good for spinnakers, where the object is always to angle the sail as much forward as possible without collapsing it.

– high-performance sailing

Modern racing boats are restricted in their sail wardrobe under various racing rules and must therefore adapt more readily than in the past. Each genoa jib on an ocean racer, for example, must be capable of being used over a wider range of wind strengths so that the restricted number of sails covers the entire range. To do this the section of the sail has to be altered; this is pre-planned by the sailmaker and instituted by the sail trimmer.

The principal controls to trim a mainsail are the halyard, the clew outhaul, the mainsheet, and the kicking strap (boom vang). In addition fine control is exercised by the luff and leech Cunninghams and the backstay and inner forestay worked in conjunction with the running backstays.

Flow is cut into the mainsail by the sailmaker and he will aim to produce a sail that will have the correct shape for light airs when the mast is held straight fore and aft and the halyard and outhaul are tensioned to remove the wrinkles from the luff and foot of the sail. This flow is removed systematically as the wind increases, the cross section of the sail becoming shallower. In addition it is necessary to move the point of maximum chord of the sail section forward in increasing wind, thereby altering the aerofoil section of the sail to suit the wind conditions. Coarse flattening of the sail is achieved by pulling the clew further out along the boom and moving the maximum chord forward by tensioning the halyard. There are, of course, limits to this – the restrictions imposed by the measurement limitations on the spars – and to overcome this Cunningham cringles are sewn into both luff and leech of the sail and each has its trimming tackle. The luff Cunningham continues the draught moving effect of the halyard; the leech Cunningham the flattening effect of the clew outhaul.

In the simplest of terms therefore the sail flattening and chord alteration are carried out together as the strength of the wind increases by hauling harder on the luff and the foot. But that is not all. The mast bend also has a dramatic effect on the shape of the sail. Much of the chord shape is cut into the sail by having a convex curve at the luff. The greater the convexity of the luff, the fuller the section. This can be reduced by inducing a bend in the mast to match the curve of the luff of the sail. Mast bend is produced by tension in the backstay and the inner forestay and control maintained by one or more running backstays. With a non-masthead rig modern yachts have two running backstays: one to the hounds and another lower down to control the bending of the spar induced by tension in the masthead single backstay.

The mast bend becomes more important in non-masthead rigs as a means of sail trim as it is possible to use it without loss of forestay tension – regrettably inevitable with a masthead forestay. The proportionally bigger mainsail of the fractional rig then becomes the more important of the two sails; greater flexibility in its trim is necessary. With a masthead rig, modern rules have reduced the mainsail to the role of a trim tab to the genoa and as such it is cut much flatter and the mast stands more or less straight in the boat. As bend of the mast reduces its vertical height above the deck, there is a natural sag in the forestay which is undesirable.

The trim of the mainsail is the way to balance the helm of a yacht. Too much power from the mainsail and the boat will have weather helm; the sail must be trimmed to provide enough weather helm for 'feel', not enough for the rudder to act as a brake.

The fine tune of a mainsail is controlled by the mainsheet, the traveller, and the kicking strap. Sails have to be trimmed to accommodate wind shear: the phenomenon that gives different angles of attack of the wind to the rig at different heights. The wind is of a slightly less acute angle to the centreline of the boat higher up the mast. For this reason some twist must be induced into the sail and the amount depends on the wind strength. There is considerable twist in light airs, which is reduced to a minimum in moderate breezes and reappears for a different reason in strong winds. In the final stages it is induced to reduce the heeling moment of the sail without losing some of its forward drive when the yacht is hard pressed.

In flat water the sail should be trimmed flatter than in a seaway as the boat will need less power to drive it through the water and it can be pointed higher. Off the wind the mainsail will be trimmed fuller, easing off the Cunninghams and some of the outhaul and halyard tensions.

To summarize the settings: in light weather to windward the halyard and outhaul are pulled to eliminate wrinkles in the sail, the traveller is up to windward of the centreline, and the mainsheet eased so that the boom is along the centreline of the boat. The leech, and therefore the twist angle, is set by the kicking-strap tension and minor adjustments to correct the set of the mainsail are made with the backstay, inner forestay, and runners. In moderate breezes the outhaul and halyard pull the sail to its maximum and the degree of flatness and chord shape is controlled with the leech and luff Cunninghams; the traveller is set on the centreline and there is much more mainsheet tension to keep the leech straight. The kicking strap controls the amount of twist and the leech can be freed by judicious use of the backstay, in conjunction with inner forestay and runners. In heavier winds the two Cunninghams will be fully trimmed in and the traveller set slightly to leeward with plenty of tension on the kicking strap. The mainsheet will then be used to feather the sail through the stronger gusts. On non-masthead rigs considerable bend will be induced in the mast by the backstay and inner forestay to remove the effect of the luff round cut into the sail and this will be controlled by the runners.

Slab reefing provides the same trimming facilities as do the Cunninghams.

All jibs and genoas are trimmed in the same basic way. It is essential to have the forestay tight to obtain the shape cut into the sail by the sailmaker. He has allowed for a small amount of sag, but more than this is detrimental as it increases the amount of draught in the sail and tends to put the maximum chord too far aft with a resultant hooking to windward of the leech.

Different weights of cloth are used for different sails, the bigger ones used in lighter weather being of lighter cloth than the smaller sails used when the wind is strong.

Greater care is therefore needed to set the light-weather sails correctly and these can be overtrimmed to their permanent detriment. Halyard tension controls the position of maximum chord, while the sheet tension controls the relative flatness of the sail and its degree of twist. In general the greater the sheet tension, the flatter the jib but the position of the sheet lead does also control the shape of the sail. Pulling the fairlead aft of its normal position would produce a sail with more twist and also keep it flatter in the lower part. The aim of obtaining the correct twist is to match the wind shear so that the angle of entry of the sail is constant throughout the luff length. The sheet lead would thus be moved aft in stronger winds and forward in light airs, but in addition it is important to match the curve of the leeward side of the mainsail with the leech of the jib to maintain constant 'slot' between the two sails.

The genoa jibs are very responsive to trim and in well-sailed racing boats one man is detailed to trim these all the time. Even as little as two knots of wind difference will demand a different sheet tension and perhaps a halyard alteration as well. The leech line too must be regularly adjusted. With greater sheet tension the leech line can be slightly eased. With less sheet, in light airs, more leech line will be needed to stop the leech from fluttering.

Off the wind sheet leads will need to go further forward and as far outboard as possible to prevent unnecessary twist in the head sails. Sails with higher-cut clews provide better average trim in off-wind conditions.

The flow of wind in a spinnaker is from leech to leech and thus the sail has the same basic trimming theory as any other. To obtain the maximum forward drive from a spinnaker, the pole should be brought aft as far as possible and the sheet trimmed against that. The sheet is eased until the weather leech begins to stall and is then trimmed home slightly.

See also HEAVY-WEATHER SAILING; HIGH-SPEED SAILING; MASTS AND RIGGING; RIGS; SAIL CARE; SAIL DESIGN AND MATERIALS.

Samson post
A strong post forward for securing the anchor cable.

Sandglass
A glass vessel with two chambers joined by a narrow channel through which a quantity of sand, powdered marble or metal filings flows from one to the other, thus measuring an interval of time, after which the vessel may be reversed to measure the next interval.
The sandglass, *dyoll*, or *horloge de mer*, is mentioned in ships' inventories as early as 1295. Before the introduction of reasonably reliable spring-driven clocks and watches in the eighteenth century, they were the standard means of timekeeping at sea and varied from 4-hour glasses to quarter-minute glasses; the most usual sizes were perhaps the half-hour glass, eight turns of which accompanied by the appropriate number of bell strokes marked the duration of a watch, and the half-minute glass for timing the run of the LOG and line. A quarter-minute glass was substituted when the ship's speed was more than about 5 knots. These 'long' and 'short' glasses continued in general use at sea until log and line themselves were superseded by the taffrail log late in the nineteenth century.

Satellite navigation
Position determination by means of artificial earth satellites. The system is an outgrowth of early satellite tracking, the Doppler effect measured at a known position being used in reverse. The Project Transit development produced the operational (U.S.) Navy Navigation Satellite System (Transit) in 1964.

The system consists of about four satellites in 108-min circular polar orbits 1100 km above the earth, four tracking stations, a computing centre and two injection stations. Global coverage is provided, with about 15–20 fixes daily. Very low and very high passes generally prove unsatisfactory. Tracking data are sent to the computing centre for updating of the orbital information. Extrapolations for the next 16 hr are sent from the injection stations to the satellites at intervals of about 12 hr. The satellites transmit current orbital data at 2-min intervals, using two frequencies, 150 and 400 mHz, to reduce the error caused by ionospheric refraction.

A suitably equipped vessel tracks a satellite during a pass (about 6 to 18 min), and an onboard computer determines the vessel's latitude and longitude. At a stationary point, error results from orbital prediction error, propagation anomalies, antenna height uncertainty, and measurement noise. The total rms (root mean square) error is about 20–30 m for a single pass and about 5 m for an average of 20–25 fixes, assuming ideal conditions. Under way, the error is greater. A maximum error of about 450 m per knot speed error occurs on a north or south course.

Because of high cost of user equipment, intermittent fix availability, and the need for accurate velocity information, navigation satellites are little used except by those requiring high accuracy, such as warships and survey vessels.

Other techniques have been proposed, to reduce cost of user equipment by transferring some of the complexities to the satellite or ground stations, to provide more frequent fixes, and surveillance capability. The techniques most frequently suggested are measurement of distance, distance difference, and elevation angle. Systems combining satellites and ground transmitters have also been proposed. Value of the existing system could be enhanced by increasing the number of satellites and adding communication capability. *See also* NAVIGATION

Scandalize
A way of temporarily shortening sail in gaff-rigged vessels by hauling up the tack and lowering the peak.

Scantlings *see* HULLS

Scend, send
Upward movement of a vessel due to wave motion in a seaway.

Schooner *see* RIGS: Fore-and-aft rigs

Scope
Length of anchor cable used by a vessel at anchor.

Scupper
A cavity in the bulwarks for the water to drain through.

Sea anchor
A canvas drogue or other arrangement designed to reduce a vessel's speed in heavy weather and keep her head-on to the seas.

Seamark
A conspicuous object serving as a guide or warning to mariners. The term may be applied to any such object, whether offshore or on land, but is generally restricted to objects in or near the water; the term landmark being applied to objects ashore. Seamarks may be either natural or man-made. A natural seamark might be a prominent rock, islet or, sometimes, a bold promontory at the water's edge. Several kinds of man-made seamarks have been established to aid navigation.

A lighthouse displays a major navigational light. The appearance depends on factors that include location, importance of the light, and its susceptibility to storm damage. The differences in appearance help in daylight identification.

A lightship is a distinctively marked vessel stationed at a designated point and displaying a prominent navigational light. The distinctive marking serves as an aid to daylight identification. A light vessel is usually anchored some distance offshore where building a lighthouse would be impractical.

A beacon is an unmanned secondary structure at a fixed point in the water or along its edge. It may be either lighted or unlighted; the latter is sometimes called a day beacon.

A buoy is a relatively small floating object anchored at a designated point to mark a channel, shoal, wreck, anchorage, or to serve some other purpose. Buoys are of various size and shape, and may be lighted or unlighted. They are the most numerous of seamarks, and are generally painted and designated in accordance with a well-established system. The two principal systems used, with local variations, are the lateral and the cardinal. The former is best adapted to an area in which channels are the principal feature; the latter is particularly appropriate in an area abounding in hazards, the types and markings of the buoys being related to the cardinal direction of the nearest danger.

A thorough knowledge of various types of seamarks and their locations, characteristics, and purposes in the area to be traversed is essential to reliable, safe navigation. *See also* BUOYAGE AND BUOYAGE SYSTEMS; LIGHTHOUSES AND LIGHT VESSELS

Sea mile *see* NAUTICAL MILE

Seawanhaka Cup *see* YACHT RACING: Major races and series

Seaway
A moderately rough sea.

Secondary port (subordinate station) *see* TIDES AND TIDAL STREAMS

Seizing
Binding together, for instance one rope to another, or parts of ropes. *See also* ROPEWORK: Splices

Self-steering gear
Essentially self-steering devices relieve the helmsman of the necessity to steer the boat in order to maintain course. This enables yachts to be sailed with much smaller crews, or even single-handed.

In the days of sail both fishermen and cargo carriers were used to balancing the sails set so that the vessel would maintain course, as was the practice of the American seaman Captain Joshua Slocum when he sailed alone around the world in the famous *Spray* in 1895–8. Today, however, the term self-steering means in effect getting the boat to steer herself by methods other than just setting the sails to obtain balance.

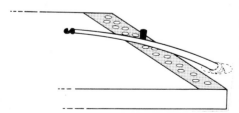

Fig. 1 A simple device used up to about 1940 was a board, with a row of holes, fitted under the tiller. By placing a peg in a suitable hole the tiller could be secured in a set position

Until World War II it was common to find in cruising yachts, as well as in small commercial vessels with tiller steering, a device, generally fitted under the tiller, that secured the tiller in a set position to enable the sails as trimmed to hold the course for perhaps half an hour or more. Such vessels required very little to keep them on course even with changes of wind strength and sea state.

– wind-vane steering gear
Model sailing yachts have long been fitted with self-steering devices, generally using either a sheet leading from the sail to the tiller or a wind vane like a small mizzen which is free to revolve and stays dead downwind, like a weathercock. The vane is linked with the tiller and when the craft goes off course the wind blows on one side of the vane applying pressure, through the linkage, to the tiller which steers the craft back to the chosen course, when the vane weathercocks once more. Sheet-to-tiller gears are not satisfactory downwind unless two headsails are used and so yacht research has concentrated on the wind-vane method.

Perhaps the first yachtsman to have produced a seaworthy wind-vane gear was the French painter and author Marin-Marie (C. de St-F. M. M. P. Durand) in his yacht *Winibelle* in 1938. H. G. Hasler, a former Royal Marine colonel, started designing vane gears in 1953. In 1957 the Amateur Yacht Research Society published *Self Steering*, a useful summary of most of the ideas put forward, including a lot of new ones, for making yachts steer themselves. It was, however, the first *Observer* Singlehanded Transatlantic Race in 1960 which brought the possibilities more to the general attention of the yachting community. For this first race, of which he was the winner, the renowned English deep-sea sailor (Sir) Francis Charles Chichester (1901–72) designed an enlarged model-yacht-type gear with a vane connected direct to the tiller.

HORIZONTAL-AXIS VANE
To overcome the loss of pressure as the vane swings towards the wind, an alternative form of vane is pivoted on a horizontal axis, like a windmill with a single sail, exactly balanced with a weight so that it stands vertical when the wind blows along its edge. When the wind blows on to one side of the vane at an angle, the vane will be blown over and power can be used as it swings, yet the angle of the wind does not change and the only loss of force is due to the slightly reducing area of vane exposed to the wind. The horizontal wind vane connected direct to the tiller will provide enough power to maintain a well-balanced yacht on course. A great number of gears of this type are in use all over the world on cruising yachts of all sizes.

WATER POWER
A wind-operated steering gear that will work

when the sails do not balance the yacht, and will maintain course while sails are changed, will have to provide more power than is obtainable from a simple wind vane. One solution is to use the power available from the water flowing past the yacht to do the work and use the wind simply to indicate direction.

One of the original and most satisfactory ways to use water power is to fit a trim tab to the main rudder. This is easy when the rudder is mounted on the transom, but much more difficult when it is below the counter; in the latter case alternative methods will probably prove more satisfactory. A trim tab is a streamlined blade fitted to the after edge of the rudder and steered in the opposite direction to the main rudder. Many designers hold that the trim tab should be a certain percentage of the area of the main rudder, but estimates vary and nearly all gears of this type seem to work well. The wind vane is coupled to the tab by links that pivot just aft of the main rudder bearings. This linkage difference is important; when the yacht swings off course the vane moves and the movement is transmitted through the linkage to the trim tab. The tab is moved out of line with the water flow and the pressure on the tab moves the main rudder to return the yacht to her chosen course. By having the axis of the tab control aft of the main rudder pintles, the angle of the tab is reduced when the rudder moves so that the main rudder does not swing hard over but only moves until the control links balance the vane and tab. If the yacht swings further off course, the vane will apply more angle to the tab. This reduction of the tab angle as the rudder moves prevents wild swinging alterations and enables the yacht to settle on course, probably with a small amount of weather helm.

When the rudder mounted below the yacht is of the balanced type it is probable that a wind vane will be able to maintain the yacht on course, especially if there is little friction in the bearings. When the rudder is mounted against a SKEG or keel below the hull other means of using the power available from the water can be used. Vane-gear manufacturers mass produce units that can be fitted to most yachts and they use a vane to move a streamlined blade in the water. Like the wind vanes there are two ways to hinge the steering servo blade. One is to have the blade as a second rudder well balanced and connected directly to the wind vane. Commercial gears of this type are made into a neat, strong unit that can be lifted off the yacht when not needed. It has the advantages that there is no connection or alteration to the usual steering gear and it can be used if the main gear is damaged or if there is wheel steering.

The other way is to pivot the servo blade horizontally, in which case a more complicated linkage is needed to connect it to the

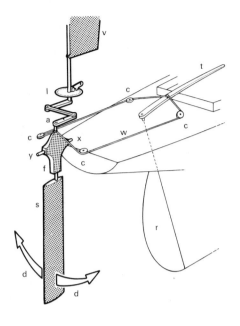

Fig. 2 The mechanics of a typical pendulum-servo gear. The servo blade (s) is hung vertically over the stern with its shaft passing through the servo frame (f). It can be turned like a rudder by the servo tiller (a). The servo frame has fore and aft bearings (x, y) that allow the whole assembly to swing from side to side like a pendulum. Steering ropes (w) are connected to the top of the servo frame and lead to the tiller (t) through sheaves (c). The vane (v) is free to weathercock in its shaft for manual steering, but when the latch (l) is engaged, any movement of the vane will cause the servo blade to turn through the linkage. The flow of water past the immersed blade forces it to swing sideways (arrows, d), pulling the steering ropes, tiller and consequently the rudder (r), thus bringing the yacht back on course

wind vane. The servo blade (sometimes described as a pendulum servo) hangs down into the water and is adjusted so that it is stable and remains fore and aft when the vane is not connected. The blade hinge has to be very strong as the loads imposed on an angled blade moving quickly through the water are huge; this means that almost un-limited power is available for steering and, unlike the trim tab on the rudder, the servo blade steers in the same direction as the main rudder so that there is no extra drag to slow the yacht. Typically a quadrant is fitted to the upper end of the swinging blade so that steering lines can convert the rocking move-ment of the blade to steering movement at the tiller and remain taut. This type of gear was designed and developed by H. G. Hasler. As with all the other gears, the links between the wind vane and the servo blade must be so

arranged that the blade comes back to the fore-and-aft position in line with the water flow as it moves from midships and vertical. When the blade reaches the hard-over posi-tion, a stop at its leading edge must remove the angle to the water flow otherwise the blade or the tiller will break.

Some gears have a servo blade with a hori-zontal pivot to provide power for steering; most popular of these is probably the Aries gear, which uses a horizontal wind vane rather than the vertical vane employed by Hasler. The Aries gear uses a neat, strong but rather heavy cast-metal housing to contain the servo-blade pivot and the rods that link the vane to the blade. Another early gear using a swinging blade and horizontal vane was developed by M. F. Gunning. Here the servo blade is divided into two parts and the vane is linked to the after part in the same way as a rudder and trim tab. Linkage allows the blade to swing sideways and steering lines are led to the yacht's normal tiller or rudder head.

CONTROLS

With all automatic self-steering devices it is essential that the gear can be disengaged and manual steering resumed immediately. The usual arrangement is a light line that holds a lock pin; this releases the wind vane so that it is free to act as a weathervane or, in the case of a horizontal pivot vane, to blow over with-out harm. With the vane disconnected, the servo blade or trim tab will line up with the water flow unless the yacht goes astern. Some gears need to have their blades locked before going astern. With a trim tab on the rudder blade there is often the choice of being able to lock the tab so that it acts as part of the rud-der area, to work the tab by hand to steer the yacht, or to secure the rudder and steer with the tab only.

To engage a wind-operated gear it is only necessary to steady the yacht onto the chosen course and connect the vane to the tab or servo blade. If the yacht settles a few degrees off course the relative position of the wind vane to the yacht is altered – usually by turning a worm gear by means of an endless line which leads to a convenient steering position. With home-built gears it is quite common to use two flat circular disks with either rows of holes in each or slots around the edge. The release pin is inserted by hand into two holes that line up when the yacht is on course and course is altered by removing the pin, altering the angle of the vane relative to the yacht, and inserting the pin through another pair of holes. This system means that someone has to go aft to alter course, but the pin can be released from the normal steering position.

To alter course using gears where the vane is connected directly to the tiller requires con-siderably more patience; in this case the

pressure available from the vane has to be matched to the pressure on the tiller needed to maintain course. The vane is set up when the sails have been adjusted so that the yacht is maintaining a reasonable course and the lines from the vane can be adjusted along the tiller to set the leverage and thus the load. Shock cord can be used to compensate for steady weather helm if necessary, but if this is used adjustments will be needed for changes in wind speed; if the vane lines only are used the course should remain steady even if the wind strength varies. A further adjustment to horizontal-wind-vane steering gears is obtain-able by altering the amount of the vane counterbalance weight or by lengthening the arm holding the weight, which has the same effect. By increasing the weight the vane will tend to return to the upright position more rapidly and this in turn brings the rudder back to midships. This slows down the swing back on to the chosen course and reduces any tendency to oversteer.

When the wind is used to steer the navigator has two problems. Since it is the angle set on the vane relative to the fore-and-aft line that maintains the course, any change in wind direction must alter the course steered. Fur-ther, it is the apparent wind blowing across the deck of the yacht and not the true wind over the sea that is used to steer. With most yachts the boat speed will not increase stead-ily in proportion to the wind speed, so that a yacht set on course and making 3 knots with a 7-knot breeze will make a different course by compass when the wind increases to 14 knots, although the relative wind direction past the vane remains constant. This applies espe-cially to a fast yacht such as a multihull, running with the wind on the quarter, for the yacht will surge forward which brings the apparent wind forward towards the beam. Any wind-controlled gear will apply helm to bear away from the wind and this will result in wild swings across the ocean and perhaps a GYBE.

A partial solution to this problem has been built into some gears by allowing the servo blade to swing aft as the yacht speed increases as she surges forward. This holds the gear and helm in the midship position until the speed drops back and the vane can again operate.

The off-course alarm is an aid that is avail-able to warn anyone using automatic steering devices of a deviation from the correct course. Most systems have a time delay and can be set to allow the yacht to swing to either side of the course in heavy weather without setting off the alarm bell.

– electric steering gear

There are nowadays a number of electrically powered steering systems in which the course to steer can either be related to the earth's magnetic field or to the wind by using a small vane to sense wind direction. Many gears

The vane steering gear used by Alec Rose on Lively Lady – *seen here arriving at Spithead at the end of his circumnavigation in 1968*

give the option to switch from magnetic to wind as required; the wind vane will be best for making progress to windward as the yacht's course will vary to take advantage of small wind changes and the yacht will settle to a more constant angle of heel. For other courses the magnetic field will keep the yacht pointing in the required direction, thus saving distance – and worry for the navigator.

The current requirement of electric steering gears can be greatly reduced by arranging the unit to steer a trim tab on the main rudder or a swinging servo blade. As the power to do the steering is now taken from the water, and the energy used is helping to steer the yacht, the power saved does not cause drag.

Semi-diameter

Half the angle at the observer subtended by the sun or moon, for which SEXTANT observations of the upper or lower limb are corrected. *See* ASTRONOMICAL NAVIGATION

Serve

A rope is served by binding marline or small stuff round it as a protection.

Set

(1) To hoist sail; (2) the direction in which a craft is moved by the water, generally due to tidal stream or current.

Sextant

An instrument for measuring angles in which one object is brought into coincidence with the image of the other in a mirror that can be rotated over a graduated arc. The great advantage of the sextant on board ship is that when this coincidence has been obtained it is not affected by small movements of the observer's eye or the instrument itself.

The sextant is a direct development of HADLEY'S QUADRANT, and in a form that could measure lunar distances in excess of 90° was suggested by Captain John Campbell of the Royal Navy in 1757. With modern improvements it has remained the standard instrument not only for astronomical observations but also for measuring horizontal angles in navigation and surveying.

The frame of the sextant carries a small telescope and the half-silvered horizon glass. When the reflecting surfaces of the index mirror and horizon glass are parallel, the direct and reflected images of a single object coincide and the pointer on the index arm should read zero. At any other setting the angle measured is double the angle traversed by the index arm; the 'sextant' arc is therefore graduated so as to read 120°, or rather more. To measure the ALTITUDE of the sun or a star its reflected image is 'brought down' to the sea horizon; tinted glass shades are interposed to reduce both to an acceptable brightness.

In the past, sextants were often used by surveyors ashore when, in the absence of a sea horizon, an 'artificial horizon', a truly horizontal reflecting surface, was employed to observe the altitude of heavenly bodies. The sextant measures the angle between the body and its reflection, i.e. twice the altitude. Such a surface is provided by levelling screws and a spirit level. An artificial horizon is occasionally useful at sea when the weather is very calm and the sea horizon obscured. Rougher measurements of altitude can be made with a bubble attachment for the sextant, a reflection of the bubble being brought into coincidence with the object reflected in the index mirror. *See also* ASTRONOMICAL NAVIGATION

Shake

A longitudinal crack in a mast or spar.

Sheave

The wheel in a block or spar.

Sheepshank *see* ROPEWORK: Bends and hitches

Sheer

The upward curve of the gunwale or top strake towards the bow and stern. *See also* HULLS: Construction components

Sheerstrake

The topmost plank of the topsides of a vessel.

Sheet *see* MASTS AND RIGGING: Glossary

Sheet (becket) bend *see* ROPEWORK: Bends and hitches

Ship

In the strict sense, a three-masted, square-rigged sailing vessel. *See also* RIGS: Square rigs

Shoulder-of-mutton sail *see* RIGS: Fore-and-aft rigs

Shroud *see* MASTS AND RIGGING: Glossary

Sidereal hour angle (SHA)

HOUR ANGLE measured westward from the First Point of ARIES

Sight

The observation of the ALTITUDE, and sometimes AZIMUTH, of a heavenly body in order to obtain a POSITION LINE.

Sight reduction *see* ASTRONOMICAL NAVIGATION; NAVIGATION: Under sail

Single-handed sailing

Single-handed passages under sail have no doubt been made ever since man first used the wind as a means of propulsion; many such

A marine sextant in use. The principles of the instrument are illustrated on p. 14

voyages were probably the result of accident or necessity. Short-handed small trading and working craft were common all over Europe, often manned by a man and a boy, and without doubt many passages were undertaken by the skipper alone. It is probable too that Polynesian and Micronesian navigators made notable solo voyages.

The first recorded single-handed ocean passage in a yacht was made in 1876 by a Danish-born American, Alfred Johnson, a Grand Banks fisherman who sailed his 20-footer *Centennial* from Nova Scotia to Abercastle in Pembrokeshire, South Wales, in 46 days. Although Johnson was not sponsored, his boat was named *Centennial* to celebrate the centenary of the American Declaration of Independence.

Centennial was a 20 ft × 5 ft 10 in (6 m × 1.8 m) dory, decked in except for a small cockpit and rigged as a gaff cutter with the addition of a small square sail and she carried internal ballast and had only a 12-in (305-mm) freeboard when laden. Johnson's crossing was not without incident. He lost many of his provisions in an early gale, was capsized and remained inverted for some time in another gale, losing his stove and soaking his bedding and the remainder of his food. After obtaining more provisions from a passing ship he finally made his landfall in South Wales, later sailing to Liverpool to

have his boat shipped back to America for the Great Philadelphia Exhibition, no doubt to benefit there from his success.

Others soon followed, many in boats that today would be considered totally unsuited to ocean crossing. In 1882, after a previous single-handed passage from British Columbia to Hawaii, the American Bernard Gilboy set off again by himself in a decked-in 18-footer *Pacific* to sail non-stop to Australia. He had, apparently, many adventures and after being at sea for 162 days was picked up, exhausted by hunger, by a ship only 160 miles from his destination.

The first single-handed transatlantic race was in 1891 and was between the Americans Si Lawlor and William Andrews (both had previously crossed the Atlantic in small craft, but with crew). Their boats, only 15 ft (4.6 m) long, were called *Sea Serpent* (Lawlor) and *Mermaid* (Andrews). Lawlor won the race, which started in Boston, in 45 days. The same pair raced again in 1892, this time to Spain. Andrews sailed a 14-ft 6-in (4.4-m) collapsible craft *Sapolio* and took 69 days, including a stop in the Azores, but Lawlor was lost at sea.

The size and type of boat sailed in these crossings make it obvious that they were stunts rather than serious single-handed sailing in seaworthy yachts. There was an air of circus about the attempts and history does not record how many single-handers did not arrive for each one who succeeded.

In 1895 a voyage took place that was to lay the foundation for future generations of single-handers. Although previous attempts had been made by some fine seamen, it was not until Captain Joshua Slocum and *Spray* came together that the reliable combination of single-handed seaman and good seaboat made numerous successful long distance single-handed passages. Slocum was not out for money or glory; he sailed single-handed because he enjoyed it. He set out from Yarmouth, Nova Scotia, on 24 April and after a very fast (29 days at sea) crossing to Gibraltar, turned back on his tracks to head across the South Atlantic toward South America. He was not attempting a non-stop circumnavigation (that would not happen for many years), but all the same he was at sea often for considerable periods of time. He sailed east to west through the Magellan Straits before heading across the Pacific. He completed the first solo circumnavigation in 1898, arriving back in Boston on 27 June after more than 46 000 miles' sailing, a feat that would still be applauded by yachtsmen today.

Spray was a heavily built 36-ft 9-in (12-m) gaff yawl (the 'jigger' mizzen was added in Brazil on the way round) with 14-ft beam, which Slocum bought as a near wreck and rebuilt before starting on his voyage. He was

able, especially after fitting the mizzen, to make her self-steer well, an ability lacked by many modern yachts, which require special self-steering gears.

On his return Slocum wrote his classic *Sailing Alone Around the World* (first published in 1901). Although he made further passages both in *Spray* and other craft, he never attempted any kind of follow-up to his circumnavigation. He was finally lost at sea sailing his beloved *Spray*.

Others followed Slocum round the world single-handed in succeeding years. By the early 1900s there was hardly a sea or ocean that had not been crossed by single-handed yachtsmen. Such men as the Canadian, John C. Voss, the American Harry Pidgeon, the Frenchman Alain Gerbault, and the American William Albert Robinson became well known in their day for their various voyages. Over shorter distances more were trying their hand at solo sailing and the single-hander became accepted as a breed of yachtsman, albeit still an unusual one.

If it was the Americans who achieved most of the firsts in single-handed sailing, it was the British who brought it more into the public eye in the mid-twentieth century. Although single-handers had been travelling the oceans and seas of the world since Slocum's time, the novelty had worn off. It was not until Colonel H. G. Hasler proposed an east to west single-handed transatlantic race in 1959 in order to 'encourage the development of craft and equipment suitable for short-handed sailing' that public interest began to increase. Among the five competitors who started the race in June 1960 – the race became the first of the Royal Western/*Observer* Singlehanded Transatlantic Races (OSTAR), run at four-yearly intervals – was Francis Chichester sailing the 39-ft 7-in (12-m) sloop *Gipsy Moth III*. He went on to win the event from Plymouth to the Ambrose Light Vessel off New York in 40 days, with 'Blondie' Hasler second in 48 days in his modified, junk-rigged Folkboat *Jester*. In 1962 Chichester again set out to try and complete the same course in under 30 days. He knocked 7 days off his previous time but still missed the magic 30-day figure. It was not until the 1964 OSTAR that Chichester was able to have another try and this time he made the crossing (the course was now to Newport, Rhode Island) with only three minutes in hand on his 30-day target. He was, however, beaten into second place by the Frenchman Eric Tabarly who had arrived nearly three days earlier, sailing the 44-ft (13.4-m) *Pen Duick II*.

By this time single-handed sailing had caught the public imagination, with Chichester becoming a household name and Tabarly being awarded the Legion of Honour. Another competitor in the 1964 race, later to become almost as well known as Chichester, was Alec Rose, who finished the race in 36 days in his solid, comfortable cruising boat *Lively Lady* in which he later completed a remarkable circumnavigation.

During the course of the 1964 OSTAR Chichester realized that in future single-handed races and fast passages would be made in a different breed of boat from *Gipsy Moth III*. Accordingly, with the backing of Lord Dulverton, a new, specialized boat, *Gipsy Moth IV* was built. At 44 ft (13.4 m) long she was larger than her predecessor and on 27 August 1967 Chichester set off from Plymouth in an attempt to circle the world, following the route of the old clippers and stopping only in Australia. The fact that he achieved the passage would be enough, but he was 65 at the time and by the time he arrived back in Plymouth he was a national hero and was knighted by the Queen.

Sir Francis Chichester rekindled interest in single-handed sailing and others since then have followed his track round the world, including Alec Rose who also received a hero's welcome on arrival in Plymouth. The French meanwhile continued to develop specialized racing single-handed craft. Tabarly entered the 1968 OSTAR in such a boat, the aluminium trimaran *Pen Duick IV*. He retired, however, after structural failures and the Briton Geoffrey Williams won in *Sir Thomas Lipton*.

It was clear that it would only be a matter of time before the next step in epic single-handed voyages would be taken, a non-stop solo circumnavigation. In 1968 the London *Sunday Times* announced a race for its Golden Globe trophy. The course was to be a west–east non-stop solo circumnavigation via the great capes of Good Hope, Leeuwin, and Horn. A number of boats were prepared for the race and yet only one actually finished the course, Robin Knox-Johnston's heavy 32-ft (9.75-m) ketch *Suhaili*, a pure cruising boat rather than an ocean greyhound. He took 313 days and despite the fact that he won the race, was not the first to 'tie the knot'. That was achieved by the Frenchman Bernard Moitessier sailing the 39-ft (12-m) steel ketch *Joshua*. He was a competitor in the Golden Globe race and by the time he had rounded Cape Horn was clearly set to win. However, instead of returning to Plymouth he chose to sail on, finally making his landfall at Tahiti after sailing non-stop one and a half times round the world. Somewhat of a 'loner' and philosopher, Moitessier abandoned the race because he wanted to reject Western values in exchange for a simpler life in the Pacific islands. *The Long Way* (London and New York 1974) is an account of his voyage and another classic of single-handed sailing.

It now seemed that the ultimate peak in single-handed sailing had been conquered; others still tried to achieve new 'firsts'. The

Scot Chay Blyth sailed the 59-ft (18-m) ketch *British Steel* non-stop round the world in the wrong direction – that is against the prevailing winds and currents. David Lewis attempted to circumnavigate Antarctica, was twice dismasted and survived only through his excellent seamanship; an account was published under the title *Ice Bird* (London and New York 1976). The Frenchman Alain Colas took the trimaran *Manureva* (Tabarly's ex *Pen Duick IV*) round the world in a record 167 days at sea. Tabarly himself was breaking records on the Pacific crossing in his revolutionary, water-ballasted monohull *Pen Duick V*, taking only 39 days. New records were being and will continue to be broken. Other yachtsmen, too numerous to mention, sailed across oceans and round the world at a more sedate pace, satisfied purely by being alone and masters of their own situation.

Although it is true that single-handed, long-distance sailing has become more popular in recent years because of the increase in numbers of people taking part in sailing, and that the success of most of the voyages is largely due to the tremendous advances in yacht design and construction since Slocum's day, it is also true that modern cruising-yacht design and cruising-equipment innovation owes a very great deal to single-handed sailing.

It was long accepted that offshore racing provided a proving ground for new ideas and designs. The sort of intensive and tough testing a craft or her equipment received during the course of an ocean race meant that any poor or inadequate boats or gear were soon weeded out and the cruising yachtsman benefited as new ideas spread from racing to cruising design. In recent years, however, racing yachts have become increasingly specialized, with the result that today the boats, equipment, and techniques developed for racing are having less and less impact on the cruising world.

The very fact that he is alone means that the single-hander has to use every method available to make the task of sailing his boat easier and thus conserve his energy, as his craft may well be designed for a crew of several. In addition, apart from a few highly developed single-handed craft, most boats undertaking long-distance solo passages are much closer to the modern cruising yacht than is today's racing yacht. Hence any ideas, designs or equipment developed are more likely to benefit the cruising yachtsman than the by-products of modern racing.

The first and most obvious single item of equipment to stem directly from single-handed sailing was the SELF-STEERING GEAR. Although model yachts had been using such gears for many years, it was H. G. Hasler who evolved systems suitable for use on offshore yachts and his ideas are still the basis of most modern self-steering gears. Having a piece of

Eric Tabarly (top left), *the French yachtsman, in one of the series of yachts he called* Pen Duick

Sir Francis Chichester's last yacht, Gypsy Moth V (left) *in which he attempted 4000 miles in 20 days, missing his target by just one day*

Robin Knox-Johnston aboard Suhaili, *a somewhat old-fashioned but very well-balanced ketch* (top)

Manureva (*ex* Pen Duick IV) *at the start of the 1978 Route du Rhum race, during which she and Alain Colas were lost at sea* (above)

equipment on board that will steer a boat accurately in all weathers is the equivalent to having another (tireless) crew member, an asset appreciated by the fully crewed yacht as much as by the single-hander. Easily handled rigs have also stemmed from single-handed sailing; Hasler provided another example of his ingenuity by adapting the CHINESE RIG for use on modern yacht hulls. His *Jester*, now owned by Michael Richey, has successfully crossed the Atlantic nine times under Chinese rig and the rig itself is gaining popularity on production cruising boats.

Less quantifiable than actual equipment (although equally important) developed through experience of single-handed sailing are the techniques and systems evolved by the single-hander. He has to find the easiest and quickest methods of doing everything on board, whether changing a sail or taking a sun sight, and in time his own systems will evolve. Perhaps the fact that he is alone makes him more analytical when considering problems, or perhaps the true single-hander is naturally more inventive than someone who sails with a crew, but there is little doubt that a well-thought-out single-handed yacht is a far more efficient, and therefore safer, machine than most crewed cruising yachts. If there is a way the single-hander can reef a sail quickly without leaving the safety of his cockpit he will find it, whereas on the crewed yacht there is enough manpower for more conventional methods to be adhered to.

Although the record of single-handed races is comparatively good, at least as far as collision is concerned, there are those who object to the sport on the grounds that it contravenes the Collision Regulations, and more particularly Rule 5, which deals with the question of lookout. Although government action, perhaps taken internationally, is possible, it seems more likely that the view will prevail that to ban single-handed sailing would make little or no contribution to safety at sea and would impose an intolerable burden on whatever forces were used to enforce the ban. The single-handed sailor, provided he is properly trained, should be able to keep alert when shipping is about, and in the open ocean the risk of an encounter is sufficiently remote to warrant some relaxation of the lookout.

No attempt has been made to try to suggest the reasons why anyone should choose to sail by himself; they are too numerous and individual. No doubt some do it for gain or glory, while others see the achievement as a challenge; many sail alone simply for the enjoyment or because they find their peace in being self-sufficient and alone for weeks or months at sea. *See also* SELF-STEERING GEAR

Skeg
Originally a short length of keel projecting beyond the sternpost to protect the rudder when grounding. Today, skegs are fitted to fin-keel yachts both to protect the rudder and stabilize steering.

Skysail
The topmost sail, above the royal, in a square-rigged ship.

Skywave
A radio signal received by one or more reflections from the ionosphere.

Slack water
The moment at the turn of the tide when the speed of the tidal stream is zero.

Slamming loading *see* HULLS: Scantlings

Sleepers *see* HULLS: Construction components

Sloop
A fore-and-aft-rigged vessel with one mast and setting a single jib.

Smack
A fore-and-aft-rigged vessel used for inshore fishing.

Snatch block
A single-SHEAVE block with a hinged opening that allows the BIGHT of a line to be taken in instead of reeving the end. Used widely for sheets that require different leads according to the sail being used.

Soldier's wind *see* FAIR WIND

Sole
The cabin floor. *See also* HULLS: Construction components

Sonic depth-finding
Sonar is an ultrasonic instrument for finding and fixing submerged objects such as submarines, fish shoals, rocks and wrecks (echo-ranging), and for recording the depth (echo-sounding). The word is an acronym for *so*und *na*vigation and *r*anging and supersedes asdic, a term that denoted echo-ranging systems only. In principle, sound pulses at some selected frequency, concentrated into a narrow beam, are transmitted into the water at regular intervals, either horizontally or vertically. The echoes returned by objects in the way of the beam are amplified and recorded against a time scale initiated with the transmission. As the speed of sound in water is constant within narrow limits the interval between transmission and echo gives the distance, or depth. Selecting the optimum frequency for any particular purpose involves a compromise between the conflicting requirements of range performance and discrimination. For the former a low frequency is needed as absorption per unit length increases with frequency. On the other hand, the latter calls for a narrow beam and a short pulse, both of which are best achieved with a high frequency.

– echo-ranging
The loss of the *Titanic* in 1912 after striking an iceberg first directed attention to the possibility of underwater detection by ultrasonic echoes, but it was the urgent problem of locating submarines in World War I that provided the real impetus. The first design, using the quartz-sandwich transducer devised by the French physicist, Paul Langevin, was undergoing sea trials when that war ended. Development continued in secret and 30 years later, after its perfection in World War II, the principle was first applied to commercial needs, initially for whale tracking and later for pelagic fish detection. It has more recently become a valuable adjunct to the echo-sounder for hydrographic and geological survey. Sonar performance, when the beam is directed horizontally, is critically affected by sea conditions because the exact speed of sound in water depends upon pressure, temperature, and salinity, the first two of which vary with depth. The outgoing wavefront is thus deflected and the beam bent downwards or upwards to be reflected from the bottom or the surface, leaving shadow zones that can alter from hour to hour. These effects can sometimes be mitigated by lowering the transducer in the water (VDS), but this involves a knowledge of the sound-velocity gradient in order to apply it to a computer for analysis of the sound-ray paths in the prevailing conditions. These aids, however, are too costly for commercial use.

The method of searching is to alter the bearing of the transducer by a few degrees between successive transmissions until the whole sector ahead of the ship has been covered; the process is then repeated. Echoes received are heterodyned to an audible frequency and amplified on a loudspeaker. They are also applied, in the form of electrical pulses, via a moving pen synchronized with the transmission, to the recorder paper, which is chemically impregnated to show a mark whenever a current is passed through it. The displacement of the pen at the moment at which the echo marks the paper gives a measure of the range of the object. The paper chart is drawn slowly forward at right angles to the pen's travel so that successive echoes from any particular target form a continuous trace, the slope of which gives the rate of approach. The rate of searching is limited by the speed of sound. It can be greatly increased, however, by a technique known as within-pulse scanning in which the whole of the search sector is covered with each transmission and then scanned for echoes by a narrow receiving beam that is electronically steered back and forth at very high speed throughout the listening period. All the echoes received are then displayed in their correct positions relative to the ship at the centre on a cathode-ray tube, as with radar. Somewhat similar results can be achieved by transmitting narrow pulses simultaneously on a group of fixed transducers that between them cover the required sector, each having a separate receiver. This is called multi-beam sonar. Another type of fixed beam, known as sidescan sonar, is widely used for surveying. In this case the transducer is long and narrow, mounted along the bilge on either or both sides, to give a vertical fan-shaped beam directed at right angles to the ship's course. When the bottom is flat each pulse, striking the seabed diagonally, returns a long-drawn-out echo which is interrupted by acoustic shadows on the further sides of any obstructions such as rocks or wrecks in line with the beam. The length of such a shadow is in proportion to the height of the object and so a series of traces on the recorder, one below the other, develop into the shape of the object as the ship passes by. In such manner acoustic maps of remarkable detail can be built up.

– echo-sounding
The first continuous recording, direct reading, ultrasonic echo-sounder underwent successful sea trials at Sheerness, Kent, in 1929. The chart recorder was of the type described above, essentially similar to the models in use commercially today. It draws a continuous profile of the seabed along the ship's track and false echoes, such as those received from fish and from layers of discontinuity in midwater, are easily identified as such. In large ships digital displays and flashing-light indicators are often used in

The display unit of this echo sounder shows the contour of the seabed beneath the vessel as a continuous trace, the depth being read off against a fathom scale on the right-hand side. The instrument illustrated is suitable for vessels exceeding about 45 ft (13.7 m) in length

addition. Yachts tend to use either a flashing-light display or a metre display. Instruments specially designed for the purpose can record the greatest depths to be found. A low-frequency, and therefore a large transducer, is needed and this must be stabilized on account of the long interval between transmission and echo.

Since the publication, in 1934, of the first echo-sounder chart to show fish echoes in midwater, this instrument has become widely used all over the world as an aid to fishing. A number of special displays to show the fish clearly under difficult conditions are in use and methods of automatic determination of the numbers of fish detected are under development. In shallow water it is possible to penetrate the seabed with a low-frequency pulse.

Southern Cross Trophy *see* YACHT RACING: Major races and series (Sydney–Hobart)

Southern Ocean Racing Conference
This body organizes the six races of what is known as the Southern Ocean Racing Circuit, which brings the cream of American, Canadian and sometimes Bermudan, British, and other ocean-racing yachts to Florida and the Bahamas at the end of January. The conference consists of the usual officers, together with representatives from the: Biscayne Bay Yacht Club; Coral Reef Yacht Club; Lauderdale Yacht Club; Miami Yacht Club; Nassau Yacht Club; St Petersburg Yacht Club.

Speed made good
The mean speed actually achieved.

Spinnaker
A large triangular sail set on the opposite side to the main when running. *See also* SAIL DESIGN AND MATERIALS; SAIL TRIM

Spitfire jib
A small jib set in heavy weather.

Splice, splicing
A method of joining or forming an eye in laid ropes. *See* MASTS AND RIGGING; ROPEWORK: Splices

Spline
A strip of wood fitted into a seam.

Spreaders (crosstrees) *see* MASTS AND RIGGING: Glossary

Spring tides
The tides that occur near the time of full and new moon when the RANGE OF TIDE tends to increase.

Spritsail *see* RIGS: Fore-and-aft rigs

Sprung
A mast is said to be sprung when it is cracked.

Square (reef) knot: *see* ROPEWORK: Bends and hitches

Square rig *see* RIGS

Standard port (reference station) *see* TIDES AND TIDAL STREAMS

Standing rigging *see* MASTS AND RIGGING

Starboard
The right side of a craft looking forward, denoted by green.

Starboard tack
A vessel is on the starboard tack when she is sailing with the wind on her starboard side.

Station pointer
A device for plotting a vessel's position as determined by measuring horizontal angles to fixed marks. In 1765 the Rev. John Michell had suggested to the Royal Society that HADLEY'S QUADRANT, which had then come into general use for measuring ALTITUDES, would be equally useful for measuring horizontal angles in hydrographic surveys. Writing in 1774, the elder Murdoch McKenzie first described the station pointer he had devised for his own extensive surveys of the British coasts. It consisted of a semicircular protractor with one fixed and two movable arms, and with a pinhole in the central pivot. The arms were set to read the angles that had been measured between the first and second, and the second and third of three landmarks already charted; the instrument was then moved over the chart until the arms touched the three fixed points. The 'resected' position was pricked through the central pinhole.

Resection from three fixed points was already a recognized method in land survey and there were several graphical and computational methods for obtaining the resected position.

The simplest method was to plot the three rays on tracing paper and manipulate this over the fixed points; the Douglas protractor has a transparent matt surface on which the rays can be drawn. But the station pointer with its longer arms and verniers reading to 1′ of arc is both more convenient in use and more accurate.

The modern station pointer differs from McKenzie's description only in having a complete circle instead of a semicircle (more appropriate for use with the sextant that measures angles up to 120°) and in having easily read micrometers instead of verniers. It is an essential tool of the hydrographic surveyor. Although resection fixes have

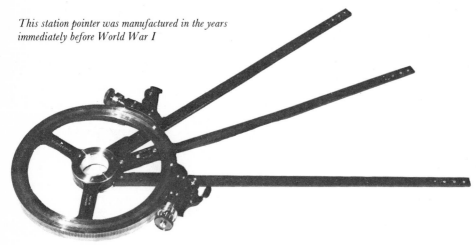

This station pointer was manufactured in the years immediately before World War I

frequently been recommended for inshore navigation, as being more reliable than compass bearings, the method is largely confined to survey work.

Stay *see* MASTS AND RIGGING: Glossary

Staysail
A triangular fore-and-aft sail set on a stay. *See also* RIGS: Fore-and-aft rigs

Stem *see* HULLS: Construction components

Sternpost
The aftermost timber to which the underwater plank ends are secured and on which the rudder is slung. *See also* HULLS: Construction components

Stiff
A vessel is said to be stiff when she does not heel easily; the opposite to tender.

Stop *see* TIER

Stopper
A short length of line or chain used to take the strain temporarily on the rigging or cable while the end is being belayed or shifted.

Strake
A line of skin planking on a wooden vessel. *See also* HULLS: Construction components

Strand
To run aground, generally more seriously than would be described by grounding.

Stringers *see* HULLS: Construction components

Subordinate station *see* TIDES AND TIDAL STREAMS

Surge
A rhythmic motion along the longitudinal axis of a craft due to wave motion.

Sweep
A long oar used in sailing vessels when the wind failed.

Swifter
(1) Rope used to connect the capstan bars in sailing vessels when weighing anchor. Swifters enabled extra hands to man the capstan. (2) the forward shroud to a lower mast.

Swig (sweat up)
To tighten a line by taking a turn and then pulling the standing part of the line at right angles and taking up the slack at the running end.

Swinging ship
Putting the ship on different HEADINGS and determining the deviation of the compass by comparing the readings with the known magnetic directions.

Sydney-Hobart *see* YACHT RACING: Major races and series

Tabernacle *see* MASTS AND RIGGING: Glossary

Tabling
Canvas sewn along the edges of a sail to give it strength.

Tack
(1) To go about by bringing the wind ahead and round on to the other bow. To work to windward close-hauled on one tack after another; (2) the lower forward corner of a fore-and-aft sail.

Tackle *see* PURCHASE

Tack tackle
A purchase used on the tack of a fore-and-aft sail to keep the LUFF taut.

Taffrail *see* HULLS: Construction components

Taffrail log *see* LOG

Take up
A vessel is said to take up when the water causes her planks to swell so that she no longer leaks.

Tang *see* MASTS AND RIGGING: Glossary

Tender
A vessel is termed tender when she heels easily; the opposite to stiff.

Thames Measurement
A formula introduced in 1855 by the ROYAL THAMES YACHT CLUB for the measurement of yachts so as to produce a fairer system of handicap, and now used to describe size. *See* HANDICAP SYSTEMS

Thole pin
A pin in the GUNWALE of a boat to which the oar can be held by means of a GROMMET; or, more usually, the oar is pivoted between two thole pins.

Thunderstorms *see* WIND AND WEATHER

Thwart
The transverse seat in a dinghy.

Tidal current *see* TIDES AND TIDAL STREAMS

Tidal prediction
For port operation, navigation, and coastal defence, predictions of times and heights of high and low water and, on occasion, of hourly elevations of the tide are required in high precision often two or more years in advance. Although the astronomical tide-generating forces are known, it is not yet possible to compute directly by theoretical principles the tidal response of the oceans and seas with sufficient accuracy, due mainly to

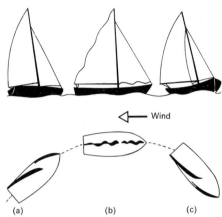

Yachts tacking (left): *the French* Gitana VI *passes astern of the Italian yacht* Il Moro de Venezia, *during the 1977 Fastnet Race*

Tacking (below): (a) *close-hauled on the starboard tack;* (b) *coming about (head to the wind, sails flapping);* (c) *close-hauled on the port tack*

the complex resonances of the marine water bodies. Tidal prediction therefore remains an empirical science relying upon the availability of an observed time series of sea level, the harmonic analysis of this series traditionally into discrete periodic elements, the projection of each element to the date of interest, and the resynthesis of the component parts.

The principles of the techniques owe much to the French astronomer Pierre Simon, Marquis de Laplace and the British mathematician and physicist Lord Kelvin (Sir William Thomson), but the main practical exploitation began in the 1920s, principally because of the efforts of A. T. Doodson and P. Schureman. Until the late 1950s the analytical basis relied upon cumbersome hand calculations, typically requiring as much as one man-month to complete, and the prediction synthesis required the construction and use of complex mechanical harmonic analogue calculators. The appearance of the electronic digital computer has since revolutionized both procedures and not only relieved the tedium but made possible the introduction of new more powerful techniques.

The analysis of a sea-level time series reveals, as expected, peaks of energy separated by approximately one cycle per day. Each peak contains a large number of tidal lines, many pairs of which are very closely spaced in frequency. The degree of separation possible is a function of the length of the series. From one month's data a dozen or more of the major constituents can be identified. Little advantage can then be gained until the series is one year in length, when more than 100 constituents can be separated. The separation of other pairs requires a nodal period of approximately 19 years and even much

longer spans, although such considerations become largely academic. The requirements for adequate predictions vary, depending upon location and in particular upon the presence or otherwise of shallow water in the line of approaching tidal progression. The results of the analysis of one month's observations are consistent with the requirements of a deep-sea locality, say an oceanic island. Most of the world's ports are, however, sited in continental-shelf areas where 50 or 60 harmonic constituents are required. For complex shallow-water areas such as the many estuarine ports, the products of an annual analysis are severely strained.

A harmonic constituent of the tide is generally expressed in the form:

$$fH \cos (\sigma t + V + u - g)$$

where

V is the phase at a selected time origin of the corresponding constituent in the equilibrium tide (the tide produced in an idealized deep-water ocean covering the entire earth)

f is a factor near to unity and u is a small phase differential, both particular to the constituent and both varying in a period of 18.61 years

σ is the speed of the constituent in solar time t

H and g are the basic constants derived from analysis representing respectively amplitude and phase lag on the corresponding equilibrium constituent.

Of the many hundreds of constituents identified, M_2, S_2, N_2, T_2 derive from variations of solar and LUNAR DISTANCES, and are all

semidiurnal in period. The main diurnal constituents are K_1, O_1, P_1, Q_1, and J_1, the first three being associated with lunisolar, lunar, and solar declinations respectively and the last two with variations of lunar distance. Other species especially 4th and higher diurnal periods, arise from shallow-water distortions where non-linear terms in the hydrodynamic equations of motions produce many combinations of the basic terms. For example, the principal lunar and solar semidiurnal constituents, M_2 and S_2, give rise, among other things, under such conditions to three quarter-diurnal constituents M_4, MS_4, and S_4. Long period constituents Mf, Mm, Ssa, Sa with periods of a fortnight, month, half-year, and year, exist but are generally perturbed by meteorological influences.

Where shallow-water distortions are unusually large, and where the requirement is for predicted maxima and minima, some success is achieved by a supplementary system of harmonic shallow-water correction constituents that deal separately with high waters and low waters, and with times and elevations. In this manner by four separate operations the harmonic departures of successive tides from a basic prediction are established. The more complex distortions of the total time profile are avoided by this technique.

Predictions for secondary locations, seaside resorts and the like, may not warrant full harmonic treatment but may be prepared by the application of variable time and height differences to predictions for a nearby standard port. These differences are likely to have been established by comparison of simultaneous observations over a short period at the two sites.

All the above principles apply equally to predictions of tidal currents except that in the case of non-rectilinear streams it will be necessary first to resolve into two directional components. After analysing and predicting each component separately the two vectors may be later combined to give current rate and direction.

The timing or elevation of the tide on a particular day is subject to possible perturbation by meteorological conditions, but it is generally possible to compute the astronomically generated tide with a precision of 1 dm and 5 min in time.

There are other prediction techniques than those described here. The so-called response method, for example, operates upon the definition by analysis and subsequent application of a response function that links the tide experienced at a place with the tide generating potential appropriate for the site and computed in terms of spherical harmonics. Application here is, however, mainly for research purposes.

Modern requirements, associated especially with the navigation of large vessels, place a premium upon prediction of tidal progression over an area rather than the conventional practice of attempting to achieve a best fit for a discrete coastal location. This requirement has promoted research into computer models. It is theoretically possible to provide solutions of the hydrodynamic equations of motion and continuity for a network of points over a sea area, in small intervals of time and space. For this purpose the computer must be provided typically with a detailed digitized hydrography, a set of initial values, specified boundary conditions, and time series representing applied forces operating on the surface. There is a real prospect of the use of such models operationally to provide sea-level forecasts some few hours in advance of real time. Such forecasts could include both tide and meteorological perturbations of level. *See also* TIDES AND TIDAL STREAMS

Tidal stream *see* TIDES AND TIDAL STREAMS

Tide-rode *see* WIND-RODE

Tides and tidal streams

Man realized very early in his history that on many coasts the level of the sea rose and fell at intervals that appeared to bear a relationship to the phases of the moon. However, it was the English scientist Sir Isaac Newton who, at the end of the seventeenth century, first attributed the rise and fall of the tides to the gravitational pull of the moon, which was large, and to that of the sun, which being far more distant was much smaller.

Newton considered the globe as completely covered in water upon which the greatest pull of the moon would be felt on the side of the

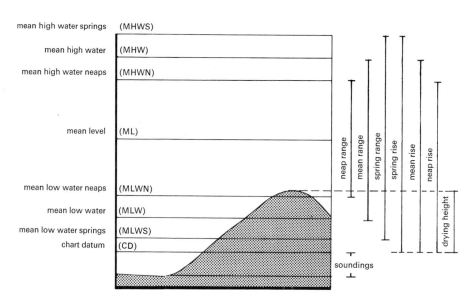

The terms and abbreviations used when describing the various tidal heights, ranges, and rises. Chart datum is fixed at a level below which the tide seldom falls, and is the reference from which soundings are taken and above which the heights of tides are calculated for use in tide tables

earth towards the moon, and the least pull on the water 180° distant on the other side of the earth. The water nearest to the moon would move towards the moon twice the distance of that on the reverse side of the earth; this had the effect of the water around the earth becoming spheroid in shape, the main access of which was directed towards the moon. This explained the twice-daily occurrence of high and low tides familiar on the British coasts, high water occurring at average intervals of 12 hr 25 min, which is half the elapsed time between one meridian passage of the moon to the next.

Newton saw the sun's influence in the varying heights of the tides during a lunar month. When the moon and sun exert their gravitation pull upon the waters of the earth in unison, as at new moon, or in opposition, as at full moon, the large 'spring' tide ranges occur; seven days after each 'spring' tide a 'neap', or small range, tide occurs owing to the sun and moon now 'pulling' at right angles.

The French astronomer Pierre Simon, Marquis de Laplace, spent the last quarter of the eighteenth and the first quarter of the nineteenth centuries in tidal research and arranged for sixteen years of tidal observations to be made at Brest. He attempted to forecast tides by formulae concerned with the movements of the sun and moon. However, the marked variations of tide from one place to another showed that the effect of the great land masses upon Newton's theoretical tide wave as it circled the earth would make

it necessary to analyse long period observations at any port where it was desired to forecast tides by dynamic formulae.

In the 1830s an Englishman, Sir John William Lubbock, with the assistance of the Hydrographic Office, was able to analyse a long series of observations of the time and height of the high water that had fortuitously been recorded in the London docks. These observations covered over 19 years, the length of a cycle of the complete lunar orbit. They enabled Lubbock to prepare tables of the effect of the moon's DECLINATION, distance from the earth and time of transit of the meridian upon the tides at a particular place, in this case the London docks, for which he was then able to prepare tables of tidal prediction of immense benefit to seamen, who required to know in advance when there would be sufficient water for their ships to enter or leave the dock.

Lubbock was subsequently able to arrange for well-type tide gauges to be installed at British naval ports. By means of a float resting on the surface of the water in the well, which had a connecting orifice to the sea, the complete tidal cycle was graphically recorded as a series of curves on a drum revolved by clockwork.

With the improvement of methods for recording the tides it became apparent that there were many complexities. The semi-diurnal tide was by no means universal. At some places the tide was diurnal, at others the heights of the two semi-diurnal tides were not equal, particularly when the declination of the moon was near its maximum; and because of the inertia of the mass of water, and friction between the water and the seabed, the crest of the tide wave lagged behind the time of passage of the moon across the meridian by varying amounts depending on the complexity of the adjacent coastline and the shallowness of the waters on the continental shelf.

It therefore became the practice to record the height of high water and the elapsed time since the moon's meridian passage for any given place at full or change of the moon, and to publish lists of these for the mariner's use in making rough forecasts of tidal conditions he might expect. These data were known as HWF&C ('high water full and change') or the ESTABLISHMENT OF THE PORT.

In the 1870s Lord Kelvin devised a machine for analysing long series of tidal records from tide gauges. The tidal curves which thus formed the data represent the tide oscillations that repeat themselves every 24 hr 50 min and may be compiled from the sum of a number of sine and cosine curves of which the wavelengths bear a harmonic relationship to each other.

The amplitudes and wavelengths of up to 20 of these different constituents could be extracted by the machine, the four most important of which concerned the principal effects of the moon and of the sun on the tides, and the effects of the changing declinations of these two heavenly bodies. From these four sets of amplitudes and wavelengths, known as the 'harmonic constants', which could be extracted from any series of tide readings of 29 days or more, calculations could be made to enable a predicted tidal curve to be drawn for any future date at the place of observation.

The seaman is largely interested only in the predicted heights and times of high and low waters, and by use of the harmonic constants such predictions have been worked out and published for the mariner in modern tide tables for a number of so-called standard ports or reference stations around the world. Also listed in tide tables are time and height differences for many secondary ports or subordinate stations, in relation to the tides at the standard ports, and at each of which sufficient observations have been made to allow the extraction of harmonic constants. Today, of course, both tidal analysis and tidal prediction from constants are performed by electronic computers. As more long-term tidal observations are made at places around the world the availability of harmonic constants is increasing; worldwide lists of them are maintained at the International Hydrographic Bureau in Monaco.

Extreme meteorological conditions, which cannot be forecast, may raise or lower the tide from its predicted height. These

differences cannot be considered in chart-making, so that the 'chart datum' is normally considered as the lowest astronomical tide.

The sea surveyor must locate this datum by reference to benchmarks, or by analysing a continuous 29-day series of tidal observations and then erecting a tide gauge with reference to this datum. This gauge must be observed, and the tidal heights recorded whenever sounding is taking place, so that all the depths shown on the chart are reduced to this common and navigationally cautious datum.

The oscillations of the sea resulting from astronomical tide-generating forces give rise to vast horizontal water movements, known in Britain as tidal streams and in the United States as tidal currents. These may flow backwards and forwards in narrow waters, reversing their direction every six hours or so; in the more open sea they may change their direction continuously, and in either case their speeds vary from maxima to minima.

Tidal streams, sometimes of 3 or 4 knots speed, if not taken into account by the navigator, may drive his vessel dangerously off course, so that the hydrographer attempts to make them predictable. Observations with a floating logship or current meter are taken from a ship at anchor over a period of 25 hours at the time of spring and neap tides; these are then analysed for the extraction of the main harmonic constants, which in turn may be used for predictions.

Sometimes the hourly predictions are shown for specific locations on navigational charts, and atlases showing the varying tidal-stream directions and rates over a wide area are published. In either case the forecast data are time-related to that of high water at an adjacent standard port.

See also TIDAL PREDICTION

Tideway
A channel or fairway through which the ebb and flow of the tide runs.

Tier (stop)
Strips of canvas or short lengths of line used to lash the sail to the boom when it is stowed.

Tight
A vessel is said to be tight when she lets no water in.

Timber
A rib steamed or bent into shape.

Time zone
An area in which the same time is kept. Time zones are generally centred on a meridian whose longitude is exactly divisible by $15°$ and are $15°$ of longitude in width.

Ton classes *see* YACHTS: Level-rating racing, Major races and series

Ton Cups *see* YACHT RACING: Major races and series

Tonnage *see* DISPLACEMENT

Topmast
The mast above the lower mast in a sailing vessel.

Topping lift *see* MASTS AND RIGGING: Glossary

Topsail
The sail set in square-rigged ships above the topsail yard and in fore-and-aft gaff vessels above the mainsail. *See also* RIGS

Topsides
The sides of a vessel above the waterline.

Tornadoes *see* WIND AND WEATHER

Track
The projection on the earth's surface of the path of a vessel.

Tracks *see* MASTS AND RIGGING: Glossary

Trade winds and currents *see* SAILING-SHIP ROUTES

Trading under sail
Within the last few years several factors have arisen which, taken together, suggest that in the near future there may be a resurgence of trading under sail.

The technology of pre-industrial society was, and still is in places, based on the harnessing of the primary, renewable, energy resources of timber, water-power, and wind. The industrial revolution changed this and technology became geared to the use of secondary, non-renewable, fossil fuels, and more recently to non-renewable uranium resources.

Of the fossil fuels oil, in particular, will be scarce by about 1990–2000 because it is unlikely that its production can continue to increase at a rate sufficient to meet the demands of the world's energy requirements. Unless supply is curtailed over the next 20 years, the world stocks of oil will start on the rapidly depleting curve from about the year 2000 onwards. Whether by control of supply or real depletion, by the 1990s there will be a general oil scarcity and consequent high prices.

The symptoms of this, and the implications for shipping, are already apparent in the rise in the prices of marine bunkers since 1972. It is likely also that with greater future competition for oil the quality of bunker fuel will decline. This may lead to less efficient conversion to propulsion energy, and more corrosion. There may similarly – as a result of low-quality fuel – be potentially more pollutants emitted from ships' exhausts into the atmosphere. And with greater pollution abatement requirements in the future shipboard equipment costs will rise. Taken together these developments might indicate the need for a shift from oil to another resource base for marine propulsion.

Reserves of coal are much greater than oil, but its weight presents obvious problems for ships and in any event its price will rise as oil becomes scarcer.

Nuclear power is more likely to increase in its application to shipping. But it too is a secondary resource, and additional sources of uranium are becoming difficult to find. As far as ships are concerned the very high capital costs of shipboard reactors, and the stringent safety requirements, dictate that nuclear fuel will be used only for very large vessels, submarines, icebreakers, and other special craft. The costs of insurance, manning, surveys etc. may be high for such ships, and the cost of accidents extremely so.

This leaves wind energy, a primary renewable resource. Before discussing the economics of utilizing wind for modern seaborne trade the types of commodities that could possibly be allocated to sailing ships should be considered.

There is no doubt a physical limit to the size of a sailing vessel. Consequently those commodities that, as a result of market and transport conditions, derive advantages from economies of scale (50 000 to 250 000 tonnes) will not be allocated to sailing ships; nor will cargoes that, because of their value or perishability, require very high speed and reliable delivery. Very approximately, the cargoes suitable for carriage in slow and moderate-sized (10 000- to 20 000-tonne) vessels under sail may be deduced as illustrated by fig. 1.

Quite clearly it is on long-distance routes that the savings in fuel costs through the substitution of wind power will be greatest. To be considered, therefore, are a range of non-perishable commodities, of relatively low value, that are required in moderate quantities, and may be carried in individually slow vessels on the interrupted-pipeline principle, and have origins and destinations widely separated in the world capable of being linked over the more reliable wind routes. Three of the commodity flows that meet these criteria are shown in figs. 2 and 3.

Another possible trade pattern for sail relates to inter-island and coastal feeder services in developing countries. The substitution of plentiful local skills and resources for high-cost imported oil will bring a return of sail, operating over relatively short distances, in these areas.

In short-distance trades in the island regions of the developing countries many people are reappraising sailing craft as a means of conveying passengers and cargoes, and it is likely

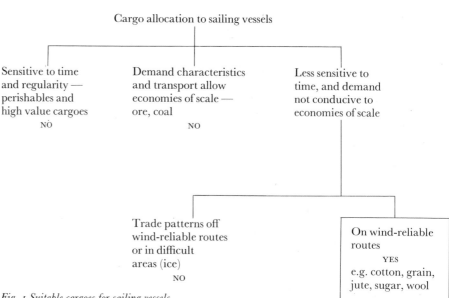

Fig. 1 Suitable cargoes for sailing vessels

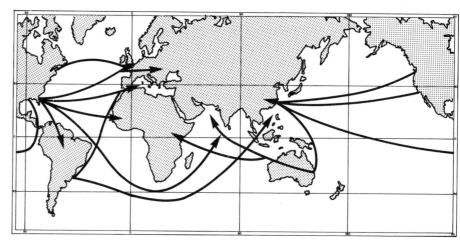

Fig. 2 Grain flow

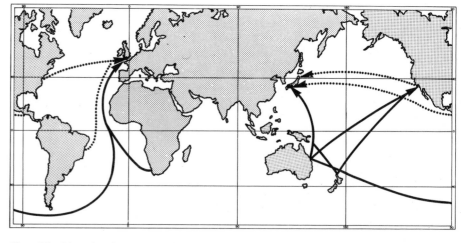

Fig. 3 Wood (——) and cotton (- - -) flow

that there will be greater use of sail in some of these areas in the future.

Several studies on the increase in freight costs due to the rise in bunker prices and optimal speeds indicate that a point may be reached when sailing vessels could compete with power-driven ships in voyage times in some ocean trades. In long-distance trading, however, the introduction of sail might mean doubling the time on passage compared with fast power-driven ships, thus presenting problems of personnel and of manning costs. These may prove a greater problem than fuel costs in the immediate future.

It would seem, then, that the motivation for a return to sail, to any appreciable extent, would come about, not from any basic desire to reduce ocean freight rates, but from a more fundamental shift to an alternative technology by industrial society in order to conserve resources.

Traffic-separation schemes
Systems, authorized by the Intergovernmental Maritime Consultative Organization (IMCO), of separating traffic at sea in areas where it converges, so as to reduce its density and lessen the incidence of end-on encounters, which can be shown to be the most dangerous. The first scheme was introduced in the Dover Strait in 1967. By the late 1970s, some 70 separation schemes had been established throughout the world in areas of dense traffic. Traffic separation was introduced as a result of recommendations put forward by an international working party set up by the Institutes of Navigation in Great Britain, France, and West Germany.

Transit (1) *see* NAVIGATION

Transit (2)
A POSITION LINE obtained by bringing two fixed objects in line. Also termed range.

Transom
A flat stern formed by bolting planks athwartship to the sternpost. *See also* HULLS: Construction components

Trapeze
A sling seat supported by a wire from the masthead, used in dinghies to get the weight of a crew member outboard to windward. The crew braces his legs against the gunwale.

Idealized diagrams of five traffic-separation schemes: (a) *by separation line and zone;* (b) *by natural obstacles;* (c) *inshore traffic zone for coastal traffic;* (d) *sectorial traffic separation at approaches to a focal point;* (e) *the meeting of several separation schemes at a roundabout*
Key: 1 – separation line; 2 – separation zone; 3 – outside limits of lanes; 4 – traffic direction arrows; 5 – circular separation zone

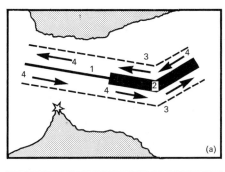

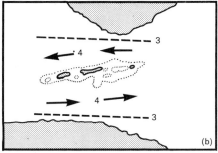

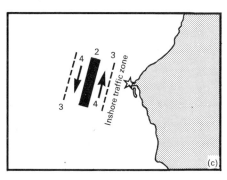

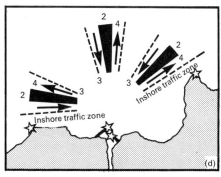

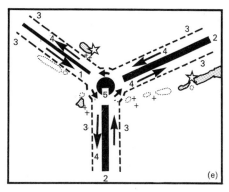

Traveller *see* MASTS AND RIGGING: Glossary

Traverse
The direction in which a sailing vessel may head is limited by the wind, so in making a long passage a craft is forced to change her course periodically. Her track, therefore, comprises a number of legs that cross and recross the course it is intended to make good. Such a zigzag track is called a traverse, and the method of sailing is known as traverse sailing. In order to estimate the ship's position at any time when traverse sailing, or to find the northing (or southing) and easting (or westing) made in a given time, and hence to find the course and distance made good, it is important that a record of the courses, and distances made on successive courses, is kept. Such a record, which in early times was made on a TRAVERSE BOARD, but more recently direct into the ship's LOGBOOK, is called the ship's reckoning. The problem of finding course and distance made good from the reckoning is called working or resolving a traverse.

The several legs of a traverse may be considered to be the hypotenuses of a succession of plane sailing triangles (*see* SAILING). For each of these triangles the corresponding difference of latitudes (d. lats) and DEPARTURES (deps) may be sailed by the plane sailing formulae. By summing the d. lats and deps, the total d. lat. (northing or southing) and the total dep. (easting or westing) is found. The solution of such problems is facilitated by a traverse table, which is merely a systematic collection of solutions of right-angled plane triangles. *See also* NAVIGATION: The practice

Traverse board
This resembled a cribbage board with holes and movable pegs, and was formerly used to record the distance or time sailed on various courses during the day. The lines of holes radiated from the centre along the points of a compass rose (*see* WIND ROSE). Traverse boards were presumably first required when long ocean voyages needed DEAD RECKONING over prolonged periods. They were evidently in use before 1574, when the English mathematician William Bourne mentioned them in *A Regiment for the Sea*.

This was the 'helmsman's' traverse board; in the seventeenth century it became more usual to record the successive courses sailed in writing, to be copied later into the ship's LOG. The traverse board was now a diagram for solving graphically the differences in latitude and DEPARTURE, or in MERIDIONAL PARTS for a Mercator chart, made good on each course sailed. Such a device, based on the simple trigonometrical ratios and known as a 'nautical square' or 'simical quadrant', had been described by the Flemish astronomer Rainer

U

Gemma Frisius and the English mathematician Leonard Digges in the mid-sixteenth century.

Traverse table
A table of the relative values of parts of plane right-angled triangles used at sea for the solution of DEAD RECKONING and other navigational problems. *See also* SAILINGS, THE; TRAVERSE

Treenails *see* HULLS: Construction components

Triatic stay
A stay between the main and fore mastheads of schooners and ketches.

Trim
The long-term attitude of a craft, particularly in pitch.

Trimaran *see* HULLS: Hull forms; MULTI-HULLS

Truck *see* MASTS AND RIGGING: Glossary

True
Related to true (as distinct from magnetic or compass) north.

True altitude
Corrected (sextant) ALTITUDE.

True wind
The wind related to a fixed as opposed to a moving body.

Trunnels (treenails) *see* HULLS: Construction components

Trysail
A small triangular sail set on the main when heaving to in heavy weather.

Tumble home
The opposite of flare. The inward curve of the sides of some vessels after they reach their maximum beam above the waterline.

Tune *see* MASTS AND RIGGING

Tunnel *see* HULLS: Hull forms

Turnbuckle (rigging screw) *see* MASTS AND RIGGING: Glossary

Two-blocked: *see* CHOCK-A-BLOCK

Typhoon *see* WIND AND WEATHER

Under bare poles *see* HEAVY-WEATHER SAILING

Under way
A vessel is said to be under way when she is not aground, at anchor, or alongside.

Uniform System of Buoyage *see* BUOYAGE SYSTEMS

United States Yacht Racing Union
The archives of the North American Yacht Racing Union, as this body was formerly known, contain a publication 'Articles of Association of the North American Yacht Racing Union as adopted October 30th 1897, and organized October 30th 1897', naming as some of the founding members the Inland Lake Yachting Association, New York Racing Association, Pacific Inter-club Yacht Racing Association, Yacht Racing Association of Long Island Sound, Yacht Racing Association of Massachusetts and the Royal St Lawrence Yacht Club. The Union apparently became dormant until it was revived in 1925 by Clifford D. Mallory, its first President.

The union's purpose was to encourage and promote yacht racing and to unify the racing and rating rules not only in the United States and Canada but throughout the yachting world. According to the original constitution its authority to do so stems from the consent of the members and member associations over which it exercises its jurisdiction in an advisory capacity.

In 1927 President Mallory and Clinton H. Crane, who became President in 1942, attended a conference held by the Permanent Committee of the INTERNATIONAL YACHT RACING UNION to consider changes in the measurement rule of the IYRU – known as the International Rule – which was beginning to replace the Universal Rule. Two years later NAYRU sent delegates to London to a USYRU conference at which a uniform code of right-of-way rules for racing was agreed upon which prevailed until 1948, when NAYRU adopted a new code conceived by Harold S. Vanderbilt. Although NAYRU did not become a fully fledged member of the IYRU until 1952, an accomplishment achieved largely through the efforts of President Henry S. Morgan, it has had a long and continuous association with the IYRU and initiated moves that led to the reunification of the racing rules in 1960, and the offshore rating rules in 1970 and in developing strong international class organizations.

In its home territory NAYRU initiated a succession of North American Championships, beginning with the Junior Sailing Championship for the Sears Cup in 1931; the Women's Championship for the Mrs Charles

Francis Adams Trophy in 1933; the North American Sailing Championship for the Clifford D. Mallory Club in 1952; the Single-handed Championships for the George O'Day Trophy in 1962; the Inter-Club Match Race Championship for the Prince of Wales Bowl in 1965; and 'Ton Cup' Championships in 1972.

The passage of time has demonstrated that the concept of the Union, considered essential in 1896 and imperative in 1925, has more than justified the objectives of its founders in furthering the best interests of yachtsmen not only in North America but throughout the world.

The Canadian Yachting Association was formed in 1931 and has subsequently grown into a dynamic national sports federation serving the needs of Canadian sailors. By 1974 it became apparent that United States sailors were in need of a similar organization, as was dramatically highlighted, for example, by the reorganization at the end of the year of the US Olympic Committee.

After conferring with officials of the CYA, it was unanimously resolved at the January 1975 annual meeting of the union to change its name to the United States Yacht Racing Union and to proceed with restructuring, the better to fulfil its new role as the United States sports federation for yacht racing. Concurrently a North American Coordinating Committee composed of three United States and three Canadian members was formed with Paul J. Phelan of the CYA as its first chairman.

The USYRU has 36 member associations covering various yachting regions of the United States. It has 552 member yacht clubs, as well as 15 affiliated associations, one of these being the Canadian Yachting Association. There are also 66 class associations.

Unreeve
To pull a line out of a sheave, block etc.

Unship
To remove an object from its proper position.

Up helm
To put the helm to windward so that the vessel bears away.

Courageous, the American 12-Metre yacht that successfully held the America's Cup *against the Australian challenger,* Australia, *in 1977 (the most recent year of the event).* Courageous *won the first four of the seven-race series. Despite many worthy attempts the cup has yet to be won by a challenger*

V

Vane steering gear *see* SELF-STEERING GEAR

Vang *see* MASTS AND RIGGING: Glossary

Variation
The horizontal angle between true and magnetic north, measured east or west of true north. *See also* MARINER'S COMPASS; NAVIGATION: Practice

Varnishing *see* MAINTENANCE

Veer
(1) The wind is said to veer when it shifts in a clockwise direction in the northern hemisphere or anti-clockwise in the southern; (2) to pay out.

Vertical danger angle
The angle between the top and bottom of an object of known height that indicates the limits of safe approach to an outlying danger at sea.

Velocity loading *see* HULLS: Scantlings

Ventilation systems *see* HULLS: Hull and accommodation systems

Mirror dinghies racing in the Thames Estuary. Designed in 1960, the Mirror is probably the most successful small racing dinghy in the world. Gunter-rigged, built of wood with glass tape reinforcement on its seams, it has built-in buoyancy and an LOA of 10 ft 10 in (3.3 m)

W

Wale
A protective extra thickness of wood bolted to the sides of a vessel where she might be damaged.

Wall knot *see* ROPEWORK: Splices

Warm front *see* WIND AND WEATHER

Warp
A heavy rope used for walking a vessel in and out of dock. Nowadays generally the line bent on to the kedge anchor.

Waste systems *see* HULLS: Hull and accommodation systems

Waterspouts *see* WIND AND WEATHER: Tornadoes and waterspouts

Water-supply systems *see* HULLS: Hull and accommodation systems

Waves
Wind-generated ocean waves have been of interest to scientists and engineers for over one hundred years, but a comprehensive understanding of the properties of such motions has only been achieved in the last twenty-five.

Waves generated by the wind on the ocean surface have lengths from about 1 cm to 1000 m. The heights of waves vary considerably: a wave of 5 m height is fairly common in oceanic conditions; extreme wave heights may reach 20 m or more. The earliest, mainly theoretical, studies of surface waves were discussed in *Hydrodynamics* (Cambridge 1932) by H. Lamb. In these studies waves were represented by simple periodic (or repeatable) forms such as trigonometric functions with a single height, period, and length. In deep water the speed, C, of a surface wave depends on the wavelength, L, and the acceleration due to gravity, g, and is given by the formula $C^2 = gL/2\pi$. Thus, a wave of length 200 m has a speed of 17 m/sec[1]. When waves reach shallow water their energy is lost through friction with the bottom and the speed of the wave becomes dependent on the local depth and 'g'. The fastest ocean surface waves are known by their Japanese name, tsunami; these waves (often wrongly referred to as tidal waves) are generated by earthquakes under the ocean. They are shallow-water waves with wavelengths of many thousands of metres and speeds of several hundreds of metres per second. Very short waves with lengths less than about 2 cm are called capillary waves and are influenced by surface tension and gravity.

Surface waves are progressive waves on the surface of the ocean – the body of the water does not move with the wave speed. In deep water the particles of water below the wave move in circular paths whose radii decrease rapidly with depth so that, at a depth of half the wavelength, almost all the energy of the wave has disappeared. (This is why submarines are not influenced by sea waves at depths greater than about 100 m.) In fact the orbits of the wave particles are not quite closed, with the result that there is a small but significant motion in the direction of the wave.

The surface of the sea is very complex and clearly cannot be described by a simple wave with a given height and length. Following the work on random noise by telecommunications engineers such as S. O. Rice, oceanographers have attempted to describe the sea surface as a random process. In this description the changing surface of the sea is represented by the addition of a large number of simple waves each of specified height, length, and direction of movement. The combination of a large number of waves of different height and length gives the ocean surface its characteristic irregularity, and the combination of different directions gives the sea its short-crested appearance. This statistical model of ocean waves has proved remarkably effective and useful to oceanographers and engineers. From some basic assumptions on the nature of the random process a comprehensive statistical framework for the probability distribution of wave heights and other wave properties has been derived. For example, it is now possible to say what proportion of a sample of wave heights measured with a wave recorder exceeds a prescribed value and what the probable value of the maximum wave height is in a given time interval. One of the most important features of this model is the representation of sea waves by an energy or power spectrum. If waves can be regarded as the superposition of a large number of simple waves, then the energy spectrum shows how the energy of these elementary waves is distributed with wave frequency:

$$\text{Frequency} = \frac{1}{\text{Period}} \times \text{Period} = L/C$$

The main scientific interest in sea waves is in the processes of their generation. Two main theories have been advanced for the generation of waves by the wind; the theories are complementary rather than contradictory. The first theory, developed by O. M. Phillips, concerns the generation of waves on a calm sea. In this process waves are generated by resonance between those wave components that travel at the same speed as pressure fluctuations in the air above the sea. The second theory, originated by J. W. Miles, shows that there can be a feedback from the waves already formed on the surface of the sea to the turbulence in the air. The resulting wave growth is very rapid and leads to the development of the main part of the wave spectrum. Field measurements of wave growth are not in agreement with Miles' theory. Scientific research on waves is therefore concerned with the measurement of wave growth in special experiments together with theoretical studies of wave generation and non-linear interaction effects.

Ultimately the energy in a wave is limited by wave breaking. This process is not yet understood in detail but a useful relation established by O. M. Phillips shows that the spectrum of waves in the 'equilibrium range', where the energy input from the wind is balanced by energy losses due to wave breaking, varies as the -5th power of the wave frequency.

In the past, the prediction of wind waves was made using empirical relationships between wave height and period and properties of the wind field such as wind speed, duration, and fetch (the distance over which the wind blows). Recently advanced numerical prediction methods based on a fundamental understanding of the processes of wave generation, interaction, and decay are being developed in a number of countries. These newer methods should be capable of forecasting the spectrum of the waves in addition to the simpler statistics of wave height and period.

– statistics
The statistical properties of sea waves can to a large extent be described by the properties of a random process with an energy spectrum (*see* Ocean waves *above*). Most measurements of waves are obtained from recorders at a fixed position in the sea and, in these cases, the wave elevation varies with time. Simple methods for the analysis of wave records have been developed on the basis of the statistical theory of sea waves by M. J. Tucker in 1963 in 'Analysis of Records of Sea Waves', *Proceedings of the Institute of Civil Engineers*, vol. 26, and others. These methods usually consist of measuring the highest wave height in a record and the average number of waves in a given time interval. A statistic which is often used in applications of wave data is 'the mean of the one-third highest waves', that for historical reasons is called the 'significant wave height'. Both the highest wave height and the significant wave height are related to the total energy in the wave system (which is equal to the area under the energy spectrum), D. E. Cartwright (1966) 'Waves, Analysis and Statistics, The Sea', vol. 1, New York.

Although the statistical properties of sea waves can be established quite well on the assumption of random process theory, these properties are valid only while wave and wind conditions remain unchanged. Sea waves are statistically 'stationary' for periods

of less than one or two hours. For longer time intervals it is not possible to predict the probability of occurrence of wave heights, and wave data must be collected at a fixed position for several years before the statistics of high waves can be established. Measurements of this kind define the 'wave climate' of a sea area. The wave climate around the British Isles is quite well-known from measurements made over many years by the Institute of Oceanographic Sciences in London using wave recorders on weather ships and light vessels.

Measurements are the most reliable source of wave statistics, but they are not yet available in sufficient density to define conditions on all the oceans and seas. Instead naval architects and oceanographical engineers have used the large amount of wave data that is available in the form of visual observations made by seamen on merchant ships during their passage over the oceans. Another source of wave data is available in the form of predictions of waves obtained from the retrospective, or hindcast, analysis of past meteorological events using either numerical wave-prediction methods on high-speed computers or simpler empirical methods. In many locations this is often the only source of wave information when no measurements or visual observations are available. Measurements of waves and winds on a global scale may be possible in future using remote sensing methods from earth satellites.

Exceptionally high waves have always interested oceanographers and those engineers concerned with the design of ships and structures. There have been many visual reports of high waves including the well-known report of the USS *Ramapo* of a wave 34 m high. Measurements of very high waves are comparatively rare because of the limited number of recorders in routine use, but the UK Institute of Oceanographic Sciences have measured a wave height of 20 m from a weather ship in the North Atlantic Ocean in 1961 and more recently a wave height of 18.5 m has been recorded by the ocean weather ship *Famita* in the northern North Sea. An extreme wave of height 24 m was filmed and measured from the spar buoy 'Flip' in the Pacific Ocean near Hawaii in 1969. It seems very possible therefore that wave heights in excess of 30 m must occur at times in certain unpredictable locations as the *Ramapo* report indicates.
See also WAVES; WIND AND WEATHER

WC systems *see* HULLS: Hull and accommodation systems

Wear
To wear ship is to put a vessel about on the other tack by bringing the wind around the stern instead of tacking.

Weather (1) *see* WIND AND WEATHER

Weather (2)
A vessel is said to weather a point or mark when she passes to weather, or windward, of it without tacking.

Weather cloth *see* DODGER

Weatherly
A vessel is said to be weatherly when she can sail close to the wind.

Weather shore
A shore to windward, which can thus offer shelter.

Weigh
To weigh anchor is to raise it from the bottom.

Well
Cockpit.

West Indies Yachting Association
Formed in 1961 with the object of promoting yacht racing in the eastern Caribbean. Initially activities were confined to Trinidad, Barbados, Guyana, and Grenada, but since then the association has grown, to include territories from St Thomas in the north, to Venezuela in the south.

It established its own rating rule for offshore yachts, devised and developed by Al Rapier of Trinidad. Although based on IOR, it is much simpler to measure and calculate. An experienced measurer can measure a 40-ft boat in about 30 minutes, and complete the calculation in 15. The close results achieved in the many regattas where the rule has been used show that it works extremely well.

Safety regulations are based on RYA regulations, but in view of weather conditions they are less stringent. Meeting the full RYA requirements would be too costly and would eliminate many local yachts, who only race occasionally.

For 1974/5 an offshore championship was established. This has one compulsory event, Antigua Sailing Week, for which 50% points were awarded.

On the dinghy scene, the Fireball, Mirror, Sunfish and Kingfish have been established, but this does not preclude individual territories from developing other classes of their choice – Martinique held championships in 1974 and 1975 for 470s, OKs and Moths.

Whip (1)
A single-block purchase.

Whip (2), **whipping** *see* ROPEWORK

Whipstaff
A vertical lever used to steer early ships when

the helmsman was placed some distance
above the tiller.

Whisker pole
A spar used to boom out the jib on the opposite side to the main when running.

Windage
The drag created by the parts of a vessel that
are exposed to the wind; or, the extent of
those parts that create wind drag.

Wind and weather
Modern yachtsmen and other navigators of
small craft rely on the timely forecasting of
changes in weather provided by national and
international meteorological services. This
dependable aid to sailing is based on past,
and continuing, scientific study of weather
patterns, and the prompt gathering of
meteorological reports from a wide area.

– world weather systems
The wind and weather system of the globe
can be simplified as shown in fig. 1. Winds
blow out of two major high-pressure belts
(the polar and subtropical highs) into two
low-pressure belts (the temperate and equatorial lows), and the effect of the earth's
rotation gives these winds an average cant to
blow either from the northeast or the southwest.

The primary air masses of each hemisphere
are divided from one another by two global
frontal systems. The polar front divides the
polar easterlies from the temperate westerlies,
and this front is more or less continuous
round the hemisphere. It is along this front
that most of the temperate cyclones (depressions or lows) develop. By comparison the
intertropical front is weak and ill-defined and
as shown in fig. 1 divides the northeast trades
from the southeast trades in the region of the
equator. In the figure it is shown in the
northern hemisphere, but it tends to follow
the sun.

The upper winds of the world are westerlies,
which reach their highest speeds in jet-
streams. Jetstreams are tubes of high-velocity
wind found around 6 miles (10 km) up and
are associated with the polar and intertropical fronts. They tend to be continuous round
the hemisphere and are important in that
new depressions form on their equatorial
sides.

The belts shown in fig. 1 are those that
would exist if the earth were uniformly covered in ocean. The generally north–south

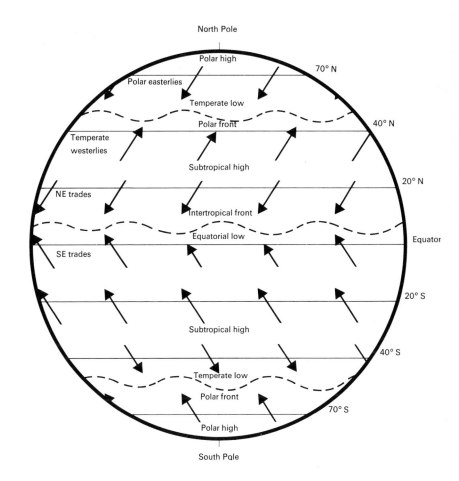

Fig. 1 (top) *The global wind and weather system*

Fig. 2 (right) *The average pressure and major
ocean currents of the North Atlantic Ocean in July.
The permanent cell of the Azores anticyclone
stabilizes the most important winds*

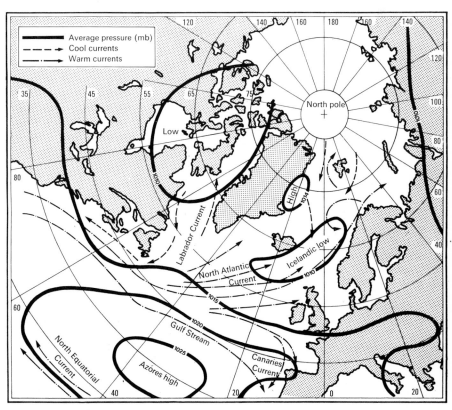

orientation of the continental masses, such as Euro-Africa and the Americas, plus the vast land mass of Asia, break up the general flow of the westerlies into more or less permanent cells. These cells form over the Atlantic (the Azores high) and the Pacific. In either hemisphere the Coriolis force, due to the earth's rotation acting on both water and air, leads to circulations of winds and currents that tend to be linked (fig. 2). These circulations enclose slack areas of weather and water (the Sargasso Sea, for example, in the Atlantic) and here air stagnates and acquires the characteristics of the sea surface under it. Such areas are air-mass source regions. The subtropical oceanic ones lead to the airmass called maritime Tropical (mT) which is warm, humid and prone to fog.

The polar source region is a semi-stagnant high-pressure region where air acquires the characteristics of the maritime Polar (mP) air mass when it is advected (or drawn out) from its source region over an ocean.

The continental source regions are only semi-permanent in that they change their characteristics between summer and winter. The continental high of central Europe-Asia reaches its maximum intensity over Siberia in midwinter. Air drawn from this source region is dry and intensely cold. It is continental Arctic (cA) air. In summer the continental low replaces the continental high and there is a monsoonal tendency for winds to blow into the continents from the oceans. This tendency is at its most obvious in the monsoons of the Indian Ocean, but is still definite on the coastline of Europe in summer.

The continental source regions of America are not so definite in their characteristics as those of Eurasia but the central United States is highly influenced by the barrier of the Rockies. The Rockies follow the general tendency for high land along the seaboard facing the westerlies that is found right through the Americas and also in Britain. Such barriers produce orographic rain on their windward slopes making the west coasts wet and robbing lands further east of moisture. In the Mediterranean it is the barriers of mountains such as the Pyrenees, Alps, and the Balkan mountains etc. that greatly modify the weather regimes in those areas.

Winds of the Mediterranean Sea are strongly influenced by local conditions and have many local names. They tend to be extensive land and sea-breeze types together with mountain-enhanced winds such as the Mistral and the Bora. Although not so strong or definite as in lower latitudes the sea and land breezes of the temperate latitudes are universal and important in that they affect the coasts where most people sail. They also have a much greater influence on the weather regimes or coastal belts than is generally realized.

– air masses and weather
The air masses of any venue are going to fall under a relatively few main headings. In temperate regions maritime Tropical (mT) air and its derivatives will be advected more or less directly from a warm southern sea area. Thus on the Atlantic coasts of Europe mT air comes mainly on southwest winds when pressure is low over the Atlantic and high over the Continent. A similar situation exists on the western coasts of North America when pressure is low over the North Pacific. On the eastern seaboard of the United States such air masses come on southeast winds, or winds that were mainly southeast before becoming locally diverted by some pressure system. In Australia similar air masses will come from the Indian Ocean.

The characteristics of mT air are high humidity and stability. This follows because they are advected over decreasing sea isotherms. When the air temperature is higher than the sea temperature then the tendency is for the air to sink and produce a stable stratified atmosphere. Coupled with high humidity this airstream is prone to fog, stratus, and other forms of cloud. In cyclonic situations it produces rain and drizzle and very poor visibility. There is also much orographic rain on slopes facing the wind, but the airstream loses much of its moisture after traversing a land mass and in summer often breaks up into conditions of extreme heat away from windward coasts. It may under these conditions become thundery. Maritime tropical air that has travelled over a land mass can be pleasant and warm, but is closely associated with depressions and so is generally an airstream of a changeable situation.

The maritime Polar (mP) air mass and its derivatives is the most prevalent air mass in Britain and northern Europe generally and often is brought southwards towards low latitudes by the action of a family of depressions. An airstream that starts in a polar region and comes equatorwards over increasing sea isotherms will have the characteristics of the mP air mass. These include instability and showers. However, visibility is (outside of showers) excellent and the characteristic weather of such airstreams is half the sky covered by cumulonimbus and associated clouds with several showers in sight and visibility further than the sea horizon.

In association with a cyclonic situation the mP air mass develops troughs that look rather like fronts, but are not fronts in that there is no change in air mass as the trough passes. Showers and more continuous rain build in linear form across the wind and there are squalls that at times may be vicious (line squalls) and may be accompanied by thunder. Such troughs usually pass in times that are measured in an hour or so and often there are fewer showers after the trough has passed

(and in the period before it arrives).

Over land the mP air mass has a diurnal variation in shower activity that grows to maximum in the early afternoon from a generally clear and cloudless early forenoon. Again troughs tend to concentrate the shower activity making it unusual to have an even distribution of showers through the day. In coastal regions a secondary shower maximum occurs in the early hours.

The advection of mP air down over an ocean like the North Atlantic and its subsequent return via a more southerly route means that the immense shower potential of such an airstream has been released already, and much warmth has been released aloft so that the airstream becomes stable at a higher level leaving the lower layers with cumulus clouds that do not grow very deep (fair-weather Cu). This is called Returning maritime Polar (RmP) air and is the benign westerly airstream of Britain and Europe that often accompanies fair anticyclonic weather.

An air mass that originates in a warm latitude such as a desert or similar region and is brought up on a mainly land track will have the characteristics of continental Tropical (cT) air. It will be dry and very warm and visibility will be poor with heat haze. What cloud there is is often at a high level. The desert wind of the Mediterranean, the Scirocco, is typical, producing extreme heat in southern Italy for example. This airstream brought up over Europe when low pressure occupies the Bay of Biscay and the Iberian peninsula produces temperature extremes in seasons when it is not expected.

Air from polar regions brought on a mainly land track (often through the agency of a blocking anticyclone) will have the characteristics of the continental Polar (cP) air mass. It will be dry and generally fair in summer, but extremely cold in winter. The intrusion of depressions into the edges of such air masses can lead to extensive blizzards. Visibility will usually be good, but in spring only a small sea-fetch is required to make cP air unstable and produce showers on windward-facing coasts.

Meteorologists recognize many variations in these air masses and often introduce others. For the non-specialist the five air masses described above will be sufficient.

– clouds and their formation
Clouds occur in two main shapes: heap clouds (cumuliform) and layer clouds (stratiform), but to these we must add an important ice cloud that does not have either of these shapes, i.e. cirrus.

Clouds form mainly in three decks:
LOW CLOUDS (BELOW 2 KM [7000 FT])
Cumulus (Cu)
Individual cloud elements with a flat base and of small vertical extent. These usually denote fair weather.

Stratocumulus (Sc)
Cumulus so closely packed as to form a layer.
The cloud may cover the whole sky or exist in
islands and Cu can transform into it.
Stratus (St)
Low foglike cloud that envelops hills and
may be associated with sea fog and poor
visibility generally. In mT air masses St may
form in fair conditions after traversing
100–200 miles of sea and can become sea fog.
MEDIUM CLOUDS (2–7 KM [7000–23 000 FT])
Altocumulus (Ac)
Small globular masses arranged in groups,
lines or waves. Ac is water-vapour cloud (as
opposed to Cc which is ice-crystal cloud) and
shows shadows. It also shows coloured
patches at times (irisations).
Altostratus (As)
An important weather-forecasting cloud as it
preceeds the nimbostratus (Ns) of warm-
frontal weather. It often has a flat grey appearance; the sun shines wanly through it at
first as if through ground glass.
HIGH CLOUDS (5–15KM [17 000–50 000 FT])
Cirrus (Ci)
An ice cloud consisting of a fairly dense head
out of which an ice shower falls (a fallstreak).
The sudden angling of these fallstreaks
(hooked cirrus) shows strong wind shear with
height and is characteristic of conditions near
jetstreams with bad weather to follow. Cirrus
assumes many forms, including the familiar
'mare's tails'. Individual elements are formed
as above, but when really bad weather is to
follow vast numbers of elements combine to
form dense banners stretching along the wind
at their level (jetstream cirrus). Cirrus streaks
crossed to one another at different heights
indicate light wind aloft and no marked
deterioration in conditions.
Cirrocumulus (Cc)
These clouds are often difficult to tell from
small Ac, but being ice clouds they show no
shading. They are, together with Ac, the
clouds of the mackerel sky of weather lore.
Cirrostratus (Cs)
A high white sheet of cloud that forms rings
(haloes) about the sun or moon. This is prognostic when it follows Ci progressively and,
in its turn is followed by As.
CLOUDS THAT SPAN THE ABOVE HEIGHT DECKS
Nimbostratus (Ns)
Deep rain-bearing layer clouds associated
with fronts and giving continuous rain. The
altostratus of a warm front or occlusion
thickens into this and the Ns only passes
when the front passes. It also accompanies
the cold front.
Cumulonimbus (Cb)
Deep shower and thunder clouds associated
with unstable conditions. The clouds usually
develop characteristic 'anvils' of false cirrus
cloud as they flatten against the tropopause.

There are many variations on the above
classification, but the list is sufficient for most

Top: *cumulus (Cu) The individual element in the
foreground is characteristic of fair-weather cumulus.
The somewhat ragged form is typical of sea Cu
rather than the more formed variety usually observed
over land*

Above: *stratocumulus (Sc). This is typical Sc
with some gaps in it and cumulus below it*

Right: *stratus (St). At evening stratus will form on leeward coasts and move inland. The first signs of this formation – which could become fog later – are shown*

Below, centre: *cirrostratus (Cs) above altostratus (As). The halo is characteristic of Cs cloud that follows cirrus when a warm front or occlusion is approaching. However, Cs is a milky veil, often across the whole sky. This sky is too dark for it to be entirely Cs and a very thin layer of As (the third cloud of the warm-front sequence) exists below the Cs. The combination suggests deterioration*

Bottom: *cirrus (Ci). In the foreground individual Ci fallstreaks can be seen while in the background denser banners of Ci are being formed. A sky that suggests strong wind later*

Far right: *nimbostratus (Ns). The darkness and solidity of this cloud are characteristic. The linear feature across the wind must be suspected of being a line where squalls or at least a wind can be expected*

Far right, centre: *cumulonimbus (Cb). A shower in the centre of the picture indicates that the cloud is Cb. Often, ashore, the true extent of Cb is masked by lower and nearer cloud around the periphery of the shower or thunderstorm*

Far right, bottom: *thunderstorm (Cb). The threatening roll cloud at the leading edge of a thunderstorm is illustrated. Sight of this cloud indicates the risk of sudden intense squalls easily up to force 8 in strength*

purposes. Any process that leads to the ascent of air forms cloud and may lead to rain. The main processes include:

1. warm air lifted over cold as happens at warm and cold fronts thus leading to Ci, Cs, As and Ns i.e. layer clouds
2. cool air flowing over a warmer surface leading to heap clouds and showers
3. turbulent eddies produced by wind friction producing low billowlike clouds
4. wave motion between two air layers moving at different speeds leading to Sc, Ac, etc.
5. orographic lifting of mainly mT air over hills and mountains
6. waves induced in an otherwise stable airstream by hill and mountain ridges; these lead to stationary, lens-shaped clouds (Ac lenticularis and Cc lenticularis)

Cloudiness over the oceans is governed by the temperature of the sea surface and by the cloud-producing agencies of weather systems. The typical cloud of the oceans is cumulus as on average the sea surface tends to be a degree or two warmer than the overlaying air.

Cloudiness over the land (and water in the lee of land) follows a diurnal variation. There is least cloud around dawn and most in the afternoon. As the sun sinks so the clouds of the day tend to die out. Cloud that offends against this rule can be due to a front. Cloud that is not thick will often 'burn off' in summer but will remain in winter.

– atmospheric pressure and weather systems

The atmospheric pressure at any place is due to the whole weight of the atmosphere above that place distributed over unit area. Usually temperature and pressure fall off with height and thus the density of the air aloft is subject to many variations. Sometimes temperature increases temporarily with height (an inversion of temperature) and this again complicates the sum total of the mass of air above any place.

In general, if the air aloft is cold, pressure will be higher at the surface and if it is warm aloft then surface pressure decreases. However, a further complication ensues when more air enters the column above the observer than leaves it (convergence). Convergence increases surface pressure. Divergence is the opposite – more air leaves the column than enters it. Divergence decreases surface pressure.

Between them the temperature variations of the air masses in an air column, and convergence into or divergence out of it, produce the changes in surface pressure as measured by a barometer. The mercury barometer 'balances' the pressure of the atmosphere against the pressure of a column of mercury. The aneroid (non-liquid) barometer, which is the only practicable device for yachts, works on a different principle (*see* Meteorological instruments *below*).

The world's pressure variations fall between 950 and 1050 millibars (mb). The deepest lows do not fall below 950 mb (28.50 in of mercury [Hg.]) nor do the most intense highs go above 1050 mb (31 in). Standard atmospheric pressure is taken to be 1013.6 mb (29.92 in or 760 mm Hg) and the value is not the average (1000 mb) of the highest and lowest, as the time for which pressure is high exceeds that for which it is low.

Low-pressure areas (depressions or cyclones) are regions where air is mainly ascending from low levels to higher ones and high-pressure regions (anticyclones or highs) occur where air is sinking from very high levels. Ascending air cools and condenses its water vapour so that lows are regions of cloudiness and precipitation. Descending air warms so that clouds tend to disperse and precipitation ceases or is inhibited.

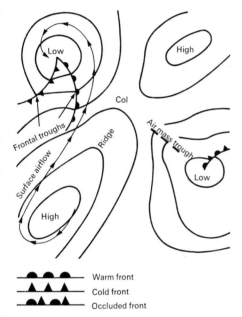

●●●	Warm front
▲▲▲	Cold front
▲●▲●	Occluded front

Fig. 3 Lows and highs, as depicted on a weather map

By taking many simultaneous pressure readings it is found that lines of equal pressure (isobars) enclose lows and highs as shown in fig. 3. This diagram shows frontal troughs and an air mass trough as they appear on the weather map. In these regions weather is deteriorated with cloud, precipitation, and squalls. The opposite of a trough is a ridge of high pressure, which is a more or less long extension of a high. Between two lows and two highs is the 'saddle-backed' pressure region called a col after the similar feature in mountains. The weather in cols tends to be variable, but winds are light and they can become the seat of thundery activity in summer.

On a stationary globe, air would flow directly from where pressure is high to where

it is low, but the effect of the earth's rotation is to form a balance of forces on moving air such that the tendency to flow from high to low is balanced by an opposite tendency that depends on the angular velocity of the earth at the point and the wind speed. The result is that wind blows along the direction of the isobars keeping low pressure on its left in the northern hemisphere and on its right in the southern.

The lowest level on average at which the surface wind is clear of the effects of surface friction is 2000 ft (600 m) and this is the level at which the wind blows directly parallel to the isobars. At the surface it blows at an angle out of high and in towards low (fig. 3). The wind that blows along the isobars is called the gradient wind. The strength of the gradient wind (and so the surface wind) is inversely proportional to the distance apart of the isobars. Thus a 'steep' gradient spanning a region means that winds must be strong there; equally, where the gradient is weak so the winds will be light. Obviously the centres of highs, lows, and cols are regions of zero gradient and so tend to be calm.

The pressure patterns tend to move as if embedded in the circumpolar westerlies (of either hemisphere), but the control of the circulation about the pressure centres decreases towards the equator (where it is zero) and so equatorial meteorology is often a difficult and perplexing study as the models that work so well in temperate latitudes fail in the tropics. There convection is the major weather factor at work and air tends to move directly from high to low and is greatly influenced by local conditions.

– fronts and frontal depressions

The model of the frontal depression is one of the most useful forecasting tools available, as it provides a framework on which to hang the details of the onset and passage of lows. Not all depressions are frontal, but the vast majority are and again the most likely places for their formation is along the Polar Front.

Without going into too much detail as to how it occurs, consider the juxtaposition of a warm mT air mass and a cold mP air mass along the Polar Front (fig. 4). The dynamics of the situation lead to the simultaneous undercutting of the warm air by the cold near the surface and the lifting and sloping-over of the warm air mass above the cold. At a point such as A, originally entirely in the cold air mass, the pressure falls and air blows in directly in an attempt to restore the situation (fig. 5). In a matter of six hours the effect of the earth's rotation has begun to develop a surface circulation about the incipient wave low (fig. 6). Such waves develop on long lengths of undisturbed front and can run along them at speeds up to 60 knots (30 m/sec). A wave may never develop into a full-scale depression, but it may have the effect of

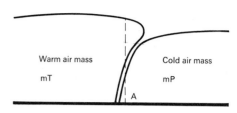

Fig. 4

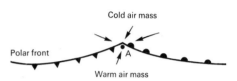

Fig. 5

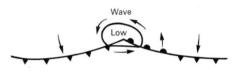

Fig. 6

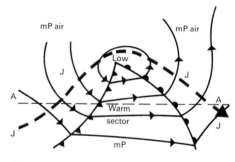

Fig. 7

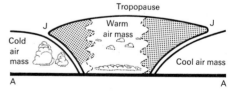

Fig. 8

delaying for some hours the passage of a cold front as a depression moves away.

Assuming that the wave does develop, the depression deepens with time and after a day or two the surface pressure pattern resembles fig. 7. The mP air continues to drive down undercutting the warm and lifting it so that there are intense weather changes along the cold front. There will often be heavy showers, thunder, squalls, and sharp and sudden veers of wind as the front passes (northern hemisphere). For VEER read BACK in the southern hemisphere. The gentler process of the lifting of the warm air over the cold along the warm frontal surface leads to much more extensive cloud layers, continuous rain, and increasing wind ahead of it, but there will be a veer of wind on the passage of the warm front, a kick in the barometer, a cessation of rain, and a change of weather type to air with tropical characteristics such as with low cloud and possibly fog and drizzle.

A cross section along A-A in fig. 7 leads to fig. 8 and shows that the warm front has about half the slope of the cold front, but the former is only about 1 in 150 so that cirrus occuring near the jetstream (J), say at 6 miles (10 km) up may be 900 miles (1500 km) ahead of the warm front at the surface. At a typical depression speed of 30–40 knots the time interval between first seeing Ci and the passage of the warm front is of the order of 24 hours, but this is only a guide. The time can be much shorter and sometimes longer. The 'short forecast – soon past' principle is applicable to such observations.

In fig. 7 the jetstream is shown curving round the low following the general direction of the upper winds over the developing depression. The depression moves under the impetus of the upper winds, which normally have a strong westerly component. Thus almost all depressions move west to east regardless of hemisphere. Because the surface winds are circulatory they have to shift with height to develop the general westerly tendency of the upper winds. Thus in the developing depression in particular, and depressions in general, the upper winds must be in a different direction from those at the surface both ahead (where the upper wind comes from the left of the surface wind) and behind (where the upper wind must come from the right of the surface wind). Recognition of this difference in direction between surface and upper winds is a very useful forecasting tool to the single observer. The above remarks apply to the northern hemisphere and in the southern hemisphere the rules work if left is replaced by right and vice versa.

New polar-front depressions form on the equatorial side of the jet-streams and remain on that side as long as they are deepening and developing. Once the low centre moves under the jet the process of filling starts. This is accompanied by the process of occlusion (fig. 9). The point of occlusion tends to stay under the jet while the low centre curves polewards as the occlusion and filling processes continue. A vertical cross section along B-B in fig. 9 would look like fig. 10. Intense depressions are accompanied by a strong jet and the recognition of jetstream cirrus (*see* Clouds and their formation *above*) in a regime that is likely to be subject to

deterioration is a timely and important pointer to the probable onset of winds that may grow to gale, or even storm force within 24 hours.

Fig. 11 is a three-dimensional schematic of a warm front and illustrates the important sequence of cloud types that precede the deteriorating weather associated with the onset of depressions: cirrus (mares' tails), cirrostratus (haloes about sun or moon), altostratus (watery sun disappears), and finally nimbostratus when the rain begins. The actual base of the Ns is often quite high,

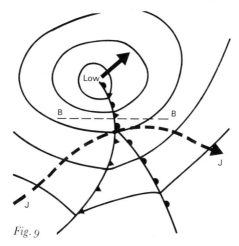

Fig. 9

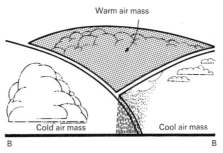

Fig. 10

but a low cloud cover forms below it (stratus pannus) that obscures the true cloudbase. This low cloud is often referred to as scud because turbulence can make it full of lumps and wisps. Pannus is not to be confused with stratus fractus (fracto-stratus), which hangs curtainlike below the cloudbase along the line of the clearance of a front.

After a certain period of time the cold front passes. This time may vary from zero, when a front is occluded, to days or even weeks, when a strong ridge of high pressure grows behind a passing depression. The intervening conditions are typical of the mT air mass and its derivatives. Weather along cold fronts is more intense than along warm ones. In opposition to the warm front where rain starts lightly and develops in intensity, the rain of the cold

front starts sharply and tails off with time. It may, because of the strong lifting action of the cold air under the warm, be very squally and showery with local thunder. Winds may veer through 90° or more in a matter of seconds and increase. However, pressure usually begins to climb behind the cold front. The Ns and Cb at first are followed by As and finally by Ci, after which, when the cold air has grown sufficiently deep, Cb with showers develop eventually to be replaced by a more stable airstream with Cu. If showers do not develop, or develop and then rapidly tail away, suspect the onset of another depression. This secondary depression may be more intense than the primary that has just passed.

The occlusion process illustrated in figs. 9 and 10 is that of cold occlusion. Because of its history the air ahead of many occlusions is cool compared to the cold air behind the front. Thus the cold air mass drives under this cool mass and the warm air mass is now lifted clear off the surface. A warm occlusion occurs when the air ahead is colder than that behind the depression.

The occlusion is a front that has the characteristics of a warm front ahead of the line of occlusion and that of a cold front behind. Thus warm frontal rain that suddenly goes showery (with other signs of the passage of a front) indicates an occlusion. The filling

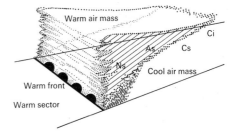

Fig. 11

process is accompanied by subsidence of air over the depression and leads to upper-level clouds being eroded with time. Such fronts where the upper air is sinking are termed katafronts, whereas the developing frontal systems of deepening depressions are called anafronts (*kata* 'down', *ana* 'up'). The final stages of katafronts need only be a more than usually thick bank of Sc cloud from which light rain (or no rain) falls.

Apart from depressions that form over the Atlantic and Pacific along the Polar Front, there are other regions where cyclogenesis occurs preferentially. Such centres for the production of new lows can for example be identified in Alberta, Canada, and in the Gulf of Genoa in the Mediterranean. Such cyclogenetic areas act as melting pots for old depressions and their rebirth as developing systems.

Older depressions can be rejuvenated by absorbing a new blast of polar air into their circulation and in the autumn, when the hurricane season is just past its maximum, old hurricanes that track across the Atlantic degenerate into depressions, but on approaching Europe they can regain some of their original vigour with winds approaching 100 knots in the worst, and luckily infrequent, cases. The Southerly Buster of southeast Australia is a violent squall that develops along the clearing cold front of a depression. It is recognized by the appearance of Cc and Cb clouds to the south or southwest; and often within an hour, after a temporary calm, it suddenly blows gale force from the south.

Depressions on the open ocean will track eastwards while developing and then curve polewards as they fill. However, when near to land the orientation of waterways will steer them. For example, many depressions from the Atlantic recurve into the area of the Kattegat on meeting the high land of Norway and Sweden. Depressions that come close to the entrance to the English Channel steer along it producing 'Channel depressions'. Similar 'steering' effects are to be found wherever a waterway exists in the general direction of the prevailing wind, e.g. in the Bass Strait north of Tasmania, and Cook Strait between the North and South Islands of New Zealand. Unfortunately, when thwarted by a mountain barrier, the energy of a depression seems to be converted into that of wind. Thus where the wind can escape along a waterway it may lead to severe gales even in the height of summer.

– non-frontal depressions

Polar lows are depressions that generate without fronts and derive their energy from convection over a warm sea surface. They are likely whenever cold air is advected directly southwards and are most likely during unseasonal outbreaks of cold air in summer and autumn. The weather is very cyclonic in type, but continuous and heavy (perhaps wintry) showers occur and it is extremely cold for the time of year. The psychological effect of the cold, wet weather coming in a season when good weather is expected is perhaps one of the worst features of polar lows.

The weather map will sometimes reveal lows without fronts. Some of these are old lows that still have not quite filled, but whose fronts have a long time since been swept out of their circulation or have disappeared due to erosion by subsidence. On the other hand large areas of quasi-stationary low pressure occur and these can cover thousands of square miles and remain largely immobile for weeks. They are normally complex in that they have more than one centre. These centres tend to revolve about their common centre of gravity and an upper-air chart will reveal that a closed circulation of upper winds exists concentrically with the centre of the surface lows. This form of 'blocking' low may act as a melting pot for other depressions that are absorbed by it. It also denies the regions under its aegis the benefit of anticyclonic weather for as long as it remains.

Heat lows form inland in summer and a map of where pressure is falling in the middle of the day will reveal low-pressure centres over local land masses. Into these centres sea breezes will transport vast amounts of cool, moist air and will often trigger thundery outbreaks inland while weather remains sunny and warm on the coast. Large continental areas become permanent heat lows in summer and monsoonal winds blow from the coasts to feed them. The Iberian peninsula, for example, develops a semi-permanent low over the High Sierras and contributes to the Portuguese trades that blow consistently down the Atlantic coast of Spain.

These are examples of depressions formed by agencies other than the Polar Front and it is worth remembering that the modern weather map will show many examples where the basic depression model is very difficult to equate to the actual situation shown. However, weather maps are drawn today with the models in mind, but also allow for the actual observations that reveal double warm and cold fronts and other oddities. The mariner must do as the meteorologist and take what nature confers whether it fits the theory or not.

– anticyclones and ridges

Anticyclones are generally areas of fair conditions with winds that are light to moderate, and reasonable visibility. However, weather in the region of anticyclones can be very variable and even when apparently set fair, hardly any two days are exactly the same. This follows because the upper air is stratified into decks, and processes of cloud building that occur between these decks are often little affected by surface conditions or by conditions at altitude. Anticyclonic conditions over the sea when the airstream is humid can lead to extensive cloud cover and over land in winter the central region of a quasi-stationary anticyclone will experience 'anticyclonic gloom' with total cover of amorphous Sc cloud. The airspace above these low cloud decks is probably almost clear of cloud, but the surface mariner sees only the cloud cover he has. Thus the idea that anticyclones always mean clear skies and sunshine by day and stars for making sights at night is by no means universally true.

The winds in the centre of an anticyclone are going to be light and local winds will be the most important wind-building processes at work. (*see* Local winds *below*). However, the winds on the edges of ridges and highs when depressions are trying to invade the territory of the more immobile anticyclonic systems can be strong and persistent and form very heavy sailing conditions, particularly as wave building depends on the time for which a particular wind has blown from more or less one direction. Should that direction have a long sea fetch, as for example with winds blowing up the English Channel, between the extension of the Azores High and a quasi-stationary depression system over northern Britain, then the small-yacht skipper should consider whether the combination of wind and seaway will not be too much for his crew (assuming that his craft is well found).

In general anticyclones divide into two main groups. There are the travelling anticyclones of relatively minor extent that move with the general movement of the circumpolar westerlies and then there are the blocking anticyclones. The latter are so-called because they form blocks to the normal run of the westerlies and mean that unusual weather types appear in different venues surrounding the blocking high. The exceptional summers experienced in Europe in 1959 and 1976 were both due to extensive blocks, the former with its axis running up the middle of the Atlantic and the latter centred over the Atlantic coastal regions.

It would seem that over long periods, measured perhaps in tens of years or even centuries, the pattern of the westerlies goes through a cycle starting, say, with a very long period of disturbed weather with very few anticyclones and an almost constant succession of depressions which then gradually, and with many perturbations, transforms into a pattern with an excess of blocks.

The blocking anticyclone is such that it will persist rather than move and a long period of unseasonal weather in a particular locality can usually be traced to the action of a block that is diverting depressions around its edges.

– prevailing winds of the oceans

The directions and relative speeds of the winds over the oceans in January and July are shown in figs. 12 and 13 and are based on *Meteorology for Mariners* (HMSO, Meteorological Office, London).

The North Atlantic circulation about the Azores anticyclone is apparent at both seasons, but has a more pronounced rotational effect in the summer although the winds are lighter. The winter pattern shows a much more pronounced trend to westerlies in the northern North Atlantic and easterlies in the southern North Atlantic. It is instructive to see the opposite circulation in the South Atlantic. A similar pattern emerges in the Pacific, but here the intertropical convergence zone migrates much further between January and July than does the similar feature in the Atlantic. The Indian Ocean shows a completely different face between

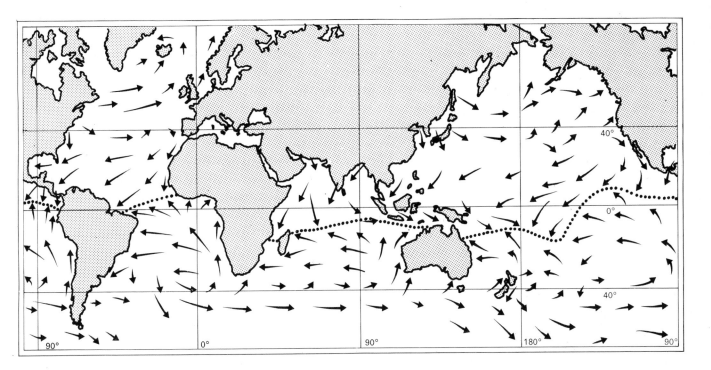

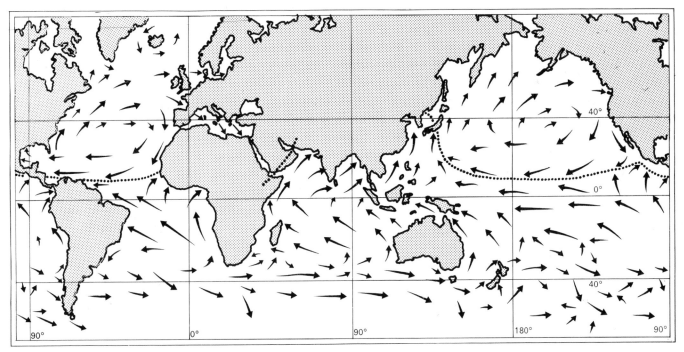

Figs. 12 and 13 The direction of winds over the seas and oceans in January (above) and July (below). The dotted line marks the intertropical *convergence zone, and the relative speeds of the winds are indicated by the length of the arrows – the longer the arrow, the higher the wind speed*

January and July because of the monsoon, which blows offshore in January, but onshore in July. What is left of the intertropical convergence zone in the Indian Ocean in July is later found across southern Arabia, but only in winter is this feature truly in evidence.

Whereas the prevailing winds of the Atlantic coasts of Europe are the same in both seasons the eastern seaboard of North America experiences a complete switch from a general direction of northwest in winter to south or southwest in summer. The enhanced

wind field from the north along the Iberian coast is the Portuguese trade wind.

The general trend of wind in the Mediterranean at both seasons is from the Gironde gap between the Pyrenees and the Alps down through the Red Sea. However, the local winds of the Mediterranean are many and varied, and make a distinct impression on any attempt of larger winds to dominate this sea area.

– large-scale winds

Large-scale winds are due to pressure systems and obey the law of C.H.D. Buys Ballot, the nineteenth-century Dutch meteorologist:

Northern hemisphere – Stand back to the wind and pressure is low on your left.

Southern hemisphere – Stand facing the wind and pressure is low on your left.

The wind at the surface is not in the direction of the gradient wind (i.e. parallel to the isobars) but blows at an angle across the isobars in towards low pressure. This angle depends on the roughness of the terrain, but it is approximately 15° over the sea and twice as much (30°) over the land.

The wind experienced by a yacht at any moment is due to the gradient wind modified in direction and speed by friction and made unsteady by large convectional, and small, turbulent eddies. Light winds tend to be more variable in speed and direction than stronger winds and they are subject to the effects of local winds such as sea breezes and nocturnal winds. Thus light winds may not obey Buys Ballot's law.

Wind is in general least around dawn and blows most strongly in the afternoon, going down in the evening. Even strong winds tend to mute during the night, but these effects are only experienced over the land, or in waters under the influence of the land. The above diurnal variation in wind speed obtains on most days, but can be greatly modified by the tightening of a pressure gradient in, say, the evening after a quiet day when the normal variation is upset and the strongest wind will then blow during the night.

On leaving the shelter of the land the mariner should allow for the wind speed to increase by one to two Beaufort forces (see BEAUFORT SCALE OF WIND FORCES) from that experienced in harbour and the difference is greatest at night when what may appear as almost calm conditions in a sheltered anchorage are suddenly replaced by a 10- to 15-knot wind at sea.

The long period wind shifts that occur as pressure systems traverse an area obey certain rules, although such rules will not cover all such wind shifts.

In general winds will back (shift anti-clockwise) in the northern hemisphere when a depression is advancing towards an area following a ridge of high pressure. The rule is most likely to be obeyed when the low centre is going to track to the north of the observer (fig. 14a). In this case wind typically from west or northwest will back through south-west towards south or southeast. Such a shift will often be accompanied by an increase in speed and the cloud sequence associated with

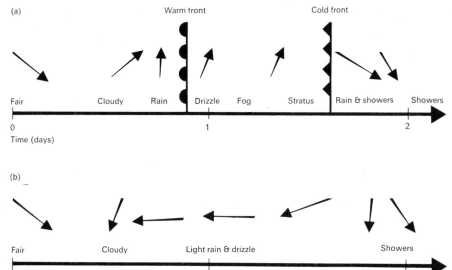

Fig. 14 Long period wind shifts during the movement of a pressure system in the northern hemisphere as experienced (a) to the south of a travelling depression centre, and (b) to the north of it

the onset of a warm front or occlusion. The wind will veer either suddenly, or in a series of shifts, as fronts pass and will eventually gain a direction for the advent of polar air behind the depression.

If the depression is to track to the south of the observer the wind is likely to continue to back, but will eventually gain the polar direction in the rear of the depression (fig. 14b).

Winds will often increase suddenly in precipitation as occurs in squalls but other sudden increases are possibly due to fronts. The normal sequence of gusts and lulls that will fill a convective airstream (Cu clouds) is due to the appearance at the surface of higher speed air from a higher level replacing temporarily the true surface air.

– local winds

Whenever the pressure gradient is slack local winds may blow. Most local winds can be traced to nearby pressure differences created by temperature differences.

Thus sea breezes will blow in coastal regions in spring and summer particularly because the sun warms the land, but not the water. The air over the land expands with the morning thus creating higher pressure aloft over the land compared to that over the sea. Thus air drifts seawards at altitude. This creates divergence over the land and so pressure falls at the surface and a surface current (the sea breeze) blows from sea to land in an attempt to equalize the difference.

In most coastal regions the sea temperature is such that the land must warm above the sea

whenever the sun shines in the morning. Therefore sea breezes will blow if other conditions allow. These conditions include the slack pressure gradient and the light winds already mentioned aided by sunshine and some convection (Cu clouds) over the land. Given these conditions a sea breeze will blow ashore in the later forenoon and will probably last into the evening before going calm. Days with light offshore gradient winds will mean that the morning wind will have to be reversed by the sea breeze and it does so behind a sea-breeze front. Wind shifts when sea-breeze fronts pass may be very marked and shifts of 180° may occur in some cases. A sea-breeze 'antifront' exists to seaward separating the onshore breeze from the offshore wind that is still blowing above and to seaward of the sea-breeze zone. Both front and antifront travel inland and seaward respectively with the day.

Sea breezes usually blow at 10–15 knots in temperate latitudes, but can be as strong as 20–30 knots on shores such as those in North Africa. In the Gulf of Mexico, for example, sea breezes may be drawn in against the gradient direction from hundreds of miles offshore and can be drawn from 20 to 30 miles offshore even in temperate latitudes.

The sea-breeze front may, in the most advantageous cases, travel 50 miles inland with the day although 30 miles is more normal.

The wind statistics of coastal places indicate that the archetypal wind regime of the coast is for the wind to blow ashore by day and from the land during the night. This regime is most marked in spring and summer in temperate latitudes and is hardly in evidence in the autumn. In the tropics or similar places sea breezes may blow throughout the year and contribute greatly to the climate of the regions under their sway.

The wind that blows from the land during the night may be the only wind for passage making on quiet nights. It is called the nocturnal wind and is a mixture of two effects. The first is the land-breeze effect, which is the reverse of the sea-breeze effect but weaker. The second is the katabatic wind that sinks under gravity off coastal slopes and adds to the land breeze. Together the land breeze and the katabatic form the nocturnal wind. Mountains inland from a coastal station will produce strong katabatics and these reach their apogee in the coastal slope winds of the Mediterranean north shores. Here the Mistral blows around the Gulf of Lions and the Bora around the shores of the Adriatic. Both winds can be gale force or stronger in the coastal belt and are a direct threat to small craft cruising these waters.

Katabatics and anabatics will contribute to the wind regime in valleys and in mountainous sailing areas will produce very local and curious conditions that only local knowledge will unravel. Anabatics (upslope winds) will blow on slopes in the morning sunshine and draw air away from slopes left in shadow. As the sun shifts with the day, slopes that were sunlit will develop anabatics as they come into sunshine. Then winds blowing one way on a lake in the morning may well be replaced by winds blowing in the reverse direction in the late afternoon.

Valleys that look out from lakes towards mountains will develop valley winds where winds blow up the valleys in the early afternoon following a sideways flow onto the flanking slopes during the forenoon. The sideways flow up the flanking slopes is maintained during the afternoon, but falters as the afternoon wears on, leaving the wind to blow up the valley with the evening. The katabatic effect means that air sinks off the slopes into the valley bottoms during the night and contributes to a night flow down the valleys that still persists at sunrise.

Such valley winds need very quiet conditions and clear skies to reach their maximum development. When stronger gradient winds blow, then winds tend to steer along the lakes either one way or the other depending on their orientation to the gradient wind blowing overhead.

– tropical cyclones

Tropical cyclones differ from depressions in the way their winds vary with height. In the temperate-latitude cyclone the vortex at the surface is inhibited and controlled by the upper westerlies into which the surface winds have to transform with height. In the tropical cyclone no such inhibition occurs and the winds rotate anti-clockwise (northern hemisphere) at all levels.

The winds blow at hurricane force round the centre or eye of the tropical cyclone in which there is a temporary calm, but the strongest winds tend to be on the polewards side of the eye towards which the storm will be tracking.

Tropical cyclones of the world have different names as follows:
Hurricanes: Caribbean and North Atlantic, eastern North Pacific, western South Pacific
Cyclones: Arabian Sea, Bay of Bengal, south Indian Ocean
Typhoons: China Sea, western North Pacific
Willy-willys: Northwest Australia.

In the northern hemisphere the season is from June to November, but odd examples turn up in most months. The West Indies saying

> June – too soon
> July – stand by
> August – look out you must
> September – remember
> October – all over

sums up the situation in the North Atlantic and the North Pacific. In the southern hemisphere the season is from November to April, with January and February the worst months. In the South Atlantic hurricanes do not occur.

Since the advent of meteorological satellites most tropical cyclones are now detectable in their breeding grounds and adequate warning can be given. This particularly applies to North Atlantic hurricanes. Before satellite coverage, storms bred in low latitudes unfrequented by ships went undetected for days.

The typical hurricane track is northwest between 10° and 30° north and a point furthest west is reached where the storm begins to come under the entrainment of the westerlies and recurves onto a northeast track. Much older hurricanes can be found in mid-Atlantic, especially in August-September, and can become intense depressions on the Atlantic coasts in Europe and particularly Britain.

The LAW OF STORMS is given in all Admiralty Pilots and similar publications of the various maritime nations and so will not be repeated here, but the sailing yacht is not, due to its low speed, able to sail to avoid hurricanes in the same way that steamships can do. Attention is drawn to practical hints and actual experiences such as appear in *Heavy Weather Sailing* by K. Adlard Coles (London and Tuckahoe, N.Y. 1968).

The best warning of impending hurricanes comes via a hurricane warning service, such as that of the U.S. Weather Bureau, which covers the Gulf–Atlantic areas and also the Pacific coast and Hawaii. As the movement of some hurricanes is erratic so the tracking of their movement by land-based radar when within 200 miles of land is important and the mariner's own observations are only a secondary adjunct to that unless his radio has failed. In the latter case the growth of swell or a confused sea, even if not of great height, must be suspected of indicating a hurricane when the other conditions make it likely. These conditions include highly coloured sunsets and sunrises, plus dense banners of cirrus that converge perspectively towards the vortex of the coming storm. The barometer may rise abnormally on the periphery of the storm area and then fall rapidly. In addition to the state of the sky and the abnormal rise of the barometer other factors such as the changes of wind direction must be taken into account. Yachts can survive hurricane conditions so long as they take adequate precautions such as battening hatches, removing ventilator cowls etc. and then run under bare poles at a natural speed keeping the waves on the quarter (*see also* HEAVY-WEATHER SAILING).

– thunderstorms and associated phenomena

It is estimated that on average there are 2000 thunderstorms erupting throughout the world at any one time and each results in a net flow of negative current from the ionosphere to the ground of about 1 Amp. There is, to offset this, a net negative current from the ground to the ionosphere in the fine areas of the world's weather of about 2000 Amps. Therefore the function of thunderstorms in the balance of the world's electricity is to offset the effect of the fine-weather atmospheric current so that the earth is not continually being charged up.

Thunderstorms are mainly confined to the tropics where they are more or less continuous when considered on a global basis. In temperate latitudes storms occur when an air mass becomes unstable to great heights. This presupposes that the upper air is unusually cold compared to the surface over which it finds itself, although air that is not initially unstable can become so by lifting either along fronts or over hills or mountains. Storms are least prevalent at sea and most prevalent over land that is fed with moist air. Thus sea breezes aid the production of thunderstorms by providing the 'fuel' for them.

Temperate-latitude storms may be either:
1. *Air-mass storms* – sometimes single cells that blow by on the wind, or in stagnant conditions in cols and quasi-stationary depressions, they may be extensive areas consisting of many cells.
2. *Frontal storms* – mainly along cold fronts where the lifting as the cold air drives under the warm may produce an extensive line of storms across the wind. Warm-frontal thunderstorms in summer often produce medium-level eruptions where the cloudbase may be

as high as 6000–10 000 ft (2–5 km) up, and the activity occurs above this level.

Each thunderstorm area consists of individual cells and these cells have an active life of about half an hour. The life cycle consists of the production of an embryonic cell as a cumulus cloud that grows rapidly and shows solidity (thin, tall cumulus clouds like chimneys cannot produce thunder). The tops can be easily seen to be growing and they will be hard and knobbly like a cauliflower head when the cell is in its prime. At this time the top will be driving well above the $-13°C$ isotherm (which is the level at which the cloud population becomes mainly ice crystals or similar particles) and supercooled water droplets will freeze on being carried up enclosing a small nucleus of liquid water. Such drops shatter and the effect of the shattering is to give a positive charge to the light ice splinters, while the heavier remnants of the ice casing are left negative. The updraught thus carries positive charge upwards and the heavier casings fall taking the negative charge downwards. This is one of the ways in which storms may be electrified and the charge separated.

At this time when the cloud tops are still growing upward and are hard in appearance there will be heavy rain and often hail falling from the thunder cell. In stagnant air conditions such cells will occupy grid squares of about 15 miles (24 km) side, but as the wind increases they elongate along the wind and diminish in size across it. However, only isolated single cells can grow when the wind is strong, as the wind shear with height breaks up the processes by which the charge can be separated. If thunder is heard in gale or near gale conditions the observer suspects immediately that a cold front is responsible and that a squall with a sharp veer of wind (northern hemisphere) is in the offing, together with a confused seaway.

Accompanying the heavy rain will be a downdraught squall which means that the wind may go from 10 to 15 knots or less to 30 to 40 knots or more. This squall often occurs under the dark roll cloud that can be seen along the leading edge of the more severe storms. The worst storms of all come up against their own wind. The wind before the storm is drawn towards it by the process of feeding it and so the storm comes up against the wind. This wind will be in some diametrically opposite direction to the downdraught squall to come.

Towards the end of its active life the cell will grow to its highest levels and will spread the characteristic anvil-shaped false-cirrus cloud under the tropopause. However, when the anvil appears the worst of the rain is over in that cell, hail will have ceased, and the winds will be ameliorating. It is only because young active daughter storms grow on the flanks of the parents that are past their prime that the false-cirrus anvil is a characteristic sign of thunder. It is these cells that carry on the storm, growing and ageing and initiating new cells for the duration of the storm.

Winds behind thunderstorms are often quite light and usually blow from the right of the storm's path (northern hemisphere). Rain at this time will have become light. In the late evening when the heat supply to a storm is cut off cloudbursts may occur because the updraughts are unable any longer to support the immense weight of precipitation products above. Such cloudbursts occurring over foothills or mountain slopes can produce flash floods on sailing waters lower down. The time lag between the cloudburst and the arrival of the flood often makes it occur during the hours of darkness with consequent risk to moored craft and dwellers near the banks of rivers and finger lakes fed by such rivers.

On mountain lakes and tarns storms may suddenly appear over local heights whose slopes look directly down onto the sailing venue. Such storms can produce falling winds (downdraught winds) that may temporarily create squalls of gale proportions on the water.

Thunder is the result of the pressure waves generated along a lightning stroke by the sudden and intense heating of the air. It rolls because of reflections of the sound waves off varied parts of the storm cells. Anyone who has been very nearly struck knows that the 'thunder' is then just an intense and sudden bang. Thus rolling thunder indicates conditions that at the moment are not likely to be dangerous.

The chances of being struck at sea are luckily small, but yachts are struck, so it is wise to take precautions. Such precautions include the efficient earthing of the mast (if metal) to a metal plate that is in contact with the sea. Such earthing must be a heavy and direct metal connection that will carry the current likely to be generated. In dinghies with metal masts it is best, if caught in a storm, to lower the mainsail (against the weight of the wind from the downdraught squall) and use the metal boom draped over the side into the water. If the boom is wooden such a form of lightning conductor will not be feasible. Masts stepped on the keelson if struck may rupture the hull whether wood or glass-reinforced plastic (GRP). Masts stepped on deck will be more dangerous to their crews as the electric potential built at the base of the mast by any flash may attempt to escape to earth via jumping to a close crew member. Dinghy construction will continue to accept the low risk of being struck and include no form of earthing to the sea. The owners of deep-keel craft would be advised to get expert help if they feel they have a problem.

The approximate distance of a storm can be found from timing the interval between seeing lightning and hearing the resultant thunder and dividing the interval in seconds by 5. This gives the approximate distance in miles. If lightning is seen and no thunder heard (summer lightning) the storms are usually more than 10 miles away. If thunder is heard and no lightning seen although a good watch is kept the storms may well be of the medium-level variety where much of the lightning occurs from cloud to cloud above the cloudbase. By night it is very unusual not to see lightning that results in thunder.

Storm areas usually move at about 20–30 knots and so no conventional craft can hope to run before them. The best course is a broad reach across the face of the storm to leave its centre (if that can be detected) to port.

– tornadoes and waterspouts

The tornado is the most violent example of a funnel cloud, but in unstable weather many smaller twisters can be produced that have an effect on sailing. The waterspout occurs mainly in association with visible thunderstorms or other Cb clouds, but spouts have been observed in the Mediterranean with no apparent cloud to give them origin, as have tornado funnels on land.

Waterspouts are quite common even in temperate latitudes and are usually purely tubes of spray. It is very rare for craft actually to encounter them. In the worst cases, however, ships are damaged and upper decks are flooded. The winds may locally be up to 100 knots in the most violent of such spouts, but these are usually degraded forms of tornadoes that originated over the land and have invaded the coastal waters.

The tornado is a land-generated funnel spout of immense power and sometimes weird effects. Tornadoes have been known to levitate immensely heavy things like railway engines and carry humans and animals through the air, sometimes with fatal results, and at others without harming them in any way. The central and southwestern regions of the United States are most prone to tornadoes, but they also appear elsewhere with lower frequency. It is very rare for tornadoes to penetrate coastal waters, but if they do they can be very dangerous indeed.

– fog and related conditions

Fog is atmospheric obscuration mainly due to water droplets when the visibility falls below about 1100 yd (1 km). When the obscuration is due mainly to water droplets and the visibility lies between 1100 and 2200 yd (1–2 km) it is mist; and it is haze when the obscuration is mainly due to solid particulates.

These limits are set for the specific use of aircraft landing and taking off; they are generally applicable to yachts because of the necessity to make landfalls. However, it may seem foggy to the small-craft mariner when visibility is in fact technically greater than the above official limits. On the open ocean there is no sure way of knowing the extent of the visibility. Only when objects at known distances become visible and the yachtsman's own position is accurately known can the limit of visibility be assessed. Therefore actual visibility limits are of little practical value to the yachtsman. His limits are fixed by the necessity of the moment. He may consider it foggy if when three miles off he cannot see the expected light he hopes to pick up. On the other hand, if threatened by merchantmen close to a shipping lane a limit of less than 1000 yd may seem a more appropriate criterion for fog.

Fog is possible if the surface underlying an air mass is colder than the air mass. However, that does not mean there will be fog. The air must also be wet enough for its temperature to fall to below its dew point. The dew point is the temperature at which air is saturated with water vapour and some must condense if the temperature falls any lower. A further complication is that a certain amount of mixing or stirring of the surface layers is essential so that the temperature and humidity of the layer near the sea surface can be spread upwards to create a homogeneity in the lowest atmospheric deck.

Sea fog is almost invariably advection fog. Advection means transfer of conditions by horizontal motion, whereas convection is via vertical motion. Around the coasts of Britain sea fog is most prevalent in spring and early summer, but it can occur at any time of year. Warm continental air with winds in the southern or easterly quadrants are particularly likely to produce fog. However, the fog conditions are only gradually assumed by the air as it leaves the land. Thus the windward coasts are often clear while the leeward ones are foggy. Winds of between force 2 and 4 are usually the most likely to result in fog when other conditions favour its formation, but with stronger winds the fog deck will lift off the surface into low stratus. Should the wind speed go down the latter may become surface fog.

Radiation fog is a land phenomenon of importance to yachtsmen who frequent landlocked waters. It is most likely around dawn when the land has radiated throughout the night and the surface has become chilled, but the obscuration may become greatest around 0900 local time when domestic and factory fires etc. have started up. In summer the dawn period is about the only one likely to have fog, but in winter any time of day or night may have fog if the conditions are right. In autumn the risk of radiation fog increases sharply from its summer minimum and in spring its incidence only decreases slowly.

Where cold currents or upwellings occur the sea area involved will be very prone to fog. The most obvious example is the Grand Banks off Newfoundland. There is a similar effect in the northwest Pacific.

Having covered the main types of fog it still remains that fog is most likely when maritime Tropical (mT) air advects northwards across decreasing sea isotherms. Thus on the south coasts of Britain for example the warm moist southwest wind is very likely to produce sea fog. In quiet conditions sea fog may exist in banks off the coast and not be visible other than as a strange line of 'low cloud' on the horizon, or even be entirely invisible over the horizon. Local winds, and in particular sea breezes, can advect this fog in to coastal areas on otherwise fine, sunny mornings.

If the mariner suspects sea fog then he should carefully consider the advisability of crossing shipping lanes on a passage, and should he have to do so he should take the most direct and fastest route even if it means resorting temporarily to the motor. Merchantmen and other big ships will have radar, but they may lose a yacht, or perhaps the radar watchkeeping is not all it should be. Further, where TRAFFIC-SEPARATION SCHEMES exist, as in the Strait of Dover, the small-craft skipper should consult Coastguards as to the best way to proceed in any weather conditions.

HUMIDITY

The humidity of the air is a quantity that is variously measured. The humidity mixing ratio as used by the professional meteorologists is the actual mass of water vapour in grams per kilogram of dry air in which the water vapour finds itself. The absolute humidity is the mass of water vapour in unit volume of air. The usual unit for this is grams per cubic metre (g/m^3).

Consider a sample of moist air in a closed space. Cool the air down and eventually the dew-point temperature is reached. The mass of water vapour in the space is now sufficient to saturate it and further cooling must lead to condensation occurring onto any solid surfaces or particulates that exist. In nature the result of this process is dew, although a proportion of the water recognized as dew is in fact evolved by plants in evapotranspiration.

The other way of saturating the space is to add water vapour until condensation is on the point of occurring. The mass m_s to saturate the space at temperature of the air divided into the mass actually existing m yields the relative humidity (RH):

$$RH = \frac{m}{m_s} \times 100\%$$

When the relative humidity is very high, as it may often be close to the sea surface, the cooling of deckheads etc. will lead to condensation on them in sympathy with the principle that condensation takes place preferentially on the coldest parts of a closed space. Such condensation will, unless protection is sought, make the whole interior of the cabin damp. Such cooling will obviously be most pronounced on nights when clearing skies lead to radiation. In temperate climates the humidity in a cabin flat or similar will usually not be so excessive as to produce conditions that coupled with the heat of the day could lead to heat exhaustion. However, it must be remembered that a combination of heat and humidity approaching the dangerous values found in the tropics can be met with when, for instance, intensely hard work is required near to bilges. As a guide, heat stroke is considered likely for a resting person when the relative humidity is 90% and the ambient temperature is 95° F (35° C). When working in such humidity heat exhaustion can set in at lower temperatures.

ICING

In winter conditions with top hamper chilled to below freezing point, rime icing due to spray etc. can be a real danger to small craft, building up to create an increase in top weight that cannot be tolerated with safety. Such rime must be removed with a chipping hammer before it grows to dangerous proportions.

On rarer occasions clear ice (of the kind that ashore is called glazed frost) forms on stanchions, pulpit etc. Rime icing is of the white opaque type and being full of air cavities is not so dense as clear ice, which is solid and therefore the more dangerous.

– meteorological instruments

The instruments that can be carried on small craft must be practical and for most an aneroid barometer is all that will be considered necessary.

The aneroid barometer has a sensing element for pressure that consists of one or more metal capsules that are slightly evacuated to place them in a state of tension. As pressure falls the capsules expand and a linkage to an indicating pointer makes the latter move anti-clockwise. In this sense the aneroid barometer 'falls' just as its more accurate, but impractical, counterpart the standard Fortin barometer does (fig. 15).

Every so often the aneroid should be taken ashore and checked against an accurate reading. This can be obtained by telephoning a local weather office and asking for a spot check on the barometric pressure.

The meteorological unit of pressure is the millibar (mb), but many aneroid barometers are calibrated in inches of mercury (in Hg). The conversion between these units follows from:

1 mb = 0.0295 in Hg

The normal range of atmospheric pressure is from that of the deepest depression (950 mb) to that of the most intense anticyclone (1050 mb). Lower values are found in tropical storms, tornadoes etc. and higher in the

255

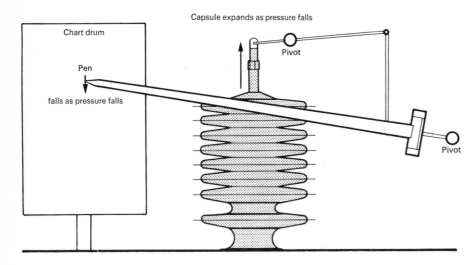

Fig. 15 The linkage system of a barograph

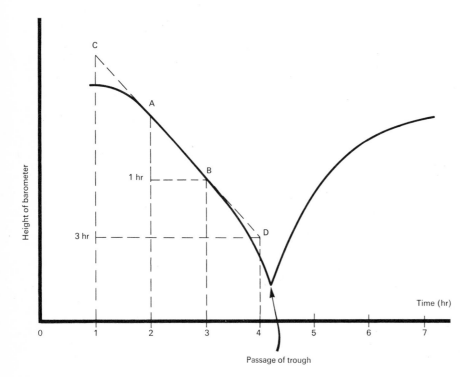

Fig. 16 A barograph trace to illustrate tendency

more often when conditions are bad) and the value subtracted from the previous hour. Multiplying this value by 3 will give the standard tendency. However, the hourly tendency is of more immediate value when the tendency is altering rapidly with time. In fig. 16 a barograph trace starts at an arbitrary time zero when the pressure is relatively high and a very deep trough passes. The height A of the barometer at hour 2 is subtracted from that of hour 3 (B) and when this tendency is extended (as if it covered a three-hour period) to C and D the standard tendency is obtained. If that standard tendency should approach 10 mb (0.3 in Hg) then a gale is almost inevitable. With storm-force winds the tendency may approach 30–40 mb/3hr or even more.

Sharply rising pressure is also just as prognostic of wind as sharply falling pressure and this is particularly so when a deep trough has just passed.

A marine-pattern barograph is an important instrument for cruising and offshore-going yachts. It shows the tendency at a glance and may, together with other signs, contribute to any early warning of strong wind to come. Specific modifications that should be looked for are that the pen is oil-damped so that it does not leave the chart in a seaway. It should be mounted ATHWART-SHIPS so that it cannot slide and small variations due to the wind-increased pressure in the cabin should be ignored.

A well-protected thermometer secured in a ventilated but sheltered part of the craft can be useful, but a specially protected seawater thermometer is also needed for comparison. The latter can be bought from the more comprehensive yacht chandlers. This should not be used directly over the side, but immersed in a bucket of water. If the air temperature is higher than the sea temperature then the risk of fog should be considered. If the sea temperature is greater than the air temperature then fog is unlikely, but showers are possible.

For small craft the wet-and-dry bulb thermometer or any other form of humidity-measuring device is of little practical value as the degree of saturation of the first few feet above the sea is often over 85% relative humidity even with relatively dry airstreams.

Wind direction can be assessed from the apparent wind triangle assuming the speed of the craft is known. To this can be added masthead anemometry equipment. In the absence of the above, wind speed must be

The Windsurfer, shown here off Sardinia, is a plastic una-rigged boardboat designed in 1968. With an LOA of 12 ft (3.66 m) and weighing only 60 lb (27.2 kg) it caught the imagination of young people everywhere

Siberian high in winter, but for practical purposes 950–1050 mb can be taken as the usual range.

The standard atmospheric pressure is: 1013.6 mb = 760 mm Hg — 29.92 in Hg.

The actual height of the barometer, although of interest, is not very important for forecasting wind. It is the change in the barometric reading over a set period of time that has prognostic value. This rate of fall or rise of the barometer is called the tendency and only tendency is of value. Therefore even a wrongly calibrated aneroid is still a useful

instrument because it will give the correct tendency. The standard period over which tendency is measured is 3 hours and the tendency given in observations and quoted by meteorologists will be the fall or rise over that period. Note that when a sharp trough passes it is possible to have exactly the same barometric reading after 3 hours as at the beginning and yet the downward tendency and following upward tendency have been such as to indicate gale-force winds. For the small-craft mariner the height of the barometer should be noted every hour (perhaps

judged from the state of sea as given in the Beaufort scale of wind force.

Devices for detecting the wind direction are many and varied, but practical indicators for dinghies include racing flags that are supported along their upper edges by wire stiffeners. Such indicators are usually statically balanced in some way and all such devices must be similarly balanced for by not having their centre of inertia coincident with the axis about which they rotate or they will oscillate in sympathy with the constant and varied motions of the masthead. Telltales that can be clipped to spars or attached to shrouds may have feathers to indicate the slightest zephyr, and also yarn for heavier airs. Lengths of wool tied to the shrouds act just as effectively.

No efficient sailing can be done in any wind speed without a reliable wind-direction indicator, as every shift is important in dinghy sailing.

See also BAROMETER; HEAVY-WEATHER SAILING; TIDES AND TIDAL STREAMS

Windlasses *see* DECK FITTINGS

Wind-rode

A vessel is said to be wind-rode when she is at anchor and lying at the command of the wind rather than the tide. Tide-rode describes the opposite situation.

Wind rose

Also called the compass rose; the starlike representation of the points of the compass on chart or compass card. Names were at first those of seasonal winds and were applied to arcs of the horizon rather than to narrow directions. Four winds were mentioned by Homer in about 900 BC. By the beginning of the Christian era, two systems of points were in use in the Mediterranean, one based on the original four winds, the other on six points obtained from the directions of the Pole Star and of the sun at midday and at rising and setting at the summer and winter solstices. In both Greece and Italy, names emerged for eight points; some of those in Italy were named from geographical directions, such as *greco* for northeast (from Greece). With the need for more points these names were compounded.

In northwest Europe, in the Germanic languages, only four basic names were used. Being monosyllabic, these were conveniently compounded to give 32 points: 4 cardinal (north, south, east, and west); 4 half-cardinal (northeast etc.); 8 intermediate (north-

northeast etc.); and 16 by-points (north by east etc.).

In the second half of the fourteenth century the wind rose appeared on both compass cards and charts. When colours were used it became customary to have the cardinal points painted blue and the half-cardinal red. This made it easier to avoid mistakes.

Among many nations the north point is distinguished by the fleur-de-lis. Its origin is obscure, but it came into use about 1500, very shortly after the appearance of a chart with a wind rose on which directions were initialled for Italian names; the letter T, for

tramontana (north), had very drooping arms. Viewed upside down, from the centre of the card, it resembles a fleur-de-lis. *See also* COMPASS CARD; MARINER'S COMPASS

Wind-vane steering gear *see* SELF-STEERING GEAR

Wire rope

Wire rope is used for a variety of purposes in sailing vessels: for standing rigging, halyards, and sheets in large vessels and for hawsers in smaller ones. Its construction and the metal used will vary with the requirements for

Breaking loads of wire rope

SIZE DIAMETER		GALVANIZED 7 × 7		STAINLESS STEEL 1 × 19		GALVANIZED 6 × 19	
in	mm	lb	kg	lb	kg	lb	kg
5/64	2	627	284	705	320	—	—
	2.5	—	—	1 100	500	—	—
1/8	3	1 388	630	1 590	720	1 098	490
5/32	4	2 464	1 117	2 820	1 280	1 950	880
3/16	5	3 852	1 746	4 410	2 000	3 040	1 378
1/4	6	5 555	2 519	6 350	2 880	4 390	2 001
9/32	7	7 571	3 433	8 640	3 290	5 980	3 211
5/16	8	9 094	4 124	10 200	4 640	7 795	3 535
11/32	9	—	—	—	—	—	—
3/8	9.5	11 514	5 221	12 900	5 870	9 878	4 480
13/32	10	14 246	6 460	16 000	7 250	12 186	5 526
7/16	11	17 226	7 812	—	—	14 739	6 684
15/32	12	20 474	9 285	22 900	10 400	17 562	7 955
1/2	13	23 968	10 869	—	—	20 608	9 346
9/16	14	27 776	12 596	31 300	14 200	23 744	10 755
5/8	16	36 512	16 558	41 000	18 600	31 360	13 768
11/16	18	46 144	20 926			39 424	17 879
3/4	19	51 520	23 364	50 848	24 544	44 128	20 012
13/16	21	62 720	28 443	—	—	48 832	22 145
7/8	22	68 544	31 085	67 200	30 825	59 136	26 818
15/16	24	81 984	37 179	—	—	70 336	31 897
1	25	96 320	43 681	89 600	41 684	82 432	37 383
1 1/16	27	—	—			—	—
1 1/8	29	111 104	50 385			95 648	43 376
1 3/16	30	—	—			—	—
1 1/4	32	145 600	66 029			124 768	56 582
1 5/16	33	—	—			—	—
1 3/8	35	174 272	79 032			149 408	67 756
1 7/16	37	184 576	83 705			158 144	71 718
1 1/2	38	205 632	92 254			176 064	79 845
1 5/8	41					195 104	88 479

Champagne, one of the German contenders in the Admiral's Cup of 1977, when the German team came fourth. Britain, United States and Hong Kong took the first three places

Note: Traditionally, sizes have been quoted as either circumference in inches, or diameter in millimetres or centimetres. The latter form is now accepted with the more general use of metric units.

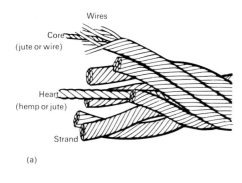

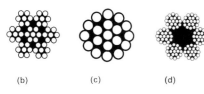

Wire rope. The components of 7 × 7 wire rope (a) *and a cross section* (b); *cross sections of 1 × 19 and 6 × 19 are shown at* (c) *and* (d), *respectively; the strengths of these three types are given in the table on the previous page*

strength, flexibility etc. It is made of wires twisted left-handed round a core to form strands that are laid up right-handed round a steel, fibre, or plastic core. It owes its great strength not only to the metal but also to the fact that the wires are continuous throughout

its length. The best construction used today is one in which the wires are preformed so that they do not untwist when the rope is opened out; this gives the rope a balanced loading.

For standing rigging the most general construction is 7 × 7, that is to say seven strands of seven wires each, six strands being laid up over the seventh as a core.

There is a range of wire ropes suitable for running rigging for which different constructions will be appropriate: the most typical construction is 6 × 19, that is, six strands each made up of nineteen wires.

The ends of wire rope may be terminated temporarily by whipping, by swaged terminals, or by Talurit splices. The ends may also be formed into eyes by hand splicing or with bulldog grips. A splice reduces the strength of wire rope by about 15 per cent.

The strength of wire rope depends on the metal used and the construction, a general principle being that flexibility can only be bought at the expense of strength. Some typical strengths are tabulated on p.257.

Wishbone
A spar shaped like a wishbone between which a sail is hoisted; the idea is to extend the CLEW.

Worm
To fill the lays of a rope by winding small stuff spirally round it. Preparatory to parcelling and serving.

Wracking *see* HULLS: Scantlings

XYZ

Yacht racing
Yacht racing is one of the world's major sports: it has numerous international fixtures, patronage by governments and national sporting bodies and frequent press coverage. It is not in the very front rank in the same way as soccer, tennis, and horse racing. The reason for this is the absence of any appreciable numbers of spectators. Its adherents are participators. Racing is invariably conducted by yacht and sailing clubs, though they vary immensely in prestige and in the standard of event run. Events become established as major for a variety of reasons and the big events outshine the names of the clubs that actually run them; the term 'Grand Prix', borrowed from motor racing, is sometimes used in description. 'Club Racing' implies a more relaxed type of event to local requirements and standards of competition.

There are no leagues or tours in sailing races of the front rank, the longest run of principal events being a series lasting for up to two weeks, or perhaps stretched over weekends during a season for a particular locality. Professionals, such as exist in sailing, are not performers as in many major sports, again because there is no gate, which could generate income for the sport. Those persons who are paid for racing are almost all in the ocean-racing and big-boat world. Some are paid to crew the big boats; young men who are maintained and paid pocket money. They enjoy the life they like and the owner of the big boat is assured of a permanent and skilled crew. The old-type paid hand is also in this category, though he is more of a retainer and is likely to be bosun or cook. The other sort of professional is formally an amateur when racing, but does it in order to promote the equipment, or very often sails, which are on the boat. It is important to him that the boat should win in order that his product can be 'proved' best and then promoted as a result. Sailmaking lofts in particular employ persons who are expert sailors (rather than commercially useful within the business) who can then go aboard boats using their products and try to project them into the prize list.

Some of the great stars of sailing races are by the nature of the sport wealthy business men and therefore genuine amateurs with no incentive ever to become professional. In this category would come Ted Turner (*America*'s Cup winning helmsman in 1977), with his television network and baseball team. His rivals in the trials, Ted Hood and Lowell North, were presidents of sailmaking firms with the reputation of their products at stake.

Influence upon the growth and conduct of the sport by the international authority is limited. The INTERNATIONAL YACHT RACING UNION lays down the rules of racing (right-of-way, entries, protests and so on) and it also promulgates policy for the Olympic classes

An engraving by Henry Williams of the Cumberland Fleet racing on the River Thames in 1782. This 'fleet' was formed in 1775 under the patronage of the Duke of Cumberland

and a certain number of other dinghy and small classes. Sailors, being individualists, look after the growth of new and improved and enjoyable ways of racing themselves.

Racing in sailing boats is carried on everywhere that it is physically possible to do so, with the proviso that the venue must be accessible to people with a certain standard of living and leisure time. Ponds, lakes large and small, rivers and particularly protected waters whether fresh or salt, such as estuaries, all see racing. Open coasts can be used by offshore racing boats and, of course, the great oceans themselves, where the basic racing rules are the same as on a flooded gravel pit. Essentially the sport is for the participants: as already pointed out, there is no reward. Yet it

costs appreciable sums of money and therefore it is not inappropriate to analyse the reasons. These might be the following:
1. Though sailing is enjoyable, just 'sailing about' can pall and is not 'cost effective' for such an expensive toy.
2. The common motive power – the wind – makes everyone feel that he should be able to go as fast as someone else in a boat nearby.
3. The sport is possible for all ages, from 10 to 70. The boats, and the antics of the crew, may be different, but they are in the same sport, indeed on the same stretch of water.
4. A sailing race is enjoyable to take part in, even when not winning. Very often there is a duel with someone else among the competitors who is not at the front.

5. There is a shared experience against the elements, as well as against the competitors.
6. There is a strong social incentive, competitors forming or joining clubs or making friends across international barriers.

-origins
The earliest yacht racing is part of the origins of yachting itself. The race between King Charles II and his brother, the Duke of York (later James II), is widely recorded. It took place on 1 October 1661 on the Thames from Greenwich to Gravesend and back. The king's yacht was better off the wind, because he lost on the beat down river but won on the run home. After that famous race, there is no more news of sailing races, though, of course, warships and pilot cutters in the course of

their business 'raced' each other in a sense. Therefore fast sailing techniques were in use, but not for sport. There were races on the Thames, probably not more than a couple each year, towards the end of the eighteenth century, by the Cumberland Fleet, now the ROYAL THAMES YACHT CLUB, whose members raced small boats on certain holidays. Almost certainly, too, there were races on festive occasions among working boats (fishing vessels, ferry boats and other small sailing craft) at scattered ports.

Such sailing races were but part of wider celebrations. To find early yacht races of anything like the intensity of the sport today, and raced for their own sake, we have to go to 1815, the year in which the Yacht Club was founded (*see* ROYAL YACHT SQUADRON). These first yacht races were matches between private, wealthy, persons each out to prove that his yacht was the faster. On 23 August 1815 *Charlotte* (60 tons) and owned by Joseph Weld raced against Thomas Assheton-Smith's *Elizabeth* (65 tons). The wager was 500 guineas, a considerable sum in those days. A local paper, *The Hampshire Telegraph*, reported: 'The match is likely to afford as much sport as any race that was ever contested by the high-mettled coursers at Newmarket. Both yachts are of beautiful model and construction and of celerity as sailors, and each gentleman confident of his vessel's superiority.' These matches were not common, possibly because of the size of the wagers, but they continued intermittently for 11 years. It was not until 1826 that the first race for more than two yachts was held at Cowes. It is interesting that the origins of one of the few match races remaining today, the *America*'s Cup, was not in match racing, but was in races where a number of boats participated. That was some years ahead still, 1851. Meanwhile from 1826, the events were such a success that the Royal Yacht Club voted several cups, including a 'Challenge Cup of 250 guineas subscribed by the ladies' for annual races every August at Cowes.

– match racing

Match racing is therefore no longer a widespread regular part of the sport, but there is nothing to prevent it. Indeed there are three prominent events that comprise match racing. These are the *America*'s Cup, the Canada Cup, and the Congressional Cup. Each is somewhat different in the way it is run. The first (*see* Major races and series *below*) is pure inshore racing with an Olympic-type course. The Canada Cup includes offshore racing – the only known offshore match race. In other words the boats can at times sail at night and out of sight of one another. It has Olympic

The 2-ton yacht Evergreen, *winner of the 1978 Canada Cup*

circles as well. The Congressional Cup is a league competition to which leading helmsmen are invited from all parts of the United States. The cup was presented by Congress. Sometimes there is an invited foreign helmsman. The boats are sent off at regular intervals, say five minutes, so duelling around the course.

Match-race tactics are the same in principle for all three variations, though in the case of the offshore race, there is a possibility that the boats may get out of touch with one another. This could be risky for the leading boat, who would then be failing to cover his opponent. Match racing is distinct from other forms of racing in that it is only essential to beat one other boat. The speed of the boat is not of prime importance, what is necessary is just to keep ahead of the opponent. Starting tactics therefore become of even more importance than usual. It does not matter if your boat is late across the line in relation to the starting gun. The only thing is to be ahead (in a commanding position) of the other boat.

The classic pre-start tactic in matches is tailing. It is proven that the boat that gets on the other's tail is in charge of the situation. IYRU rule 41 states that a yacht that is tacking or gybing shall keep clear of another that is 'on a tack' (i.e. just sailing along). When the leading boat wants to tack or gybe for the starting line, the tailer prevents her, thus driving her into the wrong bit of water. The tailer on the other hand breaks away for the line whenever he wants. Of course it is not quite as simple as this, but it is a powerful pre-start tactic and so the boats will be seen circling one another before the start in match races.

In a match race the start is invariably to windward. The object of course, is to reach that weather mark first. The boat ahead must cover. Her helmsman is not interested in getting to the mark quickly: he is interested in rounding it with his opponent astern. When the boat astern tacks, the leading helmsman tacks on top of her. Sometimes the boat astern tacks in furious succession and every time the leader responds. This is where the fitness of the crew is tested, the men behind hoping that they can wear out the resolve of the leader and break away from his control. The vagaries of the wind can upset the best-laid drills, for one advantage for the back marker is that he can see if the leader runs into light air or soft patches. Then he can attempt to avoid the same fate by sailing round the unfavourable area.

Once round the windward mark and on a reach, spinnaker drill is all important, but there is less tactical scope as both boats are making straight for the GYBE (jibe) mark (the second mark of the course). What becomes paramount is the ability to hold the inside position, either by being astern but with an overlap, or by being clear ahead, in which case under rule 42.2, the leading yacht has a clear field. The boat that rounds on the inside or ahead at this gybe mark is once again to windward and almost impossible to pass (though once again funny effects can occur in light air). Because of the customary tactics and the constraints of the rules of racing, match racing easily becomes a 'procession', a complaint frequently heard about *America*'s Cup. It will continue to be heard. The Congressional Cup may also be a series of processions but it is bound to be of more immediate appeal, if only because at least one of the pairs is probably involved in some unusual tactical battle.

– inshore racing

This term covers all 'ordinary' racing, which goes on as a recreation for thousands at innumerable yachting stations. It does not often hit the headlines in comparison with such events as sponsored races across oceans or trials for national teams, but it is ageless yacht racing. Any sort of boat can race in this way from 7-ft children's dinghies to 80-ft ocean racing boats, from Windsurfers to multihulls. The physical basics for a collection of boats to race together are: (1) the boats must belong to a common class, or be rated, or be handicapped in some way (*see* HANDICAP SYSTEMS); (2) there must be marks to round to make a course; (3) starting and finishing arrangements must exist; (4) sailing instructions must be available. The helmsmen and crews always abide by the racing rules of the IYRU. Among many other items, these call for the owner of every boat to be a member of a club (or the owner to be the club) that is recognized by the national authority. Also on board the yacht must be such a member (if the owner is not himself present). Since national authorities mean those recognized by the IYRU, a structure is thus woven for the enforcement of common rules in the world. Many club members who sail every weekend probably do not ever realize this condition under which they race.

HISTORY

In the nineteenth century, clubs enforced their own rules, which often supplemented the ancient sailing customs of the locality, but as racing became more prominent these gave way to simple national rules. International rules were proposed by Brooke Heckstall-Smith, secretary of the British Yacht Racing Association, in 1906. This proposal together with the plan for a common yacht-measurement rule resulted in the formation of the IYRU, whose racing rules have been used since among the European countries that were founder members. The United States did not join the IYRU until 1952 and North America had its own system of racing rules until 1960. The present IYRU rules are based on the American right-of-way rules.

Now that the IYRU embraces all major countries, and countries that have any sailing races, the rules are universal. They are revised once every four years and frozen in between. The first year of the revised rules is always that immediately following each Olympic Games.

RACING COURSES

There is no restriction on the shape of a sailing course. The bigger the boat, the further the distance between marks. An inshore race lasts anything between 45 minutes and 10 hours, but it can be longer. A time limit may be set in the sailing instructions: if yachts do not finish within a set time (owing to lack of wind) the race becomes void.

The Olympic course as used for all boats in the Olympic Games is widely employed for other events, since it is designed to give a high proportion of windward work. The system of setting it also means that whatever the wind on the day of the race, the start will be to windward. The Olympic 'circle' has the buoys on its circumference and the three marks can, as it were, be slid round it so that the first leg is always dead to windward. The marks are invariably left to port. The reason for this is that it means the approach to the weather mark is then finally on the starboard (right-of-way) tack. If it was the other way round, right-of-way yachts could attack a line of boats on their final approach to the mark. It has been done and, in close racing, chaos results. The legs are in the following order: windward–reach–reach–windward–run–windward. The committee boat (which gives the start) moves up the windward leg at some stage during the race and is in time to judge the finish. One further refinement of the Olympic course occurs if the wind changes any time after the first windward leg. Then the windward mark can be moved by the race officers to maintain a true beat. This is notified to competitors as they round the leeward mark.

The disadvantages of the Olympic course are that it requires enough open water to lay marks anywhere on an Olympic circle and that the race officers are involved in setting the course and laying buoys for every race. It is therefore reserved for big events where there are adequate facilities and time. Many sailing races are therefore round existing marks. In this case all marks may not be passed on the same side, a figure of eight sometimes being desirable where there are two opposite shores. Courses naming the marks can be issued well in advance, perhaps a number of them being listed and a single letter or signal indicating which one the race officers have chosen shortly before the start. A compromise is to lay a single mark to windward, so that the boats start on a beat, though after that revert to the permanent marks. This avoids the undesirable scene of a mass of

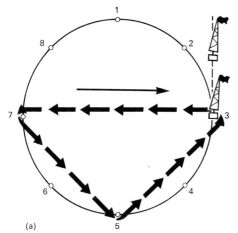

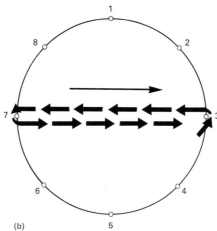

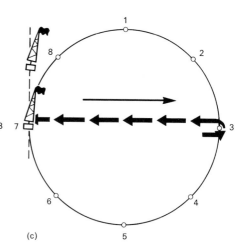

The Olympic Games courses. Eight buoys (1–8) are positioned on a circle with a radius of one nautical mile. The starting point and the rounding buoys used depend upon the wind direction which, in the diagrams above, is assumed to be from the west,

so the boats start at No. 3 buoy. A triangular course (a) is sailed first, using buoys numbered 3, 7, 5, and 3, followed by a windward and leeward course (b), and finally a windward course (c), finishing at No. 7 buoy

competitors running down to the first mark with severe crowding there.

The marks themselves can be chosen from any object attached to the sea bed. This can include navigational buoys, specially laid racing buoys, light towers and light ships, specially moored vessels or boats. Mobile marks such as those used for the windward mark mentioned above are often today fluorescent-painted inflatables of large diameter, which are light to tow but conspicuous from a considerable distance.

STARTS AND FINISHES

Communications are more difficult than in other sports. Especially in heavy weather when the water is breaking and the wind howling, only prearranged visual signals are of any use. Indeed apart from guns or distinct sound signals such as klaxons to draw attention to them, they are the only communication on the course allowed under the rules. (More recently VHF radio has been used to count down the start for ocean-racing boats so equipped.) Timing is taken from visual signals. One method of starting is to hoist a white shape when there is 10 minutes to go, a blue shape when there is 5 minutes to go and a red shape at the start time. Each shape is lowered exactly 1 minute before the next is hoisted. The other system uses flags with a distinctive class flag hoisted at 10 minutes, flag P hoisted at 5 minutes and both lowered at the starting time. The first system is used mainly in North America, the second in Europe. The European method distinguishes between different classes when several are being started in succession, but it has the disadvantage that flags in certain conditions are very difficult to read.

Olympic courses and important races are started from a 'committee boat' and the line

may be between it and another boat or buoy. There may be a further mark (inner distance mark) to keep competitors clear of the committee boat. Many weekend and club races are also started by this means. Some clubs with shore-side premises prefer the convenience (for the officials) of a shore starting box, the line being found by lining up two posts, one of which is on the box. This method may or may not use an outer distance mark.

Since racing boats in risk of collision with each other are under a different set of rules from other boats on the water, there ought

Soling yachts at the start of a race at Weymouth, England, during an Olympic Week

to be some way of distinguishing a boat that is racing. However, there is no uniform signal. Clearly a number of boats on a similar course and of similar design are racing, while stray ones can often be identified by the aspect of the crew who are attentive rather than relaxed. Possibly the only sure sign is a negative one, in that when racing the boat never carries her national ensign: on the other hand a boat cruising about does not have to do so.

DISCIPLINE AND PROTESTS

There are no referees in yacht racing, therefore any breach of the rules should result in one of three events. The offender realizing his mistake retires (i.e. disqualifies himself), or he expunges his offence. This can be done, for instance, after striking a buoy by re-rounding it in the approved manner. Failing this self-discipline, any other competitor can hoist a flag when he sees the incident, signifying that a protest will be lodged. Then the case is settled after the race by the sailing committee (or special protest committee or jury). There is a laid-down procedure for protests. So that competitors do not think up grievances after a race, the protest flag (as defined) must be hoisted 'at the first reasonable opportunity' and the protestee must be informed if this is at all possible. The IYRU attempts to prevent shoving and pushing on the course by ruling that if any boats touch or collide, then 'the two yachts shall be disqualified unless one of them retires or one or both protest'.

THE IYRU RIGHT-OF-WAY RULES

As in other sports, what started as a few simple rules to enjoy a boat race has become a truly complex web of constantly rewritten regulations and case law. The IYRU racing rules run to 6 main sections and 78 laws, most with plenty of subsections. The main sections are: Definitions; Management of Races; General Requirements; Right-of-way Rules; Other Sailing Rules; and Protests, Disqualifications and Appeals. It is fair to say that the majority of sailors who race regularly can only know that the various rules exist and look them up if necessary, but they do have a rudimentary knowledge of the right-of-way rules. Those that have a close knowledge are at an advantage in the cut and thrust of racing. A non-technical but fair summary is worth attempting and is of interest even to non-racing men, or perhaps occasional spectators from nearby craft:

1. A right-of-way boat under the rules must not mislead or baulk another which is obliged to give way.
2. The right-of-way boat should hail or give some sort of warning.
3. A port-tack boat gives way to a starboard-tack boat on all points of sailing.
4. When boats are on the same tack, the boat to windward keeps clear.
5. A helmsman may luff up to prevent a boat passing to windward (a sailing privilege of ancient custom) but not bear away, to prevent an overtaker to leeward.
6. An initially non-right-of-way boat may call for room to sail past an obstruction (e.g. shoal water).
7. A boat may not tack so as to obstruct another that is on a tack.
8. When on the same tack a boat clear astern has to keep clear of one ahead.
9. When rounding a mark this proviso also applies.
10. But if a yacht has an inside overlap as she approaches the mark, the yacht outside must

give her room to round it, which includes tacking or gybing.

BOATS FOR INSHORE RACING

It was suggested above that inshore racing can be indulged in regardless of the type of boat, yet the theoretical ideal craft is not usually the most popular. The paradox is simply explained: modern sailors do not simply want to race their boats round courses and then leave them on moorings. They want to cruise and sleep aboard, so they have cruiser-racers. Or they want to be able to pick the boat out of the water and take it home, or to other sailing waters, behind the car. In this case they have centreboard dinghies (see below). Small sailing boats with no cabin, but with a fixed ballast keel rendering them extremely unlikely to capsize are known as keelboats. The terminology is reserved for the type and not applied to cruising sail boats, though they do have keels for the same purpose. By small in this case is meant between 20 ft (6 m) and 30 ft (9 m); 12-Metre class boats are an exception.

Some keelboats do have semi-cabins or shelters and verge on the cruiser-racer. If a class does not have a watertight cockpit and does have pretensions to racing ability, such as an established class organization and a regular racing programme, it would count as a keelboat. The Dragon class in its early days had a cabin and the boats still have a low coachroof without hatches or windows, but they are pure racing boats and have no accommodation.

Since the intention in the yachting section of the Olympic Games is 'pure' racing, it is not surprising that two of its six classes should be

keelboats (the other classes are three for centre-board dinghies and one for multi-hulls). These are (for 1980 because changes can sometimes occur between Olympics) the Soling and the Star classes. The Soling was chosen by the IYRU after trials in 1967 to find an international three-man keelboat. It was first used in the 1972 Olympic Games and before that attracted top-rate competition. This had the effect of forcing rapid new techniques into the sailing of the class. For instance, as there is no trapeze, the crew has to hang over the side with legs across the side deck and feet under straps in the cockpit. It is 26 ft 9 in (8.15 m) and designed by Jan Linge of Norway. The Star class is very old established; it was started in Long Island Sound in 1911. Fibreglass hulls were first allowed in 1967. The boat has been used in every Olympic Games since 1932, except for 1976. This 23-ft (7-m) boat with big mainsail, small jib, hard-chine hull and bulb keel has a racing crew of two.

Most keelboats are, however, local in character, if only because of their lack of mobility in a wider sense. Ocean racers can make a fast passage to another port, dinghies are towed away by land, but keelboats, even where a class may be widespread in a number of stations, will usually return to their moorings after every race. There are many local classes that thrive, but the following, which continue to give good racing, are of particular interest:

Dragon Until 1972 this was an Olympic class. Designed by Johan Anker of Norway in the late 1920s, as a cruiser-racer, it was rapidly refined into a precision-built yacht for

Star-class yachts racing at the 1972 Olympic Games held at Kiel, West Germany

The three-man, sloop-rigged Dragon (above) has, over many years of development, become a deservedly popular racer

Daring-class yachts (opposite) racing during Cowes week

top-class international racing. It was carvel-planked for most of its existence; fibreglass was allowed under class rules in 1975.

Etchells 22 This 30-ft (9-m) boat was an unsuccessful contender in the IYRU three-man trials, but the class took root in the United States, and has since spread to many countries. A popular choice when a club is looking for a modern established pure keel-boat of big size.

International One-Design This rather sweepingly named class was designed in 1935 by Bjarne Aas (Norway) when rated boats were still prominent in international racing. They were a sort of 'frozen' 6-Metre in design (33 ft 4 in or 10 m LOA). Fleets gave fine racing in Long Island Sound, Bermuda, Norway, and in the Solent. The last-named class disbanded in 1973 and the boats were taken over by yachtsmen on the Firth of Forth.

Daring class The IODs clearly left a void at Cowes, because a fibreglass design was adopted that was in effect a 'frozen' 5.5-Metre boat. The class races only at Cowes, but typifies the classic local one-design keelboat.

International 110 and 210 These narrow, low-freeboard boats are popular in American waters only despite their name.

Shields Named after veteran sailor Cornelius Shields, who introduced this 30-ft (9-m) class on Long Island Sound, this is another 'frozen' 5.5 in fibreglass. It has spread to other American centres.

Flying Fifteen This 1948 design by Uffa Fox is a British 'national' class, one of a number specially recognized by the national authority. It is 20 ft (6 m) LOA; the number in the name comes from the modest days when waterline length was often used as a key figure. There are fleets in several parts of Britain and a number elsewhere.

Squib This is the second national keelboat class in Britain, has a small shelter forward, but is a sporty inexpensive modern boat (designed by Oliver Lee in 1966). (The third and last British national keelboat is the Swallow, established as a national class but never accepted, but it remains on the list.)

Sunbeam This is mentioned here as a fairly typical local class, which neither expands nor contracts in numbers, but gives good racing year after year. The boat was designed in 1922, no new ones have been built since 1938, and there are just under 40 in existence. Half the fleet sails at Itchenor, Sussex, and one half at Falmouth, Cornwall. They show no sign of flagging.

The boats mentioned are all one-design classes, though some may allow minor variations in rig. Rated and formula keelboats now belong mainly to history. There are pockets, however, where 6-Metres and 5.5-Metres are still sailed (notably Seattle, Washington) and even occasionally built. The *America*'s Cup 12-Metre is a keelboat, but used only for its unique type of racing.

– dinghy racing

Dinghy or centreboard boat racing abides by the same rules as inshore racing. The fundamental difference, if it is to be defined, is one of naval architecture. Although the keelboat may have crew sitting on the weather rail to aid stability and power to carry sail, her main stiffness comes from the iron or lead ballast keel. A centreboarder on the other hand has no ballast and stability under sail depends mostly on the crew, with a small initial stiffness given by the hull form. Dinghies can and do therefore capsize and this is a normal hazard of dinghy racing.

The Flying Fifteen, several of which are shown (left) at Cowes, may be of GRP or wood, and has a fixed keel

The GRP Squib (bottom) has an overall length of 19 ft (5.79 m) is suitable for trailing, and will accept an outboard engine

The Sunbeam (below), with an overall length of 17.5 ft (5.33 m) is a wooden centreboard boat with, for its size, a large sail area

Dinghies should be able to be righted by their crew, the hull having adequate buoyancy installed to support them. The advantage in sailing without a ballast keel is that the ratio of sail area to total weight is immense and the boats can be made to *plane*, i.e. exceed the technical limits of speed of a displacement hull. As a bonus, a racing dinghy can therefore be manhandled, kept ashore, and be launched and hauled out as required. Modern centreboarders are highly developed, sensitive and exciting sailing machines. There are innumerable different classes. These are mostly one-design, but a few are restricted classes, which means that designers can work within limits on shape of hull and rig.

HISTORY

Informal racing began between the sailing dinghies that were tenders to large yachts, the length of 14 ft (4 m) often being considered the minimum size to sail safely in a breezy anchorage, and take two men sailing or more when rowing. Several local builders in Britain and Ireland constructed 14-footers, which became classes. By the first decade of this century these included the West of England Conference dinghy, the Norfolk dinghy and the Dublin Bay Water Wag. The first Water Wag class had been established in 1878, but the 'new' class began building in 1899: 14 ft 3 in (4.33 m) LOA, beam 5 ft 6 in (1.68 m) with a lug mainsail, jib and spinnaker. Like all centreboard boats of the time the board itself was a heavy metal plate. Many classes at the time also carried inside ballast, so were no different in principle from keelboats. In 1923 the Yacht Racing Association drew up restricted class rules that were structured to include several of these established classes. Soon boats were designed and built specially to the rule and the first racing dinghy proper was under way – the International 14 dinghy class. Today it remains as the elite among racing dinghies and new designs to its rules are still produced.

By about 1947, the sport of dinghy sailing was based mainly on local classes, many of which have since died out with the advent of mass-produced boats. Most of these were built by a local yard in small quantities and had names like the Island One Design or RNSA 14: these two were heavy clinker (lapstrake) boats and the classes have disappeared; others have remained for one reason or another, such as the West Wight Scow. The International 14 was the foundation of British dinghy sailing and British dinghy sailing was the root of high-speed planing centreboard sailing as a world sport. Looking very much like the 14s were the Merlin class and the National 12; both were restricted classes, with rules for designers to tilt at. The straight ends that characterized them were the result of the maximum length rule, for designers wanted the longest waterline for overall length. The result was a plumb stem and straight-up transom.

A different type of centreboarder developed on the Continent and in America was the Sharpie. This was heavier, rather flat looking, with low freeboard, and it did not plane. It was not hauled out, but lay on a mooring in a dock. Examples of this *Jolle* type are still found active on German and Dutch inland waters. The British idea of classes designed to a rule was not generally favoured elsewhere and the American dinghy sailors preferred one-designs. The supreme example of this was the Snipe, 15 ft 6 in (4.7 m) long (first promoted by the yachting magazine *Rudder*), which rapidly became the world's numerically largest one-design. It still thrives today. Other American centreboarders tended to be large and heavy: first built in 1938 were the Lightning, 19 ft (5.8 m) and the Thistle, 17 ft (5 m). All these boats had hulls of wood, solid or hollow wooden spars, and cotton sails.

In the early 1950s the small-boat explosion began and this was primarily due to the introduction of new and more suitable materials combined with a rising standard of living. Both numbers of classes and actual boats are now enormous and uncounted: few countries have any system of recording all of such boats. Class Associations may know

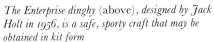

The Enterprise dinghy (above), *designed by Jack Holt in 1956, is a safe, sporty craft that may be obtained in kit form*

The centreboard Mirror dinghy (left) *is gunter-rigged, has built-in bouyancy, and is, perhaps, one of the most successful craft of its type in the world*

how many boats are registered, but not how many are built. In addition, Communist countries build boats without notice or payment of royalties on the design. The new classes have originated from clubs looking for a suitable boat, from manufacturers sensing a demand (the Fireball), from yachting magazines (GP 14; Cadet) and from daily newspapers (Enterprise, Mirror). Often the reason for the introduction of the class was an easier method of building by amateurs, or because it was lighter, or more rugged, or planed better. New classes continue to be introduced, though only a small proportion eventually thrive. *See* DINGHIES AND CENTREBOARD CLASSES: The modern sailing dinghy

RACING TODAY

The increasing importance of dinghy racing is shown by the high proportion of centreboarders in the Olympic Games. Originally the yachting Olympics were for keelboats only and it has been a long struggle to make the classes more representative. Because competition is intense and the standard high, Olympic dinghies are not necessarily popular types. They meet a certain requirement at the top of the dinghy ladder. They are the following:

Flying Dutchman (Olympic since 1960) In a way this is a modern coming together of the planing English boat and the Continental big centreboarder. Designed by Van Essen of Holland, it is just under 20 ft (6 m) long and planes at very high speed. Every sort of modern dinghy device is in use on it and the interior appears a cat's cradle of control lines to the uninitiated. A Flying Dutchman World Championship has been held since 1956.

470 (Olympic since 1976) Typical very modern lightweight, two-man centreboarder (*see* DINGHIES AND CENTREBOARD CLASSES: The modern sailing dinghy). Numbers had reached over 17 000 before Olympic selection; 15 ft 5 in (4.69 m) long, it is a strict one-design, designed by André Cornu and first built in France in 1964.

Finn (Olympic since 1952) This 14-ft 9-in (4.5-m) craft was specifically designed in Finland for the Helsinki Olympic Games and has been the Olympic single-handed class ever since. It has been considerably developed to keep it interesting in comparison with more modern classes.

The Finn Dinghy Gold Cup was presented by F. G. Mitchell to be sailed in Britain every Olympic year. It was recognized as an unofficial world championship; then in 1967 the International Finn Association recognized it as the official world championship and it can now be competed for anywhere.

Tornado (Olympic since 1976) The Olympic multihull is its role and consequently this 20-ft (6-m) catamaran with a crew of two, designed in England by Rodney March, is a thoroughbred of high performance needing expert handling. Total beam of the Tornado is 10 ft (3 m).

The following classes are just a few out of the vast mass of other designs.

5-0-5 One of the first of the new breed of 'big' planing dinghies, this design dating from 1955 was a happy blend of British and French ideas developed from earlier projected classes. Just under 17 ft (5 m) long, it is a 'rival' of the Flying Dutchman as a type, but perhaps benefits by having more freedom and less intensity than an Olympic class. There are more than 5000 in the world.

Fireball A scow type just over 16 ft (4.9 m) long, this design by Peter Milne was intended for amateur building. It is used all over the world and its performance is comparable to the 470.

International Optimist This little 7-ft 6-in box is the children's single-handed racing dinghy

that is raced all over the world (*see* DINGHIES AND CENTREBOARD CLASSES: The modern sailing dinghy). The class association claims over 120 000 boats, but the figures are uncertain and many early boats are probably destroyed and disused.

Laser Another single-hander, but this one is for keen adult racing. This is an example of a class largely promoted by the designer, Bruce Kirby, and builder, Performance Sailcraft, who originated in Canada, but now have plants in many yachting countries. Introduced in 1972, it struck a chord in its simplicity: for instance the mast comes into two and the single sail slips over it by a sleeve. Yet the light fibreglass moulding is fast, and

The una-rigged Finn dinghy (above), *designed by Richard Sarby, has a flexible mast and has gained worldwide popularity since its introduction in 1952*

5-0-5 dinghies (above right) *taking part in the European Championships in 1976. This dinghy can be built of wood or GRP, and has a plywood foredeck*

Centreboard Lasers (right) *taking part in the Women's World Championships, 1977. With an overall length of nearly 14 ft (4.25 m), this type is suitable for carrying on a car roof*

the world and national championships are now major events. Hull, rig, and sail are rigidly controlled in manufacture to produce identical boats built under licence.

Wayfarer This 1958 design is quite a different kind of dinghy. It is raced, but the main attraction is family sailing in safety with good performance. It is a favourite among sailing schools. Individuals have cruised this 16-ft (4.9-m) boat, designed by Ian Proctor, far afield, though it is not intended for such a purpose.

Sunfish This is a sailing boardboat that is so much fun that there are over 140 000 of them, mainly in the United States: *see* DINGHIES AND CENTREBOARD CLASSES: The modern sailing dinghy (Single-handers and boardboats).

Windsurfer This is also a board, but quite different, having no rudder and the sail held by the lone 'rider'. It is essentially for fun from a beach on a warm day, but it has developed into a sport in its own right, with championships held and enthusiasts in colder climates sailing in wet suits. The new sort of craft was initiated by Hoyle Schweitzer in California. Because of its cheapness, ease of transportation, and difference from normally masted sailing, it has become something of a world craze.

TECHNIQUES

As can be seen, there is now no resemblance left to those early yacht tenders, which could be rowed by oars when not used for sailing. The modern sailing machine is made for speed, excitement, and style. Among the devices seen in advanced boats are: lightweight centreboards – the board has long since ceased to be ballast and is for performance only, weight is the last thing required; hulls that include materials of very high strength and/or rigidity against weight such as Kevlar and carbon fibre; self-bailers, so that water cannot collect when the boat is sailing; chutes for quick handling of the spinnaker, which can double the sail area; trapezes, which increase power without extra weight (it depends on the rules of each class whether these are allowed): bending spars, which when controlled can give thrust while coping with strong winds, adding yet more power; ever-improving metal spars and synthetic sails, which (unlike the old materials) have little uncontrolled 'give' and so do not waste any thrust – in turn this puts strains on hulls, which have to be strong; the clothing of the crew, which is specially designed for low windage, easy movement, and comfortable body temperature.

– offshore racing, ocean and cruiser racing

The terminology to describe this branch of the sport is neither clear nor established. Ocean racing does not necessarily imply sailing across the ocean. It is used of races in the open sea and out of sight of land, such as

Jean-Louis Fabry's Revolootion *(formerly* Revolotion*), one of the great ocean racing boats of all time. Designed by Finot, she was RORC Yacht of the Year in 1977 and 1978, won her class in the 1979 Fastnet, and was top scorer in Class III*

The start (above right) *of the 1974 Newport-to-Bermuda race in a typical Newport fog*

America's Salty Goose *(right) pictured here soon after the start of the 1973 Channel race*

have the capability, are not continually making use of it and races can vary from a transatlantic to a local event along the shore spanning six hours or less. The boats use the International Offshore Rule (IOR) or other methods of handicapping.

HISTORY

The New York-to-Bermuda race was first sailed in 1906 and was then sailed three more times until firmly established under the newly formed CRUISING CLUB OF AMERICA (CCA) by races in 1923, 1924 and thereafter. (Now the Newport-to-Bermuda race on alternate even years). Weston Martyr, a British yachting writer who took part in the 1924 race, determined an equivalent event should be sailed in England. The first Fastnet race was as a consequence sailed in 1925 and the (ROYAL) OCEAN RACING CLUB formed. It very quickly became a leading influence in offshore racing. Other courses were developed: among the early races to become regular were the Channel race, North Sea race, Miami-to-Nassau, transpacific (Los Angeles-to-Honolulu), and various trans-atlantic courses from North American ports to Britain or the Continent. After 1945, the increasing number of people coming into sailing were attracted to racing boats that were habitable. Offshore racing boats were built in growing numbers, race entries swelled, and fixtures multiplied. Boats were built mainly to the CCA rule in the United States and to the RORC rule in Britain, the rest of Europe, and Australasia; in 1971 the two rules were combined in the International Offshore rule. Since the inception in 1957 of the Admiral's Cup (see Major races and series *below*), there has been an increasing trend to holding series that are a combination, for teams of boats or single entries, of some in-shore races and one or two offshore events. A points system determines the winner of such series, which have become prestigious. Local organizations have also tended to go in for series, perhaps on successive weekends of a season, or shorter span of time. The most influential kind of series on ocean racing in the 1970s has been the level-rating or Ton Cup event (see Level-rating racing).

– level-rating racing

This extension of offshore racing has become the tail that now wags the dog. Ocean racers having developed from collections of different-sized cruising boats, offshore races were invariably on time allowance – until 1965, when the One Ton Cup (see Major races *below*) was presented for ocean racers to compete for without time allowance. Now boats are built and designed to the ratings under the IOR of the Two Ton, One Ton, Three Quarter Ton, Half Ton and Quarter Ton rules. The world championship of each class is a combination offshore/inshore series, and national and local competitions take

across the North Sea or from Newport to Halifax. The ocean racer is the boat that does this, being equipped for open-sea work. It also means the person in the sport. Passage racing is sometimes used to describe short events, or overnight racing (say 100 miles). Deep-water or blue-water racing implies longer events. An offshore race means something shorter. A cruiser-racer is much the same as an ocean racer (boat) or offshore racer, but the term would not be used when speaking of the latest top boats: cruiser racing would be on a lower key, unless the term was distinguishing between it and, say, dinghy racing. It is rather a question of 'You know what it is when you see it' – and 'it' is all to do with the sort of race, which rather than being around marks within a few miles of each other, is over a course beyond the immediate control of the race officers, with the boats depending entirely upon their own crews at sea.

The offshore yacht is more elaborate and expensive for its length than all other sailing craft. It has a complex rig with various combinations of sails, engine, and electrical system, electronic aids, navigational equipment, plumbing of the various sorts, and living

accommodation. This is all part of the appeal: the boat becomes a total commitment over its period of use and to some extent before and after. Once on board it is life at sea in a way that does not pertain to day racing craft. The boat can be cruised, or sailed quickly from port to port, in order to start a race or for other purposes such as holidays. There is, however, an increasingly wide gap between the racer that is fully equipped below with cruising facilities and the out-and-out 'stripped-out' racer that is bearable for the period of the race, but too stark to live in once moored in the dock. This is due to the increasing competitive spirit, where boats are lightened as much as they can be under the rules. Extensive lists of equipment and safety precautions are usually stipulated, for offshore, passage or ocean races, by administering bodies.

A characteristic of the offshore yacht, in contrast to other sorts of racer, is its ability to keep the sea in all weather and, except in extreme conditions, even to make headway. This quality has been bred by the development of the type in races since the 1920s, designers learning how to make fast but seaworthy boats. The boats, though they

their cue from this. In the 1970s these races have set the pace in the design and crewing standards of ocean racing and kept it at an international level. The world championships are held annually in different countries, so a lively interest in one class or another in the leading yachting countries is kept up.

The inshore races are Olympic courses; each class has its own scale of length of offshore races, one 'short' and one 'long': the latter is the final climax of each series and scores the highest points of any race. However, because there are three inshore races included, there is great emphasis on close tactics: so top dinghy sailors, used to the cut and thrust of racing round the buoys, are attracted to the level-rating events. Such people had previously found ocean racing not to their liking, perhaps even boring. Here is the clue to the position now occupied by level-rating racing. The latest ideas on design and handling are now first seen in these Ton Cup events. Designer's names are made – and broken – on them. Other offshore racing follows the lead. Very innovative designs always appear extreme to those used to the conventional boats of the time, and features of the winners in the year's level-rating events may attract penalization when the IOR and its supporting

The yacht Orient *nearing the finishing line at Diamond Head, during a Transpacific race (Los Angeles to Honolulu)*

safety and other rules are revised. One problem that has spread out from the level-rating events is that light boats of doubtful construction are needed to squeeze the last fraction of a knot of speed in the inshore races. Sometimes owners of these boats then hope that the longer races will not bring any heavy weather. A boat built to withstand gales and heavy weather may be too slow to succeed in average conditions. Once the series is over the specially built light boat can be dispensed with, though this scheme has an adverse effect on the design of offshore boats as a whole.

Among rules used in level-rating events is a maximum crew limit. For instance a One

Tonner, say 35 ft (about 11 m) LOA, can have no more than seven, a Quarter Tonner (25 ft; about 8 m) four. This prevents the use of human ballast, which would give dinghy-type advantage. In the level-rating boats, alone among ocean racers, the interior volume is controlled to ensure there is adequate space below, so that the boats retain at least some value for conversion to cruising after their prime. Minimum numbers of bunks, minimum water capacity, galleys, and chart-table requirements all help towards sea-going propensities. Electronic aids and the number of sails are limited in the interests of sport and cost saving. The keen competition means that owners and designers

keep to the letter of the rule but no more than that. Boats are always scrutinized before the first race of a series.

Despite all these pressures, many believe that the level-rating events, with a flavour unknown before the 1970s, are the ultimate expression of yacht racing. Contributing to this opinion are the camaraderie of the crews; the mix from different countries, often within a boat or as rivals; the knowledge that the yachts are the very latest in design and technique; the invariably close racing; the hospitable yachting ports of the world where such events are held; and the unequalled life to be enjoyed on so many successive days of racing on the sea.

– major races and series
ADMIRAL'S CUP
This has been described as a 'world championship of ocean racing' but, although it is a most prominent fixture, it cannot rate as this because it is a team challenge of three boats per nation. The boats are designed and built to the current leading ocean-racing rating rule: at present the INTERNATIONAL OFFSHORE RULE. The limits for 1979 were 30.0-ft rating to 40.0-ft rating; time allowances are applied under the current Royal Ocean Racing Club system. These conditions may vary, but the basis of the series is the pattern of courses: three (it was formerly two) inshore courses in the Solent of about 30 miles and two offshore courses. One of the latter is the Channel Race, a 225-mile course from the Solent over a triangle in the English Channel, taking in a mark on the French coast: the precise course can vary. The climax of the series is the Fastnet race (*see below*), so when this is completed at Plymouth, the winning team is known. The series is held on every 'Fastnet year': 1979, 1981, 1983 and so on. In 1975 and again in 1977, a total of 19 national teams took part. In those years the winning team was British, but in the past the Admiral's Cup has been won by teams from Australia, Germany, and the United States.

The series originated in 1957, when the Admiral of the RORC and some colleagues donated the large gold cup to be sailed between a three-boat British team and visiting American yachtsmen, as an informal match during Cowes Week and the Fastnet. Since then the participating teams have expanded in numbers and the series has become an event in its own right. Since the Admiral's Cup became popular, a number of events have started that are run along the same lines, combining inshore and offshore races in a series. These include the Southern Cross in Australia, the Rio circuit in Brazil, the Onion Patch (*see below*) on the American east coast, and a series organized by the Aga Khan at Porto Cervo, in the Mediterranean.
AMERICA'S CUP
The undisputed major yacht race is the

*One Ton Cup boats hovering on the start line of the
150-mile offshore race during the World
Championships at Torbay in 1974*

America's Cup; some would say it is the senior
international sporting event in the world.
Certainly it was the world's first regular
international sporting contest for yachts. It is
now a seven-race series between 12-Metre
class sloops; the first boat to win four races
takes the cup. The venue is always at Newport, Rhode Island, where a yacht selected
by the NEW YORK YACHT CLUB, holder of the
cup, defends against a foreign challenge.
Since 1870, when the cup was first defended
by *Magic* (United States) against *Cambria*
(Britain), the challenger has never managed
to win any of the 23 series.

In recent years, the challenger has always
been Australian. The races are normally held

every three years: 1967, 1970, 1974, 1977. But
this depends on the challenges made, which
may not come at exactly regular intervals
(e.g. 1974). A modern feature is elimination
races between the challengers from different
countries. For instance, in 1977 French and
Swedish boats were first eliminated. On the
defender's side there is invariably fierce
rivalry between the boats from different
'syndicates', sometimes from different parts of
the United States and with rival designers
and sailmakers. This sharpens up the defend-
ing boat to such an extent that the record of
the races shows that even few individual
courses can be won against the Americans.
Since 1962, only two actual races have in

fact been won by a challenging boat.

The cup originated as a Royal Yacht
Squadron challenge cup, which was won by
the schooner *America* in a race against the best
of the British yachting fleet in a race round
the Isle of Wight (east-about) on 22 August
1851. The *America* syndicate members
presented the cup to their club, the NYYC,
in 1857 as a perpetual challenge trophy.
BERMUDA RACE
The Newport-to-Bermuda race is the oldest
regular ocean race for other than very large
vessels. The Fastnet was copied from it and
since 1924 it has alternated with the Fastnet,
being held on even years. The early races (the
first was in 1906) were from New York, then

273

from New London, but since 1936 it has always started from Newport, Rhode Island. The organizing club is the Cruising Club of America, which, as its name says, is primarily a club for cruising (more akin to the Royal Cruising Club in Britain than to the RORC).

The key to success in the 635-mile race is a peculiar navigational one, since it is necessary to find the best part of the meandering Gulf Stream, which may be either east or west of the RHUMB-LINE course. To find this, navi-

The Alan Payne-designed Gretel, *the first Australian challenger for the* America's Cup *in 1962. She only just missed winning the cup, proving to be a very worthy challenger*

gators take the sea temperature at regular intervals and detect where they are in the gradient of the stream. Although sailed in midsummer, the fleet quite often meets gale-force winds. On the other hand, it is not unknown for the wind to be a reach the whole way (a virtual impossibility in the Fastnet). The Cruising Club Bermuda Race committee is of noted independence of mind. The rules, including even that of rating, are changed for every race. After earlier rough-and-ready

systems, the CCA used the same rule as the Fastnet for 1928, but in 1932 drew up its own rule of rating (the 'CCA rule'). This, with amendments, was used until 1970, when the CCA again united with the rest of the world by adopting the IOR. After 1974, however, the Bermuda Race committee began making its own alterations to the IOR for the rating of boats over the course. American boats have always won the race, with the exception of the 1972 victory of the British 48-ft (15-m) sloop *Noryema*, owned by Ron Amey.

BRITISH–AMERICAN CUP
Though still raced for (recently in the Soling class) this trophy had its heyday when the 6-Metres were the leading class. In the early part of the century there were no common classes between the main yachting areas of Europe and North America and the United States was not a member of the International Yacht Racing Union, which consisted of European countries. It was therefore a major step for the Seawanhaka Corinthian Yacht Club on Long Island Sound to support the (European) 6-Metre class. The British–American Cup was sailed in the United States and Britain alternately and created a standard of international yacht racing not known before that date (the unique *America*'s Cup – *see above* – had been the only regular international series), the races being most years from 1921 onwards. Because the 6-Metres were built to a formula (the International Rule: *see* HANDICAP SYSTEMS), their latest designs were followed as leaders in racing-yacht design; 6-Metres were raced also at national and club level so interest was widespread. Details of the year's new Sixes were eagerly awaited (as are those of ocean-racing boats today). The last British-American Cup in 6-Metres was in 1955.

CANADA CUP
This race dating from 1895 is on the lines of the *America*'s Cup (*see above*), being a challenge for a match race. The boats are not, however, the biggest available and various rules of rating and types of yacht have been utilized. The races are always between an owner with a yacht under the burgee of the Royal Canadian Yacht Club and an American club on the Great Lakes, where the matches are held. At the present time Two Tonners, IOR boats of 32-ft rating, are used and the races are an inshore/offshore combination.

Up to 1978, when the latest race was due, 13 events had been held, of which Canada had won 4 and the United States yacht all the others.

CAPE TOWN TO RIO RACE
This promising race across the South Atlantic with the attraction of a finish in time for the Rio carnival has recently suffered from political troubles. The uncertainty of the relations of other countries with South Africa makes it

unlikely that entries will be forthcoming. At one stage just before the start of the 1976 race, the harbour of Rio was banned to the contestants, but the order was rescinded after pressure from independent competitors. This emphasizes one point about ocean racing. It is regarded as a link between the ports of call (rather like a naval visit), so if for some reason the link is not wanted by the authorities, the route cannot be used with certainty.

FASTNET RACE

Once considered a testing course for the few, moderate weather (in the 1970s) and the development of all-weather ocean racers have made this a popular event with very large entries: there were over 300 starters in 1977. Now firmly fixed as the climax of Cowes Week in odd-numbered years, the course is down the Solent, through the Needles channel, past the tidal headlands of Portland, Start, Lizard and out into the Atlantic around the Fastnet Rock. The return course passes outside the Bishop Rock (Scilly Islands), the Lizard again and ends at Plymouth, a distance of 605 miles. The tidal and coastal conditions pose numerous navigational problems. A little luck as well as skill is needed to make the decisions that bring success. If an anticyclone prevails for some of the course, then finding wind and avoiding calms is a major race winner. The RORC is the organizer and always has been since 1925, when the club was founded by those who participated in the first race. A single Fastnet course completed (or two other nominated races) remains an essential qualification for membership of the RORC.

The fleet in the race is divided into numerous classes, giving scope for winning prizes other than the overall awards. The RORC rule of measurement and rating (as amended) was used from 1925 to 1969; since then the IOR has been used. Various time-allowance systems have been adopted from time to time by the RORC. The competitors are to be found from numerous countries: the Admiral's Cup entries are also able to compete for the individual prizes in the Fastnet. British yachts have been overall winners 12 times in the 27 races up to 1977. American yachts have won eight times and the Dutch twice.

LITTLE AMERICA'S CUP

This phrase is used for the International Catamaran Challenge, which is a match race between C-Class catamarans each representing its country. Like so many other of these international races, it began as a challenge between a British and an American club. The first race was in 1961 on Long Island Sound when the British *Hellcat* took the trophy from the American *Wildcat*. There followed a string of British victories off Thorpe Bay in the Thames estuary, when American and Australian challenges were repulsed. But in

1969, the Danish *Opus III* won the trophy. The Danes lost it the next year to an Australian boat, but since then it has been captured by a United States West Coast syndicate, which defended successfully in 1977 against an Australian challenge. The original British enthusiasm for the class has waned.

Chief interest in this contest is the advanced sailing technology seen on the boats. The rules allow great freedom, especially in the

Lady Helmsman, the C-Class catamaran, built and sailed by Reg White seen here off Thorpe Bay, England, where he won the Little America's Cup in 1966

rig, so 'wingsails' looking more like an aircraft wing than a sail are seen. The mast is buried inside the wing with variable camber and trim operated mechanically. With the twin-hull configuration the result is very high speed. There is considerable difference in appearance between the two competitors, as each experiments with his separate ideas on what makes for the best speed.

ONION PATCH SERIES

This is the American equivalent of the

Admiral's Cup (*see above*), the 'Onion Patch' being the island and reefs of Bermuda. It is not so well supported because of the geographical distance from Europe, and possibly because it lacks the unique atmosphere of Cowes Week. In 1976, for instance, five nations contested. The first inshore race was from Oyster Bay to Newport, followed by two inshore races in the islands and under the bridges and around the buoys off Newport. Then the Newport–Bermuda race was the long offshore event of the series. As well as the Americans, a British team of three boats invariably competes. Other nations that have taken part include France, Germany, Canada, Brazil, and Argentina.

OSTAR

This well-established mnemonic, for *Observer* Single-handed Transatlantic Race, refers to the race sponsored by the London *Observer* and sailed under the flag of the ROYAL WESTERN YACHT CLUB of England. The course

is from Plymouth, England, to Newport, Rhode Island. The race, which originated in a private challenge, was first sailed in June 1960. There were five competitors: Francis Chichester in *Gipsy Moth* III (the winner), H. G. Hasler (the race was his idea), David Lewis (New Zealander), Valentine Howells, and Jean Lacombe (French). Subsequently the race has been held every fourth year with increasing numbers and high public interest. The entry has become international and in 1976 there were 73 finishers, 46 retirements, and 2 deaths.

The race has developed quite a different sort of boat from the ocean racer of the IOR. The originators expected that the limitation of the crew to one person would develop useful small cruisers that could be easily handled without the expensive equipment of ocean racing. But to the contrary, without a rating rule the boats became ever larger, far bigger than ever permitted under the IOR. Almost

unbelievably, the four-master *Club Méditer-ranée*, 236 ft (72 m) long, was entered by the Frenchman Alain Colas for the 1976 race. She had been specially designed but in the event proved too large for one man to handle. She put into a port in Newfoundland for repairs and the race was won by Colas' fellow countryman Eric Tabarly in *Pen Duick VI*. Tabarly had won before in 1964: the only person to win twice. The race would appear to be very firmly established with a significant number of the entrants returning each time for the experience. There are to be races in 1980, 1984, and so on. The *Observer* Round Britain Race is held every four years (1978, 1982 etc.) but is for a crew of two. Many of the very same boats are to be found in this event; the extra man is considered advisable in coastal waters. *See also* SINGLE-HANDED SAILING

PRE-OLYMPIC REGATTAS

Because the sailing Olympics are held in the

Yachts in the inshore race of the 1974 Onion Patch series passing under one of the Newport bridges

country of the host nation, though at a venue away from the main (land) events, aspirants in these classes need to practise at the Olympic base. For this purpose major regattas are given in the years leading up to the Olympics. When the Olympics were at Kiel, West Germany (1972), Kiel Week was already established and so made a useful practice regatta. Prior to the 1976 Olympic sailing at Kingston, Ontario, the Canadian Olympic Regatta Kingston (CORK), became popular, not only for the six Olympic classes but for others such as the Fireball. The 1980 sailing Olympics are to take place at Tallinn, Estonia, so that the USSR will become an unaccustomed attraction for the six classes.

PRINCE OF WALES CUP

In 1927, when dinghy racing was in its infancy, the Prince of Wales (later Edward VIII) presented a cup to the International 14-ft class (it was then only National). The

Flying Dutchman (above) *racing during Kiel Week*

Overleaf: *the start of the 1976* Observer *Single-handed Transatlantic Race at Plymouth. Dominating the scene is the four-masted French yacht* Club Méditerranée

first race for the trophy was on 1 August 1927. Since then, except for the World War II years, the 14-footers have raced for the Cup. The 14s are the aristocrats of dinghy racing, being a restricted class able to move with the times, so that the boats may have changed, but the spirit of the class has remained.

In those early days it was Uffa Fox who won the trophy, while for others his designs were essential in order to gain any success. Many of them were also built at his yard, of carvel planking to just the right weight. After 1945 came new designers such as Ian Proctor and Bruce Kirby (of Canada) and also fresh

construction methods and materials, including cold-moulded plywood. The outstanding personality of the class and of the Prince of Wales Cup is Stewart H. Morris. In different boats of the class he won the Cup 12 times in all; the first time was in 1932 and the last was in 1965.

International 14s at the start of a Prince of Wales Cup race

ROUND-THE-WORLD RACES

Publicity given to single-handed sailors in the 1960s (such as Francis Chichester, Bernard Moitessier, and Alec Rose) stimulated the *Sunday Times* of London to initiate a single-handed sailing race around the world. This began in about October 1968 (the actual date of the start was optional), but out of the nine declared starters only the English yachtsman Robin Knox-Johnston completed the course. Some years later a British yachting magazine began to promote a race round the world for fully crewed yachts with a minimum size around 45 ft (14 m) LOA. This was taken over by Whitbread and the Royal Naval Sailing Association and began in September 1973 under its control. The route meant stopping for a few weeks at each of Cape Town, Sydney, and Rio de Janeiro. The race began and ended at Portsmouth, England. The winner was the Mexican yacht *Sayula* of 64 ft (19.5 m) LOA. In 1975 another race was held, sponsored by the London *Financial Times*, this time stopping only at Sydney, but it only attracted five competitors. Again it began and finished in England. In 1977, the RNSA ran a second Whitbread Round-the-World race on the same lines as its first, but stopping at Auckland, New Zealand, instead of in Australia. Fifteen competitors took part; the winner was *Flyer*, a 65-ft (19.8-m) Dutch ketch. The main significance for the yachting scene of these events is that a standard ocean racer, albeit carefully prepared, is able to sail the ocean in this way. It says much for the development of the sport from its beginnings in coastal cruisers in the 1920s. Speeds often exceed those of the old square-rigged vessels on the same routes, though the yachts are, of course, built for speed and do not carry a cargo. A modern yacht is the racing car; a cargo sailing ship is the freight truck. *See also* SINGLE-HANDED SAILING

THE SEAWANHAKA CUP

The Seawanhaka Cup was also turned over to the 6-Metre class in 1922; it was often sailed consecutively with the British–American Cup (*see above*), when the latter was held at the Seawanhaka Corinthian Yacht Club in Long Island Sound. But its origins were earlier – in 1895. It was established as an international challenge trophy under the rating rules of the time, but interest centred on the fact that it was for a small boat – very small by the standards then prevailing. More recently the Cup has been revived, but like the British–American, it can never recover its former status: it is overshadowed by so many newer international events, especially for ocean-racing yachts. The French were cleverer when they presented the old One Ton Cup for a new form of ocean racing.

SYDNEY-HOBART RACE AND SOUTHERN CROSS TROPHY

The offshore race from Sydney, New South

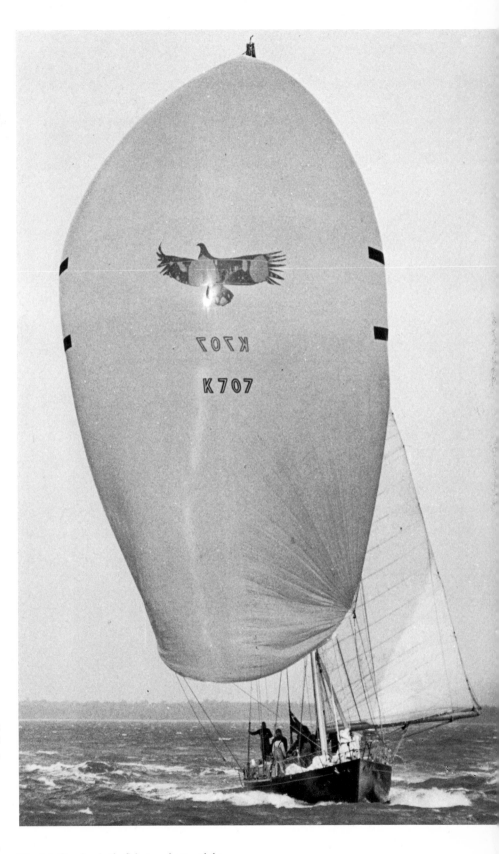

Heath's Condor in the Solent as she neared the end of the 4th leg of the 1978 Round-the-World race. She took line honours for the leg

*Yachts making their way down Sydney Harbour
soon after the start of a Sydney – Hobart race*

Wales, to Hobart, Tasmania, is held annually and has a reputation as a tough course across the Tasman Sea. It began in 1945 and, being about 630 miles long, was intended as an Australian equivalent to the Fastnet and Bermuda (*see above*) events. It has indeed become this and more recently has incorporated the Southern Cross Trophy, an international inshore/offshore series with exactly the same format as the Admiral's Cup (*see above*). The Southern Cross is open to teams from the Australian states – to ensure a reasonable entry, for international participation is limited by geography. British, American, and New Zealand teams usually take part. Others to have sent teams include France, Hong Kong, and Japan.

The Sydney–Hobart always begins on 26 December, a holiday date that attracts considerable numbers of spectator boats at the start.

THE TON CUP EVENTS

(*See also* Level-rating racing *above*; HANDICAP SYSTEMS.) A leading French club, the Cercle de la Voile de Paris (CVP), owns the One Ton Cup. The cost of the solid silver cup was met by the sale in 1898 of a yacht that has been defeated in the Coupe de France. Various classes have raced for the One Ton Cup over the years, the most notable being the International 6-Metres. The latter class was not widely enough supported after 1962 for the cup races to continue. So it was that in 1965 at the initiative of the CVP, and particularly Jean Peytel, a leading figure in the club and in international yachting matters, that the cup was raced in RORC-rated boats of 22-ft rating, but without time allowance – a novelty in ocean racing. Since then every year, except for 1970 when the RORC rule was in the process of change to IOR, the One Ton Cup has attracted the best and newest of ocean racers. The venue of the race changes each time to a major yachting nation. Because there is no time allowance, the racing is very close; and the system has brought ocean-racing boats into the forefront of all yacht racing, a position that boats racing under time allowance could never hold.

Different sizes have evolved from the original One Ton (now 27.5-ft rating). There is Two Ton (32-ft rating); Three Quarter Ton (24.5-ft); Half Ton (21.7-ft); Quarter Ton

Yachts racing for the Three Quarter Ton Cup at Plymouth in 1976

The spinnaker run during a Half Ton Cup off Poole, England

(18.0-ft); Mini Ton (16.0-ft). Unlike the Admiral's Cup (*see above*) there are no teams: instead a single yacht wins each trophy. But the number of boats from each nation is limited to keep total numbers under control, so there is still stiff competition to be nationally selected. This has the secondary effect of encouraging 'national' Ton Cup or level-rating championships. Further awards for the classes are often given as part of more general races. In Europe (except for the Admiral's Cup rating range) few competition boats are now built that are not to one of the level ratings.

Unfortunately this has had the result of driving out of the racing world a number of boats that are not so extreme and race oriented. Yet the Ton Cup boats are now the aristocrats of yacht racing – the inheritors of the mantle of the 'metre boats' that reigned from about 1910 to 1950. Designers make and break their reputations on them: their hull shape, rig, and fittings are swiftly aped by

other racers and eventually percolate through to all types of sailing boat.

TRANSATLANTIC RACES
Fully crewed races for 'ordinary' ocean-racing boats are held most years across the North Atlantic, invariably from west to east in the prevailing westerly winds. The starting and finishing points vary. Starting points can be Bermuda, or Newport, Gloucester, and other east-coast ports in the United States; finishes might be at San Sebastian, Plymouth, the Skaw, Bergen, and any other suitable points in western Europe. Because the races are from west to east, the entrants are predominantly from the United States; they vary in number from half a dozen to a score.

TRANSPACIFIC RACE
This could well claim to be the greatest of all ocean races. Whatever rating rule is in force, the real interest centres on which boat arrives first at Honolulu after sailing with a fair wind the 2225 miles from Los Angeles. Because the race is in the northeast trade winds,

boats can be designed and built to be down-wind flyers. For instance, at the time of writing the record is held by a boat called *Merlin*, 67 ft (20.4 m) LOA, which won 1977, covering the distance at an average of 11.1 knots. Up to 1977, the event had been held 30 times; the first occasion was in 1906. Dates of the race are 1979, 1981, and so on, and multihulls are accepted as competitors.

Yacht racing

Participants in the Quarter Ton Cup racing off Japan in 1978

Yankee
A medium-sized high-clewed jib that may be used in conjunction with a STAYSAIL.

Yard *see* MASTS AND RIGGING: Glossary

Yaw
Rotation about the normal axis of a craft.

Yawl
A fore-and-aft-rigged vessel with two masts, the mizzen being stepped abaft the stern-post.

Zenith
The point on the celestial sphere vertically above the observer.

Zenith distance
The angular distance from the zenith; the complement of the ALTITUDE.

Zone time
The local mean time within a TIME ZONE.

**Anglo-American Units of Measure
used in this encyclopedia
with their metric equivalents**

Picture Credits

The line diagrams were drawn by Bob Ledger from roughs supplied by the contributors to whom the producer's sincere thanks are due. The half-tone and line illustrations were supplied by the individuals, agencies, companies, museums and other institutions listed below. The producer is grateful to all of them for their kind co-operation.